THE LAWMAKERS

Judicial Power and the Shaping of Canadian Federalism

THE LAWMAKERS

Judicial Power and
the Shaping of
Canadian Federalism

JOHN T. SAYWELL

Published for The Osgoode Society for Canadian Legal History by
University of Toronto Press
Toronto Buffalo London

ISBN 0-8020-3751-8

Printed on acid-free paper

National Library of Canadian Cataloguing in Publication

Saywell, John, 1929–
The lawmakers : judicial power and the shaping of Canadian
federalism / John T. Saywell.

(Osgoode Society for Canadian Legal History series)
Includes bibliographical references and index.
ISBN 0-8020-3751-8

1. Judicial power – Canada – History.   2. Constitutional history –
Canada.   3. Canada. Supreme Court – History.   I. Title.   II. Series.

KE4248.S29 2002   347.71'012   C2002-901890-0

University of Toronto Press acknowledges the financial assistance to its
publishing program of the Canada Council for the Arts and the Ontario
Arts Council.

University of Toronto Press acknowledges the financial support for its
publishing activities of the Government of Canada through the Book
Publishing Industry Development Program (BPIDP).

... I have thought very often that an attempt to reconcile the provisions of the 91st and the 92nd sections of the British North America Act, with reference to many matters, was very much like a plunge into the thickets of free will and predestination. Looking at the matter from one point of view, it seems to be perfectly clear that we can if we will, and looking at it from another standpoint, it is just as certain that we cannot if we would.

Alexander McNeil, MP Bruce North, House of Commons, 27 February 1885

I do not think there is anything so obscure in the construction of the Act, with regard to the distribution of power, and the *dominium* given to the Dominion of Canada, that renders it necessary to go into the history of it.

Sir Montague Smith, oral argument, *Russell* v. *The Queen*, 1882

To regard Canadian constitutional law as a matter of statutory interpretation of the British North America Act ... overlooks the fact that the British North America Act will have whatever meaning the courts choose to ascribe to it ...

Professor F.E. LaBrie, 1950, *University of Toronto Law Journal*

Empiricism not dogmatism, imagination rather than literalness, are the qualities through which judges can give their Court the stamp of personality.

Bora Laskin, 1951, *Canadian Bar Review*

I never found it necessary to limit myself to purely incremental changes and while some of my former colleagues on the Supreme Court paid lip-service to incrementalism, they frequently followed me on distant voyages of discovery. Indeed, if I may be permitted to mix metaphors, they sometimes go off on frolics of their own.

G.V. La Forest, 'Judicial Law Making,' 2000

Contents

Foreword

THE OSGOODE SOCIETY
FOR CANADIAN LEGAL HISTORY

Anyone who has ever studied Canadian history at the university level has puzzled over the decisions of the Judicial Committee of the Privy Council on the British North America Act. As a student of Professor Saywell's several decades ago at the University of Toronto, Osgoode Society editor Peter Oliver was among the many undergraduates who laboured diligently to understand the apparently tortuous ways of British judges as they laid violent hands on the Macdonald constitution. Years later, as a colleague of Saywell's in York's history department, Oliver observed 'with considerable amazement the sheer audacity of Professor Saywell as he offered a rigorous and hugely demanding course on the law of the Canadian constitution to a somewhat motley assortment of undergraduates. But for those who persevered with this course, Professor Saywell set the highest of standards and always got the best from his students.'

And so too with this book. Tackling a subject of the greatest complexity, one that has been much written about and hotly debated, Saywell offers us a book – no doubt controversial – which will excite and engage every reader. He begins his analysis by offering new evidence and insights on the structure of the 1867 constitution. Relying heavily on the voices of the actors themselves, his study moves beyond a simple examination of previously published reports. He analyses oral arguments before the Judicial Committee, largely drawn from manuscripts, to determine how members of the committee interacted with counsel, developed their arguments, and came to their conclusions. His finely drawn portraits of the judges, Canadian as well as British, take us behind the scenes of judicial decision making with an immediacy and intimacy seldom if ever achieved in histories of our judicial system.

Critical of the jurisprudence of the Judicial Committee, which he argues virtually eliminated some of the essential legislative powers of the federal government, thereby destroying its capacity to act on the economic and social problems of the twentieth century, Saywell credits the Supreme Court of Canada with restoring the balance in the federation and strengthening the national government. Comprehensive, ambitious, and detailed, *The Lawmakers* will be the definitive work on the evolution of the law of Canadian federalism.

The purpose of The Osgoode Society for Canadian Legal History is to encourage research and writing in the history of Canadian law. The Society, which was incorporated in 1979 and is registered as a charity, was founded at the initiative of the Honourable R. Roy McMurtry, a former attorney general for Ontario, now chief justice of Ontario, and officials of the Law Society of Upper Canada. Its efforts to stimulate the study of legal history in Canada include a research-support program, a graduate student research-assistance program, and work in the fields of oral history and legal archives. The Society publishes volumes of interest to the Society's members that contribute to legal-historical scholarship in Canada, including studies of the courts, the judiciary, and the legal profession, biographies, collections of documents, studies in criminology and penology, accounts of significant trials, and work in the social and economic history of the law.

Current directors of The Osgoode Society for Canadian Legal History are Robert Armstrong, Jane Banfield, Kenneth Binks, Patrick Brode, Brian Bucknall, Archie Campbell, Kirby Chown, J. Douglas Ewart, Martin Friedland, Elizabeth Goldberg, John Honsberger, Horace Krever, Vern Krishna, Virginia MacLean, Wendy Matheson, Roy McMurtry, Brendan O'Brien, Peter Oliver, Paul Reinhardt, Joel Richler, James Spence, Richard Tinsley, and David Young.

The annual report and information about membership may be obtained by writing: The Osgoode Society for Canadian Legal History, Osgoode Hall, 130 Queen Street West, Toronto, Ontario. M5H 2N6. Telephone: 416-947-3321. E-Mail: mmacfarl@lsuc.on.ca.

R. Roy McMurtry
President

Peter N. Oliver
Editor-in-Chief

Acknowledgments

My first debt is to a professor who taught Government 400 at the University of British Columbia in 1949. The source of his lectures was a mystery to many of us until a senior graduate student told me it was the 1940 Rowell-Sirois Report, officially known as *The Report of the Royal Commission on Dominion Provincial Relations*. That was not surprising, for the professor was Henry Angus, one of the five commissioners. It was clear that the *Report* and Angus laid much of the blame for the sorry state of the Canadian federation in the 1930s at the door of the Judicial Committee of the Privy Council. As a child of the Depression, I found it reassuring to find some of the villains.

Four decades later I started to teach a course at York University on law, politics, and the constitution. There was not a moment, that I can remember, when I decided to write this book. One question led to another, and by the mid-1990s there was clearly a work in progress, although exactly what form it would take remained unclear in my own mind. It was not until the end of the decade that I decided that the work of the Supreme Court in judicially reshaping Canadian federalism was the only fitting conclusion to a study of the lawmakers.

The research could not have been done without the assistance of a small army of research assistants, largely made possible by the wise policy of York's graduate-history program of funding graduate students with research assistantships. In particular, I would like to thank Xavier Gélinas, Marcel Martel, Adele Perry, Mark Kuhlberg, and

Stephen Henderson. Michelle Geller not only assisted with the research but helped to put the early chapters into shape. Although not from York, Ailsa Henderson examined the Haldane Papers in the National Library of Scotland while a graduate student at the University of Edinburgh. Blake Brown was a graduate student, a research assistant, and a conscientious critic of an early draft of the manuscript.

Teaching assistants can be an invaluable resource, and mine were superb. The first, Penny Bryden, constantly appealed to me on behalf of the students to be 'user friendly,' and Graham Rawlinson and Mark Kuhlberg were not hesitant to suggest that better teaching would lead to better results. As both a teaching assistant and a research assistant, Dimitry Anastakis was in a class by himself. He taught with me for three years and worked with me over many a summer. In the end, he contributed his superior computer skills to putting the manuscript in its final shape. He was not only an assistant but the most helpful of critics.

The three assessors of the manuscript for the Osgoode Society were most encouraging and helpful. I revelled in their flattering comments and tried my best to respond to their criticisms. I think I penetrated the anonymity of one assessor; the appeal to simplify and clarify and be 'user friendly' sounded faintly familiar. Peter Russell confessed to me that he had been one of the assessors, and I thank him most warmly for his gracious comments and helpful suggestions. I waited with trepidation for the assessment by a member of the academic legal establishment, expecting to be shot down as an untutored interloper. Such was not the case, but I did attempt to answer the questions and remedy the deficiencies. But as s/he observed, to respond to some comments would have required another book, or at least substantial additions to one already too long. Although she was not officially an assessor, Jacqueline Krikorian, a published Judicial Committee scholar, kindly read the manuscript with a friendly but critical eye. Curtis Fahey, much more than a copy editor, performed miracles on the manuscript.

Peter Oliver is partly responsible for this book. Years ago the Osgoode Society gave me a small grant to work on an article – which ultimately became this book. Marilyn MacFarlane runs Peter, the society, and its authors with a firm but understanding hand.

Copies of the correspondence from the Cardwell, Carnarvon, Monck, and Langevin papers used in Chapter 1 are on deposit in the Fonds Saywell in the York University Archives. Copies of the manuscript oral arguments before the Judicial Committee have been placed in the library of the Faculty of Law, York University.

Since the 1950s I have worked on many books and projects with my close friend John Ricker. This book is no exception. John read the manuscript many times, training his eyes and ears on the grammar and syntax, and, by forcing me to explain and to clarify, made the book more comprehensible and readable. No amount of thirty-year-old Islay can repay him.

This book has been long in the making. I thank Suzanne for keeping me alive and allowing me to live on the third floor and Tupper and his ball for keeping me company.

Introduction

The Lawmakers is the story of the role of the courts in shaping the evolution of jurisdictional federalism. It is not a study of constitutional law; rather, its focus is on the law of the constitution. My concern is not whether the federal or provincial governments should have the power to police Canadians' right to drink, but how the courts defined their respective powers in reaching a decision.

I more or less slid into this study as my search for information on or explanation of specific jurists and judicial decisions proved elusive and unsatisfactory – but tantalizing. When old friends and colleagues learned that this initial dabbling was in danger of becoming an obsession and even a book, they were not encouraging. Surely nothing could be added to the literature on the Judicial Committee and the Supreme Court of Canada – or at least much that was worth knowing. I was also reminded of Peter Hogg's comment about the Judicial Committee: 'One can only debate a fait accompli for so long.'[1] Others observed that the Supreme Court was so irrelevant – at least before the Charter of Rights and Freedoms – that my time would be better spent on almost anything else.

I agreed that the course of Canadian federalism has been determined largely by the political dynamics found in the interaction of economic, cultural, and regional forces, as well as the raw elements of partisan politics, on the federal-provincial battleground. But underlying this dynamic there has always been an identifiable, if not quantifiable, ten-sion between perceptions of Canada as a strongly integrated federation or a loose confederacy of largely independent provinces. Whether judges shared in one or the other of these perceptions may be debated, but there is no question that their decisions and reasoning pushed the law of the constitution in one direction or the other.

Moreover, the courts have not been allowed to be indifferent bystanders. In a variety of ways and at different times, they have staked out the jurisdictional boundaries of the political battleground and dictated the terms of engagement. And at critical times in the near past, the Supreme Court has laboured to find formulas combining principles of law, convention, and democratic practice to aid embattled politicians in solving problems they could not. I could not agree that the history of judicial review was or is intellectually or politically irrelevant.

Many scholars have written on aspects of the subject, but most have done so to serve a unique intellectual pursuit. Paul Romney found the Judicial Committee a congenial ally in giving legal sanction to Oliver Mowat's quest for provincial sovereignty.[2] In an influential 1971 essay, Alan Cairns contended that, whether good or bad law, the decentralist jurisprudence of the Judicial Committee appropriately, if not necessarily responsively, reflected the cultural and political diversity of Canada.[3] Robert Vipond found that the jurisprudence of the committee, whatever its flaws, was congruent with and supported the constitutional doctrines of Ontario Liberals about nineteenth-century legal and political liberalism.[4] French-Canadian scholars have universally praised the Judicial Committee for federalizing a centralist constitution. 'It has long been the custom in English Canada to denounce the Privy Council for its provincialist bias,' Pierre Trudeau told an academic audience in 1964, 'but it should perhaps be considered that if the law lords had not leaned in that direction, Quebec separatism might not be a threat to-day; it might be an accomplished fact.'[5] Indeed, the jurisprudence of the Judicial Committee has always been a controversial subject – in terms of both the law and the politics of federalism. Much of the debate focuses on Richard Risk's question, 'Was the villain, or the saviour, Watson and Haldane?'[6] These two men dominated the Judicial Committee in Canadian appeals from the 1880s until 1928 and embedded their personal views of the history and structure of Canadian federalism in the law of the constitution.

Controversy did not end with the abolition of appeals to the Judicial

Committee. Even as the Supreme Court was about to experience its freedom, there was a fundamental disagreement over whether it could or should escape from the legacy of the Judicial Committee; neither in Parliament nor in statute was it given a mandate to rewrite the law of the constitution. Within a decade, however, court-watchers noted a distinct tendency of the court to enhance federal jurisdiction, without overtly declaring its independence of Judicial Committee doctrine. By the 1970s, Peter Russell warned that if the pattern continued, the court's future as a neutral umpire of the federal system would be in jeopardy. French-Canadians scholars found that the provincial autonomy seemingly guaranteed by the Judicial Committee was being legally undermined.[7]

Outraged by the frequent charge that appointment by the federal government explained the court's 'centralist bias,' Chief Justice Bora Laskin angrily lashed back with an assertion of judicial independence. 'Do we lean? Of course we do, in the direction in which the commands of the constitution take us according to our individual understandings.'[8] But the leaning, if such it was, continued, as did the suspicions or accusations.

Politically, there were attempts throughout the constitutional turmoil of the last decades of the twentieth century to create a truly independent constitutional court, or at least to offset some of the criticism by providing for provincial participation in the appointment of Supreme Court judges. Two distinguished academics, however, concluded for slightly different reasons that, whatever the case might have been in 1867, there no longer existed any sound, rational, doctrinal, or theoretical basis for judicial review of federalism disputes. All questions are political, all decisions are ad hoc, contended Paul Weiler and Patrick Monahan, and all reasoning ultimately rests on competing visions of the Canadian state. Visions are not really justiciable. Therefore, federalism adjudication should be through the political process.[9] Weiler's argument that in 1867 there was a shared purpose in the language used and in the ends to which power was allocated, but that the 'original written understanding' had eroded over time and become irrelevant to judicial review, was disputed by William Lederman in a classic defence of judicial lawmaking, although he may have objected to the word:

I consider Professor Weiler has got his history backwards. I consider the true history of the development of the B.N.A. Act by judicial interpretation to be almost the complete reverse of what Professor Weiler says it is. The greatest uncertainty about the meaning of the power-conferring words and phrases of the constitution occurs at the beginning. As time goes on and precedents accumulate, many years of judicial interpretation greatly reduces this uncertainty and makes the distribution-of-powers system much more meaningful. In other words, judicial interpretation puts flesh on the original constitutional skeleton; over the years it refines and develops the meaning of words used. So that over 100 years of authoritative interpretation, the B.N.A. Act becomes more meaningful than it was in 1867, and of course it was by no means devoid of meaning in 1867.[10]

Lederman's remarks can be translated fairly as the constitution is what the courts have said it is, not what it was when it left the hands of its authors. It was Lord Haldane who had boasted that Lord Watson had put flesh on Canadian skeleton and 'in a series of masterly judgements he expounded and established the real constitution of Canada.'[11] Not surprisingly, Lederman considered Watson to be 'the greatest of the Privy Council judges concerned with the Canadian constitution'[12] and commended the Judicial Committee for reducing uncertainty and making 'the distribution-of-powers system more meaningful.' Watson, it seems, was a 'saviour.'

The Weiler-Lederman exchange reveals that the debate is not just about judicial review but about the objectives, language, and structure of the division of powers in the British North America Act, as I prefer still to call it. Most historians have traditionally accepted and propagated the 'centralist' interpretation of Confederation, finding their evidence in the historical background and the text of the act. Paul Romney, however, has denounced the centralist version as 'a vast fabric of myth' both as history and as constitutional text.[13] Many others have simply hidden behind the conclusion that history is irrelevant and the text too obscure or ambiguous to provide any basis for an analysis of the legal quality of the work of the lawmakers. Without suggesting that the text should be determinative, certainly not for all time, I believe that it is possible to reach conclusions about language and intentions that are less obscure, ambiguous, or mythical.

The story, therefore, begins with an analysis of the division of powers in the 1867 constitution and a survey of the history of judicial review until the end of the millenium. The books relies heavily on the voices of the protagonists in argument and decision, for their words, not mine, are the stuff of which law was made. The interaction of counsel and jurist during the oral arguments before the Judicial Committee, many of which exist only as archival manuscripts, is particularly enlightening because it reveals that the decisions and rhetorical reasoning were often disturbingly idiosyncratic and problematic. It is much more difficult to go beyond the published opinions in the Supreme Court, but it is sufficient for my purpose to see to what extent the Supreme Court rewrote the law of the constitution and in the process created what Chief Justice Brian Dickson described as 'a distinctively Canadian jurisprudence.'[14]

Although I believe that an understanding of the context and text of the original constitution is an essential beginning to the history of judicial review, this study is not based on the assumption that there is one preferred approach to judicial review of a federal constitution – by either court or historian. Each of the approaches to judicial review identified in Philip Bobbitt's typology will be found in reasoning, decision, and *obiter*, often in a sometimes bewildering combination: *historical* arguments that seek to determine the intentions of the framers as revealed in evidence external to the text itself; *textual* arguments that rely on the explicit words in their plain and ordinary meaning, or by necessary implication; *doctrinal* arguments derived from previous case law; *structural* arguments based on perceived (or desirable) relationships of the two orders of government; and *prudential* arguments that, covertly or implicitly, are based on policy considerations.[15]

These approaches cannot be separated in theory, nor were they in practice. Before they became hostages to the precedents and doctrine of the Judicial Committee, Canadian courts drew on history, text, structure, and policy considerations in their reasoning and decisions. The law lords dismissed history and claimed to be blind to policy, professing instead to rely on the strict application of the rules of statutory interpretation applied to the text and ultimately to their own precedents and doctrine. But the rules were applied when convenient, and neglected when necessary. With Lord Watson it is impossible to escape the conclusion that structural arguments underlay the decisions, with text manipulated and history rewritten. Lord Haldane's law was a sometimes bizarre amalgam of historical revisionism, Watsonian structuralism, twisted doctrine, and deliberate policy considerations. Lord Atkin veered from the application of precedent only when it served his purpose, but in finding congenial the doctrinal and structural conceptions bequeathed by Watson and Haldane, provoked the demise of the law lords and judicial imperialism.

In 1949 the Supreme Court of Canada inherited the legacy of the Judicial Committee. Although conservative by training, the Canadian jurists were soon compelled to find some accommodation between that doctrinal and structural inheritance and the imperatives of the modern Canadian state. Often driven by policy considerations, they increasingly distanced themselves from Judicial Committee law, distinguishing precedent when desirable, ignoring it when convenient, and finally rejecting it when necessary. History, text, and doctrine were conveniently and pragmatically blended as the court invented a body of constitutional law to find a workable balance between functionalism and federalism. But that 'distinctively Canadian jurisprudence' was based on a conception of the Canadian state and society that continued to alarm those who had found the Judicial Committee's decentralized federalism, with an almost impotent central government, much more congenial.

There is no agreement about the 1867 beginnings and there is controversy today. My hope is that this study may illuminate some of the story and help to identify the villains and the saviours.

THE LAWMAKERS

Judicial Power and the Shaping of Canadian Federalism

1

The Genesis of Sections 91 and 92, 1864–1867

And we shall all be quite safe ...

– *Globe*, 30 Aug. 1864

Although much has been written about the division of legislative powers in the 1867 constitution, there is little agreement about the intention of the framers as expressed in the language of the act. During the argument in *Russell* v. *The Queen* in 1882, Sir Montague Smith assured counsel that 'I do not think there is anything so obscure in the construction of the Act, with regard to the distribution of power, and the dominium given to the Dominion of Canada, that renders it necessary to go into the history of it.'[1] Less than a century later, however, given the 'violently opposed positions among serious scholars,' Alan Cairns was 'tempted to ask if the pursuit of the real meaning of the act is not a meaningless game, incapable of a decisive outcome.'[2] Peter Russell concluded that it was difficult to find 'documentary evidence strong enough to throw definite light' on the terms of the act,[3] and the distinguished legal scholar W.R. Lederman declared that the 'truth is that the B.N.A. Act was simply ambiguous or incomplete in many respects as originally drafted and the answers just were not in the Act as to how these ambiguities were to be resolved and the gaps filled.'[4] Although most scholars agree that the 1867 constitution was centralist in its intent and language, Paul Romney has insisted, as we have seen, that the centralist interpretation 'is not history but a vast fabric of myth.'[5]

The conclusion that there is no standard by which to judge the judges is a temptation to be resisted. The decisions themselves are 'the flesh and blood of constitutional law,' to borrow Albert Abel's analogy. 'But flesh and blood need a skeleton ... X-raying the Act to see its bony structure is not wholly pointless. Even if the course of evolution has been such that the Act as written is only the extinct ancestor of our existing constitution, examination gratifies at least an intellectual curiosity.'[6] And in so doing, it may provide a less uncertain, more evidential, understanding of the structure of the distribution of powers in the 1867 constitution.

Whatever other purposes it served, the federal constitution of 1867 was not the product of a grand dream of a British North American nationality inhabiting a transcontinental state. Paradoxically, it was driven and drawn by the inability of French and English to live together in the unitary state imposed by the British a quarter of a century earlier. Dissolution of the union was a denial of the essential geographic and economic unity of the region, but a legislative union, with or without representation by population, was unacceptable. The preferred, if not the ideal, solution was a divorce and remarriage, with a new federal contract that would satisfy both Ontario's demands for self-government and, as *La Minerve* put it, 'Lower Canada's special interests, its religion, and its nationality.'[7]

Although the political reconstruction of the colonies had long been discussed, by 1864 'such was the opposition between the two sections of the province, such was the danger of impending anarchy,' said John A. Macdonald, that some solution was imperative.[8] When the ninth ministry in a decade tottered to its fall in the spring of 1864, ancient animosities were set aside as George Brown agreed to a coalition with Macdonald and George-Étienne Cartier, whose purpose was to seek a federal union of all British North America or, that failing, a federal union of the Canadas.[9] In less than ten days the new government issued a brief statement outlining the broad federal principles upon which it would proceed:

... in introducing the Federal Principle into the proposed federation of all the British American Provinces or of the Canadas, as the case may be, it was understood that to the local Governments and Legislatures would be entrusted the protection of all local laws, interests, and institutions ... that in the general or federal government, which would have the sovereign power and would deal with all subjects of government and legislation common to all the sections composing the federation ...[10]

Although the cabinet drafting committee did not begin work until 4 August, Brown's *Globe* reported on 1 August that 'they propose that the local governments shall be delegated governments, and that the "sovereign" power shall be vested in the general or federal Government ... Within their own sphere, of course, the local Governments must be supreme, but they possess only definite and expressly delegated powers. They will possess no *implied* power. That will attach to the general government ... ' The suggestion that the 'sovereign power,' whatever that meant, would rest with the central government alarmed the French-Canadian press. 'Where then will be the guarantee for Lower Canada when this sovereign power will reside permanently in the hands of a majority systematically hostile to our interests; what liberty will be preserved even for the acts of the local legislature, when those acts will be subject to the prerogative of the central sovereign power?' asked the *Franco-Canadian* editorially.[11]

Editorially, the *Globe* reassured French-Canadian opponents that vesting the 'sovereign' power at the centre would not threaten 'the peculiar institutions of Lower Canada ... When we speak of local provinces under a federal form of government, we do not mean mere County Councils, but legislatures empowered by the Imperial Legislature and the Crown to deal with specified matters, and enjoying a prescribed authority, with which "Congress" will not be allowed to interfere. Such legislatures would be beyond the control of the central power, set apart from it, untouchable by it. Where, then, is the danger?' The crucial issue was really the distribution of legislative power. 'In this fact lies the danger against which both Upper and Lower Canada have to guard. Both sections must take care that nothing is given to the local legislatures which ought to be reserved for the federal authority, and *vice versa*. Let us see also, that the federal authority – whether it be recognized as the "sovereign" power or not – is precluded from any interference with the legislation of local bodies, so long as they keep within constitutional limits, and we shall all be quite safe.'[12] *Le Courier de St-Hyacinthe* seemed reassured: 'The federal powers will be sovereign, no doubt, but it will have powers over certain general questions defined by the constitution. This is the only plan of confederation which Lower Canada can accept ... The two levels of government must be sovereign each within its jurisdiction as clearly defined by the constitution.'[13]

By the end of August the federal scheme was sufficiently well developed to be placed before the Maritime delegations who coincidentally had gathered at Charlottetown to discuss Maritime union. Press reports suggest that the proposed distribution of legislative powers anticipated the enumerations that would emerge in the Quebec Resolutions. The Canadians were also emphatic that the federal government would possess the residual power. When E.B. Chandler of New Brunswick proposed the reverse at Quebec, Charles Tupper interjected:

I have heard Mr. Chandler's argument with surprise. Powers undefined must rest somewhere. Those who were at Charlottetown will remember that it was fully specified that all the powers not given to the Local should be reserved to the Federal Government. This was stated as being a prominent feature of the Canadian scheme, and it was said then that it was desirable to have a plan contrary to that adopted by the United States. It was a fundamental principle laid down by Canada and the basis of our deliberations.[14]

Publicly, Macdonald stated in a speech at Halifax after the conference that all the dangers inherent in the American system would be avoided 'if we can agree upon forming a strong central government – a great central legislature – a constitution for a Union which will have all the rights of sovereignty except those given to the local governments.'[15]

The Maritimers were at least sufficiently intrigued to give further consideration to the Canadian proposal for a broader federal union. For two weeks in October 1864, delegates from the four colonies put the finishing touches on what was essentially a Canadian agreement. Apart from some debate over the location of the residual authority, even the wisdom of adding the enumerations to the federal residual authority, there was surprisingly little discussion about the distribution of legislative jurisdiction.[16] There seemed to be general agreement with the principles Macdonald outlined when the conference opened that the 'primary error' in the American constitution must be reversed 'by strengthening the General Government and conferring on the provincial bodies only such powers as may be required for local purposes. All sectional prejudices and interests can be legislated by local legislatures' while the minority would be protected 'by having a powerful central government.' But 'great caution' was necessary for 'the people of every section must feel they are protected, and by no overstraining of central authority should such guarantees be overrriden.' The constitution would be based on an imperial act, and 'any question as to overriding sectional matters determined by "[i]s it legal or not?" The judicial tribunals of Great Britain would settle any such difficulties should they occur.'[17]

What became the first version of sections 91 and 92 of the 1867 constitution emerged in the Quebec Resolutions as follows:[18]

29. The General Parliament shall have power to make Laws for the peace, welfare and good Government of the Federated Provinces (saving the Sovereignty of England), and especially Laws respecting the following subjects: –
[then followed a list of subjects, numbers 1 through 36, much like those in section 91 and including what became section 94]
37. And Generally respecting all matters of a general character, not specially and exclusively reserved for the Local Governments and Legislatures.

43. The Local Legislatures shall have power to make Laws respecting the following subjects: –
[then followed a list similar to that in section 92 and including the following subjects]
15. Property and civil rights, excepting those portions thereof assigned to the General Parliament.
16. And generally all matters of a private or local nature, not assigned to the General Parliament.

The heads of the two sections are distinct, with the federal government's enumerations unqualified and prefaced by the word 'especially,' but the tails are identical in providing a home for matters either general or local not otherwise captured by the preceding enumerations and not to be found among those reserved for the other jurisdiction. (The so-called 'sovereignty' of the central government apparently was to be found in the head with the traditional enacting clause in which the imperial government had conveyed legislative power to colonial legislatures, although Macdonald seemed to find it in the tail or more generally in the breadth and importance of federal jurisdiction.)

The debate on the Quebec Resolutions in the Canadian Legislative Assembly in 1865 casts less light than shadow on precisely what had been accomplished, perhaps because amendments were prohibited: it was all or nothing. Macdonald maintained that the federal government had 'all the great subjects of legislation. We have conferred on them, not only specifically and in detail, all the powers which are incident to sovereignty, but we have expressly declared that all subjects of general interest not distinctly and exclusively conferred upon the local governments and local legislatures, shall be conferred upon the General Government and Legislature.' The 37th subsection, he added, 'confers on the General Legislature the general mass of sovereign legislation ... This is precisely the provision which is wanting in the Constitution of the United States.'[19]

Although Macdonald maintained that they had 'avoided all conflict of jurisdiction and authority,' Christopher Dunkin found the opposite: 'Do we follow the American example, and give so much to the Union and the rest to the provinces; or so much to them, and the rest to it? Either rule would be plain; but this plan follows neither. It simply gives a sort of special list for each; making much common to both, and as to much more, not showing what belongs to either.'[20] Antoine-Aimé Dorion concluded that federal jurisdiction was not limited by the 29th section and there was 'not a word in these resolutions' to prevent the federal government from legislating within provincial jurisdiction 'because all the sovereignty is vested in the General Government, and there is no authority to define its functions and attributes and those of the local governments.'[21]

It remained for Joseph Cauchon to lecture Dorion, the future chief justice of Quebec, as well as Macdonald, on the nature of sovereignty in the new federation. If sovereignty existed, 'it must be in the Constitution. If it is not to be found there, it is because it does not exist.' In the proposed federation 'there will be no absolute sovereign power, each legislature having its distinct and independent attributes, not proceeding from one to the other by delegation, either from above or from below. The Federal Parliament will have legislative sovereign power in all questions submitted to its control in the Constitution. So also the local legislatures will be sovereign in all matters which are specially assigned to them.' And, as in the United States, disputes between them would be settled by the courts.[22]

After six weeks of partisan debate in February and March 1865, the Quebec Resolutions were approved by a vote of forty-five to fifteen in the Legislative Council and ninety-one to thirty-three in the Assembly. It was not until December 1866, however, that the delegates from Canada, New Brunswick, and Nova Scotia were able to meet in London to draft the final resolutions for submission to the imperial government. On Boxing Day 1866, after three weeks of work and play, but with the Quebec Resolutions virtually unchanged,[23] Macdonald sent the London Resolutions to Lord Carnarvon, the colonial secretary, to be embodied in an act creating the Canadian federation.

From the outset, the Colonial Office, the *Times*, the *Edinburgh Review*, and the *Economist* were sharply critical of the proposed federation. What Canada needed, they agreed, was, if not a legislative union, at least a highly centralized federation.[24] 'The hinge of the whole matter is, I think, this: Has the Central Power complete control over the Local Powers?' wrote Edward Cardwell, the colonial secretary, on receipt of the Quebec Resolutions. 'If not,' he privately warned the governor general, 'anarchy is to be apprehended as the result, sooner or later.' Assuming that Quebec was the obstacle to a more complete 'fusion,' he wondered whether it was not 'possible to recognize more pointedly the difficulty about Lower Canada: and to provide in more express terms for the autonomy of the French population in all such respects as the Union with Scotland provided for the independence of Worship, Tribunal etc etc.'[25] Cardwell continued to believe that 'Lower Canada would have a better guarantee, & not a worse, for her specialities if they are specifically enacted in the new Constitution Act: and the general scheme would be free from the numerous imperfections, which at present attach to it.'[26]

The greatest imperfection was provincial jurisdiction over property and civil rights. As discussion on the drafts began late in January 1867, Cartier and Hector Langevin were summoned to a meeting to face Lord Carnarvon, the new colonial secretary, Lord Monck, the governor general, and senior officials of the Colonial Office in a futile attempt to get them to agree to some special guarantees for their distinct society, presumably in return for some weakening of provincial jurisdiction over property and civil rights (or conceivably even its removal from the provincial enumerations).[27] As Langevin wrote to his wife: 'L'effort est fait, la victoire nous reste.'[28] All that remained was the diplomacy of drafting.

Shortly after receiving the Quebec Resolutions, Cardwell had set Sir Francis Reilly, 'our best draughtsman,' to work on a bill. Reilly was instructed to 'get rid of some of the ambiguities' and was unquestionably made aware that Cardwell and the cabinet wanted 'the Local Legislatures to dwindle down towards the Municipal as much as possible.'[29] Lord Carnarvon, who succeeded Cardwell in the summer of 1866, informed Cardwell (and certainly Reilly) that 'my foremost object wd. be to strengthen, as far as is practicable, the central govt.

against the exclusive power or encroachments of the local administration.'[30] Reilly had completed most of his first draft before the London Conference began in December 1866.

Reilly radically altered the structure of what became section 91. At its head he placed the now familiar enacting clause, an unambiguous assertion of residual legislative jurisdiction:

It shall be lawful for Her Majesty, Her Heirs and Successors, by and with the Advice and Consent of the Houses of Parliament of the United Colony, to make laws for the Peace, Order and good Government of the United Colony and of the several Provinces, in relation to all Matters not coming within the Classes of Subjects by this Act assigned exclusively to Provincial Legislation.

He followed this with a *declaratory* clause:

and for greater Certainty, but not so as to restrict the Generality of the foregoing Terms of this Section, it is hereby declared that the Legislative Authority of the Parliament of the United Colony extends to all Matters coming within the Classes of Subjects next hereinafter enumerated; that is to say ...

The federal enumerations remained largely as they were in the resolutions. However, Reilly made two significant changes in the provincial enumerations. He removed the limitation on 'property and civil rights'–'*excepting those portions thereof assigned to the General Parliament*' (which had been in the resolutions) – and completely eliminated the enumeration 'matters of a local or private nature.' Obviously well aware of the enormous potential of the breadth of property and civil rights with the qualification removed, Reilly added a very emphatic *deeming* clause at the end of what became section 91:

And any Matter coming within any of the Classes of Subjects enumerated in this Section shall not be deemed to come within the Subject of Property and Civil Rights comprised in the enumeration of the Classes of Subjects by this Act assigned exclusively to Provincial Legislation.

After receiving the London Resolutions, Reilly touched up his draft and sent it to Carnarvon on 17 January 1867.[31]

For two weeks, draft followed draft. 'The difficulties, the suggestions, the amendments during the last week have been endless,' Carnarvon informed the prime minister on 6 February.[32] Three days later, the draughtsmen, Reilly and the colonial attorneys general, finished what Sir Joseph Pope called the 'final draft.' The enacting and declaratory clauses remained as in Reilly's draft; the deeming clause, which had been in and out, was in to protect against an interpretation of property and civil rights which could encroach on the federal enumerations; and matters 'local and private,' which had been in and out, was out.[33] However, it was not until six o'clock on 12 February, when Carnarvon moved first reading in the House of Lords, that the real final draft was completed. 'Oh! Si tu savais, si tu savais,' Langevin exclaimed to his brother when the bill finally went to Parliament, for it had been necessary to 'y revoir, y revoir encore, et puis revoir quand d'autres y avaient vu ou y avaient mis la main.'[34]

In the three days after 9 February, three unquestionably interrelated changes were made to sections 91 and 92. Provincial jurisdiction over 'generally matters of a merely local and private nature' had reappeared without the qualification in the Quebec and London resolutions but with the addition of the word 'merely.' Provincial jurisdiction over property and civil rights was listed without qualification. There were, however, two critically important additions and alterations in section 91. The exclusivity and paramountcy of the federal enumerations had been reinforced in the declaratory clause by the addition of italicized words:

... and for greater certainty, but not so as to restrict the Generality of the foregoing Terms of this Section, it is hereby declared that (*notwithstanding anything in this Act*) the *exclusive* Legislative Authority of the Parliament of Canada extends to all Matters coming within the Classes of Subjects next hereinafter enumerated ...

The second was an alteration in the application of the deeming clause, which had previously been used to protect against property and civil rights. The draftsmen obviously believed that the reinforced declaratory clause adequately protected all federal enumerations against all provincial enumerations, including property and civil rights. Although it may not have been necessary, they used the deeming clause as an additional safeguard – with the singular 'Class' and the words 'comprised in' unchanged – to refer explicitly to 'Class of Matters of a local or private Nature comprised in the Enumerations of the Classes of Subjects assigned exclusively to the Legislatures of the Provinces.' No other plausible conclusions about the purpose and the interrelationship of the new provisions of the act can be reached on the basis of the drafting history and the language used.[35]

The drafting in London had provided a structural coherence, or logic, to the relationship between sections 91 and 92. Moreover, Reilly had also created a sequential approach to determining the appropriate home for federal or provincial legislation. The Quebec Resolutions had given each jurisdiction power to make laws 'respecting subjects' at the head of their respective sections and also 'generally respecting all matters' of either a general or local nature at the tail. In his first draft Reilly had empowered governments to make laws 'in relation to matters,' not subjects, 'coming within' the enumerated powers which he categorized as 'Classes of Subjects.' The sequence was first to identify the matter and then determine the 'class of subjects' within which it came. Only at that stage might the relationship of sections 91 and 92 be critical in the allocation of jurisdiction.[36]

Reilly and his Canadian associates in London had also made the exclusivity of the legislative jurisdiction of both levels of government much clearer than in the Quebec Resolutions. Within their allocated sphere, however they might be determined, both were autonomous and supreme. Jurisdictionally, coordinate or classical federalism was written into the constitution. The provision, based on the imperial model but with an undefined purpose, that the federal government could disallow provincial legislation qualified that legislative autonomy, but it could be exercised only at the discretion of the executive and was thus a matter of politics or policy, not of law, and its use was not justiciable. It would be the function of the courts to police the boundaries separating provincial and federal legislative jurisdiction.

There had been surprisingly little discussion of the enumerated heads or classes of subjects at the Quebec Conference or during the debate in the Canadian Assembly. As the jurisdictional allocation had been crafted by the Canadians, it obviously reflected their history and mirrored the broad terms on which the English and French majorities could live together in one state and apart as distinct societies. Collectively there was no mystery to the broad distribution of legislative authority, and presumably the terms used were well enough understood for immediate purposes and could be left for later dissection.[37]

The federal government was endowed with the capacity, the institutions, and the resources to develop and manage a national economy and ensure the expansion and viability of the new state. Although not exhaustive,[38] its enumerated powers included the unqualified regulation of trade and commerce,[39] fiscal and monetary policy, control of major financial institutions, navigation and shipping, the fisheries, interprovincial transportation, and communication. Most unusual, and apparently a radical departure from the Quebec Resolutions, was a provision removing from provincial jurisdiction any local work which the federal government unilaterally deemed to be for the general advantage of Canada.[40] Federal paramountcy in the shared fields of agriculture and immigration was consistent with the objective, as was federal jurisdiction over 'Indians, and Lands reserved for Indians' and 'Naturalization and Aliens.'[41]

To carry out its mandate, the federal government was given unlimited powers of taxation and capacity to borrow. Federal jurisdiction over criminal law and procedure was praised as a great improvement over the American state-centred system, balanced as it was on the one hand by provincial control over the administration of justice (including courts of criminal as well as civil jurisdiction) and, on the other, by the federal appointment of the judges of senior provincial courts.

The provinces retained their responsibility for the social, cultural, and, to some extent, business life of the community: local government, education, social services, reformatories, local transportation, the administration of justice, the enforcement of provincial laws by fines or imprisonment, the incorporation of companies with provincial objects, and 'generally all Matters of a merely local or private Nature in the Province.'[42] To finance their responsibilities, the provinces had to rely on direct taxation (then of little consequence), local licences, the returns from the management and sale of their public lands, and federal subsidies of $2.5 million annually.

'Property and civil rights,' qualified as it was from the outset, was not necessarily an exception to the local and private categorization of provincial powers. The phrase had come to Canada in the Quebec Act of 1774 as a guarantor of French law and custom, and it retained that broad significance, as 'a compendious description of the entire body of private law which governs the relationships between subject and subject, as opposed to the law which governs the relationships between the subject and the institutions of government,' in the Canadas before Confederation.[43]

Provincial jurisdiction over property and civil rights was not a matter of choice. As George Brown stated publicly, 'we have given nothing to the local bodies which did not necessarily belong to the localities, except education and the rights of property, and the civil law, which we were compelled to leave to the local governments in order to afford that protection which the Lower Canadians claim for their language and their laws, and their peculiar institutions.'[44] Charles Fisher, a New Brunswick delegate to Quebec and London, later observed that 'we know that while each Province evinced a justifiable jealousy on the subject, and a determination to reserve to the Local Legislature the exclusive right to deal with it, one Province made it a condition upon which alone it would enter the Union ... This subject ... was the primary question to be solved before any terms of Union could be agreed upon.'[45]

However, the 'justifiable jealousy' was apparently secondary to the agreement of the common law provinces at Quebec to add to the federal enumerations the power of 'rendering uniform all or any of the laws relative to property and civil rights ... And rendering uniform the procedure of all or any of the Courts in these provinces; but any Statute for this purpose shall have no force or authority in any province until sanctioned by the Legislature thereof.'[46] At London, the delegation added that 'the power of repealing, amending, or altering such Laws shall henceforward remain with the General Parliament only.'[47] Reilly removed the provision from the enumerations and, with his new wording, it emerged as section 94 of the constitution. This section declared that, after any such law was passed and adopted by a provincial legislature, the power of the federal government 'to make Laws in relation to any matter comprised in any such Act shall, not withstanding anything in this Act, be unrestricted.'

During the debate on the Quebec Resolutions, Macdonald had emphasized the importance of the provision and stated that it was 'understood, so far as we could influence the future, that the first act of the Confederate Government should be to procure an assimilation of the statutory law of all those provinces which has, at its root and foundation, the common law of England.' But he also drew applause when he added that 'no change in this respect should have the force and authority of law in any province until sanctioned by the Legislature of that Province.'[48]

Macdonald wasted little time. By the spring of 1868 he had decided on a commission for the purpose of preparing a measure for the assimilation of provincial laws. As he wrote to Sandfield Macdonald, premier of Ontario, given the similar foundation of the common law, 'there will be little difficulty in consolidating and assimilating their several Statute Laws.' Sandfield agreed that the 'project you have in view with reference to the assimilation of the laws is one of great importance and I agree with you that the task should be well executed.'[49]

However, when Macdonald included a budget for the proposed commission in 1869 and appointed John Henry Gray to undertake a preliminary study, David Mills opposed the move as one which 'would destroy the power of the Local Legislatures' and 'the present system of Federal Government' and declared that 'if it was a question whether Federal or Local Legislatures would be destroyed, the country would suffer far less by the destruction of the Federal power.' Edward Blake agreed that it was against 'sound policy' and warned that in Ontario 'his voice would be raised against such an occurrence.'[50] After a short debate, Mills's motion was lost eighty-one to thirty-three. In February 1871 Gray reported that, although the task would be enormous, 'an excellent Code of Law, simple in language, easily understood, expeditious and economical in its administration, could be formed from a judicious selection of the best of the Laws of each of the Provinces, by men who were severally acquainted with each.'[51] There the attempt died.

Despite his assurance during the debate on the Quebec Resolutions that 'we have avoided all conflict of jurisdiction and authority,' Macdonald was concerned about the conflict before the first constitutional decisions had emerged from the courts.[52] In addition to the commission, he also thought it would be

a good coup to get together the different Attorney Generals of the Dominion to discuss the great questions of the uniformity of the laws ... and we might settle some general system for future legislation, & endeavour to dispose of the questions of conflict of jurisdiction that will from time to time arise. I imagine that it will be found that in some cases the specification of the respective jurisdictions of the Local and Federal Parliaments, in the Union Act, is so indefinite as to prevent us coming to any satisfactory conclusion as to where the jurisdiction lies. In such cases by comparison of opinions we might settle where it *ought* to be, and apply to the Imperial Parliament for a declaratory Act settling the disputed points. This is the only way to prevent contradictory and embarrassing decisions of the various tribunals of the Dominion.[53]

The attorney generals never met.

The federal constitution was uniquely designed to accommodate the need for national cohesion and the preservation of local autonomy. To describe it as 'centralist' is to suggest that there is some normative or ideal federal system against which it can be measured. Jurisdictionally, the federal government was endowed with more power than the American. The transfer of the power of disallowance and the appointment of the provincial lieutenant governors from the imperial to the federal government even suggested to some a quasi-federal, hierarchical structure. Yet, politically, and constitutionally, the power of disallowance and the utility of the lieutenant governor as a federal officer proved to be incompatible with responsible government and provincial autonomy.[54] The evolution of Canadian federalism was to be largely driven by the tensions between regionalism and pluralism and between interdependence and pan-Canadianism as expressed on the battleground of politics.

Jurisdictionally, however, the law of the constitution was to be determined by the courts, regardless of how 'contradictory and embarrassing' their decisions might be. In the result, the failure to persuade Quebec to accept its constitutionalization as a distinct society and to implement section 94 proved for a long time to be decisive in the courtroom. As the American Paul Freund put it in a memorable analogy in 1953 just as appeals to the Judicial Committee had ended, the 'Canadian founders sought to effect a Copernican revolution in terms of their constitution. But the local power over property and civil rights in the province has turned out, after all, to be the central planet around which the sun of Dominion authority must rotate.'[55]

2

Made in Canada: The Provincial Courts, 1867–1881

Clearly the intentions of the framers ...
– Justice Charles Fisher, Supreme Court of New Brunswick, 1879

For a decade, the provincial superior courts, without benefit of precedent or authority, faced the challenge of judicial review of the federal constitution. The courts remained as they were on 1 July 1867. Members of the bench had been appointed by a variety of colonial governments and reflected all shades of political opinion. They were not necessarily men of exceptional talent. But as politicians, lawyers, and judges, they, and those appointed in the following decade, had directly participated, on both sides, in the debate over Confederation.[1]

In the first constitutional case to come before the courts, William Ritchie, chief justice of the Supreme Court of New Brunswick, more confident than prescient, asserted that 'it is difficult to conceive how the Imperial Parliament, in the distribution of legislative power, could have more clearly or more strongly secured, to the respective legislative bodies, the legislative jurisdiction they were respectively exclusively to exercise.'[2] However, within three years, Thomas Ramsay of the Quebec Court of Queen's Bench warned that until a general court of appeal was established 'we may fairly anticipate to see the most conflicting jurisdiction arising in the different provinces, and perhaps in the same province.'[3] Ramsay was unduly pessimistic. Although

there were inevitably differences in result, the federalism jurisprudence that emerged from the provincial courts in the first decade
revealed an intelligent and reasonable understanding of the language
and construction of   the constitution – even, one might suggest, of the
'intentions' of the designers.

Provincial court judges summarily dismissed the argument, infrequently made, that judicial review of provincial legislation was not
legitimate.[4] When the question first arose in *Chandler*, Chief Justice
Ritchie of New Brunswick stated that, put simply, the question before
the court was the supremacy of a constitution enacted by an imperial
statute. Pre-Confederation case law concerning insolvency was irrelevant because the 'British North America Act entirely changed the legislative constitution of the province ... The subordinate legislative body
of this Province, in defiance of this statute, has undertaken to legislate
on this subject ... Their right to do so is now contested, and under these
circumstances can there be any doubt as to what we are bound to do?
We think not.'[5]

The issue was thoroughly discussed in 1874 when William Badgley
of the Quebec Court of Queen's Bench questioned the legitimacy of a
judicial declaration that a provincial act was *ultra vires*. His brother
judges disagreed. The chief justice, Jean-François Duval, asked, 'Can
this Court interfere? I can have no hesitation in answering: "Yes." The
same law which has prescribed boundaries to the Legislative power
has imposed upon judges the duty of seeing that power is not exceeded.' Samuel Monck and Louis Drummond agreed that the court
had not only the 'right' but the 'duty' to declare a provincial statute
unconstitutional 'if it be in conflict with the Imperial Act which confers
a Constitution upon the Dominion.'[6] By 1875, Thomas Ramsay could
state categorically, with the approval of Chief Justice Antoine-Aimé
Dorion, that the 'question as to whether we can look into the constitutionality of a local law seems to suffer no difficulty, if an almost unanimous expression of opinion of those best qualified to judge be considered as authoritative for the decision of a practical matter.'[7]

The courts were also not impressed by the argument, frequently
made, that the federal power of disallowance somehow made judicial
review unnecessary and that an act not disallowed should therefore be
deemed *intra vires*. 'No power is given to the Governor General to
extend the power of the Local Legislature or enable it to override the
Imperial Statute,' said Ritchie in *Chandler*.[8] Chief Justice Duval was

equally dismissive: 'It has been argued that the power of disallowing Acts of the Local Legislature is given by the Imperial Parliament to the Governor General, and therefore that the Courts of Justice have no other duty to perform than that of yielding obedience to the Act. I confess that the extreme weakness of the argument on this point struck me as soon as the words were spoken ... On reference to the Imperial Act, I find it affords not the slightest ground for such an argument.'[9] In the Ontario Court of Queen's Bench, Adam Wilson dismissed the argument of counsel for Oliver Mowat, premier and attorney general, that because the power of disallowance existed the courts should adhere to the doctrine of the presumption of constitutionality:

The Courts under such constitutions which the Dominion and the Provinces possess will be obliged to declare when in their opinion, the Dominion has encroached upon the exclusive powers of the Provinces, and when the latter have usurped the higher powers of the Dominion ... There can be no restraint put upon the due exercise of the judicial power by any authority, Dominion or Provincial, for that would be to place these bodies above the law which created them, and granted them powers which are not absolute, and which no legislation of theirs can make so.[10]

But counsel for Ontario persisted with the argument that, with its power of disallowance, the federal government did not need the courts to protect its interests. In the Court of Queen's Bench, Chief Justice Robert Harrison bluntly replied that the failure 'to disallow is not to be deemed in any manner as making valid an Act ... which is essentially void as being against the constitution.'[11] Hearing the same argument on appeal, George Burton of the Court of Appeal agreed that the power of disallowance existed 'to prevent any legislation which tends to obstruct, defeat or impede the Dominion legislation. No doubt there is this additional check ... but whether allowed or not, to the extent that the Provincial Acts transcend the competence of the Provincial legislature they are void.'[12] Thomas Ramsay best summarized judicial opinion in 1882 when he observed that the 'true check for the abuse of powers, as distinguished from the unlawful exercise of them, is the power of the central Government to disallow laws open to the former reproach. Probably to a certain class of mind this interference appears harsh and provocative of grave complications as has been said; but this is hardly an argument in favour of the Courts extending their jurisdiction to relieve the central government of its responsibilities.'[13]

Judges in the provincial courts were thoroughly familiar with the well-established principles of statutory construction and, within limits, applied them to their new federalism jurisprudence. As Chief Justice John Allen of the New Brunswick Supreme Court stated, 'where the words of an Act of Parliament are plain and unambiguous, and without anything in the Act to limit or control them, Courts are bound to construe them in their plain and ordinary sense. In such a case, we can look to nothing but the language of the Act, giving the words of the Statute their ordinary meaning, to carry out what the Legislature in words enacts.' Responding to counsel's argument about the applicability of section 92(10) to the local railway in question, Allen replied that 'it is unnecessary for us to speculate on what may have influenced the Parliament, or to discuss the policy of the Act. It is sufficient that the language of the Act is, in our opinion, clear and unambiguous; and in such a case, its provisions must be respected and obeyed by all.'[14] But judges often reasoned with the knowledge, as C.K. Allen put it in his critique of British jurisprudence, that words 'mean nothing in themselves: the very conception of interpretation connotes the introduction of elements which are necessarily extrinsic to the words themselves.'[15]

The extrinsic elements, or context, most frequently appealed to were a history through which the judges had lived and sometimes helped to shape. The most personal was the observation of Charles Fisher of the New Brunswick Supreme Court: 'As I was party to the various discussions relating to the Union [at Quebec and London], and know the object of placing the fisheries under the control of the Dominion, I may have allowed myself to be influenced by that consideration.'[16] Many judges referred to the political context of Confederation itself, particularly to the 'melancholy warfare' in the United States which made the framers 'determined that there should be no question as to the supremacy of the General Government, or the subordinate position of our Provinces. It was intended that the General Legislature should be stronger, far stronger than the Federal Legislature of the United States in relation to the State Governments.'[17]

Although aware of their limited validity, judges nonetheless used the Confederation debates in 1865 and the opinions of the 'fathers' in rendering their decisions. Seeking evidence for his conclusion that a Quebec tax on insurance policies was *ultra vires*, Henri-Elzéar Taschereau of the Quebec Superior Court asked: 'Can the Constitution have intended this? I do not think so; and in support of my opinion I will take the liberty of referring to the history of our Constitution, and of citing two or three extracts which took place in our Parliament at the time of the debate on Confederation.' Of course, he continued, 'the Imperial statute must, as any other statute, be construed by itself, and the opinions I have referred to are not legal authorities ... But can it be said that a commentary on a law by the author of that law should have no weight?'[18] Long after the Judicial Committee had barred any reference to history, Canadian courts continued to admit such evidence in argument and even use it in decision. As Oliver Mowat commented in argument before the Supreme Court of Canada in 1888: 'In various cases that have been decided, I am not quite sure whether in this Court, or in other Courts, reference has been made to the resolutions upon which the British North America Act was founded. What degree of importance should be attached to them has not been stated, but at all events it is reasonable for judges to look at them, and if they do find that they throw any light on the subject, they should avail themselves of that light.'[19]

Explicitly, but more often implicitly, context was found in pre-Confederation practices and institutions.[20] The clearest exposition of this – sometimes problematic – extrinsic aid was provided by William Buell Richards, chief justice of the Ontario Court of Queen's Bench. 'We must assume, what is not probably at all doubted,' that the terms used in the constitution were those determined by the Canadians. Therefore, he argued, when the BNA Act used the word 'Municipal Institutions,' the very words of a Canadian statute of 1866, 'can there be any reasonable doubt that it was expected and intended that the "municipal institutions" which were to be constituted under that authority, would possess the same powers as those which were then in existence, under the same name, in the Province? I should think not.' On those grounds, Ontario legislation prohibiting the retail sale of liquor was upheld.

Speaking of language more generally and perhaps more accurately, Richards added: 'And when words and expressions are imported into this Act which have been in common use in legislating for these Provinces, we must continue interpreting these words in the same manner and to mean the same thing as we decided they meant in statutes passed by our own Legislatures. It would create great difficulties and inconvenience if we did not act on this rule.'[21] Chief Justice Dorion agreed in finding that the regulation or prohibition of retail liquor sales was a matter of local regulation: 'In the absence of any expression to restrict the powers so conferred, they must be understood to comprise all those matters, which at the time the union was effected, had been considered by the then existing legislatures as belonging to municipal institutions and as being of a local or provincial character.'[22]

Judges and counsel also relied heavily on American jurisprudence. In all the major licensing and taxing cases and those involving the scope of trade and commerce, American case law was discussed at length, the similarities and differences in the federal structures being explained to justify the argument or the decision. As John Ritchie of the Nova Scotia Supreme Court stated in 1876, although 'the decisions in these cases are not binding upon us, the opinion of the Judges of a Court of so high a character as that of the Supreme Court of the United States, are entitled to the greatest respect; and the reasoning on which their decisions are founded commends itself very much to my judgement.'[23] American commentary on the doctrines governing judicial review, as well as the distribution of powers, was also frequently introduced in argument and decision. John Hagarty of the Ontario Court of Queen's Bench made no apologies for his use of American jurisprudence:

Whether the governing principles be set forth in the written constitution of the United States, or be embodied in an Act of Parliament, as in our case, creates no difficulty in my mind ... as to the application of the broad principles laid down by the distinguished American jurists so often referred to in this discussion. Our law books are necessarily almost barren of authority on the subject of limited Parliamentary jurisdiction. It is to the Marshalls and the Storys of the neighbouring Republic ... that we have to look for guidance and assistance on a subject most familiar to them – most unfamiliar to us.[24]

There are few greater fictions in the history of Canadian constitutional law than the statement, so often repeated, that the Judicial Committee imposed 'coordinate' or 'classical' federalism on the constitution or, as some would say, 'discovered' the principle.[25] When they examined the macro-structure of the federal constitution, Canadian judges agreed that the central government, with its power of disallowance, the appointment of the lieutenant governor, and the residual power, had been given a constitutional and political status superior to that of the provinces, and that politically the provinces were subordinate. Few went as far as Thomas Ramsay, usually given to decisions upholding provincial legislation, in his contemptuous dismissal of the pretensions of the provincial governments, but few would have disagreed. 'It was asserted that the Local Legislatures were not of a subordinate character,' he observed in 1875.

I do not desire to say unnecessarily what may be offensive ... but since the comparison (proverbially odious) is thrust upon us in argument, I shall not avoid saying what is evidently true. Its inferior rank and dignity to those of Parliament are marked in every way – by the appointment of the highest branch by the Executive of the Dominion, by its powers being special and not general, by its territorial jurisdiction being less extensive, and above all by its legislation being subject to disallowance by the Governor-General.[26]

In the law governing the distribution of legislative authority, 'coordinate' or 'classical' federalism was explicit in the constitution. However, there was no suggestion of 'equal' sovereignty, of parallel residual powers, or powers possessed by the provinces other than those specifically stated in the constitution. As Adam Wilson of the Ontario Court of Queen's Bench emphasized:

The Provinces have properly a written and defined constitution, limited as to purposes and objects. The Dominion has in part a written and defined constitution, but it is not wholly limited by it. It possesses powers which are neither defined nor limited ... It may be said to have general jurisdiction, or, in the language of constitutional writers, general sovereignty, in all matters but those in which it is expressly excluded, or in which from the inherent condition of a dependency it is necessarily or impliedly restricted.[27]

In that sense the courts upheld the view expressed in the Confederation debates that whatever 'sovereignty' there was lay in the residual clause. And although the words 'compact' or 'treaty' were used frequently, they were not so read as to endorse any legal view of the compact theory. John Hagarty observed that, unlike the American states, 'Ontario can never be looked on as a Sovereign State surrendering certain of her rights to the Government of a Federation of which she consents to form a part. Our Province is the creation of the Imperial Parliament.'[28]

There was, however, no dissent from the doctrine that provincial subordination did not extend to legislation that fell within their jurisdiction. Canada was a federation, not a legislative union, John Spragge, chancellor of Ontario, emphasized in 1872: 'To the Provincial Legislature is committed the power to legislate upon a wide range of subjects which is indeed limited, but that within the limits prescribed the right of legislation is absolute.'[29] Chief Justice Dorion concurred: 'In their respective sphere the authority of the Dominion and Local

Parliaments are co-extensive, that is, the one is not inferior nor sub-ordinate to the other.'[30] By 1880, Thomas Ramsay could state cate-gorically that 'it appears to me that it is undeniable that the local Legislature, acting within the scope of its powers, has a right to legis-late as absolute as the Dominion Parliament legislating within the scope of its powers. Indeed, this doctrine as to the respective powers of the Dominion and local Legislatures seems to me to be almost the only one on which there has been entire unanimity of opinion.'[31]

The courts were equally unequivocal about the meaning and rela-tionship of the enacting and declaratory clauses of section 91. There was no doubt that the enacting clause was truly residual. As Francis Johnson of the Quebec Superior Court stated, 'the Imperial Act seems in effect to have said: Notwithstanding anything in this Act, notwith-standing that we have enumerated the most salient subjects on which the Dominion Legislature may make laws, it must be clearly under-stood that there is nothing at all to prevent them from legislating for the whole Dominion in matters not to be found in the list of those given to them, and not assigned to the provinces.'[32] As a result, declared Henri-Elzéar Taschereau, to determine the home of chal-lenged legislation 'it is sufficient to refer to the 92nd section, and see if by that section the subject-matter is or is not put under the control of the Provincial Power. If not, it comes within the legislative authority of the Federal Parliament even if it is not one of the classes of subjects specially enumerated.'[33]

Robert Harrison, chief justice of Ontario, agreed: 'The inference which I draw from the reading of these two sections is, that unless a legislative power be found clearly to have been conferred on the Pro-vincial Legislatures by sec. 92, it remains an unenumerated power with the Legislature of the Dominion.'[34] Like so many others, Harrison emphasized that the enumerations were not exhaustive. 'No words used in reference to legislation could be more comprehensive' than those in the enacting clause. 'Examples, however, are given of the exclusive legislative powers as to different classes of subjects intended to be vested in the Dominion Parliament. These it is expressly declared are not "to restrict the generality of the foregoing terms" of the sec-tion.'[35] In short, the residual and declaratory clauses meant exactly what they said.[36]

However, there was a lack of clarity when the courts attempted to define the application, not the purpose, of the deeming clause at the end of section 91. Frequently the clause was simply quoted directly, or when paraphrased both the words 'class' or 'classes' of matters of a local or private nature were used. As a result, it was not clear whether judges believed it applied to all of section 92 or only to 92(16). But its purpose was clear. As Frederick Torrance of the Quebec Superior Court stated, citing the declaratory and deeming clauses: 'In other words, the Imperial Act declares, first, what the Parliament of Canada alone can do, and then, to make its meaning plainer declares what the Local Legislature shall not do.'[37] This correct distinction between the affirmative and negative purpose of the two clauses was often made.

Christopher Dunkin, also of the Quebec Superior Court, believed that the deeming clause was added 'unnecessarily' in view of 'the plain and strong enactment' at the head of section 91.[38] But many judges regarded it as the ultimate protector of federal paramountcy in case of conflict, perhaps because most challenged legislation was provincial. Ramsay repeatedly observed that, in cases of what he called 'clashing' between matters that seemed to fall within two enumerations, the deeming clause was conclusive. As he wrote, the 'inconvenience' of apparently overlapping powers 'did not escape the observations of the framers of the bill, for they have terminated section 91 by a saving clause of great importance which makes section 92 subordinate to section 91.'[39]

With general agreement in all provinces on the double protection for the federal enumerations and the residuality of the enacting clause, questions before the courts turned on the scope of the enumerated powers. Although the jurisdictional location of many 'matters' came before the courts – insolvency, insurance, taxation, liquor licensing (including regulation and prohibition) and fisheries – the issue was often the location of matter within, and the relative scope of, either the regulation of trade and commerce or property and civil rights. Courts generally agreed on what became known as 'mutual modification'; both had to be limited to allow room for the other. But on the whole – certainly in view of later doctrine – trade and commerce was given a relatively broad and property and civil rights a narrow scope. There was seldom a suggestion that the federal power over trade and commerce excluded intra-provincial activities.

In 1875 Chief Justice Ritchie, speaking for the Supreme Court of New Brunswick, gave an impossibly broad definition of trade and commerce. Echoing John Marshall's comments in *Gibbon v. Ogden*, Ritchie stated:

The regulation of trade and commerce must involve full power over the matter to be regulated, and must necessarily exclude the interference of all other bodies that would attempt to intermeddle with the same thing. The power thus given to the Dominion Parliament is general, without limitation or restriction, and therefore must include traffic in articles of merchandise, not only in connection with foreign countries, but also that which is internal between different Provinces of the Dominion, as well as that which is carried on within the limits of an individual Province.

Ritchie thus denied the province the power to prohibit the sale of liquor but, with an early version of the 'aspect' doctrine, he added that the regulation of sale of liquor by retail 'would have nothing to do with trade and commerce, but with good order and Local Government, matters of municipal police and not of commerce ...'[40]

Four years later, the same court found the Canada Temperance Act unconstitutional because of its impact on a wide variety of provincial powers and revenues, not because of the limited scope of trade and commerce. 'It was clearly the intention of the framers of the Act,' declared Charles Fisher, one of the framers, 'that Parliament should have power to regulate the trade between the several Provinces, and the internal trade of each Province as well as the foreign trade of the whole Dominion.'[41]

In 1875 the Ontario Court of Queen's Bench heard concurrent challenges to provincial legislation licensing brewers and empowering municipalities to prohibit the retail sale of liquor. In *R. v. Taylor* the court denied the province the power to license brewers, who were already licensed by the federal government. 'It does relate to property and civil rights,' wrote Adam Wilson, 'but it does so by restraining and in that way regulating trade and commerce, and to that extent it usurps the power it should be subordinated to.'[42] However, in *Re Slavin and the Corporation of the Village of Orillia*, Chief Justice Richards, speaking for the court, upheld the prohibitory power as matter historically falling within 'Municipal Institutions' and inherently a matter of a local or private nature.[43] Endorsing Richard's comments, Wilson added in his decision in *Taylor*: 'And I think so, although the Dominion Government has the absolute power to regulate trade and commerce internal in each Province, as well as the foreign trade and commerce and the trade and commerce between the separate provinces, which is a far greater power than is possessed by the United States Government, for the supreme power there does not extend to the internal

trade of any of the States of the Union.' But in this instance, he concluded, the federal power was 'modified' by the 'right to exercise
the municipal powers which were possessed at the time of Confederation ... and which are not actually repugnant to the newly constituted authority of the Dominion.'[44]

In Quebec, the provincial power to prohibit the sale of liquor was
initially denied because it conflicted with the federal power over trade
and commerce. Louis Caron and Christopher Dunkin of the Superior
Court were agreed, as Caron stated, that the federal power 'is general,
and without restriction, and must of necessity include as well the internal trade and commerce of each Province as that of the whole Dominion.'[45] The decision was appealed, and a unanimous Quebec Supreme
Court found provincial prohibition essentially a matter of local regulation which historically had belonged to local institutions. However, to
dismiss the argument that it conflicted with trade and commerce, Chief
Justice Dorion offered a much narrower scope for trade and commerce
than most of the bench. The federal power, he suggested, 'ought to be
restricted to those branches of commerce of a broader application than
those already enumerated, and which are specially provided for in section 91, such as the import and export trade of the country, customs
and excise duties, and generally all those matters of trade affecting the
whole Dominion, or more than one of the provinces, or their trade relations with one another, or with the Empire, or any of its possessions.'[46]

In most of the liquor cases, the federal power over trade and commerce faced history as much as law because many judges found the
pre-Confederation practice irresistible. In several other cases, however,
the courts tested the power more on its own terms. When Quebec
imposed a tax on federally or British-incorporated insurance companies, the province claimed jurisdiction under its licensing power 92(9)
while the companies argued for immunity under 91(2). In a decision
laden with American precedents, Frederick Torrance of the Superior
Court concluded that, if the American government had legislated
respecting insurance companies as Ottawa had done in 1868, 'the
State would not be allowed to impose a further tax.' The reasoning was
even more conclusive in Canada where 'our Dominion Legislature
has greater powers in that it has exclusive control over trade and
commerce.'[47]

The province failed in its appeal to the Court of Queen's Bench. In a
lengthy judgment, H.-E. Taschereau decided that the tax could not be
upheld under either direct taxation or licensing. 'But I will go one step

further, and, taking into consideration that the respondents' company (and all similar companies) is a commercial company, and that its contracts are entirely of a commercial character (C.C. 24, 70), I find that, by the Imperial Statutes, these companies and such companies, in express and clear terms, are subject to the legislative authority and are under the exclusive control of the Federal Parliament' under 91(2).

Dismissing the appeal on the grounds that it was not a direct tax, Chief Justice Dorion observed that the regulation of insurance companies could be a difficult constitutional question. On the one hand, the local government had licensed the companies before 1867 and the power would appear to have been continued under section 129. 'On the other hand, it is urged with considerable force that a license means a permit, and if they have a right to permit, this implies a right to prohibit, and, therefore, to regulate a matter affecting the trade of the country, which the Provincial Legislatures undoubtedly have not. But I have already said we are not at present called upon to give an opinion on this point.' In dissent, Ramsay maintained that, while it 'is admitted that the business of insurance belongs to trade and commerce,' the tax itself fell within 92(9), the provincial licensing power, and was valid although 'subject always ... as all other legislation, to the controlling power of the Dominion Government.'[48]

In Ontario, where the issue was the power of the province to determine the statutory conditions on insurance policies in order to protect the insured, the courts had no difficulty locating the legislation within property and civil rights and dismissing the trade and commerce argument. In *Parsons* v. *Citizens Insurance Company* – a federally incorporated company – the Court of Queen's Bench and the Court of Appeal upheld the legislation. George Burton stated bluntly that

policies of insurance, being more contracts of indemnity against loss by fire, are like any other personal contracts between parties governed by the local or provincial law, can, I assume admit of no question ... The point that policies were transactions coming within the words trade and commerce, and so within the exclusive jurisdiction of the Dominion Parliament, was not taken in the reasons of appeal, nor I believe pressed on the argument, and would appear to be clearly untenable.[49]

In *Parsons* v. *Queen Insurance Company*, heard at the same time, the trade and commerce argument was more deliberately made. Speaking for a unanimous court, Thomas Moss declared that it could 'not be sustained.' As authority he cited *Paul* v. *Virginia* where Justice Stephen Johnson Field of the U.S. Supreme Court, stated categorically that 'issuing a policy of insurance is not a transaction of commerce. The policies are simply contracts of indemnity against loss by fire.'[50]

The determination of the difference between legislation that was 'in relation to' from that which 'affected' or 'interfered with' was implicitly and explicitly before the courts in many cases where the federal enumerated powers – and even the residual clause – were pitted against provincial enumerations, particularly property and civil rights. In *Chandler*, Ritchie had confidently stated that, where a subject was exclusively assigned to one legislature, 'the subject so exclusively assigned is as completely taken away from the others, as if they had been expressly forbidden to act upon it.'[51] The effect of that decision, Chief Justice John Allen of New Brunswick concluded, 'is that the Local Legislature has no right to deal with any subject which, even indirectly, relates to a matter over which the Dominion Parliament has the exclusive power of legislation.'[52]

But it was soon evident that it was impossible to draw such a sharp line with enumerations of broad scope and indefinite boundaries. As Wilson wrote in *Taylor*, property and civil rights are 'subjects of a very comprehensive range. Everything may be said to be embraced within the generality of these terms ... There is no law which does not, and none that can be passed which will not relate to property and civil rights.' Their scope, therefore, 'must be limited by the powers which are expressly or necessarily by implication vested in the Dominion Parliament, for that body has exclusive power over many subjects of property and civil rights, and also general sovereignty.[53] Chief Justice Allen agreed: 'In no other way, that I can see, can full effect be given to the positive and unambiguous words of the 91st section, and the two sections be made consistent.'[54] Legislating under its enumerated powers could not be held to 'be an invasion of' property and civil rights, observed John Spragge, chief justice of Ontario. 'To hold otherwise would be to nullify the powers of Parliament.'[55] Acalus Palmer of the Supreme Court of New Brunswick agreed that, if the matter was not in pith and substance within section 92, the federal government could legislate under the residual power even if it might affect or interfere with enumerated provincial powers.[56]

As Wilson discussed at length in *Taylor*, the question was one of pith and substance, not incidental interference or encroachment. If every law affected property and civil rights, so too would most provincial enactments affect trade and commerce. Citing many provincial statutes that *affected* trade and commerce but were not in pith and substance a *regulation* of it, he observed: 'All these are lawful objects, and if they can be properly adopted they do not become unlawful because they cannot be wholly separated from every other matter, and because they are attended with their inevitable consequences.' In an early, and somewhat confusing, version of the 'aspect' doctrine,[57] Wilson argued that there could be instances where both had legislated 'with respect to the same subject, and each with equal force and power, and when the subject dealt with may or may not be a regulation of trade, according to which of the two bodies is legislating upon it.' No statute, he declared, 'is ever held to be an excess of power and unconstitutional unless on the clearest proof that it is so.' The true doctrine, he suggested, was to be found in *Story*: 'In cases of implied limitations or prohibition of power, it is not sufficient to show a possible or potential inconvenience. There must be plain incompatibility, a direct repugnancy, or an extreme or practical inconvenience leading irresistibly to the same conclusion.'[58]

By the 1880s, two similar doctrines seem to have been established by the provincial courts. One was summarized by Chief Justice Dorion of Quebec in 1881: 'We consider as a proper rule of interpretation, in all these cases, that, when a power is given, either to the Dominion or to the provincial legislatures, to legislate on certain subjects coming clearly within the class of subjects which either legislature has a right to deal with, such power includes all the incidental subjects of legislation which are necessary to carry on the subject which the B.N.A. act declared should be carried on by the legislature.'[59] The second was expressed by Thomas Ramsay when he pointed to a rule of interpretation

which has been frequently recognized, and which it is important to keep in view; namely, that where a power is specially granted to one or the other legislature, that power will not be nullified by the fact that, *indirectly*, it affects a special power granted to the other legislature. This is incontestable as to the power granted to Parliament (Sect. 91 last *aliena*, B.N.A. Act), and probably it is equally so as to the power granted to the local legislature. In other words, it is only in the case of absolute incompatibility that the special power granted to the local legislature gives way.[60]

Although the doctrines emerging from the provincial courts were comparable, a judiciary so territorially divided could not provide

authoritative precedents for either a common template for the application of sections 91 and 92 or definitions of scope to guide the courts in
policing the boundaries of the enumerated powers. As early as 1870,
when Macdonald proposed the establishment of a Supreme Court,
Chief Justice Ritchie of New Brunswick observed that an 'efficient
appellate tribunal as a Court of *dernier ressort*, and whose precedents
would be a rule of decision for the Courts of all the Provinces, is without doubt much required.'[61] From the Quebec bench, Thomas Ramsay
and Louis Drummond agreed. While a general court of appeal would
not relieve the provincial courts of deciding constitutional cases, wrote
Ramsay, appeals to a new court 'will have the effect of making the
jurisprudence certain and uniform on these important questions.'[62]
Drummond even suggested that whenever 'the constitutionality of a
law is called in question, let it be immediately evoked to the Supreme
Tribunal.'[63]

Such a court was unquestionably a necessity. However, in the decade
before they were captive to the doctrines and precedents of the
Supreme Court and the Judicial Committee, the provincial superior
courts had done no injustice to the language or structure of the federal
constitution they had inherited.

3

Made in Canada:
The Supreme Court of Canada,
1875–1881

For the harmonious working of our young constitution ...
– Télésphore Fourmer, 1875

Soon after Confederation, Sir John A. Macdonald began to consider how best to fulfil the promise of section 101 of the BNA Act which authorized the government to establish a 'General Court of Appeal for Canada.'[1] But pacifying Nova Scotia and Red River, acquiring the west, and planning a railway to the Pacific were matters demanding more immediate attention, and nothing had been accomplished before his defeat in 1873. Two years later, the Liberals announced in the throne speech that a Supreme Court was 'essential to our system of jurisprudence and to the settlement of constitutional questions.'[2] The court would hear appeals from the highest court of last resort in the provinces, as well as appeals *per saltum* (directly) from provincial courts of original jurisdiction with the consent of both parties. If a province passed enabling legislation, constitutional cases in lower courts could be removed to the Supreme Court for determination. The bill provided that the federal cabinet could also apply to the court for advisory opinions on 'any matter whatever.' Its opinion, however, according to Télésphore Fournier, the minister of justice, would have no legal standing and 'would merely have its moral weight in assisting the Government to arrive at a determination.'[3]

The establishment of the court, Fournier said, 'had for its sole object the harmonious working of our young constitution.' Judicial review by an 'independent, neutral and impartial court' was much more satisfactory than the review of provincial legislation by the minister of justice and 'would prevent difficulties with the Provinces, some of which infringed on the rights of the Dominion, as the Dominion sometimes interfered with their rights.' As a result, the provinces 'would accept the court as suggested, because they entertained the same desire as this Government to refer all cases of this kind to a tribunal whose decisions would be accepted by all parties.' Moreover, 'it was very important that the Federal Government should have an institution of its own in order to secure the due execution of its laws. There might perhaps come a time when it would not be very safe for the Federal Government to be at the mercy of the tribunals of the Provinces. He believed this to be an anomaly contrary to the spirit of our Constitution.'[4]

To David Mills, however, the anomaly was a federal court empowered to hear appeals on matters within provincial jurisdiction. In his pure classical federal state, the judiciary should mirror the same divisions as executive and legislative authority.[5] But with the exception of Mills and some Quebec members concerned about civil-law appeals, there was little opposition and the bill was approved.[6] No one suggested that a court created and staffed by the federal government would not be an impartial constitutional umpire.

The early jurisprudence of the Supreme Court, limited as it was, has been criticized or condemned for the centralist 'bias' in its federalism decisions. In 1900 Richard Haldane stated that the 'judges took, or were supposed to take, the view that the meaning of the Confederation Act was that the largest interpretation was to be put upon the powers of the Central or Dominion Government ... and a series of decisions ... certainly gave colour to that view.'[7] A century later, Paul Romney, an equally passionate advocate of provincial sovereignty, lamented that even a bench appointed by Liberals 'had turned out to be unreliable' and 'insensitive to the limits on Ottawa's legislative power.'[8] However, Professor Bora Laskin, an ardent centralist, found that although there were individual disagreements over jurisdiction, a court composed of judges 'for whom Confederation was a personal experience with an evident meaning' had displayed a uniquely Canadian 'sensitivity' for the British North America Act, admittedly in decisions usually favourable to the federal government.[9]

The Supreme Court's freedom to set its own course, unbound by the precedents and doctrines of the Judicial Committee of the Privy Council, was short-lived. By the early 1880s, its subservience to the Judicial Committee was increasing, and by the end of the century the Judicial Committee had thrown its decisions and doctrines into the ashcan of history.

The Supreme Court heard six federalism appeals in the four years before it was overtaken by the Judicial Committee. Not surprisingly, both its approach to judicial review and its jurisprudence were similar to those in the provincial courts since four of its six initial appointments and two replacements in 1878 and 1879 had sat on constitutional cases in the provincial courts.[10] Of the two who had not, William Henry had been at the Quebec and London conferences where, as attorney general of Nova Scotia, he had worked on the drafting committee. As minister of justice in the Alexander Mackenzie government, Fournier had one year's experience reviewing provincial legislation.

Although five of the six decisions favoured the federal government and later led to the charge that the court had a centralist bias, all but one of the eight judges involved had been appointed by the Liberal government of Alexander Mackenzie. However, there is nothing to suggest that in making these appointments either Mackenzie or Edward Blake, when minister of justice, considered their views on federalism. Similarly, Macdonald's selection of John Wellington Gwynne in 1879 has recently been attributed to his centralist views,[11] but contemporaries applauded the appointment of the senior puisne judge of the Court of Common Pleas, in whom 'the profession and public in Ontario have such entire confidence,' and pointed to his equity expertise rather than to his constitutional views.[12] Ironically, rivalling Gwynne in his strongly centralist interpretation of the constitution was Henri-Elzéar Taschereau, a Liberal appointee in 1878 who, as a Bleu member of the Assembly, had deserted his party in 1865 to oppose Confederation as 'the ruin of our nationality.'[13]

The Supreme Court was acutely conscious of its nation-building task and, initially at least, seemed to feel that its decisions would be the law of the land. Ritchie made the point most eloquently in his first decision after succeeding Richards as chief justice in 1879:

In view of the great diversity of judicial opinion that has characterized the decisions of the provincial tribunals in some provinces, and the judges in all, while it would seem to justify the wisdom of the Dominion Parliament, in providing for the establishment of a Court of Appeal such as this, where such diversity shall be considered and an authoritative declaration of the law be enunciated, so it enhances the responsibility of those called on in the midst of such conflict of opinion to declare authoritatively the principles by which both federal and local legislation are governed.[14]

Whether upholding or rejecting provincial or federal claims to jurisdiction, few of the several dozen opinions of individual judges in the six constitutional cases heard in the first four years reflected an obsession with a narrow or technical approach to statutory interpretation. Rather, in the full knowledge that they were somehow defining a new federal constitution, the judges were overtly conscious that their task was to find its meaning by placing that constitutional text in its historical context. In the first constitutional case to come before the court, Chief Justice Richards began his decision with the observation that in 'deciding important questions' it was essential that they 'consider the circumstances' surrounding the creation of the new state and the determination of the founders to avoid the 'evils' of states' rights. 'It may be that I do not take a sufficiently technical view of the matter, that I look too much to the surrounding circumstances ... and that my mind is too much influenced by those circumstances,' he admitted,

but I consider the question to be decided is of the very greatest importance to the well working of the system of government under which we now live. I consider the power now claimed [by Ontario to license brewers and distillers licensed by Canada] to interfere with the paramount authority of the Dominion Parliament in matters of trade and commerce and indirect taxation, so pregnant with evil, and so contrary to what appears to me to be the manifest intention of the framers of the *British North America Act*, that I cannot come to the conclusion that it is conferred by the language cited as giving that power.[15]

A year later, in dismissing the argument in *Valin* that the federal government could not impose a mode of procedure on provincial courts in matters under federal jurisdiction, Ritchie also stepped outside the boundaries of the BNA Act. 'The Statutes of Parliament, from its first session to the last,' he stated, 'show that such an idea has never been entertained by those who took the most active part in the establishment of Confederation, and who had most to do with framing the *British North America Act*, the large majority of whom sat in the first Parliament.'[16]

This appeal to history and the testimony of men and documents relevant to that history often informed the reasoning in the court. Long after the Judicial Committee had barred any reference to history (often preferring its own historical assumptions), the Supreme Court, like the provincial courts, continued to admit such evidence in argument and use it in decision. As Samuel Strong wrote in 1887

In construing this enactment ['lands reserved for Indians'] we are not only entitled but bound to apply that well established rule which requires us, in placing a meaning upon descriptive terms and definitions contained in statutes, to have recourse to external aids derived from the surrounding circumstances and the history of the subject-matter dealt with, and to construe the enactment by the light derived from such sources, and so to put ourselves as far as possible in the position of the legislature whose language we have to expound. If this rule were rejected and the language of the statute were considered without such assistance from extrinsic facts, it is manifest that the task of interpretation would degenerate into mere speculation and guess work.[17]

Oliver Mowat agreed. He observed a year later, as we have seen, that if the judges found that the Quebec Resolutions 'throw any light on the subject, they should avail themselves of that light.'[18]

As they had in the provincial courts, both counsel and judges made frequent reference to American case law and authorities. Yet, as they acknowledged, the distribution of jurisdiction was structured differently in the two countries, with the issue often being the applicability, not the relevance or legitimacy, of introducing comparative federal constitutional law in a Canadian court. Pre-Confederation practices also influenced, and sometimes seemed to determine, reasoning and decision. However, counsel and judges realized that practices had differed in the colonies, and Ritchie bluntly took exception to Richard's examination 'by the light of an *Ontario* candle alone.'[19]

In its first constitutional case, the Supreme Court heard arguments based less on the facts of the dispute than on an inspired version of the law and theory of Canadian federalism. *Severn* v. *The Queen* was a challenge to Ontario legislation compelling brewers and distillers, already licensed by the federal government, to have an Ontario licence as well.[20] In 1874 the Mowat government had deliberately removed an earlier exemption for federally licensed brewers, presumably to test the power.[21] The Court of Queen's Bench had found the legislation *ultra vires* but was overruled by the Court of Error and Appeal.[22] When a similar facts case came before it in *Severn*, the Court of Queen's Bench bluntly said that it did not agree with the higher court, but, since the case was going to the Supreme Court, accepted it as precedent.[23] The facts of the case pitted the federal power of trade and commerce against the provincial licensing power for purposes of local revenue. But that was not the issue Premier Oliver Mowat placed before the court.

In a lengthy factum and in argument before the court, Mowat drew on his version of Confederation to support his contention that the distribution of power was almost the reverse of what the BNA Act said, and that the true location of the residual power lay with the provinces:

I claim for the Provinces the largest power which they can be given: it is the spirit of the *B.N.A. Act*, and it is the spirit under which Confederation was agreed to. If there was one point which all parties agreed upon, it was that all local powers should be left to the Provinces and that all powers previously possessed by the Local Legislatures should be continued unless expressly repealed by the *B.N.A. Act*. The larger powers given to the Dominion were for the purposes of nationality, so that in construing the *B.N.A. Act*, the intention was not to take from Provincial authorities any more than what was necessary.[24]

The factum outlined the constitutional doctrines on which Mowat based his argument. The province possessed 'inherent constitutional power to enact all such laws as it thinks best for the welfare of the people of the Province,' and 'with respect to such matters its powers are as full and complete as those of the Dominion and Imperial Parliaments in relation to matters Canadian and Imperial respectively.' Section 92, particularly subsections 13 and 16, he contended, confirmed the argument that 'in each Province was constituted a *plenum imperium* and not a subordinate authority, or one only with such powers as were specially conferred.' Finally, the jurisdiction conferred by section 92 was such as 'to exclude the authority of the Parliament of Canada in relation to matters coming within the classes of subjects enumerated in that section, and where the Legislature possesses jurisdiction the Court has no power to review the exercise of it.'[25]

Three years later, Mowat elaborated the last doctrine to admit, and interpret, the existence of the declaratory clause. In his brief for counsel before the Judicial Committee in *Parsons*, Mowat insisted that, despite the 'notwithstanding' clause, the federal enumerations were restrained by the enacting clause: 'The enumeration may contain some particulars which, unless so specified, would not have been held to be included in the general words but, having reference to the general object which is so stated, and to the form of the section, each article in the enumeration is, where possible and as far as possible, to be construed as not to include the powers assigned exclusively to the Legislatures of the Provinces.'[26] By 1885, Mowat was explicit that the federal government had jurisdiction only in matters not within section 92. One exception was article 16, 'if that article is such an exception,' because of the deeming clause in section 91.[27]

Addressing the specific issue before the court in *Severn*, Mowat argued that the challenged legislation fell within 92(9), which included all licences, that it was a direct tax, and that the provisions were not repugnant to federal jurisdiction over the regulation of trade and commerce. The argument relied heavily on American case law, as well as commentaries by Joseph Story and Thomas Cooley and particularly U.S. Chief Justice John Marshall's authoritative opinion that the taxing power was 'commensurate with, and essential to, the existence of the Government.'[28] Finally, Mowat reminded the court of one essential difference between the Canadian and American constitutions. 'There Courts alone have power to declare when the States have usurped the higher powers of Congress, whilst here ample power is given to the Dominion Parliament of protecting itself ... This power of disallowance should be taken into consideration when the policy of the Act is urged against us.'[29]

The court divided 4–2 (Samuel Strong and Ritchie dissenting) in denying the provincial claim and, in so doing, explicitly or implicitly rejected Mowat's version of the distribution of power. 'I should be very much surprised to learn,' wrote Richards, 'that any gentleman concerned in preparing or revising the *British North America Act* ever supposed that under the term "and other licenses" it was intended to confer on the Local Legislatures the power of interfering with every Statute passed by the Dominion Parliament for regulating trade and commerce, or for raising money under customs and excise laws.'[30] Taschereau and William Henry agreed, both citing the deeming clause, which they applied to all of section 92, rather than the declaratory clause, to buttress the argument about the scope and supremacy of the federal enumerations. If Mowat were right, Taschereau declared, the deeming clause was 'nonsensical, and should be struck out of the statute.'[31] To Henry, the purpose of the clause was obvious: 'Every constituent, therefore, of trade and commerce, and the subject of indirect taxation, is thus, as I submit, withdrawn from the consideration of the Local Legislatures, even if it should otherwise be *apparently* included. The Imperial Act fences in those twenty-eight subjects wholesale and in detail, and the Local Legislatures were intended to be, and are, kept out of the inclosure.'[32]

Fournier was the most explicit in rejecting Mowat's argument. The constitution could not have intended to expand provincial licensing power as Mowat contended, but rather 'the intention was no doubt that they should have a limited signification in accordance with the distinct powers so carefully allotted to the Federal and Local Governments.' And was there not, he asked, 'a mode of solving this question conformably to the spirit of the Act, rather than according to the views of the learned counsel of Her Majesty?' Indeed there was, for section 91 gave the federal government exclusive control over the regulation of trade and commerce, and 'this power, being full and complete, cannot be restricted unless by some specific provisions to be found in the *British North American Act*.' Fournier cited Marshall's decision in *Brown v. Maryland* that the power of the states to tax 'cannot reach and restrain the action of the National Government within its proper sphere ... It cannot interfere with any regulation of commerce.' Marshall's reasoning, he observed, 'is not only applicable to the present question, but should have more weight from the fact that under our system the Federal Government has the *exclusive* power over commerce,' and was 'such a complete answer' to Mowat's claim for the scope of property and civil rights 'that I need but refer to it.'

Mowat's other arguments fared no better. The fact that legislative power was divided, Fournier stated, disposed of the *plenum imperium* claim. The matter was not local or private because it was a regulation of trade that could affect all provinces. It was not a direct tax, but an indirect tax paid by consumers. It could not be justified under the police power because it was levied to raise revenue, and not under the licensing power because 'other licenses' must read as if they were followed by the words 'not incompatible with the power of regulating trade and commerce.' In short, if Mowat's construction of the BNA Act were accepted, it 'would no doubt, be the means of promptly and surely creating disorder and finally break up the Constitution.'[33]

In dissent, Ritchie was content to argue that 'other licenses' should be read broadly to enhance provincial revenues. But Strong went further and, for the purposes of this decision at least, offered a unique view of the distribution of powers. It was the duty of the court, Strong began, 'to make every possible presumption in favour of such Legislative Acts ... before taking upon ourselves to declare that, in assuming to pass it, the Provincial Legislature usurped powers which did not legally belong to it.' Strong agreed. That 'the regulation of trade and commerce in the Provinces, domestic and internal, as well as foreign and external, is by the *British North America Act*, exclusively conferred upon the Parliament of the Dominion, calls for no demonstration, for the language of the Act is explicit.' But, faithful to his decision in the appeal on *Taylor*, Strong held that 'other' licences meant 'any' or 'all' licences 'standing alone, unconnected with any specific words.'

A construction that would resolve the apparent conflict between a power that was both exclusive and not exclusive, Strong contended, was to read all powers conferred in section 92 as exceptions to those in section 91: 'That section 92 was, therefore, to be construed as if it has been contained in an Act of the Imperial Parliament, separate and apart from section 91, and is, therefore, to be read independently of that section.' So read, federal jurisdiction over the regulation of trade and commerce 'must be construed to mean the regulation of trade and commerce, save in so far as power to interfere with it is by section 92, conferred upon the Provinces.' Despite his claim that no 'violence' had been done to the BNA Act, the existence of the declaratory and deeming clauses in section 91, neither of which he mentioned, clearly weakened his structural contention that the enumerations in section 92 could somehow stand alone.[34]

Although Mowat had claimed jurisdiction over prohibition in his factum, the court did not address that issue. Sooner or later, however, the location of jurisdiction had to be resolved. The question had been before the provincial courts, and local prohibition of retail sale had been upheld in Ontario, Nova Scotia, and, after some conflicting decisions, in Quebec, but had been denied in New Brunswick as an interference with trade and commerce. In response to temperance pressure, Mowat had stated in the provincial legislature that he had 'most reluctantly' formed 'the deliberate and confident opinion' that the

buying and selling of liquor was a matter of trade and commerce which was beyond our jurisdiction. Then, too, the Dominion Parliament has jurisdiction over criminal law. More than this, the Dominion Parliament has jurisdiction over all classes of subjects not specially assigned to the Provinces. The Dominion Parliament has a much larger and more exclusive jurisdiction over trade and commerce than the Congress of the United States, and therefore there was no analogy between our position and that of the individual states of the Union.[35]

But Mowat did retain the 1864 Dunkin Act, with its local prohibition options, in the 1876 consolidation. As he wrote to Blake, 'I had at first excluded this Act from the Consolidation' but, on the advice of the liquor commissioners, 'decided that although *Prohibition* for the Province may be such an interference with Trade and Commerce as we have no right to make, yet that the right of prohibiting being part of the authority of Municipal Councils previous to Confederation, the Act, if not already within our jurisdiction, is not already out of it.'[36]

By this time the temperance forces had put the question firmly on the agenda of the federal Liberal Party, and, after two years of equivocation, the Mackenzie government concluded that it was desirable to have 'an effective permissive measure placed in the hands of the people of all the Provinces, with its machinery adapted to a quick and prompt response to public opinion, where it should declare itself by a majority in favour of this measure.' With an election approaching, most members were happy not to participate. Indeed, the government had astutely introduced the bill in the Senate, and left debate in the House until the end of the session.[37]

The preamble to the Canada Temperance Act (commonly known as the Scott Act) stated that 'it is very desirable to promote temperance in the dominion and that there should be uniform legislation in all the provinces,' but the procedure to bring it into force was by local option. Introducing the measure in the Senate, Senator Richard Scott stated that he had not consulted members of the Supreme Court although he did admit that 'in conversation I may have spoken of it in a general way, but I have taken no regular opinion on it from anyone.' However, the decisions in *Taylor* and *Severn*, and Strong's opinion in the *Taylor* appeal, proved

that, although there is a licensing power under the Confederation Act, in the Provincial Legislature, yet, as a branch of trade and commerce, the Federal Parliament has absolute control over the liquor question – that is, it may prohibit its importation or manufacture. The greater includes the less. If it can do that it can restrict or prohibit it in localities if thought wise and proper. The licensing power is entirely subservient and subordinate to the powers of the Federal Parliament.[38]

Senator R.B. Dickey led the attack on the bill's constitutionality and suggested that it should be referred to the Supreme Court, and Alexander Campbell, soon to be Macdonald's minister of justice, disliked the principle of the bill and also doubted its constitutionality.[39]

The Temperance Act was first challenged in New Brunswick, where the Supreme Court confirmed a decision of the Court of Appeal that the legislation was *ultra vires*.[40] The majority held that, given its stated objective, the act could not be regarded as in relation to trade and commerce; rather, it related to property and civil rights, or local and private matters, affected the provincial licensing power, and, as Charles Fisher put it, denied a citizen's 'natural right' to drink.[41] In dissent, Acalus Palmer found that the power could not be located anywhere in section 92 and was thus within the federal residual power. He dismissed the argument that it interfered with property and civil rights with the observation that everything affected property and civil rights and to apply the doctrine of interference would be to deny the federal government power over anything.[42]

The federal government had not been represented in the case, but Macdonald, victorious in the 1878 election, agreed to pay counsel for the city of Fredericton to appeal to the Supreme Court. Z.A. Lash, deputy minister of justice, acted for the city and the federal government, and John Maclaren was retained by the Dominion Alliance after Edward Blake had refused.[43]

In his factum, and before the court, Lash argued that the legislation did not fall within section 92 and therefore lay with the federal government under its residual power.[44] The respondents had failed to prove that the legislation could have been passed within the provincial jurisdiction over licences, municipal institutions, local police powers, or property and civil rights. The critical question, he continued, was not whether the object of the act was within federal or provincial powers, but 'are the means used within those powers? The means used in this case are certainly not in the local authority.' The act was valid not only under the residual clause, he continued, but under trade and commerce and the criminal law.

Admitting that the act 'interfered' with some provincial enumerations, Lash contended that this interference did not 'affect the general powers of Parliament, and if there be such interference the powers of the Local Legislatures must give way.' The respondents were, therefore, pressed back on 92(16). But the deeming clause, he observed, 'expressly provided that any matter coming within sec. 91 shall not be deemed to come within the class included in sub-section 16 of sec. 92.'[45] Subsequently, in his rebuttal of the respondents' arguments, Lash belatedly cited the declaratory clause as evidence that Parliament 'has under that section absolute and complete power over the subject-matters defined in the section notwithstanding anything in sec. 92.'

Counsel for the respondents dwelt on the interference with a wide range of provincial powers, powers that precluded 'any like power in the Parliament of Canada,' the stated object of the act, and the delegation to local authorities. If Ottawa could so legislate under the guise of trade and commerce or the criminal law, it could 'get possession of all *civil rights*' in the province or even pass laws to make people follow a certain religion.[46]

Richards had resigned in January 1879 and Ritchie had replaced him as chief justice. Throughout the argument, Ritchie, who had denied the prohibitory power to the provinces in *Kings* in 1875, seemed sympathetic to Lash and Maclaren, and he gave the lead judgment in a 4–1 decision upholding the legislation. The issue before the court was one of jurisdiction, not motive, he insisted: 'The power to make law is all we can judge of.' Citing the residual clause, the declaratory clause, which extended exclusive power to the enumerations, of which trade and commerce was one, and the protection provided by the deeming clause against (in his wording) all of section 92, he concluded that 'if then, Parliament in its wisdom, deems it expedient for the peace, order and good government of *Canada* so to regulate trade and commerce,' internal or external, 'it matters not, so far as we are judicially concerned,' to inquire into the motives which may have prompted the legislation or any other 'enactments within the scope of the legislative powers confided to Parliament, [which] tend to the peace, order and good government of *Canada*.'

From those clauses in section 91, Ritchie concluded that 'it seems very clear that the general jurisdiction or sovereignty which is thus conferred emphatically negatives the idea that there is not within the Dominion legislative power or authority to deal with the question of prohibition in respect to the sale or traffic in intoxicating liquor, or any other articles of trade or commerce.' Moreover, the possibility that the provinces, under their licensing or police powers, could deprive the federal government of 'a branch of trade and commerce from which so large a part of the public revenue was at the time of confederation raised in all the provinces, and has since been in the Dominion, never could have been contemplated by the framers of the *B.N.A. Act*.' In short, the power lay with the Dominion under its residual power and its jurisdiction over trade and commerce.[47] Fournier approved Ritchie's decision without comment.

Henri-Elzéar Taschereau was brief and to the point. If the power did not lay with the provinces, 'that power necessarily falls under the control of the Dominion Parliament ... Section 91 of the Imperial Act is clear on this ... and enacts in express terms, that the enumeration given of the classes of subjects falling under the control of the Federal Parliament is given for greater certainty, but not so as to restrict the rights of the Federal Parliament generally over *all* matters *not* expressly delegated to the Provincial Legislatures.' But, even if provincial incapacity was not accepted, he continued, the power was explicitly given in 91(2) and the declaratory clause expressly stated that '*notwithstanding* anything in this Act ... the Dominion Parliament has the right to legislate on all the matters left under its control by the Constitution, though, in doing so, it may interfere with some of the powers left to the Local Legislatures.'[48] Gwynne's judgment, characteristically verbose, found that the construction and language of the enacting, declaratory, and deeming clauses clearly established the 'proper canons of construction':

All subjects of whatever nature, *not exclusively* assigned to the Local Legislatures, are placed under the supreme control of the Dominion Parliament, and no matter is exclusively assigned to the Local Legislatures, unless it be within one of the subjects expressly enumerated in sec. 92, *and is at the same time outside of* all of the items enumerated in sec. 91, by which term '*outside of*' I mean does not involve any interference with any of the subjects comprehended in any of such items.

There was no question in Gwynne's mind that the Canada Temperance Act lay outside section 92 and inside 91 whatever interference there may be with the provincial powers.[49]

William Henry had given a broad scope to trade and commerce in *Severn*, but in *Fredericton* he seemed to change course completely. To declare an act of the federal government *ultra vires* was a serious matter, he stated, 'but it is much more serious and unfortunate to destroy the constitution of the country.' Confederation was accomplished by 'a surrender of the local legislative power, to the extent agreed upon, that the powers of Parliament were agreed to be given. It was in the nature of a solemn compact, to be inviolably kept that the rights and prerogatives of both were adopted.' In the drafting of the constitution, 'the leading idea was that in the large and extensive subjects affecting all the Provinces the General Parliament should legislate, and the smaller and less important subjects should be left to the Local Legislatures.' Provincial licensing power was an exception to federal power over trade and commerce and for Ottawa to legislate on what he described as 'minute and trifling' matters was 'an usurpation of power, and an inroad upon the constitution and prerogatives of the Local Legislatures, and results in depriving them of one of the reservations for local objects intended and provided for by the compact and act of union.'[50]

Fredericton is always cited, including the head note in the *Supreme Court Reports*, as having been based *only* on the trade and commerce power.[51] In fact, Gwynne and Taschereau, and less explicitly Ritchie with Fournier concurring, also found authority in the residual clause. Indeed, during the oral argument in *Russell*, Sir Robert Collier observed that the chief justice had in part found its validity in the peace, order, and good government clause.[52]

The court was even more emphatic in rejecting the doctrine of interference in *Valin* v. *Langlois*, a challenge to federal legislation conferring jurisdiction in contested elections on the provincial superior courts.[53] Section 41 of the BNA Act gave the federal government power to create the jurisdiction, but it was argued (both in Quebec and Ontario) that conferring it on the provincial courts infringed on provincial control over property and civil rights and the administration of justice in the province. Finding the legislation valid, the court unanimously agreed that the federal government had the right to interfere with property and civil rights 'when necessary for the purpose of legislating generally and effectually in relation to matters confided to the Parliament of *Canada*,' whether those matters fell within the enumerations or not.[54]

But *Valin* was not a good test of the scope of property and civil rights, for the matter in question was so clearly within the jurisdiction of the federal parliament that its interference with 91(13) or 92(14) was, in one sense, irrelevant. A year later, however, the court had to consider the scope and content of property and civil rights and its connection to trade and commerce when Ontario legislation imposing statutory conditions on insurance policies was challenged as an infringement of the federal power over trade and commerce.

The regulation of the insurance industry has had a long and troubled legislative and judicial history.[55] The jurisdictional question arose as early as 1868 when the minister of finance introduced a bill to compel insurance companies to secure a federal licence and deposit $50,000.[56] Luther Holton, the maverick Liberal MP from Quebec, denounced the legislation as a 'complete revolution' in the regulation of insurance which raised 'in the sharpest way that which had been raised before this session, the limit between the General and Provincial Governments.' Alexander Mackenzie added that if 'there was any matter that peculiarly belongs to [the] Local Legislature it was the business of insurance.' The bill was amended to exclude provincially incorporated companies operating exclusively within a province, although they could avail themselves of the provisions of the act. Edward Blake endorsed the amendment but objected to the principle of concurrent jurisdiction as a 'most dangerous proposition.'[57]

In 1875 the Liberals consolidated the insurance acts and created a Department of Insurance. Asked if he proposed to exempt provincially incorporated companies operating within the province from its operation, Richard Cartwight, the finance minister, replied:

As a general thing I may say that it is not the intention of the Government to interfere with Local Corporations, incorporated by the Provincial Legislatures, and doing business within the limits of their own Province; but as the question of Insurance is one among those specially relegated to the care of the Dominion Parliament I am not prepared to say that in some respects it may not be found necessary to extend superintendence over them. Our general object, however, is to deal with those companies only that do business throughout the whole Dominion.[58]

As with the earlier legislation, the act was concerned with the solvency of the companies, not with the nature of their policies.

However, the companies often proved reluctant to pay claims and, after a judicial investigation, Mowat passed an act in 1876 to impose statutory conditions on insurance policies.[59] Canadian and British companies soon challenged the act, when contesting the claims for indemnity of one William Parsons. Although the constitutionality of the legislation was not initially central to the case, two judgments of the Ontario Court of Appeal unanimously found the act *intra vires*.[60]

The central question in the appeal to the Supreme Court, however, was the constitutional validity of the act. The appellants argued that insurance was a major trade and that 'under the general as well as the special powers of the legislature, vested in the Canadian Parliament, it was and is competent for the Parliament and for the Parliament exclusively, to regulate the terms on which the Appellants may contract with those who desire to insure in their company.'[61] Mowat contended that, while the federal government might have power to incorporate the companies under the residual clause, the power was limited to their creation and did not extend to the regulation of their contracts, which fell within the exclusive provincial jurisdiction over property and civil rights as well as in 92(11) and 92(16).

Although it was not directly attributed to Mowat, the argument that the provincial legislatures 'are not in any accurate sense subordinate to the parliament of *Canada*' was a repetition of his doctrine in *Severn*: 'Each body is independent and supreme within the limits of its own jurisdiction: so that even if contracts are considered a kind of commerce, they are still governed by sec. 92, the powers in which should be read as exceptions to those conferred upon Parliament by sec. 91 ... If the local legislature has jurisdiction respecting the subject-matter of insurance contracts at all, it has the most full and ample jurisdiction – *plenum imperium* – it has sovereign power within its own limits.' The fact that the federal government had 'assumed' to legislate on insurance, the argument continued, 'prove[s] little, for the provinces have not power to disallow these Acts, and can only look to the courts for defence against the encroachments of the Federal power.'[62]

Chief Justice Ritchie began his judgment with the statement that 'there never, probably, was an Act, the validity of which was questioned, that came before a Court so strongly supported by judicial and legislative authority as this Act.' He admitted that, under its residual power, the federal government could create companies with Dominion objects, but those objects had to be reconciled with the distribution of powers. Responding to the argument that the regulation of insurance companies fell within trade and commerce, Ritchie stated:

The power of the Dominion parliament to regulate trade and commerce ought not to be held to be necessarily inconsistent with those of the local legislatures to regulate property and civil rights in respect to all matters of a merely local and private nature ... although the exercise by the local legislatures of such powers may be said remotely to affect matters connected with trade and commerce, unless, indeed, the laws of the provincial legislatures should conflict with those of the Dominion Parliament passed for the general regulation of trade and commerce.

However, the act was not a regulation of trade and commerce but a regulation of contracts which fell clearly within property and civil rights.[63] Absent for the judgment, Strong authorized Ritchie to state that he concurred.

Fournier also located insurance contracts within the civil law. Accepting the trade and commerce argument would mean that 'the greater portion of the powers of the provinces would thus become of no avail, for commerce in its most comprehensive meaning extends to everything,' and like others he read the section 91 enumerations as necessarily restricting the all-inclusive meaning of trade and commerce. In exercising its power over trade and commerce, the federal government 'a sans doute le pouvoir de toucher incidemment à des matières qui sont de la juridiction des provinces, – mais ce pouvoir ne s'étend pas au-delà de ce qui est raisonnable et nécessaire à une législation pour les fins du commerce seulement.' Given their objects, he did not find the federal and provincial legislation incompatible.[64]

Gwynne, however, maintained that upholding the Ontario legislation would not only invalidate all federal insurance legislation, for the subject had to be placed 'exclusively either under the one or the other,' but would turn over control of all trades, of all persons and corporations carrying on business in Ontario, to the provincial government. That the 'Act in question,' he concluded, 'does usurp the jurisdiction of the Dominion parliament, I must say I entertain no doubt. The logical result of a contrary decision would afford just grounds to despair of the stability of the Dominion.'[65]

Taschereau also found anomalous the argument that the federal government could incorporate companies but not regulate insurance contracts. There was no doubt in his mind, as there seldom was, that the Ontario act was *ultra vires* as a regulation 'of commercial corporations and commercial operations, and the words "regulation of trade and commerce" in section 91 ... means "all regulations on all branches of trade and commerce."' Indeed, a contrary interpretation would be against the very letter of the act. 'We cannot, it seems to me, find restrictions and limitations where the words used by the law-giver are so clear and general.'

Taschereau rejected Mowat's rendering of the structure of sections 91 and 92 and of the purpose and nature of Confederation. Like Gwynne, he also repudiated the possibility of concurrent powers (and what would become the 'aspect' doctrine) and the ability of the provinces 'to retard and impede, burden and impair, obstruct, and even defeat the enactments of the federal authority.' To the Bleu who had opposed Confederation, the issue at hand was nothing less than the constitutional supremacy of the central government:

It is of the very essence of supremacy to remove all obstacles to its action within its own sphere, and so to modify every power vested in subordinate governments so as to exempt its own operations from their influence, and it cannot be that the framers of our constitution, who determined to give to the central power of this Dominion the supremacy and strength which, in the hour of trial, were found to be so much wanting in the federal power in the United States, have thus given to a province, or to all the provinces uniting in a common legislation, the power to annihilate, either directly or indirectly, the corporation which the central power is authorized by the Act to create; that they have thus rendered inevitable in this Dominion, that conflict of powers under which a federation must always, sooner or later, crumble and break down.[66]

Following two decisions favouring a broad scope for trade and commerce, the majority had found it necessary to restrict its scope to allow for what seemed a matter of civil law or property and civil rights. But it left the duality of insurance regulation in place and could, as Gwynne had forecast, if upheld and misconstrued, place much of the normal business life of the country, other than in areas specifically mentioned in section 91, within provincial hands.

Like the provincial courts, the Supreme Court faced the challenge of deciphering the constitutional code for the location of the prerogative rights of the crown in a federal state where both levels of government were in some respects constitutional monarchies.[67] The constitution itself was hopelessly vague and ambiguous. On the one hand, the constitution explicitly stated that 'the Executive Government and Authority of and over Canada is hereby declared to continue and be vested in the Queen' and the governor general was to act 'on behalf of and in the Name of the Queen.'[68] The BNA Act made no explicit statement of the relationship of the lieutenant governor to the queen, and absent such a provision it seemed that the link between the crown and the imperial government with the provinces had been broken. However, although they were appointed by the governor general and were to assent to bills in the governor general's name, the lieutenant governors of Ontario and Quebec were to summon the legislature 'in the Queen's name, by Instrument under the Great Seal,'[69] and the executive authorities of all provinces were to continue as they had been, 'as far as the same are capable of being exercised.'[70] Politically, the lieutenant governors were appointed, paid, and liable to dismissal by the federal government.[71]

The question had arisen during the drafting of the constitution. The Quebec resolutions had vested the power of pardon and cummutation, 'which belongs of right to the Queen,' in the lieutenant governors. But the British government refused to accept this provision, despite Macdonald's view that he had 'the best of the argument,'[72] on the grounds that the prerogative power could be exercised only by 'Her Majesty's Representative holding her Majesty's direct authority for the exercise.'[73] When the issue arose soon after Confederation, the Colonial Office stood by its earlier decision. The law officers advised that the British North America Act had revoked 'all the authorities' possessed by the colonial governors other than those explicitly stated, and since the lieutenant governors were no longer appointed by the queen they would not have 'the power of pardoning *virtute officii* unless it were so given to them by the Act. The whole constitution of the Provinces was changed by the Act of Union, and the delegated Powers of Government necessarily ceased.'[74]

The determination of the relationship of the lieutenant governor, and thus the province, to the crown had two dimensions of enormous consequences for the future of Canadian federalism. The first was status or the degree of sovereignty the provinces possessed within the federation. If the crown was represented directly within the provincial government, coordinate rather than subordinate status would be achieved in the executive branch as it was in the legislative. This issue of status also raised the question of whether the provinces were new creations or the old colonies somewhat reconfigured. The second, not unrelated, dimension was the distribution of legislative jurisdiction, for what under responsible government was in theory an exercise of the royal prerogative was often in practice simply the formal confirmation of executive or legislative actions.[75]

The case to come before the Supreme Court began in 1872 when the government of Nova Scotia raised the question of the appointment of queen's counsel. Macdonald believed that, although there was some question that the lieutenant governor possessed the prerogative power, the province could, under section 92(14), confer it by statute. The law officers of the crown agreed and, so advised,[76] Nova Scotia passed the enabling legislation in 1874.

J.N. Ritchie successfully appealed to the Supreme Court of Nova Scotia for a ruling that the legislation could not affect his precedence as a federally appointed QC, whereupon the disgruntled provincial QCs appealed to the Supreme Court of Canada. Although the validity of the law itself was unsuccessfully challenged in Nova Scotia,[77] counsel for Ritchie made the legislation the central issue in the Supreme Court. Citing the dispatches from the Colonial Office and the wording of the BNA Act, he argued that 'unless this officer has power conferred upon him by the Constitutional Act to represent Her Majesty in the exercise of her prerogative powers, he can neither do so now, nor can he at any time be empowered to do so by the Legislature of the Provinces.'[78] Counsel for the appellants argued (mistakenly) that the question of validity, involving as it did the 'status hitherto claimed and enjoyed by Lieutenant-Governors,' had not been before the lower court and was 'of such grave public importance that it is to be hoped it will not be necessary under the circumstances for the court to consider it.'[79]

Adhering to the doctrine that the court should not pronounce upon the legitimacy of legislation unless it was necessary in reaching a decision, Strong and Fournier agreed that the issue was one of precedence, which was not affected by the act, and dismissed the appeal without commenting on the constitutional question. However, Fournier did wonder whether the opinion of the law officers was 'suffisant de la part de Sa Majesté pour autoriser la législation qui s'en est suivie,' an observation that suggested he could have found the legislation unconstitutional.'[80]

In Paul Romney's opinion, three judges of the Supreme Court of Canada 'declared war on provincial rights' when they decided that the issue of precedence could not be separate from the act.[81] Henry was emphatic that the local governments were 'simply the creatures of a statute, and under it alone have they any legislative powers' and any act beyond the prescribed powers must necessarily be *ultra vires*. Nor was a dispatch from the Colonial Office sufficient to extend federal or provincial powers as conferred by an imperial statute. Moreover, the queen had not assented to the act in question for the queen was not part of the local legislature, nor were the lieutenant governors her representatives.[82]

Taschereau also felt compelled to decide the broader constitutional question, 'the determination of which this court has been more specially created for.' He was already on record as stating that only in Ottawa was the queen directly represented and the lieutenant governors acted only in the name of the queen when explicitly empowered in the constitution, and 'nowhere in the Act, can a single expression be found to sustain the contention that the Lieutenant-Governor has such a power. Well if he has not this power in virtue of the *British North America Act*, how can the Provincial Legislature give it to him?' Nor could it be pretended, 'as it seems to have been in this case, indirectly at least,' that a Colonial Office dispatch could add to provincial powers: 'An interpretation of the law in a despatch from *Downing Street* is not binding on this, or any Court of Justice, and is not given as such.'[83] In a long and spirited judgment, Gwynne reiterated the views of Henry and Taschereau on the position and prerogatives of lieutenant governors and the irrelevance of the views of Downing Street.[84]

The question of prerogative, and what properly was prerogative, was more fully argued in *Mercer*, which involved the location of the right of escheat for want of heirs.[85] The case that finally came before the Supreme Court involved the estate of Andrew Mercer, who died in Ontario in 1871 without heirs or a will. His concubine and natural son took possession of some of his property and contested the claim of the province of Ontario that it had escheated to the crown in the right of the province. To strengthen his position, Oliver Mowat passed an act in 1874 declaring that escheats were to be taken by the attorney general in the name of the crown. Before his legislation was tested in the courts, the same question had arisen in Quebec where Judge Henri-Elzéar Taschereau, then of the Quebec Superior Court, found that the prerogative was the determining factor:

Je l'ai dit: ces droits appartiennent au souverain. Or, sous notre constitution, la souveraineté est à Ottawa. Il n'y a que là que Sa Majesté soit directement représentée ... Cette souveraineté du gouvernement fédéral est le principe fondamental de notre constitution ... Ici le gouvernement général a tous les droits, pouvoirs et priviléges, toutes attributions de la souveraineté, qui ... n'ont pas été expressément réservés aux gouvernements provinciaux.

Thus, if escheats were not reserved to the provinces, as Taschereau concluded, they belonged to the federal government.[86]

However, on appeal, the Court of Queen's Bench unanimously

found for the province on the grounds that escheat as a minor prerogative had been and remained part of the revenues of the provinces; that
escheats were royalties which, by section 109 of the BNA Act,
remained with the provinces; and finally, that jurisdiction over the law
of descent fell within property and civil rights.[87] Following the decision, Edward Blake, the federal minister of justice, with Mowat's concurrence, recommended that unless there were further litigation the
decision should stand, and escheats for want of heirs be provincial, but
that property forfeited to the crown in the case of treason be within
federal legislative competence.[88]

Meanwhile, the Mercers continued the battle, finally losing in the
Ontario Court of Appeal (which followed the Quebec decision).[89] With
an appeal pending to the Supreme Court, Macdonald agreed that
Mowat could keep the money – an insignificant few thousand dollars a
year – 'subject to the final decision of the Question.' Both agreed that
the appeal should be limited to the broad question of provincial or federal jurisdiction.[90]

It was an impressive array of legal talent that delivered eighty-five
pages of oral argument before the court. Zebulon Lash, deputy minister of justice, appeared for Ottawa and William McDougall represented
the same side for the family. Lash argued that escheats were revenues
and that unless specially given to the provinces remained with the federal government under section 102. Obviously unhappy with the prerogative argument, he simply stated that even assuming escheats were
a royal prerogative did not mean that this prerogative belonged to the
provinces.[91] McDougall took a similar position but argued, more fully
and with greater conviction, that the lieutenant governor did not possess the prerogative.[92]

Edward Blake and James Bethune appeared for Ontario. In his first
appearance before the court as counsel in a constitutional case, Blake
appealed for a construction of the act 'with due consideration to the
condition of the different parties who entered into the compact of Confederation.' Given the complexity of writing a new constitution, he
observed, 'it would be a fatal error to stick to the letter of the act ... The
rule of general intent and the rule of public convenience are of vital
consequence in dealing with this act.'[93] The proper approach was to
ask 'What is the real nature of the union?' and to read all sections
together 'in order that, by a broad, liberal and quasi-political interpretation the true meaning may be gathered.' So viewed, section 12 and
sections 64 and 65 made it clear 'that whatever might have been done

by any governor fell to the Governor-General of *Canada* if the subject-matter related to the Dominion of *Canada*, and fell to the lieutenant-governor if the subject-matter related to the province.' However, he contended, the central issue was not one of prerogative but of the constitutional distribution of land and property, of which escheat was a species of reversion, a casual profit. All lands and property not specially given to Ottawa were, by sections 109 and 117, retained by the provinces. 'It would be absurd to suppose that authority over the whole question of granting and transferring property was given to the local legislatures, and yet one of the smallest and least significant matters incident to it, that of escheats, should be withheld. Can it be said such a little, thwarting, vexatious question, serving no high political interest, was not given to the provinces?'[94]

The majority found, in varying degrees, that escheat was a prerogative and that unless it had been specifically transferred to the province it would fall to the Dominion under section 102 as part of the pre-Confederation revenues, and dismissed the relevance of sections 109, 117, and 92(13). On the question of the degrees of representation of the crown, Henry reiterated his decision in *Lenoir*: 'I may add that in that case they were not alone my views, but those of all my learned brethren who heard and decided it; and I have heard nothing since tending to change or weaken them.'[95] Taschereau held to his views in *Church v. Blake*, but he was relieved that it had been agreed by both parties that regardless of the outcome the case would go to the Judicial Committee, for although it was a trifling matter, it was 'right for obvious reasons that the final authoritative determination of controversies on the construction of the *British North America Act*, which is an Imperial statute, should emanate from an Imperial judicial authority.'[96]

In a long, technical decision, supported by Fournier and Taschereau, Gwynne rejected the argument for sections 109, 117, and 92(13) in favour of sections 102 and 91(1) and the prerogative power. But he could not resist the temptation to reject Blake's view of the difficulties of interpretation of the act or the general argument in favor of a broad interpretation of provincial rights:

In my judgment it expresses in sufficiently clear language the plain intent of the framers of the Act to ... confer upon the Dominion so formed a *quasi* national existence – to sow in *its* constitution the seeds of national power ... and to constitute within that national power so constituted and called 'the Dominion of *Canada*,' certain subordinate bodies called provinces having jurisdiction *exclusive* though not 'Sovereign.'..of whose legislatures Her Majesty does not, as she does of the Dominion, and as she did of the old provinces, constitute a component part, and to the validity of whose Acts, the Act which constitutes their charter does not even contemplate the assent of her Majesty as necessary.[97]

Ritchie wrote the sole dissenting opinion, with Strong apparently indicating his concurrence. Ritchie found the relevant provisions to be sections 109 and 117 rather than 102, and that section 92 (5, 13, and 16) would appear to locate the jurisdiction in the provinces. More generally, he observed that, while the duty of the court was to 'give full force and effect' to federal authority, it was also essential to preserve the powers of the provinces and not to permit them 'to be deprived of their local and territorial rights on the plea that Lieutenant-Governors in no sense represent the crown and therefore all seignorial or prerogative rights ... of necessity belong to the Dominion.' Ritchie admitted that the representative nature of the lieutenant governors had changed with Confederation but believed 'it must be conceded that Lieutenant-Governors, since confederation do represent the crown, though doubtless in a modified manner.'[98]

Ritchie's dissent was, as Blake urged, an opinion that attempted to place the narrow and technical question of the prerogative into a broader, more quasi-political context. For it did seem anomalous that revenues or powers that seemed to be within the province's jurisdiction should be denied them because of the limited representation of the crown by the lieutenant governor. That lack of congruity between legislative and executive authority continued to plague the courts and the politicians, until Lord Watson settled the matter in 1892 to the satisfaction of the courts if not the politicians, Canadian and British.[99]

It would be impossible on the basis of the first six decisions to conclude that the Supreme Court had fashioned a distinctive constitutional jurisprudence either in reasoning or result. Only in *Valin* was the court unanimous. Although five of the six decisions either upheld federal or rejected provincial jurisdiction, majorities and minorities reached decisions by different routes. Gwynne and Taschereau were consistently centralist in reasoning and result, while Strong and Ritchie were usually provincialist in result and more moderately so in reasoning. Henry decided with the majority in every case but *Fredericton*.

On balance, both the BNA Act's structure and its distribution of jurisdiction were remarkably similar to the opinions in the provincial courts. The Supreme Court gave full force and effect to the residual clause and did not separate it from the powerful declaratory clause which restricted the scope of the provincial enumerations. All members of the court were convinced that the purpose of the deeming clause was also to place limits on provincial power, but most applied it to all of section 92, either directly or implicitly. Even including *Parsons*, the federal power over trade and commerce was interpreted sufficiently broadly to include internal trade, while property and civil rights were bounded by the federal enumerations and in two instances by the residual clause. The court believed that its task was to determine the 'pith and substance,' and never suggested that interference or encroachment on provincial enumerations invalidated federal legislation under the enumerations or the residual clause.

There was some criticism that the determination of most judges to write their own decisions not only slowed down the work of the court but did little to settle the law. D'Alton McCarthy suggested that, if the court adopted the practice of a single decision, 'we should be now saved the necessity of having to wade through thirty or forty pages of judgments, which, instead of settling rather confuses the law.' Blake also suggested that it might be better to adopt 'to a large extent' the single-decision practice of the Judicial Committee of the Privy Council.[100]

In time, the Supreme Court, in spite of its shortcomings, would have shaped the federal constitution. But there was no time. Already, even Taschereau had strangely concluded that 'the final authoritative determination of controversies' arising from an 'Imperial statue' should 'emanate from an Imperial judicial authority.' More practically, as Alexander Campbell informed Macdonald, Mowat wanted several appeals to go directly to the Judicial Committee, 'saying that a decision in the Supreme Court, whatever way it went, would satisfy neither party – that whoever was defeated would appeal to the Judicial Committee.'[101]

By the 1880s, the long imprisonment had begun.

4

The Appeal to Caesar

Exercising the Authority of the Crown over its Possessions Abroad ...
– Henry Reeve, registrar, Judicial Committee, 1876

'I would very well like to see a clause introduced declaring that this right of appeal to the Privy Council existed no longer,' stated Télésephore Fournier upon introducing the bill to create the Supreme Court of Canada in 1875. The government hoped that the creation of the new court would end appeals to the Privy Council but had made no explicit provision to this effect in the bill, leaving it to be disposed of at some 'future time.' Fournier observed that legislation pending at Westminster would lead to the creation of a new imperial court of appeal and the abolition of the Judicial Committee. Although the Judicial Committee was in fact a court, in theory it entertained appeals under the prerogative and its decisions were cast in the guise of advisory opinions to the crown. With the proposed new court of appeal, however, the prerogative would not be at issue and appeals could more easily be abolished.[1]

But Aemilius Irving, the Liberal member from Hamilton, was not disposed to leave the abolition of appeals until some future time. Late in the debate, he moved an amendment that the decision of the Supreme Court 'shall in all cases be final and conclusive' and there could be no appeal to any court established by the British parliament, 'saving any right which Her Royal Majesty may be graciously pleased to exercise as her royal prerogative.' Fournier stated at once that the government accepted the amendment, and after a short debate it (clause 47) passed 112–40.[2] Sir John A. Macdonald warned Fournier that the amendment would ensure the disallowance of the act and, after the vote, vainly pleaded with the Mackenzie government to delay passage of the bill. The abolition of appeals would not only wound the loyal sentiment of the people, he argued, but would raise the question in England 'as to whether there was an impatience in this country of even the semblance of Imperial authority.'[3]

Macdonald was right. The amendment aroused great excitement in the offices of Lord Cairns, the lord chancellor, and the Judicial Committee. Lord Dufferin, the governor general, hesitated before giving assent but recommended against disallowance. As he informed Lord Carnarvon, the colonial secretary, he did not 'attach any weight' to Macdonald's objection and believed the less friction the better for the Imperial connection.[4] The question was 'one of *very* great difficulty,' replied Carnavon, for Cairns was 'dead against the Act' and 'in many quarters a much greater – and as it seems to me a somewhat undue – stress is laid upon the *judicial* bond of union.'[5] Indeed, Cairns insisted that 'what is desired appears to me to be the equivalent to a complete severance of the strongest tie between our Colonies and the Mother Country.'[6] Carnarvon had no success with Cairns and wrote in exasperation to Dufferin that 'I have no respect for lawyers or the language with which they delight to darken common sense.'[7]

By the time the act reached London, Fournier had been appointed to the Supreme Court and Edward Blake had become minister of justice. Blake was as determined to abolish appeals as Cairns was opposed, an attitude that Dufferin attributed to 'a morbid hatred of the legal authority of England, engendered probably by the frequency with which it had over-ruled his own opinion and decisions in respect of points of constitutional law.'[8] The transatlantic correspondence was heated, and Blake's personal interview with Cairns was ineffectual. In the end, Blake lost because clause 47 presupposed that the new imperial court of appeal, which was not a prerogative court, would replace the Judicial Committee. But the Disraeli government did not pass the expected legislation and the Judicial Committee, which entertained the prerogative appeals permitted by the amendment, remained alive. As Blake explained to David Mills, with the prerogative unaffected 'we are really fighting about nothing or less than nothing.'[9]

Nevertheless, Blake seized the opportunity to reject the grounds on which the British opposed abolition. The British arguments were detailed in a long memorandum by Henry Reeve, who had been clerk of appeals in the Judicial Committee since 1837 and registrar since 1857. Reeve had opposed the attempt of the Australian colony of Victoria to abolish appeals in 1871 and warmed to his task once again.[10]

The Canadian determination to abolish appeals, Reeve believed, was nothing less than a threat to the empire, for the 'Supreme Appellate authority of the Empire or the realm is unquestionably one of the highest functions and duties of sovereignty' and the 'power of constituting, determining, and enforcing the law in the last resort, is, in truth, a power which overrides all other powers.' If Canada had its way, other colonies would follow. 'To abolish this controlling power, and to abandon each Colonial dependency to a separate Court of Final Appeal of its own,' he warned, 'is obviously to destroy one of the most important ties which still connects all parts of the Empire in common obedience to the source of law, and to renounce the last and most essential mode of exercising the authority of the Crown over its possessions abroad.'[11]

There were equally important and unique reasons, Reeve contended, why it was essential to maintain appeals from Canada:

The Dominion of Canada has recently been erected on a federal basis, including several provinces. Questions of great nicety must arise under such a constitution between the federal and provincial legislatures and judicatures. These are precisely questions upon which the decision of a Court of Final Appeal, not included within the Confederation, would be most impartial and valuable. Again, in Canada strong divisions of race, religion, and party are known to exist. The policy and duty of the British Government, and especially the Last Court of Appeal, has been to secure absolute impartiality to the rights or claims of the minority of the population. Laws passed by a strong political majority, and administered by Judges and Courts appointed by the representatives of the same majority, are less likely to ensure an entire respect for the rights of all classes than the decisions of a perfectly impartial and independent tribunal. Accordingly, a very strong opposition manifested itself in Parliament against this Bill, and a protest was signed by no less than seventeen members of the Legislature.[12]

Blake was incensed. If Canadians were fit to make their laws, he replied, 'they should be fit to expound the law. If they are unfit to expound the law, its creation should also be by the same process of reasoning the work of the highest judicial authority and legal capacity existing in the metropolis.'[13] Nor was it necessary or desirable that Reeve's 'perfectly impartial and independent tribunal' police the federal system and protect the provinces and minorities against an overpowering central government and its Supreme Court:

I would observe that with the practical operation of the Federal Constitution of Canada, with the customs and systems which may have grown out of its working with many of the elements which have been found most valuable if not absolutely necessary to a sound decision in that class of cases, a Court composed of English Judges cannot possibly be thoroughly acquainted. They may indeed learn from the argument in an isolated case the view of a particular Counsel upon the matter; but the daily learning and experience which Canadians living under the Canadian Constitution acquire, is not theirs, nor can it be effectively instilled into them for the purpose of a particular appeal. I maintain that this training and learning, which can be given only by residence on the spot, is of such vital consequence as to overbalance the advantages flowing from the probably superior mental capacity of the Judges of the London Tribunal.[14]

And, as he had written earlier about Canadian judges, 'such as they are, *they are our own*.'[15]

Judicial imperialism had defeated Canadian nationalism, and the imperial authority had imposed appeals to the Judicial Committee on a government and a House of Commons openly and overwhelmingly opposed. The committee began its task of constitutional review with the conviction that its mission was to maintain the authority of the crown and the law in the interests of imperial sovereignty and unity. More specifically, it was to be the impartial umpire for a federal system, divided by race, religion, and party, where the local judicial policing was in the hands of judges appointed by the same 'strong political majority' in the federal government that passed the laws.[16]

The Judicial Committee could, of course, severely restrict appeals just as it could advise Her Majesty not to entertain appeals directly from the provincial superior courts. Accepting Blake's admission of defeat, Lord Carnarvon, personally sympathetic to the Canadian position, expressed the belief and the hope that it was not 'perhaps probable that there will be many occasions on which suitors before the new

Supreme Court will be desirous of appealing to Her Majesty in Council from its decisions.'[17]

Lord Carnarvon was too optimistic. The question was not only, or perhaps mainly, whether Canadians could afford to trek to London, but whether the Judicial Committee would easily grant appeals from Canadian courts. Dismissing the first petition to appeal, Lord Chancellor Cairns established guidelines for the committee. There was no doubt, he stated, that the 'prerogative to allow an appeal, is left untouched ... and their Lordships would have no hesitation in a proper case in advising Her Majesty to allow an appeal upon a judgment of this Court.' However, the sum involved – only $300 – was not an amount that justified 'any special interposition of the prerogative' and the decision of the Supreme Court, 'whether right or wrong,' was not one which could 'have any bearing, or which can occasion any inconvenience with respect to a large number of cases.'[18]

Rejecting a petition for special leave to appeal in 1879, Lord Selborne stated that leave should not be 'lightly or very easily granted: that it is necessary to show both that the matter is one of importance, and that there is really a substantial question to be determined.'[19] Denying an appeal three years later, Lord Fitzgerald observed that the Supreme Court Act prohibited all but prerogative appeals, 'and their Lordships are not prepared to advise Her Majesty to exercise her prerogative ... save when the case is of gravity involving a matter of public interest or some important question of law, or affecting property of a considerable amount, or where the case is otherwise of some importance or of a very substantial character.'[20]

However, as Lord Watson observed in 1889, there were no strict criteria for the Judicial Committee to follow. Its members were 'bound to apply their judicial discretion to the circumstances of each case as presented to them' during the hearing on the appeal and must examine the 'importance and effect of the judgement complained of ... No rule can be laid down which would not necessarily be subject to future qualification, and an attempt to formulate any such rule might therefore prove to be misleading.' What Selborne implied in *Valin*, Watson made explicit – the decision to entertain an appeal was in part, at least, a judgment on the quality of Canadian jurisprudence:

Cases vary so widely in their circumstances that the principles upon which an appeal ought to be allowed do not admit of anything approaching to exhaus-

tive definition. No rule can be laid down which would not necessarily be subject to future qualification, and an attempt to formulate any such rule might
therefore prove misleading. In some cases, as in *Prince v. Gagnon*, their Lordships have had occasion to indicate certain particulars, the absence of which
will have a strong influence in inducing them to advise that leave should not
be given, but it by no means follows that leave will be recommended in all
cases in which these features occur. A case may be of substantial character, may
involve a matter of great public interest, and may raise an important question
of law, and yet the judgement from which leave to appeal is sought may
appear to be plainly right, or at least unattended with sufficient doubt to justify
their Lordships in advising Her Majesty to grant leave to appeal.[21]

The combination of subjective criteria (including reflections on the
Supreme Court decision) was apparent in the decision to allow the
appeal in the celebrated rivers and streams case in 1883. Sir Barnes
Peacock, for the committee, decided that the case fell 'entirely within
the rules laid down' in *Prince v. Gagnon* as a matter of 'grave public
interest.'[22] The unanimous decision of the Supreme Court might have
deterred the committee, but Peacock observed that the Supreme Court
had overruled a 3–1 decision in the Ontario Court of Appeal (neglect-
ing to add that the latter court had overruled a decision in the Court of
Chancery). Thus, 'looking at all the circumstances of the case, without
expressing the slightest opinion as to what may be the result of the
decision,' he granted the appeal.[23] In several of his decisions on application to appeal, Lord Watson also made special references to the decisions in the Canadian courts: the unanimity of nine judges in the
Canadian courts was sufficient reason to dismiss the application in
one; the division of opinion in Canadian courts was reason to allow in
another; and the division of opinion in reason and result in the
Supreme Court, making it impossible for the decision to be regarded as
precedent, was sufficient reason for the committee to reject the application in a third.[24]

In the end, without firm criteria, the Judicial Committee was free to
determine what was a grave matter of law or an important question of
public interest, and whether the decisions in the Canadian courts were
an adequate determination of what should be Canadian law.

Between 1879 and 1899, there were 103 appeals from Canadian
courts and 175 from all the other self-governing colonies. The Supreme
Court was not the court of final appeal: 36 of its decisions were
appealed, 18 of which were reversed. Nor was it a necessary interme-

diate court as 67 appeals went directly from provincial courts to the Judicial Committee, and 50 were affirmed.[25] Well before the end of the century, the Supreme Court had become a captive court. 'Indeed, as the case is to go to the Privy Council whatever the judgement may be,' wrote Oliver Mowat to the federal deputy minister of justice in 1895, 'it is of no real consequence to any of us on which side there be a majority of the judges, though their respective judgement may have considerable value to both sides for the assistance of the Judicial Committee and of English counsel who argue the case.'[26]

There was a palpable sense of fatality on the court. As Strong observed at an opening argument in 1896, the case before them 'was only a matter of form' and its 'only object was to seize the Privy Council with jurisdiction,' to which Taschereau added that it was a pity it had not gone directly to London.[27] Years before, however, the judges of the Supreme Court of Canada had concluded that their judgments were of no value at the Judicial Committee. As Strong angrily observed during the argument on the *McCarthy Act Reference*, 'our judgment will not make any difference there: as a matter of fact, they never do. They do not appear to be read or considered there, and if they are alluded to, it is only for the purpose of offensive criticism.'[28]

However central to the supremacy of the imperial idea, the Judicial Committee of the Privy Council in 1875 was not a body of eminent jurists, nor did it have a setting appropriate to the role portrayed by Reeve and Cairns. During the debate on the Australian constitution, one MP said that he had enquired of his friends, 'Where is the Privy Council?' and no one knew. 'He then conceived the idea of starting at the top of Parliament street and knocking at every door and enquiring if the Privy council was at home, and in the course of his peregrinations he came to a door at which a policemen was standing, who, in answer to his inquiry directed him up a small back staircase, and upon entering a small room on the second floor he found himself in the presence of the august assembly.'[29]

The surroundings certainly were unpretentious. Judah Benjamin took a friend to hear him argue a case before a court which, Benjamin said, was one 'above all others in Christendom in which one can practice law like a gentleman.' This court, the friend learned, 'had the widest jurisdiction of any in the world ... and yet it presented the anomaly of not having any authority to pronounce any judgments whatsoever. In theory, the judges merely advise the Queen. In carrying out this fiction they sit at a large table, they wear neither robes or wigs and there were no tip-staves or usual court functionaries but only liveried servants.'[30] Members of the Judicial Committee sat at a long table with a vacant chair for the monarch at the end, until Lord Haldane replaced it with a semi-circular piece of mahogany, with no vacant place.[31]

In the 1870s the composition of the Judicial Committee was as unpretentious as its surroundings. The 1833 act formally creating the committee provided that its membership was to consist of the president of the Privy Council and other members of the Privy Council who held or had held high judicial office, the lord chancellor, the master of the rolls, the chief justices of the three common law courts, and others who had held high legal office. The crown was authorized to appoint two other persons, and summon others as required.[32] But the membership could be misleading, for most members were busy in the House of Lords or other courts.

Few apparently relished their work on the committee, and Henry Reeve often found it difficult to constitute a board. As Lord Westbury, the lord chancellor, once wrote to Reeve, after reluctantly agreeing to sit with the committee, 'Pray if you can, give us a paper with some variety and not wholly composed of dreary Indian appeals, the hearing of which always reminded me of the toil of Pharaoh's charioteers when they drove heavily their wheelless chariots in the deep sands of the Red Sea.'[33] Anecdotal as it might be, Westbury's view of the requisite legal talent was shared by his contemporaries. When he asked Sir William Erle why he did not attend the Judicial Committee, Erle replied that he was old and deaf and stupid. 'That is not a sufficient excuse,' replied Westbury, 'for Chelsford and I are very old, Napier is very deaf, Colvile is very stupid; but we four make an excellent tribunal.'[34] Wallace Graham, a Nova Scotian who appeared before the committee in 1887, was not quite as severe: 'The Judges are all kinds, deaf and impatient, talkative and jumping at conclusions, keen and sarcastic in a humorous way.' Graham also felt that the board would not take kindly to the 'oratorical way' of Canadian counsel who 'made gestures or raised the tone of their voice' but he found the 'Oh my Lord may I venture to – briefly my Lord of course' a little too much for his taste.[35]

By 1870, with 329 appeals pending and general agreement that the Judicial Committee was a disgrace, the government restructured the committee by adding four paid judges who had served either as a judge in a superior court or as chief justice of the High Court of Bengal, Bombay, or Madras. The first four to be appointed were Sir James

Colvile, a former chief justice of Bengal, who had been appointed in 1865 to hear Indian appeals; Sir Montague Smith, a one-time Conservative MP and a judge since 1865; Sir Barnes Peacock, who had succeeded Colvile in Bengal; and Sir Richard Collier, a Liberal MP whom Gladstone had made a judge for two days to enable him to qualify. In attendance, if not in writing the decisions, these four dominated the hearings on Canadian appeals for more than a decade.[36]

Additional reforms in 1875 created the lord of appeals in ordinary, chosen from the judges of the supreme courts or members of the bar with fifteen years' standing of England, Scotland, and Ireland. Not until the late 1880s, however, did the lords of appeal dominate the committee. The lord chancellor determined the composition of the board for each session or appeal, although the registrar, certainly until Reeve retired in 1887, and probably thereafter, appears to have had the day-to-day responsibility.[37] The presiding judge was the lord chancellor, if he attended, or the senior paid judge if no law lords were in attendance (which meant that Colvile and then Peacock presided over many of the early cases). However, after 1882, a law lord was always the presiding judge. The order of precedence was the lord chancellor, ex-lord chancellor, and then law lords in order of appointment (which, if Selborne, Herschell, or Halsbury were all absent, made Lord Watson the presiding judge).[38] In the twentieth century, if not earlier, the presiding judge, even if he were in a minority of one, decided who was to write the decision, although in practice the decision was more collegial and took account of the various interests and workloads of the members.[39]

There was little in the Judicial Committee's earliest decisions to indicate that its analysis of the distribution of legislative power or the nature of Canadian federalism would differ radically from the doctrines, however inchoate they might have appeared, emerging from the Canadian courts. No indications of indecisiveness, such as the multiple judgments and dissenting opinions in the Canadian courts, marked the decisions of the Judicial Committee. Their practice of rendering a single decision, reaffirmed in 1878, gave the appearance of a court supremely self-confident, almost arrogant, in its analysis and decisions. 'It is a most solemn part of the oath not to reveal what has passed in deliberation,' Lord Haldane wrote in 1923. 'If any Judge were to say that he had not agreed with his colleagues, the sword of the Constitution would descend on him. It never happens.'[40] Without dissent in reasons or result, it seemed that the law was so clear that all could agree.[41]

If certainty was desirable, there was great merit in the single decision. Officers of the Judicial Department of the Privy Council praised the procedure. 'It should not be forgotten,' they wrote in 1901, 'that although only one judgment is read, that one is submitted to all members of the court for revision before it is delivered in open court. Each judge makes his own amendments. The result is that the judgments of the Privy Council are remarkably free from dicta, which frequently occur where members of the court deliver separate judgments.'[42]

The law lords themselves had mixed opinions. Lord Radcliffe, appointed in 1949, believed it was one of the strengths of the Judicial Committee that the 'people who were accustomed to being in the Council got rather good at rendering one judgment that reflected the opinions of the others. There was a sort of a tradition that you didn't take a strong line unless it was one that could be shared by the others.'[43] Lord Pearce, on the other hand, suggested that the practice led to muddled law: 'We all know that in the Privy Council it gave quite a bit of weakness over the centuries to a Privy Council judgment that sentences were put in for the man who thought the appeal was doubtful as to whether it should succeed, and felt that it was more likely that it should fail, as against the man who wrote it, who was certain it should succeed, and so he put in the sentences ... You are getting a compromise judgement in a sense.'[44]

Less complimentary comments reveal that although the single judgment was not fiction, the court was occasionally, perhaps more than occasionally, divided on reasons and/or result. Before 1966, dissents could not be published, but sometimes they were recorded in the judgment book.[45] Lord Wright, who intimated later that he had dissented in a decision on a piece of R.B. Bennett's New Deal legislation, observed that the 'opinion does not necessarily represent the opinion of every member; it may be only that of a majority.'[46] And Lord Morton of Henryton, who admitted that opinion was often divided and unanimity impossible, confessed that 'infallibility is always rather a burden since no one is entitled to say, no matter what he might think, that the ultimate decision is wrong.'[47] Nor, what was even more important, could it be said that the *obiter*, so frequently embedded in the decision and not extracted from the result as precedent, expressed the judgment of any one other than he who wrote it. Sir Ivor Jennings, an apologist for the Judicial Committee's Canadian jurisprudence, wrote that while 'the substance is, no doubt, agreed to by the rest of the majority ... it is never certain that all expressions would have been accepted by the majority if they had fully considered them.'[48]

Many decisions, or more particularly the *ratio decidendi* and *obiter* contained in them, suggest that the collegial procedure described by Lord Morton and others was not taken very seriously by busy members of the board. It is impossible, for example, to reconcile many of the freewheeling judgments of Lord Watson and Viscount Haldane with the opinions of their colleagues expressed during the oral argument. Although it is difficult to penetrate the inner workings of the committee, Edward McWhinney's query is much to the point: 'Is a simple vote taken and the matter then left to the unfettered discretion of an individual judge appointed by the lord chancellor to write the opinion? The more notable Watson-Haldane opinions, for example, bear all the hallmarks of such a procedure.'[49]

The answer, in most Canadian cases, is probably that once the decision had been reached, members of the committee cared little for the argument developed by the judge chosen to write the decision. Moreover, although it cannot be documented for the law lords as it can for counsel, cases in the House of Lords were far more prestigious and noteworthy than those in the Judicial Committee, and well into the twentieth century 'the complaint could still be heard that the law lords treated their duties on the Board as a holiday from the duties in the House.'[50] While he was commenting on his own experience, Lord Denning's comments are likely even more true of Canadian appeals earlier in their history:

You had a case, then six weeks later [or in the instance of *Local Prohibition*, nine months] some chap comes up with his judgement. Well by that time you've forgotten all about it and you can't be bothered with the details and you don't take all that interest, or at least at all events I didn't by that time. I think if you leave it to one, you have to leave it to him and don't go through that judgement critically in the ordinary way. That's human nature, you've got other things to do.[51]

It is significant that on two occasions when the single-decision rule was questioned, it was retained not because it was a necessary corollary to the theory that the judgment was an advisory opinion to the crown, or even because it made certain the law, but because it was good for the empire. In 1878, when a dispute occurred over a dissenting opinion in an ecclesiastical case and led to an order-in-council reaffirming the ancient rule that 'no disclosure be made by any man how the particular voices went,'[52] Lord Selborne wrote that in the colonies 'the decisions of Her Majesty in Council have hitherto spoken with undivided voice and unquestioned authority' and that it would be unwise, perhaps, to invite 'controversies as to the soundness and finality of those decisions' by permitting dissenting opinions.[53]

Ten years later, when the chief justices of the Australian states recommended that members of the Judicial Committee should at least be free to deliver separate judgments, Lord Bramswell commented sarcastically to Halsbury, the lord chancellor, that he supposed 'the Australian judges think that sometimes their credit would be saved by a minority opinion.' Halsbury sought the opinion of thirteen jurists, nine of whom favoured retaining the single-decision practice on the grounds, as Lord Ashbourne put it, that 'this must tend to maintain a greater influence and prestige with the tribunals appealed from, and with the countries where they are situated.'[54] The Judicial Committee was still seen, as it had been with Cairns and Reeve in 1875, as a bond of imperial unity and guarantor of imperial legal supremacy which could be threatened by the appearance of disunity in the upper echelons of the imperial judiciary.

Oral arguments provide by far the most revealing insight into the workings of the Judicial Committee, as well as the problematic nature of the single opinion. When both counsel and judges in the Supreme Court made use of the oral arguments before the Judicial Committee in the seemingly contradictory cases of *Russell* and *Hodge*, Gwynne insisted that 'what they say there, in the argument, is of no consequence, because they all concur in the judgement, but one,' a number he must have deduced from the argument itself. Ritchie agreed that the court 'cannot pay serious attention to what is said in argument unless it is embodied in the judgement.' He also observed that, when *Hodge* was later cited in the Privy Council, one judge said, 'Yes, but there was a very strong minority in the judgment. It seems a very unsatisfactory way to deal with a decision.'[55] However, despite their questionable admissibility, Canadians continued to use the oral arguments when they were available.

Cautioned about their use in 1921, Wallace Nesbitt, briefly a judge of the Supreme Court of Canada (1903–5), informed Viscount Haldane that 'in our courts it has become a little fashionable of late to practically make use of all the observations of your Lordships, the whole argument. One is met on the other side the greater part of the time with the statement that their Lordships thought this, or thought that, or thought the other, not as evidenced by the ultimate judgement, but by casual observations made probably for the purpose of eliciting information ... and treated almost as solemnly as the judgment.' After whispered conversations with his colleagues, Haldane informed Nesbitt that

the decision of my colleagues and myself [is] that it is a disastrous practice. There is no settled opinion until you come to the judgement, and for the purpose of eliciting points it is very valuable in conversation to put to counsel the difficulties from time to time, but they are not settled observations, and taken in this fashion they are very misleading ... I hope you will make use of your very great position at the Bar in Canada to make it known that we do not attach importance to these interlocutory observations.[56]

However unacceptable in court, evidence from the oral argument is real evidence for the legal historian. As E.R. Cameron, registrar of the Supreme Court of Canada, commented, 'the remarks are illuminative, indicating as they do the individual views of the members of the Committee. They give the atmosphere, so to speak, of the case.'[57] They also suggest that the burden of infallibility must have been heavy indeed on the conscience of those who clearly were not of the majority in decision or reason, and who could not have accepted the *obiter* often embedded in the judgment.

Review of Canadian federalism by the Judicial Committee coincided with the gradual emergence in England in the latter part of the nineteenth century of a more literal or formal approach to the determination of the law. The characteristics of *formalism*, a term adopted from American legal history where it is used to distinguish it from the realist movement that followed, has been best described by P.S. Atiyah as 'an attitude of mind rather than anything else':[58]

... in particular, it involved rejection of the law-making power of the judge; rejection of the relevance of policy issues to legal questions, belief that law was a deductive science of principles, and that the one 'true' answer to legal questions could be found by a strictly logical process ... The notion that legal concepts and categories were merely tools by which lawyers could arrive at a range of justifiable decisions was not so much rejected, as simply not enter-

tained by most English lawyers. And inextricably involved in this development was the gradual decline of the influence of external factors or bodies of
thought on the law.[59]

In theory at least, formalism dictated a strict adherence to narrow
principles of statutory interpretation, particularly the literal rendering
of the text or the 'plain meaning' rule. As Lord Esher stated bluntly in
1891: 'If the words of an Act are clear, you must follow them, even
though they lead to a manifest absurdity. The Court has nothing to do
with the question whether the Legislature has committed an absurdity.'[60] In rare cases of obvious absurdity, however, the application of
the so-called 'golden' rule, as stated in 1857, permitted the court to
modify 'the grammatical and ordinary sense of the words ... so as to
avoid the absurdity and inconsistency, but no farther.'[61] As late as 1910,
Lord Chancellor Loreburn could state that 'we are not entitled to read
words into an Act of Parliament unless clear reason is to be found
within the four corners of the Act itself.'[62]

A second characteristic of formalism was the doctrine of precedent
and adherence to the principle of *stare decisis*. The doctrine was
asserted by Lord Campbell in 1861: 'The law laid down as your *ratio
decedendi*, being obviously binding upon inferior tribunals, and on all
the rest of the Queen's subjects, if it were not considered as equally
binding upon your Lordships, this House would be arrogating to itself
the right of altering the law, and legislating by its own separate authority.'[63] Whether the Judicial Committee was bound by its own decisions
led to a revealing exchange during the oral argument in the *McCarthy
Act Reference* in 1885, when the committee was confronted by decisions
in *Russell* and *Hodge* that seemed difficult to reconcile:[64]

Sir Barnes Peacock: Do I understand you correctly to admit that *Russell* v. *The
Queen* is not overruled by *Hodge* v. *The Queen*?
Horace Davey: Certainly. I do not know that your Lordships can overrule a
previous decision of your Lordships. The House of Lords cannot!
Sir Barnes Peacock: Some of the decisions have been varied by subsequent
decisions in the Privy Council.
Horace Davey: Your Lordships do not overrule; you explain.

Whether the committee was bound by its own decisions was never
authoritatively settled. Asked in 1946 to overrule *Russell*, Viscount
Simon expressed the opinion that 'their Lordships do not doubt that in

tendering advice to His Majesty that they are not absolutely bound by previous decisions of the Board as is the House of Lords by its own judgements.' However, he added, 'on constitutional questions it must be seldom indeed that the Board would depart from a previous decision which it may be assumed will have been acted on both by government and subjects.'[65] In practice, in spite of the authority of the single decision, the committee did find it convenient to distinguish *ratio* and *obiter*, or ignore the plain-meaning rule in reviewing its own decisions, to explain why an opinion should or should not be regarded as a binding precedent.

Although formalism was becoming the dominant characteristic of English law in the late nineteenth century, as Atiyah has observed, the differences between the formalist and realist judge could be deceptive for both tended 'to justify their decisions by a similar judicial process' and both generally accepted 'the conventions of the judicial style. And if the realist is more willing on some occasions to declare his open allegiance to some policy, the formalist is just as likely to be influenced by the same policy in an unconscious manner.'[66] Put less respectfully, policy considerations could be conveniently disguised by a mask of formalism.

While the lower courts were increasingly dominated by a professionalized judiciary, appointments to the highest legal offices were openly political. Asked to veto the appointment of an unsuitable candidate, Lord Salisbury informed the lord chancellor in 1897 that it would be 'at variance with the unwritten law of our party system ... that party claims should always weigh heavily in the disposal of the highest legal appointments.'[67] Moreover, the law lords were valued for their political experience. During the discussion of court reform in 1873, Lord Salisbury insisted that the judges of any final court of appeal should sit in the House of Lords. He explained that 'since they often had to make law as judges they should be trained for it by sitting part of the time as legislators.' Such experience, he said, saved the judges from 'too technical and professional a spirit; and their decision gained in breadth.'[68] The situation had not changed by the end of the century. Lord Chancellor Halsbury believed that political experience (as well as a congenial ideology) were essential and protested 'violently against the notion of the law of England being crystallized by the paste and scissors lawyers.'[69] As a result, in contrast to the lower courts, wrote Robert Stevens, 'the law lords took a remarkably casual approach to precedent and *stare decisis*'.[70]

Certainly there was an increasing discussion in the Lords about legal doctrines being objective and derived from the logic of the common law; and, at its core, this was an undoubted truth. Those who ran the House of Lords and the Privy Council, however, were well aware that the appeals reaching them were not dealing with core situations, but with those competing policies and doctrines inevitably operating at the penumbra. Both in administration and decision making, the political dominated over the professional.[71]

Moreover, prior to 1900, in the Judicial Committee's most formative lawmaking period, most of its members came to maturity long before the triumph of legal formalism. They also came from a variety of traditions – English, Scottish, Irish – had been groomed in practitioners' chambers, and had no exposure to academic legal education or the nascent school of textbook writers. They represented an earlier tradition, and although elements of formalism and strict textualism appeared in the language of their opinions, the underlying reasoning was often heavily structural, prudential, or even based on imaginative transatlantic assumptions about Canadian history and language.

On the other hand, the view that powers, including legislative powers, were 'paradigmatically spheres that had sharp boundaries' within which 'powers could be exercised without restraint or fear,' also a characteristic of formalism or mechanical jurisprudence, provided both a practical and theoretical approach to judicial review of divided jurisdiction.[72] The outstanding feature of the British North America Act was the attempt to draw sharp and mutually exclusive divisions of legislative authority between the Dominion and the provinces. The task of the courts was to police these boundaries. Conceptual boundary maps and jurisdictional recipes differed. And as revealed in the Canadian courts, boundaries and recipes were often determined more by subjective historical, structural, and prudential considerations than by text or doctrine. Although text and doctrine may have constrained the courts, they seldom tied them down. If so, the critical question was which subjective considerations influenced reasoning and decision.

Unlike Canadian courts, the Judicial Committee did not adopt the view that the interpretation of a federal constitution was somehow different than determining the ownership of land in Bengal: the principles of statutory construction in which they were trained were applied to both. The editor of the *Legal News* objected to applying the accepted rules of statutory interpretation: 'We should think that a statute which gives a constitution to a people should be dealt with in a wider and more comprehensive manner than an ordinary act. It has a well-considered policy and a history.'[73] But, as Lord Hobhouse authoritatively wrote in his first Canadian decision, after returning from a career in the governor general's council in India: regardless of the constitutional importance of the case, 'questions of this class have been left to the ordinary Courts of Law, which must treat the provisions of the Act in question by the same methods of construction which they apply to other statutes.'[74]

In an early case, counsel pointed out that in Canada we 'have now as they have in the United States a written constitution and would like it if it had been possible to have had the assistance of some of the legal minds in the United States to govern us in the construction of this Act, such men as Mr. Justice Story or Mr. Kent.' Encountering federalism for the first time, however, Lord Justice Mellish assured him that the board needed no such assistance: 'I think you may assume we can construe a statute.'[75]

The Judicial Committee was not prepared to hear argument based on policy or history, pre-Confederation practice, or the Canadian use of language. In one of the first cases to come before the committee, counsel was attempting to cite Lord Carnarvon's remarks introducing the BNA bill in 1867 when Lord Justice James abruptly cut him off: 'You do not suppose that we shall be influenced in construing the section by any thing that the Earl of Carnarvon said, and it is no use our having any history which is not to affect us.'[76] During the oral argument in *Russell*, counsel for the Dominion attempted to refute Judah Benjamin's heretical 'Home Rule' argument by discussing the formation of the federation. Sir Montague Smith immediately interjected, 'The Act is what we have to look at,' and, when counsel continued, Smith stated with supreme self-confidence: 'I do not think there is anything so obscure in the construction of the Act, with regard to the distribution of power, and the dominium given to the Dominion of Canada, that renders it necessary to go into the history of it.'[77]

Later, as counsel attempted to introduce pre-Confederation debates and statutes to shed light on the meaning of the words 'the regulation of trade and commerce,' Sir Robert Collier asked whether such extrinsic materials should be allowed, and answered his own question: 'We take the Act and what appears on the face of it; we do not go into any interpretation of it by referring to what took place when it was passed.' To which Smith added: 'It may be that they had a wrong interpretation, for it may be that they used it in a different sense in this Act. It is a mere speculation.'[78]

It was a strange comment from a judge who the year before had speculated that the words 'the regulation of trade and commerce' may have been used in 1867 as they had been in the Act of Union between England and Scotland in 1707, and then proceeded to formulate his momentous *obiter dictum* on the scope of the trade and commerce power in part on that speculation.[79] His historical analogy was received with derision in the Supreme Court. 'Here we have statutes enacted with reference to the history and peculiar circumstances of the country, and they go home to England and they are now disposed of by a tribunal that can have no knowledge whatsoever of the minute history of our country as those who have lived in it all our lives,' exclaimed Chief Justice Ritchie during the argument on the *McCarthy Act Reference*. In the same case, Gwynne asked S.H. Blake, who was attempting to use pre-Confederation evidence to aid in construing the meaning of trade and commerce, 'You exclude the Statute of Anne altogether?' To which Blake replied: 'I will not exclude it if your Lordships can get any light from it, and all we want is light, but I think what was passed here will shed more light on it than the Acts passed in the reign of Queen Anne.'[80]

Indeed, history as a clue to the intentions of the framers or the historical context of Confederation itself were dismissed as irrelevant in the Judicial Committee. Such evidence might be 'of great historical value, but not otherwise pertinent,' Richard Haldane commented during the oral argument in *Local Prohibition* in 1895, adding, 'It does seem a little odd to refer to those things which took place and were no doubt the basis of the Act which afterwards became the Confederation Act, for that is certainly not what your Lordships have got to interpret.'[81] A similar fate awaited the historically minded judges in the Australian federation. Dismissing the historical argument of the Chief Justice of Victoria, Lord Halsbury wrote that it was 'an expansion of the canon of interpretation in question to consider the knowledge of those who framed the Constitution and their supposed preference for this or that model which might have been in their minds. Their Lordships are not able to acquiesce in any such principle of interpretation.'[82] Lord Selborne sarcastically dismissed legislative intention with the comment: 'We know nothing about the mind of the legislature, and in point of fact, no legislature has any mind, except that which is expressed in the words which it has used.'[83] Watson was equally dismissive:

'Intention of the Legislature' is a common but very slippery phrase, which, popularly understood, may signify anything from intention embodied in positive enactment to speculative opinion as to what the Legislature probably would have meant, although there has been an omission to enact it. In a Court of Law or Equity, what the Legislature intended to be done or not done can only be legitimately ascertained from that which it has chosen to enact, either in express words or by reasonable and necessary implication.[84]

It was a classic, but disconcerting, analysis from one who on occasion based his reasoning and decision on what the legislature probably would have meant, or should have meant, or had 'obviously' or 'apparently' meant.

The most infamous application of the rules of statutory construction, combined with the refusal to hear argument about history or context as a clue to the intentions of the framers, was the 1892 decision upholding Manitoba's right to abolish separate schools, a decision that reversed a unanimous judgment of the Supreme Court.[85] Adhering to the 'ordinary meaning rule' enabled the board to determine that the word 'practice' meant just that. Thus, the provision in the 1870 Manitoba Act guaranteeing the right to denominational schools which existed 'by law or practice' had not been violated by the abolition of publicly supported separate schools in 1890: the minority still had the same rights to establish and finance their own schools as they had by 'practice' in 1870. Even Watson, who seemed sympathetic to the minority, admitted that although the intention was to guarantee separate schools, the 'language may tie you down.'[86]

It was convenient to be tied down by language because the committee, with the probable exceptions of Watson and the Catholic Morris, was openly hostile to Catholic schools, particularly Lord Macnaghten, who wrote the decision. It was not the law that was at fault, he declared, but the narrow religious convictions of the minority, and a decision of *ultra vires* would fasten Catholic schools on the province forever and limit the powers of the state 'to the useful but somewhat humble office of making regulations for the sanitary conditions of schoolhouses.' The decision was blatantly the triumph of policy disguised as strict statutory interpretation. As Taschereau exploded in the Supreme Court, it was a construction of the statute so 'unreasonable, unjust, inconsistent and contrary to the intentions of the law giver' that, on the subsequent appeal on the possibility of remedial action, Lord Herschell was compelled both to justify and then repudiate the decision.

In a remarkable critique of legal formalism (and of his own court), Herschell admitted that the decision did not reflect the intention of the Manitoba Act:

It was not doubted that the object of the 1st sub-section of section 22 was to afford protection to denominational schools, or that it was proper to have regard to the intent of the Legislature and the surrounding circumstances in interpreting the enactment. But the question which had to be determined was the true construction of the language used. The function of a tribunal is limited to construing the words employed; it is not justified in forcing them into a meaning which they cannot possibly bear. Its duty is to interpret, not to enact ... The question is, not what may be supposed to have been intended, but what has been said ... While, however, it is necessary to resist any temptation to deviate from sound rules of construction in the hope of more completely satisfying the intention of the Legislature, it is quite legitimate where more than one construction of a statute is possible, to select that one which will best carry out what appears from the general scope of the legislation and the surrounding circumstances to have been its intentions.[87]

Or, one might add, what best serves the purpose at hand. As C.K. Allen has perceptively observed, 'words mean nothing in themselves; the very conception of interpretation connotes the introduction of elements which are necessarily extrinsic to the words themselves.'[88]

Reading the oral arguments and the decisions often recalls the comments of an experienced British draughtsman that 'I have certainly observed a tendency among members of the legal profession to assume as a golden rule for the interpretation of Acts that they were not intended to mean what, to a plain man, they would appear to say.'[89] In the result, it can be argued that the convenient refusal to move beyond the allegedly strict rules of statutory interpretation allowed the Judicial Committee to give a meaning to words of their own devising. Moreover, while denying the admissibility of empirical historical evidence, members of the Judicial Committee also felt free to impose their own assumptions about the context, meaning, and intentions of the 1867 constitution, the most familiar of which was Lord Watson's famous lead-in to his decision in *Local Prohibition* – 'It was apparently contemplated by the framers.'[90] There is indeed, in argument and decision, confirmation of Strong's conviction that without context and history 'the task of interpretation would degenerate into mere speculation and guess work.'[91]

In fact, in their decisions, their Lordships ranged far and wide in commenting on the objectives of Confederation, the structure of the BNA Act, and the proper determination of the scope of federal and provincial powers. The *ratio decedendi*, which, as Viscount Simon commented, was 'the true source of precedent,' was often so mixed with *obiter dicta* as to be difficult to determine. Worse, the *obiter* themselves became embedded in precedent with a profound and lasting effect on Canadian federalism.[92]

5

Caesar Speaks, 1874–1888

and the Board looked much perplexed ...
– Donald MacMaster to John A. Macdonald, 12 November 1885

As they began their long tenure as Canada's final court of appeal, the members of the Judicial Committee did not see themselves as judicial statesmen whose task it was to shape a federal constitution for a new colony. Although federalism was to them a legislative and judicial novelty, they maintained that their role was the familiar one of finding meaning in the language and thus the objects of a somewhat unusual British statute. 'In performing this difficult duty,' wrote Sir Montague Smith, 'it will be a wise course for those upon whom it is thrown, to decide each case which arises as best they can, without entering more largely upon an interpretation of the statute than is necessary for the decision of the particular question at hand.'[1] Although the advice was not always followed, and Smith himself was guilty of venturing into the forbidden territory of speculation and forced historical analogies, the committee initially was generally judicious in its reasons and decisions about the interlocking structure of sections 91 and 92 and the scope of their enumerations.

By 1887, the Judicial Committee had heard thirteen appeals involving the division of legislative jurisdiction.[2] With the exception of a reference on the validity of a federal liquor licence act in 1885, the federal and provincial governments were never directly contesting parties. In its decisions the committee appeared to endorse Lord Selborne's opinion that it 'is not to be expected that the Legislature of the Dominion has exceeded its powers unless upon grounds really of a serious character.'[3] Of the five federal statutes reviewed, only the blatantly political liquor licence act was found unconstitutional, while three of the eight challenges to provincial legislation were upheld. The committee affirmed the five appeals from the Supreme Court of Canada, and reversed four of the eight appeals from provincial courts. The composition of the boards was reasonably stable throughout the period. The paid judges were usually a majority, although seven opinions were delivered, by law lords, four by Selborne.[4] Sir Montague Smith was the most familiar presence, sitting on eleven appeals and delivering four decisions.

Selborne's decision in his first case, *L'Union St-Jacques* v. *Belisle* in 1874, delivered, as was his custom, immediately after the argument, suggested that he understood the structure and objective of sections 91 and 92. The Quebec Court of Queen's Bench had held (3–2) that a Quebec act to prevent L'Union St-Jacques from becoming insolvent was *ultra vires* be-cause it encroached on the federal government's power over bankruptcy and insolvency.[5] Selborne had little difficulty deciding that, on its face, an act to *prevent* the bankruptcy of a local society seemed to be a matter of a local or private nature within section 92 (16). However, he continued, that section was qualified by the deeming clause in section 91: 'But the *onus* is on the Respondent to show that this, being of itself of a local or private nature, does also come within one or more of the classes of subjects specially enumerated in the 91st section.' With an *obiter* often cited later, he dismissed the argument advanced by Judah Benjamin, 'with his usual ingenuity and force,' that a federal bankruptcy law *might* be passed which would bring the association within its embrace:

Their Lordships are by no means prepared to say that if any such law as that had been passed by the Dominion Legislature, it would have been beyond their competency: nor that, if it had been so passed, it would have been within the competency of the provincial legislature afterwards to take a particular association out of the scope of a general law of that kind ... But no such law ever has been passed; and to suggest the possibility of such a law as a reason why the power of the provincial legislature over this local and private association should be in abeyance or altogether taken away, is to make a suggestion which, if followed up to its consequences, would go very far to destroy that power in all cases.[6]

Benjamin was a familiar counsel in Canadian cases and appeared before Selborne a year later in the appeal on *Valin*, when he was again congratulated on his able presentation of a weak case.[7] Although leave to appeal was denied, the reasons were an important contribution to federalism jurisprudence. Immediately after the petition was heard, Selborne stated that the 'subject- matter of this controversy' was 'beyond all doubt' placed within Dominion authority by section 41 giving the federal government control over its own elections laws and procedures. He dismissed Benjamin's argument that the power had been exercised unconstitutionally in conferring jurisdiction on the provincial courts with the pronouncement that 'if the subject-matter is within the jurisdiction of the Dominion Parliament, it is not within the jurisdiction of the Provincial Parliament, and that which is excluded from the 91st section from the jurisdiction of the Dominion Parliament is not anything else than matters coming within the classes of subjects assigned exclusively to the legislature of the provinces.' Read beside section 41, section 92(14) had nothing to do with the election petitions, and, therefore, by implication the matter clearly fell within the federal residual power.[8]

The relationship of the enumerated powers in sections 91 and 92 came explicitly before the Judicial Committee in *Cushing* v. *Dupuy*, a challenge to a federal insolvency act which provided that decisions of the Quebec Court of Appeal should be final in matters of insolvency. A constitutional question had not been raised in the Quebec courts, and although the central argument of the appellants before the Judicial Committee was that the provision derogated from the prerogative right of the crown to allow such appeals, it was also 'very faintly urged,' Sir Montague Smith noted, that the act interfered with property and civil rights in the province. With the declaratory clause and section 91(21) as authority, Smith dismissed the argument:

The answer to these objections is obvious. It would be impossible to advance a step in the construction of a scheme for the administration of insolvent estates without interfering with and modifying some of the ordinary rights of property and other civil rights ... It is therefore to be presumed, and indeed it is a necessary implication, that the Imperial statute, in assigning to the Dominion

Parliament the subjects of bankruptcy and insolvency, intended to confer on it the power to interfere with property, civil rights, and procedure within the Province, so far as a general law relating to those subjects might affect them.[9]

In short, if the 'matter' clearly fell within a federal enumeration, *interference* with the provincial enumerations did not invalidate the legislation. A year later Smith made the same point when provincial legislation was challenged in part because it interfered with federal jurisdiction over trade and commerce.

Parsons was the first important case to involve a direct conflict between the enumerated heads of federal and provincial jurisdiction.[10] In decision, it embedded the dual jurisdiction over the insurance industry which still persists; in *obiter*, it provided an interpretation of the scope of the trade and commerce power which has shaped, if not determined, federal regulatory capacity and remains to this day a controversial issue in Canadian jurisprudence. Politically, it gave Oliver Mowat his first opportunity to introduce the Judicial Committee to his version of provincial autonomy and the division of powers.

The day after the Supreme Court of Canada decided in *Parsons* that an Ontario act imposing statutory conditions on insurance policies was *intra vires*, an agitated John Wellington Gwynne urged Macdonald to go to the Judicial Committee for much more was at stake than the regulation of the industry. The decision, he warned, was 'the thin edge of the wedge to bring about provincial sovereignty which I believe Mr. Mowat is labouring to do ... I confess a very strong opinion that yesterday's judgment in those cases will be made the justification for arguing openly the question of provincial sovereignty, against the Dominion authority.'[11] Macdonald was as sensitive as Gwynne to Mowat's political objectives, but apparently less aware or concerned that the courts could be his instrument. Though he did not intervene in the appeal, he was kept informed by Sir Alexander Galt, the high commissioner, who wrote that in the hearing on the appeal the judges so expressed themselves that counsel for the companies 'consider the case as good as won.'[12]

However, on the eve of the opening argument, the solicitors for the companies informed Macdonald, then in London, that their clients were concerned about the composition of the board and asked him whether, 'looking to the importance of the constitutional question involved,' he might 'have desired to make some official communica-

tion on the subject through channels which are not open to us.' But it
was too late in the day 'as the arguments will begin tomorrow and we
find that Sir Montague Smith, whose presence will certainly add
weight to the decision, is sitting this week as the Privy Council Board,
it appears to us that matters had better now be left to their course.'[13]

Characteristically, Gwynne had gone to extremes, but he had correctly anticipated Mowat's view of the importance of his first appeal to
the Judicial Committee in pursuit of provincial power. When it was
rumoured that the insurance companies had struck a deal with Parsons allowing him to keep the insurance money and permitting the
case to be argued *ex parte* – on the part of the companies only – before
the Judicial Committee, Mowat immediately asked his London solicitors if the practices of the committee would 'allow the Province to
intervene in such cases to argue constitutional questions? Such questions being new in England, it might be very important that the Provinces should have the right of appearing by Counsel even where party
to the suit in the same interest has counsel.'[14] Although leave to intervene was not granted, Mowat in effect took over his own case.[15] Since
Ontario was not party to the suit, Benjamin's Ontario retainer was not
in effect and he could act for the insurance companies, Mowat secured
Sir John Holker, a former attorney general, to represent the province.[16]

Mowat went to London for the appeal and prepared a lengthy brief
for Holker and the solicitors, which provides an invaluable insight into
Mowat's construction of the division of powers and his theory of federalism. Since section 92 gave the provinces exclusive jurisdiction over
property and civil rights, Mowat argued, the onus was on the appellants to show that insurance also came within section 91 enumerations.
To counter the argument that it fell within trade and commerce, Mowat
asserted that, trade and commerce was implicitly limited by the inclusion in section 91 of other branches of commercial law, among which
insurance was not mentioned. Mowat admitted that, although the declaratory clause indicated that the 'enumeration may contain some particulars which, unless so specified would not have been held to be
included in the general words,' the enumerated powers, in effect, were
intended to embrace 'all possible subjects of legislative action in Canada' and resort should be had to the residual clause 'in the event only
of a case happening to arise which could not by any just construction
be brought within the enumerated particulars of either section. An
unnecessary reference to the general words, in order to give or support
a wider interruption of the enumerated powers of the Federal author-

ity than they might otherwise bear, is contrary to the intention and (it is submitted) to the proper construction of the Act.' Thus, the 'supreme national sovereignty' of the federal government endorsed by Gwynne and Taschereau in the Supreme Court was pure fiction: 'The authority of the Federal Parliament, as respects the province, is confined to certain specified matters and extends to no others.'[17]

As reported, Holker argued that trade and commerce must receive a limited definition and 'should be construed as applying to all regulations of trade and commerce which do not affect civil rights.' In addition, he continued, the provinces were empowered to deal 'with all questions of a local character, and the mode in which persons carry on their business within the limits of the province is a question of a local character.' Although Mowat had never been quite as explicit, Holker contended that the 'provinces are virtually separate countries federated into one, as in the case of the United States. Each member of the Confederation is a separate state, and has the right to make its own laws, subject to those which apply to the whole Confederation.'

Sir Farrer Herschell, the solicitor general, and Benjamin argued for exclusive federal control over insurance. The federal government possessed all powers except those given to the provinces and the 'true mode of construction, is to see if the subject is exclusively given to the Provincial Parliament, if not it belongs to the Dominion Parliament.' Property and civil rights had to be construed in a narrow sense, 'civil rights which flow from the operation of the law,' and must not be construed 'as to affect or cut down the exclusive federal control over trade, commerce and contracts.' Admitting that a single contract of indemnity might not fall within trade and commerce, they argued that 'if an insurance company is formed whose business it is to make such contracts, its transactions fall within the description of trade and commerce, that is of carrying on a business for profit, which is all that is meant by trade.' Finally, the provincial contention that, although the federal government could incorporate an insurance company, 'the power to prescribe its mode of carrying on business must be split between two legislatures' was irreconcilable with the word 'exclusive' as used in the BNA Act.[18]

In spite of his admonition to stick closely to the matter at hand, Smith felt that it was necessary in his judgment to attempt an analysis of the objectives and thus the structure of the BNA Act. He concluded that the authors realized that a 'sharp and definite distinction' between the two lists of enumerated powers could not be attained 'and that some of the classes of subjects assigned to the provincial legislatures unavoidably ran into and were embraced by some of the enumerated classes of subjects in section 91.' As a result, the act contained both the notwithstanding (declaratory) and deeming clauses in an 'endeavour to give pre-eminence to the Dominion Parliament in cases of conflict of powers,' and, whatever its broader purpose, the deeming clause applied 'in its grammatical construction only to number 16 of section 92.' However, Smith contended that in some cases where there was an 'apparent conflict,' it could not have been intended that 'powers exclusively assigned to the provincial legislature should be absorbed in those given to the Dominion Parliament,' and illustrated his point by noting the obvious exclusion of the solemnization of marriage from the broader federal powers over marriage and divorce or the distribution of taxing powers.

Smith then embedded what has become known as the double-aspect and mutual-modification doctrines in the jurisprudence of the Judicial Committee: 'With regard to certain classes of subjects, therefore, generally described in Section 91, legislative power may reside as to some matters falling within the general description of these subjects in the legislatures of the provinces.' If a conflict should exist, it was the duty of the courts to determine 'in what degree, and to what extent,' authority lay with each level of government. In so doing, the two sections had to be 'read together, and the language of one interpreted, and, where necessary, modified by that of the other' in order to arrive at a 'reasonable and practical construction of the language of the sections, so as to reconcile the respective powers they contain, and give effect to all of them.'[19]

Smith then threw caution to the wind and embarked on a momentous voyage of discovery to define the scope of both property and civil rights and trade and commerce. Section 94 demonstrated to him that property and civil rights was as broad as the French civil law that had been guaranteed in the Quebec Act of 1774. From the presence of one enumeration in section 91 – 'Bills of Exchange and Promissory Notes' – that involved contracts, he concluded that contracts in general were not among federal powers. To counter the argument that the insurance industry fell within trade and commerce, Smith stated that if such a claim were true there would be no need to mention banking, bills of exchange, or interest in the section 91 enumerations. And reaching far outside the 1867 act or pre-Confederation practice – or even the American trade and commerce power frequently referred to in Canadian courts – he mused that the words may have been used 'in some such sense' as the words 'regulation of trade' were used in the Act of Union of 1707 between England and Scotland and British regulatory acts. The concluding *obiter* was ominous for the future:

Construing, therefore, the words 'regulation of trade and commerce' by the various aides to their interpretation above suggested they would include political arrangements in regard to trade requiring the sanction of Parliament, regulation of trade in matters of interprovincial concern, and it may be that they would include general regulation of trade affecting the whole Dominion. Their Lordships abstain on the present occasion from any attempt to define the limits of the authority of the Dominion Parliament in this direction.

But that authority did not include the regulation of contracts of a particular business or trade. Having reached that conclusion, it was not necessary for the committee 'to consider the question how far the general power to make regulations of trade and commerce, when competently exercised by the Dominion Parliament, might legally modify or affect property and civil rights in the provinces, or the legislative power of the provincial legislatures in relation to those subjects.'[20]

Finally, responding to Taschereau's argument that in upholding the Ontario act the court was in fact regulating the federal power to incorporate companies, Smith observed that the federal power of incorporation fell not within trade and commerce but within the residual clause as an exclusion from section 92, thus implicitly deciding that Ottawa could not necessarily regulate that which it incorporated. As he said, 'it by no means follows (unless indeed the view of the learned judge is right as to the scope of the words "the regulation of trade and commerce") that because the Dominion Parliament has alone the right to create a corporation to carry on business throughout the Dominion that it has the right to regulate its contracts in each of the provinces.'[21]

Smith's long *obiter* became embedded as a definitional precedent in case law, with its qualifications overlooked, and had a deep and long-lasting effect on the federal power over trade and commerce. The *obiter* was as unnecessary as it was problematic. Had Smith not entered 'more largely upon an interpretation of the statute than is necessary,' he would have written that, in pith and substance, contracts of indemnity were clearly a matter belonging to property and civil rights, and whatever interference there might have been with trade and commerce was incidental.[22] In fact, that is what he soon claimed to have done.

During the oral argument in *Russell* v. *The Queen* six months later, when counsel for Russell repeatedly attempted to use Smith's definition of trade and commerce as invalidating the Canada Temperance Act because of its interference with property and civil rights, Sir Montague denied that the question of interference ever arose in *Parsons*:

I think we said that it was not necessary to consider it, because what they did there was clearly within the 92nd clause & it did not come within any of the enumerated items in section 91. But we expressly said that the question did not arise whether when it was apparently within one & also within the other, the 91st section might not overbear it. That question did not arise in that case. There we held, rightly or wrongly, that what was done was not a regulation of trade and commerce. We decided that it did not [sic] [did] fall within that subsection of 92 as to property and civil rights. The question of one overriding the other did not arise. If it had been an interference with the regulation of trade & commerce, a question would have arisen which did not arise. You seem to assume that we decided the contrary to that. I think you will find that is not so, if you look at the case.[23]

Subsequently, when counsel cited his *obiter* as a definition of the scope of trade and commerce, Smith was even more emphatic: 'It is only an observation on the Acts. It is not a statement of law.' He later added, 'It only decides what they dealt with in that case, and expressly left it open.'[24]

Smith's reasons and historical analogies were ridiculed during the argument at the Supreme Court on the *McCarthy Act Reference* in 1885. 'The decisions of judges after judges and courts after courts, which have stood for twenty or thirty years, are swept away by decisions of the judges of the Privy Council who cannot possibly know anything about these matters,' exclaimed Samuel Strong. Chief Justice Ritchie echoed his outrage: 'Is there a man living in the Dominion of Canada who believes that when the Act of Confederation was agreed upon by the representatives of this country ... any one of these men had in his mind's eye the statute of Anne as the foundation of our constitution?'[25]

Yet, however absurd in reasons, however often Smith stated that his definition was not a matter of law, a matter of law it became, shaping federal public policy until it was revisited by the Supreme Court a century later.

Months before *Parsons* was heard at the Judicial Committee, an appeal was under way against the Supreme Court decision in *Fredericton*. Thomas Barker, in whose name *Fredericton* had been brought to court, had died before an appeal was launched, but the liquor interests seized the case of William Russell who had been convicted under the Canada Temperance Act. The Supreme Court of New Brunswick, on the precedent of *Fredericton*, confirmed the conviction and Russell appealed directly to the Judicial Committee.[26]

Since his return to office, Macdonald had been furiously but unsuccessfully lobbied by Eugene O'Keefe and the liquor interests to repeal the Liberals' Temperance Act or at least weaken its provisions,[27] and now, with O'Keefe and his friends on their way to the Judicial Committee, Macdonald was pressed by the temperance lobby to defend the act in London. The appeal was 'a direct attack upon the Sovereignty of Canada as expressed in an act of Parliament, confirmed by its Supreme Court, and enforced by its own officers,' warned T.T. Brown, vice-president of the Dominion Alliance. Moreover, the appellants had retained Judah Benjamin, the 'champion of State rights,' and 'the powers of the Dominion Government would be few if left to his interpretation.'[28] But Macdonald refused to intervene on the suspect grounds that there were no funds and in the end the Dominion Alliance financed the defence. John Maclaren, a leading member of the Montreal bar, acted for the Alliance, with Ralph Fullarton, an English barrister, as his junior. Benjamin was assisted by Reginald Brown.

When the hearing began on 2 May 1882, Benjamin was suddenly called to an appeal in the House of Lords, and Brown opened with the argument that the act did not fall within trade and commerce or the criminal law but within provincial powers over licensing, property, and civil rights, or local or private matters. Within minutes, Sir Montague Smith's interjection suggested the direction the court would take: 'You first say that it is not a regulation of trade and commerce, but it will be your first argument by and by to show it is within section 92 and could not be passed by the Dominion Parliament. Of course you may say it could not be passed by either, but if it could not be passed by the Provincial Parliament then the question would be, whether the Dominion could not pass it, under its general powers.' To which Sir Robert Collier, who had obviously read the Supreme Court judgment, carefully added: 'That is the view of most of the Judges. They say if you once concede it is *ultra vires* of the Provincial Parliament, then it follows it is *intra vires* of the Dominion. That is a very short way of disposing of it.'[29] That the committee was disposed to uphold the act under the residual clause could be detected early on the second day, when Sir Barnes Peacock cut off Brown:

Peacock: I wanted to ask you, might not an act for regulating the sale of intoxicating liquors, throughout the Dominion with the object of promoting temperance in the Dominion be a law for the order and good government of Canada in relation to a matter not coming within the classes of subjects, by this Act, exclusively assigned to the Legislature of the Province, supposing it did not come within the general words 'trade and commerce,' might not it come within the previous words in the introductory part of the section?

Smith: It certainly would, unless you can point out that it comes within a class of subjects which is exclusively assigned to the Province.

Peacock: That would not be a matter of a merely local or private nature in the province within subsection 16 of the 92nd section.

Brown: In the first place, it is not a law for the peace, order and good government of Canada.

Peacock: Is it good Government of Canada to promote temperance throughout the Dominion. That would be the good order and Government of Canada.

Brown: It is possible, if it were such a law, that we should not be here.

Peacock: It may not be a very good mode of doing it, or it may be. They did not do it directly, but they passed a law applicable to the whole of Canada, giving a local option ... Is that a matter exclusively within the Province; within any of the classes mentioned in section 92. I do not want to interrupt you – only to see what you say as to that – because that is the point which operates upon my mind.

Brown: I submit that it does not come within those words.

Smith: Surely everything comes within those words, which is not specially assigned to the province.

Brown: Yes, that is so.

Smith: You need not criticize the words, because they have general legislative power over all matters not specifically and exclusively assigned to the Provincial power. Well, your first step, of course, is to show that the Parliament of the Province, or the Legislature of the Province might have passed such a law. If not, and if it is to be passed at all, then it must be by the Dominion Parliament.

Brown: Yes, my Lord.

Peacock: The special classes enumerated in section 91 are expressly stated 'But not so as to restrict the generality of the foregoing terms of this section.' They are not to restrict the generality of the previous words.

Brown: No, my Lord.[30]

The committee repeatedly dismissed Brown's argument that the act was invalid because it interfered with provincial licensing powers and, particularly, with property and civil rights. 'If you take the widest possible meaning of 'property and civil rights in the Province,' it would give the province the right of Legislation with regard to everything,' Collier interjected, 'and would take from the Dominion Parliament the power of legislating about anything. You must take it with certain restrictions.' To which Smith added, 'Property and civil rights you must take it may be affected by an Act of the Dominion Legislature in some of the enumerated powers.'[31] And Peacock later went to the heart of the matter: 'The Act does not say interference with any of these classes of subjects; but they are to legislate exclusively upon those subjects.' The distinction must be drawn, he insisted, between *interfering with* and *legislating upon*, for there was nothing in the act that invalidated federal legislation because of its interference with matters within provincial jurisdiction.[32] Again and again, the committee encouraged Brown to make the 92(16) argument because of the local-option provision, but Brown informed the judges that Benjamin had agreed to make that case.

When Benjamin arrived mid-way through the second day, his arguments fared no better than Brown's. He first stated that the object of Confederation was only to form a union for 'political and commercial purposes' and create 'a common front of emulation or defence' against the United States. 'In other words, whatever was domestic, whatever was private ... whatever was Home Rule was to be left with the Provinces. Their domestic Institutions, their Home Rule was not to be interfered with, but the general purpose of an Empire, of a Confederation, of a great government were all to be given up.' The proper rule of construction of sections 91 and 92, therefore, was one that would prevent any interference with the domestic legislation of the provinces by withdrawing from section 91 all powers given to the provinces. Unwilling to let that pass, Smith quietly observed that 'it is very difficult – because the legislature would appear to have reversed the general principle. They say notwithstanding anything in the 92nd section contained, the classes that are enumerated at all events are to prevail if there is anything like a conflict.'[33]

Benjamin then argued that the local-option provision by its 'very nature' violated the principle of home rule. 'You say they cannot do it, in a matter of a purely local nature, by a contrivance for making it general,' countered Smith. 'Then what you have first to make out is, that an Act of this sort is one of a purely local nature.'[34] But Benjamin failed to address the question and, making little headway with the argument that it was legislation relating to tavern licences, or property and civil rights, abruptly ended his argument: 'I really have said all that I have to say, and before a tribunal like this, it is no use repeating it.'[35]

Counsel were then instructed to withdraw, and when they returned, Smith told John Maclaren that they wished to hear argument only about 92(16). 'If it is not within that, there is an end to the case, as far as the Respondents are concerned. If it is within it, then the further question would arise, whether it comes within any of the enumerated classes in section 91' and was thus withdrawn from 92(16) by the deeming clause.[36]

Mocking Benjamin's lecture as 'constitutional heresy,' Maclaren launched into his exposition of section 92(16). Not only was the scope of local and private qualified by the adjective 'merely,' it was still further qualified by the deeming clause 'to which your Lordships have repeatedly referred' and which served the same purpose as the declaratory notwithstanding clause did for the other provincial enumerations.[37] Thus, even if the legislation was regarded as a matter of a 'merely local or private nature,' it was removed from provincial jurisdiction by the deeming clause – which, as all on the board agreed, 'points directly to sub-section 16 and treats that as one class' – because it came within trade and commerce and the criminal law.[38]

Sir James Hannen, hearing his first Canadian appeal, was troubled by the prospect that otherwise valid provincial legislation could be removed from provincial jurisdiction 'by making it a crime to do that which the provincial legislature had the authority to say might be done.' Maclaren agreed in principle but (anticipating a version of Lord Watson's national concern doctrine) quickly added that a matter once regarded as local or private 'under altered circumstances might become of sufficient importance and sufficiently general ... that the Parliament of Canada would consider it to be conducive to the order and good government of Canada and to make it an offence under the criminal law.' Houses of ill-fame, he observed, were just such a case, and all agreed that the deeming clause would remove the matter from 92(16).[39] Maclaren later held Selborne's *dictum* in *L'Union St-Jacques* as authority for his contention that, in the absence of federal legislation, the province could legislate 'until the Parliament of Canada comes in and declares those matters to be of sufficient importance for them to take hold of them and embody them as part of the criminal law of the Dominion.'[40]

Although Maclaren had raised the evil of intemperance, it was left to Fullarton to stress the evils of what Smith and others had described as Canada's 'national vice.'[41] The controversy over drinking was of such 'general interest and importance' in Canada, he explained, that the government 'did not dare in the state of public opinion to do as I said more than tentative legislation' and thus timidly chose local opinion.[42] But the purpose was necessary and unequivocal: 'I submit that it is because drunkenness & its spread, has become a matter disgusting to the feelings & morals of the people of Canada, threatening the good order and government of the country that therefore the Dominion Legislature have had to put it into the criminal law, and to take it out of the matters of a purely local or private nature.'[43]

Six weeks after the argument, Smith delivered the Judicial Committee's decision. 'The true nature and character of the legislation in the particular instance under discussion,' he wrote, 'must always be determined in order to ascertain the class of subjects to which it really belongs.' So examined, the legislation was not in relation to licensing although it might interfere with provincial revenues. Nor was it in relation to property and civil rights. Rather, the act related

to public order and safety. That is the primary matter dealt with, and though incidentally the free use of things in which men may have property is interfered with, that incidental interference does not alter the character of the law. Upon the same considerations, the Act in question cannot be regarded as in relation to civil rights ... Laws of this nature designed for the promotion of public order, safety or morals, and which subject those who contravene them to criminal procedure and punishment, belong to the subject of public wrongs rather than to that of civil rights. They are of a nature which fall within the general authority of Parliament to make laws for the order and good government of Canada, and have direct relation to criminal law which is one of the enumerated classes of subjects assigned exclusively to the Parliament of Canada ... Few, if any, laws could be made by Parliament for the peace, order, and good government of Canada which did not in some incidental way affect property and civil rights; and it could not have been intended, when assuring to the provinces exclusive legislative authority on the subject of property and civil rights, to exclude the Parliament from the exercise of this general power whenever any such incidental interference would result from it.

Nor did the committee accept the argument that the machinery of local option was a tacit admission of its local and private nature. The object was the promotion of temperance throughout the Dominion and the machinery of local option did 'not alter its general and uniform character.'

Having concluded that the act did not fall within any of the enumerations in section 92, and was thus within the residual clause, Smith added that it was 'unnecessary to discuss the further question whether its provisions also fall within any of the classes of subjects enumerated in section 91.' However, he added, in abstaining from this discussion, they 'must not be understood as intimating any dissent' from those judges of the Supreme Court who found that the legislation fell within trade and commerce.[44]

The reasons and decision in *Russell* became the most controversial in the early jurisprudence of the Judicial Committee. Smith had upheld federal legislation under the residual power regardless of its interference with property and civil rights, thus affirming Peacock's distinction between *in relation to* and *interference with*. Public wrongs had trumped civil rights.

Unlike Mowat, Macdonald did not see the courts as a potential ally in federal-provincial jurisdictional disputes. But he did see the decision in *Russell* as a court-sent opportunity to take the political battle to Mowat for control of the liquor trade. 'Have you read the judgment of the Scott Act?' he asked Alexander Campbell, the minister of justice. 'It is pleasant to me to know that my opinions are strongly supported as to the invalidity of the Ontario Licensing Act – as to the extent and meaning of the words 'Trade and Commerce.' This decision will be a great protection to the Central Authority – a contrary one would have greatly disturbed the integrity of the Dominion. Armed with the judgment we can go at Mowat and the Secession Party at the rate of a hunt[?]'.[45] Macdonald had obviously not read the decision carefully, for it said nothing about the Crooks Act, Mowat's 1876 liquor-licensing legislation.[46]

Macdonald's objective was blatantly political. The Crooks Act had given Mowat a political weapon of terrifying breadth and efficiency by taking the control of liquor licensing and regulation away from the local governments and placing it in the hands of provincially appointed liquor commissioners and inspectors. Whether they actually constituted an army of election workers, their employment by the Liberals certainly made the owners of the 4,793 taverns and 1,307 licensed shops – traditional supporters of the Tories – hostage to the Liberal Party.[47] During the 1882 election campaign, Macdonald had boasted that he would pass an act returning to the municipalities the power they had lost. The decision in *Russell* three days after the election provided the opportunity and excuse to live up to his promise.

With a provincial election anticipated in February, Eugene O'Keefe urged Macdonald to let the 'Hotel Keepers ... know as soon as possible that Mowat and company have no further say in the licences and there will be no doubt about the course they will take.'[48] Sir John needed no urging. In the 1883 throne speech, the governor general read that he was advised that *Russell* 'goes to show, that in order to prevent the unrestricted sale of intoxicating liquors, and for that purpose to regulate the granting of shop, saloon and tavern licences, legislation by the Dominion Parliament will be necessary.'[49]

The government has been 'quite satisfied that the law as it obtains in the different provinces should be continued,' Macdonald explained during the throne speech debate, even though he had always believed that control of the trade lay with Ottawa. But the decision in *Russell* compelled them to act because it was obvious 'that the very reasons on which the Privy Council decided that this Parliament has the right to deal with the Scott Act, are the reasons that the Provincial Legislature of Ontario has not a right to deal with that subject under the Crooks Act, except as a matter of revenue for municipal or provincial purposes.'[50]

A month later, Macdonald craftily established a select committee, chaired by D'Alton McCarthy, to draft the appropriate legislation. Although the preamble to the McCarthy Act stated that the law respecting the sale of liquor should be 'uniform throughout the Dominion, and that provision should be made in regard thereto for the better provision of peace and order,' most of the provisions were similar to those in the Crooks Act. However, local control was placed in the hands of a judge, the warden or mayor, and a federal appointee. The board appointed the inspectors and approved the licences. Anticipating political opposition, the act provided that the inspectors were to be paid from the fees levied, and the revenues were to go to the local, not the provincial, government, but the provinces were permitted to impose a further tax for local revenue. Moreover, the act was not to affect powers to prohibit conferred on Quebec municipal councils as of 1867.[51]

There was no question that the McCarthy Act would wind up in court for it was a direct challenge to the provincial regulation of the retail liquor trade that had been upheld by the superior courts in all provinces. After the decision in *Fredericton*, plaintiffs vainly sought protection against provincial liquor laws by arguing that the federal government had taken possession of the field. The argument was fully canvassed and rejected by Chief Justice William Meredith in the Quebec Superior Court in 1880 when the validity of a provincial Sunday closing law was challenged. Reviewing the argument and decision in *Fredericton*, he noted that the Supreme Court had not determined that Parliament possessed the exclusive jurisdiction so as to exclude any provincial regulations. The case law, therefore, indicated that while the federal government had the power to prohibit the provinces could 'for the preservation of good order in the municipalities under their control make reasonable police regulations ... provided they do not improperly interfere with trade and commerce ... I have thought it right to endeavour to make the point under consideration plain, because some persons seem to think it impossible that Parliament, and the provincial legislatures, can for any purpose whatever, or under any circumstances whatsoever, legislate in relation to the same matter.'[52]

When provincial regulations, including the right to prohibit sale at stated times, came before the Court of Queen's Bench again, Thomas Ramsay, speaking for a unanimous court, cited Meredith with approval. The court had suspended judgment until it secured the decision in *Russell*, wrote Ramsay, 'in the hope that we might find some rule authoritatively laid down which might help us in adjudicating on this case ... In this we have been to some extent disappointed ... Their Lordships have remained strictly within the issues submitted to them' in deciding that although the Canada Temperance Act may have interfered with sections 9, 13, and 16 of section 92, it was in pith and substance an act dealing with public wrongs. The decision, Ramsay continued, 'will command general assent, not only owing to the source from which it comes, but also from its cogency.' However, the Judicial Committee 'has not either expressly or by implication maintained that the Dominion Parliament can alone pass a prohibitory liquor law.' The fact that both levels of government had legislated might be inconvenient but the federal government did have the power of disallowance and it 'seems to be fairer to leave the rule of expediency to be applied by a body responsible to the people at large, rather than to a comparatively irresponsible body like a court.'[53]

The case most directly related to the McCarthy Act was one challenging the constitutionality of the Crooks Act itself. Convicted of
operating a billiard table in his tavern at times prohibited by the regulations of the Toronto Board of Liquor Commissioners, Archibald
Hodge, secretary of the 'licensed victuallers,' challenged the validity
of the act. Assuming that the province had the authority to make
such regulations and enforce them with imprisonment at hard labour,
counsel argued that the power could not be delegated because the
province itself had only delegated powers and could not further delegate them given the maxim *delegatus non potest delegare*. Speaking for a
unanimous Court of Queen's Bench, Chief Justice Hagarty reluctantly
agreed that the province could not further delegate its powers.[54]

The decision was overturned by a unanimous Court of Appeal
where Mowat argued the case for the crown. While the issue before the
court did not explicitly involve a conflict of jurisdiction, the decision
articulated a strong statement of the powers and status of the provinces which resonated in the Judicial Committee. Chief Justice John
Spragge observed that the Dominion and the provinces 'each derive
their powers from the same source; and the power to make laws in
relation to the several classes of subjects, legislation upon which is, by
the Imperial Act, committed exclusively to the Provincial Legislature is
as large and complete as it is in the classes of subjects committed by
enumeration of subjects to the Dominion Parliament. The limits of the
subjects of jurisdiction are prescribed; but within those limits the
authority to legislate is not limited.'

It was evident from an examination of the subjects exclusively given
to the provinces that it was 'intended that their Legislatures should
possess very large and ample powers in relation to all subjects of a
local and domestic nature. They had possessed plenary powers upon
these subjects before Confederation; and the general scheme of Confederation appears to have been to leave to them the plenary control of
these subjects.' Thus, provincial legislative power was limited only by
the boundaries of section 92. Given that Ontario had plenary power
over municipal institutions and the power to enforce its laws, as well
as to delegate its authority to subordinate bodies, the Ontario act was
intra vires.[55] The decision in *Hodge* was released on 30 June 1882 but,
although the decision in *Russell* had been reported in the *Globe* on
24 June, there was no mention of it in the written decisions.

Following their defeat in the Court of Appeal, the liquor interests
'fully intended throwing the matter up,' but Macdonald, not wishing

to intervene openly, urged them to appeal to the Judicial Committee and led them to understand that they 'would not be called on to pay any more for contesting the case.'[56] And on the eve of the argument, George Burbidge, the deputy minister of justice, wired J.K. Kerr, counsel for Hodge: 'Premier desires point to be pressed. Local Act *ultra vires*. Conflicts with power of Parliament to regulate liquor traffic, to make uniform laws regarding trade therein and for the peace, order and good government of Canada. See Scott Act and Act last session, with special reference preamble.' Kerr did not need that last-minute advice. As he told Burbidge later, 'I had previously arranged to raise all these points on behalf of my clients.'[57]

For senior counsel Mowat had retained Horace Davey, the brilliant equity lawyer, who confined himself largely to cases before the Judicial Committee and the House of Lords.[58] Aemilius Irving, who prepared the brief, acted as junior counsel.[59] Mowat and J.R. Cartwright; the deputy attorney general, were also in London during the summer, and briefed Davey on the history of the liquor question. Asked during the argument what book he was using to review the case law in provincial courts, Davey replied that was Cartwright's case book: 'I possess it because the Attorney-General of Ontario presented me with a copy when he was here.'[60]

Mowat did not need a lawyer of Davey's skill. Although the hearing lasted three days, J.K. Kerr, who had lost twice in Ontario courts, lost again in the first hour. A majority of the committee had sat on *Russell* and in what was, perhaps, a desperate gamble, Kerr claimed that *Russell* effectively placed complete control of the liquor traffic in federal hands, even including the hours of sale.[61] As members of the committee who had sat on Russell repeatedly contested that interpretation of the decision, Lord Fitzgerald impatiently cut Kerr off with the declaration that there was 'no conflict' between the Canada Temperance Act and the Ontario act.

They may co-exist and do co-exist. Your position is this: that the Provincial legislature could not pass any Act at all regulating the sale of spirituous liquor within the Province. For instance, if they passed an Act in this form: Be it enacted that no licence[d] dealer in spirituous liquors shall keep his shop open from Saturday evening till Monday morning: that is *ultra* the power of the Provincial Legislature and must go to the Dominion.
Mr. Kerr: Yes.
Lord Fitzgerald: That would be carrying *Russell* v. *The Queen* a long way.
Sir Richard Couch: That was certainly not decided in *Russell*.[62]

The committee was not sympathetic to Kerr's argument that the province did not have the authority to delegate its powers to the Board of Liquor Commissioners. It seemed to agree with Fitzgerald that, if the power lay with the province, 'I apprehend that it follows from that, that it has entire power of legislation as to that particular subject,' or with Hobhouse, who felt delegation was fine as long as the province 'keeps control in its own hands.' When Kerr continued with his argument that, having power delegated to them by the imperial parliament, the provinces could not delegate further, Fitzgerald interjected: 'Would not that be reducing the Provincial Legislatures to [be] the mere delegate of the Imperial Parliament[?]'[63]

Knowing that he had the committee on his side, Horace Davey was brief and confident when he turned to the question of delegation near the end of his argument on the third day. What 'possible application' he asked, had the maxim *delegatus non potest delegare* to the case? 'The Provincial Legislature is not a delegate in any sense whatever, either of the Imperial Legislature or of the Dominion Legislature, or of Her Majesty ... It has limited power of legislation, so far as the area of legislation is concerned. It can only legislate on the classes of subjects within which its jurisdiction is confined by the Imperial Statute,' but within its jurisdiction the province 'is just as supreme and sovereign as the Imperial Parliament. I put it as high as that.'[64]

Without conceding the provincial right to prohibit, Davey wanted to avoid asking the court to repudiate *Russell* 'because I am bound to admit that if you said it was either one or the other exclusively, either proposition would be wrong, because it may belong with different aspects, to both or either.'[65] Accepting the legitimacy of *Russell*, Davey asked, 'How does that in any way interfere with the right of each Province to empower the municipal bodies within its area to make regulations in the nature of police regulations for securing decency, order, sobriety and morality within their cities[?]'[66]

Returning to the same argument that there was not a conflict between an act applying to all of Canada as a matter of peace, and order, and good government and a provincial act 'local in its character and area,' Davey observed that the deeming clause in section 91 provided for that very circumstance.

That is to say, that the provincial Legislature cannot legislate on a matter which is expressly mentioned on [*sic*] the enumeration in section 91, confirming [*sic*] their legislation to the Province, and say that it is a matter of local or private nature, but where the Dominion legislation is not on any matter which is expressly mentioned in the enumeration of section 91, but is made under the general power to make laws, for the peace, order and good government of Canada, it does not by any means follow that the provincial Legislature cannot make a local law of a similar character.[67]

Fitzgerald's decision was delivered a month later. After reviewing and explaining the reasoning in *Russell*, Fitzgerald concluded:

It appears to their Lordships that *Russell* v. *The Queen*, when properly understood, is not an authority in support of the appellant's contention, and their Lordships do not intend to vary or depart from the reasons expressed for their judgement in that case. The principle which that case and the case of *Citizens Insurance Company* illustrate is, that subjects which in one aspect and for one purpose fall within section 92, may in another aspect and for another purpose fall within section 91.[68]

When it had been observed during the argument that, before Confederation the municipalities regulated and could prohibit the sale of liquor, Collier had interjected, 'It is not a question of what they exercised before Confederation. We have only to deal with the Statute.'[69] But the argument apparently carried weight, and in the decision Fitzgerald wrote that the provisions of the Ontario act seemed to be 'similar to, though not identical in all respects with, the powers then belonging to municipal institutions' before 1867. When 'properly understood,' the act authorized municipalities to make regulations 'in the nature of police or municipal regulations of a merely local character ... and as such are calculated to preserve, in the municipality, peace and public decency, and repress drunkenness and disorderly and riotous conduct.' The regulations seemed to come within heads 8, 15, and 16 of section 92 and did not conflict with the general regulation of trade which belonged to the Dominion parliament.[70]

Praising the judgments in the Ontario Court of Appeal, Fitzgerald quickly disposed of the delegation argument with a ringing confirmation of the doctrine of coordinate federalism:

It appears to their Lordships, however, that the objection thus raised by the appellants is founded on an entire misconception of the true character and position of the Provincial Legislatures. They are in no sense delegates of or acting under any mandate from the Imperial Parliament. When the British North America Act enacted that there should be a legislature for Ontario, and that its legislative assembly should have exclusive authority to make laws for the Province and for provincial purposes in relation to matters enumerated in section 92, it conferred powers not in any sense to be exercised by delegation from or as agents of the Imperial Parliament, but authority as plenary and as ample within the limits prescribed by section 92 as the Imperial Parliament in the plenitude of its power possessed and could bestow. Within these limits of subject and area the local legislature is supreme, and has the same authority as the Imperial Parliament, or the Parliament of the Dominion, would have under like circumstances to confide to a municipal institution or body of its own relation authority to make by-laws or resolutions as to subjects specified in the enactment, and with the object of carrying the enactment into operation and effect.[71]

Provincial legislative sovereignty within the boundaries of section 92 had been legally confirmed.

The decision in *Hodge* was delivered on 15 December 1883, and early in the new year Mowat officially requested Macdonald to repeal the McCarthy Act and 'prevent groundless doubts and useless litigation.'[72] Blake also urged the great 'centralizer' to repeal the act and 'not seek now to draw us into conflict with the local Legislature on some other pretense of concurrent, paramount, enhanced or mystical power.'[73] Angrily daring Blake to stand up without a fee and declare the act unconstitutional, Macdonald replied that *Hodge* was not the last word on the question and the government had no intention of repealing the McCarthy Act.[74] But the pressure increased on Macdonald to repeal the act or go to court, and the cabinet finally agreed to refer the act 'with all convenient speed to the Supreme Court of Canada, or the Judicial Committee of the Privy Council, or both.'[75]

The Supreme Court heard the reference in September. The federal factum argued that, given the objects stated in the preamble, the law regulating the liquor traffic should be uniform across Canada, that provision should be made 'for the better preservation of peace and order,' and that jurisdiction fell within the regulation of trade and commerce and the residual clause. *Hodge* decided that local regulation fell within subsections 8 and 16 of section 92, but, reading *Hodge* beside *Russell*, the province could make such regulations only until Parliament legislated, as Selborne had indicated might be possible in *L'Union St-Jacques*. When Parliament legislated, provincial regulations 'so far as they may be inconsistent with the general regulations of Parliament respecting the traffic must give way to the paramount regulation made by Parliament.' The provinces argued that Canadian case law, supported by *Hodge*, confirmed the historical provincial jurisdiction as 'in the nature of police or municipal regulations of a merely local character,' which did not interfere with federal jurisdiction over trade and commerce.[76]

The argument before the Supreme Court took five days but could have been over in as many hours. Counsel for the other provinces added little to the argument of Aemelius Irving and Samuel Hume Blake for Ontario, and, with their exaggerated claims of federal jurisdiction, James Bethune and George Burbidge even detracted from the substance of the federal factum. The court itself was also at fault, frequently interrupting counsel and engaging in long and testy discussions along the bench. Samuel Strong was particularly gruff and outspoken while Ritchie indulged in frequent and lengthy musings. Henry offered the occasional opinion which, as apparently was customary, passed without comment. Perhaps unhappy with the case before him, Gwynne was unusually reserved, and his colleague Taschereau, who often supported federal jurisdiction, was on leave.[77] Fournier did not utter a word.

It was really a case of *Russell* v. *Hodge*. For the first time the Supreme Court found itself dissecting the decisions of the Judicial Committee. 'The expressions of the Privy Council increase the difficulty of construing the Act,' Strong complained, 'because, first, we have to construe the Act, and then we have to construe the judgments of the Privy Council.'[78] Taken alone, 'I do not hesitate to say that I think Russell and the Queen entirely authorized this Act ... If it had not been followed by *Hodge* and the Queen.'[79] And in comparing the two decisions – and referring frequently to the oral argument in *Hodge* – members of the court were less than flattering to 'judges sitting in a foreign country who know nothing about our institutions and laws.'[80]

Irving and Blake wanted to avoid placing *Russell* in conflict with *Hodge*, for if the court decided they were incompatible, it could be placed in the uncomfortable position of overruling its decision in *Fredericton*. As Ritchie observed, 'If *Russell* and the *Queen* goes, the Scott Act goes.' Strong agreed. 'This is simply a substitute for carrying on the Temperance Act. We shall have to take great care to see that any decision that we may pronounce shall be without prejudice to the Act so far as it affects the Scott Act.'[81] As a result, Irving and Blake argued that the two acts under review were of an 'entirely different character' and thus the decisions were compatible.[82] Although Gwynne agreed,[83] Strong exclaimed that it was 'beyond the power of legal argument' to reconcile the two decisions. 'If ever there emanated from one tribunal two conflicting decisions, they are these two decisions.'[84]

The court was unsympathetic to the exaggerated claims to federal jurisdiction based on *Russell*. Burbidge's observation that 'what one day, in the growth of a country, may be a police power, may another day, become a matter of national concern and importance,' and thus the jurisdiction could shift, drew the reply from Strong that the 'framers of the organic law ought to have provided for that.'[85] Bethune's arguments that federal power over trade and commerce 'extends to all trade, and the minutest divisions of it' and that, under the residual clause, parliament 'may exercise if it chooses, the whole police power of the country' seemed to insult the court.[86] 'What do you leave to the Local Legislatures at all?' asked Ritchie. Clearly exasperated, Strong exclaimed that 'it is the duty of this court not to allow any part of this Act to be reduced to a dead letter. The 92nd section gives large and important powers – powers which the very object of the Act was to conserve to the Provinces.'[87]

One of those was 'Municipal Institutions,' and the court insisted, as Canadian courts always had, that municipal institutions possessed the powers they had in 1867 unless they were explicitly withdrawn. As Ritchie commented, 'we must find out what municipal institutions means, and having done so, you must say nothing interfering with these comes within the jurisdiction of the Dominion Government.' (Gwynne's quiet interjection, 'Whatever interferes with trade and commerce shall not be deemed to come within municipal institutions,' was lost.)[88] Bethune's point that pre-Confederation practice was of little value 'because there is nothing to indicate that they intended to continue those powers' was rejected by Ritchie, who claimed, without reasons, that while some powers previously possessed by the local governments were now in section 91, 'it intended the rest to remain. Because some have been taken away we should not strive and struggle to find a reason for taking more of them away.'[89]

Sensing that the court was on his side, Blake in his rebuttal stated that the act before them clearly fell within the *Hodge* precedent, and dared to suggest that the Judicial Committee should then have said of *Russell*: 'We have more light; we were wrong and we regret it.' If they had made that admission, Strong interjected, 'they would have commanded my respect – if they had accounted for the difference in the two decisions.'[90] However, Blake continued, they 'approached it with the idea of not making any admission but endeavouring to reconcile what I consider irreconcilable.' The McCarthy Act could not stand because in *Hodge* the Judicial Committee had placed the same matter in section 92 'and being placed there it is safe, and is, as it were in a city of refuge, and even the Dominion cannot touch it when surrounded by that safeguard.'[91] The Court, he trusted, would ensure that 'nothing that is not given to the Dominion by the enactment, will be permitted to interfere with the sacred rights of the provinces upon which the solemn compact was made which resulted in the Act of Confederation.'[92]

Although the Supreme Court Act provided that members of the court could state their dissent in a reference case, the court had adopted the practice of not giving reasons.[93] When counsel suggested that the court give reasons that would assist the Judicial Committee, Strong exclaimed that a decision of the court would have no effect in an appeal to the committee and would be alluded to 'only for the purpose of offensive criticism ... I mention that as a reason why I say now, positively, for my part, that advisedly I shall not give a reason for my judgment. No powers short of the Parliament of Canada can compel me, and I will not give my reasons for my judgment.'[94] Without giving reasons, the court released its judgment in January 1885: the McCarthy Act was *ultra vires* except the sections regarding vessels and wholesale licences and those carrying into effect the Canada Temperance Act. (Henry felt that all were *ultra vires*).[95] When the House of Commons met, the government introduced an amendment to the act providing that its operation 'is and shall be suspended, unless and until the same shall be decided by the Judicial Committee of the Privy Council to be *intra vires* of the Parliament of Canada.'[96]

The appeal was heard on 11–12 November 1885. A full board of seven, graced by the presence of Lord Halsbury, was recruited for the case. With the exception of the Lord Chancellor, all were only too familiar with the jurisdictional battle over policing Canadians' right to drink.[97]

Sir Farrer Herschell, a Liberal MP and Gladstone's solicitor general, with George Burbidge as his junior, acted for the federal government. The future lord chancellor wisely did not press the claim for federal jurisdiction as far as counsel had before the Supreme Court, but he did base his argument on *Russell* with some help from *Parsons*. 'I certainly rely on *Russell* v. *The Queen* as a distinct authority in favour of the propositions for which I am contending. I shall maintain that there is no distinction between *Russell* v. *The Queen* and the present case. The scope, character and object of the Act is precisely the same in both.'[98]

Sir Montague Smith's interjection indicated the problem facing Herschell. The *ratio* in *Russell*, Smith observed, was that as a prohibitory act the Canada Temperance Act did not fall within section 92, but that this was 'sort of a Regulating Act rather than a Prohibitory Act.'[99] Similar comments were made by others, and Sir Barnes Peacock pointedly observed that the special conditions for Quebec suggested 'that these are matters of a local nature which must be regulated according to the locality.'[100] Perhaps for that reason Herschell did not base his argument on the residual clause but rather on the trade and commerce argument that had found favour in the Supreme Court in *Fredericton* and – with Smith agreeing – was not repudiated in *Russell*. And if it were authority 'that would at once maintain the position which I have to maintain, before your Lordships, because if it comes within that clause in section 91, it does not matter whether it comes within section 92 or not.'[101]

There was, he contended, no conflict between *Russell* and *Hodge* for in *Hodge* the Judicial Committee 'accepts it, approves of it, and reaffirms it; but holds that the case and the decision in question was in no way inconsistent with it.'[102] *Hodge* decided only that the province could make local regulations as long as they did not conflict with a general law passed by the Dominion. Citing the 'aspect' doctrine, laid down in other cases, he argued that 'in one aspect' the province could legislate 'even though it was a matter in relation to which the Dominion Parliament might legislate for the whole Dominion.'[103]

As Smith continued to insist that *Russell* upheld a prohibitory act and Herschell admitted that *Hodge* upheld the provincial regulatory power, Halsbury finally insisted that Herschell 'face the question' of whether the McCarthy and Crooks acts were inconsistent.[104] Intervening for the first time, Lord Fitzgerald stated: 'The Ontario Act, which we had before us in *Hodge* v. *The Queen*, was one dealing with exactly the same subjects as are now specified by the Act of 1883 ... Now as I understand this case and your present argument, if the Act of 1883 is, as a whole, within the powers of the Dominion Parliament, it supersedes the whole of the Ontario Act which we were dealing with in *Hodge* v. *The Queen*.'[105] Herschell admitted that it superseded much of it.

However, he also questioned the *ratio* in *Hodge* that jurisdiction over liquor regulation after 1867 fell within 'Municipal Institutions' because, 'of course, the very object of the Act was to take away from the Provincial Legislature some of the powers which they had heretofore possessed, and to confer those powers upon the Central Parliament, and, therefore, to say that they must necessarily have had all the power of legislation which before they could exercise through their Municipal bodies is an argument that cannot be sustained.'[106] Halsbury seemed to agree: 'I should have thought it meant the creation of them – how many they were to consist of, and how they were to elected. Surely that cannot involve anything that is now before the committee.'[107]

With Halsbury's apparent support for his 92(8) contention, Herschell continued that even if there was a prima facie section 92 argument, the declaratory clause explicitly provided that in case of conflict or inconsistency, matters within the enumerated heads of section 91 overrode those in section 92. Whatever doubt there was about other trades, 'the liquor traffic is surely a trade' and 'it raises the question distinctly, which was left with as "it may be" in *Citizens Insurance Company* v. *Parsons*, whether the Dominion Parliament has not power to make a general regulation affecting all trades, or a particular trade throughout the whole of the Provinces of Canada?' There was no authority in any cases before the committee 'to the contrary of that. There is no dictum even to the contrary of that.'

Moreover, in section 92 there was nothing 'which points to any regulation of trade and commerce except for revenue purposes.' The object of the act was the peace, order and good government of Canada, and, linking the residual clause to its extension in the enumerations, he concluded that 'all legislation for the regulation of trade, if that regulation has in view the peace, order, and good government of the country, comes distinctly within the power committed to the Dominion Parliament.'[108]

Mowat relied again on Horace Davey, assisted by Richard Haldane. Davey had been given the lengthy Ontario argument, probably prepared by Irving, which argued that all provincial powers were exclusive, with the possible exception of 92 (16); that *Hodge* had located the power in sections 8 and 16; that *Parsons*, with the exception of 'and it may be,' had restricted the federal power over trade and commerce to international and interprovincial trade, and the 'and it may be' had been stated 'in terms which intimated that they were not prepared to decide whether such a third class really exists or not'; and, although it did not dissent, the Judicial Committee did not 'express concurrence' in *Russell* with the decision of the Supreme Court that the Canada Temperance Act was *intra vires* as coming within trade and commerce. The memorandum noted the *ratio* in the decisions in *Russell* and *Hodge* as making a distinction between prohibition, which fell to the Dominion, and regulation short of prohibition which belonged to the province. It coyly added:

Some of the Judges in Canada also expressed that view, and hold it still; others have called the distinction an arbitrary one; and it appears from the shorthand writer's notes of the argument in the present case before the Supreme Court, that the inconsistency of the two decisions was supported by counsel on both sides, and by some of the learned judges; and that in the course of the discussion some observations were made which their Lordships of the Privy Council, if they should become aware of them, could not fail to regard as offensive. It is hardly necessary to say that neither the Ontario Government, nor it is believed any of the other Provincial Governments, concur in any of the disparaging remarks made in reference to their Lordships of the Judicial Committee or their decision.[109]

At the outset, Davey challenged Herschell's contention about the structure of sections 91 and 92, and put forward Mowat's view of the relationship between the residual and declaratory clauses that had never found favour in any court. If the act in question fell within section 92, he argued, the explicit language of the residual clause excluded it from federal jurisdiction:

But, my Lords, I venture to submit to your Lordships that all the enumerated matters in section 91 are subject to those words in relation to all matters not coming within the classes of subjects by this Act assigned exclusively to the Legislatures of the Province. My submission to your Lordships is that the whole section is governed by those words, and that the enumerated articles in section 91 are only an illustration inserted for greater certainty, but those words to which I referred govern the whole of the section ... and that the regulations made under the powers given by section 91 must be such as do not interfere with the exclusive jurisdiction given to the Legislatures of the provinces by section 92.[110]

The true construction of the deeming clause, he stated in reply to a query from Smith, was that the province could not legislate on matters within the federal enumerations on the ground that the legislation was of a local or provincial character, but it was equally true that the federal parliament could not legislate on matters within section 92 'on the suggestion or contention that the legislation is for the whole of Canada.'[111]

Hodge had decided that an Ontario act virtually identical to the act in question fell within sections 8 and 16 of section 92 while *Russell* had determined that prohibition was not exclusively assigned to the provinces. 'That is the ground of the decision,' Smith interjected, 'that it did not fall within any of the matters in section 92: right or wrong, that is the decision.'[112] A few moments later, Smith added: 'Both decisions, of course, are in force, and they may well stand together. The question is whether this case comes nearer to one or the other.'[113] The key, Davey continued, was: 'Is the legislation in its character local or not? "Character" is not the exact word, but I cannot find one better.'[114] The Ontario act was local in its character and so was the Dominion act, and if the latter was upheld there would be two virtually identical acts in operation.[115]

Differing with Herschell (and with Halsbury) on the meaning of 92(8), Davey claimed *Hodge* as authority for a much wider interpretation which extended to 'the creation of bodies and to the defining the rights, power, duties, and privileges of bodies created for what is called municipal purposes, that is to say, the regulation of decency, order, and so forth,' and in *Hodge* 'it was not thought out of place to refer to what was the existing state of things' in 1867.[116]

In a short argument, the thirty-year-old Richard Haldane relied on *Parsons*, *Russell*, and *Hodge* to argue that the three cases had 'laid down a principle for the construction of the Confederation Act, and that principle appears to me to be expressed in that way that the same subject, for example the drink question, may for one aspect and one purpose be within section 91, and for another aspect and for another purpose may be within section 92.' When they clashed, 'that clashing can only be of an incidental clashing.'[117] But in the present case it was not a matter of incidental clashing: 'The simple question is whether the Act which is before your Lordships is not substantially identical with the Act which was construed, and which was said to be within Provincial authority, and exclusive provincial authority, in *Hodge* v. *The Queen*.[118]

As a friend of Macdonald summarized the argument: 'In the end Herschell shouted Russell and Davey – Hodge – and the board looked much perplexed.'[119]

The analyses of the hearing by Burbidge and Donald MacMaster, who were in London and attended the hearing, were remarkably similar. Although both believed that Herschell had the better of the argument, Burbidge felt that the result was 'doubtful' while MacMaster thought that it was 'about a tossup which way it goes with the chances against the Act as far as appearance go.' As both observed, Smith was against the act from the beginning and during Herschell's rebuttal, in particular, was hostile and argumentative. Fitzgerald was also categorically opposed. The text also bears out their opinion, as MacMaster put it, that 'Peacock & Couch incline strongly in favour of the Act the former expressly so – and with cogent reasoning. Hobhouse, too, leaned to Herschell's argument I thought.' Although Lord Halsbury seemed to shift during the argument, in the end 'he seemed hesitating but if anything against the Dominion Act.' Both agreed that Lord Monkswell (Collier) was hard to read, but in all probability would oppose the act. 'I expect,' MacMaster concluded, 'there will be strong controversy between the members of the board – and the Lord Chancellor's view will likely turn the scale.'[120] Exactly a month later, the Judicial Committee certified its opinion to the queen that the McCarthy Act was in every respect *ultra vires*.

Macdonald's political vendetta had long-term jurisdictional consequences. Although no reasons were given, the reference case was often referred to in later arguments as an explicit confirmation of *Hodge* and as weakening the precedent of *Russell*. To the extent that Herschell had been unable to bring regulation within trade and commerce, it also tended to confirm the limited scope of trade and commerce as determined in *Parsons*. Moreover, in decision at least, the Judicial Committee seemed unwilling to accept the argument that the federal government could seize matters once judicially held to be local by deeming them to be a matter of national importance and expanding their scope territorially. While these were all important jurisdictional issues, the case in which they were raised was too obviously political for them to be considered by the courts on their strictly constitutional merits. But the apparent weakening of *Russell* and the confirmation of the enhanced status and powers of the provinces in *Hodge* remained in the collective memory of the Judicial Committee.

Important as they were to become doctrinally, the liquor cases did not significantly alter the power or responsibilities of the federal or provincial governments. However, in 1887 the Judicial Committee greatly widened the scope of provincial taxing powers in section 92(2): 'Direct

Taxation within the Province in order to the raising of a Revenue for provincial Purposes.' Perpetually in search of revenue without directly taxing its own citizens, the government of Quebec had first taxed insurance companies by demanding that a stamp be placed on every policy and, years later, had imposed a stamp duty on every exhibit filed in court. The Judicial Committee had confirmed a decision of the Quebec Superior Court finding the first tax unconstitutional as not being direct taxation.[121] The Supreme Court of Canada overturned a decision of the Quebec Court of Queen's Bench to find the second *ultra vires*, a decision that the Judicial Committee confirmed on similar grounds.[122]

In 1882 the Quebec government decided to test the constitutional boundaries with An Act to Impose Certain Direct Taxes on Certain Commercial Corporations, which imposed taxes on all banks, insurance companies, and other corporations doing business in the province. The taxes were not only on every place of business in Quebec but, in the case of banks, on the paid-up capital of the corporation.[123] Even before the federal Department of Justice reviewed the legislation, the matter was before the courts, and its constitutionality was therefore left to private litigation.

By a 3–2 majority (Dorion and Cross dissenting), the Court of Queen's Bench upheld the taxes either as direct or as somehow authorized by section 92(16) as a matter of a local or private nature. Dorion's cogent dissent was in part based on his assumption about what direct taxes meant in Canada in 1867 and on his opinion that, in view of the strict separation of powers and concern for local autonomy, it could never have been intended that a province could levy taxes 'calculated to reach the inhabitants of other provinces ... Such a pretence is inconsistent with the whole object and intent of the Act.' The careful provisions concerning taxing and licensing powers in section 92, he insisted, negated the idea that the taxes could be upheld under 92(16).[124]

At the Judicial Committee, Samuel Blake and W.H. Kerr were lead counsel for three banks, all of which had their head offices in Toronto. They argued that the tax was not levied 'within the province' because the head offices and the capital were outside; that the tax was not a direct tax as understood in 1867 but, as Dorion had argued, a licence tax; and, finally, that the subject matter fell within section 91 and therefore, even if prima facie it was within section 92, the powers of the Dominion were to prevail. Even before the end of the four-day pleadings, the board had obviously made up its mind, choosing neither to hear the argument against 92(16) nor counsel for Quebec who were present. Ten days after the argument, Lord Hobhouse delivered the decision for a board consisting of Macnaghten, Peacock, Couch, and Sir Richard Baggallay.[125]

Proceeding to determine first whether the tax fell within 92(2), the court adopted John Stuart Mill's definition that a direct tax was one 'which is demanded from the very person who it is intended or desired should pay it.' Hobhouse found that the tax fell within that description, although he admitted that 'in the intricacies of mercantile dealings the bank may find a way to recoup itself out of the pockets of its Quebec customers. But the way must be an obscure and circuitous one ... and if the bank does manage it, the result will not improbably disappoint the intention and the desire of the Quebec government.'[126] With reasoning equally unconvincing, Hobhouse stated that 'within the province' meant that any person may be taxed if found within the province, and the tax levied on the paid-up capital somehow brought it within the province.[127]

The apparent conflict with the federal government's power over banking was resolved by the simple assertion that the board could not see 'how the power of making banks contribute to the public objects of the provinces where they carry on their business can interfere at all with the power of making laws on the subject of banking or with the power of incorporating banks.'[128] The argument that the level of taxation could be such as to 'crush a bank out of existence, and so to nullify the power of Parliament to erect banks,' was dismissed with the comment that 'their Lordships cannot conceive that when the Imperial Parliament conferred wide powers of local self-government on great countries such as Quebec, it intended to limit them on the speculation that they would be used in an injurious manner. People who are trusted with the great power of making laws for property and civil rights may well be trusted to levy taxes.'[129]

The task of the board was straightforward, he explained in words that themselves need some explanation:

Their Lordships have to construe the express words of an Act of Parliament which makes an elaborate distribution of the whole field of legislative authority between two legislative bodies, and at the same time provides for the federated provinces a carefully balanced constitution, under which no one of the parties can pass laws for itself, except under the control of the whole acting through the Governor-General. And the question they have to answer is whether the one body or the other has power to make a given law. If they find that on the due construction of the Act a legislative power falls within sect.92, it would be quite wrong to deny its existence because by some possibility it may be abused, or may limit the range which otherwise would be open to the Dominion parliament.[130]

Hobhouse acknowledged that in *Severn* the Supreme Court had given a broad scope to the trade and commerce power:

But since that case was decided the question has been more completely sifted before the committee in *Parson's Case*, and it was found absolutely necessary that the literal meaning of the words should be restricted, in order to afford some scope for powers which are exclusively given to the provincial legislatures. It was there *thrown out* that the power of regulation given to the parliament meant some general or interprovincial regulations. No further attempt to define the subject need now be made, because their Lordships are clear that if they were to hold that this power of regulation prohibited any provincial taxation on the persons or things regulated, so far from restricting the expressions, as was found necessary in *Parson's Case*, they would be straining them to their widest conceivable extent.[131]

However, the suggestion that the provinces 'possess powers of legislation either inherent in them, or dating from a time anterior to the Federation Act and not taken away by that Act' was also dismissed with the emphatic statement that 'they adhere to the view which has always been taken by this committee, that the Federation Act exhausts the whole range of legislative power, and that whatever is not thereby given to the provincial legislatures rests with the Parliament.'[132]

The judgment, so much of which was subjective, carried a heavy explosive charge. It opened up an enormous field for provincial taxation which would not appear to have been intended or contemplated in 1867.[133] Specifically, as Peter Hogg has commented, 'while a tax levied on property outside the province would be unconstitutional,' a tax levied on a person or corporation could be based on the amount of property held outside the province.[134] More broadly, as Gérard La Forest has written, once Mill's definition was accepted 'in the way it was ... there were few intellectual buffers to prevent its progressive expansion to cover almost the whole field of taxation, in fact if not in form.'[135] Finally, the dubious authority of the *obiter* 'thrown out' in *Par-*

sons was affirmed, again in *obiter*, and the ghost of the Canadian approach to trade and commerce was laid to rest.

The death of William Henry in May 1888 provided Macdonald with the opportunity to make his first appointment to the Supreme Court since that of Gwynne in 1879. Macdonald wrote to Sir John Thompson, the minister of justice, that 'we must shortly begin to think of a Judge for the Supreme Court at Ottawa. We must endeavor to get a good man who will not throw Dominion rights away.'[136] Thompson replied that the Maritime bench was not promising, and suggested that if Macdonald wished to depart from the practice of replacing one New Brunswicker by another, now was the time.[137] Macdonald consulted D'Alton McCarthy about the federalist views of leading members of the Ontario bench. The reply was not encouraging. Whether Featherstone Osler, 'is what you term a Federalist, I could not say,' McCarthy commented. 'At present I should think his feelings are more inclined – unknown probably to himself – by his political bent – which is decidedly Tory than by Provincialism or the reverse.' George Burton would not, 'answer your requirements as being a federalist in his views. He is quite the reverse and more strongly tinged with Provincialism than any Judge on the Bench here.' Christopher Patterson 'leans that way or rather his judgments were always against the Dominion and for the Province – but he was not as provincial in drawing a line in favour of Provincialism' as was Burton. 'He is not a great judge,' concluded McCarthy, but would accept the appointment and would 'do no discredit to the Supreme Court.' 'Neither would be safe,' Macdonald noted to Thompson, but in the end Patterson was appointed.[138]

On the whole, however, Macdonald and his two key ministers of justice, Alexander Campbell and John Thompson, were only occasionally and usually reluctantly engaged in battle on the judicial field. On countless occasions, when commenting on dubious provincial legislation, they observed that the solution was best left to private litigation by those who felt aggrieved. In the major cases before the provincial appeal courts, the Supreme Court, and even the Judicial Committee, although federal jurisdiction or property was at issue, Ottawa chose not to intervene.[139] Mowat, on the other hand, as Gwynne had astutely understood, saw the courts as his preferred battleground in the pursuit of provincial power. As a result, for more than fifteen years, the Judicial Committee heard a consistent, and on its terms coherent, argument about the law of the federal constitution, prepared at Queen's Park and often presented by Horace Davey, with no equally consistent response, or no response at all, from Ottawa.

Disengagement or non-intervention was Thompson's declared policy. In 1891, when Mowat suggested a reference on the constitutionality of a provincial insolvency act, Thompson replied that 'my view on the general question of the policy of such references is that they should be made only under very exceptional circumstances, and that questions of the constitutionality of federal or provincial legislation should be left, as far as conveniently may be, to be decided in the course of litigation between persons affected by it rather than be made matter of litigation between the Federal Government and a Province.'[140]

Indeed, Thompson had been indignant when the governor general, Lord Lansdowne, had supported Mowat's proposal for a reference on the provincial authority to appoint queen's counsel. Having observed the battle between Ottawa and Queen's Park since his appointment in 1883, Lansdowne was convinced that 'whenever there is a serious misunderstanding upon a constitutional point between the Dominion Govt. and that of any of the provinces it is convenient to have recourse to the Imperial tribunal.'[141] Thompson dared to disagree with His Excellency:

I think we should not, in regard to any question which may arise between the Federal and Provincial authorities, enter into a case for reference to the Privy Council. In many respects it is the *most unsatisfactory tribunal* in the Empire. It has displayed such ignorance of our geography and our constitution that many of the sayings of its Judges, and even many passages from its judgements are treasured in the different Provinces as offering a fund of professional humour which time will make incredibly valuable.[142]

It was not only the committee's geography and history that was at fault but, even more important, its federalism jurisprudence:

When a constitutional question comes up they regard the Provincial authority as the weaker vessel – entitled to a decision on grounds of chivalry and generosity – while the fact is that the great danger of Canada is the weakness of the Federal authority – beset as it is on every side by the provinces, seeking to enlarge their powers at its expense, and seeking to make it carry all the burthens. Every decision in favour of a Province, as against a Federal claim, makes the weakness more apparent, and is accepted in Canada as an infallible decision, although it may be one which renders more conspicuous the inferiority of the Judges who constitute the tribunal. We should, I think, leave all such litigation to private suitors and avoid placing the Dominion Government in the position of an unfortunate litigant.[143]

As matters stood in 1886, Thompson's criticism seems unjustified. The three decisions that upheld provincial jurisdiction – *Parsons*, *Hodge*, and the *McCarthy Act Reference* – all confirmed the decisions in Canadian courts, and while *Mercer* was reversed on appeal from the Supreme Court, where Ritchie and Strong had dissented, it did confirm the decision in the Ontario Court of Appeal. More important, by 1886, there had been no sharp disagreement with the Canadian courts over the structure of sections 91 and 92. The residual clause had been upheld as an instrument of federal jurisdiction in *Valin* and *Russell* and implicitly in *Lambe*; the enumerated heads of section 91, protected by the powerful declaratory clause, remained exclusive but not exhaustive examples of federal legislative jurisdiction; and the deeming clause had been repeatedly confirmed in argument and decision as a restriction on the scope of section 92(16).

Nevertheless, Judicial Committee precedents increasingly confined the Canadian courts and the Supreme Court had ceased to be regarded as a final court of appeal for constitutional cases. Even the binding nature of Supreme Court decisions on lower courts was often questioned. As Ramsay stated, 'the Supreme Court is not a final Court of Appeal ... We are not, therefore, I think, disturbing hierarchical authority in disregarding an isolated judgement so compromised as that in *Severn* v. *The Queen*.'[144] And during an argument in 1893, Taschereau stated that in view of a likely appeal to the Judicial Committee the case should have been abandoned or gone directly to London: 'Constitutional questions cannot be finally determined in the court. They never have been, and can never be under the present system.'[145] By 1887, it had become clear that, in law, Canadian federalism would be shaped not in the old building at the foot of Parliament Hill but in a small room up a back staircase on Downing Street.

The judges on the Supreme Court, as Richard Risk has written, 'did not always (or even usually) reason elegantly, coherently, or consistently,' but they had 'dealt with federalism questions by thinking openly about Canada and its history and nature.'[146] That spirit gradually waned and finally disappeared as the Supreme Court of Canada became supreme in name only.

6

The Watson Era, 1889–1912*

The mind of a master and the hand of a great craftsman ...
– Lord Denning, 1963

After two decades of judicial review in the Canadian courts and the Judicial Committee, the structure of sections 91 and 92 and their interrelationship remained substantially as was intended and legislated. Differences of judicial opinion were less on the structure than on the determination of the 'matter' of challenged legislation and on the appropriate content or scope of the enumerations. Although the principle of coordinate federalism was generally accepted (with Gwynne a vocal exception), the theoretical and practical status of the lieutenant governor remained legally and politically controversial. But, by the end of the century, the Judicial Committee had imposed a radically different template on sections 91 and 92, and authoritatively asserted the independent status of the lieutenant governor as the representative of the crown for all purposes of provincial government. However mysterious the inner workings of the committee, the author of the decisions embodying the new doctrines was William Watson.

---

*The substance of this chapter was first presented at the founding conference of the Organization for the Study of the National History of Canada in Ottawa on 5 November 1995.

When Watson became a lord of appeal in 1880, wrote Richard Haldane, 'he found himself face to face with what threatened to be a critical period in the history of Canada.' The country was torn by conflicts between the advocates of federal paramountcy and provincial autonomy. The Supreme Court of Canada endorsed the principle of federal paramountcy, Haldane asserted, but in the appeals to the Judicial Committee, Lord Watson 'made the business of laying down the new law that was necessary his own. He completely altered the tendencies of the Supreme Court ... In a series of masterly judgments, he expounded and established the real constitution of Canada.'[1] Haldane's claim obviously lingered in the mind of the Judicial Committee. It fell to Watson 'to shape the destinies of Canada,' wrote Lord Denning in 1963. 'The British North America Act was a skeleton. The mind of a master and the hand of a great craftsman were needed to endow it with a lasting and expanding virtue, and at the right moment the master-mind appeared in the person of Lord Watson, a truly dominant figure. Like the prophet of old, He had the daring to ask himself: Can these dry bones "live"? and proceeded to vivify their framework with the impulse of a progressive interpretation.'[2]

Lord Watson was acclaimed on his death as one of the great jurists of his day, and among his distinguished contemporaries, the *Times* noted, 'probably none of them have so largely influenced the jurisprudence of the British Empire.'[3] Haldane found Watson to be the ideal imperial judge, whose function, 'sitting in the supreme tribunal of the Empire, is to do more than decide what abstract and familiar legal conceptions should be applied to particular cases. His function is to be a statesman as well as a jurist, to fill in the gaps which Parliament has deliberately left in the skeleton constitutions and laws that it has provided for the British Colonies.'[4] Watson was admirably fitted to be the statesman-jurist. Despite his declared commitment to the conventional principles of statutory interpretation and judicial restraint, he was cavalier in embedding his speculations and assumptions in the constitutional law of Canada as seemed to be appropriate for a jurist shouldering his imperial responsibility.

Among scholars of the law and of federalism jurisprudence, Watson remains a central and controversial figure. In a highly literalist, positivist, almost tautological verbal analysis of his decisions and doctrines, G.P. Browne maintained that they were not only consistent with, but the only possible reading of, the language and structure of the BNA Act.[5] W.F. O'Connor and Bora Laskin concluded from their historical and textual analysis that Watson's rendering of the act was either a confused or wilful distortion.[6] Paul Romney, besides insisting that the traditional centralist interpretation of Confederation is a 'vast fabric of myth,'[7] claims that in setting out the 'guidelines by which to construe the distribution of powers as a whole' Watson was right, apparently because his decisions 'were about as close' to Oliver Mowat's 'analysis as one could get without using the same words.'[8]

Other scholars have been more nuanced. William Lederman, who considered Watson 'the greatest of the Privy Council judges concerned with the Canadian Constitution,' commended the Judicial Committee for reducing uncertainty and making 'the distribution of powers system meaningful,' obviously because Watson and his colleagues had captured what Lederman believed to be the ideal balance between unity and diversity.[9] Alan Cairns accepts the 'vast fabric of myth' argument but believes that it was the constitution, not Lord Watson, that was at fault. Bad law meant good statecraft, for the decisions that 'deliberately enhanced provincial powers in partial defiance' of the constitution and revealed a 'solicitous regard for the provinces' were a necessary and thus defensible, if not conscious, response to the 'fundamental pluralism' of Canada.[10] While Cairns suggests that 'a few elderly men in London' could not have pushed the country in a direction it would not have otherwise taken,[11] Robert Vipond, in his admirably nuanced study of the provincial-rights movement in Ontario, rightly counters that Watson and the Judicial Committee gave judicial sanction to the advocates of decentralization and helped shape the political and constitutional debate over federalism.[12]

Watson's early career was as unremarkable as it was unrewarding; only the death or elevation of his seniors explained the growth of his practice and his appointment to office. Born in 1827, 'he was never an ardent politician,' wrote a contemporary, 'but by nature, taste, and conviction he was a Conservative.'[13] With Conservatives a rarity among Scots lawyers, Watson was appointed solicitor general when Disraeli returned to office in 1874. Two years later, when Lord Gordon was made the first Scots lord of appeal under the 1876 act, Watson succeeded him as lord advocate with a seat in the House of Commons as the representative of the universities of Aberdeen and Glasgow. Disraeli had regarded the Lord of appeal as a 'plumb job' and 'an appointment to make a Scotsman's mouth water.' However, after Gordon died in 1879, Lord Chancellor Cairns spent five fruitless months trying to persuade leading Scottish judges to accept the appointment. In 1880, he turned to Watson, who accepted and was given a life peerage as Baron Watson of Thankerton.[14]

Watson first sat with the Judicial Committee in the appeal from Quebec in *Dobie* in 1881 and wrote the decision.[15] He did not sit on another Canadian appeal until 1888 but often heard petitions for leave to appeal. He was also a member of the board in civil law appeals from Quebec, probably because of his civilian training in Scots law.[16] From 1888 until his death in 1899, Watson was the pre-eminent Canadian specialist on the Judicial Committee. He was a member of the board in the sixteen cases concerning the constitution and delivered the decision in ten. With one exception, these decisions advanced, or invented, interpretive doctrines.[17]

By 1888, the committee was composed largely of the law lords. Lord Herschell, lord chancellor from 1892 to 1895, sat on five cases and delivered the judgment in four, and Lord Halsbury (lord chancellor in 1885, from 1886 to 1892, and from 1895 to 1905) sat on six and wrote the decision in one. Lord Macnaghten, an Irish lord of appeal appointed in 1887, sat on fourteen appeals and, after expressing strong personal views during the argument, wrote the controversial decision upholding Manitoba's right to abolish denominational schools.[18] Lord Hobhouse sat on ten appeals and Lord Morris on nine, but neither wrote decisions.[19] Before joining the board in 1894, Horace Davey, as counsel, fought five appeals included here, all but one for the provinces. In the seven appeals for which there are transcripts of the oral arguments, Watson, Herschell, and Halsbury dominated the proceedings, with Watson usually the most persistently vocal.

Although there was considerable continuity on the board, with Watson present at all appeals and presiding in those when neither Herschell nor Halsbury was present, it is impossible to find a coherent or consistent approach to judicial review. Watson and the board professed to endorse Hobhouse's principle in *Lambe*, that cases arising under the BNA Act would be determined 'by the same methods of construction and exposition'[20] applied to any other case, pleading strict rules of statutory construction and refusing to examine extrinsic aids or Canadian context. Although Watson was emphatic that the '"intention of the Legislature" is a common but slippery phrase,' in practice he did not hesitate to provide his own version of what must have been the intention of the legislature. Similarly, Sir Montague Smith's admonition that the court should decide each case 'without entering more largely upon an interpretation of the statute'[21] than was necessary was sometimes cited in principle but usually ignored in practice. Watson in particular, in argument and decision, indulged himself in wide-ranging conclusions and speculations about language, history, intentions, and policy.

Lord Watson's first major judgment originated as a territorial dispute between Ontario and Ottawa over the Ontario-Manitoba border but became a landmark definition of the nature of aboriginal land rights.[22] The Indians had surrendered the disputed territory in the Treaty of 1873. Arbitrators had accepted Ontario's claim in 1878, but Macdonald refused to accept the decision. With an appeal to the Judicial Committee likely, Macdonald injected a new element into the controversy when he boasted during the 1882 election that its decision would be of little consequence. Although the land had belonged to the Hudson's Bay Company, he argued, 'it was subject to the Indian title. They and their ancestors had owned the land for centuries until the Dominion Government purchased them ... By seven treaties the Indians of the Northwest conveyed the lands to Canada; and every acre belongs to the people of Canada, and not to the people of Ontario.'[23]

When Macdonald refused to accept the decision of the Judicial Committee in 1884 awarding the territory to Ontario, Mowat launched a suit against the St Catherine's Milling Company which had been given a federal licence to cut timber in the disputed territory. D'Alton McCarthy, who was to act for the company (and Ottawa), had not been keen about forcing the issue, but in the end he agreed that 'if the question is to be raised it had better be as a matter of law than as a matter of politics.'[24]

The matter of law as it emerged in court depended in part on title to the surrendered land: if title was in the crown, it would pass to the province under section 109, the property provision of the 1867 BNA Act; if it was in the Indians, the federal government could claim ownership through purchase. There was also the unsettled jurisdictional question about the meaning of section 91(24), which gave the federal government jurisdiction over 'Indians, and Lands reserved for the Indians.' When Mowat won in Chancery, Sir Alexander Campbell urged Macdonald not to wage another legal battle with Mowat. Rather 'put to one side the fact that the money came from the Dominion – and ask ourselves for whom is the crown now trustee, and that the answer to that is for those who have ultimately come to be the owners of the country, and who are represented by the Government of Ontario – I think that we shall have to come to this and that we should come to it.'[25]

But Macdonald refused and, after losing in the Ontario Court of Appeal, went to the Supreme Court. For the majority, Ritchie held that the Indians had a legal right of occupancy but the crown held legal title to the land which passed to Ontario in 1867. Strong (with Gwynne concurring) dissented on the grounds that the Indians did have some legal rights and that, while unsurrendered lands were the property of the crown, they were lands reserved for Indians which passed to the Dominion in 1867.[26] Macdonald stubbornly appealed in the name of the company to the Judicial Committee.[27]

The argument at the Judicial Committee continued for seven days before Selborne, Watson, Hobhouse, Peacock, Smith, and Couch. Mowat and Blake appeared for Ontario, aided by Davey and Haldane. Mowat led off with what Blake described as a 'lamentable failure ... no judgment, no capacity for answering questions, no facility for meeting difficulties and a persistent presentation of minor unimportant and untenable points against the mind of the court.' The outcome, wrote Blake (openly worried about his £6,000 fee if they lost), 'is distinctly worse still than it was before he spoke, and is still in danger.'[28] Blake then had the polite attention of the board for two days. He conceded that the Indians had the right of occupancy but argued ownership was vested in the crown and had passed to Ontario.[29] 'Our chances of success are distinctly improved,' he wrote triumphantly to his wife, 'and poor Mowat who thought our case absolutely lost has recovered spirits and we both think we shall win ... my argument has made a sensation ... my *opponents* said it was the most brilliant piece of eloquence they had ever heard ... nevertheless the case hangs by a thread.'[30]

In a mixture of law and policy, the Judicial Committee rejected the argument of Sir Richard Webster and McCarthy that the Indians had owned the land, and confirmed the decisions in the Canadian courts. Aboriginal title to the land, wrote Watson, was only a 'personal and usufructuary right' but ownership was vested in the crown.[31] As a result, the beneficial interest in the lands surrendered in the Treaty of 1873 was transmitted to the province under section 109 of the BNA Act.

Long held as a classic statement of the nature of aboriginal tenure, as recognized by the Royal Proclamation of 1763, Watson's opinion has been largely discredited in the Supreme Court. 'The subsequent jurisprudence has attempted to grapple with this definition,' noted Chief Justice Antonio Lamer, 'and has in the process demonstrated that the Privy Council's choice of terminology is not particularly helpful to explain the various dimensions of Indian title.'[32] Although the issues remain complex, Canadian courts now recognize that aboriginal title arises from occupation of the land prior to the conquest, the assertion of British sovereignty, and the Royal Proclamation.

In decision, Watson accepted the Ontario position that section 91 (24) gave the federal government only legislative power, not proprietary rights, over 'Indians, and Lands reserved for the Indians.' However, he rejected the argument that 'lands reserved for the Indians' were simply Indian reserves created after the surrender. Again falling back on the language used, as well as grounds of public policy, he concluded that 'the words actually used are, according to their natural meaning, sufficient to include all lands reserved, upon any terms or conditions, for Indian occupation. It appears to be the plain policy of the Act that, in order to ensure uniformity of administration, all such lands, and Indian affairs generally, shall be under the legislative control of one central authority.'[33]

In the end, Canada could legislate for aboriginals in the unsurrendered lands it did not own, and the province could not legislate for or secure a surrender of lands it would own. Perhaps that was less a complication than having a huge federal enclave in northwestern Ontario and later in western Canada. It was the prospect of that outcome that Webster believed influenced the decision: 'For a long time the result seemed to be in great doubt. I think, and thought at the time, that the decision was largely governed by questions of policy, which were undoubtedly very much in favour of the view taken by Canadian Courts, as it would have been most inconvenient that there should be established a province within a province as would have been the case if the reserves had been held to be the property of the Dominion.'[34]

To complicate the outcome further, Watson gratuitously added that since the benefits of the surrendered land accrued to the province, it 'must, of course, relieve the crown, and the Dominion, of all obligations involving the payment of money which were undertaken by Her Majesty, and which are said to have been in part fulfilled by the Dominion Government.'[35] It was inevitable that Ottawa would someday attempt to recover its outlay. When it did, Lord Loreburn agreed with the majority in the Supreme Court that Ottawa had not acted as an agent of the provincial government but 'with a view to great national interests.' As a matter of 'fair play' the province might be liable but 'in point of law' it was not. Loreburn admitted that, while Watson's statement 'does give strong support to the view of those who rely on it,' it was 'quite possible that Lord Watson did not intend to pronounce upon a legal right. If he did so intend, the passage in question must be regarded as *obiter dictum.*'[36]

Blake's eloquence had been less apparent in his argument over substance than in his oratorical portrayal of the provinces as an endangered species needing the protection of the court if they were to survive. The court's preliminary task was to understand the 'general scheme' of the constitution:

In truth the Act is in many points little more than a skeleton, which is to be clothed with flesh and muscle, nerve and sinew, into which the breath of life is to be breathed by interpretation ... the word federal is the key which unlocks the clauses, and reveals their contents. It is the glass which enables us to discern what is written. By its light the Act must be construed ...

It was not the intention of Parliament to mutilate, confound and destroy the provinces mentioned in the preamble, and having done so, from their mangled remains, stewed in some legislative cauldron, to evoke by some legislative incantation absolutely new provinces into an absolutely new existence ... it was the design, I say ... by gentle and considerate treatment to preserve the vital breath and continue the political existence of the old provinces. However this may be, they were being made, as has been well said, not fractions of a unit, but units of a multiple. The Dominion is a multiple, and each province is a unit of that multiple.[37]

Blake's invitation to give the constitution a 'very large, liberal and comprehensive interpretation' in the provincial interest and to escape the narrow confines of rigid statutory interpretation may not have influenced Watson. But the history and theory of federalism he later advanced was not dissimilar, and in his decisions could be heard echoes of the need to protect that endangered species. And Blake's anatomical analogy appears to have had a lasting and agreeable effect on Richard Haldane, his junior in the case.

Watson's next judgment has aroused less attention but is equally problematic. The reasoning is not convincing historically and the argument has recently been criticized by the Canadian courts, although they did not directly question the decision. What is known as the *Precious Metals* case involved the ownership of the gold and silver in the forty-mile belt of railway land transferred from British Columbia to Canada by the 11th article in the terms of union in compensation for the construction of the Canadian Pacific Railway.[38] The terms were initially negotiated by Sir George-Étienne Cartier, a lawyer, and three laymen from British Columbia. There was no suggestion in the negotiations, in the terms themselves, in the statute authorizing the transfer, or in the 1883 revisions that precious metals were excluded or included. The legal contention that they were not included was based on a sixteenth-century English decision in which, after lengthy deliberations, the justices and barons decided that 'all mines and gold and silver' belonged to the queen, even those on the Earl of Northumberland's land.[39] The rule derived from the decision was that a grant of land to private persons would not include the prerogative ownership or 'royalties' of precious metals unless the intention of the crown was expressed, as Horace Davey said in argument at the Judicial Committee, by 'apt and precise words.'

A majority of the Supreme Court found that the rule governing private grants was inapplicable and that all mineral rights were transferred to Canada. Chief Justice Ritchie stated that the terms of union should not be regarded as a transaction between the crown and a private individual or between private parties but as a statutory arrangement 'in settlement of a constitutional question between the two governments, or rather, giving effect to, and carrying out, the constitutional compact under which British Columbia became part and parcel of the Dominion of Canada, and as a part of that arrangement the government of British Columbia relinquished to the Dominion of Canada ... all right to certain public lands belonging to the crown.'[40]

Ritchie also found persuasive – both for what it said and what it did not say – an 1883 provincial minute of council stating that one of the conditions of the transfer was that Ottawa 'shall establish a land system equally liberal as to mining and agricultural industries, as that in force in the province at the present time.'[41] Gwynne (Taschereau concurring) agreed that the ancient precedent was inapplicable: 'The case must be regarded not at all in the light of a grant of land by the crown to a subject, but in the light of a treaty between two independent contracting parties upon the faith of which alone the Province of British Columbia was received into and became part of the Dominion of Canada.'[42]

Without elaborate reasons, Watson reversed the decision of the Supreme Court. If the agreement could be regarded as either 'a separate and independent compact' or 'an independent treaty,' the conclusion reached by the Supreme Court 'would have been inevitable.' But their Lordships found that the 11th article of the terms of union simply 'embodies the terms of a commercial transaction, by which one Government undertook to make a railway, and the other to give a subsidy, by assigning part of its territorial revenues.' Section 109 of the BNA Act, which provided that 'all lands, mines, minerals, and royalties' belonging to the province would be retained, should be read to include British Columbia. The 11th article was an exception, but it did not profess to deal with the 'jura regia' and the province retained ownership of the precious metals in the railway belt.[43]

Three Canadian courts have recently criticized Watson's language, and implicitly his reasons. Chief Justice William Esson of the British Columbia Supreme Court observed in 1989 that while the decision 'must no doubt be taken as stating the law on the specific issue raised in the case,' Watson's 'crabbed view' of the 11th article 'as merely setting the terms of a commercial transaction' was unacceptable. 'That view simply ignores the enormous scope of the project to which the Dominion committed itself, and the essential part it played in creating a dominion from sea to sea. To Lord Watson, this was no more significant than, say, an agreement to extend a Glasgow tramway into an adjoining suburb. Ritchie C.J. and Gwynne J. were surely closer to the mark.'[44] The British Columbia Court of Appeal also agreed with Ritchie's characterization of the terms of union and, with reference to Watson's reasons cited above, stated that 'if we consider ourselves bound by that pronouncement we would, of course, be bound to follow it, leaving it to the Supreme Court of Canada to correct what is obviously a serious misapprehension of Canadian constitutional history.[45]

In the Supreme Court of Canada, Justice Frank Iacobucci found Watson's language 'troubling':

If Lord Watson meant to suggest that Term 11 is simply a commercial and not a constitutional provision, then the judgement of the Privy Council must be regarded as having been rendered *per incuriam* [politely, through inadvertence; less respectfully, through ignorance] for reasons I have already noted. If, then, Lord Watson erred in this fashion, the Court of Appeal below was correct to assert that the Privy Council 'seriously misapprehen[ded]' Canadian history and the learned trial judge was correct to refer to its 'crabbed' view of Term 11 (assuming without deciding that, as a matter of *stare decisis*, either court had sufficient justification to ignore the perceived authority of the Privy Council).[46]

However, Iacobucci preferred 'a more generous view of Watson's reasons,' which involved reinterpreting what Watson must have meant and elaborating the argument Watson might have made. He concluded lamely that at least in his decision Watson's 'exceptional treatment' of royalties was consistent with other judgments of the Judicial Committee.[47]

Watson's opinions in *St. Catherine's Milling* and *Precious Metals* were based in part on his interpretation of the rights of the crown in the province. And, in 1892, Watson had the opportunity to settle finally the troublesome but critical issue of the constitutional status of the lieutenant governor. The Supreme Court decisions in *Lenoir* and *Mercer*, neither of which had been argued or settled precisely on the point, suggested that the lieutenant governor did not represent the crown directly and possessed only the prerogatives expressly stated in the constitution. However, Ritchie's dissent in *Lenoir* (with Strong's apparent concurrence) that the lieutenant governor continued to represent the crown, 'though doubtless in a modified manner,' was endorsed in the provincial courts.[48] In the Ontario Court of Appeal, George Burton 'respectfully' but pointedly stated that, if 'it had not been for the expression found in some judicial utterances placing within very narrow limits the powers of the executives of the provinces, I should have thought it too clear for argument, that the powers formerly exercised by the Lieutenant-Governors of the other Provinces, and by the Governor-General of Canada in reference to provincial matters ... were now vested exclusively in the Lieutenant-Governors.'[49]

That had always been Mowat's position. The lieutenant governor, he insisted, was 'entitled *virtute officii* and without express statutory enactment, to exercise all prerogatives incident to the Executive authority in matters over which the Provincial Legislatures have jurisdiction.' This was a matter not only of law but of history, for it was the 'undoubted and unquestioned understanding on which the subject of Confederation was considered, on which the resolutions which formed the basis of the BNA Act were framed and accepted, and was the understanding which, without any express provision to this effect in the Act, has been acted upon as of course by the Dominion and Provincial authorities ever since.'[50] As the courts circled the issue and the federal minister of justice refused Mowat's request for a reference to the Judicial Committee, the Ontario premier seized the initiative.[51]

In 1888 he passed An Act respecting the Executive Administration of the Laws of this Province which in declaratory language stated that the meaning of section 65 of the BNA Act confirmed that the lieutenant governor had executive authority over all matters within provincial jurisdiction as his predecessors had before 1867, including the power of commuting and remitting sentences for offences against the laws of the province.[52] John Thompson, the federal minister of justice, found the act objectionable but, to avoid 'any unnecessary conflict,' did not recommend disallowance.[53] In the end, he and Mowat agreed to a stated reference case in the Ontario courts in the first instance rather than to the Supreme Court or the Judicial Committee where no reasons would be given.

The case was first heard in Chancery in June 1890; Edward Blake acted for Ontario. In a unanimous decision on 6 December, the court found the act *intra vires*. While the intention of section 92(1) was 'manifestly intended to keep intact the headship of the Provincial Government, forming, as it does, the link of federal power,' declared Chancellor Boyd, that did not prevent a statutory increase in the constitutional position or functions of the lieutenant governor. More broadly, he continued, although 'no direct or immediately representative coordination of queen and people may exist in the provincial Assembly, yet sovereign power must substantially operate and be manifested in Ontario legislation in order to the efficient exercise of territorial government under the sanctions of the Imperial Act.'[54] The decision was confirmed by the Court of Appeal in January 1892.[55] As the appeal was proceeding to the Supreme Court, Lord Watson made it largely unnecessary with his decision in *Liquidators of the Maritime Bank of Canada* v. *Receiver-General of New Brunswick*, delivered in July 1892.[56]

The case originated with the collapse of the Maritime Bank, which was indebted to the provincial government.[57] Arguing before the Supreme Court of New Brunswick, A.G. Blair, premier and attorney general, contended that the *Bank of Nova Scotia* case, 'which determined the crown, in the exercise of its prerogative rights in the country can claim a preference over creditors of the same class, narrows the first question down to this, whether the crown, as represented by the local government, has been bereft of its prerogative right.' Citing sections 64, 65, and 72 of the BNA Act and observing that the provinces possessed a Great Seal, Blair concluded that there was not 'a syllable in the Act excluding the crown from the exercise of its rights in respect of matters retained by the Local Executive.' Divest the crown in the province 'of its executive rights as represented by the lieutenant governor, and the whole machinery of Government would stop.' The lieutenant governor was appointed by the governor-general in the name of the queen and thus 'the whole scheme of Union is made consistent and harmonious. The Sovereign is not only the chief, but the sole magistrate of the nation, and all others act through her. The executive authority, as represented by the Federal and Provincial Governments, reaches out in both directions and covers the whole ground.'[58]

The court easily found for the provincial government. 'It is true that the prerogative rights of the crown were by the Statute apportioned between the Provinces and the Dominion,' Chief Justice John Allen stated, 'but this apportionment in no sense implies the extinguishment of any of them, and they there continue to subsist in their integrity, however their locality might be altered by the division of powers contained in the new constitutional law.' Justice John Fraser agreed that the prerogatives possessed by the lieutenant governor were co-extensive with the division of powers.[59]

The decision was immediately and unsuccessfully appealed to the Supreme Court. In the most confirming judgment, Christopher Patterson, who had joined the court in October 1888, found the decision consistent with 'the spirit and tenor of the British North America Act' and 'in accordance with the views which prevail in the bulk of the decisions under the statute although all the opinions expressed, particularly in the earlier cases, may not have been in harmony.' Patterson cited Lord Watson's decisions in the St. Catherine's Milling and the Precious Metals cases, 'not that these bear directly on the point at hand: they are merely instances of late utterances where the Provincial Governments are spoken of in the same terms as the Dominion Government as representing the queen.'[60]

Gwynne dissented vigorously and predicted that the judgment 'will no doubt give to the dispensers of the Prerogative in London ... another opportunity to indulge their favourite game ... to exalt the provinces of the Dominion of Canada at the expense of the Dominion and to neutralize or repeal the BNA Act.' Indeed, so successful had they played the game, he wrote to his old friend Judge J.R. Gowan, that 'old as I am I fully expect that both you and I shall be present as mourners at the funeral of Confederation cruelly murdered in the house of its friends.'[61]

The appeal was heard at the Judicial Committee in May 1892 when Watson presided at the two-day argument. Sir Richard Webster was retained by the liquidators and Sir Horace Davey appeared with Blair for the province. It was an uneven battle in talent and in precedent.

Foolishly adopting Gwynne's extreme centralist reasoning, which had never been accepted in the Judicial Committee (or the Supreme Court), Webster argued that the governor general alone represented the queen and that the lieutenant governor of a province, 'with functions different from the old government and legislatures, and with powers limited and defined by statute and municipal in their general character,' neither represented the crown nor possessed any prerogatives not expressly granted. Davey observed that sections 64 and 65 continued the executive authority of the provincial governments unless 'cut down by express enactment and there is nothing in the Act of 1867 or in any subsequent Act which abolishes or alters them.' More broadly and in line with decision, 'according to the true effect of that Act the provincial governments and legislatures are within their respective spheres sovereign ... The intention was that the Dominion and the provinces should have coordinate authority within their respective spheres, all subject to the control of the Imperial Parliament.'[62]

In his judgment, Watson summarily dismissed what he described as the 'sum and substance' of Webster's argument that Confederation had severed the connection between the crown and the provinces and had reduced the provinces 'to the rank of independent municipal institutions' as propositions for which 'their Lordships have been unable to find either principle or authority.'[63] The appointment by the governor general was under the Great Seal, or the 'Executive Government of the Dominion,' which, by section 9, was declared 'to continue and be vested in the Queen,' and was thus 'the act of the Crown; and a Lieutenant-Governor, when appointed, is as much the representative of Her Majesty for all purposes of provincial government as the Governor General himself is for all purposes of Dominion Government.'[64] Citing *Mercer*, *St. Catherine's Milling*, and *Precious Metals* as authority, Watson concluded: 'Seeing that successive decisions of this board, in the case of territorial revenues, are based upon the general recognition of Her Majesty's continued sovereignty under the Act of 1867, it appears to their Lordships that, so far as regards vesting in the crown, the same consequences must follow in the case of provincial revenues which are not territorial.'[65]

The legal position of the crown in the right of the province and thus of the office of the lieutenant governor had been settled. As Edward Blake commented later in the Supreme Court, during the argument in the case involving the provincial authority to appoint queen's counsel, there was nothing new in Watson's decision but 'it appears to me that

in that case the Judicial Committee had concluded to make a definite statement of their view of the position of the province, and to
place their decision upon a broad and clear view of the result of previous decisions affecting the rights of the different provinces of the
Dominion.'[66]

Watson was not content just to declare the law, but in one long *obiter*
he placed the Judicial Committee's imprimatur on his view of the history and philosophy of Canadian federalism:

The object of the Act was neither to weld the provinces into one, nor to subordinate provincial governments to a central authority, but to create a federal
government in which they should all be represented, entrusted with the exclusive administration of affairs in which they had a common interest, each province *retaining* its independence and autonomy. That object was accomplished
by distributing, between the Dominion and the provinces, *all powers executive
and legislative*, and all public property and revenues which had previously
belonged to the provinces; so that the Dominion Government should be vested
with such of these *powers*, property and revenues as were necessary for the due
performance of its constitutional functions, and that the *remainder should be
retained by the provinces* for the purposes of provincial government. But, in so
far as regards those matters which, by sect. 92, are specially reserved for provincial legislation, the legislation of each province continued to be free from
the control of the Dominion, and as supreme as it was before the passing of the
Act.[67]

Watson had, in fact, redefined, perhaps even realigned, the nature of
Canadian federalism. His long *obiter dictum*, unnecessary for the determination of the issue before the court, not only confirmed the legal
foundations for provincial sovereignty but also, in placing all residual
powers – apparently including legislative – within the province, was
an endorsement of the compact theory of the delegated capacity of the
federal government and of provincial pre-eminence.[68]

Over the next few years, Watson and his colleagues had to confront
more explicitly the task of mastering the structure of sections 91 and 92
and the scope of their enumerations. The first occasion was *Tennant* v.
Union Bank of Canada, a challenge to the provisions of the federal Bank
Act which had validated warehouse receipts as negotiable instru-
ments, unlike Ontario's *Mercantile Amendment Act* which did not.
D'Alton McCarthy, counsel for Tennant, argued that the federal gov-

ernment's jurisdiction over banking 'must be so exercised as not to interfere with property and civil rights.' Horace Davey, for the bank, argued the exclusivity of federal power over banking and, on the precedent of *Cushing*, that even if the subject could be brought within section 92, the power of the Dominion was 'paramount.'[69]

The decision, wrote Watson, turned upon the construction of sections 91 and 92. Section 91 gave the federal government power to make laws in relation to all matters not assigned exclusively to the provinces, 'and also' exclusive legislative authority in relation to certain enumerated subjects, one of which was banking. As the statutory regulations at issue 'unquestionably relate to property and civil rights,' opposition to the provisions of the act would be 'unanswerable if it could be shewn that, by the Act of 1867, the Parliament of Canada is absolutely debarred from trenching to any extent upon matters assigned to the provincial legislatures by sect. 92. But sect. 91 expressly declares that, "notwithstanding anything in this Act," the exclusive legislative authority of the Parliament of Canada *shall extend* to all matters coming within the enumerated classes; which plainly indicates that the legislation of that Parliament so long as it strictly relates to these matters, is to be of paramount authority.'[70]

In the decision, however, Watson stated that the federal power over banking was 'wide enough to embrace every transaction coming within the legitimate business of a banker' and confirmed the validity of the Bank Act.[71]

Watson's bifurcation of section 91 with the words 'and also' could be attributed to sloppy language rather than deliberate intention had it not been followed by a more explicit separation of the residual clause and the enumerations in *Local Prohibition* two years later. W.F. O'Connor and G.P. Browne, the former to denounce and the latter to praise, agreed that 'and also' represents what Browne described as the 'first incontestable precursor' of the separation of section 91 into two compartments.[72] They also agreed that the substitution of the enacting tense 'shall extend' for the declaratory 'extends' reinforced the division.[73] And while the decision confirmed the paramountcy of the section 91 enumerations, the words 'strictly relates' added a narrow interpretive dimension to the words 'in relation to.'

A few days after he delivered the decision in *Tennant*, Watson was on the board for the appeal on *Voluntary Assignments*, a challenge to Ontario legislation providing relief to insolvent debtors and enabling them to make a voluntary assignment of assets among creditors.[74] The act had been challenged as relating to 'Bankruptcy and Insolvency' (section 91(27)) although the 1875 federal insolvency act had been repealed in 1880 and there was no federal legislation on either bankruptcy or insolvency. After inconclusive judgments in the Ontario courts, E.L. Newcombe, the deputy minister of justice, agreed to facilitate an appeal to the Judicial Committee in 1893. Mowat believed that the committee would appreciate the importance of the appeal 'if informed by counsel that the Ontario Act in question is the only substitute for a bankruptcy or insolvency law which this province has; and that in consequence of the differing opinion in various sections of the Dominion, the Government has hitherto been unable to frame a law which the Canadian Parliament is prepared to accept.'[75]

The Judicial Committee was undoubtedly influenced by the absence of federal legislation. Both during the argument and in his decision, Herschell pointed to the absence of compulsion or the creation of the legal status of a bankrupt or insolvent as provisions which were common to schemes of bankruptcy and insolvency, and thus found the act a valid exercise of jurisdiction under property and civil rights. However, he added, such provisions could be contained in a federal act and the province would thus be 'precluded from interfering ... But it does not follow that such subjects, as might properly be treated as ancillary to such a law and therefore within the powers of the Dominion Parliament, are excluded from the legislative authority of the provincial legislature when there is no bankruptcy or insolvency legislation of the Dominion Parliament in existence.'[76] Herschell's suggestion of the 'unoccupied field' would soon be clarified.

The discussion during the pleadings provide important additional insights into Watson's view of the distribution of legislative jurisdiction and his theory of Canadian federalism. When the case was first heard in the Court of Appeal, E.F.B. Johnston, the deputy attorney general, advanced a proposition novel even for the Mowat government:

The Province, apart from the British North America Act, would have the power inherently to deal with property as it is dealt with by the Act in question. The British North America Act does not destroy such right, but suspends it only. The restriction as against the province is merely the result of a political arrangement whereby the provinces are united in a Federal Government without their rights being abrogated.

If the Dominion Government therefore does not exercise its rights as regards bankruptcy, the power to deal with that law may be exercised by the Local Legislatures. The reason is, that if the Dominion practically waives its right to legislate on that branch of property and civil rights, which was excepted in its favor, the Local Government would have the power under the wide term, and because that power only remained in suspense during the exercise of Dominion rights ...[77]

Opening his argument before the Judicial Committee, Blake did not go so far as to suggest that the provincial power over property and civil rights was merely suspended by the existence of federal legislation; instead, he contended that, 'even though the Dominion Parliament might by legislation passed under one or the other heads in section 91, appropriate some particular Provincial field otherwise occupied by section 92 so as to exclude the Province from its further occupation, yet it by no means follows that, in the absence of such Dominion legislation, the Provincial field is to be taken as limited by the possible range of unexercised power by the Dominion Parliament.' Watson's interjection, although somewhat impenetrable, suggests that he saw the section 91 enumerations as exceptions from section 92: if the power were exercised, provincial laws as to property and civil rights could be modified, but if not exercised they remained untouched. 'That,' replied Blake, 'is the line of argument I intend to pursue.'[78]

Watson repeatedly interjected to the same effect during Sir Richard Webster's argument that, occupied or not, federal jurisdiction was exclusive: 'If they have passed legislation which did trench quite properly an area in which the Province might exercise legislation then if it rescinded that legislation you are thrown back upon the old and prime question what is the area allowed to them and is it trenched on?'[79] Later, when Webster argued that you were to 'read out' of section 92 anything in section 91, Watson observed:

That is rather suggesting this – the area of the Legislative Power is defined and capable of definition, and is absolutely exclusive in all cases. That is not the view which has been suggested by the decisions of this board. The decisions of this board rather point to this – and at present I am rather inclined to agree with them – that there is a certain extent of that Legislation which might be reserved to the Province, but there are many ancillary regulations which might be made in carrying out their primary object and the power given to them in which they can over-ride the Provincial Authorities. But the provincial Authority is there.'[80]

Or again: 'It is not exclusive as soon as they [the federal government] retreat from it and do not occupy it by legislative means.'[81]

Watson's sentiments and his view of the appropriate constructions of sections 91 and 92 were clearly in harmony with Blake's final pleas that 'the deeper the wound Parliament can make in "Property and Civil Rights," the larger the area in which it can infringe ... the more indefinite and elastic the range of its potential action, the more important it is to decide that at any rate until Parliament chooses to act the other Legislature shall not be disabled from acting.'[82]

Watson obviously believed that as a matter of law the province could legislate within its enumerations, not only on property and civil rights, unless and until the field was occupied by federal legislation under its enumerated powers. As he restated his proposition during the oral argument in *Fielding* v. *Thomas*: 'I think you may take this as a general proposition, that the provincial legislature cannot be debarred from exercising any of the power specified by reason of the ability of the Canadian Parliament to deal with the same matter. There is no bar in the way of the provincial parliament until there is legislation by the Dominion Parliament.'[83] A few months later, during the argument in *Brewers and Malsters*, he was even more decisive:

I do not see that the powers in 91 have any effect whatever in limiting the powers of the provincial Legislature under 92 except in those circumstance where in virtue of those powers given by 91 there has been actual legislation by the Dominion Parliament ... As long as there is no legislation in the Dominion Parliament on the same subject the provincial Legislature has full power to exercise the specific rights given it by section 92. You have no power to include in 91 powers given by 92.[84]

In his judgment in the *Fisheries Reference* in 1898, however, Herschell had to correct or clarify the unoccupied-field doctrine drawn from *Voluntary Assignments*.[85] The declaratory clause unmistakably asserted the exclusivity of federal legislative authority under the enumerations, he observed, and provincial legislation in relation to any enumeration was 'incompetent.' It had been suggested during the argument, 'and this view has been adopted by some of the judges of the Supreme Court, that although any Dominion legislation dealing within the subject would override provincial legislation, the latter is nevertheless valid, unless and until the Dominion Parliament so legislates. Their Lordships think that such a view does not give due effect to the terms of s. 91, and in particular to the word "exclusively."'[86]

The decision was given in May 1898 and, in view of the 'collegial' practices of the committee, presumably had been read by Watson. Yet, during the argument in *Bonsecours* in March 1899, Watson could lecture Blake that the 'power of exclusive legislation given to the Dominion Parliament by section 91 can never take effect till the legislation exists, and until it exists and occupies the field, which is the expression that has been used aptly enough, the law of the province must subsist.'[87]

However, a few months later, in his last decision, Watson seemed to qualify his position.[88] The British Columbia Supreme Court had upheld a provincial statute prohibiting the employment of Chinese in coal mines as coming within property and civil rights, and it was on that ground that Haldane argued its validity. Blake contended that the federal government had exclusive jurisdiction over aliens by section 91(25), and as 'the Dominion Parliament had dealt with the subject as completely as it saw fit ... it was not competent to the provincial legislature to further impose restrictions and disabilities upon the Chinese alien immigrants into British Columbia.'[89]

Watson agreed that the 'whole pith and substance' of the regulations established prohibitions 'which affects aliens or naturalized subjects, and therefore trench upon the exclusive authority of the Parliament of Canada.' He rejected the argument, which had found favour in the lower court, that the federal naturalization act had established only partial control over the rights of aliens: 'The abstinence of the Dominion Parliament from legislating to the *full limit of its powers*, could not have the effect of transferring to the provincial legislature the legislative power which had been assigned to the Dominion by s.91 of the Act of 1867.'[90] Watson's decision was to be 'distinguished' (to use the legal term for 'altered') almost beyond recognition but his belated and partial denial of the unoccupied-field doctrine, even if the federal government had not legislated 'to the full limit of its powers,' was not.[91]

The Judicial Committee was also given the opportunity to write another chapter in the long political and legal battle over liquor regulations. Despite the apparent trade-off in *Russell*, *Hodge*, and the *McCarthy Act Reference*, Mowat could not escape the political pressure from the temperance forces for total prohibition. After repeatedly tightening the regulations, he passed an act in 1890 giving the municipalities their pre-Confederation local-option powers. The act was found *intra vires* in the Ontario Court of Appeal, largely under section 92(8). Chief Justice John Hagarty stated that 'it may safely be said that there is no apparent intention in the Confederation Act to curtail or interfere with the existing general powers of municipal councils unless the Act plainly transfers any of existing such powers to the Dominion jurisdiction.'[92] However, the court upheld the prohibition of retail sales only, although Burton stated that without the binding precedents of *Fredericton* and *Russell* he would have upheld total prohibition.[93]

Although Mowat professed to support total prohibition, he said in the legislature that he 'wondered whether there was any lawyer in the house who was prepared to say we had jurisdiction.'[94] Requesting Sir John Thompson to agree to a Supreme Court reference, he wrote that rather than claiming jurisdiction for the province, 'I have expressed great doubts as to whether the courts would hold that jurisdiction was in the Provinces, though it is of course my duty to uphold that view before the courts until the point is decided.'[95] Thompson finally agreed.

Before the reference reached it, the Supreme Court had heard what was in effect an appeal on the local-option act but had delayed announcing the decision until the reference itself was heard. Strong, Fournier, and Taschereau had held that the province could prohibit retail sales under 92(8); while Gwynne and Robert Sedgewick, the former deputy minister of justice, had held that pre-Confederation municipal practice was irrelevant, given the redistribution of power in 1867, and that provincial prohibition was an unconstitutional interference with trade and commerce.[96] When the reference itself was heard in May 1894, the federal government readily conceded the provincial power to prohibit retail sales but contended that only Ottawa could prohibit the manufacture or importation of liquor and also determine what was retail or wholesale.[97] Taschereau did not sit on the reference, and George King, who had recently joined the court, supported Gwynne and Sedgewick in finding the act unconstitutional.[98] In the result, two different decisions were announced on 15 January 1895: by a majority of 3–2 the court had found the Ontario legislation both *ultra* and *intra vires*. As Lord Watson sarcastically commented early in the argument before the Judicial Committee, 'they must have been right once.'[99]

The substantive question before the Judicial Committee was the right of the province to prohibit the sale of liquor, but there were other questions concerning manufacture, importation, and 'what ifs,' or, as Lord Chancellor Halsbury put it, 'all the things which may happen in the course of this world's history, which may or may not render temperance legislation or any other legislation proper.'[100] The sarcasm was understandable, for it was the fourth time the committee had been asked to determine who could stand between Canadians and their beer. Four members of the board had heard it all before; only Watson and Lord Morris had not.[101] On the other side of the table, John Maclaren, counsel for Ontario, had acted in *Fredericton, Russell* and *Local Prohibition* in the Court of Appeal and the Supreme Court, and Haldane had acted in *McCarthy.* Much to Mowat's dismay, Edward Blake had been retained by the distillers, as had Wallace Nesbitt, who had fought the legislation before the Supreme Court. E.I. Newcombe, the deputy minister of justice, was senior counsel for the federal government, but most of the burden fell on Blake.[102]

Maclaren relied almost exclusively on the section 92(8) argument which had always won favour in the Canadian courts and had been accepted by the Judicial Committee in *Hodge.* But it was evident at once that Herschell, Halsbury, and Watson believed that pre-Confederation law or practice was legally irrelevant because the province could not endow municipal institutions with powers it did not itself possess. Herschell did muse, however, that since local governments had been given the power for the 'good order and sobriety of the community ... I think there is a good deal to be said for that being one of the subjects of a local nature.'[103] Maclaren was constantly pressed, by Herschell in particular, to go to 92(16), but he was hesitant not only because of *Russell* but also because he feared the application of the deeming clause. Herschell agreed that 'if it is within the specific subjects mentioned in section 91, then clearly all matters although merely local if they are within any of those specific subjects are under section 91.'[104]

Any legislature, Blake stated, had the power to prohibit any trade for social, moral, economic, fiscal, or political reasons, and 'I am going to contend that both under the general and under the enumerated powers of the Dominion the jurisdiction to prohibit on any of these grounds rests in, and rests solely in, the Dominion.'[105] Blake's structural analysis of section 91 and the purpose of the residual, declaratory, and deeming clauses was exemplary, as were his attempts to revisit *Parsons* and re-examine the trade and commerce power. But whether it was general weariness by the third day of argument or hostility to a counsel who was by now an Irish nationalist member of parliament, the court engaged in constant interruptions and interjections as well as long irrelevant musings. Never overly deferential before the committee, Blake was often exasperated: 'Surely, when you come to the enumerated powers. Which I hope to reach some time' – or 'I ventured to assume that your Lordships would understand the language that your

Lordships used.'[106] Watson was by far the worst offender and his performance is ample witness to the comments of a contemporary: 'Recently, too, he became oblivious of the interruptions of the other judges, unceremoniously breaking in even upon interruptions, and when his brethren turned round and looked aghast, no doubt expecting the customary apology, the noble lord audibly pursued the thread of his own thoughts without deferring to his right hand or his left.'[107]

Nine months after the argument, Lord Watson delivered the decision. Agreeing to give only a qualified answer to some of the questions, describing them as 'academic rather than judicial,' the committee upheld the Ontario legislation and confirmed the provincial power to prohibit the sale of liquor. All that was necessary in decision was to determine that in 'pith and substance,' a phrase Watson was to create in *Union Colliery*, local prohibition was a local and private matter which had always been entrusted to local authorities and was not a matter in relation to trade and commerce despite its incidental effects. But, with a careful selection and revisiting of some precedents, a rejection of others, and some jurisprudential inventions, Watson seized another opportunity to reconstruct Canadian federalism to his own satisfaction, a reconstruction that could not have secured unanimity or probably even a majority.[108]

The law could not be upheld under section 92(8), wrote Watson. Despite the many decisions in the Canadian courts, the committee had properly concluded that while the province possessed the power to create municipal institutions, it could delegate only those powers it possessed. Therefore, jurisdiction had to lie in either section 92(16) or 92(13) and, since it could not be in both, Watson's preferred choice was the former. However, his difficulty was that, by its wording, reinforced by precedent and frequent and undisputed judicial comment in argument, the deeming clause withdrew from 92(16) any matter infringing on the enumerations in section 91. Moreover, there was the precedent in *Russell*, not overruled in *Hodge*, that the power to prohibit lay within the federal government's residual power and could also be said to fall within trade and commerce. With an imaginative reconstruction of sections 91 and 92, aided by equally imaginative assumptions about the intentions of the framers, Watson warmed to his task of overcoming these obstacles in what was in many ways a fifteen-page *obiter dictum*.

Watson first redefined the purpose of the deeming clause. In *Parsons*, Sir Montague Smith had observed that the declaratory and deeming clauses were both designed to give 'pre-eminence to the dominion parliament in cases of a conflict of powers' but pointed out that the latter 'applies in its grammatical construction only to No. 16 of sect. 92.'[109] Although Gwynne and the others in Supreme Court had felt that it applied to, and limited, all of section 92, the Judicial Committee never wavered from Smith's observation. Smith repeated his conviction during the argument, in *Russell* and both Horace Davey and Collier reaffirmed it during the argument in *Hodge*, as did Davey in the *McCarthy Act Reference* argument.[110]

During the argument, Maclaren and Herschell had agreed that the clause applied to 92(16), and, as Herschell stated, 'if the thing is one of the things specifically mentioned in section 91 then you are thrown.'[111] Watson seemed to agree during a brief discussion when Blake cited Smith's observation in *Parsons* and Herschell interjected: 'But more than that surely. The effect of that provision at the end of section 91 is to exclude from sub-section 16 certain things that otherwise would have come distinctly within it.' To which Blake replied, 'I do not know my Lord, that it was necessary at all,' because the declaratory clause protected the federal enumerations from all of section 92. Davey interjected, 'And for greater certainty still,' and Watson added, 'They put it for greater certainty twice over.'[112] And later no one disagreed when Blake stated that 'it is conceded that if the subject we are now dealing with is embraced within this enumeration it is withdrawn from "merely local and private" by the express terms at the close of the section.'[113]

When Blake, Davey, and Herschell were commenting on the 'sting' in both the 'head and tail' of section 91, a perplexed Watson observed, 'I am afraid there may be a difficulty which we will have to get out of in that respect.' In his decision, without apology or evidence, Watson disagreed with his own court and removed the difficulty.[114] Smith's observation 'was not material to the question arising in that case, and does not appear to their Lordships to be strictly accurate.' On the contrary, it was 'apparently contemplated by the framers ... that the due exercise of the enumerated powers conferred upon the Parliament of Canada by s. 91 might, occasionally and incidentally, involve legislation upon matters which are *prima facie* committed exclusively to the provincial legislatures by s. 92.' In order to provide for that contingency, the deeming clause was added. Not only did the clause apply to all of section 92, but its purpose was not to subtract from section 92(16) the power to legislate in relation to anything coming within the section 91 enumerations. On the contrary, it was to permit the federal government 'to deal with matters local or private in those cases where such legislation is necessarily incidental to the exercise of powers conferred upon it by the enumerative heads of clause 91.'[115] In short, its object in effect was to diminish federal jurisdiction as protected by the declaratory and deeming clauses.

The residual clause was next to be explained. Watson's comments during the argument amply confirmed Lord Macnaghten's friendly observation that he did not have 'the precision of thought and language which distinguished Lord Westbury ... or that singular facility of lucid exposition which in the hands of Lord Cairns made argument superfluous.'[116] An anonymous contemporary was less kind: 'Watson's mind, like his body and his gait, was singularly massive, and its movements deliberate. In his early days he was therefore considered slow.'[117] In fact, Watson certainly appeared to have difficulty determining the purpose of the residual clause. At one point during the argument he observed that the

effect of the original first words – they have not been a great deal considered, and may some day require considerable attention – appears to me to be to override to a certain extent nearly all the clauses giving jurisdiction. If that is thought good for one, each Province may enact for itself, because it thinks it for the benefit of the Province. The Dominion Parliament apparently have power if they are really justified, and I assume they are acting fairly and honestly in the matter, to enact it as a general regulation.[118]

Whatever may have been his expository problems, his grasp of the clause was at best uncertain. 'Every power that is not entrusted, I take it, to the Parliament of Canada, which does not belong to it, is with the province,' he commented. 'No; it is the other way,' Herschell quickly interjected. 'Everything which is not expressly enumerated to the Province is with the Canadian Parliament.' To which Watson replied: 'It belongs either to the Dominion by virtue of one of the sub-sections 1 to 29, or by virtue of it not coming under section 92, in which case the last sentence of section 91 gives it.'[119]

Watson made it all much clearer, if only to himself, in his decision. The declaratory clause simply indicated that there may 'be matters not included in the enumerations upon which the Parliament of Canada has power to legislate because they concern the peace, order and good government of the Dominion.' But since the deeming clause did not apply to such matters, any federal legislation 'ought to be strictly confined to such matters as are unquestionably of Canadian interest and importance, and ought not to trench upon provincial legislation with respect to any of the classes of subjects enumerated in s. 92.' This was a matter not only of law but of politics: 'To attach any other construction to the general power which, *in supplement* of its enumerated powers, is conferred upon the Parliament of Canada by s. 91, would, in their Lordships' opinion, not only be contrary to the intendment of the Act, but would practically destroy the autonomy of the provinces.'[120]

However, the residual clause did have a purpose. During an irrelevant discussion about the possible manufacture of cordite, Watson commented, 'It rather occurs to me that if any question arose as is now suggested, the legislature of Canada would have full power to legislate under the general words with which section 91 commences and which are not limited by the words which follow. Any subjects may be dealt with which is necessary, which, in the opinion of the Government is required for the peace, order or good government of Canada.' Later, during a rambling discussion of what was 'local,' Watson observed that what may once have been a 'local evil ... may attain such dimensions as to become a threatened danger to the whole Dominion and in that case I should be sorry to doubt that there is power, given to the Dominion Parliament to intervene.'[121] The observation passed without comment. Nevertheless, Watson decided to add his 'national concern' and 'national dimension' doctrines to the constitution:

Their Lordships do not doubt that some matters, in their origin local and provincial, might attain such dimensions as to affect the body politic of the Dominion, and to justify the Canadian Parliament in passing laws for their regulation or abolition in the interest of the Dominion. But great caution must be observed in distinguishing between that which is local and provincial, and therefore within the jurisdiction of the provincial legislature, and that which has ceased to be merely local or provincial, and has become a matter of national concern, in such sense as to bring it within the jurisdiction of the Parliament of Canada.

As an illustration, he suggested that restricting the sale of arms to young people would be a provincial matter, but traffic in arms for seditious purposes might become a matter of national concern.[122]

In his decision, Watson next turned to 'the regulation of trade and commerce,' the scope of which had been extensively discussed in argument. Arguing for federal jurisdiction over prohibition, Blake had insisted that by decision it lay within the residual clause and trade and commerce. Reminded that *Parsons* had rejected the view that the federal government had authority over 'every particular dealing,' Blake first emphasized that Smith had explicitly not defined the scope of trade and commerce. He then began to argue the greater relevance of Canadian language and practice than Smith's extrinsic aids, when Lord Davey cut him off with, 'Is that admissible?' Clearly it was not. 'I have no right to ask your Lordships to depart' from *Parsons*, Blake continued. 'And if your Lordships think that the attempt at a definition or suggestion, made *obiter* perhaps, and stated in *Lambe*'s case to be thrown out rather than otherwise, is not important to be discussed, I will not trouble your Lordships.' Obviously they felt it was not important.[123]

During the argument, Watson had admitted that he had no idea of the scope of trade and commerce. 'I do not think any of the cases afford a definition or anything like a precise definition of what precisely is meant by the expression "regulation of trade" in sub-section 2,' he had lectured Newcombe. 'There are explanations of it, but the explanations, as far as I can find, require as much explanation as the section itself.'[124] As Newcombe argued that prohibition could fall within trade and commerce, Watson anticipated his ultimate decision. 'If it had been "Trade and Commerce" I could quite well have understood that these words might have implied abolition as well as regulation,' he countered, 'but when the power given expressly is confined to the regulation of the liquor trade could they abolish it. I could quite understand their doing it in virtue of the general power at the commencement of the section.'[125] Thus, just as Blake was anxious to reopen *Parsons* to find in trade and commerce a home for prohibition, Watson was determined to close that door and keep it within the residual clause in order to leave the 92(16) door open.

No sooner had Blake begun his trade and commerce argument than Watson asked him whether the Canada Temperance Act in reality had been upheld under trade and commerce or the residual clause. 'You see the importance of the distinction between these two ... The distinction may be important when you come to consider the enactments of the last clause of section 92.'[126] Blake persisted in arguing the authority to prohibit under 91(2), and, faced with Watson's strenuous opposition, was heartened by the lord chancellor's intervention. 'I made an observation the other day which, I think, I ought to retract upon consideration,' Halsbury informed Blake. 'What occurred to me was, and it is relevant to our present discussion, that these words "Regulation of Trade" could not be satisfied by prohibition. I think I was too hasty. Trade generally may be regulated by prohibiting a particular trade.' That admission, Blake said later, seemed to make further argument on the point unnecessary.[127] In the last moments of the argument, Watson seemed to concede the possibility that the words could include prohibition, although, as usual, it was difficult to decipher his code: 'You cannot put a general meaning on them, you must refer to the context of the statute to discover what the Legislature meant in employing them. I do not doubt that the Regulation of Trade and Commerce may very fairly include prohibition. If the context gave an indication I should not be surprised at its being either way in one statute, but then being construed one way in one statute would not lead to its being similarly construed in another.'[128]

In his decision, Watson reluctantly accepted *Russell* as precedent that the Canada Temperance Act was valid under the residual clause (but ignored Smith's pointed statement that the committee did not dissent from the Supreme Court's finding that it was also valid under trade and commerce). That being so, the only remaining obstacle was the possibility that prohibition could fall within trade and commerce. 'If it were so,' wrote Watson, 'the Parliament of Canada would, under the exception from 92 which has already been noticed [the deeming clause], be at liberty to exercise its legislative authority, although in so doing it should interfere with the jurisdiction of the provinces.' No such danger need be apprehended, however, for despite Halsbury's intervention, Watson had no difficulty in asserting that a 'power to regulate, naturally, if not necessarily, assumes, unless it is enlarged by the context, the conservation of the thing which is to be made the subject of regulation.'[129] As authority, Watson reached for Davey's recent decision in *City of Toronto* v. *Virgo*, a case in which he had participated, which struck down a city by-law prohibting hawkers from plying their trade in certain sections of the city, with the argument that a 'power to regulate and govern seems to imply the continued existence of that which is to be regulated or governed.'[130]

Mowat's liquor legislation, with some qualifications, could stand.

In so deciding, Lord Watson had reconstructed sections 91 and 92 of the constitution. The path of reconstruction was tortuous indeed. Watson strayed far from precedent and ignored previous judicial comment: he reversed the application of the deeming clause, excluded any meaningful purpose for the declaratory clause, explained (almost away) the content and possible application of peace, order, and good government, and advanced the novel proposition that federal regulation excluded prohibition. The pretense that the committee's single decision was collegial was revealed as the myth it was. Given the views expressed by his colleagues during the argument, Watson's judgment in all its particulars could not have been delivered without strong dissent – if anyone cared nine months after the argument when the judgment was delivered.[131] But his reasons, doctrines, and *obiter dicta* became embedded in the law of the constitution.

With something less than the precision of a scholar, Watson had written the text for symmetrical federalism. In *Liquidators*, Watson's provinces had fathered Confederation, delegated a limited capacity to the national government, and retained a direct connection with the crown. In *Local Prohibition*, he expanded their legislative jurisdiction by the process of redefining and limiting federal jurisdiction. It is no wonder that, on his death in 1899, Richard Haldane could prophesy that 'nowhere is his memory likely to be more gratefully preserved that in those distant Canadian provinces whose rights of self-government he placed on a basis that was both intelligible and firm.'[132]

Apart from those few who maintain that Watson's jurisprudence was a reasonable and faithful rendering of the 1867 constitution, the intellectually curious have attempted to determine his motive. Unfortunately, Watson is of little assistance. Unlike his disciple, Lord Haldane, he bequeathed neither correspondence nor memoirs. Conclusions about motive must be reached on the basis of his published opinions on behalf of the committee and his participation in the arguments, although some scholars assume that his opinions were obviously derived from currents of nineteenth-century political and legal thought.

Watson's solicitude for the autonomy of the provinces has led Murray Greenwood to conclude that the motive was 'institutional self-interest.' In its support of provincial jurisdiction, Greenwood argues that the committee avoided being labelled superfluous and created a supportive political constituency in Canada. The motive was not the perfection of Canadian federalism but the preservation of appeals and the continuation of judicial imperialism. However provocative, it is impossible to find in the constitutional decisions, at least, quantitative support for this speculation.[133] Suzanne Birks also finds imperialism lurking in the committee's law. Analysing the apparent logic of the decisions, she suggests that the provincial crown served not only, or even primarily, as a vehicle to establish provincial executive autonomy or sovereignty, but was essential to establish or re-establish a direct link between the provinces and the empire. The interesting but intuitive argument is most fairly stated in her words:

At the beginning of the activist period in the 1890s, the issue of Canada's incomplete sovereignty operated as a fundamental, sustaining presumption for Lord Watson in the enunciation of the *Maritime Bank* doctrine. Lord Watson made it clear in the decision that the Canadian federal system had to be bolted to the constitutional framework of the Empire. The independence of the provinces from Ottawa's control was by no means independence from Great Britain and the sovereign, any more than Ottawa's powers could exclude the authority of London. This interweaving of the Canadian and imperial structures established a point of departure in the interpretation of the Canadian constitution which was necessarily detrimental to the federal cause ... Faced with the energetic drive of the provinces, who participated with considerable vigour in the constitutional disputes before the Judicial Committee, and given the inclination of the board to preserve the integrity of the imperial structure, the Privy Council's redirection of Confederation is entirely comprehensible.[134]

David Schneiderman looks for the roots of Watson's solicitousness in late-nineteenth-century legal thought. In his determined exclusion of prohibition from regulation, he suggests, 'Watson was faithful not necessarily to the text of the constitution but to the ideological presuppositions of the constitutional lawyer of the late nineteenth century.' Those presuppositions included a judicial penchant for limited or weak government, and the belief that personal liberty and property were best protected in 'the repositories of counter power' in a federal state. Schneiderman implies that these presuppositions explain much more than the limits of regulation: 'It is this understanding of federalism – as a means of limiting legislative authority and promoting provincial autonomy – that fits the conception of federalism as facilitative of liberty. It also makes more coherent the Privy Council's application of the common law rules of interpretation to the *British North America Act*.'[135]

Similarly, although Richard Risk finds both the reasoning and the result of *Local Prohibition* difficult to explain, he agrees in large part with Schneiderman. Although Watson's restrictions on the residual clause 'may simply have been a product of misunderstanding of the structure of sections 91 and 92,' more generally, both in the analysis of

the residual clause and throughout the judgment, Risk finds confirmation of the presence, if not the dominance, of the 'rule of law thought.'
This principle, 'with its general model of autonomous powers divided
by sharp lines policed by courts, was a foundation of Dicey's analysis
of federalism, and any reading of "peace order, and good government"
as an indefinite power or a threat to the (autonomous) powers of the
province was fundamentally inconsistent.' Risk finds further confirmation of the 'rule of law thought' in what he sees as the court's unwillingness to consider context and values, preferring to rely instead on
the supposedly plain meaning of the words in the constitution.[136]

Neither Watson's opinions nor his comments during argument provide direct confirming evidence for these and other plausible arguments. But, however much Watson may have professed to rely on the
'plain meaning of the words in the constitution,' in both argument and
decision he enthusiastically engaged in substantive, if idiosyncratic,
lawmaking, which might have had roots more personal and experien-
tial. For his comments in argument and *dicta* in decision do reveal that
he had an instinctive predisposition both to decentralization and to
judicial lawmaking, which might be expected from a partially assimi-
lated Scots lawyer trained in the civil law.

Lord Watson, wrote a contemporary, was a striking example of early
training in civil law which, with its liberal views of the law and sense
of historical development, 'furnished him when he came to sit on the
Judicial Committee, with the key to the legal puzzles which make up
the legal mosaic of our Empire.'[137] His training and experience were
not the same as those of his southern colleagues. Scots law was not
fundamentally a case-law system. Precedent and *stare decisis* were relatively recent English imports, which were still not firmly entrenched
and certainly far less rigid in Scots law and practice.

For that reason, Watson felt less restraint in disregarding precedent
or lower-court reasoning, as he indulged in speculation about the
nature of Canadian federalism and solved the legal puzzles to his satisfaction. As he once said in the House of Lords, before Halsbury's 1898
statement on the binding nature of precedent, 'so long as such revising
discretion remains in the highest tribunal in the land there is wisdom
in the practice that cobblers in less exalted places should stick to their
lasts and leave to the supreme tribunal the task of making such modifi-
cations as the times may require to previously established rulings.'[138]

Unlike other Scots lawyers who migrated south, Watson remained
what a colleague described as a 'typical and ardent Scot' whose educa-

tion and experience were exclusively Scottish until he was middle-aged, when he was drawn south by promotion not envy.[139] Watson was familiar with the unique federal system that united England and Scotland in the new state called Great Britain. Original Scottish proposals for this union had called for a version of a federal system in which their legal system, religion, and other matters of concern to a permanent minority could be guaranteed. Although the British insisted on a unitary state and, like 'whiskey polluted with soda, previous separate elements had been superseded by a new species altogether,' the union 'took effect as a skeletal, but nonetheless fundamental, written constitution for the new Kingdom of Great Britain' when it came into being. 'It does not seem to be widely realised that the basic constitution of this new kingdom was the prototype of written constitutions which expressly limit the powers of organs of government in relation to each other,' explained a leading Scottish authority, 'in particular which, by restricting the powers of the legislature which makes laws for the whole country, protect the interests of a permanent minority from being overriden by a permanent majority.'[140]

During his four years in the Commons and later in the Lords, Watson showed no interest in politics but was assiduous in protecting and promoting Scottish interests – Scot law, religion, local government, the universities. And, just as he was solicitous for Scottish interests while in parliament, so too was he solicitous for minority interests in Canada. Although he felt that the Judicial Committee might be tied by the statutory language of the Manitoba Act, Watson was almost alone in expressing sympathy for the minority in *Barrett*.[141] Trained in the civil law, he became familiar with the Civil Code of Quebec and, in a judgment overruling a decision of the Supreme Court, referred to the 'general importance to the province of Quebec of the question arising upon the construction of its Civil Code,' noting in justification that his judgment confirmed that of all seven judges who heard the case in Quebec.[142] With the civil law of the other provinces embedded in property and civil rights, it was natural that he would show, as he constantly did, a similar concern for their jurisdiction and for the significance of the stillborn section 94.

It is dangerous to draw definitive conclusions from Watson's comments during the oral arguments, for, even more than his considered opinions, they confirm the judgment of a contemporary that 'he was no grammarian or philologist. No one accustomed to listen to him could ever predict how any sentence was to end; and we are quite sure that many of his propositions ended in an entirely different manner from what their author intended or the listener expected.'[143] A modern student of his jurisprudence is much less kind: 'One of the difficulties in writing about contributions such as those of Lord Watson, is that they are – with respect – too confused to classify.'[144] However, his language in *Liquidators*, even more than the result, supports the compact theory of Confederation. As he commented during the argument in *Brophy*, Confederation was 'by consent and there were no means of compelling it. Of course the Imperial Parliament might have it in their power, but it certainly never was the intention of the imperial legislature to compel it, and certainly the adjustment of the terms were left to the contracting parties.'[145] A similar understanding of federalism would appear to explain his proposition that provincial jurisdiction was the rule and federal legislative authority the exception.

Although he did not say so in as many words, Watson seemed to anticipate Haldane's belief that the provinces were 'like independent kingdoms'[146] under the British sovereign. It followed that, in the resolution of federal-provincial disputes, the committee was involved in 'some really international questions between Canadian governments.'[147] All that was necessary was to restructure the BNA Act to fit the theory, a task made easier by Watson's view that 'bills are drawn in order that they may pass, as razors are manufactured in order that they may sell – in other words the legislator instead of clothing his purpose in plain and unambiguous language, resorts to all kinds of verbal disguises in order to make it appear colourless and innocent in the eyes of those from whom opposition is expected.'[148] On many occasions Watson admitted or revealed that sections of the BNA Act were difficult to understand and that someday the apparent ambiguities or uncertainties would have to be resolved. In *Local Prohibition* he stripped the act of its 'verbal disguises' to make it coherent and consistent with his conception of Canadian federalism.

The first decade of the twentieth century was a quiet interlude between the doctrinal turbulence of the Watson and Haldane courts. There were fourteen federalism appeals. Eleven decisions of the Canadian courts were confirmed, including all from the Supreme Court, and nine upheld federal jurisdiction. Several of the appeals fell within Watson's precedents.[149] The Judicial Committee held on five appeals that federal railways and Bell Telephone were immune from provincial or municipal regulations. Federal ownership of the foreshore in Vancouver and the right of the Canadian Pacific Railway to obstruct passage to the water were confirmed and the provincial attempt to control water rights in the railway belt was rejected.[150]

Dismissing an appeal of a Supreme Court decision finding the attempt of the Grand Trunk Railway to contract out of liability for personal injury to their employees, on the ground that a federal statute prohibiting it fell within property and civil rights, Lord Dunedin wrote that the decisions in *Voluntary Assignments* and *Tennant* established two propositions: 'First, that there can be a domain in which provincial and Dominion legislation may overlap, in which case neither legislation will be *ultra vires*, if the field is clear; and secondly, that if the field is not clear, and in such a domain the two legislations meet, then the Dominion legislation must prevail.' To the doctrine of paramountcy, Dunedin added that of ancillarity. The 'true question' was not whether the law 'deals with a civil right – which may be conceded – but whether this law is truly ancillary to railway legislation.' In his opinion it was, and because such railways were 'mere creatures of the Dominion legislature ... it cannot be considered out of the way that the Parliament which calls them into existence should prescribe the terms which were to regulate the relations of the employees to the corporation,' although the legislation did 'touch what may be described as the civil rights of those employees.'[151]

In a surprising decision, the committee found Ontario's Sunday observance legislation, which prohibited working, 'tippling,' swearing, fishing, sports and excursions, *ultra vires*. It was openly unsympathetic to arguments based on 92(13) or 92(16). After three days of argument, Halsbury, the lord chancellor, was exasperated: 'We are drowning everything in words. The Act of Parliament says you shall not work on Sunday, putting it in its broadest form, if you do you shall be indicted and punished. Is that not a criminal offence made so by Statute?'[152] Immediately after the argument, Halsbury delivered a decision, in which he stated that the 'reservation of the criminal law for the Dominion of Canada is given in clear and intelligible words which must be construed according to their natural and ordinary signification' and it was 'impossible to doubt' that an infraction of the Ontario act was 'an offence against the criminal law.'[153]

The Laurier government was as unhappy with the decision as was the Lord's Day Alliance. After prolonged negotiations with the provinces and appeals to the Supreme Court and the Judicial Committee,[154] the government passed An Act respecting the Lord's Day, which prohibited a wide variety of activities under the criminal law. But the act allowed the provinces to opt out of many provisions and left prosecution to the provincial attorney general. The act remained in force until 1985 when, in *Big M. Drug Mart*, it was deemed to be in violation of the *Charter* guarantee of freedom of religion.

However, the Judicial Committee was given the opportunity to revisit and confirm Lord Watson's doctrines in 1911 with a Quebec challenge to the federal Railway Act, which subjected provincial railways to its provisions relating to through traffic. Intervening for Ottawa, E.L. Newcombe chose to base his argument on the residual clause, national dimensions, and the regulation of trade and commerce, thus inevitably inviting the court to return to *Local Prohibition*.[155] In his decision, Lord Atkinson chose not only to reject the arguments but, seldom altering Watson's language, to extract and codify the doctrines found in Watson's decision:

1. The deeming clause did not derogate from provincial legislative authority under 92(16) except to enable the federal government to deal with 'matter, local or private, in those cases where such legislation is necessarily incidental' to the exercise of power under the section 91 enumerations.
2. The deeming clause had no application to anything but the enumerations, and, in legislating on matters not enumerated, the Dominion parliament had 'no authority to encroach' upon the classes of subjects in section 92.
3. Sections 91 and 92 indicated that, under the residual clause, federal legislation 'ought to be strictly confined to such matters as are unquestionably of Canadian interest and importance, and ought not to trench upon provincial legislation.'
4. To 'attach any other construction of the general powers which, in supplement of its enumerated powers, are conferred upon the Parliament of Canada by s. 91 would not only be contrary to the intendment of the Act, but would practically destroy the autonomy of the provinces.'
5. If the federal government had power to legislate for the whole country on matters which were in each province 'substantially of local or private interest, upon the assumption that these matters also concern the peace, order and good government of the Dominion, there is hardly a subject upon which it might not legislate to the exclusion of provincial legislation.'

The same considerations, Atkinson continued, applied to the regulation of trade and commerce. 'Taken in their widest sense these words would authorize legislation by the Parliament of Canada in respect of several of the matters specifically enumerated in s. 92 and would seriously encroach upon the local autonomy of the province.'[156]

The act could not be justified on the grounds that it concerned the peace, order, and good government of Canada, or that it dealt with the regulation of trade and commerce, or that it was necessarily incidental to the control of federal railways. It was *ultra vires* as 'an unauthorized invasion of the rights of the Legislature of the province of Quebec.'[157] Although Atkinson admitted that Watson's decision had 'little if any application,' he had embedded the latter's construction of the BNA Act even more deeply into federalism jurisprudence.[158]

The doctrinal stage was set for Viscount Haldane, eagerly waiting in the wings.

7

Viscount Haldane, 1911–1928*

It moulds and makes, as well as interprets the law ...
– Richard Haldane, 'Appellate Courts of the Empire,' 1900

'His return to active connection with the Law by being placed on the Judicial Committee afforded him great satisfaction,' noted Haldane's friend Sir Almeric Fitzroy, clerk of the Privy Council. 'His ambition is to sit on those appeals from the self-governing Dominions which raise judicial problems of the highest constitutional import, and so, as I reminded him, take up the great work of Watson, which he has so fittingly commemorated.'[1] It was Watson, Haldane had written, who had 'expanded and established the real constitution of Canada.'[2] From 1911 until his death in 1928, at least in Canadian appeals, Haldane dominated the Judicial Committee as no one had before or would afterwards. In argument and decision, he revealed that his mission was to continue to protect 'those distant Canadian provinces' from any encroachment by a marauding federal government and its Supreme Court.

*An earlier version of this chapter was presented as a paper at the Canadian History Legal Conference, 'Exploring Canada's Legal Past,' Faculty of Law, University of Toronto, 9 May 1998.

Richard Burdon Haldane was born in Edinburgh in 1856 but spent his youth and his vacations at the family estate of Cloan at Perthshire. As a teenager, Haldane lost the faith of his deeply religious parents and ultimately found solace in a mixture of philosophy, theology, natural science, and the idealism of T.H. Green and Georg Hegel. In 1877 he moved to London to study law and was called to the bar in 1879. Thereafter, except for politics and vacations, London was his home. Not unduly modest, he applied unsuccessfully for 'silk' to join the ranks of queen's counsel in 1887. Three years later he was able to boast to his mother that "I am supposed to be the youngest Q.C. made for fifty years."[3]

Haldane's practice flourished and his political ambitions grew. As a member of the Young Liberal Imperialists he lobbied for the lord chancellorship after the Liberal victory in 1905. But the prize went to Lord Loreburn and the prime minister, Henry Campbell-Bannerman, sent Schopenhauer, as he contemptuously called Haldane, to the War Office to see how long he could survive.[4] Survive he did, and brilliantly. In 1911 he accepted a peerage to lead the Asquith government in the House of Lords and enthusiastically seized the opportunity to sit as a law lord, for which the elevation qualified him under the Appellate Jurisdiction Act, although he had never held judicial office.[5] When Loreburn resigned in June 1912, Haldane was appointed at once. He was forced out of the cabinet in 1915 by a despicable newspaper campaign accusing him of being pro-German, but he continued to sit with the Judicial Committee until his death in 1928.[6]

Leo Maxse of the *National Review* was less than enthusiastic about the new occupant of the woolsack: 'He was always a prodigious gasbag, but never a great lawyer, and as he abandoned the law for nearly seven years in order to play ducks and drakes with the British army ... he is clearly unfitted for the Lord Chancellorship.' But 'won't his judgements be a study!' wrote Horatio Bottomley in *John Bull*. 'He can never say "No" to a question under 20 minutes. Still he knows something about the law.'[7] Haldane was aware of the criticism but felt assured that he had 'a long experience at the Bar of the most difficult and miscellaneous kinds of work; and memory had preserved the bulk of my knowledge, notwithstanding absence for over six years at the War Office.'[8]

Nevertheless, in spite of what Harold Laski called his 'colossal' vanity,[9] Haldane confessed that 'I never considered that I was equipped by nature for the part of a great judge.' He lacked the 'judicial temperament,' the detachment of a Lord Watson or the 'passionate absorption in the law' of a Lord Blackburn. Over time, the field of law had become much wider and politics, the 'path to the highest in the legal hierarchy,' more demanding. 'Still,' he rationalized, 'knowledge of the law, and the desire to be absolutely just, go for a good deal and I had both of these.'[10] While contemporaries spoke fondly or bitterly of his many qualities or achievements, none accused him of being a great jurist.

As Haldane realized, he was occupied with too many pursuits to be passionately absorbed in the law. He took great pride in his work in philosophy and the connection between metaphysics and modern science, although critics maintained that his essays were 'almost entirely without value' and described him as 'a Hegelian who never understood Hegel.'[11] He was devoted to improving the quality of higher, and more broadly based, social education. Overshadowing all his interests was his endless and obsessive political intrigue and social networking, which reflected, as Sidney and Beatrice Webb observed, his 'weakness – his dilettante desire to be in every set.' Another contemporary, Laski, reported after his weekly dinner with Haldane that the jurist's 'varied genius' 'enabled him to dine one night with the King and the next with Jimmy Wolfe the boxer.'[12] Haldane was the consummate host: his table graced by the finest claret, an abundance of food that shocked Beatrice Webb, and the best of port and choice cigars that he smoked to excess. It was unbecoming of him to encourage Edinburgh students to pursue a life of contemplation, chided George Bernard Shaw, when he was 'generally making the greatest possible success of the world, the flesh and the devil.'[13] Well might the Webbs and the Laskis spend a weekend together wondering why 'Haldane was so good at most things and yet not superlative in anything.'[14]

He was certainly not superlative in exposition; to follow Haldane's thought is a difficult task. Not only was he inconsistent, sometimes perhaps deliberately so, but his language and reasoning were on occasion virtually incomprehensible. Lord Birkenhead referred to his 'tiresome prolixity in exposition,'[15] while his friends Beatrice and Sidney Webb were not alone in speaking of 'his curiously wooly mind' and his 'incurable delight in mental mistiness.'[16] As the Liberal essayist A.G. Gardiner commented, no one could 'invest a subject in a more lucid fog. A lucid fog, I know, seems a contradiction in terms; but no one who has heard Mr. Haldane speak for, say, three hours will deny that there is such a thing' for 'the lucidity of his mind is as conclusive as the fog in yours. The clearer he becomes to himself, the more hopeless is your bewilderment.'[17] Others were less kind. A colleague in the War Office regarded Haldane as 'a sophistical rhetorician who has alternately cajoled and bewildered his military advisers, and has ended by convincing himself that the dexterities of the conjurer are the inspiration of genius.'[18] There are times in pursuing Haldane's thought when the words of Augustine Birrell, Liberal lawyer and man of letters, come to mind: 'Haldane's mind is full of black slush.'[19]

Haldane was a romantic, almost mystical, believer in crown and empire, an empire of persuasion not of force. Three weeks after his appointment as lord chancellor, when he first presided at the Judicial Committee, he wrote to his mother: 'I am sitting here as president of the Supreme Tribunal of the Empire at the Privy Council – carrying out as well as I can the principle I advocated many years ago in my little book *Education and Empire.*'[20] It was a revealing statement. One of his speeches reprinted in the book was in praise of the Judicial Committee, 'a most important portion of the silken bands which, with so little friction, hold our great Empire together.'[21]

The work of the committee, he lamented, was 'apt to be looked upon as a mere means of declaring, without altering, the existing law and constitution. But that is a narrow view, and mischievous pedantry when the attempt is made to enforce it in practice.'[22] Lord Watson, who had 'filled in the skeleton which the Confederation Act had established, and in large measure shaped the growth of the fibre which grew around it,' was 'the Privy Council Judge par excellence.'[23] He was the 'ideal of what a judge of the Empire ought to be ... He not only decides particular cases. Such is the weight of the decision of this Court, that its spirit extends beyond its letter, and it moulds and makes, as well as interprets the law.'[24]

The Canadian attempt in 1875 to abolish appeals had failed 'and we were more fortunate than we ought to have been, considering the littleness of the public interest at home in the Judicial Committee.' But today, he reminded his Scottish audience, danger threatened again as the Australians were determined to abolish appeals.[25] The colonials were misguided, he believed, because with its 'spirit of fearless justice,' the Judicial Committee had been 'of enormous influence in educating the Colonial Courts.' The power of appeal 'to a very strong tribunal has kept these Courts up to the mark, and caused them to take increasing trouble over the reasons for their decisions.'[26]

Haldane's belief in the 'law-changing functions' of the Judicial Committee was derived in part, at least, from his philosophical conclusions about the nature of the state and the relationship of the state and the individual.[27] While sitting on the committee, he wrote that the state 'is no static entity ... not an arbitrary creation ... the state is made, not by external acts, but by the continuous thought and action of the people who live its life. In this sense it is never perfect, for it is a process that remains always unbroken in creative activity.'[28] Thus, the law could not be static for 'law is more than mere command. It is this indeed, but it has a history which cannot be understood apart from the history and spirit of the nation whose law it is. Larger conceptions than those of a mere lawyer are required for the appreciation of that significance, conceptions which belong to the past and which fall within the province of the moralist and sociologist. Without these we are sometimes unable to determine what is and what is not part of the law.'[29]

As Jonathan Robinson has observed, Haldane clearly believed that 'law *cannot* be practiced without reference to more than the law itself' for he described himself as 'a lawyer whose almost daily duty it is to ascertain the reasons why the law has become what it is, because unless I can do so, I am bound to fail in the interpretation of its scope and authority.'[30]

Given the lawmaking functions of the Judicial Committee, Haldane maintained that 'the very political experience' of such great judges as Selborne, Cairns, and Watson (who had little in fact) 'added to their value. It is a paradox, but a very real truth, that their training as politicians had made them better judges for such a Court ... We are far away here from the Continental conception of a Judge as mere interpreter of rigid codes.'[31] Indeed, we cannot treat these questions 'as if we were a court of law,' Haldane was to comment during the argument on Manitoba's Initiative and Referendum Act. 'We are really giving administrative assistance.'[32]

It was not surprising that, in an after-dinner discussion about judges at Sir John Sankey's, Laski reported that Haldane 'seemed to look for what I may call a 'man of the world' quality in their decisions: Sankey was more interested in the endeavour to make the case emit a big, working principle.' Yet, in the same breath, Haldane appeared to contradict everything he had written about the lawmaking functions of the court. 'I was astonished to find that whereas Sankey took the obvious and sensible view that judges inevitably legislate,' wrote Laski, Haldane insisted that they merely 'declare what is already law, and not the combined efforts of all of us could move him from that.'[33]

From 1911 to his death in 1928, Haldane presided over a fluid panel and dominated the proceedings in Canadian appeals. He missed only 63 of the 204 appeals from Canada and delivered the decision in 24.[34] Many cases were not central to the jurisdictional balance between the federal and provincial governments: these cases involved such matters as separate schools, railways and other undertakings within 92(10) and 91(29), provincial succession taxes, marriage and divorce, Asian labour and the Japanese treaty in British Columbia, and the always contentious issues of fishing rights and harbour foreshores. Nine appeals, however, were pivotal to Canadian federalism.[35] Haldane sat with the committee on all, gave the decision in eight, and kept an eye on Lyman Poore Duff's decision in *Reciprocal Insurers* in 1924.[36] The oral arguments are convincing proof that Haldane dominated the proceedings, sometimes almost monopolizing them.[37]

Haldane took an intense personal interest in Canadian cases and was outraged when Sir Charles Fitzpatrick, chief justice of the Supreme Court, dared to criticize the committee's judgment in *Cotton* v. *The King*:[38]

I presided myself in *Rex* v. *Cotton*. We gave days to the hearing to which we devoted the energies of a picked tribunal ... You say there is a nasty feeling about the judgement of which I weighed every line personally. Well. It is for you in Canada to say what you want. You need not keep the Appeal to the Privy Council. But so long as you do and I have anything to do with the Supreme Court of Imperial Justice I hope it will look at nothing but law & Justice & Truth. We had better shut the Judicial Committee up than lend ourselves to any other standard ...

You speak of myself as not giving personal attention to Canadian cases. I have sat on every case of importance since I became Chancellor & have instituted the Canada 'duty.' I have lent the whole strength of our tribunal on cases from Canada even to the sacrifice of English work in the House of Lords of two judges ... And it certainly never gave more time or pains to Canadian cases ... You must take us or do what you are quite within your rights in doing by abolishing the Appeal. You must not mind my writing this freely when I have been making some of the hardest efforts of my life. I do not like to have them misinterpreted.[39]

Haldane's uniquely personal interest in Canadian appeals went as far back as 1884. He was then serving in the chambers of Horace Davey, who was, in Haldane's judgment and that of many others, 'the finest advocate on pure questions of the law' that he had witnessed.[40] Before his appointment as lord of appeal in 1894, Davey had appeared in eleven Canadian constitutional appeals, losing only *Reed*,[41] which quickly found a Quebec duty on legal documents *ultra vires* as being indirect taxation. The hearing on the petition to appeal in *Reed* was also Haldane's first appearance before the Judicial Committee and his first encounter with Lord Watson. Davey had been retained by Quebec but, learning the night before the hearing on appeal that he was scheduled to argue in the House of Lords, told Haldane to be prepared. Haldane was fond of recalling the situation. The London solicitors and the Quebec solicitor general were outraged but when the case was called

I rose, and after apologising for the absence of Davey, opened the point very carefully, and without exaggerating laid stress on the great constitutional question which underlay the apparently small stake at issue. Lord Watson, who presided, proceeded to question me. I was ready with answers, and, after a little, to my vast relief, a consultation of the judges in a low tone resulted in Lord Watson telling me that the Judicial Committee thought I had made out a case for appeal. I bowed and retired. Not one word was said by Freshfield's or the Solicitor General. They were still swelling with anger at the risk they had been forced to run.[42]

It was also the beginning of Haldane's long association with Oliver Mowat. According to Haldane, after the hearing, the Freshfields and Williams partners, who were Mowat's solicitors, had read the shorthand notes of his argument and were so impressed that they sent their clerk to his chambers with a major brief marked one hundred and fifty guineas, 'far more than I had ever dreamed of receiving as a fee,' and promised more in Privy Council cases. 'Before long,' Haldane recalled, 'I had a very large business as a Junior in the constitutional cases from Canada in the Privy Council. Ontario gave me its general retainer, and I appeared for the Prime Minister, throughout the long series of his struggles with Sir John MacDonald [sic], the Prime Minister of Canada, for the right of the province to pass its own legislation.'[43]

The association with Davey, who had held Mowat's retainer since 1883, continued, with the result that 'we had for several years an almost unbroken series of victories, which led when he left the Bar, to my succeeding him in the lead of many of the constitutional cases from Canada, and which brought me into close relation with the Canadian politicians and statesmen.'[44] The issues at stake in the legal battles with

Ottawa were so important, he told the Scottish Law Society, that while Ontario 'bore the brunt of the struggle,' other provincial premiers 'used to come over to argue in person with the assistance of English counsel.'[45]

After only three appearances in Canadian constitutional cases, Haldane was a self-proclaimed expert. Responding to Joseph Chamberlain's argument that the Canadian provinces offered a model for some degree of self-government for Ireland, Haldane wrote to the *Times* that he had listened to him in the House of Commons

with silent wonder and amazement. As one of the standing counsel for the province of Canada which has of late years been engaged in the most frequent conflicts with the Dominion on the bloodless battlefield of the Privy Council offices in Downing Street, I had come to imagine that the provisions of the British North America Act, 1867, as interpreted over and over again by the Judicial Committee, could not be misunderstood, at least in their most general terms. This illusion was dispelled by Mr. Chamberlain's speech.[46]

The conditions endorsed by Chamberlain were that the powers given to the local authority 'should be delegated and not surrendered ... clearly defined and subject to revision and control' and that the administration of justice should remain with 'an authority responsible to the Imperial Parliament.' 'The Canadian constitution,' wrote Haldane, 'is inconsistent with and flagrantly violates every one of these conditions.' Provincial powers were not delegated but were exclusive and not subject 'to revision and control.' They were enumerated in general terms and included exclusive control over property and civil rights, all matters of a local and private nature, and the administration of justice. Each province had an independent executive and the Judicial Committee had recognized 'the general principle that the executive power is derived from the legislative power, unless there is a restraining enactment.'[47] There was some truth in Chamberlain's point that the constitution provided for 'the separate treatment of provinces which are distinct in race,' but Haldane dismissed it as an 'unimportant suggestion of an analogy for the separate treatment of the provinces.'

It was not clear whether the conclusion to be drawn was that the provinces enjoyed far more independence than was proposed for Ireland or, as he wrote later, that the status of a Canadian province 'could not satisfy Irish aspirations.' Whatever its meaning, Haldane boasted that 'my letter helped to prevent the idea from being persisted in, for it was known that I was familiar with the interpretation which had been put, by a series of judicial decisions of the Privy Council, on the Imperial Statute of 1867 which had set up the Provinces.'[48]

Between 1886 and his last appearance as counsel in a Canadian constitutional case, Haldane had appeared in thirteen appeals, eleven in the provincial interest. Until Davey was appointed to the House of Lords in 1894, Haldane was always his junior. And if Edward Blake was acting for Ontario, Haldane followed him. On occasion, however, the two were rivals. Overall, he lost five appeals and owed the victory in all the others except *Bonsecours* to senior counsel. His performance in *Brophy*, where he appeared against Blake and John Ewart, was particularly inept. His argument that a paramount legislature could repeal entrenched language guarantees drew from Herschell the sarcastic comment, 'That is a very feeble protection ... against that you have no protection at all.'[49]

Haldane's career as counsel in Canadian constitutional cases was much less impressive than he later claimed. It was in these years, however, that Haldane formed his opinion of the structure and purpose of the federal system and of Canadian constitutional and political history, which he carried to the Judicial Committee. In 1900, when colonial secretary Joseph Chamberlain stated that the proposed Australian constitution was similar to the American, rather than the Canadian, Haldane was quick to correct him. 'It is true that, in Canada, the general powers of legislation are reserved to the Dominion Parliament,' he explained, 'while only specified powers are given to the Provincial Parliaments but the latter have among these specified powers the widest capacity for dealing unreservedly with property and civil rights.' As a result, the difference between Canadian and Australian federalism, where the residual powers remained with the states, was only 'technically' rather than substantively accurate.[50] It was also in this period that he became a fervent admirer of Lord Watson before whom he had argued in eleven appeals, in which Watson wrote the decision in five. And it was Watson's construction of the constitution in *Liquidators* and his reconstruction in *Local Prohibition* that Haldane took with him to the Judicial Committee and to the grave.

With Haldane's admittedly confused mixture of politics, history, and law sustaining his belief in the law-changing functions of the court, his participation in the oral argument in eleven appeals provides unique insights into his federalism jurisprudence. During the appeals, however, Haldane strenuously objected to any use of oral arguments. When Wallace Nesbitt later wanted to cite from the argument in *John Deere*, Haldane informed Nesbitt that comments during the argument 'are not settled observations, and taken in this fashion they are very misleading.'[51] And he cut off E.L. Newcombe when he attempted to use Haldane's comments in *Deere* during the argument in *Bonanza Creek*: 'What I said in the course of the discussion is only for the purpose of keeping my mind open until the end of the argument when I make it up. That is why I am listening so patiently.'[52] Although unacceptable in the Judicial Committee, the evidence from oral arguments is particularly valuable for understanding Haldane, whose interjections often took the form of lengthy and combative arguments with counsel.

Seated with the Judicial Committee, Haldane soon revealed that the 'bloodless battlefield' where 'the real contest was between Sir John Macdonald and Lord Watson' had been an apt metaphor.[53] As the arguments proceeded in his court, the battle was still raging between Mowat and Macdonald, Watson and John Gwynne. The wily Wallace Nesbitt, who had found life on the Supreme Court boring and unremunerative, knew how to strike the right chord. He reminded Haldane 'of the fight the province had to meet for years and years,' drawing from Haldane the response 'that this Bar used to be blocked with Provincial Prime Ministers who came to vindicate their own rights.'[54] Nor was he hesitant to remind counsel who disagreed with him that 'I held Sir Oliver Mowat's general retainer, so I ought to know.'[55] The proposition that, if interference with property and civil rights was merely incidental to the main object, federal legislation could be upheld under the residual clause led to an angry appeal to history:

If your doctrine were right, the position and status of the provinces would long ago have been swept away. There was a school of thought which thought that the purpose of the Act was to magnify the Dominion and bring the provinces more and more under control in the interests of unity. It was that very doctrine that was checked – and there was some countenance for it in some of the earlier decisions – and stopped by this board in the series of cases to which we are now referring. All I have to say is the checking of it is nowhere more clearly made apparent than in Lord Watson's judgment down to this point.[56]

Years later, when counsel referred to Watson's warning in *Local Prohibition* that the residual clause posed a threat to provincial autonomy,

Haldane hastened to interject: 'That sentence of Lord Watson's marked the watershed. Up to then the trend had been in favour of the Dominion under the guidance of the Supreme Court. Then Lord Watson set up a new tendency, and then it followed almost as much the other way.'[57]

The truth was that Haldane did not like the Canadian federal system; in fact, he repeatedly insisted, it was not a true federal system. During the pleadings in an Australian case he stated that 'with deference to a great many people who talk on the platform just now of the federal system in Canada there is no federal system.'[58] In the decision, he argued that

in a loose sense the word 'federal' may be used, as it is there used in the preamble of the 1867 Act to describe any arrangement under which self-contained States agree to delegate their powers to a common government with a view to an entirely new Constitution even of the States themselves. But the natural and literal interpretation of the word confines its application to cases in which these States, while agreeing on a measure of delegation, yet in the main continue to preserve their original constitutions.

Although the Canadian model 'was founded on the Quebec Resolutions and so must be accepted as a treaty of union among the then Provinces ... when once enacted by the Imperial Parliament it constituted a fresh departure, and established new Dominion and Provincial Governments with defined powers and duties both derived from the Act of the Imperial Parliament which was their legal source.'[59] Elaborating his comments during the oral argument in the *Initiative and Referendum* appeal, he explained that the provinces were 'entirely new states, so far as legal power and Constitution are concerned' and 'were given certain limited powers: they were given a purely statutory Constitution. A Dominion was set up to which was reserved all the residuary powers which had not been granted, unlike the United States and Australia, where the general power of making laws for the peace, order and good government remained to the States.'[60]

However, Haldane fought the obvious conclusions about the federal constitution that followed from his analysis. He diminished the residual clause, and the power and scope of the enumerations, and elaborated a conception of federalism based on the theoretical, historical, and legal supremacy of the provinces. At times, his observations and arguments were, if he meant or understood what he said, historically and legally absurd.

In one way or another he repeatedly stated that the provinces 'did not agree to unite as one Dominion' but 'handed themselves over to the Imperial Legislature to emerge in a new statutory form.'[61] Canada, it appeared, did not exist: 'I do not think that they ever became one state, but they did receive their legislative power from the Imperial Parliament on a bargain that the Imperial Parliament would re-create these powers fashioned forth in a manner agreed at Quebec.'[62]

Since his days as counsel, Haldane had argued that the 'absolute co-ordinate power of the provincial legislatures' (which he seemed to assume was a Judicial Committee invention, whereas it had been widely endorsed by the Canadian judiciary, with the notable exception of John Wellington Gwynne) made the word federal 'an inaccurate and inappropriate term, and how it came to be used in this statute it is diffi-cult to conceive.'[63] To Haldane, 'co-ordinate' did not refer simply to powers that lay within provincial or federal jurisdiction; rather, the provinces were 'in a sense like independent kingdoms with very little Dominion control over them.'[64] And his theory of Canadian federalism 'was that the provinces should be autonomous places as if they were autonomous kingdoms.'[65] It was essential, he lectured counsel, to understand the basic principles of the constitution: that 'each province is treated as a most important entity, as a country by itself, except that certain things are reserved. Whether it was a good form of constitution or not it was the form of constitution that was adopted in 1864 at Quebec.'[66]

Haldane believed in the compact theory in its most extreme form historically and in law and, despite the troublesome existence of the residual clause, in the 'truly federal' nature of the constitution. That seemed clear in the discussion of section 65 of the BNA Act during the argument in *Bonanza*. E.L. Newcombe was attempting to make Haldane understand that the powers of the crown in the province under section 65 (and in the Dominion under section 12) were, as the language indicated, only those capable of being exercised after 1867 within their respective legislative jurisdictions: if the legislative power belonged to Ottawa under section 91, it could not be exercised by the province.

'Where do you say they are only to be exercised by the Dominion?' Haldane exploded. 'I, on the contrary, find in the Act the new provinces are likened to the old united province of Canada, except so far as things are taken out, and the Confederation constituted. I am quite aware that the residuary powers are in the Confederation, but, for the rest, – it is a

true Confederation – it is only the things which are taken out as belonging to Confederation from its nature that operate restrictively.'[67]
Haldane revealed his hierarchy of constitutional values when he said,
'Every citizen of the province is a citizen of Canada, and has to take his
part in common Government, he has to pay taxes and do many
things.'[68]

'Peace, Order and good Government' did not fit easily within the
Haldane version of the federal constitution, and it was essential that he
diminish or destroy the clause as an effective source of federal jurisdiction. The obstacle was the decision in *Russell* which, although compromised by *Hodge* and the *McCarthy Act Reference*, as Watson reluctantly
and enigmatically stated, 'must be accepted as an authority to the
extent to which it goes.' It was obvious that *Hodge* had 'shaken' *Russell*
and 'plain that Lord Watson did not believe in the judgements of this
Board in *Russell* v. *The Queen*,' Haldane commented in two early arguments, and 'it became the custom never to cite that case ... We cannot
overrule it, but we never cite it.'[69] The decision was 'an island that
stands out in the middle of a vast ocean'[70] and 'I think I may say – I
have a long experience at the Bar in these cases in those days – that it
was a tacit rule; a convention between judges and counsel that *Russell*
v. *The Queen* was not to be cited.'[71]

   But if Watson had helped Haldane qualify *Russell*, he had also
placed another obstacle in his way by inventing the national dimensions or national concern doctrine. The misleading headnote to *Local
Prohibition* in the printed *Appeals* cases, around which so much argument has swirled because judges and counsel prefer the abbreviated
version of the decision, read that federal legislation under the residual power 'must not trench on any of the subjects in s. 92 ... *unless*
they have attained such dimensions as to affect the body politic of the
Dominion,'[72] whereas Watson's *obiter* was much more guarded.
Responding to the argument that the insurance industry had grown
to such a magnitude as to affect the body politic and come within
Watson's national concern doctrine, Haldane provided the authorized version of Watson's doctrine: 'What it meant, surely, is that the
subject must be of some great magnitude in order to bring it within
the scope of these words at all. It does not follow because of the great
magnitude, it may not also come within section 92, and I look in vain
for anything in the British North America Act which cuts down the
plain language of the Confederation Act which gives exclusive juris-

diction to the provinces in matters which fall within the enumerations of section 92 ...[73]

When counsel persisted in citing Watson, Haldane insisted that 'I think he might have said, that in order to come under 'peace, order and good government' it must have attained to a certain dimension; still it must not trench on the exclusive jurisdiction of the provinces.' There were two conditions that had to be fulfilled under the national dimension doctrine, Haldane explained: 'First of all, the question has to be a question of Canadian interest and importance and, secondly, and separately, they are not to trench upon provincial legislation.'[74] In decision he determined that only 'highly exceptional circumstances' such as 'those of a great war' could justify federal legislation under the residual clause that interfered with property and civil rights.[75]

It was during the argument in *Snider* that Haldane's version of Confederation was openly challenged by Lewis Duncan, an argumentative Toronto lawyer who, even more than most Canadians, was temperamentally unable to adopt the deferential and colonial tone expected of counsel. Duncan, who had won in the Ontario Court of Appeal, immediately launched an attack on Haldane's conception of Canadian federalism and his invention of the emergency doctrine, each of which he stated was contrary to the historical context, the intentions of framers, and the language of the BNA Act. 'There are two different conceptions of government here, or different conceptions of federalism which are struggling here for recognition, and your Lordships' decision on that matter will have a far-reaching effect on subsequent Dominion legislation.'[76] The Canadian constitution, he explained, was founded on the Quebec Resolutions and they in turn were passed during the American Civil War.

Now this is what the Canadian drafters of the Constitution did. They said: Above all things we must avoid what was probably a mistake in the American constitution that is giving the residuum of power to the States, and we will use language sufficiently clear to give that residuum to the Dominion so that in any case in which the Dominion considers the matter is for the peace, order and good government of the country, that power lies with the Dominion. That is putting it in an extreme way.[77]

The second conception of federalism was that which informed the Judicial Committee:

If the second conception of Federalism is the proper one: that there are enumerations in section 91 and other enumerations in section 92, that these cover
the whole legislative field except in cases of national emergency amounting to
war on the Dominion, and so on, then who is to find that fact? If that is the conception there is practically no residuum except in cases of national emergency,
and those words, which I suggest were most carefully drafted to give the
Dominion power to legislate for peace, order and good government of Canada,
are by that gloss, I suggest, deprived of the effect which the founders of Confederation intended.[78]

Haldane was not sympathetic. There was no question that his was
the second conception. The imperial government handed over all the
powers 'that Canada asked for. It is, however, true that Canada did
not ask for a scientific division, they said peace, order and good
government except with regard to what the Legislatures of the provinces generally do. What is not under section 92 we include today in
the numerous heads of section 91, that is all.'[79] When Duncan continued to argue that in the Quebec Resolutions, the federal government was given jurisdiction over 'all matters of a general character
not specially and exclusively reserved to the local government' and
the provinces responsibility 'for matters of a local and private
nature,' Haldane angrily insisted 'that was just what they did not
do' and, as Duncan persisted, angrily repeated 'I say that was not
carried out.'[80]

It was essential, however, that Duncan establish the authority of
peace, order, and good government, for the respondent's case in *Snider*
rested largely on the argument that the Industrial Disputes Investigation Act 'in its proper aspect' was not a law in relation to any of the
matters in section 92 but was one for the peace, order, and good government of Canada.[81] When that had become apparent early in the
argument, Haldane foretold its fate: 'That means if the subject-matter
does not come within section 92 then they can only get at it if they can
import the construction which was imported in the *Manitoba pulp case*?
... And that is a very difficult matter to import; that is for the extreme
necessities of war?'[82] A few minutes later Haldane interrupted counsel:
'Before you go into evidence, let us see what "national emergency"
means. If a hostile force is invading the country, notwithstanding its
constitution, the people of that country will rise and resist, and orga-
nize themselves in order to attain its end.' Power would not fall within
section 92 then and the federal government could act. 'That is a very

different thing from legislation as regards strikes, which is very important legislation, but each province can deal with it.'[83]

Later, there was an exchange on the board about what constituted an emergency. When Lord Dunedin said, 'To my mind the *Russell* case is not an emergency at all,' Haldane agreed: 'The *Russell* case is not an emergency.'[84] Duncan explicitly based his argument on a national concern doctrine that was not based on emergency:

Duncan: 'My submission to your Lordships is that in matters which are truly of national concern Canada is a State and not a congeries of provinces.'
Haldane: 'Would you carry that so far as to say that even where there is no emergency or peril to national life that is so?'
Duncan: 'As in *Russell* v. *The Queen*?'
Haldane: 'Then say you do not want emergency.'
Duncan: 'I say emergency is not written into the Constitution at all.'[85]

But Haldane had already written the emergency doctrine into the constitution in *Re Board of Commerce* and *Fort Frances* and he reiterated it in his decision in *Snider*. Having examined the evidence 'produced at the trial,' he wrote, their Lordships 'are of opinion that it does not prove any emergency putting the national life of Canada in unanticipated peril such as the Board which decided *Russell* v. *The Queen* may be considered to have had before their minds.'[86] The circle had been squared; Russell was no longer an anomaly.

The enumerations and the construction of section 91 and its relationship to section 92 were also reconsidered and reconstructed, a task made easier because, during the argument in *Bonanza Creek*, Haldane admitted that he did not understand the written constitution:

Why certain things should be given to the Dominion and others not given, I have never known. I have put it down to this, and indeed I think I have said so in judgement, that when they discussed the distribution of powers at Quebec in the autumn of 1864, they were discussing as a Parliament [sic] an assemblage of statesmen, not as a body of logicians, and they discussed what would be convenient and did not trouble themselves whether the things were quite consistent or overlapped or not, which was left to the Courts to determine.[87]

When Haldane joined the Judicial Committee, the powerful declaratory (or notwithstanding) clause in section 91 had virtually disappeared and had been replaced for a different purpose by the deeming clause at the end of the section. Sir Montague Smith had correctly positioned the two clauses in his decision in *Parsons*, and his understanding had been repeated by the board in every oral argument including that in *Local Prohibition*, where it was agreed that the deeming clause explicitly referred to and limited the possible scope of 92(16).[88] Nevertheless, Watson had decided otherwise in his decision.[89] Haldane repeatedly reminded counsel that Watson had corrected Smith, and that it was the deeming clause that gave whatever protection there was to section 91 enumerations. From peace, order, and good government, he lectured counsel in *Great West Saddlery*, were taken the enumerations in section 92. 'Then there is the enumeration in section 91 which per se would be merely an expression of the general words to which I have alluded, but which are given their force and validity by the concluding words of section 91 which say that everything that falls within the enumeration of section 91 is to prevail over the enumerations in section 92.'[90]

Yet, in the application of the deeming clause, Haldane was much less open to accepting even his own version of the prevailing power doctrine. Reminded of his position by Sir John Simon, Haldane altered course: 'To clear it up, surely these words at the conclusion of section 91, which were commented on very carefully in the case in 1896, simply mean that the whole of the subjects in section 92 are included as local and private and heads in section 91 are not to be construed as affecting them.'[91] And that certainly was his position in argument and decision in refusing to distinguish between 'in relation to' and 'interference with.'

Federal jurisdiction over 'the Regulation of Trade and Commerce' and the 'Criminal Law' also suffered at Haldane's hands. During the argument in *Great West Saddlery*, Wallace Nesbitt scoffed at his opponents' reliance on trade and commerce. 'Every attempted encroachment before this committee has been under the regulation of trade and commerce. I think Lord Haldane will bear me out in that statement. I have heard it argued here to justify every possible encroachment.' Haldane did agree: 'I think it has been matched by the attempts of the Committee to cut it down.'[92] Certainly, from *Parsons* to *Montreal Street Railway*, the argument had never been accepted as validating federal or invalidating provincial legislation. And in only one of the nine cases considered here where the argument was advanced was it accepted, but then it materialized less as an expansion than as a limitation of federal jurisdiction.[93]

As Haldane stated during the argument in *Board of Commerce*: 'Must it not be taken that since the 1896 case ... at all events, perhaps earlier, sub-section 2 of section 91 must be taken as containing merely ancillary powers. A power that can only be exercised so as to interfere with a provincial right only if there is some paramount Dominion purpose as to which they are applicable.' Well might E.R. Cameron exclaim, 'What is meant by this? Ancillary to what?'[94] But, although the record reveals no such doctrine, Haldane's decision turned it into law: 'Nor do the words in s. 91, the "Regulation of Trade and Commerce," if taken by themselves, assist the Dominion contention. It may well be, if the Parliament of Canada had, by reasons of an altogether exceptional situation, capacity to interfere that these words would apply so as to enable that Parliament to oust the exclusive character of the Provincial powers under s. 92.'

In *John Deere*, Haldane explained, their lordships 'expressed the opinion that the language of s. 91 head 2, could have the effect of aiding the Dominion powers conferred by the general language of s. 91. But that was because the regulation of trading of Dominion companies was sought to be invoked only in the furtherance of a general power which the Dominion Parliament possessed independently of it.' In short, trade and commerce standing alone could not justify interference in any trade in which Canadians would 'be free to engage in the Provinces.'[95] And the decision in *Snider* made absolutely explicit that 'excepting in so far as the power can be invoked in aid of capacity conferred independently under other words of s. 91, the power to regulate trade and commerce cannot be relied upon as enabling the Dominion Parliament to regulate civil rights in the Provinces.'[96]

Criminal law fared no better. That power could be exercised, Haldane stated in *Board of Commerce*, 'where the subject matter is one which by its very nature belongs to the domain of criminal jurisprudence,' such as making incest a crime. But the challenged acts, in his judgment, were simply an attempt to interfere with property and civil rights and to justify it 'by enacting ancillary provisions, designed as new phases of Dominion criminal law.'[97] During the argument in *Snider* he warned that 'if you have something substantial then you can make an amendment to the criminal law giving effect to it, but you cannot usurp power under section 92 under the title of criminal law.'[98] And in his decision Haldane simply reiterated the doctrine he laid down in *Board of Commerce*.

The conviction that property and civil rights was the operative residual clause was the basis of his federalism jurisprudence. Long before he joined the Judicial Committee, Haldane had concluded that because the provinces possessed 'the widest capacity for dealing unrestrictedly with property and civil rights,' Canadian federalism was only 'technically,' rather than substantively, different from the American or Australian. As he said during the argument in *John Deere*, 'without expressing a final opinion on it I should say "civil rights" was a residuary expression; it was intended to bring in a variety of things not comprised in the other heads, including what was not touched by section 91 in the specifically enumerated heads.'[99]

In his futile attempt to demonstrate during the argument in *Snider* that 'interference with' was not the true test, Lewis Duncan was simply echoing Smith's point in *Russell* that if it were the test 'few if any laws could be made by Parliament for the peace, order and good government of Canada.' Thus, if you extended property and civil rights 'to comprehend entire freedom from government legislation,' Duncan tried to explain, 'there is nothing whatever that can fall outside the enumeration of section 92, because by so doing "property and civil rights" becomes the greatest residuum of all. The doctrine says we are Provincial citizens, members of some independent State, free from interference by the Dominion Government under peace, order and good government, and we say you must not interfere with our freedom of action, whatever it may be.' Does it not mean, Haldane asked rhetorically, that 'what people are allowed to do or not to do, is for the province?' Yes, replied Duncan, if you adopt the 'conception of an independent State.' To which Haldane replied: 'It is an independent state, it is cut into expressly by the enumerations of section 91.'[100]

One of those civil rights, Haldane insisted, was the 'civil rights to liberty. The essence of the English common law is the right to liberty unless some process of the Court interferes with it.'[101] His court was not going to accept Duncan's argument that 'public duties' could be opposed to 'civil rights,' and he warned Duncan that 'I think you are putting a very wide proposition that under peace, order and good government, you can restrict the liberty of the subject of the province.'[102] The comment was not surprising because, in his decision in *Board of Commerce*, Haldane had stated that it could be only in the most exceptional circumstances that 'the liberty of the inhabitants of the Provinces may be restricted by the Parliament of Canada.'[103]

Haldane's judgments were the application in law of his political view of the appropriate structure of Canadian federalism. All of his important federalism decisions involved the regulatory capacity of the federal government.[104] Five of the eight concerned the contested jurisdiction over corporations, including insurance companies, and others the validity of federal wartime regulations in 1914–18, Ottawa's post-First World War attempt to control prices, and the validity of the 1907 Industrial Disputes Investigation Act. With minor qualifications, the decisions were in favour of the provinces. Even *Fort Frances*, upholding wartime regulations under the emergency doctrine, in effect confirmed the federal government's inability under other circumstances to interfere with property and civil rights.[105]

Jurisdiction over companies had been troublesome from the beginning largely because of the lack of clarity in the division of jurisdiction. The provinces were given exclusive authority over the incorporation of companies with 'Provincial Objects.'[106] It was assumed that the federal government also had the capacity to incorporate companies with other than provincial objects as well as in areas covered by its enumerated powers, but it was not until 1881 that Sir Montague Smith authoritatively declared that the power lay within the residual clause.[107] However, the question already had arisen of the meaning of 'Provincial Objects.' Federal ministers of justice insisted that the words included both a territorial and a functional limitation and strenuously opposed – to the point of disallowance – provincial attempts to incorporate companies, usually insurance companies, whose activities extended beyond the provincial boundaries.[108]

By the turn of the century, the jurisdictional squabbles had become much less benign. As national commercial activity grew, so did the number and size of corporations. And as the territorial scope of business expanded, so did the tendency of companies to seek federal incorporation. To police corporate activity within the province or increase provincial revenues, the provinces, beginning with British Columbia in 1897 and Ontario in 1900, passed legislation to control 'extra-provincial' corporations. The conditions for carrying on business in the province included a licence and a fee, disclosure of corporate activities, and the maintenance of a resident attorney. More disturbing was the provision, designed to force compliance, denying companies that were not licensed the capacity to appear in the courts. The federal government strenuously opposed this interference with federally incorporated companies, but only one Manitoba statute was disallowed.[109]

The question of company law became more complex in 1910 when the Laurier government passed amendments to the Insurance Act, among which were provisions requiring all companies not confining their business to a single province to obtain a federal licence and make a security deposit, as well as demanding some uniformity in life-insurance policies. Questioned about their constitutionality, the minister of finance replied: 'There has always been more or less contention as to the relative powers of the federal and provincial authorities in relation to this subject. We have merely acted on the best legal advice we could obtain. There is no present litigation in which the government is concerned, but my impression is that a reference will shortly be made to the Supreme Court in which the question will be included.'[110] The reference was on both jurisdiction over companies and the validity of the insurance amendments.

The Supreme Court heard the *Insurance Reference* for thirteen days in November 1912. E.L. Newcombe, deputy minister of justice, Eugene Lafleur for the insurance companies, and F.W. Wegenast for the Canadian Manufacturers' Association argued that, in size and scope, the industry had outgrown its provincial character sufficiently to satisfy Watson's national dimensions test as well as to bring jurisdiction within the general regulation of trade and commerce. Wallace Nesbitt warned on behalf of Ontario and the provinces that, if the act were upheld, 'it would go to the destruction of Provincial autonomy ... it would enable the Dominion ... to legislate upon practically every subject matter in which the people of the province engage.' Aimé Geoffrion said, in effect, that it had all been settled by Watson in 1896 and Atkinson's summary and addendum in *Montreal Street Railway*: 'What I claim is this that Privy Council has first stated as regards the residuum clause of 91 ... it can never be relied on to encroach on any subject exclusively assigned to the provinces by 92, and then they went on and said that the same rule must apply to trade and commerce.' Geoffrion and Nesbitt, with the precedents of Smith, Watson, and Atkinson, clearly had the ear of the majority, which, with Fitzpatrick and Davies dissenting, found the challenged sections of the act *ultra vires*.[111]

Before the appeals reached London, the Judicial Committee had decided *John Deere Plow Co.* v. *Wharton*, an appeal from a Supreme Court of British Columbia decision upholding a provincial statute that required every extra-provincial company to secure a licence, without which the company could not operate or sue in provincial courts.[112] In what has been described as a 'constitutional solecism,'[113] a 'suggestion replete with difficulties,'[114] and an 'exercise in judicial ingenuity,'[115] Haldane declared that the trade and commerce power enabled the federal government to prescribe 'to what extent the powers of companies the objects of which extend to the entire Dominion should be exercisable and what limits should be placed on such powers. For if it be established that the Dominion Parliament can create such companies, then it becomes a question of general interest throughout the Dominion in what fashion they should be permitted to trade.' To confound the issue further, however, Haldane quickly added that he did not mean to suggest that 'the power to regulate trade and commerce can be exercised in such a way as to trench, in the case of such companies, on the exclusive jurisdiction of the Provincial Legislatures over civil rights in general.' In the result, the province could *not* destroy the 'status and powers' of a federal company as British Columbia had done, but the provinces could, he said, regulate extra-provincial companies in a variety of ways by properly framed legislation.[116]

The appeals on the insurance and company reference followed and, together with an appeal from the Supreme Court on *Bonanza Creek Gold Mining Company* v. *R.*, were heard by Haldane for eight days in December and the decisions released in February 1916.

The insurance decision was clear-cut. Although section 3 of the BNA Act exempted companies that carried on their business wholly within the province, Haldane found the licensing provision of the federal act *ultra vires*. As a result of the decisions in *Hodge* and the *McCarthy Act Reference*, Haldane stated, 'it must now be taken that the authority to legislate for the regulation of trade and commerce does not extend to the regulation by a licensing system of a particular trade in which Canadians would be otherwise free to engage in the provinces.'[117] Nor was he sympathetic to the arguments based *on Russell* or the national dimensions test:

No doubt the business of insurance is a very important one, which has attained to great dimensions in Canada. But this is equally true of other highly important and extensive forms of business in Canada which are to-day freely transacted under provincial authority. When the British North America Act has taken such forms of business out of provincial jurisdiction, as in the case of banking, it has done so by express words which would have been unnecessary had the argument for the Dominion addressed to the Board from the Bar been well founded.[118]

Later attempts by the federal government to secure regulatory control over the insurance industry failed, regardless of the jurisdictional basis cited – be it criminal law, aliens, immigration, bankruptcy and insolvency, or taxation: 'It is really the same old attempt in another way,' wrote Viscount Dundedin in 1932.[119]

As a demonstration of judicial ingenuity, the decision in *Bonanza Creek* was Haldane at his most inventive. The gold mining company had been incorporated by letters patent under the Ontario Companies Act, which gave the lieutenant governor in council authority to incorporate companies under the Great Seal. *Bonanza* acquired some leases in the Yukon, but when a dispute arose the federal government argued that the company did not have the capacity to acquire and exercise powers and rights outside the boundaries of the province. By a 3–2 majority, the Supreme Court had found that the words 'provincial objects' confined the operations of the company to the territorial limits of the province.[120] In view of Haldane's reasoning and decision, the observations of Justice Lyman Poore Duff are significant:

It has never been doubted in this country that the doctrine of *ultra vires* applies to companies incorporated under the Ontario 'Companies Act' and that it does so apply was not disputed by the appellant's counsel and indeed it is not arguable that the reasoning of Lord Cairns in *Ashbury Railway Carriage and Iron Co.* v. *Riche*, by which his Lordship reached the conclusion that the doctrine governs companies formed under the 'Companies Act,' 1862, does not apply to the provisions of the Ontario 'Companies Act.' It results inevitably that the company had no capacity to enter into contracts upon which the action is brought unless some additional capacity over and above that imparted to the company by the Ontario 'Companies Act' has been acquired by it from some other source.[121]

At the Judicial Committee, the argument was proceeding along familiar grounds until the beginning of the seventh day on the combined references when Haldane commented to Sir Robert Finlay: 'There is one thing you have not called our attention to specifically, and that is the nature of the Ontario Companies Act. It may give a general power to the Crown in the province of Ontario to create corporations generally, analogous to common law corporations, statutory corporations, under a power so wide that the corporations are analogous to common law corporations.' Finlay made no comment, but Haldane returned to the point a few minutes later: 'From what you say there is the possible view, that the right to grant a charter at common law belongs to the prerogative of the Crown, and, unless taken away, the right is there ... The Crown has the power to create corporations at common law, and all the British North America Act did was to say, we will distribute the exercise of the prerogative.'

Haldane continued to elaborate what was to be his decision: that in effect the charter of incorporation was an executive act, a prerogative act of the crown under section 65 of the constitution which had not been abrogated, and it was by virtue of the grant under the Great Seal and not by words of the Companies Act that the authority of the corporation existed.[122] In the case of such a company created by charter, 'the doctrine of ultra vires has no real application in the absence of statutory restriction added to what is written in the charter. Such company has the capacity of a natural person to acquire powers and rights.'[123] As a result, the governing precedent was not *Ashbury Railway Carriage* but the *Sutton Hospital* case in 1613 which (apparently) decided that a company created by the prerogative, or royal charter, had all the capacities of a natural person to acquire powers and rights, and the doctrine of *ultra vires* therefore had no application.

In his judgment, Haldane ended the jurisdictional argument whether 'provincial objects' confined provincial companies to the boundaries of the province.[124] The provinces now could – and they did – incorporate, as the decision read, by 'the exercise by the Lieutenant-Governor of the prerogative power to incorporate by letters patent with the result of conferring a capacity analogous to that of a natural person.'[125]

When it became clear during the argument where Haldane was going, an astonished E.L. Newcombe was bold enough to state that the question was simply one of the construction of sections 91 and 92 and the prerogative rights of the crown were completely irrelevant. In answer to Haldane, he insisted that there was no power to create a common law corporation in Canada. The statutory power was delegated to the lieutenant governor 'for the sake of convenience' and could have been delegated to any other official.[126]

Newcombe's astonishment was echoed by lawyers, judges, and, to this day, academic commentators.[127] The best that one critic of the decision could write on Haldane's behalf was that the Judicial Committee was driven to its conclusion 'for the purpose of administering what it considered to be substantial justice: in other words, hard cases make dubious law.'[128] E.R. Cameron observed at the time that the decision had been 'severely criticized by lawyers of eminence in Canada ... Indeed, many now believe that the Judicial Committee has evolved a

Frankenstein that may have a devastating influence upon the commercial world.'[129] Lord Haldane had definitely said that 'the ultra vires
doctrine doesn't apply to common law companies,' wrote a leading
English expert who disagreed with it, 'so it is no good for me to suggest the contrary.'[130]

That same sense of fatality in the face of Judicial Committee precedent pervaded the Canadian courts: 'It is perhaps regretted that
the notion of prerogative right to create corporations by royal charter
and its consequences was introduced into Canadian company law,'
observed Frank Hodgins of the Ontario Court of Appeal. 'But as it has
been ...'[131] Chief Justice William Meredith was blunt in his condemna-
tion of the decision. As a result of this new doctrine, 'a company incorporated in this Province for the purpose of aiding in the propagation of
the Gospel may spend all its energies and means in aiding the propagation of infidelity ... Never, until very recent years, had any such
notion been advanced, if indeed imagined, in this Province.'[132]

One of the most impassioned critics, John S. Ewart, sarcastically
observed that the words 'letters patent' had 'aroused in the minds of
English judges ideas of kingly prerogative' and quoted J.H. Morgan,
ironically a friend of Haldane's, with approval: 'A French critic of great
acuteness, M. Boutmy, has remarked of the English constitution that it
is full of hibernating parts – ancient statutes, disused prerogatives, der-
elict councils which time cannot enervate nor desuetude destroy.
Should a grave emergency arise, a touch of the lawyer's wand will call
them into life and renew the vitality of their youth.'[133] So it was with
Haldane's incomprehension and magnification of the position and role
of the Crown in the 'independent kingdoms.'[134]

Haldane's decision confirmed the principle, long contended for and
established by *Liquidators*, that the legislative and executive powers
vested in the provinces were co-extensive. Moreover, whatever prerogative authority existed was not delegated by the legislature but
had their source in the crown itself. However, Haldane was too jealous of the prerogative to accept the argument that the governor
general and lieutenant governor had the right, without express delegation, to exercise the prerogative 'as though by implication completely handed over and distributed in such a fashion as to cover the
whole of the fields to which the self-government of Canada extends.'
In such a case, the governor general and lieutenant governors would
'be more clearly viceroys than representatives of the Sovereign,' but

in Canada the exercise of the prerogative was restricted to the terms of their commissions and the provisions of the British North America Act.[135] The rights of the imperial crown were thus preserved unless expressly abrogated, for there was nothing similar to the Australian constitution which provided that the executive powers, though declared to be in the sovereign, were in fact exercisable by the governor general.[136]

Two years later, the position of the lieutenant governor was again before the board.[137] Manitoba's Initiative and Referendum Act provided that laws could be made and repealed by the direct vote of the electors thus, in fact if not in form, bypassing the legislature and the lieutenant governor.[138] Citing Watson's decision in *Liquidators* and section 92(1) of the BNA Act providing that a province could amend its constitution 'except as regards the Office of Lieutenant Governor,' Haldane easily found that

the character of the office of Lieutenant-Governor, and to his position as directly representing the Sovereign in the province, renders natural the exclusion of his office from the power conferred by the Provincial Legislature to amend the constitution of the Province. The analogy of the British Constitution is that on which the entire scheme is founded, and that analogy points to the impropriety, in the absence of clear and unmistakable language, of constructing s. 92 as permitting the abrogation of power which the Crown possesses through a person who directly represents it.[139]

The conclusion was inevitable from a man who saw Canada as a federation of 'independent kingdoms' where the lieutenant governor was the *direct* representative of the crown. But perhaps Edward Blake had been closer to the intentions of the framers when he argued that the purpose of the provisions was to make certain that the lieutenant governor's 'constitutional position as a federal officer is not to be affected.' A decision in the Ontario Chancery Court in 1890 found that the section 'is to keep intact the headship of the provincial Government, forming as it does, the link of federal power.'[140]

Haldane's best-known and lasting decisions in their effect on Canadian federalism were in *Board of Commerce* and *Snider*. The Board of Commerce Act, 1919, and the Combines and Fair Prices Act, 1919 were designed to police and outlaw the post-war increase of prices which the *Canada Law Journal* described as 'without excuse and without parallel in history.'[141] The Board of Commerce was given wide powers of investigation and of restraining or prohibiting activities deemed to be in contravention of the act.[142] The legislation was an unprecedented peacetime interference with property and civil rights, and it was soon referred to the Supreme Court.[143]

The Supreme Court divided equally. Desperate to find a home for legislation that he felt to be in the national interest, Francis Anglin, writing for Chief Justice Louis Davies and Pierre Mignault (who had joined the court in 1918), argued that a decision of *intra vires* could be supported under both trade and commerce and peace, order, and good government. Drawing support from Smith's decision in *Russell* and Watson's reference to matters 'unquestionably of Canadian interest and importance,' Anglin argued that when the 'true aspect and real purpose' of the legislation was considered, it could (following Watson) be justified under the residual clause as a matter relating to 'public order, safety or morals, affects the body politic of the Dominion and is a matter of national concern' or (following Smith) as a matter falling outside section 92. However, in view of Watson's warning in 1896, repeated by Haldane in 1916, about the need to give the residual clause a narrow construction, he wrote that 'I prefer, therefore, to rest my opinion upholding its constitutional validity on the power of the Dominion Parliament to legislate for "The Regulation of Trade and Commerce" as well as on its power "to make laws for the peace, order and good government of Canada."'[144]

John Idington, Duff, and Louis-Philippe Brodeur wrote judgments denying Anglin's arguments on all counts, with Duff relying on Judicial Committee precedents to counter both the trade and commerce and residual clause arguments. Duff did not go as far as Idington in detecting a threat to individual freedom, but he did conclude that if the legislation could be sustained under the residual clause

it is not easy to put a limit to the extent to which Parliament ... may from time to time in vicissitudes of national trade, times of high prices, times of stagnation and low prices and so on, supersede the authority of the Provincial legislatures. I am not convinced that it is a proper application of the drink legislation, to draw from it conclusions which would justify Parliament in any conceivable circumstance forcing upon a Province a system of nationalization of industry.[145]

As soon as the decision was released, the attorney general of Alberta urged Ontario and Quebec to join in the appeal to the Judicial Committee. 'I find that some of the Judges who held in favour of Dominion jurisdiction have done so largely on the ground that the clause in the B.N.A. Act which states "generally for the peace, order and good government of Canada" gave the Dominion Parliament jurisdiction,' he wrote to W.E. Raney, attorney general of Ontario. He then added:

This is a new doctrine and one which as I understand it has not heretofore been considered seriously by the courts. If, however, this doctrine should prevail in the Privy Council the provinces of Canada would have little left in the way of exclusive jurisdiction and would be reduced to almost the status of municipalities of the Dominion, the Dominion having over-riding powers of legislation in fields heretofore considered fields of exclusive jurisdiction to the provinces.[146]

Premier Louis-Alexandre Taschereau became keenly interested and retained Sir John Simon and Charles Lanctot, and Ontario reluctantly agreed to join Alberta.[147]

There was little prospect of the resurrection of peace, order, and good government by Haldane's court. The arguments lasted three days and were largely a repetition of those before the Supreme Court. For Ottawa, Newcombe relied on Anglin's decision and introduced the somewhat novel doctrine that 'if and in so far as the enacting authority of Parliament depends upon the existence of any political or economic conditions which may justify its exercise there must necessarily be a presumption in favour of the legislation, or the Court should assume such conditions as may be essential to maintain the validity of the statute.'[148] Counsel for Quebec eagerly picked up Idington's statements about the 'extravagant claim' for trade and commerce and his view that federal power to legislate concerning property and civil rights 'had no existence in the residual power of Parliament, save in the extreme necessity begotten of war conditions, or in manifold ways that do not touch provincial rights.'[149]

Four months after the argument, Haldane delivered a judgment that, in a combination of reasons and outrageous *obiter*, was contemptuously dismissive of the case for validity. Not only did he deny the capacity of the trade and commerce power standing alone to interfere with property and civil rights, but, in effect, he also denied the utility of the criminal law power to enforce economic regulations. Above all, he turned property and civil rights into a jurisdictional wall to protect the liberty of the people of the province against the menace of the federal government:

It is to the Legislatures of the Provinces that the regulation and restriction of their civil rights have in general been exclusively confided, and as to these the Provincial Legislatures possess quasi-sovereign authority. It can, therefore, be only under necessity in highly exceptional circumstances, such as cannot be assumed to exist in the present case, that the liberty of the inhabitants of the Provinces may be restricted by the Parliament of Canada, and that the Dominion can intervene in the interests of Canada as a whole in questions such as the present one.[150]

Conceivably there could be circumstances 'such as war or famine when the peace, order, and good government of the Dominion might be imperilled under conditions so exceptional that they require legislation of a character in reality beyond anything provided for in the enumerated heads in either s. 92 or 91,' and, 'although great caution is required in referring to it, even in general terms, it ought not, in the view their Lordships take of the British North America Act, read as whole, to be excluded from what is possible.'[151] Not much was left of the residual clause or trade and commerce, and what there was, it seemed, could be applied only at the discretion of the Judicial Committee.

A year later, in June 1923, Haldane presided on the appeal in *Fort Frances Pulp and Paper Co.* v. *Manitoba Free Press Company,* a dispute over a newsprint contract which was challenged on the ground that the federal government's control of newsprint prices, which originated during the war but was continued afterwards, was *ultra vires.*[152] The appellants argued that the order-in-council of 1919 was passed after the war ended and the governing precedent was the *Board of Commerce.* The argument was heard for three days. 'Yesterday I had a heavy struggle in the Privy Council,' Haldane informed his mother at the end of the argument, 'but in the end had a majority of one for my interpretation of the Canadian Constitution. I am now writing the judgement with deliberation – as it is very important.'[153] His problem probably was that he wished to distinguish *Commerce,* while his colleagues, two of whom had sat on it, felt that legally at least it was not distinguishable.[154]

In his decision a month later, in language redolent of his philosophical writing, Haldane repeated that in the event of war the 'interests of individuals may have to be subordinated to that of the community in a fashion which requires s.91 to be interpreted as providing for such an emergency' because they 'concern nothing short of the peace, order, and good government of Canada as a whole.'[155] The 'kind of power' adequate to deal with the emergency 'is only to be found in that part of the constitution which establishes power in the State as a whole. For it is not one that can be reliably provided for by depending on collective action' of the provinces. Haldane's new unique version of Canadian federalism continued with the statement that 'the basic instrument on which the character of the entire constitution depends should be construed as providing for such centralised power in an emergency situation follows from the manifestation in the language of the Act of the principle that the instrument has among its purposes to provide for the State regarded as a whole, and for the expression and influence of its public opinion as such.' Such a power is implied in the United States, he observed, and such a 'scheme of interpretation is all the more to be looked for' in Canada 'where the residuary powers are given to the Dominion Central Government; and the preamble of the statute declares the intention to be that the Dominion should have a constitution similar in principle to that of the United Kingdom.'[156]

Haldane admitted that in those exceptional cases the 'line of demarcation' between property and civil rights and the 'new aspect of the business of government' was difficult to define, but it was not necessary to arrive at such a definition because 'the Dominion Government, which in its Parliament represents the people as a whole, must be deemed to be left with considerable freedom to judge.' The same was true after the war because the extent to which wartime regulations 'may have to be maintained is one on which a Court of law is loath to enter. No authority other than the central Government is in a position to deal with a problem which is essentially one of statesmanship.' Of course, there still was a role for the court when a question of *ultra vires* arose, but 'very clear evidence that the crisis had wholly passed away would be required to justify the judiciary ... in overruling the decision of the Government that exceptional measures were still requisite.'[157]

Haldane's tolerance for federal statesmanship was short-lived. Eighteen months later, more adversary than judge, he was brawling with Lewis Duncan during the argument in *Snider*. Duncan's impolitic statement that Prime Minister Mackenzie King was interested in the outcome because 'it is his own child' drew Haldane's sarcastic response that he would treat his argument 'with more reverence than we did.'[158] At issue was the validity of the federal Industrial Disputes Investigation Act of 1907 (often called the Lemieux Act after Labour Minister Rodolphe Lemieux), designed to prevent or assist in the settlement of strikes and lockouts in mines and industries connected with public utilities by giving the minister of labour, upon application, the power to appoint a board to make investigations and recommendations which, however, were not binding. After a reference to a board, a lock-out or strike was to be unlawful. 'What is my civil right if it is not to lock out?' stormed Haldane during the argument, putting his finger on what he believed to be the central point at issue.[159]

Although the act was upheld by the Superior Court in Montreal in 1913, its constitutionality was always suspect.[160] As Arthur Meighen explained in 1925, 'I well recall on more than one occasion when we in our time encountered difficulties and sought the advice of the Justice Department, ... we were told, do not get into the courts on any doubt-ful questions under this act; if you do you are very liable to come to disaster.'[161]

But the issue did come before the Ontario courts when the employ-ees of the Toronto Electric Commission applied for a board under the act and the commission sought an injunction to restrain the board. Jus-tice John Orde granted the injunction and, on the *Board of Commerce* precedent, found the act unconstitutional because it interfered 'in the most direct and positive manner' with property and civil rights and municipal institutions and could not meet the national emergency test argued by Lewis Duncan. However, he continued, the act had been beneficial and 'I ought to add that I have come to this conclusion with reluctance. I am of course merely dealing with the bald question of law.'[162]

On appeal, with the attorneys general of Canada and Ontario inter-vening, Justice Herbert Mowat found the act *intra vires*. Given the size and scope of industrial disputes, which could obliterate provincial boundaries, Mowat concluded that it satisfied the national concern test: 'If such an ill as occasional over drinking is subject to Dominion legislation, it must follow that the prevention of strikes by conciliation which conceivably might occasion the starving of people "should also be."'[163]

The Court of Appeal divided 4–1 in favour of constitutionality of the act. Writing for the majority, Thomas Ferguson found that although the act trenched upon property and civil rights, 'yet, according to its "true nature and effect," "its pith and substance,"' it was legislation to pro-vide machinery for settling disputes which could affect 'the national welfare, peace, order, and safety, and the national trade and busi-ness.'[164] After a lengthy review of Judicial Committee precedents, in which he openly contested Haldane's reading of *Russell* and pointed to inconsistencies in the *Insurance Reference* and *Fort Frances*, Ferguson concluded that the 'weight of authority' supported the proposition that only under the enumerated heads could the federal government trench upon the heads of section 92. Having said that, he immediately found that the act could be upheld under trade and commerce and the criminal law.[165] Chief Justice William Mulock added that the legislation was also competent under peace, order, and good government.[166]

In dissent, Hodgins found that the act did not meet Haldane's emergency test or Watson's national concern test because, despite its national scope, it was really designed to 'seize upon local disputes.' Judicial Committee precedents from *Russell* through Haldane, he argued, in an unadulterated repetition of Haldane's reading of Watson's 1896 *obiter*, had laid down 'a rule which must, until circumscribed by the Judicial Committee, govern this case; and that rule is to confine the powers of the Dominion Parliament, in its action under the provision as to the peace, order, and good government of the Dominion, to such matters of Canadian interest and importance as can be dealt with, without trenching upon any of the subjects specially reserved to the Provinces.' Nor did precedent offer any support for the argument that the act was valid under trade and commerce or the criminal law. Like Orde, Hodgins added that 'I very much regret having to arrive at a conclusion adverse to the validity ... of this Act. It has been a successful experiment in warding off industrial difficulties in many cases.'[167]

The argument before the Judicial Committee continued for five days. As usual, Haldane dominated the proceedings, constantly interrupting counsel and even his brother judges who dared to offer observations of which he disapproved. He was particularly abusive with Lewis Duncan and, to a lesser extent, with Sir John Simon who argued the case for validity. Duncan found Haldane difficult to handle, and Simon repeatedly had to appeal for a hearing, even attempting flattery when all else failed: 'I speak with the greatest submission to your Lordship because we all know your Lordship is a master of the subject.'[168]

It was not necessary for Stuart Bevan, acting for Ontario, to outline the arguments he would face; Haldane anticipated and rejected them for him. Trade and commerce, he interjected, 'has been so attenuated by decision of this Board that it is very difficult to rely on it.'[169] Criminal law would fare no better: 'Unfortunately for that view, we have more than once decided that the power over the criminal, which is given exclusively to the Dominion under section 91, does not enable it to trench on property and civil rights by merely using that road.'[170]

So, too, the emergency doctrine: an invasion 'is a very different thing from legislation as regards strikes, which is very important legislation, but each Province can deal with it.'[171] When Lord Atkinson dared to say that he could understand 'national convenience,' Haldane cut him off: 'That will not do ... An emergency is something so terrible and to be outside anything in section 92, such as the Dominion being in peril.'[172] Obviously, the case was lost from the outset unless Atkinson or Dunedin, the other experienced members of the committee who at times seemed sympathetic to Simon's argument, took a stronger position.

The argument ended on 24 November 1924 and Haldane wrote his mother that he had spent the following weekend 'preparing this judgment in an important case on the constitution of Canada where I am now as well known as here, in a different capacity.'[173] In his decision, citing the 'more recent decisions' of the Judicial Committee as having put an authoritative construction on the distribution of powers, Haldane easily dismissed the arguments based on trade and commerce or the criminal law. Argument based on the residual clause, which had found some favour in earlier decisions, needed a lengthy exegesis on *Russell* before it could be discarded as precedent. But in the end, having examined the evidence produced at trial, the lordships 'concur in the view taken of it by Hodgins J.A. They are of opinion that it does not prove any emergency putting the national life of Canada in unanticipated peril such as the Board which decided *Russell* v. *The Queen* may be considered to have had before them.'[174] Apparently the decision in result if not reasoning was that of the committee as a whole. 'I am being much criticized from Canada over the constitutional judgement disallowing the Lemieux Act,' Haldane reported to his mother. 'But we have none of us the least doubt about the judgement.'[175]

Although Haldane continued to sit on the Judicial Committee, *Snider* was his last important federalism decision. By the early 1920s, he was not in good health. Diagnosed as a diabetic in 1910, he had suffered several serious collapses while on the committee and attributed his recovery from the second in 1922 to the use of insulin, discovered just a year earlier.[176] Ordered by his doctor to rest for a year, Haldane missed most of the appeals in the summer of 1922 but was back at work in November. According to a close friend in 1922, "the roar of the cataract" was in his ears – he was nearing his end.'[177] In January 1927 Beatrice Webb noted that 'Haldane looks old and ill; but he is hard at work on his Privy Council judgments – they are short of Judges, and those they've got are aged – some over 80 and most over 70!'[178]

However, in 1928 he listened to nine days of argument in the famous *Tiny Township* case and three months later delivered a twenty-five-page decision.[179] The decision was written, J.H. Morgan wrote, 'with the hands of a dying man and left him exhausted. He was ordered by his medical adviser to abandon, once and for all, every form of public activity. He begged for one dispensation, namely, that he might still be allowed, after the Long Vacation, to participate, occasionally, in the sitting of the Judicial Committee. His doctor felt compelled to refuse the petition. A few days later the end came.'[180]

Two weeks after his death, Lord Sumner, appointed to the committee by Haldane in 1913, wrote to Lord Loreburn: 'All the prophecies when I came away were that we should not see Haldane again. Prophecies are not often so right. I suppose speeches will be made in the House by those who feel called upon to make them, of whom I am not one, but I think most people in the know would agree that he went on, judicially at any rate, too long.' 'This seems to be one of the less happy examples of Sumner's acute but bitter mind,' commented R.F.V. Heuston in Haldane's defence. 'As president of a tribunal Haldane in his last years may have been a little slower and more reminiscent than he had been. But his judgements show no sign of intellectual exhaustion.'[181] Sumner was a brilliant though bitter man, but he had sat with Haldane on seven of the cases considered here and his judgment must have some weight. If Haldane's increasing obstinacy, obtuseness, and judicial and historical self-assurance during the arguments were any indication, he had gone on too long.

In argument and decision, Viscount Haldane had done his best to perform radical surgery on the misshapen federal system the Canadians and Sir Francis Reilly, the Colonial Office draftsman, had produced in 1867. Lord Watson, Haldane's ideal statesman-jurist, had led the way. But it was his follower who most decisively and openly sought to assimilate Canadian federalism to the correct American and Australian model. Although he never referred to it in argument, Haldane's juxtaposition of the federal residual power and the enumerations with property and civil rights in the 'independent kingdoms' looked remarkably like the Tenth Amendment: 'The powers not delegated to the United States by the Constitution, nor prohibited by it to the States, are reserved to the States respectively, or to the people.'

Haldane was enormously pleased with his reconstruction. 'I have to write practically all the judgements in the constitutional cases,' he told his mother, 'for the good reason that since Lord Watson's time there has been no other who knew this branch of learning.'[182] At the end of the Canadian appeals in the summer of 1923, he informed her that he had 'decided as many cases for Canada as Lord Watson did,' and boasted to his sister that 'we have added a good deal to the unwritten constitution of Canada there is much good pleasant feeling.'[183] A year later, when the American and Canadian bar associations were meeting in London, the daily letter to his mother read: 'Last night we had the first of our Canadian dinner parties. The guests made me feel as if I were one of the Fathers of Canada.' The social life was tiresome, he complained the next day. 'Still they are very nice boys and they hail me as one of the fathers of the Canadian constitution.'[184]

Haldane's Canadian jurisprudence has attracted the attention of academics who have looked for an explanation of his reasoning and decisions outside the boundaries of the constitution. Fifty years ago, James Mallory suggested that, in their rejection of government intervention and hostility to executive authority, his decisions were a reflection of nineteenth-century liberalism, but admitted that the conclusion was difficult to reconcile with Haldane's sympathy for the Labour Party.[185] Among other factors, Stephen Wexler has suggested that Haldane's imperialism lay at the root of his hostility to a national government which had demonstrated its opposition to imperial unity by refusing to participate in the Boer War until compelled by public opinion. As a result, Haldane not only restricted the jurisdiction of the federal government but enhanced the status of the provinces in the empire by dividing sovereignty and making the lieutenant governor the 'direct representative' of the imperial crown. Wexler also suggested that Haldane's support for Irish Home Rule led him to draw a sympathetic parallel between Ireland and the Canadian provinces.[186]

Jonathan Robinson and David Schneiderman, professors of philosophy and public law respectively, have found the roots of Haldane's federalism jurisprudence in political theory. Robinson attributes Haldane's view of the state, as well as of the role of law and the jurist, to his understanding of Hegel, which provided him with 'a theoretical justification' for his federalism jurisprudence:

If we examine this justification we will see that Haldane's work on the Committee was neither arbitrary nor ill-considered, for it follows from his philosophical views that the different social and political elements, or 'functional parts' as he would have said, of the state must be allowed to develop and flourish if it is to survive. Among the most important of these functional parts were the provinces, and these had to be protected and allowed to develop whatever the text of the BNA Act might say.[187]

From Hegel, Haldane drew the conclusion that, since 'the source of power of the state and the reality of the state is the embodiment of common purposes entertained by the people who constitute it, that source can only be a general will ... and the true source of sovereignty must be simply public or general opinion.'[188] It would follow, Robinson argues, that 'any move to strengthen the central government would do violence to public opinion and interfere with the functioning of the different organs of government at their own level.'[189] Thus, it was not surprising that a view of a constitution which gave the widest capacity to property and civil rights was 'a faithful reflection of Haldane's interpretation of Hegel's political philosophy, with its organized hierarchy of powers and "concurrence of purpose" on the part of those institutions in which the sovereignty of the state finds expression.'[190]

David Schneiderman agrees that Hegelian theory played an important part in Haldane's constitutional thought, but, in order to develop an association between Haldane and Harold Laski, he suggests that it would be 'fruitful to situate Haldane's judicial work within other intellectual currents with which he had both an influence and an affinity.'[191] The current he identifies was political pluralism, whose advocates, such as Laski, maintained that self-government should be exercised at the local levels. In the pluralist state, therefore, power would be partitioned or functionally devolved 'so that the diversity of group life could be given expression.'[192] Although Haldane was not a pluralist, the views of the state he drew from Hegel were similar in some respects.[193] As Haldane wrote to the young Laski, 'I hope you will go on with the valuable work you are doing. The problem of decentralization requires the best thought that can be given.'[194] Reviewing a book by Laski, he wrote that it is those 'institutions which have genuine popular power expressed in them that become organs of ethical ideals and of true citizenship, and so the superiority of the pluralist state becomes evident.'[195]

Applying theory to law, Schneiderman maintains that Haldane's belief in decentralization 'is perhaps best exemplified in his subordination of federal power to provincial power, whenever the language of the 1867 Act allowed.'[196] Obviously sympathetic to the politics and apparently the law of Haldane's federalism jurisprudence, he concludes: 'Perhaps the better interpretation of Haldane's Canadian constitutional law is this: citizenship in a federal polity is advanced by favouring autonomous local government over state authority, save for those rare instances when the polity itself is under threat.'[197] The current invocation of the language of pluralism in the search for constitutional reform inevitably leads Schneiderman to suggest that it was Haldane and not his critics who best reflected the Canadian reality.[198]

Haldane's preference for the decentralized state is obvious in both his political theory and his constitutional law. The extent to which theory dictated his law cannot be determined. What is clear, however, is that, in argument and decision on the 'bloodless battlefield' of the Judicial Committee, Haldane had fought on the side of Oliver Mowat and Lord Watson, neither of whom had been immersed in Teutonic metaphysics or late-Victorian pluralism, and continued throughout his life to plead their cause in his endeavour to protect and nourish the provincial kingdoms.

8

Lord Sankey and 'Progressive Constructionism,' 1929–1935

The swing of the judicial pendulum ...
– Vincent MacDonald, 1935–6

For almost a decade after Haldane's death, a new generation on the Judicial Committee adopted a more fluid and comprehensive approach to judicial review which looked at the constitution within a contemporary context. With two exceptions, they did not reject the doctrines and dogmas of the Watson-Haldane era; rather, they 'explained' or 'distinguished' or applied them in novel ways to new circumstances. In reasoning and decision, the committee found new authority for federal jurisdiction both in the constitution itself and in the enhanced status of the national government.

The new departure could be attributed to the substance of the issues before the committee, which did not fall easily into earlier doctrine. It could also be attributed in part to John Sankey, lord chancellor from 1929 to 1935. In conversation with Haldane and Harold Laski before his elevation, Sankey had taken what Laski described as 'the obvious and sensible view that judges inevitably legislate' and claimed that he was 'interested in the endeavour to make the case emit a big working principle.'[1] Sir Ivor Jennings believed that it was 'doubtful' if Sankey had any definite views about Canadian federalism, 'but his bias was clearly against pettifogging lawyers' arguments that interfered with the effective control of social life and the freedom of Dominion action, and this led him to infuse a new spirit into the process of interpretation.'[2]

Although Haldane and Sankey were friends, it is tempting to speculate that Sankey relished the opportunity to revisit Haldane's provincialist doctrines. When Ramsay MacDonald formed a Labour government in 1924, his first choice as lord chancellor had been Sankey, at that time a judge on the Court of King's Bench and a known friend of Labour. But, as Sankey recorded in his diary, MacDonald told him that Haldane had 'held a pistol to his head and threatened to give no help, unless he was made Chancellor ... so I have lost it.' However, Sankey did become lord chancellor on the formation of MacDonald's second government in June 1929.[3]

Sankey was fortunate in having a new generation of law lords on the bench. By the late 1920s, criticism of the Judicial Committee had disturbed Arthur Balfour, lord president of the Privy Council, who believed that as a 'valuable bond of empire' the prestige of the committee had to be maintained. As the Imperial Conference of 1930 approached, he warned cabinet that 'there was a good deal of criticism of it at the [1926] Imperial Conference, and ... it became perfectly clear that when the next Conference came around, the Judicial Committee would probably become the subject of a more serious attack. I very earnestly hope that before that period arrives its position will have been made as impregnable as the legal talent at our disposal, secured by adequate salaries, can possibly make it.'[4]

Balfour noted that the most obvious weakness of the committee was age. Most boards over which Haldane presided were composed of men in their seventies and eighties who, Sir Hamar Greenwood told the House of Commons, were so old they could neither see nor hear counsel.[5] By 1932, the composition of the Judicial Committee had been transformed, with only Lord Blanesburgh, appointed in 1923, continuing to sit well into the 1930s. Dissatsifaction with the committee's decision in the Quebec-Labrador boundary dispute in March 1927, which, as Balfour had predicted, 'will get us into trouble,'[6] was the pretext for the forced resignation of the eighty-four year-old Lord Atkinson in 1928.[7] His replacement was Lord Atkin, the first of the new appointments. Over the next few years, the older, mostly political appointees were replaced by lords Tomlin, Thankerton (Watson's son), and Russell, three professional judges. When Sumnner and Dunedin retired in 1930 and 1932, to be replaced by Lord Macmillan and Lord Wright, the Haldane court had vanished. In time, Atkin became the senior member of the committee, absent the lord chancellor, and was the most diligent in attendance and prolific in decision.

The first appeal to the court did not foretell a new beginning but suggested rather that doctrines drawn from the Watson era would guide the committee's deliberations. The appeal was to determine whether a compulsory federal licence for a fish cannery was ancillary to federal jurisdiction over fisheries. The Supreme Court had held unanimously that the regulations were *ultra vires*, and the Judicial Committee agreed. Sankey asked Tomlin, described by Dunedin in 1935 as 'the best of the bunch,'[8] to write the judgment. Although it did not seem necessary for the decision, Tomlin decided to extract from the body of precedents four propositions that had been established by the committee concerning the conflict of jurisdiction between the Dominon and the provinces:[9]

(1) The legislation of the Parliament of Canada, so long as it strictly relates to subjects of legislation expressly enumerated in s. 91, is of paramount authority, even though it trenches upon matters assigned to the provincial legislatures by s. 92: see *Tennant v. Union Bank of Canada* [1894] A.C.31.

(2) The general power of legislation conferred upon the Parliament of the Dominion by s. 91 of the Act in supplement of the power to legislate upon the subjects expressly enumerated must be strictly confined to such matters as are unquestionably of national interest and importance, and must not trench on any of the subjects enumerated in s. 92 as within the scope of provincial legislation, unless these matters have attained such dimensions as to affect the body politic of the Dominion: see *Attorney-General for Ontario* v. *Attorney-General For Canada* [1896] A.C. 348.[10]

(3) It is within the competence of the Dominion Parliament to provide for matters which, though otherwise within the legislative competence of the provincial legislature, are necessarily incidental to effective legislation by the Parliament of the Dominion upon a subject of legislation expressly enumerated in s. 91: see *Attorney-General of Ontario* v. *Attorney-General for the Dominion* [1894] A.C.189; and *Attorney-General for Ontario* v. *Attorney-General for the Dominion* [1896] A.C. 348.

(4) There can be a domain in which provincial and Dominion legislation may overlap, in which case neither legislation will be ultra vires if the field is clear, but if the field is not clear and the two legislations meet the Dominion legislation must prevail: see *Grand Trunk Ry. of Canada* v. *Attorney-General of Canada* [1907] A.C.65.

Tomlin's propositions did not adopt Atkinson's far more restrictive propositions based on Watson's *dicta* or Haldane's emergency doctrine, and were thus open-ended. Although the propositions were incomplete, and the second, and most often referred to, misleading, they became a reference point for many arguments and decisions during the last quarter-century of Judicial Committee appeals.[11]

However, in his first decision, Lord Atkin suggested that the Judicial Committee would not be overly deferential to precedent as he explained away Haldane's bizarre *dicta* which had strangled the federal power over criminal law and trade and commerce. In 1923 the King government had passed the Combines Investigation Act (amended in 1927), which made it an indictable offence to be party to the formation of a combine, and added section 498 of the Criminal Code to make it an indictable offence to conspire to lessen competition unduly. Indicted under the act, the Proprietary Articles Trade Association, joined by Ontario and Quebec, challenged its constitutionality, and the government referred the matter to the Supreme Court.

The appellants relied on the *Board of Commerce* precedent and Haldane's limited scope of the criminal law and trade and commerce powers. Duff, however, found Halsbury's definition of the criminal law power in *Hamilton Street Railway* authoritative and, confronted with Haldane's definition, wrote that 'it is difficult to understand upon what justification the Dominion Parliament can be denied the power under s. 91 to declare any act to be a crime which, in its opinion, is such a violation of generally accepted standards of conduct as to deserve chastisement as a crime.'[12] Newcombe was more circumspect in stating that he was convinced that Haldane had 'never intended to suggest that Parliament might not competently find a public wrong lurking or tolerated under the head of civil rights which it is necessary or expedient, according to its will and discretion ... to suppress in the exercise of its authority over the criminal law.'[13]

On appeal, Lord Atkin declared that Haldane's *dictum* was 'of little value ... for the domain of criminal jurisprudence can only be ascertained by examining what acts at any particular period are declared by the State to be crimes.' However, as a saving collegial gesture, he added that the board agreed 'with the view expressed in the judgement of Newcombe J. that the passage in the judgement in the *Board of Commerce* case to which allusion has been made was not intended as a definition.'[14]

It had also been argued at the Supreme Court that the act could not be upheld as a regulation of trade and commerce given Haldane's decision in *Board of Commerce*, confirmed in *Snider*, that under 91(2) standing alone the federal government could not interfere with property and civil rights. The argument was not addressed directly in the Supreme Court decision, but at the Judicial Committee federal counsel argued that Haldane's observations were either misunderstood or, if not, they were *obiter*. Atkin seemed to agree. Finding the act valid under 91(27), it was unnecessary to consider whether it could also be upheld under trade and commerce. But he did find it appropriate to add:

Their Lordships merely propose to disassociate themselves from the construction suggested in argument of a passage in the judgement in the *Board of Commerce* case under which it was contended that the power to regulate trade and commerce could be invoked only in furtherance of a general power which Parliament possessed independently of it. No such restriction is properly to be inferred from that judgement. The words of the statute must receive their proper construction where they stand as giving an independent authority to Parliament over the particular subject matter ... their Lordships in the present case forbear from defining the extent of that authority. They desire, however, to guard themselves from being supposed to lay down that the present legislation could not be supported on that ground.[15]

The rationalization or dismissal of Haldane's constitutional absurdities was less revealing of a radical change in the committee's approach than the new spirit evident in *Edwards* (the *Persons* case), Sankey's first decision, where he quoted W.H.P. Clement with approval:

The Privy Council, indeed, has laid down that Courts of law must treat the provisions of this Act by the same methods of construction and exposition which they apply to other statutes. But there are statutes and statutes; and the strict construction deemed proper in the case, for example, of a penal or taxing statute or one passed to regulate the affairs of an English parish, would be often subversive *of* Parliament's real intent if applied to an Act passed to ensure the peace, order and good government of a British Colony.[16]

In *Edwards*, Sankey was not impressed by arguments based on Roman law, early English decisions, or the old common law disability of women to hold public office which had led to a unanimous decision in the Supreme Court that women were not 'persons' for purposes of eligibility to sit in the Senate.[17] 'The British North America Act planted in Canada a living tree capable of growth and expansion within its natural limits,' Sankey declared. The object was to grant Canada a constitution, and it was not 'the duty of this Board – it is certainly not their desire – to cut down the provisions of the Act by a narrow and technical construction, but rather to give it a large and liberal interpretation so that the Dominion to a great extent, but within certain fixed limits, may be mistress in her house, as the Provinces to a great extent, but within certain fixed limits, are mistresses in theirs.'[18] A 'heavy burden' lay on the committee to set aside a unanimous decision of the Supreme Court and it would do so only 'after convincing argument and anxious consideration.' However, not only were there ambiguities of language which supported such a reversal, but the board was mindful that the object of the act was 'to provide a constitution for Canada, a responsible and developing state.'[19]

In its explicit reasoning and result, the decision was a sharp break with previous Judicial Committee jurisprudence. While Canadians found it eminently sensible, Arthur Berriedale Keith, perhaps the most eminent British authority, described it as an 'unfortunate' decision and one that even the Judicial Committee's 'admirers have found difficult to reconcile with their conception of the judicial function.' The decision, he explained, 'has never carried much conviction for those who hold that the convenience of avoiding an amendment of the Canadian constitution should not have been allowed to produce a situation wholly foreign to the minds of those who framed the constitution of Canada.'[20] Ivor Jennings agreed that it was 'a most remarkable decision.'

For in effect, it wiped out the rule that the Canadian Constitution is a statute, to be interpreted like other statutes. Commonsense tells us that nobody in 1867 contemplated that women could become Senators. Yet because the Act was a Constitution it was given a progressive interpretation. This doctrine has not yet applied to disputes between the Dominion and the Provinces, but there appears to be no reason why it should not; and, if it is so applied, economic and social arguments will become almost as familiar as they are in constitutional arguments before the Supreme Court of the United States. It will involve, to put it simply, a presumption in favour of Dominion powers. Many would agree that this would be a desirable innovation; and some will agree that the strictly legal or historical method of interpretation leads often to nonsense.[21]

Sankey's approach to judicial review was quickly described as 'the rules of progressive construction' by Lucien Cannon, the federal solicitor general, in argument before the Supreme Court on the Aeronautics reference six months after the decision in *Edwards*.[22] The Aeronautics Act, giving the federal government general regulatory control over aerial navigation within Canada and its territorial waters, had been passed in 1919 (later amended) in accordance with a convention drawn up at the Paris Peace Conference, which had been signed by Canada and later ratified by His Majesty on behalf of the empire. Challenged by Quebec at the 1927 Dominion-Provincial Conference, the government referred two general questions to the Supreme Court:

1 Did the federal government have 'exclusive legislative and executive authority for performing the obligations of Canada, or any Province thereof, under the Convention?'
2 Was federal legislation 'providing for the regulation and control of aeronautics generally within Canada, including flying operations entirely within the limits of a province, necessary or proper for performing the obligations of Canada, or of any Province thereof, under the Convention aforementioned, within the meaning of s. 132 of the British North America Act, 1867?'[23]

The answers of the court, and there were many, were of little assistance. On the first question, the court unanimously held that the federal government did not have 'exclusive' legislative or executive authority and, construing the word 'generally' to mean 'in every respect,' also concluded that under section 132 the federal government did not acquire *exclusive* authority to carry out Canada's obligations under the convention. However, it appeared from the lengthy judgments (and the long headnote) that the federal government's jurisdiction was or might be '*paramount* in the exercise of its authority to carry out these obligations.'

The court did not accept the argument that aeronautics fell within the residual clause either because it was not mentioned in sections 91 or 92 or because it satisfied the national dimensions or national interest test. On the contrary, the court was unanimous in deciding that intra-provincial aviation fell within section 92(13).[24] And in holding that the jurisdiction of the provinces runs through the space above the surface as well as below, Duff, Thibaudeau Rinfret, and John Lamont apparently agreed with Aimé Geoffrion's jest that the proposition advanced in argument that a civil right 'becomes something else when it leaves the earth was in the realm of fancy ... And surely it does not depend on whether it is a machine you are using, or a horse, or whether the horse sticks to the ground, or the machine is able to fly up in the air.'[25]

On appeal to the Judicial Committee, W.N. Tilley contended for Ottawa that aviation was neither local and private nor enumerated in section 92. Jurisdiction, therefore, lay within the federal government's residual power. However, if the board felt it necessary to find a home within the section 91 enumerations, he argued for trade and commerce and navigation and shipping. Finally, under section 132, the federal parliament was 'the only legislature authorized to perform treaty obligations, whether of Canada or of the Provinces. The Convention deals with so many topics that these obligations cannot be performed effectively without some regulations not directly within its terms.'

Quebec had retained Sir John Simon to lead Geoffrion. Citing Watson and Haldane precedents, Simon argued the virtually all-encompassing authority of subsections 13 and 16 of 92 and the restriction of the residual power to an emergency such as war. Section 132 was irrelevant, he maintained, because the regulations were enacted before the convention was signed and the obligations were only those relating to international flying, 'not a vast body of regulations dealing with the whole subject.'[26]

The strong board presided over by Sankey (Dunedin, Atkin, Russell, and Macmillan) refused to adopt the piecemeal and precedent-laden approach of the Supreme Court or of counsel. Instead, Sankey reached out for his 'big, working principle' and wound up with several, one of which was his famous warning against a too rigid adherence to precedent or doctrine in the review of the Canadian constitution:

Under our system decided cases effectively construe the words of an Act of Parliament and establish principles and rules whereby its scope and effect may be interpreted. But there is always a danger that in the course of this process the terms of the statute may come to be unduly extended and attention may be diverted from what has been enacted to what has been judicially said about the enactment.

To borrow an analogy: there may be a range of sixty colours, each of which is so little different from its neighbour that it is difficult to make any distinction between the two, and yet at the one end of the range the colour may be white and at the other end of the range black. Great care must therefore be taken to consider each decision in the light of the circumstances of the case in view of which it was pronounced, especially in the interpretation of an Act such as the British North America Act, which was a great constitutional charter, and not to allow general phrases to obscure the underlying object of the Act, which was to establish a system of government upon essentially federal principles. Useful as decided cases are, it is always advisable to get back to the words of the Act itself and to remember the object with which it was passed.

Sankey cautioned that Confederation was a compromise and judicial interpretation should not 'be allowed to dim or whittle down the provisions of the original contract upon which the federation was founded. Nor is it legitimate that any judicial construction of the provisions of ss. 91 and 92 should impose a new and different contract upon the federating bodies.' At the same time, while the court 'should be jealous in upholding the charter of the Provinces as enacted in s. 92 it must no less be borne in mind that the real object of the Act was to give the central Government those high functions and almost sovereign powers by which uniformity of legislation might be secured on all questions which were of common concern to all the Provinces as members of a constituent whole.'[27]

Over the years, Sankey continued, there had 'grown up around the British North America Act a body of precedents of high authority and value as guides to its interpretation and application,' leading to the four propositions cited by Lord Tomlin in 1929. Of these, Sankey stressed the second and third. Yet he also emphasized Watson's cautionary warning that 'great caution must be observed' before justifying federal jurisdiction under the residual clause in areas once local or provincial. Further, from Haldane's decision in *Fort Frances*, Sankey drew the proposition that 'there may be cases of emergency where the Dominion is empowered to act for the whole' and 'where the Dominion is entitled to speak for the whole, and this not because of any judicial interpretation of ss. 91 and 92, but by reason of the plain terms of s. 132, where Canada as a whole, having undertaken an obligation, is given the power necessary and proper for performing that obligation.'[28] Rather than rely on 'forced analogies or piecemeal analysis,' the board therefore adopted a 'broader view' and concluded that the governing section was section 132, which conferred 'full power' on the federal government 'to do all that is legislatively necessary for the purpose.'[29]

In his summation, however, Sankey suggested that perhaps the broader view and s. 132 were not in themselves sufficient for his purpose. By the terms of section 132, the breadth of the obligations under the convention, and federal jurisdiction under the various heads of section 91, he observed, 'it would appear that substantially the whole field of legislation in regard to aerial navigation belongs to the Dominion.' Moreover, while a small portion of the remainder was not by specific words vested in the Dominion, neither was it vested in the province. And as to that small portion the board had concluded that 'it must necessarily belong to the Dominion under its power to make laws for the peace, order and good government of Canada.' The committee had also determined, Sankey concluded, that aerial navigation and the fulfilment of Canadian obligations under section 132 were 'matters of national interest and importance; and that aerial navigation is a class of subject which has attained such dimensions as to affect the body politic of the Dominion.'[30]

Liberal politician and outstanding lawyer Newton Rowell confidently believed that the decision marked 'definitely the escape of the Judicial Committee from the delusion that the determining provision in the BNA Act is that conferring control of property and civil rights upon the Provinces.'[31] John Ewart, lawyer and Canadian nationalist, believed it was the best of the Judicial Committee's decisions: 'It takes us a long way from the annoying subtleties of Lord Haldane. Its correctness of direction, its statesman's-like grasp and appreciation of actualities, and the clarity of its reasoning constitute a combination of qualities that force memory of the great American federalist, John Marshall. Curious that its spirit should have (at length) manifested itself in London rather than at Ottawa.'[32]

Before the *Aeronautics* case was heard at the Judicial Committee, Quebec, joined by Ontario and other provinces, had challenged the federal Radiotelegaph Act, which had been passed in 1927 as a result of an International Radiotelegraph Convention that Canada had signed in its own right. The questions referred to the Supreme Court were: '(1) Has the Parliament of Canada jurisdiction to regulate and control radio communication? (2) If not, in what particulars is the jurisdiction limited?'[33] The two-day argument before the court pitted the formidable W.N. Tilley, aided by Brooke Claxton, against the equally formidable Charles Lanctot and Aimé Geoffrion.

The federal factum and Tilley argued that the subject matter of radio communication did not come within section 92 and was of 'such character and such national importance that it must fall within Dominion jurisdiction, not being local to the Provinces in any sense, and that if there were not other provisions at all by way of reference to telegraphs, etc., it would certainly come within Trade and Commerce, or if not, under the Laws for the Peace, Order and good Government of Canada.'[34] Claxton added that the convention demanded national control 'in its every aspect' and observed that radio was nationally controlled in such countries as the United States, with whom Canada had signed an agreement, and Australia.[35]

Lanctot argued that, on the whole, radio fell within 92(13) because the transmitting and receiving machines were property and 'the waves which emanate from one and go towards and are captured by the other are within the exercise of a civil right which is competent to all the inhabitants of the Province to exercise.' He admitted that the jurisdiction was divided and a 'Yes' or 'No' answer to the first question would satisfy neither. However, Justice Thibaudeau Rinfret pointedly interjected, a 'Yes' decision would mean that 'the Parliament of Canada [has] jurisdiction in every respect. That would leave nothing to the provinces.'[36] Ottawa's action was typical, he continued, more advocate than judge, for ever since Confederation whenever there were matters 'which, if I may use the expression, were lying around loose and disorderly, without having been made the subject of actual legislation,' the federal government had attempted to seize them.[37]

Geoffrion vigorously attacked the proposition that the national dimensions test could encroach on property and civil rights, however many provinces were involved. Referring to Watson's doctrines, and perhaps with an eye on Sankey's 'progressive construction,' he insisted that 'you are not entitled to take something from 92 because you think it is of Canadian importance. You are not entitled to take something out of 91 because you think it is of local importance ... Our Constitution is not left loose so that courts from time to time, changing and with changing conditions, would decide what is of national importance and what is not.'[38]

The court divided 3–2 in favour of the validity of the legislation. Chief Justice Anglin (with E.L. Newcombe and Robert Smith) failed to find a home for radio in section 92 and thus, although various aspects were covered by section 92 enumerations, concluded that it fell within the residual clause. But his reasoning, perhaps influenced by Sankey, was also based on policy: 'My reasoning for so concluding is largely that overwhelming convenience – under the circumstances amounting to necessity – dictate that answer.'[39] Rinfret rejected exclusive federal control as he did the argument of convenience, preferring to endorse

Duff's position in *Eastern Elevator* that the inability of the provinces to act necessarily placed jurisdiction in federal hands.[40] Lamont also agreed that federal jurisdiction was not 'exclusive, although in some particulars, a very large measure of control admittedly belongs to it,' a position that Duff, who was hospitalized with colon cancer, was likely to have endorsed.[41]

On appeal, the Judicial Committee listened to largely the same cast and the same arguments for three days in December 1931. In light of Sankey's wide-ranging decision in *Aeronautics*, Tilley placed more emphasis on national dimensions and the residual clause, while Geoffrion countered that section 132 did not apply in any way and that aspects of radio had to be distributed under sections 91 and 92.

Viscount Dunedin's approach to law was described as 'law pure and simple, touched if anything by common sense,'[42] and he rejected at once any division of the subject between the two jurisdictions. Canada was a signatory to the convention and the only legislation that could bind all Canadians was federal legislation. Agreeing that the convention was not a section 132 treaty, Dunedin expounded a controversial legal and historical doctrine resulting from the growth of Dominion autonomy and the Statute of Westminster, which had been passed the day the hearing began:

This idea of Canada as a Dominion being bound by a convention equivalent to a treaty with foreign powers was quite unthought of in 1867. It is the outcome of the gradual development of the position of Canada vis-à-vis to the mother country, Great Britain, which is found in these later days expressed in the Statute of Westminister. It is not, therefore, to be expected that such a matter should be dealt with in explicit words in either s. 91 or s. 92. The only class of treaty which would bind Canada was thought of as a treaty by Great Britain, and that was provided for by s. 132. Being, therefore, not mentioned explicitly in either s. 91 or s. 92, such legislation falls within the general words at the opening of s. 91 which assign to the Government of the Dominion the power to make laws 'for the peace, order and good government of Canada in relation to all matters not coming within the classes of subjects by this Act assigned exclusively to the legislatures of the Provinces.' In fine, though agreeing that the Convention was not such a treaty as is defined in s. 132, their Lordships think that it comes to the same thing.[43]

Dunedin concluded that, although 'the question had obviously to be decided on the terms of the statute, it is a matter of congratulation that the result arrived at seems consonant with common sense. A divided control between transmitter and receiver could only lead to confusion and inefficiency.' Or, he might have agreed with Anglin that the decision arose from 'circumstances amounting to necessity.'[44]

Even advocates of a stronger central government were disturbed by the decision or the reasons. Like others of an older generation, John Ewart believed that decision introduced 'a new and disruptive idea ... into current conceptions of our constitution ... No Canadian lawyer, and probably no intelligent Canadian layman, could be induced to believe that if the Dominion Parliament had no power to enact certain legislation, it could acquire the power by promising a foreign state that it would enact it.'[45] Professor Vincent MacDonald of Dalhousie Law School approved the outcome but stated that the reasoning was

a bastard method which is neither the traditional method of avoiding all references to external aids or facts and construing the Act by reference solely to what has been said – for he does consider the situation existing in 1867 as to treaties. Nor is it a method of construing the Act as a living instrument adapting its terms to a new condition – for he does not consider whether the terms of sec.132 may not be sufficiently elastic to cover treaties affecting Canada to-day in the same way in essence, though in accidental features of negotiation and signature differing from those in 1867.[46]

Two other decisions, although not related to federalism, indicated that the Judicial Committee was, perhaps, reflecting the changing imperial structure in the 1920s and 1930s, endowing the Canadian government with an enhanced status and finding new content for both the residual and enumerated powers. In *Nadan* (1926), the Judicial Committee had found unconstitutional a section of the Criminal Code, first passed in 1888, prohibiting appeals in criminal cases. The prohibition was invalid as annulling the prerogative right of special petition to appeal and because the legislation could have no extra-territorial effect.[47] Although the Canadian government had intervened, it was not disturbed by the decision because it was aware that the committee had reached a political decision in order to pre-empt the abolition of appeals by Ireland. However, those less in the know had found it an affront to Canadian nationalism. 'The decision, both in what it says and what it implies, makes short work of the claim that Canada has, in law, any claim to national status,' John Dafoe editorialized. 'This is not news to anybody who has given attention to this question. It has been known, right along, that so far as the text of the law is concerned Canada's "national status" is sheer pretence.'[48]

A few years later, the Judicial Committee was given the opportunity to revise the implications of the decision in *Nadan*. At issue in *Croft* v. *Dunphy* was a section of the Customs Act which gave Customs officers authority to board and bring into port any vessel hovering in the territorial waters of Canada. The *Dorothy M. Smart*, registered in Nova Scotia, with a cargo of rum from St Pierre, was so boarded and, in subsequent litigation, the act was challenged. The Supreme Court of Nova Scotia upheld the legislation under the residual clause and as a matter of customs revenue, but was reversed on appeal to the Supreme Court of Canada.[49] Duff, with Rinfret and Lamont concurring, found authority in neither the residual clause nor the enumerations, preferring the narrow construction placed on the powers of the Canadian parliament by the Judicial Committee in *Nadan*, which, apparently, denied legislation with extra-territorial effects.[50] Newcombe, with Lawrence Cannon concurring, located jurisdiction in the enumerations and the residual clause.[51] Newcombe quoted Lord Halsbury, who had held in *Riel* v. *The Queen* that the words of the residual clause 'are apt to authorize the utmost discretion of enactment for the attainment of the objects pointed to.'[52]

On appeal, Lord Macmillan had no difficulty reversing the decision of the Supreme Court in finding that Canada had the capacity to pass legislation with extra-territorial effects:

In their Lordships' opinion the Parliament of Canada is not under any such disability. Once it is found that a particular topic of legislation is among those upon which the Dominion Parliament may competently legislate as being for the peace, order and good government of Canada or as being one of the specified subjects enumerated in s. 91 of the British North America Act, their Lordships see no reason to restrict the scope of such legislation by any other consideration than is applicable to the legislation of a fully Sovereign State.[53]

The Statute of Westminster had been passed before the argument. Rather than including it in his reasons, however, Macmillan was content to observe that in view of the decision nothing need be said about section 3 of the Statute, which gave Canada full power to make laws having extra-territorial operation, beyond observing that the question of the validity of such legislation 'cannot at least arise in the future.'[54]

Three years later, the committee directly revisisted *Nadan*. With the passage of the Statute of Westminster, the doctrines of extra-territorial-ity and repugnancy (under which Canadian statutes had been declared void on the ground that they were repugnant to British statutes) were abrogated and the government re-enacted the prohibition of criminal appeals. The issue came before the Judicial Committee again in 1935 when some coal companies convicted in Quebec under the Combines Investigation Act were denied leave to appeal. Counsel for the companies argued that the right to entertain appeals was a 'prerogative right of the King as the fountain of justice inherent in the Crown and inseparable from it,' which could be diminished only by an act of the imperial legislature in which 'there must be express words or necessary implication.' There were no such words in the BNA Act, 'peace, order and good government' being insufficient, nor did the Statute of Westminster confer such power.[55]

In what was described as a decision 'of policy rather than of law, and that policy is predicated on what is desirable from the point of view of Imperial politics,'[56] the Judicial Committee held the prohibition to be valid. After the Statute of Westminster, wrote Lord Sankey, in his last decision the day before he was replaced as lord chancellor, the only remaining question was the competence of the Canadian parliament, which must be ascertained from the words of the 1867 act. Moreover, as recently laid down in *Edwards*, 'in interpreting a constituent or organic statute such as the Act, that construction most beneficial to the widest possible amplitude of its powers must be adopted.' There was no doubt that the prerogative could not be restricted 'save by express words or by necessary intendment,' but in the view of the court, section 91 'does invest the Dominion Parliament with these powers. It does not indeed do so by express terms, but it does so by necessary intendment.'

With the fetters removed by the Statute of Westminster, section 91 'read along with the rest of the Act is, according to its true construction in their Lordships' opinion ... intended to make and is apt to make the Dominion Legislature supreme and endow it with the same authority as the imperial parliament, within the assigned limits of subject and areas, just as it was said in *Hodge* v. *The Queen* that s. 92 of the Act had that effect in regard to the Provincial Legislatures.' The legal supremacy of the imperial parliament remained unimpaired, but 'that is a theory and has no relation to realities. In truth Canada is in enjoyment of the full scope of self-government.'[57]

In both the revitalization of many areas of federal jurisdiction and in the approach to judicial review, there had been a remarkable change at the Judicial Committee after Haldanes' departure. The residual power was given content not attached to an emergency; criminal law and trade and commerce had been freed from Haldane's restrictions; Watson's national dimensions doctrine was judicially perceived to have applications far beyond what Watson intended and was emancipated from his severe qualifications; and the national government was endowed with an enhanced status with correlative functions. Most important, perhaps, the court no longer saw its task as the protection of provincial autonomy in the face of federal aggression, but one of examining the concrete issues before the court in the context of a document designed to give the country a workable modern constitution. Vincent MacDonald searched for the appropriate metaphor to describe the apparent judicial revolution: 'The ebb-tide of Dominion power having reached its lowest mark with the *Snider Case* in 1925, that power has been borne along on a flowing tide of returning vitality which, if sustained, may yet give Canada the constitution it was intended to have. This turn of the tide – or, to use a more current metaphor, this change in "the swing of the judicial pendulum" – is of particular significance in the solution of the problems of to-day.'[58]

Similar views were widely expressed in the hearings of the special committee on the British North America Act established in January 1935.[59] Indeed, the deputy minister of justice believed that amendments were unnecessary. Properly interpreted, the constitution endowed the federal government with all powers that 'are essentially national in their nature,' and, in light of the trend in recent judicial decisions, he concluded that 'I would expect to be supported in the view that anything which can be shown to be national in scope will be held to belong to this parliament.'[60] O.D. Skelton agreed that 'the pendulum is swinging somewhat in the other direction' but was uncertain of the reasons: 'How far that is due to changes in personal factors and how far it reflects the growth in national unity, the emergence of the national government in the war and post-war periods as the heir to former imperial powers, and the rise of the new problems of such magnitude as to require national action, I shall not attempt to inquire; the fact remains of a reversal in trend, though one that has not gone far yet.'[61]

Regardless of the distance travelled, the swing of the pendulum suggested to many that Prime Minister R.B. Bennett's New Deal Legislation might pass judicial scrutiny.

9

The New Deal at Court and
the End of Appeals

She still retains the water-tight compartments ...

– Lord Atkin, 1937

In January 1935 Prime Minister Bennett declared that the 'old order is gone' and promised a radical 'New Deal' to combat the Great Depression. Even before the details were revealed, it was obvious that for the first time in Canadian history an entire legislative program would end up in court. Although the ultimate test would be on Downing Street, not at the corner of Bank and Wellington in Ottawa, the initial references to the Supreme Court are of unusual interest and importance. Not only were the judgments revealing, but almost two thousand pages of oral argument provide a rare opportunity to examine the interactions of counsel and bench, and of law and politics, in what would be the dress rehearsal for the appeal to the Judicial Committee.[1] The judgments in the Supreme Court indicated that the pendulum had swung, but not very far, while the subsequent decisions of Lord Atkin for the Judicial Committee starkly indicated that the swing itself had been a naive judicial and political illusion. The illusion shattered, legal realists and Canadian nationalists joined forces to demand an end to judicial imperialism and the long reign of the Judicial Committee.

In his radio broadcasts proclaiming the New Deal, the prime minister declared that 'reform means Government intervention. It means Government control and regulation. It means the end of *laissez-faire.*' Although the legislation was less radical than the rhetoric, the package thrust the state more boldly into the regulatory arena than ever before. A farm credit act was designed to enable farmers to reach a compromise with their creditors to avoid bankruptcy. A national marketing act attempted to find a way to regulate the marketing of natural products that would pass judicial scrutiny. Three acts established standards for industrial wages and hours of work. Two measures policed unfair trade and combinations in restraint of trade. The centrepiece was the establishment of an employment and social-insurance fund with contributions from employers, employees, and government.[2]

Much of the package appeared to be unconstitutional if Haldane's doctrines and precedents in the insurance cases, *Board of Commerce*, and *Snider* were followed. However, after the swing of the pendulum, there were those like W.P.M. Kennedy who believed that for 'a nation whose constitution has been divorced by judicial decisions from its origins and historical intentions, it is, perhaps, pardonable to clutch respectfully but not without hope, at any straws thrown to us in the whirlpool of judicial chaos.'[3]

Questioned in the House of Commons, Minister of Justice Hugh Guthrie observed that 'the trend' of Judicial Committee decisions 'has in recent years changed considerably' towards 'the enlargement of the powers of the federal government rather than towards restriction of them.'[4] Asked by Mackenzie King if he believed that the legislation was valid, Bennett replied that 'I have given a great deal of study to the matter and convinced myself that the effect of the treaty statute, to which perhaps I should have directed my attention earlier than I did, and the two decisions of the Privy Council ... warrant the conclusion at which I have arrived.'[5] However, W.N. Tilley and Aimé Geoffrion, two of the country's most eminent constitutional lawyers, privately advised the Department of Justice that much of the legislation was invalid in whole or part.[6]

By March 1935, Mackenzie King had devised his political strategy. In a prepared statement he requested the government to refer the labour and unemployment-insurance bills to the Supreme Court or assure their validity with a constitutional amendment. 'The Liberal Party approves the principle of the social legislation thus far introduced and desires to see it in operation,' he solemnly declared. 'We refuse to be maneuvered into a position of opposition to this legislation. We refuse also by voting against the legislation to raise directly an issue of provincial rights.[7]

King won the October 1935 election, and within two weeks of the formation of his cabinet he referred each act to the Supreme Court with the question, 'Is this Act ultra vires of the Parliament of Canada?' Responding to the accusation that the question implied that they were, Ernest Lapointe, the minister of justice, wrote that the 'very concise form of the question means that all aspects which will have a bearing upon the matter shall be properly included in the argument and brought to the attention of the Court.' The selection of Newton Rowell and Louis St Laurent as federal counsel, he added, 'will satisfy public opinion and is a guarantee that the best possible argument will be presented to the Court.'[8] The court acted with despatch and arguments opened on 15 January 1936. 'Things are warming up around the court in anticipation of the reference,' Chief Justice Duff had written a friend,[9] and during the argument Bennett's executive secretary found that 'the atmosphere of the Court was saturated with politics – the judges talk of little else.'[10]

Lyman Poore Duff was the most experienced member of the court. Appointed by Laurier in 1906, he had finally succeeded to the throne when Anglin retired in 1933. While Anglin had been concerned about the need for an effective central government, Duff proved to be one of the 'most vigilant and vigorous judicial spokesmen' in support of provincial autonomy.[11] He was also much more respectful of the jurisprudence of the Judicial Committee: 'What a succession of giants! Including Watson and Macnaghten, the Scotsman and the Scotch-Irishman, both endowed with statesmanlike insight and, at the same time, possessed by the very genius of law and judicature.'[12] Although Duff's decisions suggest a disposition opposed to state intervention, he had insisted that the Supreme Court was not concerned with 'the ultimate social, economic or political aims of the legislator'[13] and that an appeal to such policy questions as the need to address the grievances of the Atlantic provinces 'rather assumes the possession by this court of an authority which is not vested in it as a court of law.'[14]

Second in seniority was Thibaudeau Rinfret. Appointed by King in 1924 after many years as a professor of corporate law at McGill and two years on the Quebec Superior Court, Rinfret was a Liberal with a brother in King's cabinet. He was also an uncompromising defender of provincial jurisdiction and had never found any justification for federal legislation since he joined the court. Lawrence Arthur Cannon also had impeccable Liberal credentials as the son-in-law of Sir Charles Fitzpatrick and the brother of King's solicitor-general from 1926 to 1930. Appointed to the Quebec Court of King's Bench in 1927, he joined the Supreme Court before King's defeat in 1930. Cannon did not sit on the *Radio Reference*, but in his judgment in *Aeronautics* he pointedly rejected Sankey's living-tree doctrine as applicable to Canadian federalism.[15]

Three justices were relatively recent Bennett appointees. Oswald Smith Crocket had lobbied for the appointment for years, before Bennett succumbed to the pleading of an old friend, despite his belief that to transfer a man who had been a New Brunswick trial judge for eighteen years to the Supreme Court 'and expect him within a reasonable time to acquire the habit of an Appellate Judge, is asking a great deal.'[16] It certainly was asking a great deal of Crocket. A conservative to the core, he later told friends that Bennett's New Deal had 'ruined' the party.[17] Early in 1935, Bennett had filled the two Ontario vacancies. Henry Davis had sat on the Court of Appeal for two years, and Patrick Kerwin, once a partner in Minister of Justice Hugh Guthrie's law firm in Guelph, had been a trial judge on the Ontario Supreme Court since 1932. John Lamont, the western member of the court, was ill and had requested leave, and the chief justice saw no objection. 'After all,' Duff wrote to Ernest Lapointe, 'the result of these references will finally turn upon a judgement of the Judicial Committee and that does not seem to me an inexorable objection to giving Lamont such leave as he desires.'[18] It was not a court likely to look sympathetically on government intervention and regulation.

Facing Rowell and St Laurent when the fifteen days of arguments opened on 15 January 1936 was a galaxy of provincial attorneys general and their deputies as well as the best counsel money could buy. The court turned first to section 498A of the Criminal Code which prohibited discriminatory practices designed to destroy competition. Rowell based his argument on Atkin's restoration of the federal criminal law power, while his opponents contended that section (a) in particular, which made it an offence to discriminate among purchasers, was an invasion of property and civil rights. 'If the Dominion can prohibit anything it likes by labelling it a crime,' exclaimed Arthur Roebuck, attorney general of Ontario, 'then the provinces might just as well fold their tents like the Arabs and silently steal away.'[19]

Writing for the majority, Duff (Rinfret, Davis, and Kerwin concurring) unhesitatingly found that whatever doubts may have existed about the scope of the criminal law power, none could remain after Atkin's decision: 'The jurisdiction in relation to criminal law is plenary; and enactments passed within the scope of that jurisdiction are not subject to review by the courts.'[20] Canon held that section (a) was a 'colourable attempt' to invade the provincial field. Crocket agreed: Atkin had not 'intended to disapprove of anything previously laid down in the judgements of the Board in either the *Board of Commerce* or *Reciprocal Insurers* case,' and it was 'not only their right but their clear duty' to subject such legislation to judicial scrutiny.[21]

St Laurent next argued the case for the validity of the Dominion Trade and Industry Commission Act. Section 14 gave the commission, after full investigation under the Combines Investigation Act, power to recommend industrial agreements which would not be against 'the interests of the public' in order to end 'wasteful or demoralizing competition.' The arguments consumed three days, but Duff's decision for a unanimous court took three pages. Although some provisions concerning unfair trade practices could be upheld following Atkin's precedent, section 14 could not. It was not 'necessarily incidental to any exercise of any powers of the Dominion in relation to criminal law,' nor, consistent with Haldane's decision in *Snider*, could it be sustained as in relation to trade and commerce because it contemplated actions in respect of agreements 'which may relate to trade that is entirely local.' The attempt to create a national trademark – Canada Standard or C.S. – was 'really an attempt to create a civil right of action of a novel character and to vest it in the Crown in the right of the Dominion' and was unconstitutional.[22]

The most tedious arguments concerned the three labour statutes which were passed, the order of reference stated, 'for the purpose of enacting the necessary legislation to enable Canada to discharge certain obligations declared to have been assumed by Canada under the provisions of the Treaty of Peace ... and to which Canada as part of the British Empire was a signatory,' as well as obligations under the draft conventions of the International Labour Organization adopted in 1919, 1921, and 1928 and ratified by Canada in 1935.[23] Hoping to escape the responsibility for implementing the conventions, King had referred the constitutional question to the Supreme Court in 1925. The court had decided that the federal government's only responsibility was to place the conventions before the 'competent authority,' in this case the provinces.[24] But in the following decade, law and politics appeared to have transformed the Canadian state.

The argument outlined in the federal factum and elaborated by Rowell in a two-day lecture was that Ottawa possessed both the treaty-making and treaty-implementing power under section 132 or, on the precedents of *Radio* and *Aeronautics*, under the residual power.[25] As a result of the Balfour Declaration and the Statute of Westminister, Canada had achieved a new status within the empire and internationally. On the authority of *British Coal*, Canada had 'capacity under the *British North America Act* to accept the new status and to accept all the powers incident thereto,' among which was the prerogative power of making treaties which had been transferred from the king's ministers in Britain to those in Canada.

Sankey's prismatic colours and living-tree metaphors, and the national dimension doctrine, were cited in support of the argument that the subject matter of the conventions had now become matters of national and international importance and fell within federal authority to legislate for the peace, order, and good government of Canada. Rowell further argued, but without enthusiasm, that the acts were, in pith and substance, regulations of trade and commerce to equalize the conduct of national and international trade.[26] He also stepped beyond statutory boundaries to plead with the court to open its eyes and witness the economic and political upheaval around the world. Unless conditions in Canada were 'very radically improved,' he warned, 'and young men and women coming out of colleges and schools can find an opportunity to work, we shall in this country face conditions of social unrest and upheaval.' The court was not justified 'in construing the Act on the basis of the social and economic conditions of 1867; if we did it would be unworkable. The Act must be capable of construction consonant with the changing conditions of the time, and I respectfully submit, that it is so capable.'[27]

But the court was more concerned about arguments based on the decisions in *Radio* and *Aeronautics* than with the threat to world order. Predictably, Rinfret asked Rowell whether Ottawa could secure control over the solemnization of marriage by negotiating an appropriate treaty, which drew the safe but evasive response, 'I think Your Lordships would even hold that it was a colourable use of the treaty-making power.'[28] Duff had difficulty with the argument that Dunedin's *dictum* – 'it comes to the same thing' – in *Radio* had somehow transferred the treaty power into the residual power. 'Section 132 is one thing, and the framers of the British North America Act dealt with international obligations under section 132,' he interjected. 'One understands that, and there it is; but to treat the residuary powers as giving you virtually the same authority as you have under section 132, so that you can override anything in 92, is going pretty far ... I quite sympathize with the apprehensions of the provinces to that interpretation of the residuary clause ... Of course we are bound by the decisions.'[29] Moments later, Duff admitted that 'I am trying to get the meaning of the judgement. It is certainly a novel idea of the residuary clause.'[30]

When Rowell and Duff were disagreeing over the dimensions doctrine, with Rowell arguing that in *Aeronautics* Sankey had placed some matters of property and civil rights in the residual clause, Duff replied testily: 'I was not thinking of the Aeronautics case, because I must frankly admit I do not follow it ... I understand that you are relying on the Aeronautics case, and there is something there, I confess, the scope of which I do not understand.'[31] When Rowell urged the court to follow Sankey's advice and get back to the original words and purposes of the BNA Act, Duff revealed his dilemma. 'It is a very simple matter for the Judicial Committee to say that. But does that mean that we are to pay no attention to the decisions, or that we are not bound by the clear effect of the decisions? What is the effect of that opinion so far as we are concerned?'[32]

The provinces were united in opposition to finding the legislation valid under the treaty power. Quebec and New Brunswick (which adopted the Quebec position on all cases) opposed validity on any grounds. However, Saskatchewan was interested in determining whether the Dominion or the provinces had the authority to enact the legislation. British Columbia maintained that the 1925 decision was correct, and opposed validity not on the merits of the legislation 'but only on the attempt of the Dominion to invade the domain of provincial jurisdiction.'[33]

The Mitch Hepburn government in Ontario supported the legislation but denied that either the *Radio* or *Aeronautics* decisions gave the federal government jurisdiction under the treaty power. Moreover, on the precedent of *Snider*, the subject matter fell within property and civil rights. Therefore, the only 'constitutional capacity' remaining, the province argued, was the power to make laws for the peace, order, and good government of Canada. But the language and content of that broad residual power had been interfered with by judicial interpretation until it was finally 'whittled down' by Haldane to an emergency power.

However, Sankey's references in *Aeronautics* to 'high functions and almost sovereign powers' and 'national interest and importance' and 'such dimensions as to affect the body politic of the Dominion,' the Ontario factum contended, 'showed in order to end 'wasteful or demoralizing competition' 'a disposition on the part of the Privy Council to go back to the original view as to the jurisdiction of Parliament under peace, order and good government.' With the adoption of the Sankey interpretation, justification did not depend on war or famine but on determining 'a matter to be one of national interest and importance, a matter of common importance to all the provinces, and something that has attained such dimensions as to affect the body politic of the Dominion, in which uniformity of legislation is desirable.' On those grounds, Ontario contended that the legislation was 'probably' valid under the power conferred to make laws for the peace, order, and good government of Canada.[34]

In decision, Duff overcame his concern about provincial autonomy and his reservations about *Radio* and *Aeronautics*. Writing for Kerwin and Davis, he stated that Dunedin's decision settled the location of the treaty power:

It seems hardly open to dispute that their Lordships intended to lay down that international obligations, which are strictly treaty obligations within the scope of s. 132, as well as obligations under conventions between governments not falling within s. 132, are matters which, as subject of legislation, cannot fall within s. 92 and, therefore must fall within s. 91; and since they do not fall within any of the enumerated powers of section 91, they are within the ambit of the Dominion power to make laws for the peace, order and good government of Canada.[35]

Moreover, Canada had achieved equality of status within the commonwealth and recognition as an 'international unit' with 'a status enabling her to enter into, on her own behalf, international arrangements, and to incur obligations under such arrangements.'[36] Although the 'crystallization of constitutional usage into a rule of constitutional law to which the Courts will give effect' was usually a slow process, Duff observed, the pace of change since the war had accelerated, and the right of Canada to enter into such arrangements 'must be recognized by the Courts as having the force of law.'[37]

Although their judgments varied in detail, the position of Rinfret, Canon, and Crocket was best stated by Canon:

It is not admissible that the Parliament and Government of Canada could appropriate these powers, exclusively reserved to the provinces, by the simple process of ratifying a labour convention ... The framers of our constitution, and the Privy Council by their recent judgements in the *Radio* and *Aeronautics* cases never intended to plant in its bosom the seeds of its own destruction. If such interference with provincial rights by way of international agreement is admitted as *intra vires* of the central government, we may as well say that we have in Canada a confederation in name, but a legislative union in fact. Uniformity is not the spirit of our constitution. We have not a single community in this country. We have nine commonwealths, several different communities. This is in fact embodied in the law.[38]

It was certainly the law as shaped by Watson and Haldane.

The *Labour Conventions* argument over, the court turned to the Employment and Social Insurance Act where Louis St Laurent relied almost entirely on the Watson/Atkinson/Tomlin national dimensions doctrine. Unemployment, of which the court could take judicial notice, was of such an extent and threat to the social order that it had become 'unquestionably of national interest and importance' and attained such dimensions as to fall within the residual power. Aware that his argument would encounter Haldane's emergency-power doctrine, St Laurent, though obviously uncomfortable cast as an economist, emphasized that unemployment was cyclical and structural, national and international, and while the situation was 'acute' at the moment, 'it is not a situation that we can look upon as a purely temporary situation.'[39]
    Rinfret immediately led the attack on St Laurent's argument:

Rinfret: I am trying to ascertain how the theory works out – whether the fact of its being a matter of national concern is the ground of your jurisdiction?
    St. Laurent: Yes, My Lord.
    Rinfret: Well how long does the jurisdiction last?
    St. Laurent: According to what was stated by Lord Haldane in the Fort Frances case, whenever it happens that the situation no longer exists –
    Duff: But that is the emergency power.
    St. Laurent: Yes.
    Duff: I understood you were not putting it on that ground.

St. Laurent: Not on the ground of its being a temporary emergency, but on the ground of –
Rinfret: So that the fact that at the moment a situation of that kind exists will transfer that jurisdiction to you for all time.
St. Laurent: Not necessarily ...
Rinfret: Then it must be temporary legislation; it cannot be permanent.

The chief justice attempted to assist the flailing St Laurent: 'I should have thought that the effect of what you are saying was that you were legislating to mitigate the condition – to mitigate the evils of the present situation and to prevent a recurrence of them.' Counsel was grateful. But Rinfret was not accommodating: 'If you began passing preventive legislation to meet a national crisis, you might also assume jurisdiction over everything contained in 92.'[40]

St Laurent was obviously unable to rescue the national dimensions doctrine from Haldane's grasp, and although Duff was helpful on the point, it was unlikely – given his own view of the residual power (which he was to elaborate in his decision on *Natural Products Marketing*) – that he could have endorsed St Laurent's argument. Yet, from the beginning, he appeared either to have found, or was trying to find, a way to uphold the act, and in the end he was to lead St Laurent towards the conclusion he had reached.

The factum stated that the contributions to the fund were taxes within section 91(3) but did not suggest that the act was valid on that ground. Though in argument St Laurent repeated that it was a valid tax, he added that 'we cannot get through the imposition of taxes jurisdiction over a subject matter that we should not otherwise have jurisdiction over.' Almost in passing, Duff observed, 'I do not suppose the courts have any control over the disposition which the Parliament of Canada may choose to make of public moneys.'[41]

As St Laurent laboured through his dimensions argument for the second day, Duff commented, 'I am wondering how far you have to go for this particular legislation. A good deal of it, at all events, rests upon the control by the Dominion over its own property ... And the Dominion's power of taxation.' Perhaps sensing Duff's direction, Rinfret suggested that 'you are taxing merely for the purpose of putting your scheme into operation, and not for anything else ... the taxation in this Act is exclusively ancillary to the whole scheme.' Duff disagreed. 'Is it exclusively ancillary? What is the main point of the whole scheme? It is paying money, is it not?'[42]

At last, St Laurent understood and accepted Duff's direction. Beginning his rebuttal the next day, he emphasized that his third central argument was that the act really amounted to nothing more 'than the raising of money by a mode of taxation and the appropriation of money thus raised for the purpose deemed by Parliament to be of public interest.' When Rinfret immediately observed that it was a new argument, St Laurent replied, 'I must confess I did not realize the importance it might have in connection with this legislation, until later.' Duff quickly came to his assistance: 'As I said Saturday, so far as we are concerned after our experience in the other case, I think we must feel that we have some responsibility to consider the question from all points of view whether presented in argument or not.'[43]

It was precisely on his own grounds – the authority to tax and to spend its assets – that Duff (with Davis concurring) upheld the validity of the act. Other reasons failing, wrote Rinfret for the majority, there remained the argument 'only faintly advanced by counsel' though accepted by 'my Lord the Chief Justice' that the act could be supported under federal powers to tax and spend. However, he wrote, the federal government could not thereby 'indirectly accomplish the ends sought for in this legislation. If it were otherwise, the Dominion Parliament, under colour of the taxing power, would be permitted to invade almost any of the fields exclusively reserved by the Constitution to the legislatures in each province.'[44]

The argument on the Natural Products Marketing Act was surprisingly brief. The measure was an ingenious administrative and legislative attempt to escape from the narrow construction that Watson and Haldane had placed on Smith's *obiter* in *Parsons* regarding the possible scope of the trade and commerce power. As Haldane had boasted during the argument in *Great West Saddlery,* every attempt to have federal legislation upheld as a regulation of trade and commerce had been more than matched by the efforts of the Judicial Committee to prevent it.[45] Following precedent, Canadian courts in the post-war years had, sometimes reluctantly, struck down federal attempts to regulate the marketing of natural products, even when 80 per cent of the product was for the international market, and at the same time had found provincial attempts an unconstitutional interference with trade and commerce.[46]

The Natural Products Marketing Act of 1934 (amended in 1935 to include forestry products) attempted to locate a boundary between local (property and civil rights) and extra-provincial (trade and commerce) marketing regulation. The Dominion Marketing Board was given a broad authority to regulate the flow of products to market, including withholding products from market and discouraging production or price-fixing. The constitutional incapacity of the federal government was to be overcome by the establishment of local or provincial producers boards under the laws of the province, which could exercise any or all of the powers of the Dominion board, or the boards could act conjointly. Moreover, no marketing scheme could be approved unless 'the principal market for the natural product is outside the province of production' or 'some part of the product may be exported.'[47] Finally, in an obvious attempt to salvage something, section 26 provided that 'if it be found that Parliament has exceeded its powers in the enactment of one or more of the provisions, none of the other or remaining provisions of the Act shall therefore be held to be inoperative or *ultra vires*.' Enabling legislation was passed by all the provinces, and when the act went to court there were twenty-two marketing schemes in operation.[48]

A sense of futility on St Laurent's part and of general indifference on the bench pervaded the shortest argument on all the New Deal cases. The federal factum adopted a shotgun approach – perhaps a 'Hail Mary' would be a better metaphor – arguing validity under the residual clause, trade and commerce, taxation, agriculture and fisheries, statistics, and the criminal law. The burden of St Laurent's somewhat convoluted pleading was that the act 'is in its broad features, in pith and substance, regulation with respect to foreign and interprovincial trade; and that in its effects upon other trade than foreign and interprovincial it is a general regulation, though to carry out the general policy it is necessary in an ancillary fashion to get down to minute regulations of individual trades; but the minute regulations of individual trades are merely ancillary provisions ...' At which point, before calling a luncheon break, Duff interjected: 'And you say that because it is pursuant to a general policy which applies to all commodities, or all within a very comprehensive definition at all events, it is a regulation of general trade, or a general regulation of trade – is that the way you put it?'[49]

After lunch St Laurent countered by returning to the 'Parsons case – they all go back to the Parsons case' – which had (in what later he called the second branch of Parsons) 'established the principle that there is a field of general regulation of trade and commerce outside of its international or inter-provincial aspect, which is within the federal jurisdiction under that head of section 91.' He conceded that the 'decisions so far have not determined with any degree of precision what those general regulations may be; but it is our submission that at least they go to the length of permitting the Dominion legislature, the Dominion Parliament, to determine the general trade policy of the country.'[50]

St Laurent did not justify the act under the residual clause, other than to reiterate that if it was 'in relation to something which is not within provincial jurisdiction, then I think the conclusion clear that it would be within the jurisdiction of parliament.'[51] Nor did he emphasize the obvious provincial interest, other than to insert the agreements in an appendix to the factum 'merely to show that there was all over Canada a situation necessary to be dealt with, and that Parliament attempted to deal with it to the extent that it has jurisdiction to do so. It was not attempting to take something away from the Provinces; it was merely attempting to deal with what was looked upon as an evil, and to deal with it to the extent that federal jurisdiction had to be exercised in order that it might be dealt with effectively.'[52]

The weight of precedent was much too heavy to be lifted by St Laurent's brief and weak advocacy. Indeed, Duff's uncritical summary and severe application of Judicial Committee doctrine on the trade and commerce and residual powers, with what Gerald LeDain described as his 'own touches and emphasis' added, was to earn him the highest commendations from Lord Atkin.[53] The enactment did not fall within the 'contemplation' of section 91(2) 'in the sense which has been ascribed to those words by decisions which are binding on us and which it is our duty to follow.' Watson's and Haldane's decisions proved beyond doubt, as Duff had stated in *King* v. *Eastern Terminal Elevator* in 1925, that 'Parliament cannot acquire jurisdiction to deal in the sweeping way in which these enactments operate with such local and provincial matters by legislating at the same time respecting external and interprovincial trade and committing the regulation of trade which is exclusively local and of traders and producers engaged in a trade which is exclusively local to the same authority.'[54] Duff acknowledged that, in *Parsons*, Smith had recognized the possibility of federal jurisdiction over 'general regulations of trade applicable to the whole Dominion,' but both then and since the Judicial Committee, followed by the Supreme Court, had decided that the natural scope of the words had to be limited in order to protect provincial autonomy.[55]

The only challenge facing Duff in rejecting the argument based on the residual clause was to combat the recent heterodoxy by explaining what Watson had really meant by his national concern doctrine. Watson's language, Duff wrote, was 'carefully guarded. He does not say that every matter which attains such dimensions as to effect the body politic of the Dominion falls thereby within the introductory matter of section 91. Rather, he said that "some matters" may attain such dimensions.' The application of the principle 'must always be a delicate and difficult task,' but 'Lord Watson's admonition to the courts to observe "great caution" in considering such matters is one that will not be lightly regarded by prudent judges.'[56]

Duff avoided the difficulty of countering the argument that *Aeronautics* had constituted 'a new point of departure' on the national concern doctrine by refusing to deal with it. 'One sentence is quoted from the judgement,' he wrote, 'which we will not reproduce because we do not think their Lordships can have intended in that sentence to promulgate a canon of construction for sections 91 and 92.' Duff distinguished the treaty aspects of *Radio* and *Aeronautics* from matters of domestic concern. Thus, the court was bound by Haldane's decision in *Snider*, *Commerce*, and *Fort Frances*, and 'consistently with these decisions, we do not see how it is possible that the argument now under discussion can receive effect.'[57]

Last to be heard was the argument on The Farmers' Creditors Arrangement Act of 1934. The bill had passed without division, but Premier Duff Pattullo of British Columbia secured an injunction from the provincial Supreme Court to prevent its operation in the province. Writing for the majority (Cannon dissenting), Duff held that the legislation fell generally within federal jurisdiction over bankruptcy and insolvency.[58]

Arguments ended on 5 February 1936. The decisions, written largely by the chief justice, were delivered on 17 June. By majority the court had upheld the Farm Credit Act and Section 498A of the Criminal Code. The Natural Products Marketing Act and the Trade and Industry Act had been unanimously struck down. However, on two critical cases the court had been sharply divided. The Employment and Social Insurance Act was held to be *ultra vires* by a 4–2 majority, and the court divided 3–3 over the Labour Conventions cases. Canon had opposed the entire package. Crockett had found only the Farm Credit Act acceptable, and Rinfret accepted only the Farm Credit Act and Section 498A as falling within federal jurisdiction. Given the nature of the divisions within the court it was not implausible to hope that the New Deal would fare better at the hands of the Judicial Committee.

Petitions for special leave to appeal to the Judicial Committee were filed at once, and arguments were set for the November–December term. The Canadian cast was smaller than at Ottawa. Attorneys general Roebuck and McNair represented Ontario and New Brunswick, and J.W. De B. Farris, British Columbia. Surprisingly, Quebec retained counsel only for the argument on the marketing act. Newton Rowell had been appointed chief justice of Ontario, and R.S. Robertson of Fasken, Robertson of Toronto joined Louis St Laurent and C.P. Plaxton as counsel for Canada. The arguments were much the same as before the Supreme Court, although counsel often shifted their emphasis to accommodate or counter the reasons and decisions of the Supreme Court.

Conjecturally, the fate of some of the New Deal appeals may have been the result of the intricacies of British politics and personalities. When the National Government was reconstructed in June 1935, Ramsay MacDonald could have insisted that his successor, Stanley Baldwin, continue Sankey as lord chancellor. However, MacDonald preferred that his son, Malcolm, receive a cabinet position, and Baldwin was free to appoint Viscount Hailsham, to whom he was politically indebted, who had been lord chancellor in 1928–9. After the cabinet was sworn in, Malcolm wrote to Sankey, 'It was very charming of you at Buckingham Palace on Friday to come and wish me well in the new cabinet for I know that you must be feeling that I am only in it because you are out of it.'[59] Sankey made no attempt to disguise his bitterness. As he wrote to Reading, the lord chief justice: 'Next let me thank you for your kind letter which was very welcome and a real help at a time of disappointment and disillusionment. I did not retire from the Lord-Chancellorship, quite the contrary. I was anxious to continue and had actually prepared my speech on the India Bill ... However, politicians are queer things, and devoid of gratitude, however hard you work.'[60] It was not surprising, as Heuston commented, that Sankey did 'not seem to have felt entirely bound by the conventional obligation of an ex-Lord Chancellor to earn his pension by sitting judicially when requested to do so.'[61] He did accede to one request from Hailsham to sit in a case in the House of Lords, but that was the last until 1940.

Hailsham, a devout believer 'as to the paramount importance of retaining the appeal to the Privy Council,' was well aware of the importance of the Canadian appeals.[62] In his first term as lord chancellor he had presided on all the Canadian appeals and intended to do so in his second, but a serious stroke in the fall of 1936 forced him to relinquish most of his official duties. With the appeals imminent, Lord Atkin informed Sir Claud Schuster, the permanent secretary, that he and the other law lords believed that the composition of the board would not 'command sufficient authority in the Dominions.' Hailsham immediately explained to Atkin that he had asked Schuster 'to write to Sankey, as the only available ex-Lord Chancellor, to explain the position and ask him if he would be good enough to take my place as President of the Board. Unfortunately, Sankey was unable to see his way to render me that assistance.' Under the circumstances, he wrote Atkin, 'I had chosen what I thought was as strong a Board as it is possible to compose, in yourself, Macmillan and Roche and Wright, who had kindly agreed to come up from the Court of Appeal and Sidney Rowlatt, whose merits I regard as second to none.'

In the end, Hailsham agreed that Lord Thankerton, who had 'expressed a desire to sit and his recent visit to Canada renders him a very suitable member of the Board,' could replace Roche. But he refused to remove Rowlatt, a retired King's Bench judge, who was apparently the major reason for the discontent.[63] Though still concerned, Hailsham was pleased to report to Atkin during the hearings that 'no less than four of the Canadian Counsel' had 'expressed the greatest possible satisfaction at the Constitution of the Board ... I expect the decisions, when given, will carry conviction, which, after all, is the best test of the strength of the tribunal.'[64]

With Sankey's refusal to sit, Atkin presided, as the senior law lord. Sankey had authored three of the most 'progressive' decisions in the history of the Judicial Committee, and his judgment in *Aeronautics* had influenced the Supreme Court. Atkin had sat with Sankey on *Aeronautics* and *British Coal*, and he must have been unhappy with both decisions. His biographer reports that 'he felt strongly that the Statute of Westminister had been a retrograde step, and he believed as strongly in the value of a single final determination of justice as a bond of union and a focus of impartiality unaffected by local pressures.'[65]

Moreover, he was unsympathetic to the general thrust of the Canadian legislation. As a renowned commercial lawyer, wrote Robert Stevens, Atkin 'would allow no sentimentality to interfere with what he conceived as the best over all approach of the business community.'[66] His biographer confirmed that 'his natural disposition was against extensions of power in a central government which could interfere with free commerce and the sanctity of bargains.'[67] Atkin also saw issues in terms of clear and definite divisions between the executive, the legislature, and the judiciary. As he exclaimed in an Australian decision invalidating regulations that interfered with interstate trade: 'The Constitution is not to be mocked by substituting executive or legislative interference with freedom.'[68] An academic student of his commercial law jurisprudence concluded that his 'burning belief in the fundamental liberty of the subject is reminiscent of the preferred freedoms theory adopted by Black and Douglas JJ in the United States.'[69]

The portraits of Atkin as a judge drawn by his contemporaries were remarkably similar. All his colleagues agreed with Dunedin that he was 'obstinate if he has taken a view and quite unpersuadable.'[70] Lord Denning, who often appeared as counsel before becoming a law lord, reported that Atkin always read the documents before the argument 'and I am afraid that he had often made up his mind beforehand – so the argument of Counsel did not influence him very much.'[71] Lord Radcliffe found him 'intolerable as a presiding Law Lord because he had no wish that the case should be fully and fairly explored. He'd formed a view and he was going to use whatever odds he possessed ... to try and see that he succeeded.'[72] After the argument, Atkin had 'the reputation of being unyielding in his views in the private discussions which take place after the hearing among judges of appeal.'[73] His daughter recalled that his strength as an advocate 'lay in persuading the court to see it his way' and after he became a lord of appeal he 'would come home and say that he thought he had won his brothers over to his side or so-and-so is still not convinced but I think he may be tomorrow.'[74]

Atkin's view of the importance and the varied uses of precedent are illuminating as background to the New Deal decisions. Lord Wright found that Atkin was 'a firm believer in the strict adherence to precedents' in the House of Lords. Although he believed that 'that law was indeed dynamic not static, and should adapt itself to the needs of the present,' he insisted 'as paramount the need in our common law system for having settled rules, because he felt without them certainty would be impossible as long as judge-made law in its own way and within its limitations ranked along with statutory law as part of the legal system.'[75]

Atkin was also noted for the way he used precedent. His 'intellectual distinction lay in his ability to handle precedents and rules in such a way that he could lay down principles,' Robert Stevens wrote, and 'his facility with precedents was a source of wonder even to other law lords.'[76] Although Atkin was a master manipulator of precedent, R.W. Harding concluded that he

did not subvert the doctrine of precedent; he acknowledged that where authority was precise and clear, it was not part of his judicial duty to ignore it, however unsatisfactory it might seem to be. But he was prepared to look with great care to see whether an authority stood for precisely what was generally supposed. If the end were worth achieving (and whether it could be tested by common sense) and if there were a legitimate way through, Lord Atkin would get there, when some of his brethren might not, with the aid of his tremendously powerful flair for distinguishing.[77]

There was no doubt that Atkin was a masterful judicial craftsman, and a dominant, if not domineering, presence as a presiding law lord. His biographer agrees that 'his reputation for being unpersuadable was probably well-founded. If for only this reason, it seems safe to treat the point of view revealed by the 1937 Canadian decisions as his own.'[78] There can be little doubt that a court directed by Sankey would have reached conclusions somewhat different on some of the appeals. And it could be that Ivor Jennings, writing soon after the New Deal judgments were delivered, was right when he speculated that 'it is possible, though it cannot be proved, that the desire of Mr. Ramsay MacDonald in 1935 to safeguard his son's political career, and the anxiety of Lord Hailsham to leave the lower office for the more exalted and better paid position on the Woolsack – circumstances which sent Lord Sankey into retirement – invalidated a large part of the Canadian "New Deal."'[79]

Although it may have been a strong board, there was no one who in both ability and experience was Atkin's equal.[80] Macmillan had acted as counsel in Canadian appeals and sat on twelve, all of which favoured the federal government, including *Aeronautics* and *British Coal*, and wrote the judgment in two. Dunedin, a fellow Scot, described him as 'very able, but you cannot put your best into law if you have as many irons in the fire as he has.'[81] Thankerton had sat on eight Canadian appeals and delivered the judgment in three tax cases. Dunedin informed Hailsham in 1935 that Thankerton was 'doing well as to work and law, but making himself a veritable nuisance by excessive talking.'[82] Unlike his father, Watson's son was noted for his 'abundant caution' and he once stated in decision that, faced with public-policy issues, the functions of the court was 'to expound, and not expand, such policy' and 'be watchful not to be influenced by their view of what the principle of public policy, or its limits, should be.'[83]

The strongest among them was Lord Wright, who had been a distinguished commercial lawyer before becoming a judge and later, in 1932, a law lord. He had sat on three Canadian appeals, including *British Coal*, but had not written a judgment. 'I think very well of him,' commented Dunedin, 'but as, of course, I never sat with him, he being my successor, I am not in a position to form a final judgement.'[84] Legal historian Robert Stevens believed that he 'did not equal Atkin's genius as a common lawyer' and was not 'such a subtle master of the art of doctrinal manipulation or, to put it more conventionally, of legal craftsmanship.'[85] Lord Macmillan wrote that Wright's law was founded on 'practical reason and common sense' and that he 'fought against subtle distinctions, unnecessary functions and historical survivals which are a hindrance to the proper development of the law.'[86]

Among those historical survivals was a rigid adherence to *stare decisis* and linguistic literalism. 'It seems clear,' Wright wrote in 1942, 'that, generally speaking, a rigid method of precedents is inappropriate to the construction of a constitution, which has to be applied to changing conditions of national life and public policy.' Language, too, 'might be moulded to suit the needs of the time in some aspects not unlike public policy,' because 'an application of words which might be reasonable and just at the time, might be wrong and mischievous at another time.'[87]

Sir Sydney Rowlatt had rebelled against judicial salary cuts in 1931 and threatened to resign. However, reassured by the lord chancellor that he was 'still in the full vigour of mind and body,' Rowlatt agreed to stay on for a year. His reward in retirement was appointment as a privy councillor.[88] An observer at the New Deal appeals reported that he 'sat through the ... hearings in his overcoat making neither note nor comment.'[89]

Although the arguments before the board were heard in a different order, Atkin chose to deliver his decision in *Labour Conventions* first, 'both because of the exceptional importance of the issues involved and because it affords them an opportunity of stating their opinion upon some matters which arise in the other cases.'[90] In the six-day argument, federal counsel had admitted that under normal circumstances the matters dealt with would fall within property and civil rights, but that they were removed by the operation of section 132. 'If that not be so in any event the conventions were validly entered into and the obligation to perform was an obligation of the Dominion of Canada which it could properly discharge by enacting the legislation in question, really making an application of *In re The Regulation and Control of Radio Communication in Canada*. Reliance is also placed on the peace, order and good government aspect of the matter in the same way as it was in the *Radio* case.'[91]

Developing his argument, Robertson contended that the 1925 Supreme Court decision had been wrong, and that the performance of the obligations did not depend on whether the subject matter fell within section 92, for with 'the transference of the treaty-making to the Dominion executive, and the correlative power to legislate to carry out the obligations, nothing is taken from the Provinces.'[92] As Robertson continued with the argument – 'not inconsistent with decided cases' – Atkin cut him off and made his position clear: 'That is a very far-reaching doctrine: it means that Canada could make an agreement with any State which would seriously affect Provincial rights.'[93]

Although Ontario opposed the treaty argument, Roebuck explained again that Ontario 'looks on the legislation as good, and believes that it is in the public interest, but they are unfortunate in being called upon to fight a bad principle in connection with a good measure. The Acts are of national importance, and the subject has attained such proportions as to affect the body politic.'[94] New Brunswick and British Columbia opposed the legislation on all grounds, Farris even arguing that, if the acts were upheld as laws for the peace, order, and good government of Canada, 'it will be even more fatal, even more an invasion of provincial rights than if upheld under the treaty-making powers.'[95]

Atkin's judgment was a contemptuous dismissal of the federal argument and a hymn of praise to provincial autonomy. The conventions were not empire treaties and section 132 was not at issue. He repudiated Dunedin's reasoning in *Radio* that, as a result of Canada's emergence as an international 'juristic person' the treaty power in 132 was transferred to the residual clause: 'While it is true, as was pointed out in the *Radio* case, that it was not contemplated in 1867 that the Dominion would possess treaty-making powers, it is impossible to strain the section so as to cover the uncontemplated event.'[96]

Astonishingly, although Duff (for Kerwin and Davis) had concluded that 'it follows from what has been said that this treaty obligation is an obligation within s. 132'[97] and 'the point was argued before them [the Judicial Committee] in opening and again in reply,'[98] Atkin wrote: 'It appears that all the members of the Supreme Court rejected the contention based on s. 132, and their Lordships are in full agreement with them.'[99] As Robertson wrote home, with respectful understatement, it was 'somewhat difficult to understand this lapse on the part of their Lordships.'[100]

All that remained was to deal with sections 91 and 92 and the decisions in *Aeronautics* and *Radio* which had led Duff to reverse his 1925 decision. Atkin had little difficulty with the precedents. Sankey's decision in *Aeronautics*, on which Atkin had sat, was distinguished because it applied to section 132 and, 'but for a remark at the end of the judgement, which in view of the stated ground of the decision was clearly obiter, the case could not be said to be an authority on the matter now under discussion.'[101] The *Radio* decision, Atkin admitted, 'appears to present more difficulty.' But close reading of the decision revealed to him that the 'true ground of the decision' was not that the performance of treaty obligations fell within federal jurisdiction but that the subject matter of the conventions fell within the section 91 enumerations.[102]

Assuming Atkin had studied Dunedin's decision, he had obviously decided to accept one of the *ratio decedendi* and not the other. As W.R. Lederman concluded (and most would agree), Atkin's decision on the point 'is simply not a legitimate interpretation of Viscount Dunedin's reasons for his judgement. If one reads what Viscount Dunedin said, obviously he was resting his decision on both grounds.' And, Lederman continued, as Lord Simonds stated in the House of Lords, 'if a judge states two grounds for his judgement and bases his decision on both, neither of these grounds is a dictum.'[103]

In a few paragraphs, Atkin had dismissed as *obiter* Sankey's view that aerial navigation satisfied the national dimensions doctrine and, as *dictum* or simply wrong, Dunedin's view that although a convention was not a section 132 treaty 'it comes to the same thing.' In the result, therefore, although the federal executive now had power to make treaties, there was 'no existing constitutional ground for stretching the competence of the Dominion Parliament so that it becomes enlarged to keep pace with the enlarged functions of the Dominion Executive ... In other words, the Dominion cannot, merely by making promises to foreign countries, clothe itself with legislative authority inconsistent with the constitution which gave it birth.' This was not only good law but was consistent with Atkin's view that the distribution of legislative power was 'one of the most essential conditions, probably the most essential condition, in the inter-provincial compact to which the British

North America Act gives effect.' To accept the treaty argument, which could lead to federal legislation affecting civil rights in the province, 'would appear to undermine the constitutional safeguards of Provincial constitutional autonomy.'[104]

The argument, supported by Ontario, that the matter of the statutes was of such importance by the 1930s to satisfy Watson's national dimensions test gave Atkin the opportunity to revisit *Local Prohibition*. Having decided that Sankey's application of the doctrine was 'clearly obiter,' he found it necessary to explain the status of Watson's doctrine. 'It is interesting to note how often the words used by Lord Watson,' he emphasized, 'have unsuccessfully been used in attempts to support encroachments on Provincial legislative powers given by s. 92. They laid down no principle of constitutional law, and were cautious words intended to safeguard [against] possible eventualities which no one at the time had any interest or desire to define.' That branch of constitutional law, he continued, 'had been stated with such force and clarity' by Duff in the marketing decision, where Watson's doctrine was tied to Haldane's emergency doctrine, 'that their Lordships abstain from stating it afresh ... The few pages of the Chief Justice's decision will, it is to be hoped, form the locus classicus of the law on this point, and preclude further disputes.'[105] The Canadian government possessed the power to negotiate and sign treaties, but the enumerations in sections 91 and 92 were to determine their implementation and, some were to argue later, might even be extended to the power to negotiate.[106]

The appeal on unemployment insurance was the first argued and the second delivered. St Laurent relied on Duff's opinion in the Supreme Court, followed by a variety of renderings of the 'national interest and importance' and provincial-incapacity arguments. He countered Haldane's emergency doctrine by asserting that, if the object of the act was 'to abate an evil which is a threat to the body politic of the Dominion then, though it may affect subjects which are in the enumerated classes of s. 92, it is competently enacted. The danger to the body politic of the Dominion can arise from an internal situation just as it can from a foreign enemy or other external menace.'[107] The Depression was not an emergency as Haldane had used the word but was one that 'involved a new function of government which circumstances forced on the Government of Canada.' Roebuck added that the act was in the 'public interest' of the provinces and the Dominion and hoped that it would be 'possible within the four corners of the constitution' to find a way to uphold the legislation. The obvious corner was the residual power or the 'overriding power of s. 91 taking things of extraordinary importance out of the local and private provisions of s. 92.'[108]

In his decision, Atkin dismissed the 'special importance of unemployment insurance' argument by referring to his judgment on the dimension doctrine in *Labour Conventions*, and observing that all members of the Supreme Court agreed that it could not be supported upon 'the suggested existence of any special emergency.' All that remained was the rejection of Duff's opinion based on sections 1 and 3 of 91:

That the Dominion may impose taxation for the purpose of creating a fund for special purposes, and may apply that fund for making contributions in the public interest to individuals, corporations or public authorities, could not as a general proposition be denied ... But assuming that the Dominion has collected by means of taxation a fund, it by no means follows that any legislation which disposes of it is necessarily within Dominion competence. It may still be legislation affecting the classes of subjects enumerated in s. 92, and, if so, would be ultra vires ... To hold otherwise would afford the Dominion an easy passage into the Provincial domain.[109]

In pith and substance the act was not one dealing with a nation-wide economic and social problem of unprecedented magnitude, but an insurance act, like any other, affecting property and civil rights and thus *ultra vires*.

The appeal on the Marketing Act fared no better. The federal government had decided not to appeal, but British Columbia did. At the Judicial Committee, Farris emphasized that there were 'really practical reasons' why the act should be supported because it was designed to 'fit in along' with provincial marketing acts, and experience in British Columbia had shown that the 'same Board could function in two capacities – both as a Federal and Provincial Board.' If the act could not be upheld as a whole, Farris pleaded, it should be declared invalid only to the extent that it trenched on provincial jurisdiction.[110]

Atkin held that the legislation affected property and civil rights and rejected arguments based on trade and commerce and the residual clause, citing Duff's judgment as 'conclusive.' As the sections said to be severable were 'incidental and ancillary to the main legislation,' they too were invalid. The board appreciated that federal-provincial cooperation might be the only way to circumvent the jurisdictional divide, but unlike the act before them, 'the legislation will have to be very carefully framed, and will not be achieved by either party leaving its own sphere and encroaching upon that of the other.'[111]

The final three decisions were minor victories for the federal government. The board affirmed the decision of the Supreme Court in the appeal on section 498A of the Criminal Code. The governing precedent, Atkin stated, was his decision in *Proprietary Articles*. 'The only limitation on the plenary power of the Dominion to determine what shall or shall not be criminal,' he reiterated, 'is the condition that Parliament shall not in the guise of enacting criminal legislation in truth and substance encroach on any of the classes of subjects enumerated in s. 92. It is no objection that it does in fact affect them.'[112] Atkin gave Thankerton the relatively easy task of delivering the decision affirming the validity of the farm credit act as genuine legislation relating to bankruptcy and insolvency.[113]

Ontario and New Brunswick had appealed sections of the Trade and Industry Commission Act dealing with unfair trade practices which the Supreme Court had upheld, while Ottawa appealed the rejection of the national trademark. The board dismissed the provincial appeal but upheld the federal appeal on the trademark. 'There could hardly be a more appropriate form of the exercise' of the trade and commerce power 'than the creation and regulation of a uniform law of trade marks,' wrote Atkin. 'It is perfectly true, as is said by the Chief Justice, that the method adopted in s. 18 is to create a civil right of a novel character.' However, there was no reason 'why the legislative competence of the Dominion Parliament should not extend to the creation of juristic rights in novel fields, if they can be brought fairly within the classes of subjects confided to Parliament by the constitution.' In effect, he rejected, as he had in *Proprietary Articles*, Haldane's doctrine that the regulation of trade and commerce had no independent authority.[114]

When Atkin's decisions were delivered on 28 January 1937, the pendulum swung back with devastating velocity. The approach to judicial review, heralded in *Edwards* and reinforced in *Aeronautics* and *Radio*, was not only abandoned but explicitly repudiated. Sankey's and Dunedin's reasoning was either twisted and distinguished or rejected. Watson's national dimensions doctrine was returned to the prison of Haldane's emergency test. The federal power over trade and commerce power was blocked at the provincial border, and not even the desire of all governments to cooperate could survive Atkin's rigid and selective application of *stare decisis*. The explicit words 'in relation to' were again indelibly translated as 'affecting.' Canada's recently achieved international status, in terms of its capacity to perform international obligations, was forced into the crucible or labyrinth of the enumerations. After a brief moment of freedom, the residual power had again been swallowed up by its progeny.

In explicit and unmistakable language, as well as in reasoning and decision, the Judicial Committee had assumed its historic, but self-imposed, mission to protect and nourish provincial autonomy. With undoubted conscious intent, Atkin countered Sankey's 'living tree' metaphor with his own: 'While the ship of state now sails on larger ventures and into foreign waters she still retains the water-tight compartments which are an essential part of her original structure.'[115]

It is, perhaps, a mistake to attribute the change in direction to 'the Judicial Committee.' In reasoning and in decision, Atkin could not possibly have secured unanimity. Perhaps finding justification for breaking with the convention of apparent unanimity in Atkin's declared preference for multiple judgments,[116] Lord Wright later publicly stated that he disagreed with the decision in *Labour Conventions* and with Atkin's watertight compartments. In a tribute to Sir Lyman Duff, in which he endorsed Duff's opinion in the Supreme Court, Wright stated that the problem before the board 'was really settled, it seems to me, by the Privy Council in the *Aeronautics* and *Radio* cases ... by going back to the law of the constitution.'[117]

Atkin's watertight compartment 'theory' expressed a view of sections 91 and 92 that Wright was 'unable to reconcile with the general words' of the BNA Act. Atkin seemed to believe that the federal powers were restricted to the enumerations, Wright stated, and ignored 'the whole framework of the provisions, in particular the warning that the enumerated powers are without prejudice to the generality of the power of the Dominion to make laws for the peace, order and good governments of Canada.' That 'overall obligation and power' of the Dominion was 'cut into' only by the exceptions in section 92. 'Subject only to these, it covers any duty and corresponding power necessary for the purpose of good government, even though it is not enumerated in the British North America Act.' That power, Wright contended, was more correctly called 'overriding rather than residual' and the act 'more accurately uses the word generality by way of description.'[118]

It would also have been difficult for Macmillan, who had sat with Sankey on *Aeronautics*, to accept Atkin's reasons or decision in *Labour Conventions*. Thankerton, on the other hand, apparently 'made it clear' during the argument that 'he was in complete accord with Lord Atkin's views.'[119] If Robert Stevens is right that 'most believe the swing vote was that of Rowlatt,' the intriguing possibility lingers that Sankey's refusal to preside allowed Atkin to reverse the swing of the judicial pendulum and embed his watertight compartment metaphor in Canadian constitutional jurisprudence.[120]

Lord Atkin lived long enough to know that his decisions had provoked a reaction in Canada that would lead to the abolition of appeals. However, although it would have been uncharacteristic, he may have taken comfort in Professor A. Berriedale Keith's patronizing lecture to Canadians that it was only the 'unfortunate' decision in *Edwards* and the 'unguarded phraseology' in *Aeronautics* and *Radio* that had led the naively optimistic colonials into believing that the Judicial Committee, without reversing its entire body of jurisprudence, could uphold the heart of the Bennett New Deal.[121] This lecture did not sit well with Keith's academic colleagues in Canada, many of whom, as the editor of the *Fortnightly Law Journal* sarcastically commented, had 'always pined for a method of construction of the B.N.A. Act unknown to practical jurists.'[122] The substance of the decisions may have been contentious, but the explicit finality in the judgments that Canada was not the master but the prisoner of a judicially determined seventy-year-old constitution was not.

The decisions forged an alliance between academic legal realists, who believed that because of judicial review the law had lost touch with reality, and the nationalists, who agreed that Canada needed a constitution reflecting the needs of the mid-twentieth century and that it was unseemly that the country should be governed by a constitution judicially determined by an alien court. The time had come to 'abandon tinkering with or twisting the British North America Act,' wrote W.P.M. Kennedy, one of the naively optimistic academics, and face the facts:

The federal 'general power' is gone with the wind. It can be relied upon at best when the nation is intoxicated with alcohol, at worst when the nation is intoxicated with war; but in times of sober poverty, sober financial chaos, sober unemployment, sober exploitation, it cannot be used, for these, though in fact national in the totality of their incidents, must not be allowed to leave their water-tight compartments; the social line must not obliterate the legal lines of jurisdiction – at least this is the law, and it killeth.

The constitution had to be rewritten and appeals to the Judicial Committee abolished.[123]

In the House of Commons, Charles Cahan led the demand for abolition. A venerable Tory MP from Montreal, he charged that Canadian sovereignty, in fact resided in the Judicial Committee, whose members 'although personally ignorant' of Canada dared substitute their 'political judgements' and their 'personal preferences' for the enactments of parliament. Moreover, they were guilty of grossly and deliberately misinterpreting the federal constitution. No less an authority than Lord Haldane had boasted that Watson had 'expounded and established the real constitution of Canada' and he had followed in Watson's 'footsteps.' In the end, the committee had 'so amended and redrafted the original constitution and so clothed it in fantastic conceptions of their own, that it bears the grotesque features of a jack-o'-lantern which now serves to evoke derisive comment and criticism.'[124]

Ernest Lapointe, the minister of justice, was defensive about the quality of the Judicial Committee's jurisprudence, but he agreed that the appeal practice did not fit easily with Canada's national status. He was confident that Canada possessed the power to abolish appeals, but believed that time was needed for public discussion and investigation 'and this is not to suggest procrastination – a favourite word on many occasions – before we take a step which would be very important.'[125] However, when Cahan introduced a bill in 1939 to abolish all appeals, Lapointe agreed with the 'substance and form' of the bill and referred its constitutionality to the Supreme Court.[126]

The Supreme Court decision was given in January 1940. Duff, Rinfret, Kerwin, and Albert Hudson found the abolition of all appeals constitutional. The Statute of Westminster had removed the obstacle, Duff stated, and 'there is now full authority under the powers of Parliament in relation to the peace, order and good government of Canada in respect of the objects within the purview of section 101 to enact the Bill in question.' Crocket found abolition completely unconstitutional as a rupture of the relationship of the provinces to the crown and an interference with the provincial administration of justice. Davis believed that the bill would be *intra vires* if amended to allow appeals from provincial courts on matters within provincial jurisdiction. He admitted that there 'may be some difficulty at times in working out a division of legislative authority in appeals in civil cases but that is inherent in the practical working out of any federal system.'[127]

The Canadian response was not welcome at the centre of the empire, where every effort was made to keep the Canadian judiciary within the imperial embrace. Informing a friend that Cahan had been defeated in the 1940 election, Sir Claud Schuster, permanent secretary in the lord chancellor's office, wrote, 'I hope I am not committing an indiscretion when I say that the news gave me a considerable amount of pleasure.'[128] In fact, until the Judicial Committee itself sealed the fate of appeals in 1947, the lord chancellor's office and other law lords seriously toyed with schemes to retain imperial supremacy. Cahan's attack in 1938 prompted Lord Chancellor Maugham to propose appointing more Canadians to the Judicial Committee, a strategy Lord Stanley thought would look bad under the immediate circumstances.[129] Lord Simon, the wartime lord chancellor, favoured a peripatetic court that would hear Canadian appeals in Ottawa and was encouraged by Vincent Massey, the high commissioner. 'The more I thought about this imaginative idea, the more I liked it,' Massey wrote, for 'it would remove most of the serious objections' in Canada.[130] Churchill found the idea 'an attractive one' but did not feel that the winter of 1944 was a 'suitable' time 'to raise a question of this kind.'[131]

The most determined was Lord Jowitt, who in 1945 became lord chancellor in the Labour government. As lord chancellor in the earlier Labour government, he had opposed the abolition of appeals from Ireland, and now he looked for ways to dissuade the Canadians.[132] 'I always like to think that one of the ties which binds Canada to us is the Privy Council appeal,' he wrote to Lord Addison, the commonwealth secretary. 'Of course there are those in Canada who may think this is rather derogatory ... Suppose we were to send a really strong court to Canada to sit in Ottawa, might it not appeal to the Canadian imagination.'[133] Goddard, the lord chief justice, encouraged Jowitt. After a visit to Canada late in 1945, he reported that Canadian opinion was 'by no means unanimously in favour of abolition' and that several people had told him that if the Judicial Committee were to sit in Ottawa, 'abolition would be dead.'[134]

Jowitt proposed the idea to Louis St Laurent, now minister of justice in Mackenzie King's cabinet, during his visit to London in January 1946; however, he was disappointed to find that St Laurent was 'most interested and most helpful but expressed the very clear view that as a matter of timing now was not the time to raise the question.' St Laurent explained that the appeal to the Judicial Committee 'which will be heard this summer might well result in a decision that Canada is perfectly free to abolish the right of appeal to the Privy Council by Canadian legislation. That being so, a proposal along the lines suggested, would, if made to the Dominion now, give the impression that it was a last minute effort by the UK to retain some sort of superior right.'[135]

The Judicial Committee heard the appeal for six days in October 1946. In view of what he termed the 'transcendent constitutional importance' of the issue, Jowitt assembled the most prestigious board ever to sit on a Canadian appeal, at least a majority of whom had hoped that the day might never come.[136] Ontario was joined in the appeal by British Columbia, New Brunswick, and Quebec. The provinces argued that abolition was a violation of their jurisdiction over the administration of justice and of their traditional right to bring civil appeals to the Judicial Committee. They also contended that abolition was an alteration in the terms of the BNA Act, whereas section 7 of the Statute of Westminister – 'a pact with the provinces,' as Ontario put it – had expressly stated that the statute should not be 'deemed to apply' to any amendment or alteration of the act.[137] On the contrary, after 1931, the power to abolish both prerogative appeals and appeals as of right from the provincial courts rested with the provinces. Finally, they denied the existence of federal jurisdiction in sections 91 or 101 to prevent appeals from provincial courts.

Federal counsel denied provincial capacity under 92(14), which, like all provincial jurisdiction, was bounded by the territorial limits of the province, and maintained that the Supreme Court was correct in finding that jurisdiction lay with section 101 to establish an 'ultimate' court of appeal whose decisions would be binding on all provincial courts. Even if the provinces did possess some legislative authority, 'the power of the Dominion Parliament under "peace, order and good government" to legislate in relation to matters of national concern would enable Parliament to enact this legislation. It may so provide as being a proper provision for the achievement of full national sovereignty and autonomy in Canada.'[138]

The Judicial Committee endorsed the federal argument and Duff's reasoning. After the Statute of Westminster had removed any remaining 'restriction or fetter,' wrote Jowitt, Ottawa had jurisdiction to abolish appeals.[139] He rejected the provincial contention that sections 91 and 92 should be used as a template for appeals, as Davis had decided; a 'strange result would follow' from this because the 'judicial and legislative spheres are not coterminous.'[140] In any case, it was unnecessary to 'embark on a nice discrimination' of those sections because the authority lay in section 101 to establish a final and exclusive court of appeal. Moreover, it was 'a prime element in the self-government of the Dominion, that it should be able to secure through its own courts of justice that the law should be one and the same for all its citizens.'[141] Adopting a 'somewhat wider point of view,' as had Lord Sankey, Jowitt declared that it is 'irrelevant that the question is one that might have seemed unreal at the date of the British North America Act. To such an organic statute the flexible interpretation must be given which changing circumstances require, and it would be alien to the spirit, with which the preamble to the Statute of Westminister is instinct, to concede anything less than the widest amplitude of power to the Dominion legislature under s. 101 of the Act.'[142]

The Judicial Committee had given Ottawa the authority, but Mackenzie King was reluctant to act. Combined with proposals for a Canadian governor general and talk of a Canadian flag, King was afraid that abolition would arouse pro-British and anti-French sentiment and jeopardize Louis St Laurent's anticipated coronation as his successor. Combined with the proposal to give the federal government power to amend the constitution in areas within its jurisdiction, it had aroused the suspicion of the provinces, particularly George Drew of Ontario, Maurice Duplessis of Quebec, and Angus L. Macdonald of Nova Scotia. St Laurent and the Quebec caucus supported abolition except for constitutional appeals, as did Paul Martin and some other members of the cabinet.[143] A suggestion that provincial opposition might be mollified by periodic appointments of provincial judges to the Supreme Court was apparently scotched by Duff, who said that a court was like a cabinet where solidarity was desirable, while judges from different provinces 'brought in for an occasion would regard themselves as having to follow special lines.'[144]

With the cabinet unable to reach a consensus, King decided on delay. He warned cabinet that, with a number of provincial elections approaching, as well as a Liberal convention and a federal election, abolition would be attacked as an illustration of how 'Ottawa is trying to get everything in its own hands here; take away fair play from the provinces and concentrate it in a court in Ottawa under their influence.'[145] However, the convention that elected St Laurent also passed a resolution in support of abolition, and following the government's re-election in June 1949 the legislation was passed and given royal assent on 10 December 1949. The statute provided that the Supreme Court 'shall have, hold and exercise ultimate civil and criminal jurisdiction in Canada' and that its decisions 'shall, in all cases, be final and conclusive.'[146]

After the die had been cast in 1949, the Judicial Committee continued to hear appeals already in the judicial pipeline, the last in 1954. Although there were some interesting departures from earlier doctrines and a willingness to loosen the rules of statutory interpretation and take a broader view, the committee made no obvious attempt to respond to the realist-nationalist criticisms of its jurisprudence. Indeed, the committee may even have relished reversing some judgments of the newly emancipated court.

The Judicial Committee remained unequivocal in the protection of federal jurisdiction over banking and interest, finding the entire package of Alberta's banking and debt-adjustment legislation unconstitutional.[147] In the 1939 bank-taxation case, Viscount Maugham asserted the board's right to take 'judicial notice' of legislative history and political context to determine the effect or objectives of the legislation. The act to 'regulate and control banks and banking' was obviously an attempt to prevent the banks from interfering in the attempt to create 'a new economic era in the Province' and was *ultra vires*. Maugham also laid to rest the argument based on *Bank of Toronto v. Lambe* [1887] that the possibility of abuse of power should not lead to a finding of *ultra vires*, asserting that it had never been laid down by the Judicial Committee that 'if such a use was attempted to be made of the provincial power as materially to interfere with the Dominion power, the action of the province would be intra vires.'[148]

It was also Maugham who, in the 1943 decision finding Alberta's Debt Adjustment *Act* unconstitutional, rediscovered the powerful declaratory clause as the source of the exclusivity of the federal enumerations and declared that those words 'must be given their natural effect.' (The deeming clause was 'inserted from abundant caution' but was to the same effect.) Moreover, he continued, clarifying the unoccupied-field doctrine and laying Watson's views to rest, once an act was to be found beyond provincial competence, 'it is immaterial whether the Dominion has or has not dealt with the subject by legislation, or to use the other well-known words, whether that legislative field has been or has not been occupied by the legislation of the Dominion Parliament ... and the contention that, unless and until the Dominion Parliament legislates on any such matter, the provinces are competent to legislate is, therefore, unsound.'[149]

In other less familiar areas, the Judicial Committee upheld federal jurisdiction. The Supreme Court had divided 3–3 on the validity of federal orders-in-council of 1945 under the National Emergency Transition Powers Act 1945 (NEPTA) regarding the deportation of Japanese whether naturalized or natural-born. On appeal, Lord Wright found in *Fort Frances* precedent for the federal government's authority to suspend provincial jurisdiction over property and civil rights to deal with an emergency, adding that the committee was not concerned about wisdom or effectiveness.[150]

The committee also upheld the expropriation of grains under the same statute as the federal government attempted to control post-war profiteering. In 1950 the Supreme Court, by majority, found that expropriation was not specifically authorized by the NEPTA. At the Judicial Committee, Lord Radcliffe declared that the best way of approaching the interpretation of the act 'was to endeavour to appreciate the general object that it serves to give its words their natural meaning in the light of that object.' Having done so, the committee found that expropriation 'would be a likely incident' of the realization of powers under the act.[151]

Undoubtedly the decision with the greatest potential for an expansion of federal jurisdiction, if followed in the Supreme Court, was Viscount Simon's wide-ranging judgment of 1946 upholding the 1878 Canada Temperance Act (consolidated in 1927). At issue was the decision and reasoning in *Russell v. The Queen* and Haldane's explanation in *Snider*. The New Brunswick Supreme Court found that, since Haldane's emergency justification had passed, the temperance act was no longer valid.[152] In 1939 the Ontario government referred the question to the Court of Appeal with the argument that provincial jurisdiction 'should not be ousted by a fifty year old interpretation of the B.N.A. Act, especially as Ontario and the Dominion were unrepresented by counsel, and the decision was based on an assumed condition which no longer exists.' The Court of Appeal held that the temperance act was valid. W.R. Riddell reflected the views of the majority when he stated, 'We are not at liberty to disregard what the Judicial Committee has declared in a judgement to be law. And I conceive it makes no difference on what ground they proceeded – they gave an authoritative statement of what the law is.'[153]

At the Judicial Committee, the appellants argued that 'the time has come ... for the Board to review *Russell v. The Queen* ... and declare it not a good decision; it has been losing strength.' Aimé Geoffrion replied for the federal government that it 'is not a question of overruling *Russell's* case, but of reversing it, and if that is to be done the whole matter should be reopened. There is the same controversy about "trade and commerce" and so on; in other words, the slate must be wiped clean and a start made again to build a new jurisdiction on the constitution.'[154]

Ironically, Viscount Simon had been counsel in *Snider* when, during the argument, it was agreed that *Russell* had not been decided on the grounds of an emergency. After citing Haldane's explanation in *Snider*, he observed that there was 'nothing in the judgement of the Board in 1882 which suggests that it proceeded on the grounds of an emergency; there was certainly no evidence before the Board that one existed.' Moreover, nowhere in the BNA act was Parliament given the power 'to legislate in matters which are properly to be regarded as exclusively within the competence of the provincial legislatures merely because of the existence of an emergency.'[155]

In their lordship's opinion, the true test must be found in the real subject matter of the legislation: 'If it is such that it goes beyond local or provincial concern or interests and must from its inherent nature be the concern of the Dominion as a whole (as, for example, in the *Aeronautics* case and the *Radio* case) then it will fall within the competence of the Dominion Parliament as a matter affecting the peace, order and good government of Canada, though it may in another aspect touch on matters specially reserved to the provincial legislatures.'[156] Haldane's emergency doctrine, therefore, had no basis in law and the national concern doctrine, as liberally applied by Sankey and Dunedin, had been rescued from Watson's restrictions and Atkin's clarification.

Although the Judicial Committee was not bound by its previous decisions, Simon concluded, there had been many occasions when the board 'might have overruled the decision had it thought it wrong. Accordingly ... the decision must be regarded as firmly embedded in the constitutional law of Canada, and it is impossible now to depart from it ... so far as the Canada Temperance Act is concerned the question must be considered as settled once and for all.' Moreover, Simon continued, outlining a new doctrine of reasonable potential, if the matter lay within federal jurisdiction, so did the power to re-enact its provisions 'with the object of preventing a recurrence of a state of affairs which was deemed to necessitate the earlier statute. To legislate for prevention appears to be on the same basis as legislation for cure.'[157]

However, Simon's colleagues on the Judicial Committee were less willing to loosen the shackles of Haldane's emergency doctrine and the Watson-Atkin restraints on the residual clause. In 1949 the committee rejected the absurd proposition (as had the Supreme Court) that the Canadian Pacific's Empress Hotel was an integral part of a unified national system of such enormous scope and national importance as to fall within federal jurisdiction under the residual clause, and thus be immune from provincial labour regulations. Lord Reid emphasized that Watson's national concern *dicta* had to be read in the context of his warning that to allow the federal government under the residual clause to encroach on subjects in section 92 'would not only be contrary to the intendment of the Act, but would practically destroy the autonomy of the provinces.' He believed it important to repeat Atkin's sarcastic comment as to how often Watson's words 'have unsuccessfully been used in attempts to support encroachments on the provincial legislative powers given by s. 92.'[158]

In 1950 Lord Morton also found it necessary to cite Atkin's comments in finding the federal prohibition, with penal sanctions, against the manufacture and sale of margarine or other butter substitutes *ultra vires*, as had the Supreme Court. Federal counsel admitted that the purpose of the act was to protect the dairy industry, but argued that it could be upheld under the criminal law, agriculture, trade and commerce, and peace, order, and good government.[159] The Judicial Committee found no substance in any of the arguments, and in rejecting them it consolidated the jurisprudence on trade and commerce and the residual clause.

A decision accepting the trade and commerce argument, wrote Morton, 'would be contrary to the current of authority and, in particular, to certain recent decisions of the Board,' citing as authority Atkin's enthusiastic and unequivocal endorsement of Duff's review of the case law. 'The truth is,' Morton continued, that 'the present case is typical of the many cases in which the Board has felt bound to put some limit on the scope of the words used in head 2 of s. 91,' as Duff had repeated, '"in order to preserve from serious curtailment, if not from virtual extinction, the degree of autonomy which, as appears from the scheme of the Act as a whole, the provinces were intended to possess."'[160]

Morton relied completely on Atkin (and Duff) to refute the argument that, because the legislation did not come within any of the provincial enumerations, it fell within the residual clause as legislation for the peace, order, and good government of Canada. He noted that federal counsel had relied on *Russell* and *Canada Temperance*, but stated that passages from those decisions relating to matters of national concern had to be read in the context of Atkin's decision in *Labour Conventions* where he qualified Watson's national concern doctrine and endorsed Haldane's emergency doctrine as the only justification for federal legislation which could override the normal distribution of power in the enumerations. So read, the act was in relation to property and civil rights and, absent an emergency, could not be upheld under the residual clause.[161]

By the time Lords Reid and Morton had delivered their decisions, the Supreme Court of Canada had begun life as the final court of appeal. With their judgments, the Supreme Court inherited a legacy of doctrine and precedent much as it had been developed by Watson, Atkin, and, to a lesser extent, Haldane.

10

Restoring the Balance:
The Supreme Court of Canada,
1949–1979

We have been charged with bias ...
– Chief Justice Bora Laskin, 1978

'The legacy of the Privy Council was not an easy one,' recalled Justice
Brian Dickson in 1979. 'A wave of anticipation attended the abolition
of appeals to the colonial court; the Supreme Court was arguably not
bound by its precedents; was unhampered by its style of statutory
interpretation; was freed from the threat of review.'[1] Thirty years earlier, however, the anticipation was tempered by suspicion and doubts.
There was legitimate concern that the institutional practices and intellectual capacity of the bench would not enable the Supreme Court to
be an acceptable final court of appeal. There was widespread scepti-
cism in the provinces, as Mackenzie King had foreseen, that a federally
appointed court could be trusted to be an impartial umpire of a sometimes volatile federal system. Nor was it clear that the Supreme Court
would or even should abandon the doctrinal legacy and style of statutory interpretation bequeathed by the Judicial Committee. In 1949 the
only certainty was that, as the court of last resort, the Supreme Court
would be free of the threat of review.

The more substantial and contentious jurisprudential issue was
whether the powerful doctrine of *stare decisis* would or should cast a

Privy Council shadow over the deliberations of the politically emancipated court. Among the academic critics, the abolition of appeals and the abandonment of Judicial Committee law had been synonymous. Unless 'we get rid of the past decisions of the Judicial Committee,' W.P.M. Kennedy had written, 'they will hang around the necks of the judiciary ... in that uncanny reality with which *stare decisis* seems doomed to rob the law of creative vitality.'[2]

However, many politicians did not share the views of the professoriate. When M.J. Coldwell had demanded a special committee to recommend changes to the BNA Act in 1938, Ernest Lapointe, the minister of justice, replied that the committee could do nothing 'except read these decisions. It could not define powers and jurisdiction other than as they exist and they have been defined by the courts.'[3] Indeed, throughout the 1938 and 1939 debate on abolition, Lapointe was defensive about the quality of Judicial Committee decisions, agreeing only that the appeal did not fit easily with Canada's national status. And it was on those grounds that the government agreed to refer the draft bill for abolition to the Supreme Court in 1939.

As the moment of abolition approached, it became clearer that the practitioners did not share the academic hostility to Judicial Committee law. At a special conference organized by the Department of Justice in December 1948, a majority of the leading lawyers from all the provinces concluded that although *stare decisis* ought to obtain, the rule should not be mentioned in the legislation establishing the Supreme Court as the final court of appeal.[4] The Canadian Bar Association made its decision public just weeks before the abolition bill was introduced in the Commons. The association requested time for public discussion and consultation with the provinces on both the wisdom of abolition and the powers of the Supreme Court, but, if appeals were abolished, there was unanimous agreement 'that the rule of *stare decisis* ought to continue to be applied with respect to past decisions of the Court, as well as with respect to past decisions of the Judicial Committee.'[5]

The Conservative opposition in the Commons also appealed for delay and for the explicit adoption of the rule of *stare decisis* in the legislation. George Drew warned of the political dangers of ending the reign of the Judicial Committee as the 'referee' of federalism, and stated that if past decisions were set aside, 'there would be endless confusion, and the whole structure of government would to some extent lose its defined form.'[6] Prime Minister St Laurent emphasized that, although the fundamental issue was whether the law should be made in Canada, the rule of *stare decisis* 'is something with which I entirely agree.'[7] If so, replied David Fulton, more than sceptical about the interaction of law and politics in Ottawa, why not preserve the principle with his amendment, which read that 'the Supreme Court of Canada shall be bound by the law as declared in all orders of His Majesty in council hitherto made on the advice of the judicial committee of his privy council and the reasons assigned therefor by the said judicial committee, in so far as the said law is applicable to Canada.'[8]

Fulton's amendment was rejected without a recorded vote, but it was obvious that there was little support for the view that the Supreme Court should begin its new life with a blank page. Although some agreed with Charles Arthur Cannon that the court should not be 'bound and gagged,' the minister of justice, Stuart Garson, may have best expressed the opinion of the House when he declared that the basic question was whether we 'have enough confidence in the Supreme Court of Canada as a court of last resort that we think it competent and willing to apply the Privy Council decisions as an integral part of the law of Canada.' If not, 'I think there is a grave question whether we should continue it at all as an institution of the country.'[9]

Neither in politics nor in law had the Supreme Court been given a legislative mandate to abandon *stare decisis* and escape from the jurisprudential shadow cast by the Judicial Committee, or the freedom to rewrite the constitutional law of Canada. Canadian nationalism, with the help of Lord Atkin, had brought the institution embodying judicial imperialism to an end, but not necessarily the judicial conservatism and theory of federalism embedded in the doctrines and 'style of statutory interpretation' of the imperial court.[10]

The issue of *stare decisis* mirrored a debate over the nature and future of federalism which was captured in 1951 in articles by two men who decades later would sit together on the Supreme Court. Louis-Philippe Pigeon, professor of constitutional law at Laval, embraced what he described as the 'autonomist conception of federalism.' The opponents of provincial autonomy, he maintained, relied on a fallacious view of the peace, order, and good government clause, or the 'so-called' historical reconstruction of the act which was 'a pretended inquiry into the intentions of the framers of the Canadian constitution, otherwise than by a consideration of the meaning of the words used in the final document.'[11]

While the courts, particularly the Judicial Committee, had 'recognized the implicit fluidity of any constitution by allowing for emergencies and by resting distinctions on questions of degree,' their 'great value' was that they firmly 'uphold the fundamental principle of provincial autonomy; they staunchly refuse to let our federal constitution be changed gradually, by one device or anther, to a legislative union. In so doing they are preserving the essential condition of the Canadian confederation.'[12] Strict adherence to Judicial Committee precedent was thus essential to the preservation of provincial autonomy and Canadian federalism.

Known for his advocacy of an expansive interpretation of the federal residual power, Professor Bora Laskin appealed for a truly emancipated court. 'It is hardly credible that the Supreme Court will seek to walk in the shadow of the Privy Council,' he wrote, 'asking itself not only what Privy Council decisions are controlling but striving to reflect the Privy Council's approach to problems of interpretation. Such a final court would be merely a judicial "zombie," without soul or character.'[13] The court could not accept *stare decisis* as 'an inflexible rule of conduct,' particularly in constitutional cases.[14] What was required was 'the same free range of inquiry which animated the court in its early days of existence, especially in constitutional cases when it took its inspiration from Canadian sources. Empiricism not dogmatism, imagination rather than literalness, are the qualities through which the judges can give their court the stamp of personality.'[15]

However, the burden of precedent was not easily shed. For decades the Supreme Court seemed content to chip away at the doctrinal legacy of the Judicial Committee without openly asserting its emancipation. The first, very qualified, suggestion that the court was as free as the Judicial Committee to modify previous decisions was made in an *obiter* by Ivan Rand in 1957. The Judicial Committee, he observed, had occasionally 'modified the language' used to describe sections 91 and 92 'in its general interpretative formulations' and that 'incident of judicial power must, now, in the same manner and with the same authority be exercised in revising or restating the formulations that have come down to us.' The exercise, he continued, 'involves no departure from the basic principles of judicial distribution' but was only a 'refinement of interpretation in application to the particularized and evolving features and aspects of matters which the intensive and extensive application of the life of the country inevitably presents.'[16]

The deep potential of the *obiter*, if applied and followed, was enormous. But the court in principle refused to take a position. As John

Cartwright declared in 1966, 'I do not propose to enter on the question, which since 1949 has been raised from time to time by authors, whether this Court ... is, as in the case of the House of Lords, bound by its own previous decisions on the questions of law or whether, as in the case of the Judicial Committee or the Supreme Court of the United States, it is free under certain circumstances to re-consider them.'[17]

In the same year, however, Lord Chancellor Gardiner issued a 'Practice Statement' declaring that 'too rigid adherence to precedent may lead to injustice in a particular case and also unduly restrict the development of the law. They propose therefore to modify their present practice and, while treating former decisions of this House as normally binding, to depart from a previous decision when it appears right to do so.'[18] With the House of Lords on side, Emmett Hall, while a member of the Supreme Court, wrote, 'So much for the doctrine of *stare decisis*.' The court was now free to shed the legacy of the Judicial Committee: 'The way is open: should it be used? This brings us to an academic or philosophical consideration of the question.'[19]

In fact, from the beginning, the court had quietly revisited the decisions and doctrines of the Judicial Committee, but only in 1978 did it openly state that Judicial Committee decisions would no longer be regarded as of binding authority. A unanimous court agreed with Pigeon, who found 'it quite proper for us to overrule what may be left in the judgement,' and with Laskin, who, after observing that the court had recently 'departed' from previous decisions in three cases, stated that there 'are equally compelling reasons here to set aside the *Crystal Dairy* doctrine and I would unhesitatingly do so.'[20] Later in 1978, Chief Justice Laskin stated in decision that 'this court has asserted its freedom not only to depart from its own decisions but from Canadian decisions of the Privy Council as well.'[21]

Gordon Bales wrote shortly afterwards that the statements 'may indicate that the court is prepared to leave the safe harbour of binding precedent and to commence an exciting voyage dedicated to the rejuvenation of the law.'[22] However, as Dickson cautioned, while the court was no longer bound by prior decisions, 'it is not free wheeling. A judge of the Court does not have any mandate to mount a white horse and go off in search of his personal holy grail, his own notion of social or economic justice.'[23] Justice Gérard La Forest's observation undoubtedly reflected the practice, if not the theory, of the court by the 1990s. After fifteen years on the court, he could state that given 'the fact-centric nature of litigation and the multiplicity of principles available for resolving disputes in any given context, *stare decisis* seems to me less of a constraint on judicial lawmaking than is generally supposed. Certainly, in my attempts to move the law forward, I have only rarely found it necessary to overrule cases.'[24]

The Supreme Court was also hostage to the Judicial Committee's theoretical, if not always, or even usually, applied, approach to judicial review. A major limitation of the committee, as Chief Justice Dickson contended, was 'its reluctance to permit extrinsic evidence of any kind to aid constitutional interpretation. Thus the decisions were rendered without any reference to the social, economic and political context in which the issues arose.'[25] Unlike the Judicial Committee, the Supreme Court had never been as blind to context or deaf to argument based on history in constitutional cases, as the New Deal hearings revealed. But, in general, the use of such extrinsic aids as parliamentary debates, government reports, economic statistics, and the labours of academics was, following the example of the Judicial Committee, either discouraged or prohibited. The practice, it seemed, would persist. When in 1950 counsel attempted to use an academic article in support of his argument that 'proven facts' were admissible, Chief Justice Rinfret immediately interjected: 'The Canadian Bar Review is not an authority in this court.'[26] But Rinfret's was the voice of the past and after 1950 the court gradually opened the door to almost all forms of extrinsic aids.

The most quantifiable was, in fact, the increasing citation of scholarly studies. In 1957 there were ten references to secondary literature in sixty decisions,[27] while from 1991 to 1996 there were 2,817 academic citations in 680 decisions.[28] The growing number of references to academic authorities, as well as the inclusion in decisions of bibliographies of authors cited (a practice that began in 1985), unquestionably owed a good deal to the appearance in 1967 of law clerks who usually came directly from law school.[29] Their assistance, Laskin admitted, has 'enabled the Judges to infuse their reasons for judgement with a wider range of supporting references than the pressure of their work loads would otherwise have permitted.'[30]

Dickson welcomed the infusion of scholarship into the reasons. 'Happily those days are behind us' when juristic writings were kept out of court, he said, for the court benefited from legal scholarship, the weight of which 'depends on the cogency of the argument, the intellectual honesty of the scholarship, the thoroughness of the research and, yes, the reputation of the author.'[31] 'I can assure you,' Chief Justice

Lamer added in 1992, 'that good scholarship plays an important role in shaping the legal principles that evolve through the judicial process.'[32]

The court also became more liberal in taking judicial notice of, or listening to, argument based on extrinsic factual or contextual evidence. The 'major breakthrough,' said Dickson, was the *Anti-Inflation Reference* of 1976, when counsel on both sides presented a wide range of statistical evidence to support or deny that socio-economic circumstances justified the legislation. Although Chief Justice Laskin had concluded that such evidence could be considered by the court, he cautioned that 'no general principle of admissibility or inadmissibility can or ought to be propounded by this court and that questions of resort to extrinsic evidence and what kind of extrinsic evidence may be admitted must depend on the constitutional issue on which it is sought to adduce such evidence.'[33]

Four years later, Dickson observed, off the bench, that in subsequent cases 'extrinsic evidence has been admitted to assist in the task of interpretation. Decisions no longer need be rendered in a vacuum – currents in social, economic and political thought can now assist in the resolution of constitutional disputes.' Justice, he added, 'must not be blind to the purposes of Parliament' and resort to legislative history, 'including Hansard, committee minutes and White Papers ... might well be considered to be admissible,' subject always to the court's determination of relevance and weight.[34] The issue was settled when Justice John Sopinka wrote authoritatively for the court in *R. v. Morgentaler* in 1993:

The former exclusionary rule regarding evidence of legislative history has gradually been relaxed but until recently the courts have balked at admitting evidence of legislative debates and speeches ... The main criticism of such evidence has been that it cannot represent the 'intent' of the legislature, an incorporated body, but that is equally true of other forms of legislative history. Provided that the court remains mindful of the limited reliability and weight of Hansard evidence it should be admitted as relevant to both the background and purposes of legislation. Indeed, its admissibility in constitutional cases to aid in determining the background and purpose of legislation now appears to be well established.[35]

Shedding the Judicial Committee's precedents, doctrines, and rules of statutory interpretation lay in the future when the Supreme Court began life as the final court of appeal. Decades from now, when the papers of the Supreme Court justices, now in the National Archives, are opened for research, forensic legal historians will be able to understand better how the court reached its decisions. Chief Justice Dickson explained the process within the court which will ultimately enable the historian to penetrate the institutional politics of law or accommodation as the court worked its way towards its opinion(s). After the post-argument conference at which all members spoke, the junior first, Dickson said, 'it was always my practice when I went back to the office, to my chambers, to dictate a memorandum – one, two, three, four, five pages – setting out briefly what the facts were, what were the main arguments, how each of the members of the court felt about the outcome, how the case should be decided. Then if some other member of the court was writing, when he or she circulated it I would check it against my notes, and sometimes it would alter one's opinion.'[36]

Papers like Dickson's will reveal the process of decision making as initial drafts are written, commented upon, revised, and rewritten, until the final decisions are released. For now, however, the published opinions, reinforced by judicial comments off the bench and subjected to academic dissection, must serve as a guide to how, if not always why, the Supreme Court shaped the law of Canadian federalism. The terrain will be familiar to students of the Supreme Court's federalism jurisprudence but it is to be hoped that even they will find the cumulative body of law, largely abandoning Judicial Committee precedent and doctrine and inventing a distinctively Canadian jurisprudence, as Dickson was to describe it, interesting and informative.

Court watchers after 1949 found the reversal of some of the Supreme Court's early decisions by the Judicial Committee discomfitting. Much more distressing, however, than loss of face was the judicial defeat of an ingenious scheme to punch holes in Atkin's watertight compartments. To facilitate the establishment of old age pensions, a scheme was devised whereby the province delegated authority to make laws in relation to employment to the federal government, which would in turn delegate power to levy an indirect sales tax to the province. A bill to that effect in Nova Scotia was referred to the Nova Scotia Supreme Court which, by majority, found it *ultra vires*. At the Supreme Court of Canada in 1950, decisions and opinions from Smith to Atkin were cited to demonstrate that the legislatures were sovereign within their sphere. If the attempt to break down the watertight compartments succeeded, a unanimous court agreed with Ivan Rand, 'the whole scheme of the

Canadian constitution would be entirely defeated.'[37] For good measure, five judges found authority in Watson's *obiter* during the oral
argument in *Bonsecours* that the division of power was absolute: 'If they
have it, either one or the other of them, they have it by virtue of the Act
of 1867. I think we must get rid of the idea that either one or the other
can enlarge the jurisdiction of the other or surrender jurisdiction.'[38]

Two years later, however, the court reversed field in *Willis*, when it
decided that *administrative* inter-delegation was valid, and approved a
scheme where a provincial marketing board was empowered by
Ottawa to exercise powers to regulate interprovincial and export trade
conferred by Ottawa. The court now found authority in Judicial Committee decisions as early as *Valin* v. *Langlois* in 1879, which, Chief Justice Rinfret stated, established beyond 'the slightest doubt' the
principle later affirmed by Lord Atkin that it was competent for Parliament to 'employ its own executive officers for the purpose of carrying
out legislation which is within its constitutional authority.'[39]

Citing Atkin's *dicta* about 'co-operation' in the 1937 marketing case,
Kerwin observed that the Nova Scotia inter-delegation case did not
meet his criteria for breaching the watertight compartments, but this
attempt 'to carry out Lord Atkins' suggestion is an entirely different
matter' because it did not involve the transfer of legislative authority.[40]
Most commentators found the distinction between administrative and
legislative inter-delegation unpersuasive, but applauded the result as
introducing a much-needed element of flexibility and efficiency into
the constitution. It seemed obvious, as well, as Paul Weiler wrote, that
the court had been 'worried about the practicality of its earlier absolute
ban and wanted to relax it without giving the appearance of retreat.'[41]

After the *Willis* decision, various forms of inter-delegation were
accepted by the court, although the prohibition of legislative inter-
delegation was never formally rescinded. Perhaps the most significant
example was the approval of the federal Motor Vehicle Transport Act
(1953–4). In 1951 the Supreme Court had declared that a New Brunswick licence for the operation of a bus line from Boston to Glace Bay
was *intra vires* but, reasoning from 92 (10) (a), *ultra vires* when the bus
line crossed provincial borders. In *Winner* (1954) the Judicial Committee rejected this surgical test (as had Sankey and Dunedin in *Aeronautics* and *Radio*), finding that the undertaking was one and indivisible
and thus within federal jurisdiction. After the decision, the federal
government in effect turned regulatory authority over such interprovincial highway operations to provincial boards. In *Coughlin* (1968) a

majority of the Supreme Court found that the constitutional prohibition on inter-delegation had not been violated. As Cartwright wrote in the majority opinion, 'it is satisfactory to find that there is nothing which compels us to hold that the object sought by this co-operative effort is constitutionally unattainable.'[42]

Atkin's watertight compartments had been breached by judicially approved legislative techniques which may not have satisfied legal purists or classical federalists. Indeed, as late as 1986, Chief Justice Dickson could state that the prohibition of legislative inter-delegation was essential to safeguard federalism. 'If the provinces began to bargain away their spheres of legislative competence in return, perhaps for a favourable and special fiscal arrangement with the federal government,' he explained, 'those provinces who wished to maintain their legislative autonomy might be pressured by fiscal constraint to abandon it.'[43]

However, the court apparently preferred a functional to a literal or mechanistic approach to an issue on which the constitution was silent. There was even justification for Weiler's comment that the court 'has recognized that the political agencies of Canadian governments are primarily responsible for the distribution of legislative authority, at least when they are mutually agreed.'[44] That recognition was also congruent with the prevailing trend by the 1960s to circumvent the distribution of legislative jurisdiction by a variety of conditional grants and shared-cost programs.

The Supreme Court soon revealed that it was much less apprehensive than many of the law lords had been of a broader scope of federal jurisdiction under both the residual clause and the enumerations. In 1958 Ivan Rand, who joined the court in 1943, seized an opportunity to assert his conception of Canadian federalism when counsel based an argument on an Australian decision. In Australia, Rand explained, autonomous states conferred some powers on the central government and retained those not transferred. But in Canada 'a converse formulation was effected: in constitutional authority a new and paramount Dominion was created to which was attributed power to legislate for the peace, order, and good government generally.' Although the residual power was 'subject to certain local and private powers exclusively vested in the provinces when created,' those powers in turn 'were made subordinate to the paramount and exclusive authority specifically defined and reserved to the Dominion.' Rand's conception may not have been that of the court, but not since the days of Ritchie, Strong, and Gwynne had such language been expressed in decision.[45]

After he had left the court, Rand suggested that the 'scope of the federal residual power presents a fertile field for judicial cultivation' because 'divergences' in the jurisprudence 'evidence a fluid area where judgement has not crystallized and presents an opportunity for fresh consideration of residual resources.'[46] In fact, before he retired, the court had an occasion for a fresh consideration of the residual clause when the municipality of St Paul, Manitoba, under the authority of the Municipal Act, passed a by-law prohibiting the Johannessons, who held a federal air-transport licence, from building an airstrip. The Manitoba Court of Appeal had upheld the prohibition.

On appeal in 1952, the Supreme Court, after much revisiting of the judgments of Watson, Sankey, Dunedin, and Simon, unanimously held that aeronautics was exclusively within federal jurisdiction as a matter of national dimensions or concern which transcended provincial boundaries. All but Rinfret, who found Sankey's decision in *Aeronautics* decisive, cited as authoritative Viscount Simon's statement that 'the true test must be found in the real subject matter of the legislation.' Moreover, as Roy Lindsay Kellock wrote: 'Once the decision is made that a matter is of national interest and importance, so as to fall within the peace, order, and good government clause, the provinces cease to have any legislative jurisdiction thereto and the Dominion legislation is exclusive.'[47]

Simon's test was again determinative in the 1956 decision of Justice James McLennan of the Ontario High Court that the Atomic Energy Control Act of 1952, asserting federal jurisdiction over the production and use of atomic energy, 'from its inherent nature is of concern to the nation as a whole ... and within the powers of Parliament to make laws for the peace, order, and good government of Canada.' McLennan found that 'it would be incompatible with the power of Parliament to legislate for the peace, order, and good government of Canada if labour relations in the production of atomic energy did not lie within the regulation of Parliament.'[48]

The court also expanded federal jurisdiction over labour relations when the revised federal Industrial Relations and Disputes Investigation Act was challenged. Initially passed in 1925 as a consequence of the *Snider* decision, the act asserted federal jurisdiction over those employed in 'connection with any works, undertakings, or business that is within the legislative authority of the Parliament of Canada,' including, among others, navigation and shipping, and over the exclusions from provincial jurisdiction by section 92(10)(a-c). When two rival unions sought to be the bargaining agents for the Eastern Terminal Stevedoring company, which operated terminals in many ports, including Toronto, the act was referred to the Supreme Court.

In 1955 the court unanimously found the act *intra vires* (but with Rand and Locke excluding strictly local undertakings from its operations) and by majority ruled that the act applied to the company. Rand dismissed Haldane's reasoning in *Snider* that the legislation then at issue could have been passed by the provincial legislature as 'quite unrealistic as applied to these undertakings.'[49] The decision had the potential of significantly enlarging federal jurisdiction over labour relations, a potential that was realized as the court adopted a usually sensible functional test to determine whether labour relations were sufficiently integral to a federal undertaking to bring them within federal jurisdiction.[50]

The court also removed some of the shackles from the trade and commerce power. Ironically, the first sign that the Supreme Court would take a less restrictive view of the trade and commerce power was revealed in a complicated decision of 1957 generally upholding Ontario's 1950 Farm Products Marketing Act which stated that it covered only marketing 'within the province.' But, in so doing, Kerwin, Rand, Charles Locke, and Henry Nolan reflected on the nature and weight of precedent, and the circumstances in which federal jurisdiction could reach transactions within the province.

Rand accepted Duff's precedent in *Eastern Terminal Elevator* in 1925 (approved by Atkin in his 1937 marketing decision) that 'Dominion regulation cannot embrace local trade merely because in undifferentiated subject matter the external interest is dominant.' But he then proceeded to devise a rule: 'That if in a trade activity, including manufacture or production, there is involved a matter of extraprovincial interest or concern its regulation thereafter in that aspect of trade is by that fact put beyond provincial power.' Moreover, federal jurisdiction had to be placed in a context broader than that in the case law from Smith to Atkin because 'trade agreements reaching the dimensions of world agreements are now a commonplace; interprovincial trade in which the Dominion is a single market, is of similar importance, and equally vital to the functioning of the country as a whole. The Dominion power implies responsibility for promoting and maintaining the vigour and growth of trade beyond Provincial confines, and the discharge of this duty must remain unembarrassed by local trade impediments.'

Finally, Rand disputed the classification of provincial jurisdiction over local trade as a matter of property and civil rights. 'The production and exchange of goods as an economic activity,' he contended, did not take place 'by virtue of positive law or civil right' but had 'an identity of its own recognized by head 2 of s. 91. I cannot agree that its regulation under that head was intended as a species of matter under head 13 from which by the language of s. 91 it has been withdrawn.' The meaning of the reasoning in *Parsons* had to be reconsidered, for while the location of contracts in 92(13) 'seemed obvious,' the 'true conception of trade (in contradistinction to the static nature of rights, civil or property) is that of a dynamic, the creation and flow of goods from production to consumption or utilization, as an individual activity.'

Whereas the Judicial Committee had found section 94 evidence of the broad scope of property and civil rights, Rand found it conclusive of a narrower conception because uniformity in the internal economy of each province could not have been expected. Rand concluded that it was within 92(16), 'what may be called the residuary power of the Province,' that 'the autonomy of the province in local matters, so far as it might be affected by trade regulation, is to be found.'[51] Although it was *obiter*, his reconstruction of the nature of trade and commerce and the location of local trade could, if followed in decision, restore a balance in the jurisdiction over trade and commerce.

The implications of the *obiters* were soon translated into law. In 1958 the court heard a challenge to the Canadian Wheat Board Act (1952), which provided that no one other than the board could export grain from a province. To contest the provisions, Stephen Murphy bought grain in Manitoba but the Canadian Pacific refused to ship it to British Columbia. Murphy argued that the provision was a violation of section 92(13) and of section 121 (providing for free trade among the provinces) and also contended that the 1926 declaration that grain elevators were for the general advantage of Canada was invalid. Without falling back on authority, Locke held that it was 'too clear for argument' that the provisions dealing with the export of grain fell within 91(2) and that authorities, including the 1957 reference, determined that it was 'immaterial' that it interfered with property and civil rights.[52]

Similarly, Rand emphasized that 'apart from matters of purely local and private concerns, this country is one economic unit; in freedom of movement its business interests are in an extra-provincial dimension, and among other things, are deeply involved in trade and commerce between and beyond provinces.' In 1867 the regulation of trade and commerce in Canada was exclusively confided to parliament 'notwithstanding anything in this Act. However, by what has been considered the necessary corollary of the scheme of the [BNA] Act as a whole ... this authority has been curtailed so far but only so far as necessary to avoid the infringement, if not "the virtual extinction," of provincial jurisdiction over local and private matters including intra-provincial trade; but the paramount authority of Parliament is trenched upon expressly only as it may be affected by s. 121.'[53]

The old compartmentalized approach to trade and commerce was completely abandoned when in *Klassen* (1959) the Manitoba Court of Appeal considered whether a Wheat Board quota scheme applied to a mill which bought, processed, and sold locally. Following *Murphy*, which settled that the purpose of the Wheat Board Act fell within trade and commerce (and much that was said there in *obiter* was relevant to the question at issue), the court held that the undoubted interference with property and civil rights 'is incidental and ancillary to the achievement of the purpose of the Act, the pith and substance of which is the provision of an export market for surplus grains, a matter which has undoubtedly assumed a national importance.'[54]

Bora Laskin was ecstatic: 'Not only are "mechanical applications of legal formulas no longer feasible" if the *Klassen* case survives, but we will have to withdraw Iddington J.'s portrait of the federal trade and commerce power as "the old forlorn hope, so many times tried unsuccessfully."'[55] *Klassen* indeed survived, for the Supreme Court refused leave to appeal and embedded it in the 91(2) jurisprudence. Looking back in 1973, Paul Weiler believed that *Klassen* was 'perhaps' the most important 91(2) decision since 1949: 'For the first time a Canadian court saw that once having discerned the main thrust or "aspect" of the legislation as valid federal regulation of the marketing of a product beyond provincial borders, it should then uphold the related controls on intra-provincial activity if they are functionally desirable in the over-all scheme. Given such an approach there is very little in the way of federal legislation which could not be validated on the same pragmatic reasoning.'[56]

Although the results were not as dramatic, the Supreme Court also adopted an expansive view of the criminal law power. In *Goodyear Tire* (1956) the court upheld provisions of the Combines Investigation Act

(1952) prohibiting the continuation of illegal acts. Rand seized the occasion for another of his extended essays:

It is accepted that head 27 of s.91 of the Confederation statute is to be interpreted in the widest sense, but that breadth of scope contemplates neither a static catalogue of offences nor order of sanctions. The evolving and transforming types and patterns of social and economic activities are constantly calling for new penal controls and limitations and that new modes of enforcement and punishment adapted to the changing conditions are not to be taken as being equally within the ambit of parliamentary power is, in my opinion, not seriously arguable.[57]

In other appeals, the criminal law power was held to extend to provisions for the forfeiture of a vehicle used in connection with a narcotic drug offence.[58] Provincial slot-machine legislation was held to be in conflict with the criminal law regarding gaming.[59] Compulsory closing, with penal sanctions, on six Catholic holidays was viewed as legislation regarding religious observance, not working hours, and thus within the criminal law.[60] The purpose of Quebec's Padlock Act was found to be in pith and substance the suppression of communism and beyond provincial jurisdiction, with the majority of the court referring to the criminal law as the constitutional basis for legislation on civil liberties.[61]

The court remained protective of any encroachment on federal jurisdiction over bankruptcy and insolvency. The 1894 Judicial Committee decision in *Voluntary Assignments*, already qualified, was easily distinguished to find Alberta's personal insolvency legislation unconstitutional.[62] Saskatchewan's debt-moratorium legislation was quickly found unconstitutional on the basis of a Judicial Committee decision in 1943 on comparable Alberta legislation.[63]

The 1950s were truly a remarkable decade in federalism jurisprudence. Although the court generally reasoned within flexible parameters of precedent, the doctrines and decisions portrayed a strikingly different view of Canadian federalism than the constructions offered by the Watson-Haldane-Atkin school. No longer was the federal government the beast to be caged, as the court, in Dale Gibson's opinion, 'displayed unusual vigour and imagination, and an unprecedented determination to adapt the law to Canadian conditions, even if this meant departing from the paths previously trodden by the Judicial Committee of the Privy Council.'[64] After the Canadian Wheat Board decision in 1950, the court rejected every challenge to federal jurisdiction, while about half of the challenges to provincial legislation were successful.[65] Through all of this, the court may well have reflected the growing nationalism of the 'elites' in post-war Canada, a group that included business leaders, politicians, bureaucrats, and academics.[66] Indeed, it would have been remarkable if the judiciary had remained unaffected by this trend.

In the 1960s, Dale Gibson lamented, the 'open activism of the fifties was succeeded by a cautious pragmatism.' The tendency to articulate policy arguments was 'largely abandoned' and opinions offered 'little justification for the court's decisions beyond formal legal reasoning.'[67] Paul Weiler agreed that, in contrast to the jurisprudence of the 1950s, the decisions of the 1960s did not examine the issues or the arguments in depth but rather summarized the 'doctrines and cases which support the conclusion which is reached and then only in very sketchy form.'[68] Weiler concluded that the 'philosophical orientation' of the court, from a policy-oriented to a more formalist style, 'changed direction sharply, somewhere around the year 1960,'[69] a reflection un-questionably of the changed composition of the bench. Roy Lindsay Kellock and Rand had retired in 1958 and 1959 (and Locke and Kerwin were to follow in 1962 and 1963). Joining the court in 1958 were three Diefenbaker appointments: Ronald Martland, Roland Ritchie, and Wilfred Judson. Martland and Ritchie had been very active in the Conservative Party and were appointed directly from practice with no judicial experience.[70] Ritchie's biographer describes them as 'black-letter advocates for whom *stare decisis* was all important.' Of Ritchie he writes: 'There is a sense of an overwhelming hesitance, an unwillingness to push or to dig deep, a reluctance to think seriously about what the law should be. The law is to be read, the precedents are to be found, and they are to be followed.' By the time he left the court in 1984, Ritchie 'was one of the few remaining examples of a judge who almost inherently deferred to *stare decisis* and legislative authority.'[71]

If Rand embodied the spirit of the 1950s, writes Gibson, Martland 'seems to have been the archetypal judge of the sixties.'[72] Archetypal or not, Martland became what Peter McCormick terms the 'centre of gravity' at least by the late 1960s[73] and, with Ritchie, remained at the centre well into the era of the Laskin court. 'I rather share the view that it is not the task of judges to make law,' Martland told an interviewer, 'but essentially it is to apply it as it exists, and leave it to the people's elected representatives to determine whether they want change.'[74] He translated this philosophy into constitutional law: 'My feeling was well the *B.N.A. Act* was there, good or bad, and it had to be applied.'[75] At other times, however, Mantland observed that constitutional appeals 'do lend themselves more than others to the possibility of making new law, because you are dealing with situations that haven't arisen before and you have no precedent. You have some leeway there, and must have it in a growing constitution.' There was not a great deal of research into the issues, he admitted, but 'you may have certain ideas about what is proper in a federal constitution that have a bearing on your reaction to the argument.'[76]

The most striking feature of much of the jurisprudence of the 1960s was the court's apparent determination to uphold provincial legislation which on its face seemed unconstitutional, a task it performed by preferring the concurrency doctrine to federal paramountcy. Although a precedent had been set in the Saskatchewan *Breathalyzer* appeal in 1958, when the court found that a provincial law mandating the suspension of a driver's licence for refusal to take the test was not in conflict with a federal law stating that no one was required to take the test,[77] Weiler believed that three decisions in 1960 established 'the new attitude' of the court for the 1960s.[78] Two were highway-related cases in which provincial laws were upheld although in conflict with provisions of the Criminal Code.[79] In the third, the court upheld a provincial law creating an offence of issuing a false prospectus, although Locke and Cartwright found that the law was in conflict with a comparable section of the Criminal Code.[80]

Throughout the following decades, the court continued to give a narrow scope to federal parmountcy, with the result, Peter Hogg concluded, that the 'sole test of inconsistency in Canadian constitutional law is express contradiction. This is the course of judicial restraint, allowing the fullest possible play to provincial legislation.'[81] However, the court rejected concurrency in finding two provincial acts in conflict with federal criminal law. In 1967 the B.C. Motor Vehicle Act, as it might affect juvenile delinquents, was found invalid because it conflicted with federal juvenile delinquency law which was 'of paramount authority' even though it trenched upon matters assigned to the provincial legislatures by section 92.[82] Thus, it might also be argued that concurrency in some cases reflected judicial balance since in an earlier era provincial legislation often might have trumped federal law.

The court also appeared to seek a functional balance in rejecting challenges to provincial taxes or levies. In a decision of 1960 that 'distinguished' (virtually to the point of overruling) Judicial Committee and Supreme Court decisions, the court upheld a British Columbia milk-marketing scheme involving financial pooling arrangements on the grounds that it related to trade, which fell within sections 92(16 and 13), and was not indirect taxation or an interference with trade and commerce.[83] The court also rejected challenges to provincial sales and profits taxes on the grounds that they were indirect.[84] However, when British Columbia attempted by means of taxation to force mining companies to smelt the ore in the province rather than export it, the court found it *ultra vires* as in relation to trade and commerce.[85]

But the federal government's jurisdiction as defined in *Murphy* and *Klassen* was cut back in a unanimous but highly controversial decision of 1968 upholding a Quebec marketing scheme which forced Carnation Milk to pay higher prices for raw milk than other processors. With Ottawa intervening in support, Carnation contended that because it shipped the bulk of its processed milk out of the province, the scheme was an interference with interprovincial trade. For the court, Martland found the authoritative precedent in Duff's 1936 judgment in the marketing case, approved by Atkin on appeal, and in Atkin's opinion in *Shannon* in 1938, to hold that the law was in relation to intra-provincial trade. Martland acknowledged the several *obiter dicta* in the Ontario marketing reference, but wrote that while 'I agree with the view of the four judges ... that a trade transaction, completed in a province, is not necessarily, by that fact alone, subject only to provincial control, I also hold the view that the fact that such a transaction incidentally has some effect upon a company engaged in interprovincial trade does not necessarily prevent it being subject to such control.'[86]

The Judicial Committee, with the exception of *Voluntary Assignments*, had studiously protected federal jurisdiction over interest and bankruptcy and insolvency. However, in 1963, the Supreme Court upheld Ontario legislation which enabled a court to determine whether the terms of a loan, including interest, were excessive or unconscionable. The narrow definition of interest used by the court – 'day to day accrual' – served the purpose of the majority decision but seriously narrowed federal jurisdiction.[87] (However, in 1978, the court again widened the definition without expressly repudiating the earlier decision.)[88] On the other hand, in a controversial 5–4 decision of 1969, the court found Ontario legislation regulating insolvent insurance companies an unconstitutional encroachment on the federal Winding-Up Act. 'In this case,' Weiler commented, 'the majority of the court tacitly overruled a long sequence of decisions by the Privy Council and the Supreme Court – extending from 1910 to 1945 – which had denied parliament the jurisdiction to regulate the insurance business.'[89]

With one exception the court rigorously upheld the immunity of federally regulated undertakings from provincial encroachment.[90] Although it seemed a stretch, Ontario's Go-Train commuter service, which used its own rolling stock, was held to fall within federal jurisdiction because it ran on the Canadian National Railway's interprovincial line. In a joint opinion of 1967, the court determined that the 'constitutional jurisdiction depends on the character of the railway line and not on the character of a particular service provided on that railway line ... From a physical point of view, the commuter service trains are part of the overall operations of the line over which they run.'[91] More disturbing to the provinces was a unanimous decision of 1966 that Bell Telephone was immune from Quebec's minimum wage legislation, although there was no federal wage legislation in effect. Immunity for Bell and other similar federally regulated undertakings had been based on the supposition that provincial or municipal regulations could impair or paralyse their operations. The court extended the immunity to include a law which only 'affects a vital part of the management and operation of the undertaking.'[92]

Politically, the two most controversial decisions involved the application of the federal residual power. When the National Capital Commission Act, giving the commission the power to expropriate land for the capital region, was challenged in *Munro* (1966), the court found that the matter did not fall within the enumerations of sections 91 or 92 and, therefore, fell within the residual clause. Citing the judgments and *dicta* of Dunedin and Simon, and the *Canada Temperance* and *Johannesson* precedents, Cartwright stated that 'I find it difficult to suggest a matter of legislation which more easily goes beyond local or provincial interests and is the concern of Canada as a whole than the development, conservation and improvement of the National Capital Region.'[93] The decision, proclaimed André Tremblay of the University of Ottawa, was 'un triomphe incomparable' for 'l'un des pouvoirs les plus centralisateurs' of the BNA Act and should reinforce the determination of Quebec to secure a constitutional court. Anticipating later criticism of the court, he concluded that there were at least three lessons to be drawn:

Le premier est que la Cour suprême paraît de moins en moins attachée aux décisions du Conseil privé, lesquelles décisions, nous l'avouons, avaient transformé une constitution très centralisée en un document plus fédéral. Le deux-ième, c'est que les pouvoirs législatifs résiduaires ou généraux serviront probablement de plus en plus base juridique à des mesures législatives fédérales. Le troisième, c'est que le Québec aura de moins en moins confiance à la Cour suprême pour protéger son autonomie et pour faire valider les lois qu'il pourrait éventuellement passer pour agrandir le cadre de ses activités.[94]

Professor Gil Rémillard lamented that, with the decision, the limita-tion 'des pouvoirs fédéraux d'empiètement – que le Comité judiciaire avait judicieusement elaborée' – in Watson's 1896 decision, among oth-ers, 'n'existe plus.'[95]

For the first time since 1949, the Supreme Court was thrown into the political battlefield when federal-provincial diplomacy failed to resolve the ownership of the offshore mineral rights in the territorial sea adjacent to British Columbia. The 1967 reference by the Pearson government was obviously expected to uphold federal ownership, and Premier W.A.C. Bennett denounced the move as the first step to plun-der provincial resources and the cabinet discussed secession.[96] With six provinces (excluding Quebec, which characteristically maintained that the question had to be settled by political negotiations, not the courts) intervening in support of provincial ownership, the court agreed with the federal government that Canada was the sovereign state recog-nized in international law, and that British Columbia, as colony or province, never had possession of the territory in question. The lands did not fall within section 92 since they were outside provincial bound-aries, and therefore fell within exclusive federal jurisdiction as a 'mat-ter affecting Canada generally and covered by the expression, "the peace, order, and good government of Canada."' Moreover, 'the min-eral resources of these lands are of concern to Canada as a whole and go beyond local or provincial concerns or interests.'[97] To alarm the provinces further, the decision suggested again that the controversial decision in *Labour Conventions* fragmenting the treaty power could be overruled.[98]

The direction of the Supreme Court's jurisprudence in the 1960s was uncertain and it may have been inconsistent and doctrinally vacuous, but it was not all 'backward.' When the court upheld provincial juris-diction, it did so without restricting federal authority. In judicially authorizing concurrency and confirming inter-delegation in *Cough-lin*, it abandoned, when necessary to reach the desired outcome, the watertight paradigm in favour of a more functional and permissive approach to divided jurisdiction. As Gibson concluded: 'Rather than stressing the exclusivity of federal powers, the court tended to encourage jurisdictional co-existence, with federal priority reserved chiefly for situations of actual conflict.'[99] And although *Carnation* made the scope of trade and commerce less certain, in 1966 the court confirmed the decision of the Ontario Court of Appeal that a new criminal offence dealing with resale price maintenance – the regulation of contracts for sale and resale – was valid as a protection against harmful consequences of commercial activities, although contracts had traditionally been held to fall within 92(13).[100] Finally, the immunity of federal undertakings was enlarged and strengthened, and the residual power was strikingly enhanced in *Munro* and *Offshore Minerals*.

Although some found a dramatic change in approach, the results were not nearly as dramatic. No challenge to a federal statute was upheld and, although fewer, there were several major landmark decisions expanding federal jurisdiction. At the same time, 70 per cent of the challenges to provincial jurisdiction were rejected. Reflecting on the jurisprudence of the 1960s, François Chevrette concludes with some justice: 'On pouvait avoir l'impression d'être en présence d'un fédéralisme rigide pour les provinces et souple pour le pouvoir central.'[101]

The Supreme Court was transformed in the 1970s and whatever centre of gravity there had been, disappeared. Martland, Ritchie, Judson, and Wishart Spence remained from the Diefenbaker-Pearson years. But Pierre Trudeau had transformed the court with the appointments of Pigeon in 1967, Laskin (1970), Dickson (1973), Jean Beetz, and Philippe de Grandpré (1974). In the selection of a new chief justice in 1973, Trudeau's catapulting of Laskin over five senior justices was obviously designed to strengthen the intellectual leadership of the court. There was also the suspicion that the prime minister had political motives. Professor Laskin was renowned for his criticism of the Judicial Committee and his advocacy of a strong central government, and as a justice of the Ontario Court of Appeal he had made no secret of his position on judicial review. With politicians reluctant to change the constitutional *status quo*, Laskin believed that the courts could not be passive bystanders:

I do not question the political logic of this position, given the assumption that the constitutional division of powers must remain untouched, either by the molar process of amendment or by the molecular process of judicial review. The assumption is, however, unacceptable to an evolving society, whatever may be the political postures of the moment. A federal state is a legal expression of a politically-agreed balance of centralizing and decentralizing features, and of a political agreed means of adjusting that balance from time to time without destroying the state in the course of any such adjustment. The responsibility of the courts, and especially of the Supreme Court of Canada, as an agency of adjustment is, of course, a heavy one; but we strike at the legal roots of the country if we deprecate the exercise of this constitutional function or seek to paralyze it when it has achieved a power balance that is particularly congenial to either provincial or federal proponents, as the case may be.[102]

But, if Trudeau's purpose was also to direct its jurisprudence, the appointments of Beetz and de Grandpré (as well as Pigeon) seemed calculated to assure some balance in federalism jurisprudence.

Throughout the 1970s the court seemed more sharply divided, if not polarized, than before, with the Martland-Ritchie-Judson bloc often allied with the Quebec trio. Laskin, who dissented in 50 per cent of the appeals between 1970 and 1973 and 42 per cent between 1973 and 1978, became known as the 'Great Dissenter' and, with Dickson and Spence, formed the 'L-S-D connection.'[103] Dickson recalled that in post-argument conferences, Laskin

felt strongly on certain issues and pressed and expressed them with vigour and elegance. I don't think he cared very much to what extent he was supported by other members of the Court ... Pigeon, depending on the topic, was always very direct and finite. De Grandpré had his point of view, which he always expressed quite firmly. Ritchie was never too aggressive at conference. Judson rarely said anything at conference. Martland always had an opinion, usually quite succinct, and concise, definite, which he would stick to normally.[104]

Opinions in federalism appeals more obviously reflected individual conceptions of the appropriate balance of power between federal and provincial jurisdiction than the specific matters before the court. Philippe de Grandpré was to leave the court within four years, 'complaining of court's direction on constitutional matters' and what he regarded as Laskin's 'mindless centralization.'[105]

Although the Supreme Court's record on trade and commerce was mixed, the jurisdictional balance tipped in favour of the federal government. In 1971 the court adopted the functional approach in *Murphy* and *Klassen* when it unanimously upheld a National Energy Board licence to Caloil of Montreal on condition that its imported oil could be sold only east of the Ottawa River. The policy, designed to protect the Ontario market for western producers, was to foster the development of western oil resources. Pigeon found that the condition was 'an integral part of a scheme for the regulation of international and interprovincial trade, a purpose that is clearly outside provincial jurisdiction and within the exclusive federal field of action.'[106] If followed, the decision could permit Ottawa to expand its jurisdiction over trade and commerce whenever the object was to protect or foster some domestic resource.

Two appeals concerned the always complicated provincial marketing schemes. In a contrived case to test the protective chicken- and egg-marketing policies in Quebec and Ontario, Manitoba gave local boards the power to market all eggs sold in the province, whatever their origin. In a surprising 1971 decision, which seemed to contradict Judicial Committee precedents and even his own decision in *Carnation*, Martland delivered the court's opinion that the scheme was unconstitutional for 'it not only affects interprovincial trade in eggs, but ... aims at the regulation of such trade ... It is designed to restrict or limit the free flow of trade between provinces as such. Because of that it constitutes an invasion of the exclusive legislative authority of Canada over the matter of the regulation of trade and commerce.'[107]

In response to the obvious need for some regulation of the egg market, Ottawa and all the provinces established the Canadian Egg Marketing Agency, which assigned each province a share of the national market. The complicated plan was administered by a national and ten provincial boards which were granted powers by inter-delegation from the other level of government. In 1978 the court unanimously found inter-delegation within the principles established in *Willis*, and although the boundaries between local and interprovincial trade were too blurred to have been accepted by Duff and Atkin, it agreed with Pigeon that the scheme represented 'a sincere cooperative effort' and 'it would be really unfortunate if this all was brought to nought.'[108]

However, in two highly controversial decisions, the court not only 'brought to nought' two federal statutes but threatened to turn the trade and commerce clock back to 1937 or beyond. In *Dominion Stores v. The Queen* (1980), Willard Estey (appointed in 1977), writing for a 5–4 majority, found unconstitutional a provision in the Agricultural Standards Act providing that if federal grade names for goods in interprovincial trade were to be used locally they must meet the same standards. In a decision that overturned two Ontario courts, Estey took as authority all the Judicial Committee decisions from Smith to Atkin (and ignored all Supreme Court decisions since 1949) to conclude that the federal government was not empowered 'to regulate local trade simply as part of a scheme for the regulation of international and interprovincial trade.'[109]

'There is a two-fold problem with this passage,' commented James C. MacPherson. 'First, the roll call of relevant cases gives the impression that time has stopped in 1937,' which may have marked the end of the Depression but certainly 'did not signal the end of constitutional law. The Supreme Court of Canada picked up the torch laid down by the Privy Council and immersed itself in the intricacies of Canadian constitutional law, including the trade and commerce power. It is astonishing that a majority of the current court would completely ignore these efforts and wrap itself in the musty doctrinal cloak of "the ancients" – the Privy Council.' Moreover, in ignoring recent case law, the court had not only 'enunciated doctrinal principles completely at variance with the principles stated in these cases,' but had apparently narrowed the first branch of *Parsons* to its 'pre-Depression anemia' and added new restrictions to the necessarily incidental doctrine which 'may make it very difficult for the federal government to establish an integrated national marketing scheme.' The consequences for Canadian constitutional law, he concluded, 'are worrisome – rarely has the court used relevant precedents in such a perplexing way, and with such unfortunate results.'[110]

In 1979 the court by a 6–3 majority also struck down a section of the Food and Drugs Act which prohibited labelling that could be misleading.[111] The court readily found that Labatt's 'Special Lite Beer,' which exceeded the alcoholic content for 'light beer' in the regulations, could mislead, and turned to Labatt's second argument that the section was unconstitutional. The federal government's arguments that the regulation could be upheld under 91(2), the criminal law, or peace, order, and good government were rejected with reasons which, if followed, could have dramatically reversed the direction of Supreme Court jurisprudence.

In his judgment, Estey again returned to *Parsons*. He agreed with Smith that, without 'judicial restraint' in the interpretation of the trade and commerce power, 'provincial areas of jurisdiction would be seriously truncated,' and he then continued with a recitation of opinion limiting the scope of section 91(2), including Watson's clarification of *Russell*, Haldane in *Board of Commerce*, and Duff and Atkin in the 1937 marketing decisions. More recent decisions, he noted, had recognized 'a federal competence in marketing legislation, provided the principal purpose and thrust of the legislation was the regulation of interprovincial or international trade.'[112]

But, in Estey's opinion, there was no extra-provincial trade involved; the brewing industry consisted of a number of discrete provincial operations. He dismissed Laskin's argument that the second branch of *Parsons* could justify the power 'to fix standards that are common to all manufacturers of food, including beer'[113] with a clarifying explanation that Smith's 'it may be' *obiter* (or 'afterthought,' as he termed it) 'and all the subsequent references thereto are all predicated upon the requirement that the purported trade and commerce legislation affected industry and commerce at large or in a sweeping general sense,' which obviously misleading labelling did not.[114]

Although Hogg believed that the regulations *should have*,[115] and MacPherson *might have*,[116] been upheld under the criminal law power, Estey disagreed: the content of beer had nothing to do with health or the advertising with deception. Finally, a cursory review of Judicial Committee authorities was sufficient to enable Estey to conclude that 'the brewing and labelling of beer has not been said to have given rise either to a national emergency or a new problem not existing at the time of Confederation, nor to a matter of national concern transcending the local authorities' power to meet and solve it by legislation.' Thus, he could find no basis for the regulations within peace, order, and good government.[117]

Although Estey's archaic reasoning, if not the decisions themselves, threatened to turn the clock back, in 1977 the court did protect the trade and commerce power against attempts by Saskatchewan to regulate the production and pricing of its natural resources.[118] With the escalation of oil prices in the 1970s, the province attempted to capture the increased economic rents from the producing companies by levying a surcharge at the well-head equal to the difference between the old and new price. Although the case arose in private litigation, the federal government outraged the provinces by intervening to support the challenge and protect its jurisdiction. For the majority, Martland wrote that, not only was the surcharge an unconstitutional indirect tax, but, in fixing the price of a product of which 98 per cent was exported, the province had interfered with the regulation of trade and commerce. Dickson (with de Grandpré concurring) dissented on the grounds that the tax was direct and not a device for assuming control of the export trade, whose undoubted incidental effect on trade and commerce was not disabling.[119]

A year later, the court heard a challenge to Saskatchewan's use of quotas to regulate the production of potash, most of which was exported, to stabilize the market and increase prices. Once again, to protect its jurisdiction, the federal government joined the corporation as co-plaintiff. For a unanimous court, Laskin stated that, although 'production controls and conservation measures with respect to natural resources' were ordinarily within provincial jurisdiction, the 'true nature and character' of the scheme was clearly an attempt to fix the price of goods in the export market and was thus beyond provincial jurisdiction.[120]

Since the decision reversed that of the provincial Supreme Court, Laskin felt compelled to counter the statement of provincial chief justice Edward Cullitin that the consequence of invalidating the legislation would be to give the federal government the power to control production and pricing. 'There is no accretion at all to federal power in this case, which does not involve federal legislation, but simply a determination by this court, in obedience to its duty, of a limitation on provincial legislative power for it does not follow that legislation of a Province held to be invalid may *ipso facto* be validly enacted by Parliament in its very terms.'[121] He also added a lecture to justify judicial review, however controversial the outcome:

Where governments in good faith, as in this case, invoke authority to realize desirable economic policies, they must know that they have no open-ended means of achieving their goals when there are constitutional limitations on the legislative power under which they purport to act. They are entitled to expect that the Courts, and especially this Court, will approach the task of appraisal of the constitutionality of social and economic programs with sympathy and regard for the serious consequences of holding them *ultra vires*. Yet, if the appraisal results in a clash with the Constitution it is the latter which must govern. This is the situation here.[122]

The Supreme Court considered the always controversial scope of the residual clause in four decisions during the 1970s. In 1975 there was no disagreement, on the court at least, that the Official Languages Act of 1969 was outside provincial jurisdiction.[123] More controversial was the 4–3 decision of 1976 that, although the argument had not been advanced, river pollution affecting more than one province fell within federal jurisdiction. Writing for the majority, Pigeon declared that 'the same view ought to be taken in respect of the pollution of interprovincial waters as with respect to interprovincial trade.' The enumerated powers in section 91, he emphasized, were only 'for greater certainty' and 'the basic rule is that general legislative authority in respect of all that is not within the provincial field is federal. Here, we are faced with a pollution problem that is not really local in scope but truly interprovincial.'[124]

The most important decision since 1949 was the reference on Trudeau's Anti-Inflation Act of 1975, which imposed national wage and price controls in an attempt to curb inflation. It was the first time since 1949 that a major federal policy had been challenged in court, and the first time that the historical variations on peace, order, and good government were thoroughly dissected. In the result, three opinions reflected very different assumptions about the fundamental nature of Canadian federalism. [125]

The federal government's argument was based on the preamble to the act. This preamble stated that 'the containment and reduction of inflation has become a matter of serious national concern' which, from its inherent nature as a matter of concern to the entire country, could be upheld as a law for the peace, order, and good government of Canada under Simon's 'true test' in *Canada Temperance*. The alternative basis, best described as a fall-back position, was that the economic crisis so threatened Canadian economic stability as to justify federal intervention.

Chief Justice Laskin (writing for Dickson, Judson, and Spence) sought authority in *Russell*, *Local Prohibition*, and *Canada Temperance* to support the national concern or dimensions doctrine. Noting Atkin's caution that Watson's words in 1896 'laid down no principle of constitutional law, and were cautious words intended to safeguard possible eventualities which no one at the time had any interest or desire to define,' Laskin (of course, knowing he had lost the point), offered his own defensive *dicta* to protect the future:

It is my view that a similar approach of caution is demanded even today, both against a loose and unrestricted scope of the general power and against a fixity of its scope that would preclude resort to it in circumstances now unforseen.

Indeed, I do not see how this court can, consistently with its supervisory function in respect of the distribution of legislative power, preclude in advance and irrespective of any supervening situations a resort to the general power or, for that matter, to any other head of legislative authority. This is not to say that clear situations are to be unsettled, but only that a Constitution designed to serve the country in years ahead ought to be regarded as a resilient instrument capable of adaptation to changing circumstances.[126]

However, without admitting defeat, Laskin wrote that since there was a 'general concession' by the opposition that the act 'would be valid if it were what I may call crisis legislation,' and since that was the alternative argued by its proponents, the wise course was to determine whether it could be supported on that ground. If sustainable as crisis legislation, it was unnecessary 'to consider the broader ground advanced in its support, and this because, especially in constitutional cases, courts should not, as a rule, go any further than is necessary to determine the main issue before them.'[127] Without difficulty, but carefully choosing his words, he found that the court 'would be unjustified in concluding ... that the Parliament of Canada did not have a rational basis for regarding the *Anti-Inflation Act* as a measure which, in its judgement, was temporarily necessary to meet a situation of economic crisis imperilling the well-being of the people of Canada and requiring Parliament's stern intervention in the interests of the country as a whole.'[128]

Ritchie (for Martland and Louis-Philippe Pigeon) rejected the national concern doctrine as legitimatizing the act under the residual clause and stated that 'the aura of federal authority can in my view only be extended so as to invade the provincial arena when the legislation is directed to coping with a genuine emergency ...' In his judgment, the evidence before the court supported the conclusion that parliament was 'motivated by a sense of urgent necessity created by highly exceptional circumstances.'[129] Beetz (with de Grandpré) undertook an extensive critical analysis of the judicial historiography of the residual power and outlined rigorous criteria to justify its use, approved by Ritchie, which was to condition application of the clause in the future.

Beetz agreed that the residual power could be used in extraordinary circumstances, but he contended that parliament must explicitly signal, as it had not, that it was acting pursuant to that extraordinary authority. In normal circumstances, however, the national concern doctrine had been narrowly defined, and must constitute a 'matter' which did not fall within provincial jurisdiction and was clearly a matter of national concern. To so qualify, a matter must have 'a degree of unity that made it indivisible, an identity which made it distinct from provincial matters and a sufficient consistence to retain the bounds of form.' Moreover, the scale of the impact on provincial jurisdiction had to be considered. In the end, Beetz wrote, the containment of inflation 'does not pass muster as a new subject matter. It is an aggregate of several subjects some of which form a substantial part of provincial jurisdiction. It is totally lacking in specificity. It is so pervasive that it knows no bounds. Its recognition as a federal head of power would render most provincial powers nugatory.'[130]

The federal government had gambled and both won and lost. The court upheld the act but rejected the national concern justification and partially revived Haldane's emergency doctrine after its setback in Simon's judgment. Moreover, Beetz had written new and compelling doctrine on the possible potential of peace, order, and good government. On the other hand, the court had accepted the existence of an emergency or 'crisis imperilling the well-being' of the nation as authorizing peacetime legislation under the residual clause, and placed the onus of rejection on the appellants.[131] And there lingered in Laskin's opinion an eloquent plea for judicial resiliency in recognizing the legitimacy of the exercise of federal jurisdiction in matters affecting the peace, order, and good government of Canada in circumstances unforeseen.

Commentators found it difficult to assess the consequences of the decision(s) for federalism although all agreed they were, or could be, of enormous significance. While there was disappointment and criticism regarding the reasoning and results from all sides, there seemed to be a consensus among anglophones that the issue was framed 'in terms sufficiently narrow to prevent the decision from having far-reaching implications in terms of the federal balance of powers.'[132] Peter Russell, for example, was relieved that the court had not liberated the residual clause 'from the shackles placed upon it by the Privy Council's jurisprudence and thereby provide[d] the constitutional underpinning for a revolutionary readjustment of the balance of power in Canadian federalism.'[133]

However, francophone scholars were less certain that the shackles remained. Gérald Beaudoin was reassured that the law was upheld under the emergency, rather than the national dimension, doctrine, even if the latter theory 'n'a pas été reléguée aux oubliettes.'[134] Recalling that Professor Laskin had written that Simon's judgment in *Canada Temperance* 'may be likened to the removal of shutters from a house which has been kept dark for many years,'[135] Pierre Patenaude worried that the 'shutters are closed but the back door is wide open.'[136] His fellow academics, François Chevrette and Herbert Marx of the Université de Montréal, were not content that peace, order, and good government 'has now been examined, considered, re-examined and finally buried. Will it be resurrected? The Chief Justice has provided the necessary rationalization for would-be resurrectionists. It should also be noted that the burial was essentially by way of *obiter dictum* and not by a formal *ratio decidendi*. Consequently, a resurrection of the clause – in effect the national dimension doctrine – should not be completely ruled out.'[137]

Ironically, the first door to be opened owed more to a debatable application of Beetz's criteria of 'new' and 'distinctive' than to the national concern doctrine. In 1978 the court faced a challenge to a conviction under the Narcotic Control Act on the grounds that the section of the Criminal Code authorizing the federal attorney general to prosecute was an unconstitutional violation of the provincial prosecutorial authority under 92(14). Perhaps to avoid the prosecutorial issue, on which the court was deeply split, Pigeon for the majority conveniently (but imaginatively) found that the act itself was valid under the residual power, and thus within federal enforcement authority, because narcotics was a 'genuinely new problem which did not exist at the time of Confederation and clearly cannot be put in the class of 'Matters of a merely local and private nature.'[138]

Fundamental differences over the boundaries of federal jurisdiction were apparent in two 1978 decisions in both of which Pigeon, Beetz, and de Grandpré dissented. In *Capital Cities*, Laskin for the majority rejected the argument that the Canadian Radio-Television Commission lacked authority to enforce the deletion of American commercials on cable television: 'This submission amounts to a denial of any effective federal legislative jurisdiction of what passes in interprovincial or international communication, whether by radio or television, and is in truth an invitation to recant the *Radio* case ... Although this court is not bound by the judgements of the Privy Council any more than it is bound by its own judgements, I hold the view that the *Radio* case was correctly decided under the terms of ss. 91 and 92(10)(a).'[139]

Federal jurisdiction extended to the regulation of television signals from outside Canada and the transmission of the signals inside Canada and it would, Laskin opined, be incongruous 'to deny the continuation of regulatory authority because the signals are intercepted and sent on to ultimate viewers through a different technology.'[140]

In *Dionne*, delivered the same day, the court reaffirmed federal jurisdiction over cable television and denied the possibility of any 'divided constitutional control of what is a functionally inter-related system.'[141] However, in *Kellog* (1978), the court did leave some room for provincial regulatory authority when it determined that television content was not in pith and substance about broadcasting, despite its undoubted effects. In upholding a Quebec law prohibiting the use of cartoon advertising directed at children, Martland found that the law related to the control of commercial activity within the province and was valid within section 92(13).[142]

Although most of the major federalism decisions enhanced or protected federal jurisdiction,[143] there were decisions that protected or extended provincial legislative or regulatory authority. In 1979 the court finally placed boundaries around the inter-jurisdictional immunity of federal works when it determined by majority that the contractor working on the federal Mirabel airport was subject to Quebec minimum-wage law.[144] It also considered the boundaries of federal jurisdictional immunity in areas under its legislative authority. In the 1974 appeal on the application of the Alberta Wildlife Act to Indians living on a reserve, the decision was framed by Laskin in dissent. Section 91(24) gave the federal government exclusive legislative authority over Indians and lands reserved for Indians. Such reserves, Laskin insisted, were 'enclaves,' which, so long as they exist as Reserves, are withdrawn from provincial regulatory power. The majority, however, found that the natural-resources agreement between Canada and Alberta made the provisions of the act applicable to all Indians wherever they lived. Rejecting the 'enclave' proposition, the majority found that the act did not relate to Indians, qua Indians, and was applicable to all Indians including those on reserves.[145] The decision was strengthened at the end of the decade when, in a 7–2 decision (Laskin and Ritchie dissenting), the court ruled that a shoe manufacturing company, owned by Indians incorporated in Ontario, funded by the federal Department of Indian Affairs, and located on a reserve, fell within provincial labour laws of general application.[146]

The provinces also benefited from decisions based on concurrency. In 1978 provincial law concerning fraudulent preferences was held (5–4) not to be directly repugnant to federal bankruptcy law.[147] In 1973 the court twice upheld provincial drunk-driving laws although they conflicted with the more lenient provisions in the Criminal Code.[148] The court, in 1977, also rejected a challenge to British Columbia's monopoly of automobile insurance by a company engaged in national and international operations despite the incidental impact on interprovincial trade and commerce.[149]

In two controversial and divisive decisions of 1978, the court relaxed the limitations on provincial jurisdiction in the field of criminal law. Citing Strong in *Severn* in 1878 that provincial legislation should be approached on the assumption that it was validly enacted, Ritchie, for a 5–4 majority, upheld Nova Scotia's prohibition of the public exhibition of films deemed to be immoral as a matter relating to the regulation of the provincial film business and within 92(13 or 92(16).[150] In *Dupond*, Beetz reached back to *Hodge* in 1883, in which Ontario's liquor regulations were upheld as designed to prevent disorderly conduct, to reject a challenge to a Montreal by-law prohibiting assemblies in public streets on the grounds that its purpose was to prevent public disturbances.[151] In another case, in 1977, the majority of the court concluded that the administration of justice in the province included criminal justice and upheld the validity of a Quebec commission to inquire into organized crime.[152] And in 1978 the court determined that Quebec could establish a commission to inquire into the activities of the RCMP but not into the management of the force itself.[153]

By the end of the 1970s, the Supreme Court had heard more than one hundred federalism appeals. Almost 40 per cent of the challenges to provincial legislation were upheld, but federal legislation seemed legally immune until four federal statutes were held *ultra vires* in whole or part in the late 1970s.[154] Substantively and doctrinally, the tendency was the same. As a result, the Supreme Court was subjected to increasing academic and political scrutiny and criticism. Although opinions differed on the quality of the decisions and reasoning, the unanimous verdict was that the cumulative result of its decisions had been favourable to the federal government. Stealing a line from Maurice Duplessis, René Lévesque put it best: 'Comme la Tour de Pise, la Cour penche toujours du même bord.'[155]

By 1975, Peter Russell, admittedly an anti-centralist, had concluded that there were 'strong grounds' for 'doubting whether the Supreme Court can continue to be respected as a reasonably impartial arbiter of dominion-provincial disputes, given the federal government's monopoly in appointing its judges and the fact that the central government has not lost a constitutional case decided by the court since 1949.'[156] However, Russell wrote, although the court had been 'relatively generous in its treatment of the major sources of federal power,' the decisions had not 'significantly altered the balance of power in Canadian federalism.' Nevertheless, he observed, some of the provinces were alarmed, and if 'the undermining of the Supreme Court's legitimacy as a constitutional arbiter goes too much further it could pose certain dangers to the future of confederation.'[157]

Dean K.M. Lysyk of the University of British Columbia's Faculty of Law, admittedly an admirer of the 'balance' achieved by the Judicial Committee, found the numbers troubling, and the expansion of federal jurisdiction over trade and commerce particularly ominous. Lysyk chose not to question the merit of the decisions: 'What is relevant for present purposes is the cumulative effect of these decisions in giving rise to the perception, and in so far as the provinces are concerned the apprehension, that the court is not as sensitive to the importance of guarding provincial autonomy as was the Privy Council, or as they (the provinces) might wish a future constitutional court of last resort to be.'[158] Provincial apprehension was well documented when the *Report of the Western Premiers' Task Force on Constitutional Trends* observed that 'there is an increasing tendency on the part of Ottawa to oppose the constitutionality of provincial legislation,' and listed eleven cases decided or pending since 1973.[159]

The scholarly and political criticism led Peter Hogg to ask: 'Is the Supreme Court Biased in Constitutional Cases?'[160] Hogg admitted that 'over the past few years ... the federal interest has fared much better than the provincial interest.' However, given the impotence of the residual clause at the hands of the Judicial Committee, its resurrection would not 'surprise a visitor from another planet'[161] and the expansion of trade and commerce was 'very cautious,' although as a barrier to provincial jurisdiction it had been 'applied more boldly.'[162] The natural resource and communication decisions were arguable, but after a review of other jurisdictional areas, including the court's narrow definition of inconsistency to trigger federal paramountcy, Hogg concluded that the Supreme Court 'has generally adhered to the doctrine laid down by the Privy Council precedents; and that where the court has departed from those precedents, or has been without close precedents, the choices between competing lines of reasoning have favoured the provincial interest at least as often as they have favoured the federal interest. There is no basis for the claim that the court has been biased in favour of the federal interest in constitutional litigation.'[163]

Gilbert L'Écuyer, in a massive study for the Parti Québécois government, reached the same conclusion about bias, but for quite different reasons. He found that the Supreme Court decisions were generally more favourable to the federal government than those of the Judicial Committee. However, he concluded, other than on rare occasions, the decisions were well founded in law and faithful to the text of the BNA Act and the intentions of the authors. 'Il semble en effet que les décisions de la Cour Suprême auront généralement tendance à être favorable au gouvernement fédéral tant et aussi longtemps que le tribunal devra interpréter un texte qui prête essentiellement, par son libellé et l'intention de ses auteurs, à une vision centralisatrice.'[164]

There is a surprising unanimity among francophone authorities. Without exception, as far as I can determine, they agree that the division of jurisdiction in 1867 was more than tilted towards Ottawa; that the decisions of the Judicial Committee 'ont rendu la constitution canadienne plus conforme au principes du fédéralisme';[165] and that the decisions of the Supreme Court (at least until the end of the 1970s) conformed to the language of the text.[166] Indeed, as Jean Beetz acknowledged in 1965, before his appointment to the court, the Judicial Committee had given property and civil rights 'une extension si grande' that it became 'le site du pouvoir résiduel' and had so restricted the federal enumerations, particularly trade and commerce, 'allant jusqu'à compléter, et peut-être jusqu'à trahir, la lettre de l'article 91.' Section 92 had been enlarged as much as was 'humainement possible' and a province could not 'sans modification constitutionnelle, espérer voir sa compétence augmenter.'[167] Gil Rémillard agreed:

Il faut bien avouer que plusieurs des décisions du Comité judiciaire, parmi les plus provincialistes, tiennent d'un véritable tour de prestidigitation quant à leur fondement juridique. Avec un pragmatisme tout à fait anglo-saxon, le haut tribunal anglais a su donner à la constitution canadienne ce caractère fédéraliste que la lettre de la Loi constitutionnelle de 1867 ne réflétait pas toujours. La Cour suprême, pour sa part, s'en est tenue beaucoup plus à la lettre qu'à l'esprit de l'Acte de 1867. Ainsi n'a-t-elle pu que confirmer son caractère quasi fédératif.[168]

Beetz and all francophone scholars liked the progeny bequeathed by the Judicial Committee, but were concerned, as Jacques Brossard put it, that 'l'évolution politique de ces dernières années soutenue par la Cour suprême du Canada, le ramène – de façon régressive – à ses origines.' Without arguing that the court was (necessarily) biased, they emphasized the expansion of federal jurisdiction with the resurrection and extension of the national dimensions doctrine; the broadened scope of trade and commerce; new judicial doctrines justifying interjurisdictional immunity and a more liberal view of ancillarity or incidental powers; and a more functional approach which led to inter-delegation and concurrency.[169] The common thread in all critiques was the critical importance to Quebec (and to federalism) of maintaining intact Atkin's watertight compartments. Pierre Patenaude, dean of Law at the University of Moncton, expressed the widespread concern in the title of his article: 'L'érosion graduelle de la règle de l'étanchéité: une nouvelle menace à l'autonomie du Québec.'[170]

The criticism of the *nationalistes* was more directly political. The court had become the final court of appeal, wrote Jacques-Yvan Morin, 'with all the hopes of English-Canada hanging around the necks of its judges.' Although it took a few years, French Canadians soon realized that the Supreme Court was in a position 'to correct the trends of the past' and that 'the guarantees they had come to expect from the imperial institutions had come to an end.' That realization, he speculated in 1965, 'may have been one of the initial factors that launched the profound movement for self-determination which is developing in Quebec.'[171]

Explicitly or implicitly, scholarly and political critics of the court's federalism jurisprudence attributed its centralist tendency to appointment by the federal government. As Henri Brun and Guy Tremblay phrased it, 'la justice doit non seulement être rendue, mais elle doit apparaître avoir été rendue. Force est de constater que le dernier pôle de cette alternative n'est pas présent en ce qui regarde la Cour suprême, dont tous les juges sont nommés par le gouvernement fédéral: lorsqu'une province se plaint de la Cour suprême, c'est qu'à ses yeux justice ne parait pas être faite ou pouvoir être faite dans l'état actuel des choses.'[172] The criticism did not go unanswered. In a public *ex cathedra* statement, Chief Justice Laskin attacked the accusers:

We have ... been charged with bias, with manifesting a tendency to lean in a particular direction. The bill of particulars on this allegation is very selective. There has been no attempt to strike any balance on an overall assessment of our performance; no attempt to measure our performance against the constitutional prescriptions which we are obliged to respect and which we do respect. The allegation is reckless in its implication that we have considerable freedom to give voice to our personal predilections and thus to have political preferences.

We have no such freedom, and it is a disservice to the present members of this Court and to the work of those who have gone before us to suggest a federal bias because of federal appointment. Do we lean? Of course, we do, in the direction in which the commands of the constitution take us, according to our individual understandings.[173]

Concern about federalist leaning by the Supreme Court led the provinces to put restructuring of the court on the agenda when the process of constitutional reform began in the 1960s. But all proposals for provincial participation in the selection process died with the death of the Victoria Charter in 1970 and the Meech Lake and the Charlottetown accords in the 1990s. And the leaning, if such it was, continued in the last decades of the century.

11

Consolidation and Innovation
1980-2000

A distinctively Canadian jurisprudence ...

–Justice Brian Dickson, 1984

Academic and political criticism did not deflect the direction, or notice-ably restrain the momentum, of the Supreme Court's jurisprudence in the 1980s and 1990s. Although there was little or no diminution of existing provincial jurisdictional powers, the expansion or enhance-ment of federal jurisdiction of the previous decades was consolidated. Federal paramountcy prevented encroachment on the enumerated heads and the sweep of the interjurisdictional immunity doctrine was broadened. Confronted by new issues or variations of the old, the court was innovative in finding new uses for the major sources of fed-eral jurisdiction: the criminal law, trade and commerce, and the resid-ual clause. By the end of the century, the Supreme Court had created a 'distinctively Canadian jurisprudence' and the legacy of the Judicial Committee had become a faint juristic memory to be recalled when convenient. More fundamentally, by the 1980s the court was accepted as a legitimate lawmaking institution.

The critical moment was the amendment to the Supreme Court Act in 1975 which abolished most appeals as of right. The court was now in charge of its own agenda and would hear appeals only if 'the Supreme Court is of the opinion that any question involved therein is, by reason of its public importance or the importance of any issue of mixed law and fact involved in such question, one that ought to be decided by the Supreme Court or is, for any other reason, of such a nature or significance to warrant decision by it.' Initially proposed as a means of reducing the workload, the amendment was, in effect, a parliamentary mandate for judicial lawmaking.[1] As Chief Justice Laskin said, the amendment finally sealed 'the Court's status as Canada's ultimate appellate Court.'[2] In 1983, a few months before his elevation, Dickson stated that it was difficult

to overestimate the importance of this provision. The criterion for the court granting leave to appeal is now the 'public importance' of the legal issues raised by a given case, a standard which allows the court to concentrate its efforts where it feels they are most needed and where they will have the most widespread – and we hope beneficial impact. The very concept of 'public importance' invites a consideration of underlying principles and practical consequences, and in a growing number of decisions these factors play a prominent part in the analysis.

Federalism jurisprudence had always been concerned with the delicate equilibrium in the Canadian state and society, with the listings in sections 91 and 92 subject to varying interpretations. Although the words and phrases continued to pose interpretive problems, Dickson continued, a notable feature of recent decisions was 'a new willingness to engage the questions of the proper meaning of ss 91 and 92, not as an abstract exercise in statutory interpretation, but as a practical problem with foreseeable political consequences. Whether not one agrees with the solutions offered in these judgements, this conceptualization of the court's role in such cases is an important and I think positive development for Canadian jurisprudence.'[3] Judicial lawmaking was now an accepted fact.

Critically important also was the mandate given to the Supreme Court to fashion the law relating to rights and freedoms when the Charter became law in 1982. There were no sections 91 and 92 to provide guidance or precedent, and the court had a clean slate on which to write its constitutional prescriptions. This is not the occasion to discuss the possible effect of the Charter on federalism,[4] but it is appropriate to suggest that there was an inevitable spillover from the necessarily innovative approach to Charter interpretation to the more traditional federalism jurisprudence. Certainly, the principles enunciated in Chief

Justice Dickson's approach to Charter review in *Hunter* v. *Southam* could not be easily distinguished from federalism review.

> The task of expounding a constitution is crucially different from that of construing a statute ... A constitution ... is drafted with an eye to the future. Its function is to provide a continuing framework for the legitimate exercise of government power ... It must, therefore, be capable of growth and development over time to meet new social, political and historical realities often unimagined by its framers. The judiciary is the guardian of the constitution and must, in interpreting its provisions, bear these considerations in mind.[5]

For these and other reasons – including perhaps academic criticism of the somewhat closed style of reasoning[6] and the changing composition and leadership of the court – there were changes in both the style and the substance of Supreme Court jurisprudence in the 1980s. The court did attempt to articulate more deliberately its reasoning, and the policy considerations that lay behind it. On occasion it created what might be called procedural and jurisdictional recipes to assist in the determination of validity. The most familiar example is Dickson's sequential criteria for the determination of section 1 of the Charter justification in *Oakes*. There were others for the residual power, trade and commerce, and interjurisdictional immunity. In spite of the political ferment outside the courtroom, or perhaps because of it, judgments and decisions seemed more often flavoured, if not decided, by references to the *national* union or *national* interests or necessities and to the functional inability of the provinces, singly or collectively, to act in the national interest.

An academic tone was increasingly evident in the judgments, where the bibliography of 'Authors Cited' was at times as long as the list of 'Cases Cited.' Judgments often read like academic historiographical essays, and judges occasionally engaged in spirited combat with dissenting academics or flattered others with their concurrence.[7] As Dickson commented in 1984, 'what was once largely a monologue has now turned into a dialogue, with the courts welcoming and often incorporating academic research and opinion.'[8]

The research was facilitated by the three law clerks employed by each judge by the 1990s.[9] Their utilization, however, was undoubtedly a reflection of the changing membership of the court. When Martland and Ritchie retired in the early 1980s, the court of the 1950s and 1960s went with them. Of the twenty-two puisne judges who sat on the court between 1980 and 2000, eleven were or had been full-time law professors at one stage of their careers and many others had lectured part-time. Other than John Sopinka (who had combined full-time legal studies with full-time professional football), the other justices had had extensive experience on the provincial superior courts or with government, or both. Academician Laskin was replaced by the scholarly Dickson as chief justice in 1984, and he was succeeded in 1990 by Antonio Lamer, a criminal law specialist and professor of law at the Université de Montréal.

There was no one better positioned than Dickson to suggest in 1983 that, for all these reasons, a new era had arrived in the evolution of the court:

In my opinion the mandate of the Supreme Court of Canada is to oversee the development of a distinctive Canadian jurisprudence. Our ability to do this was sharply circumscribed in the days of appeals as of right and in an era predominated by a reflexive deference to British legal opinion. I think we have now emerged from that era. As I see it the challenge currently before our courts is to develop a jurisprudence that combines a respect for recognized rules and established principles with sufficient flexibility to meet the specific needs of an evolving Canadian reality. Change need not, and should not, take place at break-neck speed. *Stare decisis* is still alive and well, but blind obedience to the antiquity of disembodied precedence will no longer sway our court.[10]

In 1991 the Supreme Court made what was in many ways the most important decision in the history of modern judicial review. At issue was nothing less than the core of post-war federalism – the federal spending power and the device of shared-cost programs. When Ottawa capped its payments under the Canada Assistance Plan to the three richest provinces in 1990, the government of British Columbia asked the provincial Court of Appeal to determine whether Canada had the authority to limit its obligations under the plan, and if the province had the 'legitimate expectation' that no change would be made in the agreement without its consent. The court replied 'No' to the first question and 'Yes' to the second.

Before the Supreme Court, where three provinces intervened, the federal government argued that the issue was non-justiciable because, 'to answer the question would be to draw the court into a political controversy and involve it in the legislative process.' For a unanimous court, Sopinka replied that the court's 'primary concern is to retain its proper role within the constitutional framework of our democratic form of government.' It was for the court to determine 'whether the question is purely political in nature and should, therefore, be determined in another forum or whether it has a sufficient legal component to warrant the intervention of the judicial branch.'[11] Judicial intervention warranted, the court held that a sovereign parliament could amend payments regardless of any agreement with the provinces. Nor was there any support

in Canadian or English cases for the position that the doctrine of legitimate expectations can create substantive rights. It is part of the rules of procedural fairness which can govern administrative bodies. Where it is applicable, it can create a right to make representations or to be consulted. It does not fetter the decision following the representations or consultation. Moreover, the rules governing procedural fairness do not apply to a body exercising purely legislative functions.[12]

In response to Manitoba's more fundamental argument that the use of the federal spending power in areas of provincial jurisdiction was unconstitutional, Sopinka replied, 'I disagree. The Agreement under the Plan set up an open-ended cost sharing scheme, which left it to British Columbia to decide which programs it would establish and fund. The simple withholding of federal money which had previously been granted to fund such a matter within provincial jurisdiction does not amount to the regulation of that matter.'[13] Had the decision been otherwise on either issue, the entire structure of post-war health and social-security programs could have collapsed, or at least become the subject of fractious federal-provincial negotiations.

The court heard more than a dozen appeals on variations of interjurisdictional immunity of federal works and undertakings from provincial regulation in the 1980s and 1990s. With the exception of three relatively unimportant appeals, the immunity of federal works and undertakings from provincial regulation was protected or expanded in all but one of the significant decisions.[14] Although the court had, after the surprising 1966 decision in *Bell*, placed some boundaries on the application of the doctrine in *Montcalm*, it held in 1983 that Northern Telecom was immune because its installation of telephones was an integral part of Bell's operations.[15] However, the court adopted the narrow approach when Ontario's Public Service Act, which prohibited public servants from participating in provincial and federal elections, was challenged because the latter fell within the exclusive domain of the federal government. The court found the prohibition was firmly grounded in section 92(1 and 4). In a concurring judgment, Dickson admitted that he shared with Peter Hogg the view that interjurisdictional immunity was not 'a particularly compelling doctrine' and he welcomed the limitations placed on it in *Montcalm* by a liberal application of the pith-and-substance doctrine:

The history of Canadian constitutional law has been to allow for a fair amount of interplay and indeed overlap between federal and provincial powers. It is true that doctrines like interjurisdictional and Crown immunity and concepts like 'watertight compartments' qualify the extent of that interplay. But it must be recognized that these doctrines and concepts have not been the dominant tide of constitutional doctrines; rather, they have been an undertow against the strong pull of pith and substance, the aspect doctrine and, in recent years, a very restrained approach to concurrency and paramountcy issues.[16]

Although federal-provincial agreement is not 'conclusive of the demarcation' of jurisdictional boundaries, Dickson added, the court should be 'particularly cautious' when, as in the present case, the federal government did not oppose validity but actually intervened to support it.[17]

In spite of his appeal for caution and restraint, Dickson sat with a unanimous court that applied the immunity doctrine in three consolidated appeals a year later. The leading decision was given by Beetz at great length in *Bell Canada* v. *Quebec*, which held that provincial health and safety laws could not apply to an interprovincial undertaking such as Bell. For the court, Beetz observed that 'it is sufficient that the provincial statute which purports to apply to the federal undertaking affects a vital or essential part of that undertaking, without necessarily going as far as impairing or paralyzing it.' Beetz rejected the concurrency or double aspect rule. He insisted that 'a basic minimum of unassailable content' had to be exclusively assigned to each enumerated head of section 91 which provincial legislation could not affect. Moreover, concurrent jurisdiction would lead to a proliferation of regulations, and the application of the paramountcy rule between rival 'systems of regulation' would be a 'source of uncertainty and endless disputes.'[18]

In a surprising 1989 decision, the court unanimously found that

Alberta Government Telephones (AGT), whose facilities existed solely within the province and which had been provincially regulated, was a federal undertaking and subject to exclusive federal jurisdiction. The court held that, because the AGT system had extra-provincial connections, it fell within the provisions of 92(10)(a). The location of the facilities or the residence of subscribers, Dickson wrote, 'will not preclude a finding that an undertaking is interprovincial in scope' because the 'primary concern is ... rather the service which is provided by the undertaking through the use of its physical equipment.' In short, as Dickson said, 'it is an all or nothing affair.'[19]

The legitimacy, or at least the use or abuse, of the declaratory power itself was fully canvassed in 1993 when the court had to determine whether employees at Ontario Hydro's nuclear-generation stations were subject to provincial or federal jurisdiction. For the majority, La Forest found that the nuclear plants fell under the provisions of the Atomic Energy Control Act and thus under federal jurisdiction. But he felt compelled to lecture his dissident colleagues (and perhaps academic critics as well) about the nature and purpose of the declaratory power and its cousin, interjurisdictional immunity, as well as the difference between law and politics:

It was argued that the declaratory power must be read narrowly to make it conform to principles of federalism. There is no doubt that the declaratory power is an unusual one that fits uncomfortably in an ideal conceptual view of federalism. But the Constitution must be read as it is, and not in accordance with abstract notions of theorists ...'[20] The restricted view advanced here for the first time appears to be based on the danger thought to be posed to the structure of Canadian federalism if the courts do not confine federal power in this area ... But more fundamentally, I think the argument evinces a misunderstanding of the respective roles of law and politics in the specifically Canadian form of federalism established by the Constitution.[21]

The declaratory power was not the only 'draconian power vested in the federal authorities,' La Forest continued, for the powers of disallowance and reservation gave it 'unrestricted authority' to veto provincial legislation. All were frequently used after Confederation to accomplish 'the original constitutional mandate by establishing the authority of the central government and its policies, and in particular to ensure the construction of the intercontinental railway. Later, the declaratory power was effectively used as a tool to regulate the national grain market in pursuit of the constitutional vision of integrating the western region of Canada into the country.' The powers were ultimately challenged and 'faded almost into desuetude when these large constitutional and national tasks had been accomplished.' Disallowance had not been used since 1942, and the declaratory power only twice since the 1960s. 'It is the very breadth of these powers that protects against their frequent or inappropriate use. It was not the courts but political forces that dictated their near demise ... In a word, protection against abuse of these draconian powers is left to the inchoate but very real and effective force that undergirds federalism.'[22]

Admitting that bifurcation of jurisdiction over labour relations in a single enterprise might be inconvenient, La Forest did not accept arguments for concurrency or provincial jurisdiction. If the problems seemed 'sufficiently acute,' and if parliament deemed it 'appropriate,' resort could be had to the technique of administrative inter-delegation.[23]

In a lengthy dissent, Iacobucci (for Sopinka and Peter Cory) contended that federal jurisdiction over such works and undertakings was not plenary but confined to aspects that are 'integral to the federal interest in the work,' which in the present case they were not. The 1867 constitution created a 'federalist system of government' and should be so interpreted as not to allow the powers of Parliament or the provincial legislatures to subsume the powers of the other. To allow the federal government, under either the declaratory or the residual clause, 'to control labour relations at these facilities would not be reconcilable with the distribution of legislative powers under which the provinces are accorded jurisdiction over property and civil rights, including labour relations, and the management of electrical generating stations' (in section 92A of the 1982 constitution).[24]

However, Iacobucci and Cory were in the majority in the last such case of the century when the court found in 1998 that the processing plants of West Coast Energy, as well as the interprovincial and international pipelines, were an integral part of an undertaking already under federal jurisdiction.[25] In a lengthy dissent, Beverley McLachlin emerged as the staunch defender of the 'federalist system.' The answer to the question whether there was the necessary 'functional integration' of a provincial enterprise to bring it within 'the realm of federal regulation,' she insisted, lay in the framework of the constitution, and the test for a transfer under section 92(10)(a) 'must conform to this constitutional framework, not deform it.' Because the power was 'exceptional, it follows that it should be extended as far as required for the purpose that animates it, and no further.' Extending federal jurisdiction to the production stage of primary resources 'under the guise' of regulating the pipelines was inconsistent with reading the constitution as 'a harmonious whole' and was, in her judgment, going too far.[26]

Jurisdiction over criminal law prosecutions, rather than the substance of the law itself, was the most contentious issue as the court began to hear criminal law appeals in the 1980s. The controversial decision in *Hauser* had placed the Narcotic Control Act within the residual clause and thus permitted federal prosecution, but the decision had not determined that federal prosecutorial authority could extend to criminal law. Dickson had dissented on the grounds that the act fell within criminal law, and prosecution, therefore, lay within provincial jurisdiction. Laskin had not sat on the case, but when the court found British Columbia's Heroin Treatment Act within provincial jurisdiction under a number of enumerated heads (92(7, 13, 16)), Laskin seized the opportunity to observe that 'unless we revert to a long abandoned view of the peace, order and good government power as embracing the entire catalogue of federal legislative power, I would myself have viewed the *Narcotic Control Act* as an exercise of the federal criminal law power,' as well as referable to the trade and commerce power, and within federal prosecutorial authority.[27]

The fundamentally different views held by Laskin and Dickson were starkly revealed in two 1983 decisions. Charged with a violation under the Combines Investigation Act, the Canadian National Railway countered with the plea that the 1969 amendment to the Criminal Code providing for prosecution by the federal attorney general was unconstitutional. For the majority, Laskin (Ritchie, Estey, and McIntyre concurring) refused to make any distinction between offences under criminal and non-criminal laws and, even assuming that the act rested only on the criminal law, wrote that the federal attorney general could prosecute without provincial consent.

Laskin maintained that, after Confederation, only federal abstention from interfering in the prosecution of offences under federal law, including criminal law, had led to the view that prosecution was embraced only in 92(14). 'Language and logic inform constitutional interpretation' and by 'no stretch of the imagination' could the language of section 92(14) 'be construed to include jurisdiction over the conduct of criminal prosecutions. Moreover, as a matter of conjunctive assessment of the two constitutional provisions, the express inclusion of procedure in civil matters in provincial courts point to an express provincial exclusion of procedure in criminal matters specified in s.91(27).'[28]

Dickson (Beetz and Lamer concurring) concurred in the result because he found the provisions of the act valid under both criminal law and trade and commerce and therefore there was concurrent prosecutorial authority. But he emphatically declared that, as 'to prosecutorial authority by virtue of the characterization of S. 32(1)(c) as criminal law, I am still of the opinion that only the provincial Attorney General can validly prosecute criminal enactments.'[29]

In a decision released the same day involving a similar federal prosecution under the Food and Drugs Act, the same majority endorsed the *Canadian National* decision, and Beetz and Lamer declared that it was binding. But in dissent, Dickson concluded that it rested solely on the criminal law power and thus relied on provincial prosecution. To Laskin's appeal to language and logic, Dickson replied that 'a page of history may illuminate more than a book of logic,'[30] flavouring his rebuttal with a touch of sarcasm:

If, as the Attorney-General of Canada contends, the provinces have for over 100 years been exercising, if not usurping, a jurisdiction not properly theirs, the provinces would seem to have been blissfully unaware of the fact, so also the federal Crown. One can look in vain among the Confederation debates, subsequent case law, the text books, other writings on the Constitution for any firm assertion on the part of the Attorney-General of Canada that the primary and, indeed, exclusive prosecutorial authority in criminal cases rests, and has always rested, with the federal Crown.[31]

Moreover, the geographical extent of the country and the 'primitive state of communications, all combine to make it clear that it was not within the contemplation of the Fathers of Confederation that ultimate constitutional authority for the control and prosecution of all criminal offences – the multitude of cases arising daily in the hundreds of communities in what was then Canada – would centre in Ottawa.'[32] In short: 'Blind centralism can be no answer.'[33] Provincial authority to administer the criminal justice system was 'a matter of constitutional law, not of federally delegated administrative powers,' and the amendment to the Criminal Code was to that extent *ultra vires*.[34]

The Laskin-Dickson debate over history and logic was essentially an argument about federalism, a conflict between Laskin's centralized model and Dickson's search for balance and moderation. Dickson's history probably had the better of the argument, but Laskin's model was more responsive to the needs of a modern regulatory state that could not always depend on provincial prosecutions for federal offences.[35]

The court also broadened and strengthened the boundaries of the criminal law power itself. In 1983 Laskin was able to persuade a unanimous court to undermine the decision in *Dupond* in which he had dissented. The Alberta Court of Appeal had upheld a municipal by-law prohibiting street solicitation for purposes of prostitution, but Laskin held that its purpose was 'so patently an attempt to control or punish prostitution as to be beyond question.'[36] A decade later, in 1993, the court struck down Nova Scotia's attempt to prohibit abortions outside designated medical institutions. For the court, Sopinka held that the prohibition had little to do with its stated object of maintaining 'a single high-quality of health-care delivery system' but was in effect an attempt to legislate in the area of criminal law. In so determining, Sopinka claimed for the court the right 'to refer to extrinsic evidence of various kinds provided it is relevant and not inherently unreliable. This clearly includes related legislation ... and evidence of the "mischief" at which the legislation is directed. It also includes legislative history.'[37] The debate in the legislature, he concluded, demonstrated that members of all parties understood the purpose of the legislation 'to be the prohibition of the respondent's proposed clinic on the basis of a common and almost unanimous opposition to abortion clinics,' which were seen as a public evil to be eliminated.[38]

Although the disposition ultimately rested on the Charter, the challenge to the Tobacco Products Control Act (1988) underlined the wide scope and potential of the criminal law power. The law did not criminalize the sale of tobacco, but prohibited, with penal sanctions, advertising and sale without health warnings. The Quebec Superior Court had found the act *ultra vires*, but the Court of Appeal, while denying its validity as criminal law, upheld it as a matter of national concern which met all the tests for the doctrine established in *Crown Zellerbach* in 1988.[39]

'Put bluntly, tobacco kills,' wrote La Forest for seven members of the court. 'Given this fact, can Parliament employ the criminal law to prohibit tobacco manufacturers from inducing Canadians to consume these products, and to increase public awareness concerning the hazards of their use? In my view, there is no question that it can.'[40] The power was plenary in nature and, in developing its definition of criminal law, 'this Court has been careful not to freeze the definition in time or to confine it to a fixed domain of activity.'[41] Although parliament could have chosen to prohibit the manufacture and sale of tobacco products, it chose not to do so given the widespread addiction and the impossibility of enforcement, but 'the wisdom of Parliament's choice of method cannot be determinative with respect to Parliament's power to legislate.'[42]

In dissent, John C. Major (Sopinka concurring) argued that, although the criminal law test was elusive, the sections limiting commercial expression, when the activity itself was not criminalized, did not fall within the boundaries of criminal law. However, in *obiter*, Major agreed with the Quebec Court of Appeal that the act met the national dimensions test for legislation under 'peace, order and good government.'[43]

The test became even more 'elusive' two years later when the court rendered a decision which, if followed, could establish criminal law as a power almost without borders. The issue was a challenge to the Canadian Environmental Protection Act (1985) which established a screening mechanism for identifying toxic substances and authorized the federal cabinet to determine how they might be used by industry. Hydro-Québec responded to the charge that it had dumped prohibited substances into a river with the argument that the act was *ultra vires* as not falling within any of the federal enumerated powers or the residual clause, and was a colourable attempt to invade provincial jurisdiction under the criminal law. Three Quebec courts agreed that provisions of the act could not be upheld under peace, order, and good government or the criminal law.

On appeal, the federal government sought support under both, but the principal focus before the court was the national concern doctrine. However, by a 5-4 majority, the court upheld the provisions under the criminal law power, and La Forest wrote a long, and somewhat laboured, justification of the decision.[44] Perhaps the national concern doctrine had been emphasized in argument, La Forest purposefully mused, because *RJR-MacDonald* had not yet been decided. As a result, he found much of the discussion 'not altogether apt to a consideration of the criminal law power.' Nevertheless, having found validity in the criminal law power, the court had 'to deal with the national concern doctrine, which inevitably raises profound issues respecting the federal structure of our constitution which do not arise with anything like the same intensity in relation to the criminal law power.'[45] Not surprisingly, the author of the dissent in *Crown Zellerbach*, opposing a broad application of the national concern doctrine, explained why the criminal law was the preferred (if not necessarily the only) choice:

The national concern doctrine operates by assigning full power to regulate an area to Parliament. Criminal law does not work that way. Rather it seeks by discrete prohibitions to prevent evils falling within a broad purpose, such as, for example, the protection of health. In the criminal law area, reference to such broad policy objectives is simply a means of ensuring that the prohibition is legitimately aimed at some public evil Parliament wishes to suppress and so is not a colourable attempt to deal with a matter falling within an area of provincial jurisdiction.[46]

La Forest found authority from Halsbury in *Hamilton Street Railway* in 1903 through Atkin and Rand to *Morgentaler* and *RJR-MacDonald*, to support the proposition that the criminal law was conferred in its 'widest sense' (Halsbury) and not 'frozen in time' (*RJR-MacDondald*). An abundance of unnecessary documentation was introduced to demonstrate that 'protection of the environment is a major challenge of our time. It is an international problem, one that requires action by government at all levels.'[47] Although the residual clause might seem to be the home for action at all levels, La Forest was convinced that Canada could meet its obligations by use of the criminal power. 'The purpose of the criminal law is to underline and protect our fundamental values ... stewardship of the environment is a fundamental value to our society and Parliament may use its criminal law power to underline that value. The criminal law must be able to keep pace with and protect our emerging values.'[48]

Since the decision would in no way preclude the provinces from exercising their powers 'to regulate and control the pollution of the environment either independently or to supplement federal action,' La Forest maintained that the fear that it would 'distort the federal-provincial balance seems to me to be overstated.' The problem was to find the appropriate federal balance:

In *Crown Zellerbach*, I expressed concern with the possibility of allocating legislative power respecting environmental pollution exclusively to Parliament. I would be equally concerned with an interpretation of the Constitution that effectively allocated to the provinces, under general powers such as property and civil rights, control over the environment in a manner that prevented Parliament from exercising the leadership role expected of it by the international community and its role in protecting the basic values of Canadians regarding the environment through the instrumentality of the criminal law.[49]

In a powerful dissent, Lamer and Iacobucci (Sopinka and Major concurring) rejected all the arguments for validity. Although protection of the environment was a valid criminal law purpose, an examination of the impugned provisions demonstrated that the focus of the legislation was regulation not prohibition. Even assuming that the protection against harmful substances could be described as 'new matter,' it did not have the required singleness, distinctiveness, and indivisibility to bring it within the embrace of peace, order, and good government.

While the dissent weakened the force of the decision, La Forest's sweeping expansion of the scope of the criminal law power to protect 'fundamental values' and include an unprecedented role for the federal government in environmental management was disturbing in its potential. As Graeme G. Mitchell wrote, La Forest's 'loose reformulation of the test for ascertaining if an impugned law is criminal in nature, combined with his willingness to accept an aggressive regulatory function for the criminal law power invite increasingly invasive forays by Parliament into areas of legitimate provincial jurisdiction.' However, he suggested that the forthcoming *Firearms Reference* 'will not only delineate the parameters of the criminal law's regulatory aspect but also test the elasticity of the balance of legislative powers in our federal system.'[50]

The *Firearms Reference*, on the validity of federal legislation in 1995 which required the licensing and registration of guns, did test the elasticity of the criminal law power with a result that dismayed the seven provinces and the territories that opposed the act. The Alberta Court of Appeal had upheld the legislation as a valid exercise of the criminal law power by a 3-2 majority. The full Supreme Court, in the first constitutional case to be presided over by Chief Justice McLachlin and heard by two recent appointees, Louise Arbour and Louis LeBel, sat on the appeal for two days in February 2000, before a courtroom packed with interveners. A short, unanimous, and anonymous decision on 15 June stated unequivocally at the beginning:

We conclude that the gun law control comes within Parliament's jurisdiction over criminal law. The law in 'pith and substance' is directed to enhancing public safety by controlling access to firearms through prohibitions and penalties. This brings it under the criminal law power. While the law has regulatory aspects, they are secondary to its criminal law purpose. The intrusion of the law into the provincial jurisdiction over property and civil rights is not so excessive as to upset the balance of federalism.[51]

Justifying its decision, the court explained that the first task was to determine the 'matter' of the law: 'What is its true meaning or essential character, its core?'[52] That determination involved an examination of purpose and effect. A wide range of extrinsic material – including Parliamentary debates, ministerial statements, and American studies – was introduced to determine the 'mischief' sought to be remedied and thus the purpose of the law. To the frequent argument that the law would have little effect because it would not be obeyed, the court replied that 'Parliament is the judge whether a measure is likely to achieve its intended purpose; efficaciousness is not relevant to the Court's division of powers analysis.'[53] Viewed from both purpose and effect, the law was in '"pith and substance" directed to public safety' and, having a valid purpose connected to a prohibition backed by a penalty, fell within the criminal law power.[54]

Finally, although the law removed from provincial jurisdiction regulations concerning the ownership of guns, it did not hinder the provincial right to continue to regulate the property and civil-rights aspects of guns. Nor did it allow the federal government 'to significantly expand its jurisdictional powers to the detriment of the provinces ... While we are sensitive to the concern of provincial governments that the federal jurisdiction over criminal law not be permitted such an unlimited scope that it erodes the constitutional balance of powers, we do not believe that this legislation poses such a threat.'[55] Having found the law a valid exercise of the criminal law power, the court found it 'unnecessary to consider whether the legislation can also be justified as an exercise of its peace, order and good government power.'[56]

Peace, order, and good government was referred to often in the last decades of the century, and was finally freed from the grasp of Watson and Haldane. While Laskin was on the court, he continually promoted the possibilities of the residual power and the second branch of *Parsons*. For example, although a majority of the court found *ultra vires* the federal export tax on natural gas, an important but politically divisive component of Trudeau's 1982 National Energy Policy (NEP),[57] Laskin did not. In an opinion that was clearly his (though written jointly with Lamer and McIntrye), Laskin emphasized that the court must take the broad view of the NEP as a comprehensive program designed to equalize economic benefits across the country

and thus as engaging the power of Parliament to legislate for the peace, order and good government of Canada. It may be that it would be sufficient in this context to embrace the trade and commerce power in that somewhat neglected dimension described in the *Parsons* case ... as 'general regulation of trade affecting the whole dominion.' The power to legislate for the peace order and good government of Canada is to us a more apt repository of authority for the proposed legislation of the scope and extent envisaged by the National Energy Program.[58]

Like other sections of the constitution, the residual clause had to be given 'a contemporary exposition ... Sterilizing grants of constitutional power does a disservice to a living constitution.' Had the Supreme Court 'accepted sterility after the Privy Council pointed to an evolutionary path in *Edwards*,' Laskin continued, it might not have reached the decision it did in *Johannesson* or relaxed 'the structures thought to limit resort to the peace, order and good government power' in *Anti-Inflation*, which 'laid to rest once and for all the idea that the general power could be invoked (apart from its purely residual scope) only in a time of emergency.' Haldane's explanation in *Snider* that *Russell* was decided 'on an emergency footing ... to save the nation from the disaster of convulsing alcoholism did no credit to the judicial process and, in our view, demeaned the Privy Council. We need only call in aid that body's corrective judgement in the *Canada Temperance Federation Case.*'[59]

This dissent did not move the majority. It found the export tax a violation of section 125, which trumped federal taxing power, rather than as part of a regulatory system whose national objectives might be supported under both branches of trade and commerce or the residual clause.

The major substantive revisiting of the residual clause came in the 1988 decision in *Crown Zellerbach* in which Gerald LeDain outlined a recipe for the application of the national concern doctrine.[60] *Northwest Falling*[61] had upheld federal prohibitions in the Fisheries Act against dumping deleterious substances in waters frequented by fish. However, in *Zellerbach* the challenged Ocean Dumping Control Act prohibited dumping in provincial waters even if it could not be shown to pollute extra-provincial waters. Since the act did not fall within any enumerated power, the federal government relied on the argument that the prevention of marine pollution was a matter of 'inherent national importance.' For the majority, LeDain agreed (Dickson, William McIntyre, and Bertha Wilson concurring). On the basis of Simon's 'true test' doctrine and the decisions and opinions of the court since 1949 regarding the national concern doctrine, including Beetz's formula in his dissent in Anti-Inflation, LeDain drew the following conclusions 'as to what now appears to be firmly established':

1. The national concern doctrine is separate and distinct from the national emergency doctrine of the peace, order and good government power, which is chiefly distinguishable by the fact that it provides a constitutional basis for what is necessarily legislation of a temporary nature;
2. The national concern doctrine applies to both new matters which did not exist at Confederation and to matters which, although originally matters of a local or private nature in a province, have since, in the absence of national emergency, become matters of national concern;
3. For a matter to qualify as a matter of national concern in either sense it must have a singleness, distinctiveness and indivisibility that clearly distinguishes it from matters of provincial concern and a scale of impact on provincial jurisdiction that is reconcilable with the fundamental distribution of legislative power under the Constitution;
4. In determining whether a matter has attained the required degree of singleness, distinctiveness and indivisibility that clearly distinguishes it from matters of provincial concern it is relevant to consider what would be the effect on extra-provincial interests of a provincial failure to deal effectively with the control or regulation of the intra-provincial aspects of the matter.[62]

Given the potential of the 'provincial inability' test, LeDain cautioned that its application 'must not, however, go so far as to provide a rationale for the general notion, hitherto rejected in the cases, that there must be a plenary jurisdiction in one order of government or the other to deal with any legislative problem.' Rather, its utility lay 'in assisting in the determination whether a matter has the requisite singleness or indivisibility from a functional as well as a conceptual point of view' to satisfy the national concern test.[63]

   In a powerful dissent, La Forest (for Lamer and Beetz) contended that marine pollution was not a single, indivisible subject that could fit easily into LeDain's national concern doctrine, nor was it related to any enumerated head as were some of the cases LeDain cited. La Forest acknowledged that it was impossible to demarcate boundaries between marine and fresh-water pollution or between federal and provincial responsibilities, and that without some regulatory model there could be no regulation of marine pollution. But he warned that 'the potential breadth of the federal power to control pollution by use of its general power is so great that ... the constitutional challenge in the end may be the development of judicial strategies to confine its ambit.'[64]

In spite of LeDain's cautionary *obiter*, some commentators were alarmed by the potential of the recipe for the national concern doctrine. Micheline Patenaude believed that LeDain had 'fait d'un agrégat d'agrégats une matière au nom de l'intérêt national. Elle donne tort à ceux qui croyaient peu probable une remise en question de sa décision dans *Re Loi anti-inflation.*'[65] André Tremblay marked the decision as 'le plus indicatif des risques que représente la théorie des dimensions nationales.' 'Elle autorise par voie judiciaire des transferts permanents de compétences législatives provinciales au profit du Parlement fédéral.'[66] There was no doubt that the decision articulated broadened criteria for the application of the national concern doctrine in general and for its application to the environment in particular. As Professor Alastair Lucas commented, 'the ill-defined bounds of this environmental jurisdiction have caused provincial unease about the security of provincial jurisdiction over natural resources and pubic property.'[67]

The undoubted concern was somewhat relieved by La Forest's decision in *Friends of the Oldman River* (1992).[68] The appeal involved the authority of the minister of transport to subject a dam authorized by the Alberta government to an environmental assessment under the Navigable Waters Protection Act, which provided that no such damn could be built without ministerial approval. The minister had approved the dam, but without an environmental assessment. The Friends argued that the federal 'Environmental Assessment and Review Process Guidelines Order' compelled the government to undertake a review in any area of federal responsibility.[69]

La Forest seized the opportunity to pick up where he had left off in his dissent in *Crown Zellerbach* and clarify federal and provincial jurisdiction over the environment. The task was made easier because the only other member remaining from the *Zellerbach* court was (now) Chief Justice Lamer, who had also dissented. La Forest noted first that the 'environment' had not been assigned *sui generis* to either level of government. Quoting Professor Dale Gibson, he stated that manage-ment of the environment 'does not, under the existing situation, consti-tute a homogeneous constitutional unit. Instead, it cuts across many different areas of constitutional responsibility, some federal and some provincial.'[70]

La Forest then recalled that in *Crown Zellerbach* he had argued that 'environmental control, as a subject matter, does not have the requisite distinctiveness' to meet the Beetz test for the national concern doctrine. 'Although I was writing for the minority in *Crown Zellerbach*, this opin-ion was not contested by the majority. The majority simply decided that marine pollution was a matter of national concern because it was predominantly extra-provincial and international in character and implications, and possessed sufficiently distinct and separate charac-teristics as to make it subject to Parliament's residual power.'[71]

Such a 'constitutionally abstruse matter' as the environment did not 'comfortably fit within the existing division of powers without consid-erable overlap and uncertainty,' La Forest continued. Analytical con-cepts such as functionalism and conceptualism had been applied, but none was 'suitable in every instance.' Therefore, the preferred solution was the tried and true examination of 'the catalogue of powers' in the 1867 constitution to determine 'how they may be employed to meet or avoid environmental concerns. When viewed in this manner it will be seen that in exercising their respective legislative powers, both levels of government may affect the environment, either by acting or not act-ing.' So applied, the federal government had the responsibility under its exclusive jurisdiction over navigation and shipping and was not only authorized but compelled to undertake an environmental assess-ment of the Oldman River dam.[72] A regulatory scheme for inland nav-igable waters was essential and under federal jurisdiction,[73] while a dam, as a local undertaking, was subject to provincial control. For the moment, at least, the environment had been returned to the comfort-able fold of sections 91 and 92.

However, in two other decisions, La Forest struck a judicial blow for the utility of peace, order, and good government and the trade and commerce power to serve the imperatives of national unity, and in the process he made new law. In 1990, facing the issue of the interprovin-cial recognition of court judgments, La Forest (for the court) stated that Canadian courts had made 'a serious error in transposing the rules developed for the enforcement of foreign to the enforcement of judge-ments from sister-provinces.'[74]

In language that recalls that of John Wellington Gwynne, La Forest wrote that the rule 'seems to fly in the face of the obvious intention of the Constitution to create a single country. This presupposes a basic goal of stability and unity where many aspects of life are not confined to one jurisdiction.' The creation of a common market presupposed the importance of the national regulation of trade and commerce to the country as a whole. The unitary nature of the superior court system meant that 'any concerns about differential quality of justice can have no real foundation.' In short, what he described as the 'integrating character of our constitutional arrangements as they apply to interprovincial mobility is such that some writers have suggested that a "full faith and credit" clause must be read into the Constitution and that the federal Parliament is, under the "Peace, Order and good Government" clause empowered to legislate respecting the recognition of enforcements of judgements throughout Canada ... The present was not, however, argued on that basis, and I need not go that far.'[75]

But a 1993 challenge to a Quebec act prohibiting the removal of business documents as the result of a court order outside the province was argued on constitutional terms, allowing La Forest to refine his analysis and conclusion. '*Morguard* was not argued on constitutional terms, so it was sufficient there to infuse the constitutional considerations into the rules that might otherwise have governed issues of enforcement and recognition of judgement,' he observed. But those infusions were now 'constitutional imperatives and apply to the provincial legislatures as well as to the courts.'[76] The 'integrating character of the constitutional arrangements' of 1867 compels the courts to give 'full faith and credit' to judgments of courts in other provinces. 'This, as is also noted in *Morguard*, is inherent in the structure of the Canadian federation, and, as such is beyond the power of provincial legislatures to override.'[77] Ultimately, the issue was related to 'the rights of the citizen, trade and commerce and other federal legislative powers, including that encompassed in the peace, order and good government clause.'[78]

The decisions in *Hunt* and *Morguard* may not have surprised those who remembered La Forest's speech soon after his appointment to the Supreme Court. 'But most of all I enjoy writing judgements, particularly where one can move the law forward for the better,' he said. 'In this I sometimes follow my colleagues, sometimes they follow me. But leader or follower, whenever I come across a case where the law can be refashioned for the public good and private justice, I shall continue to do so – with relish.'[79] Robert Sharpe, a member of the Ontario Court of

Appeal, described the decision as a 'tour de force remodelling of the regime for the recognition and enforcement of judgements' and found 'it difficult to think of a more significant exercise of the power of judicial lawmaking.'[80]

It is also almost impossible to think of a justice of the Supreme Court who so soon after retirement declared that judges must not confine themselves to 'minor incremental changes' in the law. As he said in another public speech, 'I never found it necessary to limit myself to purely incremental changes and while some of my former colleagues on the Supreme Court paid lip-service to incrementalism, they frequently followed me on distant voyages of discovery. Indeed, if I may be permitted to mix the metaphors, they themselves go off on frolics of their own.' His decisions in *Hunt* and *Morguard*, he stated in an astonishing admission of judicial lawmaking,

resulted in cataclysmic changes to the recognition and enforcement of judgments across the country and ultimately of foreign judgements. Reliance on Parliament or the Provincial Legislatures to affect changes in this area was simply unrealistic ... I was aware, of course, that such a drastic judicial change seriously affected the values of certainty and continuity in the law. However, a law aimed at justice and order is surely to be preferred to an arcane rule-oriented approach that often bred injustice and which, moreover, was fundamentally at odds not only with the common market underlying the federal structure of our constitution but also, for that matter, with the comity that should prevail among judicial authorities at the international level.[81]

If La Forest led, all his colleagues followed as they frolicked together in a rewriting of the law.

The Supreme Court was also inventive in finding new roles for the trade and commerce power. In one celebrated case of 1982, the court appeared to invite the federal government to enter the securities field at a time when the question was a matter of some dispute. Writing for the majority (Laskin, Ritchie, Martland, McIntyre, and Lamer), Dickson found that both federal and provincial insider-trading laws could stand. However, he noted that, unlike the United States, the provinces had 'taken control' of the industry and added that 'I should not wish by anything said in this case to affect prejudicially the right of Parliament to enact a genuine scheme pursuant to its power to make laws in relation to international trade and commerce.' This is of particular significance considering the international and interprovincial character of the securities industry.[82]

Rejecting a 1994 appeal against a National Energy Board environmental assessment of a Hydro-Québec project for the export of power to the United States, Iacobucci (for the court) stated that the critical question was whether the project was to meet the demands of the export contract. If the answer was in the affirmative, 'it becomes appropriate for the Board to consider the source of the electrical power to be exported, and the environmental costs that are associated with the generation of that power.' Aware of the concern that such a broad inquiry would 'have ramifications for the operations of provincial undertakings or matters under provincial jurisdiction,' Iacobucci cautioned that in defining the jurisdictional limits of the board, the court must ensure that it is 'truly limited to matters of federal concern. At the same time, however, the scope of its enquiry must not be narrowed to such a degree that the function of the Board is rendered meaningless or ineffective.'[83]

However, the invention with the most potential for the expansion of federal regulatory jurisdiction was the practical application of the second branch of *Parsons*. Sir Montague Smith's musing – 'and it may be' that the regulation of trade and commerce 'would include general regulation of trade affecting the whole Dominion' – had never been accepted by the Judicial Committee or the Supreme Court as a substantive component of section 91(2).[84]

The process of discovery began soon after Bora Laskin became chief justice. In a deliberate *obiter* in the *Anti-Inflation Reference, 1975*, Laskin observed that 'since no argument was addressed to the trade and commerce power I content myself with observing that it provides the Parliament of Canada with a foothold in respect of "the general regulation of trade affecting the whole Dominion,"' and given the scope of the act indicated that he would have supported it under that branch of section 91(2).[85]

In fact, six months earlier, with deliberate and unconcealed intent, Laskin had begun the process of reviving the second branch when the court held that a section of the federal Trade Mark Act providing a civil remedy for 'any business practice contrary to honest industrial or commercial usage' was unconstitutional as a matter of property and civil rights.[86] Although it was unnecessary to the decision, Laskin (for the court) wrote that 'I do not find anything in the case law on s.91(2) that prevents this court, even if it would retain a cautious concern for *stare decisis*, from taking the words of the Privy Council in the *Parsons* case, as providing the guide or lead to the issue of validity that arises here.' Quoting the second branch, Laskin pointedly observed that the 'plain fact' was that the section in question was *not* a regulation and was *not* concerned with 'trade as a whole' or with 'general trade and commerce.'[87] Even more conclusively:

Its enforcement is left to the chance of private redress without public monitoring by the continuing oversight of a regulatory agency which would at least lend some colour to the alleged national or Canada-wide sweep of s. 7(e). The provision is not directed to trade but to the ethical conduct of persons engaged in trade or in business, and, in my view, such a detached provision cannot survive alone unconnected to a general regulatory scheme to govern trading relations going beyond merely local concerns. Even on the footing of being concerned with practices in the conduct of trade, its private enforcement by civil action gives it a local cast because it is applicable in its terms to local or interprovincial competitors as it is to competitors in interprovincial trade.[88]

Defining what the challenged section was not, Laskin had deliberately indicated what could be the criteria for validity under the second branch.

Dickson accepted the obvious invitation to write a positive recipe for the second branch in *Canadian National* in 1983.[89] Although the majority found sections of the Combines Investigation Act valid under the criminal law power, Dickson also found it valid under the second branch of *Parsons*. Noting references to the second branch in case law and Laskin's *dicta* in *Vapor*, Dickson emphasized that 'every general enactment will necessarily have some local impact, and if it is true that an overly literal conception of "general interest" will endanger the very idea of the local there are equal dangers in swinging the telescope the other way around. The forest is no less a forest for being made up of individual trees.'[90]

Although the regulation of local trade or business lay at the 'very heart of local autonomy,' wrote Dickson, a 'different situation obtains ... when what is at issue is general legislation aimed at the economy as a single integrated national unit rather than a collection of local enterprises.'[91] Laskin had indicated three criteria for a valid exercise of the general power, and Dickson added 'what to my mind would be even stronger indications of valid general regulation of trade and commerce, namely (i) that the provinces jointly or severally would be con-stitutionally incapable of passing such an enactment and (ii) that failure to include one or more provinces or localities would jeopardize successful operation in other parts of the country.' The list was not exhaustive, nor was the presence of any or all of 'these *indicia* necessar-ily decisive ... Nevertheless, the presence of such factors does at least make it far more probable that what is being addressed in a federal enactment is genuinely a national economic concern and not just a col-lection of local ones.'[92]

Although Dickson's judgment was not that of the court, incorporat-ing as it did Laskin's opinion in *Vapor*, it was hailed as a momentous stage in the history of the trade and commerce power. Professor H. Scott Fairly commented that 'the Dickson test for the neglected branch of *Parsons* commends a purposive division of powers analysis in pref-erence to the continued application of disconnected doctrinal rules of thumb, which have thwarted the development of consistent jurispru-dence in federalism cases. It is hoped that the newer trend will con-tinue to grow.'[93] Neil Finkelstein was equally enthusiastic because the decision envisaged a 'real scope for national economic regulation which need not be hinged on extra-provinciality.' Because Dickson did not speak for the majority, the 'matter is still technically open. If, how-ever, *Vapor Canada* and the analysis adopted by Dickson J. in *Canadian National Transportation* are accepted, many previously arguable ques-tions are now resolved.'[94]

The analysis in the two decisions was followed when Dickson, for a unanimous court, wrote Laskin's dicta and his own opinion in *Cana-dian National* indelibly into federalism jurisprudence in the decision in *General Motors* (1989) which upheld a section of the Combines Investi-gation Act. Consistent with his search for balance, Dickson wrote that when the general power is advanced 'as a ground for constitutional validity, a careful case by case approach remains appropriate. The five factors articulated in *Canadian National Transportation* merely represent a principled way to begin the difficult task of distinguishing between matters relating to trade and commerce and those of a more local nature.'[95]

Then followed a Dicksonian formula for determining constitutional-ity: the extent or seriousness of encroachment on provincial jurisdic-tion; the presence of a regulatory scheme; the functional relationship of the impugned sections to the act as a whole; testing the validity of the scheme against the criteria for the general power established in

Canadian National; and, finally, testing the integration of the impugned provision into the regulatory scheme.[96] Painstakingly applying his formula, Dickson found that the Combines Investigation Act was 'a complex scheme of competition regulation aimed at improving the economic welfare of the nation as a whole. It operates under a regulatory agency. It is designed to control an aspect of the economy that must be regulated nationally if it is to be successfully regulated at all.'[97] Although the challenged section undoubtedly intruded on property and civil rights, it easily passed the 'functionally related test' as it would have passed the stricter 'necessarily incidental' test.[98]

Acknowledging that the act had 'existed for decades' without the section which created a civil cause of action for infractions, Dickson opined that 'I see no reason why remedies available for violations of the Act should be frozen in time' rather than amended 'to conform to changing economic realities.'[99] He disagreed that the decision 'tilts the constitutional balance between the federal domain and the domain of the provinces. Satisfying all of the concerns which I have discussed ensures that the constitutional balance will not be upset.'[100]

Sir Montague Smith's speculative 'and it may be' had finally found a home in section 92(1).

Since the 1950s, the danger that had seemed most threatening to provincial autonomy was the possibility that the court would reverse Atkin's decision in *Labour Conventions*, which had been regarded, in Quebec at least, as 'un bastion provincial impregnable.'[101] Politically, nationalists in the rest of the country had condemned the decision, and legally many found it impossible to accept Atkin's dismissal of Dunedin's decision in the *Radio* case (and Sankey's *obiter* in *Aeronautics*). While two 'inconsistent decisions may both be wrong,' W.R. Lederman wrote in 1963, 'they cannot both be right.' Since neither was superior as precedent, he argued, the Supreme Court 'is free as a matter of the principles of precedent to overrule one of these cases and follow the other, or, indeed, the court is free to strike out on a new line that is not complete approval or disapproval of either of the extreme positions involved.'[102]

Confirming federal control over aeronautics as a matter of inherent national concern in *Johannesson*, all seven members of the Supreme Court had endorsed Simon's 'true test' doctrine as well as the *dicta* of Dunedin and Sankey.[103] Four years later, in 1956. Chief Justice Kerwin stepped outside the necessities of the case to declare 'that it may be necessary with other matters to consider in the future the judgement of the Judicial Committee in the *Labour Conventions* case,' and Rand added ominously that 'provisions that give recognition to incidents of sovereignty or deal with matters in exclusive sovereign aspects, do not require legislative confirmation.'[104] After leaving the court, he wrote that the legislative power to implement treaties had been transferred to Ottawa as 'an inherent faculty of an independent state.'[105]

The decision in the 1967 *Offshore Mineral Rights* case seemed to confirm Rand's opinion, and in Edward McWhinney's judgment it looked as if the court was making the 'fatal equation' between international and internal jurisdiction.[106] In 1974 then Professor La Forest observed that 'little notice has been taken of a gradually evolving doctrine in the Supreme Court of Canada that should facilitate the exercise of Canada's sovereign status in the international sphere, whatever the ultimate fate of the *Labour Conventions* case.' In the end, La Forest predicted that 'policy grounds, not technicalities, will, however, dictate the future of the *Labour Conventions* case, and these policy grounds are far more evenly balanced than both supporters and critics of the decision are willing to admit. These may be looked at from several points of view: from an international perspective, from the perspective of those emphasizing strong national authority, and from that of those emphasizing a more even balance of power between the federal government and the provinces.'[107]

Suspicion that the court was quietly undermining *Labour Conventions* was fuelled by Laskin and Dickson *obiters*. In *Vapor*, confronted with the argument that a section of the federal Trade Marks Act was valid because it had been enacted to implement an international obligation, Laskin observed that although case law and comment, including Rand's *ex cathedra* statement, 'would support a reconsideration of the *Labour Conventions* case, I find it unnecessary to do that here because, assuming that it was open to Parliament to pass legislation in implementation of an international obligation by Canada under treaty or Convention (being legislation which would be otherwise beyond its competence),' there was no evidence that the legislation was enacted on that basis.[108] In such a case, Laskin proposed two tests: Did the legislation explicitly state that it was passed to implement an international obligation? And did the legislation remain within the scope of the obligation?

In *Schneider v. The Queen* (1982), Dickson (for the majority) appeared to confirm both the assumption and the tests. Rejecting the argument that, in adopting the convention on *Narcotic Drugs*, the federal government had occupied the field and that British Columbia's Heroin Treatment Act was thus *ultra vires*, Dickson repeated Laskin's comments. Applying Laskin's first test, he concluded that because there was nothing in the federal Narcotics Control Act to indicate that it was passed to implement a treaty obligation, British Columbia's Act was not 'legislation falling within the scope of any federal power to legislate for the implementation of international treaties.'[109] The Laskin-Dickson opinions led a perplexed Professor A.L.C. de Mestral of McGill to ask, 'Where do we stand now? Do we have two *obiter dicta* or do we have a new rule based upon an *obiter dictum*?' Critical of both reasoning and result, de Mestral warned that with the comments in the two cases concerning the treaty-implementing power, the Supreme Court 'has taken itself very far out on a limb. If the court is not careful the branch will soon break and the country will be the worse for it. There is still time to climb down.'[110]

The court, it appeared, had no intention of climbing down. In *Crown Zellerbach*, Le Dain did not rely on the treaty power. But he did rely on the existence of international obligations to demonstrate that federal jurisdiction over marine pollution met his criteria for validity under the residual clause. In dissent, La Forest seemed to accept the existence of a federal implementing power but saw it as one limited by Laskin's tests.[111] Moreover, the decision in *General Motors* and Dickson's recipe for validity under the second branch of *Parsons* could enhance the federal capacity to negotiate and implement international trade agreements.[112]

Writing before either case had been decided, Professor Jacob Ziegel wrote that 'whatever its members' own intellectual convictions, it is difficult to see the Supreme Court braving the almost inevitable provincial storm that would follow the reversal of a constitutional doctrine that the federal government itself has respected for the past 50 years.' However, the court could follow routes provided by both the residual clause and the trade and commerce power, and given the court's judgments suggesting an appreciation of the importance of the federal government's role in directing the national economy, he felt that the second was more likely.[113]

In the result, the court seemed to be following both routes. And if the Laskin-Dickson *obiters* were taken as precedent, the court appeared to have determined that if Canada's obligations under an international treaty or convention met their two tests, the federal government could legislate within areas of provincial jurisdiction. There had been no frontal attacks against Atkin's impregnable provincial bastion; it had simply been circumvented. But Atkin's compartments were no longer watertight.

Not surprisingly, the judgments and doctrine of the Supreme Court troubled francophone commentators. Critics had already questioned the thrust and tenor of decisions in the first three decades after 1949, but by the end of the century the criticism had become more political and often focused on the legitimacy of the court itself. For almost thirty years, the Supreme Court had attempted to preserve the equilibrium achieved by the Judicial Committee, wrote Brun and Tremblay in 1997, but the court 'démontre de plus en plus qu'elle est destinée, comme plusieurs le craignaient, à dilapider ou dénaturer l'héritage du Conseil privé.'[114] Their review of the case law of the 1980s and 1990s was a constant reiteration of the court's relentless centralism and was best summarized in the critique of the flexible criteria in the new national concern doctrine: 'La Cour suprême est ainsi plus certaine de pouvoir parvenir au résultat désiré. Or, la théorie des dimensions nationales ne peut jouer qu'à sens unique, dans le sens des intérêts fédéraux et de la centralisation. En se gardant le loisir de se prêter à un tel jeu politique, la Cour suprême déborde radicalement de son rôle judiciaire de gardienne du fédéralisme au Canada.'[115]

In 1997, after surveying the work of the court since the 1970s, Vilaysoun Loungnarath concluded that 'le *statu quo* n'existe pas, c'est un mythe; plutôt, le fédéralisme constitutionnel s'est engagé, irrésistiblement, sur une pente centralisatrice.'[116] That the court's jurisprudence was diametrically opposed to the decentralizing demands of Quebec was obvious, but more important was its legitimacy: 'L'idéologie centralisatrice de la Cour suprême du Canada porte des valeurs politiques. Ce qui soulève une question plus large, celle de la légitimité d'une intervention judiciaire animée par des valeurs politiques.'[117] Micheline Patenaude stated that it was 'incontestable' that the *obiter* and judgments in *Crown Zellerbach* and *General Motors* 'marquent un pas important vers l'unification du pays du moins sur le plan juridique.' Recalling that, before his appointment to the Supreme Court, Jean Beetz had cautioned that if the rest of Canada opted for centralization, Quebec would resist assimilation and dream of leaving, she warned: 'C'est l'avenir du pays même qui est en jeu en ce moment. Et ce pays ressemblera ou ne ressemblera pas à l'image que s'en fait la

Cour suprême. Mais ce n'est pas elle qui rendra le jugement définitif à ce sujet.'[118]

Among anglophone scholars there was little criticism of the thrust of the court's jurisprudence, although there was an abundance of technical academic analysis of decisions and reasoning. Professor Katherine Swinton, before her elevation to the bench, was one of the exceptions. 'The endorsement of the national concern and general regulation of trade and commerce doctrines,' she warned, 'should cause uneasiness among those satisfied with the present arrangement of powers or interested in a less, rather than more, centralized system of government.'[119] Before applying the new doctrines to allow further shifts towards the centre, she argued,

the court should have a strong empirical base for its decision to reallocate powers. In addition, it must finally come to terms with the values that influence the balance of powers in the federal system. If there is to be a greater emphasis on economic efficiency and spillover concerns, then the court should consider the evidence on these issues in a much more rigorous way. Finally, in this process of power allocation, the court must also come to terms with the difficult issue of the legitimacy of judicial review of federalism.[120]

Although politics more than law separated the Supreme Court watchers, there could be no argument about the direction of its federalism jurisprudence. During the last two decades of the century, the Supreme Court had continued on its course of rebalancing the structure of the federation by expanding the field of activity of the federal government without narrowing the traditional enclaves of provincial power. The dogmatic centralism of Bora Laskin – expressed more often in dissent or *obiter* than in decision – was absent after 1984, but the seminal and innovative decisions of Dickson, Le Dain, and La Forest – all justices of moderation – invented new content for trade and commerce, the national concern doctrine, and the criminal law.

Federal jurisdiction embraced new aspects of environmental policing and protection, competition policy, health, and social security. Prosecutions for offences under the criminal law were no longer dependent on provincial initiatives. The interjurisdictional immunity was broadened beyond what many critics and judges believed was reasonable or necessary, and concurrency was rejected to protect federal undertakings from the slightest provincial encroachment. The court unequivocally endorsed the legitimacy of the federal spending power, as well as the federal government's authority in law to alter unilaterally the financial terms of shared-cost programs. The federal declaratory power, however Draconian it might seem in a federal context, was declared to be beyond judicial surveillance.

The court continued to use the language of balance and moderation to emphasize its respect for a federalism responsive to the regional and social diversity of the country. But decision, reasoning and *obiter* seemed to reflect the functional imperatives of the national interest and of the provincial inability to develop policies, as Dickson said, 'aimed at improving the economic welfare of the nation as a whole.'[121] Provincial incapacity did not become the litmus test to broaden the scope of federal jurisdiction, but it was a critical consideration when the court wrote recipes for the national concern doctrine and the second branch of *Parsons*.

Provincial unwillingness to respect the judgments in other provinces was declared 'to fly in the face of the obvious intention of the Constitution to create a single country.' Interprovincial 'full faith and credit' was a constitutional imperative inherent in the integrating structure of the constitution and ultimately was related to 'the rights of the citizen, trade and commerce and other federal legislative powers, including that encompassed in the peace, order, and good government clause.'[122]

Indeed, more than ever before, reference to the peace, order, and good government of Canada often underlay decisions based on more specific jurisdictional grounds. Once laughed out of the court, like the regulation of trade and commerce, the primary grant of federal legislative power 'to make laws for the Peace, order and good government of Canada' had, as intended, become symbolic of the national purposes that underlay the federation.

Rebalancing jurisdictional federalism may not have threatened the country, but the political and constitutional turbulence of the last decades of the century did. On four famous and much analysed occasions, the Supreme Court was asked to leave the field of traditional jurisprudence and confront issues on which political agreement was impossible and to which there were no obvious, or even possible, legal answers. A court less committed to the national interests at stake could have decided that the issues were non justiciable; in the result, however, the court reached far beyond the law to place a judicial stamp on what it considered were the fundamental principles and values of Canadian federalism and the Canadian state. As never before, the

court determined the rules of engagement on the political battleground.

Among the consistent proposals to make intra-state federalism more
effective were the attempts to provide for provincial participation in
the selection of senators. The Trudeau government proposed such an
amendment in 1978, believing that it fell within the terms of the 1949
constitutional amendment which gave the federal government authority to amend the constitution except for matters assigned exclusively to
the provinces. However, on a reference, the Supreme Court found that
in 1867 the Senate had been established 'as a means of ensuring
regional and provincial representation in the federal legislative process' and Parliament could not alter its 'fundamental features, or
essential characteristics.'[123]

More ominous was the October 1980 threat by Pierre Trudeau to
request the British government to patriate the 1867 constitution with
amendments to entrench a charter and an amending formula without
the consent of the provinces. Surprisingly, a committee of the United
Kingdom House of Commons concluded that, however 'anachronistic'
its 'surviving role,' its responsibility was to ensure that the request
'conveys the clearly expressed wishes of Canada as a whole, bearing in
mind the federal character of Canada's constitutional system.'[124] The
provinces launched three challenges. The Manitoba Court of Appeal
(3–2) and the Quebec Court of Appeal (4–1) held that neither by law
nor by convention was provincial consent required. The Newfoundland Court of Appeal, however, decided unanimously (3–0) that unilateralism was a denial of provincial sovereignty and contrary to both
law and convention. As a result of the British decision and the narrow
7-6 victory in the courts, Trudeau had no alternative but to seek a decision from the Supreme Court.[125]

Dickson later recalled that there were more post-argument conferences in this case than in any other 'I can recall – very many more. Not
only conferences with all members of the court, but also with group-
ings within the court in order to try and decide the best manner of
resolving the issue.'[126] Unanimity was impossible. Seven members
concurred in finding that 'law knows nothing of any requirement of
provincial consent.'[127] Martland and Ritchie, the two senior members
of the court, however, emphasized that on each occasion in the past
when the court had to consider questions for which the BNA Act provided no answer, 'this Court has denied the assertion of any power
which would offend against the basic principles of the Constitution.'

Unilateral amendment was an assertion of a power 'which could disturb and even destroy the federal system of constitutional government in Canada. We are not aware of any possible legal source of such power.' There was, they maintained, a convention arising from clear and consistent historical practice that such amendments affecting provincial powers required a substantial 'degree' of provincial consent.

With Dickson, Beetz, Lamer, and Julien Chouinard concurring, the majority found that unilateralism would violate convention and 'to violate a convention is to do something which is unconstitutional although it entails no direct legal consequences.' However, the convention could be neither quantified nor enforced by the courts: 'Conventions by their nature develop in the political field and it will be for the political actors, not the Court, to determine the degree of provincial consent required.'[128] Within six weeks, the political actors, with the exception of Quebec, had found a resolution to the political impasse.[129]

The Parti Québécois government immediately challenged the decision and the political result on the grounds that, by historical convention, the agreement of Quebec was required. The Quebec Court of Appeal found that the agreement of nine provinces represented the 'substantial' measure of provincial consent, and rejected the argument that the distinctions in civil law, language, and religion recognized in law endowed Quebec with the power of veto.[130]

On appeal, the Supreme Court reaffirmed that no requirement of unanimous consent existed. The court agreed that the principle of duality included recognition not only of linguistic and cultural differences but also of the proposition that 'the two founding peoples of Canada are fundamentally equal' and that Quebec possessed 'all the attributes of a distinct national community.' However, although the principle had been accepted historically by statesmen and constitutional experts, neither the federal nor the other provincial governments had ever accepted the convention of a Quebec veto: 'We know of no example of a convention being born while remaining unspoken, and none was cited to us.'[131] In law or by convention, the Supreme Court had upheld certain fundamental principles of federalism but had denied that the constitution was either a compact of all the provinces or of two nations.

Finally, and almost inevitably, the Supreme Court was asked to give an advisory opinion on the ground rules governing the secession of Quebec before the possible separatist victory in a referendum. The primary question before the court was whether, under the constitution,

Quebec had the legal right to secede unilaterally, with secondary questions concerning unilateral secession and the right to self-determination under international law. The government of Quebec refused to participate, and the court appointed an *amicus curiae*. On 20 August 1999 the decision was released as an opinion of the court.

In a long and sometimes elegant essay, blending law and political culture, the court argued that secession must be examined in the light of four basic principles – federalism, democracy, constitutionalism and the rule of law, and respect for minority rights – that 'inform and sustain the constitutional text; they are the vital assumptions upon which the text is based.' Those 'defining principles function in symbiosis. No single principle can be defined in isolation from the others, nor does any one principle trump or exclude the operation of the other.'[132] What remained was to create an algebraic formula on the constitutional law of secession.

Federalism and democracy dictated that the 'clear repudiation of the existing constitutional order and the clear expression of the desire to pursue secession by the population of a province would give rise to a reciprocal obligation on all parties to Confederation to negotiate constitutional change to respond to that desire.' But the repudiation must be 'free of ambiguity' in terms both of the question asked and of the support it received. Moreover, the principles of the rule of law and constitutionalism entrenched the constitution 'beyond the reach of simple majority rule,' and, combined with democracy, required broad support in the form of an 'enhanced majority' to achieve constitutional change.[133] Unafraid of the minefield, the court insisted that the rights of minorities, including aboriginals, would have to be resolved 'within the overall framework of the rule of law ... Nobody seriously suggests that our national existence, seamless in so many respects, could be effortlessly separated along what are now the provincial boundaries of Quebec.'[134]

The issue had been clearly joined. The government of Canada accepted the Supreme Court's opinion that unilateral secession was illegal and its conditions and provisions for political negotiations, reserving to itself the determination of what was an unambiguous question and enhanced majority. Quebec insisted on its right to determine unilaterally its political and legal future. But, in enshrining the principles of federalism, democracy, constitutionalism and the rule of law, as well as respect for minorities, in the constitution, the court had both acknowledged the legitimacy of the desire to secede and established the ground rules which protected those fundamental principles.

In clarifying the legal framework 'within which political decisions had to be taken under the Constitution' and 'identifying binding obligations under the Constitution,' the court had made new constitutional law governing secession. The responsibility of statecraft was then returned to the political actors. It was for them to decide what was a clear majority on an unambiguous question, and to determine the process and content of negotiations. The reconciliation of the various legitimate interests could be achieved only politically and, concluded the court, to the extent that the issues were political, 'the Courts, appreciating their proper role in the constitutional scheme, would have no supervisory role.'[135]

It could do no more.

Afterword

The judicial lawmakers, not John A. Macdonald or Sir Francis Reilly, are the real authors of Canadian constitutional law. Sometimes they have made law almost imperceptibly at the margin; sometimes radically at the centre. In fact, one among them rewrote the fundamental structure of the federal division of powers. Judicial power is a frightening third estate in a federal system.

There is an awful finality about judicial decisions, for there is no easy legislative override and constitutional amendments are almost impossible. Each case declares the victors, and to them belong the spoils, or at least the responsibilties, while the vanquished can only plead for equity.

Occasionally the decisions of the judicial lawmakers have encouraged the political actors to seek compromise solutions. But on the whole it has been the judges themselves who have decided or been forced by circumstance to rewrite the law they have written.

Legislatures tried imaginatively but unsuccessfully to circumvent the misapplication of Sir Montague Smith's trade and commerce doctrine for almost a century before a court less blinded by precedent found a path. Peace, order, and good government was hostage to the Watson-Haldane doctrines until judicial common sense found innovative use for the words when no others in the constitutional text seemed judicially appropriate to contemporary necessities. Property and civil rights, though limited to the provinces by the text of the BNA Act, remained an almost insuperable barrier to any form of national regulatory peacetime action until the Supreme Court itself diminished the mantra of 'interfered with,' broadened interjurisdictional immunity, and discovered the capacity of the criminal law to protect the public good.

This book has its villains and its saviours. But its fundamental objective has been less to cast blame than to show that the law of the constitution is what the judicial lawmakers have said it is, and will be what they say it may be.

Appendix

The British North America Act, 1867
(The Constitution Act, 1867)
Relevant Sections

WHEREAS the Provinces of Canada, Nova Scotia and New Brunswick have expressed their desire to be federally united into One Dominion under the Crown of the United Kingdom of Great Britain and Ireland, with a Constitution similar in Principle to that of the United Kingdom:

III. EXECUTIVE POWER

9. The Executive Government and authority of and over Canada is hereby declared to continue and to be vested in the Queen.

12. All Powers, Authorities and Functions which under any Act of the Parliament of Great Britain, or of the Parliament of the United Kingdom of Great Britain and Ireland, or of the Legislature of Upper Canada, Lower Canada, Canada, Nova Scotia, or New Brunswick, are at the Union vested in or exercisable by the respective Governors or Lieutenant Governors of those Provinces, with the Advice, or with the Advice and Consent, of the respective Executive Councils thereof, or in conjunction with those Councils, or with any Number of Members thereof, or by these Governors and Lieutenant Governors individually, shall, as far the same continue in existence and be capable of being

exercised after the Union in relation to the Government of Canada be vested in and be exercisable by the Governor General, with the Advice or with the Advice and Consent of or in conjunction with the Queen's Privy Council for Canada, or any Member thereof, of by the Governor General individually, as the Case requires, subject nevertheless (except with respect to such as exist under Acts of the Parliament of Great Britain or of the Parliament of the United Kingdom of Great Britain and Ireland) to be abolished or altered by the Parliament of Canada.

V. PROVINCIAL CONSTITUTIONS

Executive Power

58. For Each Province there shall be an Officer, styled the Lieutenant Governor, appointed by the Governor General in Council by Instrument under the Great Seal of Canada.

59. A Lieutenant Governor shall hold office during the pleasure of the Governor General; but any Lieutenant Governor appointed after the Commencement of the First Session of the Parliament of Canada shall not be removeable within five years from his Appointment, except for Cause assigned, which shall be communicated to him in Writing within One Month after the Order for his Removal is made, and shall be communicated by Message to the Senate and the House of Commons within One Week thereafter if Parliament is then sitting,, and if not then within One Week after the Commencement of the next Session of Parliament.

60. The Salaries of the Lieutenant Governor shall be fixed and provided by the Parliament of Canada.

64. The Constitution of the Executive Authority in each of the Provinces of Nova Scotia and New Brunswick shall, subject to the Provisions of this Act, continue as it exists at the Union until altered under the Authority of this Act.

65. All Powers, Authorities and Functions which under any Act of the Parliament of Great Britain, or of the Parliament of the United Kingdom of Great Britain and Ireland, or of the Legislature of Upper Canada, Lower Canada, or Canada, were or are before or at the time of the Union vested in or exercisable by the respective Governors or Lieutenant Governors of those Provinces, with the Advice or with the Advice and Consent of the respective Legislative Councils thereof, or in conjunction with those Councils, or with any number of Members

thereof, or by those Governors or Lieutenant Governors individually, shall, as far as the same are capable of being exercised after the Union in relation to the Government of Ontario and Quebec respectively, be vested in and shall or may be exercised by the Lieutenant Governor of Ontario and Quebec respectively, with the Advice or with the Advice and Consent or in conjunction with the respective Executive Councils, or any Members thereof, or by the Lieutenant Governors individually, as the Case requires, subject nevertheless (except with respect to such as exist under Acts of the Parliament of Grear Britain or of the United Kingdom of Great Britain and Ireland) to be abolished or altered by the respective Legislatures of Ontario and Quebec.

VI. DISTRIBUTION OF LEGISLATIVE POWERS

Powers of the Parliament

91. It shall be lawful for the Queen, by and with the Advice and Consent of the Senate and House of Commons, to make Laws for the Peace, Order and good Government of Canada, in relation to all Matters not coming within the Classes of Subjects by this Act assigned exclusively to the Legislatures of the Provinces; and for greater Certainty, but not so as to restrict the Generality of the foregoing Terms of this Section, it is hereby declared that (notwithstanding anything in this Act) the exclusive Legislative Authority of the Parliament of Canada extends to all Matters coming within the Classes of Subjects next hereinafter enumerated; that is to say, –

1 The Public Debt and Property
2 The Regulation of Trade and Commerce
3 The raising of Money by any Mode or System of Taxation.
4 The borrowing of Money on the Public Credit.
5 Postal Service.
6 The Census and Statistics.
7 Militia, Military and Naval Service, and Defence.
8 The fixing of and providing for the Salaries and Allowances of Civil and other Officers of the Government of Canada.
9 Beacons, Buoys, Lighthouses, and Sable Island.
10 Navigation and Shipping.
11 Quarantine and the Establishment and Maintenance of Marine Hospitals.

12 Sea Coast and Inland Fisheries.
13 Ferries between a Province and any British or Foreign Country or between Two Provinces.
14 Currency and Coinage
15 Banking, Incorporation of Banks, and the Issue of Paper Money.
16 Savings Banks.
17 Weights and Measures.
18 Bills of Exchange and Promissory Notes.
19 Interest.
20 Legal Tender.
21 Bankruptcy and Insolvency.
22 Patents of Invention and Discovery,
23 Copyrights.
24 Indians, and Lands reserved for the Indians.
25 Naturalization and Aliens.
26 Marriage and Divorce.
27 The Criminal Law, except for the Constitution of Courts of Criminal Jurisdiction, but including the Procedure in Criminal Matters.
28 The Establishment, Maintenance, and Management of Penitentiaries.
29 Such Classes of Subjects as are expressly excepted in the Enumeration of the Classes of Subjects by this Act assigned exclusively to the Legislatures of the Provinces.

And any Matter coming within any of the Classes of Subjects enumerated in this Section shall not be deemed to come within the Class of Matters of a local or private Nature comprised in the Enumeration of the Classes of Subjects by this Act assigned exclusively to the legislatures of the Provinces.

Exclusive Powers of the Provincial Legislatures

92. In each Province the Legislature may exclusively make Laws in relation to Matters coming within the Classes of Subjects next hereinafter enumerated; that is to say, –

1 The Amendment from Time to Time, notwithstanding anything in this Act, of the Constitution of the Province, except as regards the Office of Lieutenant Governor.

2   Direct Taxation within the Province in order to the raising of revenue for Provincial Purposes.

3   The borrowing of Money on the sole Credit of the Province.

4   The Establishment and Tenure of Provincial Offices and the Appointment and Payment of provincial Officers.

5   The Management and Sale of Public Lands belonging to the Province and of the timber and Wood thereon.

6   The Establishment, Maintenance, and Management of Public and Reformatory Prisons in and for the Province.

7   The Establishment, Maintenance, and Management of Hospitals, Asylums, Charities, and Eleemosynary Institutions in and for the Province, other than Marine Hospitals.

8   Municipal Institutions in the Province.

9   Shop, Saloon, Tavern, Auctioneer, and other Licenses in order to the raising of a Revenue for Provincial, Local, or Municipal Purposes.

10   Local Works and Undertakings other than such as are of the following Classes: –

(a) Lines of Steam or other Ships, Railways, Canals, Telegraphs, and other Works and Undertakings connecting the Province with any other or others of the Provinces, or extending beyond the Limits of the Province:

(b) Lines of Steam Ships between the Province and any British or Foreign Country.

(c) Such Works as, although wholly situate within the Province, are before or after their Execution declared by the Parliament of Canada to be for the general advantage of Canada or for the Advantage of Two or more of the Provinces.

11   The Incorporation of Companies with Provincial Objects.

12   The Solemnization of Marriage in the Province.

13   Property and Civil Rights in the Province.

14   The Administration of Justice in the Province, including the Constitution, Maintenance, and Organization of Provincial Courts, both of Civil and of Criminal Jurisdiction, and including Procedure in Civil Matters in those Courts.

15   The Imposition of Punishment by Fine, Penalty, or Imprisonment for enforcing any Law of the Province made in relation to any Matters coming within any of the Classes of Subjects enumerated in this Section.

16 Generally all Matters of a merely local or private Nature in the Province.

Uniformity of Laws in Ontario, Nova Scotia and New Brunswick

94. Notwithstanding anything in this Act, the Parliament of Canada may make Provision for the Uniformity of all or any of the Laws relative to Property and Civil Rights in Ontario, Nova Scotia and New Brunswick, and of the Procedure of all or any of the Courts in these Three Provinces, and from the passing of any Act in that Behalf the Power of the Parliament of Canada to make Laws in relation to any Matter comprised in any such Act shall, notwithstanding anything in this Act, be unrestricted; but any Act of the Parliament of Canada making provision for such Uniformity shall not have effect in any Province unless and until it is adopted and enacted as Law by the Legislature thereof.

Agriculture and Immigration

95. In each Province the Legislature may make Laws in relation to Agriculture in the Province, and to Immigration into the Province; and it is hereby declared that the Parliament of Canada may from Time to Time make Laws in relation to Agriculture in all or any of the Provinces, and to Immigration into all or any of the Provinces; and any Law of the Province relative to Agriculture or Immigration shall have effect in and for the Province as long and as long only as it is not repugnant to any Act of the Parliament of Canada.

VII. JUDICATURE

96. The Governor General shall appoint the Judges of the Superior, District and County Courts in each province, except those of the Courts of Probate in Nova Scotia and New Brunswick.

101. The Parliament of Canada may, notwithstanding anything in this Act, from Time to Time provide for the Constitution, Maintenance, and Organization of a General Court of Appeal for Canada, and for the Establishment if any additional Courts for the better Administration of the Laws of Canada.

VIII. REVENUES; DEBTS; ASSETS; TAXATION

102. All Duties and Revenues over which the respective Legislatures of Canada, Nova Scotia, and New Brunswick before and at the Union had and have Power of Appropriation, except such Portions thereof as are by this Act reserved to the respective Legislatures of the provinces, or raised by them in accordance with the special Powers conferred on them by this Act, shall form One Consolidated Revenue Fund, to be appropriated for the Public Service of Canada in the Manner and subject to the Charges in this Act provided.

109. All Lands, Mines, Minerals, and Royalties belonging to the several Provinces of Canada, Nova Scotia, and New Brunswick at the Union, and all Sums then due or payable for such Lands, Mines, Minerals, or Royalties, shall belong to the several Provinces of Ontario, Quebec, Nova Scotia, and New Brunswick in which the same are situate or arise, subject to any Trusts existing in respect thereof, and to any Interest other than that of the Provinces in the same.

117. The several Provinces shall retain all their respective Public Property not otherwise disposed of in this Act, subject to the Right of Canada to assume any Lands or Public Property required for Fortifications or for the Defence of the Country.

121. All Articles of the Growth, Produce, or Manufacture of any one of the Provinces shall, from and after the Union, be admitted free into each of the other Provinces.

IX. MISCELLANEOUS PROVISIONS

General

132. The Parliament and Government of Canada shall have all Powers necessary or proper for performing the Obligations of Canada or any Province thereof, as Part of the British Empire, towards Foreign Countries, arising under Treaties between the Empire and such Foreign Countries.

Notes

Introduction

1 *Constitutional Law* (Toronto: Carswell 1999), 432.
2 *Mr Attorney: The Attorney General of Ontario, in Court, Cabinet, and Legislature, 1791–1899* (Toronto: Osgoode Society / University of Toronto Press 1986).
3 'The Judicial Committee and Its Critics' (1971) 4 *Canadian Journal of Political Science*, 301 at 334.
4 *Liberty and Community: Canadian Federalism and the Failure of the Constitution* (Albany: State University of New York Press 1991).
5 'Federalism, Nationalism and Reason,' in P.-A. Crepeau and C.B. Macpherson, *The Future of Canadian Federalism* (Toronto: University of Toronto Press 1965), 16 at 30.
6 'The Scholars and the Constitution: P.O.G.G. and the Privy Council' (1996) *Manitoba Law Journal*, 496 at 500.
7 'The Political Role of the Supreme Court in Its First Century' (1975) 53 *Canadian Bar Review*, 576.
8 'Judicial Integrity and the Supreme Court of Canada' (1978) 12 *Law Society of Upper Canada Gazette*, 116 at 118.
9 Paul Weiler, 'The Supreme Court of Canada and Canadian Federalism,' in *Law and Social Change* (Toronto: Osgoode Hall Law School 1973); Weiler, *In the Last Resort: A Critical Study of the Supreme Court of Canada* (Toronto: Carswell/Methuen 1974); Patrick Monahan, 'At Doctrine's Twilight: The

Structure of Canadian Federalism' (1984) 34 *University of Toronto Law Journal*, 47.

10 'Comment,' in *Law and Social Change*, 73–4.

11 'Lord Watson' (1899) 11 *Juridical Review*, 272 at 279.

12 'Unity and Diversity in Canadian Federalism' (1975) 53 *Canadian Bar Review*, 597 at 607–8.

13 'The Nature and Scope of Provincial Autonomy: Oliver Mowat, the Quebec Resolutions and the Construction of the *British North America Act*' (1992) 25 *Canadian Journal of Political Science*, 3 at 28.

14 'The Development of a Distinctively Canadian Jurisprudence,' Address to the Faculty of Law, Dalhousie University, 29 October 1983 (Transcript of Speeches Delivered by the Right Honourable Brian Dickson, Supreme Court of Canada, vol. 1).

15 *Constitutional Fate: Theory of the Constitution* (New York: Oxford University Press 1982), 7.

1 The Genesis of Sections 91 and 92, 1864–1867

1 Supreme Court of Canada Library, oral argument, second day, 68.

2 'The Judicial Committee and Its Critics' (1971) 4 *Canadian Journal of Political Science*, 301 at 332.

3 *Leading Constitutional Decisions*, 4th ed. (Ottawa: Carleton University Press 1987), 12. Russell's difficulty results in part from his belief that ' little was added or changed [to the Quebec Resolutions] in the subsequent negotiations and enactment in London.' (*Constitutional Odyssey: Can Canadians Become a Sovereign People?* [Toronto: University of Toronto Press 1993], 32.

4 'Thoughts on the Reform of the Supreme Court of Canada' (1970) 8 *Alberta Law Review*, 1 at 2.

5 'The Nature and Scope of Provincial Autonomy: Oliver Mowat, the Quebec Resolutions and the Construction of the *British North America Act*' (1992) 25 *Canadian Journal of Political Science*, 3 at 28. In a heavily technical, almost tautological, study, G.P. Browne argued that given the rules of statutory construction, the doctrine of precedent, and judicial restraint, the Judicial Committee was faithful to the text of the BNA Act. Admitting that some law lords began with 'certain assumptions,' he maintained that 'that does not preclude the framers of the act from having held those same assumptions.' *The Judicial Committee and the British North America Act: An Analysis of the Interpretative Scheme for the Distribution of Legislative Powers* (Toronto: University of Toronto Press 1967), 32.

6 'The Neglected Logic of 91 and 92' (1969) 19 *University of Toronto Law Journal*, 487 at 520.

7 9 September 1864, cited in A.I. Silver, *The French Canadian Idea of Confederation, 1864–1900* (Toronto: University of Toronto Press 1982), 33. George Brown expressed the Ontario viewpoint in a letter to his wife at the end of the Quebec conference: 'All right!! Conference through at six this evening – Constitution adopted – a most creditable document -a complete reform of all the abuses and injustices we have complained of!! Is it not wonderful? The old French Canadianism entirely extinguished.' Brown later changed the 'old French Canadianism' to 'The old Domination.' National Archives of Canada (NAC), Brown Papers, Brown to Anne Brown, 27 October 1864.

8 Canada, Provincial Parliament, *Parliamentary Debates on the Subject of the Confederation of the British North American Provinces, 3rd Session, 8th Provincial Parliament of Canada* (Quebec: Hunter, Rose 1865), 26 (hereafter *Confederation Debates*).

9 In March, Brown had persuaded the government to establish a committee of the Legislative Assembly to study the constitutional problem. Just hours before the government fell, his committee reported that 'a strong feeling was found to exist among members of the committee in favour of changes in the direction of a federative system, applied either to Canada alone, or to the whole British North American Provinces.' Canada, Legislative Assembly, *Journals*, 14 June 1864, 384.

10 *Globe*, 25 June 1864.

11 *Globe*, 30 August 1864.

12 Ibid.

13 2 September 1864, cited in Silver, *Idea of Confederation*, 36. The best account of the debate over sovereignty and the distinction between 'political federalism' based on the imperial model and 'constitutional federalism' is Robert C. Vipond, '1787 and 1867: The Federal Principle and Canadian Confederation Reconsidered' (1989) 22 *Canadian Journal of Political Science*, 3. See also Paul Romney, 'Provincial Equality, Special Status and the Compact Theory of Canadian Confederation' (1999) 32 *Canadian Journal of Political Science*, 21.

14 Hewitt Bernard's notes on the Quebec Conference, 24 October 1864, cited in G.P. Browne, *Documents on the Confederation of British North America* (Toronto: McClelland and Stewart 1969), 147 (hereafter *Documents*).

15 Montreal *Gazette*, 26 September 1864.

16 William Henry of Nova Scotia, later a judge of the Supreme Court of Canada, asked Quebec 'not to fight for a shadow' and agree that the federal government should have undefined residual powers. 'Anything beyond

that is hampering the case with difficulties' (Browne, *Documents*, 125). After failing again at London, Henry formally noted his objections in a note to Macdonald: 'As to the clauses which provide for the powers of the general and local Legislatures – the former should, I think, have the general power of Legislation awarded to it to be restrained only as to the specific measures given by name to the local Legislatures' (NAC, Macdonald Papers, 26 December 1866).

17 Browne, *Documents*, 94–5.
18 Ibid., 158–61.
19 *Confederation Debates*, 33, 41.
20 Ibid., 33, 505.
21 Ibid., 505.
22 Ibid., 697.
23 The only substantive addition was that of the remedial clauses of section 93 which had been a condition of Galt's joining the delegation. Langevin had secured the addition of the 'solemnization of Marriage' to the provincial enumerations. Control of penitentiaries was transferred from provincial to federal jurisdiction, leaving the provinces with public and reformatory prisons.
24 *The Times* (10 December 1864), *Edinburgh Review* (January 1965), *The Economist* (27 August, 26 November 1864).
25 NAC, Monck Papers, Cardwell to Monck, Private, 18 November 1864.
26 Ibid., Private, 11 August 1865. The efforts by the Colonial Office to change the Quebec Resolutions (and Macdonald's alleged conspiracy) is more fully elaborated in John T. Saywell, 'Backstage at London, 1864–1867: Constitutionalizing the Distinct Society' (2000) 1 *National History*, 331.
27 On 13 January, Monck had informed Carnarvon that 'Macdonald apprehends a good deal of difficulty with Mess. Cartier and Langevin on the proposed change to Property and Civil rights and suggests that your Lordship and I should see them apart from the general discussion' (Browne, *Documents*, 230).
28 Archives of Quebec (AQ), Fonds Langevin, Langevin to Justine, 24 January 1867.
29 Ibid., 3 December 1864. Reilly was probably also advised to examine the 1853 New Zealand constitution, a legislative union with some quasi-federal features. Cardwell stated in the House of Commons that he would have liked to see 'the overriding and controlling powers' given to the central government as in New Zealand. But he agreed with Carnarvon that matters should not be pressed 'at the moment' since 'it is, as he justly said, not our arrangement but theirs.' (U.K., *Parliamentary Debates*, 3rd series, vol. 185,

1178, 28 February 1867.) In Reilly's first draft he called the lieutenant governor 'Superintendent' and gave the Assembly the power to pass 'Ordinances' similar to Article 18 of the New Zealand constitution.

30 Public Record Office (PRO), 30/48/40, Cardwell Papers, Carnarvon to Cardwell, 19 July 1866.

31 PRO, 30/6/154, Carnarvon Papers, Reilly to Graham, 17 January 1867. This was undoubtedly the draft dated 'Revise 23 Jan. 1867,' in Joseph Pope's *Confederation: Being a Series of Hitherto Unpublished Documents Bearing on the British North America Act* (Toronto: Carswell 1895), 141; and Browne, *Documents*, 247. Emphasis added.

32 PRO, 30/6/139, Carnarvon to Derby, 6 February 1867. 'I have had a meeting with Mr Reilly over his and your drafts,' Sir Frederick Rogers, the under-secretary, wrote to Macdonald on the same day, 'which he seems pretty much to have in shape, or so nearly so that they could be placed in a few hours in the printer's hands. But there is still a good deal wanting from you – particularly the Local Constitutions – the powers of the Local Legislatures – and the Education clause. I hope you will be able to furnish them to him soon, as Lord Carnarvon is very anxious to get on with the bill, so as to distribute it on Saturday [9 February] – the possibility of which seems to be getting more and more doubtful.' (Sir Joseph Pope, ed., *Correspondence of Sir John Macdonald: Selections from the Correspondence of Sir John Alexander Macdonald* [Toronto: Doubleday 1921]), 41).

33 Pope, *Confederation Documents*, 214. Section 16 in that draft read: 'Such other Classes of Subjects (if any) as are from Time to Time added to the Enumeration in this Section by any Act of the Parliament of the United Colony.'

34 AQ, Fonds Langevin, Langevin to Édouard Langevin, 12 February 1867.

35 André Tremblay noted these last-minute alterations. What puzzled him was the use of the deeming clause to protect against 92(16) rather than 92(13). 'Voulait-il d'une part limiter l'exercice des compétences découlant de 92(16) et d'autre part faire jouer un rôle plus important à l'article 92(13)? Cela est possible [which in my judgment was clearly not possible], mais il reste que le paragraphe final était inutile et n'avait de sens que comme garantie supplémentaire de la supériorité, prépondérance et exclusivité de la législation fédérale sur la législation provinciale, et comme moyen de limiter la mise en œuvre de l'article 92(16) (*Les compétences législatives au Canada et les pouvoirs provinciaux en matière de propriété et de droits civils* (Ottawa: Éditions de l'Université d'Ottawa 1967), 48–9. By 1993, Tremblay had concluded that the addition of the two clauses meant that 'le principe d'égalité des deux paliers de gouvernement, propre au fédéralisme, n'était donc pas respecté. (*Droit constitutionnel: Principes* [Montreal: Les Éditions

Thémis 1993], 181.) See also the extended discussion in Browne, *The Judicial Committee*, 158ff. and passim.

36 See the superb analysis of Abel, 'Neglected Logic of 91 and 92.'

37 'We in Canada already know something of the advantages and disadvantages of a Federal Union,' Macdonald observed, and 'we know, as a matter of fact, that since the Union of 1841, we have had a Federal Union.' (*Confederation Debates*, 30.) For two views that the 1867 constitution, particularly the division of powers, was ideologically based, see Peter J. Smith, 'The Ideological Origins of Canadian Confederation' (1987) 20 *Canadian Journal of Political Science*, 3; and Bryce Weber, 'The Public, the Private and the Ideological Character of the Division of Powers in Sections 91 and 92 of the Constitutional Act of 1867' (1991) 26 *Journal of Canadian Studies*, 88.

38 The precise status of the enumerations in relation to the residual clause has been a subject of scholarly, jurisprudential, and polemical debate. For Laskin and others, they were 'merely illustrations' of what was included in the power to make laws for peace, order, and good government of Canada. ('"Peace, Order and Good Government" Re-Examined' [1947] 25 *Canadian Bar Review*, 1054.) Albert Abel termed them 'an illustrative specification' of the range of federal jurisdiction. The declaratory clause, he argued, 'provides illustrations: it removes doubts about the complete and unconditional inclusion of the named items in the class to which they relate; but it does not cut down the full and natural context of the class.' Nor did it 'properly generate an implication of any restrictive construction whatever tending to confine the general language to a limited or exceptional operation. To treat the "peace, order and good government of Canada" as in some way diminished by the enumeration of classes of subjects "for greater Certainty" was a construction heresy on the part of the Judicial Committee.' ('What Peace, Order and Good Government?' [1969] 7 *Western Ontario Law Review*, 1 at 4, 10.) W.R. Lederman infers from a comparison of the resolutions and the final text that the declaratory and deeming clauses together were 'designed to ensure that the twenty-nine specific categories in the original federal list were to taken as withdrawn from the historic scope of the provincial property and civil rights clause, and withdrawn also from the new provincial category of things generally of a local or private nature.' ('University and Diversity in Canadian Federalism' [1975] 53 *Canadian Bar Review*, 597 at 602). André Tremblay concluded that the enumerations, prefaced by the declaratory clause, indicated that federal jurisdiction was 'non limitée, exclusive et prépondérante.' (*Les competénces législatives au Canada*, 48.)

39 Or as George Brown described it, 'control over all questions of trade and

commerce.' E. Whelan, *The Union of the British Provinces: A brief Account of the Several Conferences Held in the Maritime Provinces and in Canada, in September and October 1864, on the Proposed Confederation of the Provinces, together with a Report of the Speeches Delivered by the Delegates from the Provinces, on Important Public Occasions* (Charlottetown: G.T. Hazard, 1865), 195.

40 Section 92(10)(c). Section 29(11) of the Quebec Resolutions gave the federal government jurisdiction over 'all such works as shall, although lying within any province, be specially declared by the Acts authorizing them to be for the general advantage.' (Brown, *Documents*, 158.) The revised version first appeared in the draft of 23 January. (Ibid., 257.) The initial version was ambiguous. The Interprovincial Conference of 1887 passed a resolution stating that 'it was not the intention that local works should be so withdrawn without the concurrence of the Provincial Legislature' and the constitution should be amended in accordance with the Quebec Resolutions. ('Minutes of the Interprovincial Conference,' in *Dominion, Provincial and Interprovincial Conferences from 1887 to 1926* [Ottawa: King's Printer, 1951], 21.) See Kenneth Hanssen, 'The Federal Declaratory Power under the British North America Act' (1968) 3 *Manitoba Law Journal*, 87.

41 Section 45 of the Quebec Resolutions had stated: 'In regard to all subjects over which jurisdiction belongs to both the General and Local Legislatures, the laws of the General Parliament shall control and supersede those made by the Local Legislature, and the latter shall be void so far as they are repugnant to or inconsistent with the former.' This section was repeated as section 44 in the London Resolutions. Reilly had removed it in the first British draft except for the explicit reference to the concurrent powers over agriculture and immigration. My personal but unsubstantiated opinion is that the Canadians intended it to be a general paramountcy in overlapping areas, but that Reilly correctly felt the same objective was achieved when he added the declaratory and deeming clauses to his first draft. Macdonald certainly suggested a broader application of paramountcy during the debate on the resolutions when he stated that there were 'numerous subjects which belong, of right, both to the Local and General Parliament' and that in 'all these cases ... the same rule should apply as now applies in the cases where there is jurisdiction in the Imperial and the Provincial Parliaments, and that when the legislation of one is adverse or contradictory to the legislation of the other, in all such cases the action of the General Parliament must over-rule, ex necessitate, the action of the Local Legislature.' (*Confederation Debates*, 42)

42 An exception was federal jurisdiction over marriage and divorce, except for the 'Solemnization of Marriage' which Langevin, without difficulty, added

to the provincial powers at London. However, marriage was deemed to concern the legal status and the allocation of divorce was the answer to a political/religious problem. As Langevin explained in the Assembly, 'we found this power existing in the constitutions of the different provinces, and not being able to get rid of it, we wished to banish it as far from us as possible' (*Confederation Debates*, 389.)

43 Peter Hogg, *Constitutional Law of Canada* (Toronto: Carswell 1992), 538.

44 In Toronto on 2 November 1864, quoted in Whelan, *British Provinces*, 197.

45 *R. v. Fredericton* (1879), 19 N.B.R. 139 at 168 (S.C.).

46 Browne, *Documents*, 159. What became section 94 was not among the initial list of federal powers, but was moved by Macdonald on the second-to-last day of the conference. The minutes of the conference do not record its adoption. However, number 34 of the Quebec Resolutions provided that, until the consolidation of the laws of the three provinces, the judges would be selected from their respective bars, and this provision remained as section 97 of the 1867 act.

47 Ibid., 222.

48 *Confederation Debates*, 41.

49 NAC, Macdonald Papers, Macdonald to Sandfield Macdonald, 26 May 1868; ibid., Sandfield Macdonald to Macdonald, 29 May 1868.

50 House of Commons, *Debates*, 1869, 17 June 1869, 641, 853, 854. Blake anticipated later arguments against asymmetry by opposing a situation where Parliament could control the laws of three provinces when one-third of its members were from Quebec. Both men obviously saw the proposed uniformity, as does Samuel V. LaSelva, who suggests that section 94 could best be looked on as 'transferring constitutional jurisdiction' rather than uniformity of laws. 'Federalism and Unanimity: The Supreme Court and Constitutional Amendment' (1983) 16 *Canadian Journal of Political Science*, 757.

51 Canada, *Sessional Papers* (no. 16), 1871, 'Preliminary Report,' 9 February 1871. Gray had been premier of New Brunswick (1856–7) and a delegate to Charlottetown and Quebec. Macdonald had also proceeded at once with the consolidation of the statute law within federal jurisdiction, including criminal law, under the direction of Judge Robert Gowan. Many statutes were passed in 1868–9.

52 *Confederation Debates*, 33.

53 NAC, Macdonald Papers, vol. 572, Macdonald to Sandfield Macdonald, 30 May 1868.

54 These issues will not be discussed here. See Robert Vipond, *Liberty and Community: Canadian Federalism and the Failure of the Constitution* (Albany:

State University of New York Press, 1991), and John T. Saywell, *The Office of Lieutenant Governor: A Study in Canadian Government and Politics* (Toronto: University of Toronto Press, 1957).

55 'A Supreme Court in a Federation: Some Lessons from History' (1953) 53 *Columbia Law Review*, 597 at 601.

2 Made in Canada: The Provincial Courts, 1867–1881

1 The most prominent was Charles Fisher who, before his appointment to the Supreme Court of New Brunswick in 1867, had been at Quebec and London where as attorney general he had worked on the drafting committee. W.J. Ritchie of the Supreme Court of Nova Scotia and William Henry, later appointed to the Supreme Court of Canada, had also been at London. Antoine-Aimé Dorion, Christopher Dunkin, H.E. Taschereau, M.C. Cameron, and John Sanborn had participated in the 1865 debate: all but Sanborn had been opposed and he was critical. John Allen of the New Brunswick Supreme Court had been a member of a delegation to London in 1865 opposing Confederation. Hugh McDonald and Henry Smith of the Supreme Court of Nova Scotia had actively opposed Confederation.

2 *R. v. Chandler* (1869), 12 N.B.R. 556 at 560 (hereafter *Chandler*).

3 *Pope v. Griffith* (1872), 16 L.C.J. 169 at 170 (Q.B.) (hereafter *Pope*).

4 The only federal acts to be challenged in the early years were the Canada Temperance Act, S.C. 1878, c. 16, and the Dominion Controverted Elections Act, S.C. 1874, c. 10. On the academic debate over the origins of judicial review, see: B.L. Strayer, *Judicial Review of Legislation in Canada* (Toronto: University of Toronto Press 1968); W.E.R. Lederman, 'The Independence of the Judiciary' (1956) 34 *Canadian Bar Review*, 769; Jennifer Smith, 'The Origins of Judicial Review in Canada' (1983) 26 *Canadian Journal of Political Science*, 115; Norman Siebrasse, 'The Doctrinal Origin of Judicial Review and the *Colonial Laws Validity Act*' (1993) 1 *Review of Constitutional Studies*, 75; Peter W. Hogg, *Constitutional Law of Canada* (Toronto: Carswell 1992), 117. Although the discussions in the *Confederation Debates*, as with much else, are indeterminate, there seemed to be the presumption that the courts, particularly the Judicial Committee, would determine constitutionality. At one point Cartier stated: 'Neither the Imperial Government nor the General Government will interfere, but the courts of justice will decide all questions in relation to which there may be differences between the two powers.' (*Confederation Debates*, 1865, 690.) On the whole, the early decisions support Strayer's contention that the 'constitutional law of the Empire in 1867 apparently embraced the convention that where legislative powers were

granted subject to limitation the courts would enforce those limitations.'
(Strayer, *Judicial Review,* 15.)

5 *Chandler* at 566. 'I have no doubt that it is competent for this court, or
indeed for any court in this Province, incidentally to determine whether
any Act passed by the Legislature of the Province be an act in excess of its
powers,' wrote Ramsay of the Quebec Superior Court. 'This is a necessary
incident of the partition of the legislative power under the B.N.A. Act,
without reserving to any special court the jurisdiction to decide as to the
constitutionality of any of the Legislatures.' (*Pope* at 170.) The questions of
legitimacy was raised by a county court judge in New Brunswick and in the
legislature. See Gordon Bale, *Chief Justice William Ritchie* (Ottawa: Carleton
University Press 1991), 107.

6 *L'Union St-Jacques* v. *Belisle* (1874), 20 L.C.J. 29 at 34 (Badgley), at 38 (Duval),
at 39 (Monck), at 40 (Drummond) (P.C.) (hereafter *Belisle*).

7 *Ex parte Dansereau* (1875), 19 L.C.J. 210 at 226, 231 (Dorion) (Q.B.) (hereafter
Dansereau).

8 *Chandler* at 567.

9 *Belisle* at 39. A.V. Dicey wrongly speculated that the power of disallowance
'was possibly given with a view to obviate altogether the necessity of
invoking the law Courts as interpreters of the Constitution.' (A.V. Dicey,
Introduction to the Study of the Law of the Constitution [London: Macmillan
Press, 1893], 158).

10 *R.* v. *Taylor* (1875), 36 U.C.Q.B. 183 at 192 (hereafter *Taylor*). Mowat personally made the same argument, with a little twist, before the Supreme Court
of Canada, when he stated that in Canada, unlike the United States, 'ample
power is given to the Dominion Parliament of protecting itself ... The power
of disallowance should be taken into consideration when the policy of the
Act is urged against us.' (*Severn* v. *R.* (1878), [1979] 2 S.C.R. 70 at 81 [hereaf-
ter *Severn*]). See also his *Factum* for *Severn* discussed below. Romney maintains that Mowat's argument was an attempt not to evade judicial review,
but to assert provincial sovereignty. Since the province was 'omnipotent
within its jurisdiction' and disallowance enabled the federal government
power to protect 'its own jurisdiction and the integrity of the dominion,'
Mowat argued, the 'courts, therefore, could not constitutionally strike
down valid provincial legislation merely on the ground of conflict with
federal jurisdiction.' Of course, the courts could not strike down 'valid'
provincial legislation in any case. ('The Nature and Scope of Provincial
Autonomy: Oliver Mowat, the Quebec Resolutions and the Construction of
the *British North America Act*' [1992] 25 *Canadian Journal of Political Science,* 3
at 16.)

11 *Leprohon* v. *The Corporation of the City of Ottawa* (1877), 40 U.C.Q.B. 478 at 490 (hereafter *Leprohon* [U.C.Q.B.]).

12 *Leprohon* v. *The Corporation of the City of Ottawa* (1878), 2 O.A.R. 522 at 547 (hereafter *Leprohon* [O.A.R.]).

13 *The Corporation of Three Rivers* v. *Sulte* (1882), 5 *Legal News* 330 at 334 (Q.B.) (hereafter *Sulte*).

14 *R.* v. *Dow* (1873), 14 N.B.R. 300 at 308 (S.C.).

15 C.K. Allen, *Law in the Making* (Oxford, U.K.: Oxford University Press 1964), 417.

16 *Robertson* v. *Steadman* (1876), 16 N.B.R. 621 at 635 (S.C.) (hereafter *Robertson*).

17 *Angers* v. *The Queen Insurance Company* (1877), 21 L.C.J. 77 at 80 (Sup. Ct.) (hereafter *Angers* (Sup. Ct.]).

18 *Angers* as cited in J.R. Cartwright, ed., *Cases Decided on the British North America Act, 1867, in the Privy Council, the Supreme Court of Canada, and the Provincial Courts* (Toronto: Blackett Robinson 1882), 117 at 145. Citing Macdonald's opinion as minister of justice on a Quebec statute, Ramsay observed that 'it must be borne in mind that Sir John Macdonald was one of the authors' of the constitution 'and from the high and responsible position he held at the time of Confederation, his opinion is entitled to a great weight on a question of this sort.' (*Dansereau* at 217.) There was, however, a general acceptance of the rule of statutory interpretation which held that language used in the legislature was not to be judicially noticed. As Burton said, 'I apprehend that in this as in the case of any ordinary enactment little or no weight could be attached to the language or opinions of individual members of the Legislature or Government, even if there were any mode of bringing that language under our notice judicially.' But, he continued, 'if it were allowable to refer to the remarks of Lord Carnarvon when introducing the measure, I should say that it seems to favour the view which I have expressed.' Moss agreed that Carnarvon's words could not be introduced but then added that if they could 'I agree with my brother Burton, that it does not aid the appellants.' (*Smiles* v. *Bedford et al.* (1877), 1 O.A.R. 436 at 445, 451.)

19 Oral argument in *Re Portage Extension of the Red River Railway*, reported in extenso by Holland Brothers, Senate reporters, and printed by A.S. Woodburn 1888. As cited in A.H.F. Lefroy, *The Law of Legislative Power in Canada* (Toronto: Toronto Law Book and Publishing 1897–8), 4.

20 This was particularly true in all provinces in the troublesome liquor cases. For an excellent analysis, see R.C. Risk, 'Canadian Courts under the Influence' (1990) 40 *University of Toronto Law Journal*, 687.

21 *In Re Slavin and the Corporation of the Village of Orillia* (1875), 36 U.C.Q.B. 159

at 176 (hereafter *Slavin*). The same court, in a concurrent decision, used pre-Confederation practice to declare taxing brewers *ultra vires* as falling within the federal trade and commerce power. (*Taylor* at 183.) With the redistribution of power in 1867, the law and logic of the argument were questionable. Macdonald and Blake, Fournier and Laflamme, as ministers of justice, had questioned provincial legislation regulating the sale of liquor which seemed to go beyond the section 92(9) power of licensing for the purposes of raising revenue, and did not feel that the power automatically fell within municipal institutions (92[8]). But rather than disallow, they chose, as Macdonald wrote, to leave it for 'persons feeling aggrieved by any action under the statutes, to test the question of its validity in the courts. (W.E. Hodgins, *Correspondence, Reports of the Ministers of Justice and Orders in Council upon the Subject of Dominion and Provincial Legislation 1867–1896: Compiled under the Direction of the Honourable the Minister of Justice* (Ottawa: Government Printing Bureau 1896), 102, 147, 152, 257, 281.)

22 *Cooey* v. *The County of Brome* (unreported) cited in *Lepine* v. *Laurent* (1892), 14 *Leg. News* 369 at 370 (C.Q.). When Richards made the same argument in the Supreme Court of Canada, Ritchie of New Brunswick objected to his reading the act 'by the light of an Ontario candle alone' for the facts did not apply to New Brunswick (*Severn* at 99). Ramsay later noted that 'we have not found any Statute conferring such powers' in New Brunswick; 'but at any rate we have the two great Provinces of Confederation, and one of the smaller ones, persistently including amongst municipal institutions the right to prohibit the sale of strong drink.' (*Sulte* at 332.) The head-note to the decision in *Sulte* expressed the views of the unanimous Court of Queen's Bench: 'The state of things as existing in the confederated provinces at the time of Confederation, and more particularly that which was recognized by law in all or most of the Provinces, is a useful guide in the interpretation of the meaning attached by the Imperial Parliament to indefinite expressions employed in the B.N.A. Act of 1867.' (*Sulte* at 331.)

23 *Keefe* v. *McClennan* (1876), 11 N.S.R. 5 at 13 (S.C.).

24 *Leprohon* (O.A.R.) at 533. The question before the court was the capacity of a province or municipality to tax the income of federal civil servants, a power the court rejected. The classic American case, heavily relied on in this case, was Marshall's decision in *McCulloch* v. *State of Maryland*, 17 U.S. (4 Wheat.) 316 (1819). Stating that, unlike the American states, Canadian provinces had only enumerated powers, Spragge argued that the 'principle is, if anything, more free from difficulty in its application to our constitution than to that of the United States.' Leaving to others the analysis of American case law, Spragge expressed his 'high appreciation of their great merits and

value, adding only this, that the process of reasoning upon which the Judges in these cases proceed is in my humble judgement incontrovertible' (*Leprohon* at 529). John Weldon of the New Brunswick Supreme Court cited Spragge and Hagarty with approval, adding that 'in the infancy of our Federal Constitution, I cannot but think it fortunate that we have the decisions of these distinguished jurists to aid and guide us in its construction.' (*Ex parte Owen* (1881), 20 N.B.R. 487 at 497 [S.C.].)

25 Indeed, Lord Fitzgerald's much quoted statement that 'within these limits of subject and area the local legislature is supreme, and has the same authority as the Imperial Parliament, or the Parliament of the Dominion' echoed the decisions of Spragge and Burton in the Ontario Court of Appeal. *Hodge* v. *R.* (1883), 9 A.C. 117 at 132 (P.C.).

26 *Dansereau* at 224.

27 *Taylor* at 191.

28 *Leprohon* (O.A.R.) at 536.

29 *Re Goodhue* (1872), 19 Grant Ch. 366 at 418 (Spragge), at 385 (Draper) (hereafter *Goodhue*).

30 *Dansereau* at 231.

31 *Dobie* v. *Board for the Management of the Temporalities Fund of the Presbyterian Church of Canada in Connection with the Church of Scotland, et al.* (1880), 3 *Leg. News* 244 at 250 (Q.B.). See also *Goodhue* at 368 (Spragge), at 418 (Draper); *Dansereau* at 231 (Dorion).

32 *Ryan* v. *Devlin* (1875), 20 L.C.J. 77 at 83 (Ct. Rev.) (hereafter *Ryan*). The issue was a challenge to the validity of the Elections Act assigning jurisdiction to the provincial courts on the grounds that it interfered with 92 (13 and 14). The decision in *Ryan* which upheld the act was confirmed in *Valin* v. *Langlois* (1879), 5 Q.L.R. 1 at 2 (Sup. Ct). Chief Justice Meredith simply stated: 'That subject not being one of those placed by the act of confederation within the exclusive power of the provincial legislatures, is, therefore, within the general powers of the dominion parliament.' The decision in *Ryan* was approved in *Re Niagara Election Case* (1878), 29 U.C.C.P 261.

33 *Anger* (Q.B.), cited in Cartwright, *Cases*, 138.

34 *Leprohon* (U.C.Q.B.) at 488.

35 *Ulrich* v. *The National Insurance Company* (1877), 42 U.C.Q.B. 141 at 155.

36 Chief Justice Draper seemed magnificently unclear about the meaning of the declaratory clause. 'Exclusive of what?' he asked. 'Surely not of the subordinate Provincial Legislatures, whose powers had yet to be conferred, and who would have no absolute powers until they were in some form granted and defined. Would not this declaration seem rather intended as a

more definite or extended renunciation on the part of the Parliament of Great Britain of its power over the internal affairs of the New Dominion, than was contained in the Imperial Statute 18.' Geo. 111, ch. 12, and 28–9 Vic. ch. 63, sec. 3–4–5' (*Taylor* at 220).

37 *Belisle* v. *L'Union St. Jacques* (1870), 15 L.C.J. 212 at 215 (Cir. Ct.).

38 *Ex parte Cooey* v. *The Municipality of the County of Brome* (1877), 21 L.C.J. 182 at 185 (Cir. Ct.).

39 *A.G. Quebec* v. *A.G. Canada* (1876), 2 Q.L.R. 236 at 243 (Q.B.). By virtue of the deeming clause, Ramsay believed that the 'exclusive authority of Parliament is absolute, while that of the several Legislatures is only so when the matter does not clash with the powers specially conferred upon Parliament.' (*Angers* v. *Queen Insurance Company* (1877), 22 L.C.J. 307 at 308 [P.C.] [hereafter *Angers*] [P.C.].) Ramsay clearly confused the purposes of the declaratory and deeming clauses.

40 *R.* v. *The Justices of the Peace of the County of Kings* (1875), 15 N.B.R. 535 at 539, 541 (S.C.).

41 *R.* v. *Fredericton* (1879), 19 N.B.R. 139 at 168 (S.C.) [hereafter *Fredericton*].

42 *Taylor* at 200. On appeal, Chief Justice Draper and Samuel Strong held that licences in 92(9) basically meant *any* licences for purposes of revenue. However, Strong stated, 'I only desire to add that I am of opinion that a license which would amount to prohibition would be an undue influence with the exclusive power of the Dominion Parliament as to trade and commerce, as has been in effect lately decided by the Supreme Court of New Brunswick on the case of *Regina* v. *the Justices of the Peace of the County of Kings*.' ([1875] 36 U.C.Q.B. 218 at 224). When a similar facts case came before it, the lower court openly disagreed with the Court of Appeal. (See also Chapter 7.)

43 *Slavin* at 159.

44 *Taylor* at 212, 213. Wilson used the decision in *Taylor* to comment on the problem of judicial review. 'It is in the nature of things almost unavoidable to prevent a conflict arising between two Legislative bodies in the due exercise of their respective powers, most of which from necessity are described in general and comprehensive terms, as it is impossible to express the details in any other way less than a code. But the code itself would have to be supplemented from time to time, and even then, with all the elaboration it received, it would not be so convenient or practical or comprehensive, or useful for all purposes, as the simple enumeration of the rights and powers intended to be exercised under the general terms by which they are commonly known, and which are quite as well understood as, and perhaps better than, they could be if it were attempted specially to define them.' (*Taylor* at 191.)

45 *Hart* v. *Missisquoi* (1876), 3 Q.L.R. 170 at 172 (Cir. Ct.); *Cooey,* ibid., at 182.

46 *Lepine* v. *Laurent* (1891), 17 Q.L.R. 226 at 229 (Sup. Ct.).

47 *Angers* (Sup. Ct.) at 81.

48 *Angers* (Q.B.), 22 L.C.J. at 307 at 311 (Dorion), at 308 (Ramsay). Taschereau's judgment is reported in Cartwright, *Cases,* 134.

49 *Parsons* v. *The Citizens' Insurance Company* (1879), 4 O.A.R. 96 at 100.

50 *Parsons* v. *The Queen Insurance Company* (1879), 4 O.A.R. 103 at 109.

51 *Chandler* at 566.

52 *Robertson* at 632.

53 *Taylor* at 199.

54 *Robertson* at 631.

55 *Smith* v. *The Merchant's Bank* (1881), 28 Grant Ch. 629 at 638. Spragge had Sir Montague Smith's decision in *Cushing* v. *Dupuy* (1880), 5 A.C. 409 at 410 (P.C.) as precedent but stated that it only confirmed his own judgment.

56 *Fredericton* at 146ff.

57 As stated by Lord Fitzgerald in *Hodge* v. *The Queen* (1883), 9 A.C. 117 at 130: 'Subjects which in one aspect and for one purpose fall within sect. 92, may in another aspect and for another purpose fall within sect. 91.'

58 *Taylor* at 206, 207. The aspect doctrine would appear to have originated with Chief Justice Marshall in *Gibbons* v. *Ogden* 22 U.S. (9 Wheat.) 1 (1824) at 204. 'So, if a state, in passing laws on subjects acknowledged to be within its control, and with a view to those subjects, shall adopt a measure of the same character with one which congress may adopt, it does not derive its authority from the particular power which has been granted, but from some other, which remains with the state, and may be executed by the same means. All experience shows, that the same measures, or measures scarcely distinguishable from each other, may flow from distinct powers; but this does not prove that the powers themselves are identical.'

59 *Bennett* v. *The Pharmaceutical Association of the Province of Quebec* (1881), 1 Q.B.R. 336 at 340.

60 *Sulte* at 333.

61 Gordon Bale, *Chief Justice William Johnstone Ritchie: Responsible Government and Judicial Review* (Ottawa: Carleton University Press 1991), 343. Ritchie had written a long critique of Macdonald's draft bill of 1869 in which he, like others, strenuously opposed granting the court original jurisdiction. The critique is reprinted in Bale.

62 *Pope* at 170.

63 *Belisle* (P.C.) at 45.

3 Made in Canada: The Supreme Court of Canada, 1875–1881

1 On the creation of the court, see: Peter Russell, *The Supreme Court of Canada as a Bilingual and Bicultural Institution* (Ottawa: Queen's Printer 1969); Ian Bushnell, *The Captive Court: A Study of the Supreme Court* (Montreal: McGill-Queen's University Press 1992); Jennifer Smith, 'The Origins of Judicial Review' (1983) 16 *Canadian Journal of Political Science*, 115; Michael John Herman, 'The Founding of the Supreme Court and the Abolition of the Appeal to the Privy Council' (1976) 8 *Ottawa Law Review*, 7; James Snell and Frederick Vaughan, *The Supreme Court of Canada: History of the Institution* (Toronto: University of Toronto Press 1985), Chapter 1.

2 House of Commons, *Debates*, 4 February 1875, 3.

3 Ibid., 23 February 1875, 286.

4 Ibid., 23 February 1875, 288; 16 March 1875, 755; 23 February 1875, 288.

5 Ibid., 16 March 1875, 741. Although Edward Blake made no comment, on later occasions he declared that, theoretically at least, in a federal system judicial and legislative authority should be identical. (See House of Commons, *Debates*, 1885, 158–9.)

6 In the Commons, Mousseau's amendment that the Supreme Court could not hear appeals from Quebec regarding 'property, civil rights, and civil procedure' was defeated 106–10. (House of Commons, *Journals*, 1875, 312.) Francophone senators first moved that the court should have no jurisdiction over matters assigned to the provinces and, that failing, moved that the act not come into force in Quebec 'unless and until this Act is adopted and approved by the Legislature of the Province of Quebec, as to the appellate jurisdiction of 'The Supreme Court,' in cases relating to Property, Civil Rights and Civil Procedure in the said Province of Quebec.' The amendment was defeated 35–18. (Senate, *Journals*, 1877, 27–8.) Opposition to the attempted abolition of appeals to the Judicial Committee is discussed in Chapter 4.

7 'The Appellate Courts of the Empire' (1900) 12 *Juridical Review*, 1 at 4.

8 *Getting It Wrong: How Canadians Forgot Their Past and Imperilled Confederation* (Toronto: University of Toronto Press 1999), 154.

9 'The Supreme Court of Canada: A Final Court of and for Canadians' (1951) 29 *Canadian Bar Review*, 1038 at 1058

10 The Chief Justice, William Buell Richards, an active Reformer in politics before his appointment to the bench in 1853, was appointed chief justice of the Court of Queen's Bench by Macdonald in 1868; Samuel Henry Strong had advised Macdonald on an early draft of a Supreme Court bill, and was appointed by him to the Court of Chancery and later was elevated to the

Supreme Court of Ontario by Mackenzie; William Johnstone Ritchie had been chief justice of New Brunswick since 1865 after ten years on the bench; Jean-Thomas Taschereau, a Bleu in politics, was appointed from the Quebec Court of Queen's Bench. Taschereau retired in two years and Mackenzie appointed Henri-Elzéar Taschereau. Richards retired in 1879 and Macdonald selected John Wellington Gwynne.

11 Paul Romney, 'From Railway Construction to Constitutional Construction: John Wellington Gwynne's National Dream' (1991) 20 *Manitoba Law Journal*, 91 at 101n.27. Romney attributed the appointment to Gwynne's centralist decision the day before his appointment in *Re Niagara Election Case: Plumb v. Hughes* (1878), 29 U.C.C.P. 261. His argument is not convincing. In fact, Gwynne had been promoted to the Court of Appeal by the Liberals. But, as Romney observes, Macdonald may have known about his constitutional views. However, despite the fact that several key constitutional decisions were pending in the Supreme Court, Gwynne wished to delay his appointment to clean up some cases in his own court.

12 'The Supreme Court Bench' *15 Canada Law Journal* (February 1879), 41.

13 Defeated in the 1867 election, Taschereau was appointed to the Quebec Superior Court by Macdonald in 1871. On the Supreme Court he replaced his uncle, Jean-Thomas Taschereau, a Conservative appointed by the Liberals in 1875, who found Ottawa distasteful and resigned in 1878. He had also opposed the establishment of a Supreme Court administered by common law judges. (*Confederation Debates*, 1865, 897.)

14 *Valin* v. *Langlois* (1879), 3 S.C.R. 1 at 9–10 (hereafter *Valin*).

15 *Severn* v. *The Queen* (1878), [1879] 2 S.C.R. 70 at 95 (hereafter *Severn*).

16 *Valin* at 22.

17 *St. Catherine's Milling and Lumber Co.* v. *The Queen* (1887), 13 S.C.R. 577 at 606–7.

18 Oral argument in *Re Portage Extension of the Red River Railway*, reported in extenso by Holland Brothers, Senate reporters and printed by A.S. Woodburn in 1888. As cited in A.H.F. Lefroy, *The Law of Legislative Power in Canada* (Toronto: Toronto Law Book Publishing 1897–8), 4. As late as 1912, Justice Idington insisted that the BNA Act was not 'an ordinary instrument. It is but the outline of what was meant to found and form the government for a great state. And as I have heretofore said, we must in the interpretation of its terms and construction of it as a whole, view it if we can as statesmen should, even if we be not such. We must summon to our aid history and especially constitutional history, and some knowledge of the social structure if we would understand aright how to harmonize the various parts when apparently conflicting, as here by the literal meaning of the

terms, even in actual conflict.' *In Re Marriage Laws* (1912), 46 S.C.R. 132 at 383.

19 *Severn* at 99.

20 See R.C.B. Risk, 'Canadian Courts under the Influence' (1990) 40 *University of Toronto Law Journal*, 687.

21 An Act to Amend and Consolidate the Law for the Sale of Fermented or Spiritous Liquors, 37 Vict. c. 32.

22 *R. v. Taylor* (1875), 36 U.C.Q.B. 183.

23 *Severn* at 73. Interestingly, Richards had sat on *Taylor* in the initial decision and Strong had been on the Court of Appeal.

24 Ibid. at 80.

25 NAC, RG 125, vol. 4, file 126, *Factum of the Respondent between the Queen and John Severn* (Toronto 1877).

26 'Report of the Attorney-General of Ontario with respect to certain proceedings before the Privy Council ...,' Ontario, *Sessional Papers*, 1882, no. 31, 3.

27 Archives of Ontario (AO), Irving Papers, MU 1493, 'Memorandum by the Attorney-General of Ontario in the Privy Council. In the matter of the Liquor License Act, 1883, of the Province of Canada, and an Act Amending the Same.' (Toronto, 12 October 1885.)

28 *Factum of the Respondent*, 4, 5; *Severn* at 82.

29 *Severn* at 81.

30 Ibid. at 94.

31 Ibid. at 115.

32 Ibid. at 138.

33 Ibid. at 118–25. The Canadian constitution, Fourner added, 'does not acknowledge as in the United States, a division of power as to commerce' (at 121).

34 Ibid. at 103–10. Significantly, both Ritchie and Strong had argued that, if the licence was unreasonable or injurious to trade and commerce, it should be disallowed as Mowat had suggested. Richards and Fournier rejected the proposition. Disallowance would always be regarded as a 'harsh exercise of power, unless in cases of great and manifest necessity,' Richards stated. Fournier dismissed the argument with the comment that 'it is precisely on account of its extraordinary and exceptional character that the exercise of this prerogative will always be a delicate matter. It will always be very difficult for the Federal Government to substitute its opinion instead of that of the Legislative Assemblies in regard to matters within their province, without exposing themselves to be reproached with threatening the independence of the Provinces ... It cannot, therefore, be argued that because this

right exists we must adopt an interpretation which would lead to the necessity of having recourse to it.' (Ibid., at 96, 131–2.)

35 *Globe*, 11 March 1873.

36 AO, Blake Papers, Mowat to Blake, 30 December 1876.

37 An Act Respecting the Traffic in Intoxicating Liquor, 41 Vict. c. 16, cited as the Canada Temperance Act, 1878.

38 Senate, *Debates*, 1878, 342. For Strong's *obiter*, see Chapter 2, n.42.

39 Senate, *Debates*, 1878, 356 (Dickey), 375 (Campbell).

40 *The Queen on the Prosecution of Thomas Barker* v. *The Mayor of Fredericton* (1879), 19 N.B.R. 139. (In *Kings*, the Nova Scotia Supreme Court had denied the provincial prohibitory power. See Chapter 2, n.40).

41 Ibid. at 173.

42 Ibid. at 141ff.

43 NAC, RG 13, vol. 2239, file 89/1880, Harrison and Burbidge to the mayor of Fredericton, 14 October 1879; ibid., Lash to Campbell 6 January 1880. E.H. Dewart to Lash, 11 February 1880.

44 NAC, RG 125, vol. 15, file 157, *Appellant's Factum*; *City of Fredericton* v. *The Queen* (1880), 3 S.C.R. 505 at 508.

45 Ibid. at 510–12.

46 Ibid. at 518, 520–5.

47 Ibid. at 533–42.

48 Ibid. at 558.

49 Gwynne did apply the deeming clause to all of section 92, but, responding to the argument that it applied only to 92(16), replied that 'it would make no difference in the result ... for the previous part of the 91st section in the most precise and imperative terms declares that, "*notwithstanding any thing in the Act*," notwithstanding, therefore, any thing whether of a local or private nature, or of any other character, if there be anything of any other character enumerated in the 92nd section, the exclusive legislative authority of the Parliament of Canada extends to all matters coming within the classes of subjects enumerated in the 91st section.' (Ibid., 568.) Gwynne is Paul Romney's surrogate for John A. Macdonald: 'Perhaps the most authoritative statement of the centralist position was that of John Wellington Gynn, the foremost judicial exponent of Macdonald's idea of Confederation.' ('Why Lord Watson Was Right,' in Janet Ajzenstat, ed., *Canadian Constitutionalism* [Ottawa: Canadian Study of Parliament Group 1991], 177 at 191.) Although it is useful to juxtapose his extreme centralism against Mowat's extreme view of provincial sovereignty, Gwynne did not speak for Macdonald or for any other judge on the Supreme Court.

50 *City of Fredericton* at 545, 552, 555.

51 See, for example, Peter Russell, Rainer Knopff, and Ted Morton, *Federalism and the Charter: Leading Constitutional Decisions* (Ottawa: Carleton University Press 1989), 44.

52 Supreme Court Library, *Russell* v. *The Queen* (1882), MSS oral argument, second day, 9. See also the discussion of the decision during the oral argument on the McCarthy Act Reference in 1885 (Canada, *Sessional Papers*, 1885, no. 85, 125–6.)

53 (1879), 3 S.C.R. 1. Strong attended the argument but was absent when the judgment was delivered and, apparently, did not bother to indicate concurrence or dissent. (Gwynne had upheld the legislation in *Re Niagara Election Case: Plumb v. Hughes* (1878), 29 U.C.C.P. 261.)

54 Ibid. at 2.

55 The intentions would have been much clearer if the records of the Quebec Conference were more complete. On 25 October 1864 Mowat introduced the section outlining federal legislative jurisdiction, which included: 'For the regulation and incorporation of fire and life insurance companies.' However, the delegates agreed to 'strike out' that provision. (G.P. Browne, *Documents on the Confederation of British North America* [Toronto: McClelland and Stewart 1969], 85, 125). In the absence of a record of the discussion, we cannot be certain whether it was deemed superfluous as covered by other federal enumerations or whether the delegates agreed it should be left to the provinces under either 92(13) or 92(11), the incorporation of companies with provincial objects. The latter is the most likely, but Mowat's silence on the matter when he appeared before the courts might suggest to some that the historical answer might not have served his plea.

56 An Act Respecting Insurance Companies, 31 Vict. c. 48.

57 House of Commons, *Debates*, 1868, 744, 756, 757.

58 Regrettably, Cartwright did not state why it was 'specially relegated to the care of the Dominion.' Ibid., 1875, 453.

59 An Act to Insure Uniform Conditions in Policies of Fire Insurance, 39 Vict. c. 24.

60 See Chapter 2, nn.52, 53.

61 NAC, RG 125, vol. 74, file 852, *Appellant's Factum in the Supreme Court of Canada between William Parsons (Respondent) and the Citizens Insurance Company (Appellants)*.

62 *The Citizens Insurance Company* v. *Parsons* (1879), [1880] 4 S.C.R. 215 at 229–30 (hereafter *Parsons*). Taschereau noted that Mowat had conceded the federal power to create under the residual clause. (Ibid. at 309.)

63 *Parsons* at 243. Strong concurred without writing a judgment. Henry's decision was much the same as Ritchie's. As Gordon Bale has noted, Ritchie

carefully did not alter his definition of the scope of the trade and commerce power. (Gordon Bale, *Chief Justice William Johnstone Ritchie: Responsible Government and Judicial Review* [Ottawa: Carleton University Press 1991], 203.)

64 *Parsons* at 270, 257. The French text (257) is slightly different from the English. Fournier, of course, had been minister of justice when the 1875 act was passed. Here he observed that the federal act was to protect the public from irresponsible companies and drew its power from trade and commerce, while provincial legislation regarding contracts fell within property and civil rights. Fournier also cited Marshall in *Gibbons* v. *Ogden* in support of the double-aspect doctrine (275).

65 *Parsons* at 329, 330–1, 347.

66 Ibid. at 306–7, 295, 312–14. See also his decision in *Angers*, Chapter 2, n.48.

67 An interesting account of the issue from the point of both law and constitutional theory is Suzanne Marthe Birks, 'The Survival of the Crown in the Canadian State: The Political Components of Monarchy' (LLM thesis, Osgoode Hall, 1980).

68 Constitution Act, 1867, sections 9, 10.

69 Ibid., sections 56, 90, 82.

70 Ibid., sections 64, 65. Section 65 first appeared in the fourth draft, undated, as section 96, 'Miscellaneous Sections respecting Ontario and Quebec,' and Section 64 as Section 89 of the same draft. (Browne, *Documents*, 292–4.) What became section 12, with similar provisions concerning the federal government, first appeared in the 2 February draft. (Ibid., 266.)

71 Ibid., sections 59, 60.

72 Joseph Pope, *Memoirs of Sir John A. Macdonald* (Toronto: Musson 1894), 291.

73 NAC, Orders in Council, 1868, no. 175 A., Report of the Minister of Justice, 31 December 1868.

74 Granville to Young [Lisgar], 24 February 1869, Canada, *Sessional Papers*, 1869, no. 16, 5. (See also Carnarvon to Dufferin, 7 January 1875, ibid., no. 11, 38.) The early decisions in the provincial courts seemed to confirm the decision of the law officers. Harrison of the Ontario Court of Queen's Bench denied the province, through the lieutenant governor, the right to issue commissions for special courts: 'the power being a prerogative one, can only be exercised by the Queen or her representative. The Governor-General is the only executive officer provided for by the Act who answers this description.' (*Regina v. Amer* (1878), 42 U.C.Q.B. New Series, 391, at 407–8). Henri-Elzéar Taschereau agreed that 'sous notre constitution, la souveraineté est à Ottawa. Il n'y a que là que Sa Majesté soit directement représentée.' Lieutenant governors could act only in the name of the

Queen, he added, 'dans le cas, où par voie d'exception' the B.N.A. Act explicitly conferred the power. (*Church v. Blake* (1875), 1 Q.L.R. [Sup. Court], 177 at 180, 181.) On appeal it was determined that the prerogative did not apply to escheats, but the court observed that in those particular aspects mentioned in the act, 'il est aussi bien le représentant du Souverain que l'est le Gouverneur-général dans les siennes.' (*A.G. Quebec v. A.G. Canada* (1876), 2 Q.L.R. [Queen's Bench Appeal Side], 236 at 242.)

75 Paul Romney, *Mr Attorney: The Attorney General for Ontario in Court, Cabinet, and Legislature, 1791–1899* (Toronto: Osgoode Society / University of Toronto Press 1986), 242–59. Contemporaries also saw the determination of the place of the crown as critical to the status and jurisdiction of the province. See, for example, D.A. O'Sullivan, *Government in Canada: The Principles and Institutions of our Federal and Provincial Constitutions; the B.N.A. Act, 1867, Compared with the United States Constitution, with a Sketch of the Constitutional History of Canada* (Toronto: Carswell 1887), and W.H.P. Clement, *The Law of the Canadian Constitution* (Toronto: Carswell 1892). See also R.B. Risk, 'Constitutional Scholarship in the late Nineteenth Century: Making Federalism Work,' (1996) 46 *University of Toronto Law Journal*, 427. The history of the controversy between Ontario and Ottawa is documented in Ontario, *Sessional Papers*, 1888, no. 37 'Correspondence relative to the appointment of Queen's Counsel by the Federal and Provincial Governments.' The final resolution is discussed below in chapter 6.

76 Canada, *Sessional Papers*, 1873, no. 50, 2. Lisgar to Kimberley, 4 January 1872, enclosing report of the minister of justice, 2 January 1872; Kimberley to Lisgar, 1 February 1872.

77 In re *Precedence of Ritchie, Q.C.* (1877), [1876–7] 11 N.S.R. 450 at 452. Challenging the statute and the status of the lieutenant governor was John Thompson, the minister of justice in the later battle with Mowat.

78 *Lenoir v. Ritchie* (1879), 3 S.C.R. 575 at 596. Chief Justice Ritchie declined to sit on a case involving his brother!

79 Ibid. at 594–5.

80 Ibid. at 606.

81 Romney, *Mr Attorney*, 250.

82 *Lenoir v. Ritchie*, 610–13.

83 Ibid. at 618, 620, 625, and n.74 above.

84 Ibid. 630ff.

85 *Mercer v. A.G. Ontario* (1881), 5 S.C.R. 538.

86 *Church v. Blake* (1875), 1 Q.L.R. 177 at 180–1.

87 *A.G. Quebec v. A.G. Canada* (1876), 2 Q.L.R. 236.

88 Hodgins, *Correspondence*, 123.

89 *A.G. Ontario* v. *O'Reilly* (1880), 26 Grant's Chancery Reports 126; 6 O.A.R. [1880] 576.
90 House of Commons, *Debates*, 1884, 26; *Mercer v. A.G. Ontario* (1881), 5 S.C.R. 538 at 540.
91 Ibid. at 542.
92 Ibid. at 552.
93 Ibid. at 577.
94 Ibid. at 578–9, 583. Bethune contended that 'it would certainly require very strong words to abolish the prerogative right of Her Majesty in respect of which it existed before Confederation, I submit that the true construction is that the executive authority of the Queen continues, and was to be carried out, in every part of Canada after Confederation, by the Governor-General in respect of Dominion matters and by the Lieutenant-Governors as her representatives in Provincial matters.' (Ibid. at 589.) T.J.J. Loranger, intervening for Quebec, provided the court with a long rambling version of the compact theory, anticipating almost word for word much of his book *Letters upon the Interpretation of the Federal Constitution Known as the British North America Act, 1867* (Quebec: Morning Chronicle 1884).
95 5 S.C.R. at 667.
96 Ibid. at 667, 672–3.
97 Ibid. at 710–11.
98 Ibid. at 643–4.
99 *Liquidators of the Maritime Bank of Canada* v. *Receiver-General of New Brunswick*, [1892] A.C. 437. See John T. Saywell, *The Office of Lieutenant-Governor* (Toronto: University of Toronto Press 1957), 15ff.
100 House of Commons, *Debates*, 1880, 261 (McCarthy), 253 (Blake).
101 NAC, Macdonald Papers, Campbell to Macdonald, 5 April 1884.

4 The Appeal to Caesar

1 House of Commons, *Debates*, 1875, 286. The Judicial Committee of the Privy Council was created by statute in 1833, although it had a much longer history as a court of appeal from the colonies. Its role was embedded in the constitutional fact and theory of imperial supremacy which was made explicit in such statutes as the Colonial Laws Validity Act of 1865, a measure that, while removing conflict with the common law as grounds for invalidating colonial legislation, reaffirmed the supremacy of imperial statutes over colonial legislation. The British North America Act was just such an imperial statute, as Ritchie had noted in *Chandler*. (See Chapter 2, n.5.)

On the proposed restructuring of the appellate courts, see Robert Steven, *Law and Politics: The House of Lords as a Judicial Body*, 1800–1976 (Chapel Hill: University of North Carolina Press 1978), Chapter 2.

2 *Debates*, 1875, 976, 980. Nine Quebec members opposed the amendment because they believed civil law appeals were safer in the hands of judges familiar with Roman law than with the predominantly common law judges on the Supreme Court. The bill passed without a recorded division. In the Senate an amendment to remove clause 47 was defeated only with the casting vote of the speaker. However, seventeen senators, most of them anglophone, entered their dissent in the Senate, stating that the bill 'interferes with the right of appeal to the Judicial Committee of the Privy Council, hitherto enjoyed by the people of Canada, and thus tends to weaken the connection between the Dominion and the Mother country' (Senate, *Journals*, 1875, 282). Irving had failed to secure support for an amendment abolishing appeals from the provincial superior courts, in part because Fournier said it would mean the abrogation of provincial laws but could come later (943). Blake agreed with Irving. (F.H. Underhill, 'Edward Blake's Interview with Lord Cairns on the Supreme Court Act, July 5, 1876' [1938] 19 *Canadian Historical Review*, 294.) Canadian appeals had come largely from Quebec. Between 1867 and 1876, there were forty-one decisions on Canadian appeals of which thirty-four were from Quebec. See Albert S. Abel, 'The Role of the Supreme Court in Private Law Cases' (1965) 4 *Alberta Law Review*, 43 n.11.

3 Ibid., 981.

4 Dufferin to Carnarvon, 11 November, 1875, in C.W. de Kiewiet and F.H. Underhill, *The Dufferin-Carnarvon Correspondence, 1874–1878* (Toronto: Champlain Society 1955), 163.

5 Ibid., 167. Carnarvon to Dufferin, 4 November, 25 November, 1875. Hugh McCalmont Cairns was a Scots/Irish Ulsterman. A Belfast MP, he was fiercely Tory in politics and one of Disraeli's most trusted colleagues.

6 Cairns to Carnarvon, 2 November 1875, in David M.L. Farr, *The Colonial Office and Canada, 1867–1887* (Toronto: University of Toronto Press 1955), 144. Farr's account is the most complete, but see also David B. Swinfen, *Imperial Appeal: The Debate on the Appeal to the Privy Council, 1833–1986* (Manchester, U.K.: University of Manchester Press 1897), 35.

7 *Dufferin-Carnarvon Correspondence*, Carnarvon to Dufferin, 15 December 1875, 173.

8 Ibid., Dufferin to Carnarvon, 3 November, 11 November 1875, 160, 162.

9 Blake to Mills, 29 May 1876, in F.H. Underhill, 'Edward Blake, the Supreme Court Act, and the Appeal to the Privy Council, 1875–1876' (1938) 19 *Canadian Historical Review*, 257.

10 Swinfen, *Imperial Appeal*, 51n.37, 55. There were in fact two British memo-

randa, one by Reeve and a second prepared for the lord chancellor which was largely on the specific application of clause 47. These and Blake's rejoinder were printed by Blake for the cabinet. (National Archives of Canada [NAC], Laurier Papers, *Correspondence respecting the Supreme and Exchequer Court of Canada*, confidentially printed for the use of the Privy Council [n.d.].) Much of Blake's masterful state paper was reprinted in L.A. Cannon, 'Some Data relating to the Appeal to the Privy Council' (1925) 8 *Canadian Bar Review*, 455. Swinfen is the best account of the controversy from the British side. See also his 'Henry Reeve and the Judicial Department of the Privy Council' (1984) *Dundee Review of Modern Studies*, 55. Unfortunately, the only biography of Reeve is lamentably thin on his work at the Judicial Committee. It seems clear, however, that he was opposed to the creation of the imperial court of appeal and the abolition of the Judicial Committee. (J.K. Laughton, *Memoirs of the Life and Correspondence of Henry Reeve*, vol. 2 [London: Longmans, Green 1898], 209.)

11 'Memorandum upon the Supreme Court and Exchequer Act of Canada and the right of Appeal from the Colonial Courts to Her Majesty in Council,' *Correspondence*, 13.

12 Ibid., 14.

13 'Observations on the Confidential Memoranda on the Subject of the 47th Clause of the Supreme Court, transmitted by Lord Carnarvon, 9th March 1876,' *Correspondence*, 26.

14 Ibid., 31.

15 Ibid., 26.

16 By the end of the century, Blake endorsed much of what Reeve had written. During the debate on the Australian constitution in 1900, with its controversial attempt to abolish appeals, Blake declared in the British House of Commons that 'it was found with us that where bitter controversies had been excited, where political passions had been engendered, where considerable disputations had prevailed, where men eminent in power and politics had ranged themselves on opposite sides, it was a great advantage to have an opportunity of appealing to an external tribunal such as the Judicial Committee for the interpretations of the Constitution on such matters.' Obviously, like his colleague Mowat, Blake had found the 'federal spirit' in the Judicial Committee much to his liking. (U.K., House of Commons, *Parliamentary Debates*, 1900, 774.)

17 *Correspondence*, 40. Carnarvon to Dufferin, 29 August, 1876.

18 *James Johnston* v. *St. Andrew's Church* (1877), 3 A.C. 159 at 162–3. The Supreme Court reversed decisions in two Quebec courts by a 4–2 margin and refused leave to appeal (1877), 1 S.C.R. 235.

19 *Valin* v. *Langlois* (1879), 5 A.C. 115 at 117–18.

20 *Prince* v. *Gagnon* (1882), 8 A.C. 103 at 105.
21 *Cite de Montréal* v. *Les Ecclésiastiques du Seminaire St. Sulpice de Montréal*
   (1889), 14 A.C. 660 at 662. Quoting Selborne's *dicta*, Lord Davey stated in
   1903 that 'those principles have been consistently acted on by this Board.
   And in the case of *Consumer's Cordage Co., Ltd.* v. *Connolly* which was a petition for special leave to appeal from a judgement of the Supreme Court of
   Canada, (heard by this Committee on June 27, 1901), it was said that where
   a person has elected to go to the Supreme Court, it is not the practice to
   allow him to come to this Board, except in a very strong case. It is different
   where a man is taken before the Supreme Court, because he cannot help it.
   But where a man elects to go to the Supreme Court, having his choice
   whether he will go there or not, this Board will not give him assistance
   except under special circumstances.' (*Clergue* v. *Murray*, [1903] A.C. 521 at
   522.) A note appended to the report observed that, in two other cases of
   nearly the same date, both involving the rights of the crown, the principle
   had been ignored.
22 *The Times*, 7 March 1883.
23 Wheeler, *Confederation Law of Canada*, 450. The appeal was from *McLaren* v.
   Caldwell (1883), 7 S.C.R. 435. However, the committee refused to hear arguments concerning the constitutionality of the Supreme Court Act or the
   right of the Supreme court to entertain appeals which involved the construction of a provincial act.
24 *Dumoulin* v. *Langtrey* (1887), *Robinson* v. *Canadian Pacific Railway* (1891), and
   MacMillan v. *Grand Trunk Railway* (1889), in George Wheeler, *Privy Council
   Law* (London: Stevens and Son 1893), 970, 991, 982. Between 1877 and 1891,
   there were thirty petitions for appeal from the Supreme Court; only eight
   were rejected. (Ibid., 957ff.). The hearing on the leave to appeal in *St. Catherine's Milling* v. *The Queen* was an instance where the appeal was against the
   decisions of the Chancery and Court of Appeal in Ontario and the Supreme
   Court of Canada (Strong and Gwynne dissenting). D'Alton McCarthy acted
   for the company and Richard Haldane with Irving for Ontario. 'I should
   like to know,' said Lord Hobhouse, 'that it is a matter of general importance
   but that the judgment is apparently wrong. There are three Courts deciding in one way only that there are two judges of the Supreme Court[,] the
   other and you were the Appellants to the Supreme Court, whereas you
   might have brought the case here at once.' McCarthy replied, 'It was
   thought desirable in a case of this kind where so much depended upon
   local knowledge to go to the Supreme Court because of the local knowledge which it is rather difficult or impossible for your Lordship to have,'
   drawing from Sir Barnes Peacock the query, 'If we have not local knowl-

edge why come here?' All seemed to agree that, with the ownership of 55,000 square miles of Indian lands at stake, the matter was of general importance and would in some form or other come before the committee for a final decision. Haldane argued that the appeal should be denied, but, if litigated, should be by the Dominion government, whose proprietary interest in 'lands reserved for Indians' was at issue. Hobhouse agreed and, after some opposition, the federal government agreed to intervene. (Archives of Ontario [AO], Irving Papers, MU 1480, 41/06/02, Transcript for hearing for leave to appeal 22 July 1887.) Argument before the committee took seven days in 1888. Mowat and Blake, with Horace Davey and Haldane, appeared for Ontario. Lord Watson delivered the judgment in Ontario's favour (14 A.C. 46).

25 There were twelve appeals in constitutional cases including two on the Manitoba schools question and two on local prohibition. Eight of the decisions were confirmed. The four reversals included the two schools decisions. F. Murray Greenwood, 'Lord Watson, Institutional Self-interest, and the Decentralization of Canadian Federalism in the 1890's' (1974) 9 *University of British Columbia Law Review*, 244, Table I at 266.

26 NAC, RG 13, vol. 2272, file 204/98, Mowat to E.L. Newcombe, 16 May 1895.

27 Supreme Court of Canada Library, oral argument, *Provincial Fisheries* 1894 [sic 1896], 3.

28 Canada, *Sessional Papers*, 1885, no. 85, oral argument, *McCarthy Act Reference*, 212.

29 U.K., *Parliamentary Debates*, 1900, 103.

30 Robert D. Meade, *Judah P. Benjamin: Confederate Statesman* (New York: Oxford University Press 1943), 372.

31 R.F.V. Heuston, *Lives of the Lord Chancellors, 1995–1940* (Oxford, U.K.: Clarendon Press 1964), 218.

32 Sir William Holdsworth, *A History of English Law*, 7th ed., vol. 1 (London: Methuen 1956), 516.

33 T.A. Nash, *The Life of Lord Westbury*, vol. 2 (London: Bentley and Son 1888), 174.

34 Ibid., 174. An English legal historian has commented that there 'were times in the latter half of the nineteenth century when the reputation of the Judicial Committee was not high. The personnel of the board was often senile and undistinguished; and it was said that the single-judgement rule had been providentially devised to enable all but the member who was going to write the judgement to sleep during the hearing.' (R.T.E. Latham, 'The Law and the Commonwealth,' in W.K. Hancock, *Survey of the British Common-*

wealth Affairs, vol. 1, *Problems of Nationalism, 1918–1936* [London: Oxford University Press 1964], 554.)

35 NAC, Thompson Papers, Wallace Graham to John Thompson, 13 July 1887.

36 The addition of the paid judges did not commend itself to the editor of the *Legal News* (4 [1881], 73) who commented that, although the decisions of the committee 'have been received with a certain kind of deference, greater perhaps that their intrinsic merits deserved,' the 'Lyndhursts, St. Leonards and Wensleydales could hardly make any serious mistake. The old Judicial Committee had then something more than *prestige* to make up for its very obvious defect. The alteration of its composition, by the appointment of paid councillors, has, at any rate, destroyed its *prestige*. It would be invidious to carry the comparison further.'

37 Laughton, *Reeve*, passim. Two lords of appeal were appointed at once: Blackburn and Gordon, a Scots Lord. Regarded by many as the country's leading lawyer by the time he died in 1887, Blackburn presided in *Dobie* in 1881 and wrote the decision in *Caldwell* v. *McLaren* in which the Judicial Committee upheld Mowat's rivers and streams legislation. After Gordon died in 1879, he was replaced by William Watson. When Colvile died, Fitzgerald, a former Liberal MP, was appointed as an Irish Lord. In 1891, when the final vacancy occurred, Lord Hannen became the fourth lord of appeal. The 1875 reform caused some misgivings among older members of the committee. When Reeve contemplated resigning, Sir Lawrence Peel, a veteran of the board, urged him against it. 'One word about your "resignation." "Don't." The weaker the thing is, the more your value will be felt. Sir Montague will go. He had as much as told me so, not very lately. It will be a new Court, not the old P.C., nor can it have the character of the House of Lords. It will have its entire way to make and where is the stuff? It may in time win approval; but it will be a child at first.' (Peel to Reeve, 11 December, 1880, in Laughton, *Reeve*, vol. 2, 281.)

38 The order of precedence is somewhat more complicated. 'The rules were, and are, that in the absence of the Lord Chancellor of the day, an ex-Lord Chancellor takes precedence over the other Law Lords not of higher rank in the peerage. But as between ex-Lord Chancellors, precedence is according to their rank in the peerage.' Heuston, *Lord Chancellors*, 301.

39 Alan Paterson, *The Law Lords* (London: Macmillan 1982), 93.

40 'The Work for the Empire of the Judicial Committee of the Privy Council' 1 *Cambridge Law Journal* (1923), 145.

41 The single decision, which was not the case in the House of Lords, was that in theory the judgment was an advisory opinion to the crown. The best

study is D.B. Swinfen, 'The single judgement in the Privy Council 1833–1966' *Juridical Review* (1975), 153.

42 F. Stafford and G. Wheeler, *Practices of the Privy Council in Judicial Matters* (London: Sweet and Maxwell 1901), 876.

43 Paterson, *Law Lords*, 98.

44 Ibid., 99. Pearce was appointed in 1962.

45 In 1966 the practice changed to allow dissents to be written and published. Before 1966 they could be written but not published. (A.V. Lowe and J.R. Young, 'An Executive Attempt to Rewrite a Judgement' (1978) 94 *Law Quarterly Review*, 255 at 272n.40.) In that period, concluded Alan Paterson, 'it is difficult to tell how frequently written dissents were produced ... because they were not usually kept, their existence was not always recorded in the judgement books, and in any event the judgement books before the mid-30s were destroyed by fire in a bombing raid in the Second World War.' (Paterson, *Law Lords*, 241n.64.) Examples can be found. 'I am sorry that Sumner has written a dissenting Memo in *James* v. *Davis Bay Rlwy*' ([1914] A.C. 1043), Lord Moulton wrote to Haldane. (National Library of Scotland [NLS], Haldane Papers, MS 5910, 12 June 1914.) After the argument in *Fort Frances Pulp and Paper* v. *Manitoba Free Press Company* in 1923, Haldane wrote to his mother that he had 'a heavy struggle in the Privy Council ... but in the end had a majority of one for my interpretation of the Canadian Constitution.' (Ibid., MS 6006, 27 June 1923.)

46 Wright, 'Precedents,' 4 *University of Toronto Law Journal* (1942), 265.

47 Lord Morton, who sat on a number of Canadian constitutional appeals after his appointment in 1947, described the process followed after the argument: 'A very full discussion takes place and we all state our personal views. I do not think it is a breach of confidence to say that the junior member of the Board is invited to state his views first. The discussion may be prolonged. If it turns out that we are unanimous, we go on to decide who shall draft the judgement and what form it shall take. If, however, for the moment, we are three to two or four to one, further discussions follow either then or at a later stage, at which our various views are fully disclosed. It may be that unanimity is thus achieved. If it is not, at least the points of divergence emerge clearly. If we are still divided in opinion, a member of the majority drafts the judgement, but our task is by no means finished at that stage, as you can well appreciate. When the draft judgement has been prepared it is fully considered and fully criticized by the other four members of the Board. That accounts, I think, for what sometimes seems a long delay before judgement is finally issued. We are most anxious to ensure, if possible, that no words are used which may be mis-

understood.' Address of the Right Hon. Lord Morton of Henryton, *Year Book of the Canadian Bar Association* (1949), 107 at 109. In a tribute to Sir Lyman Duff, Lord Wright observed that 'no record is kept of difference or dissents on the Board and the Privy Councillor's oath of secrecy prevents disclosure, so that a particular member's view may be known only to his colleagues.' He then proceeded to differ with the judgment in the *Labour Conventions* case of 1937 although he had sat on the case. (33 *Canadian Bar Review* [1955], 1124.)

48 Jennings, 'Constitutional Interpretation: The Experience of Canada' 51 *Harvard Law Review* (1937), 22.

49 McWhinney, *Judicial Review* (Toronto: University of Toronto Press 1956), 53.

50 Latham, 'The Law of the Commonwealth,' in Hancock, *Survey,* 554.

51 Paterson, *Law Lords*, 99. Denning was appointed in 1957. Lyman Duff's correspondence with Sir Charles Nash, registrar of the Privy Council, does indicate that the judgments were circulated and efforts, not always successful, were made to secure agreement. In one instance Duff replied, 'I have not suggested any changes, because the points on which I do not agree seem to involve the substance of the reasoning, and upon them, in effect, I intimated orally my view before leaving.' (10 September 1924.) Duff's own judgment in *Reciprocal Insurers* was approved without alteration. (Neish to Duff), 25 January 1924.) Haldane accepted the lord chancellor's amendments in *City of Montreal v. Harbour Commission of Montreal*, [1926] A.C. 298, and Duff was asked if he accepted the changes on pages 7 to 9 'which had been substantially rewritten' and to reply by telegram. (Neish to Duff, 23 October, 1925.) NAC, Duff Papers, Duff to Neish, 10 September 1924; Neish to Duff, 25 January 1924 and 23 October 1925.

52 Holdsworth, *History of English Law*, vol. 1, 519, no. 10.

53 Cited in Swinfen, *Imperial Appeal*, 233. The fullest discussion and apology for the single decision is Lord Selborne's *Judicial Procedure in the Privy Council* (London: Macmillan 1891). Among his comments were: 'No rational argument has been, or can be, advanced in favour of the disclosure of difference of opinion in the Judicial Committee, of which is not a necessary, or at least a legitimate consequence, that dissentient Judges ought also publicly to state the reasons for their dissent. If we have not already sufficient security for judicial purity, there as well as elsewhere, it can hardly be obtained by the declaration of dissents without reasons ... In the absence of those reasons, nothing can result from the publication of the mere fact of dissent, except some possible disparagement, proportionate to the personal reputation of the dissenting Judges, of the decision of the Court; which, nevertheless, in a Court of last resort, must be final and conclusive' (58–9).

However, Selborne added, whether 'it is expedient when a judgement is not unanimous, to declare that it is that of a majority, without any indication of the opinions of particular members of the Court is a different question. This seems to be absolutely within the discretion of the Judicial Committee, in each particular case; it involves no departure from any known rule' (61). I have found no instance where such a declaration was made.

54 Ibid., 235.
55 I have been unable to find any reference in the decision or the literature to a minority on *Hodge*, but, given the precedent of *Russell*, it would have been unlikely that the committee was unanimous. *Sessional Papers*, 1885, no. 85, Oral argument, Supreme Court of Canada, *McCarthy Act Reference*, 76.
56 *Great West Saddlery* v. *R.*, [1921] 2 A.C. 91. The oral argument is printed in E.R. Cameron, *Canadian Companies and the Judicial Committee* (Toronto: Carswell 1922), 182. Nesbitt replied: 'Your Lordships's observations will be in print, and I will see that they are diffused.' He then proceeded to continue reading from the oral argument in *John Deere*.
57 Ibid., 3.
58 P.S. Atiyah, *The Rise and Fall of Freedom of Contract* (Oxford, U.K.: Clarendon Press 1979), 388.
59 Ibid., 660. See also P.S. Atiyah and Robert Summers, *Form and Substance in Anglo-American Law: A Comparative Study of Legal Reasoning, Legal Theory, and Legal Institutions* (Oxford, U.K.: Clarendon Press 1987), Chapter 9; and David Sugarman, 'Legal Training, the Common Law Mind and the Making of the Textbook Tradition,' in William Twining, ed., *Legal Theory and Common Law* (Oxford, U.K.: Blackwell 1986), 26.
60 *R.* v. *Judge of the City of London Court* (1892), 1 Q.B. 273 at 290, cited in Michael Zander, *The Law-Making Process* (London: Butterworths 1999) 109.
61 Cited in Sir Rupert Cross, *Statutory Interpretation*, 2nd ed. (London: Butterworths 1987), 16.
62 Ibid., 17.
63 Cited in Rupert Cross, *Precedent in English Law* (Oxford, U.K.: Clarendon Press 1977), 9
64 Supreme Court of Canada Library, 'Report of the Proceedings before the Judicial Committee of the Privy Council on the Hearing of the Petition of the Governor-General of Canada in relation to the Dominion License Acts of 1883 and 1884,' Manuscript Oral Argument, 189 (hereafter *McCarthy Act Reference*).
65 *A.G. Ontario* v. *Canada Temperance Federation*, [1946] A.C. 193 at 206. See Chapter 9, n.152.
66 Atiyah, *Freedom of Contract*, 660.

67 Cited in Daniel Duman, *The English and Colonial Bars in the Nineteenth Century* (London: Croom and Helms 1993), 181.

68 Brian Abel-Smith and Robert Stevens, *Lawyers and the Courts* (London: Heinemann 1967), 122.

69 Cited in Raymond Cocks, *Foundations of the Modern Bar* (London: Sweet and Maxwell 1983), 122.

70 *The House of Lords as a Judicial Body, 1800–1976* (Chapel Hill: University of North Carolina Press, 1978), 100.

71 Ibid., 183.

72 Richard Risk, 'Canadian Courts under the Influence' (1990) 40 *University of Toronto Law Journal*, 687 at 713. Risk's analysis is, perhaps, more similar to that of American scholars than of English. See Morton Horwitz, who writes that later nineteenth-century legal thought was dominated by 'categorical thinking – by clear, distinct, bright-line classification of legal phenomena' (*The Transformation of American Law* 1870–1960 [New York: Oxford University Press 1992], 17).

73 'Local and Federal Jurisdiction' (1882) 5 *Legal News*, 1.

74 *Bank of Toronto v. Lambe* (1887), 12 A.C. 575 at 579.

75 *Maher v. The Town Council of Portland*, 'The argument before the Judicial Committee of the Privy Council July 17, 1874' (Canadian Institute for Historical Microreproductions [CIHM] 09657 at 9).

76 Ibid. at 3.

77 Supreme Court of Canada Library, oral argument, *Russell v. The Queen*, second day, 68.

78 Ibid., 116.

79 *Citizens Insurance Company v. Parsons* (1881), 7 A.C. 96 at 112.

80 *Sessional Papers*, 1885, no. 85, oral argument, *McCarthy Act Reference*, 202, 82.

81 *The Liquor Prohibition Appeal* 1895 (London: William Brown 1895), 90.

82 *Webb v. Outrim*, [1906] A.C. 81 at 90.

83 Selborne's dicta is a colourful paraphrase of the opening sentence in P.B. Maxwell's classic nineteenth-century text, *On the Interpretation of Statutes* (London: Methuen 1875): 'Statute law is the will of the Legislature; and the object of all judicial interpretation is to determine what intention is either expressly or by implication conveyed by the language used.' (*St. Catherine's Milling Lumber Co. v. The Queen* [1889].) Blake's oral argument, during which Selborne made the statement, is in *The St. Catherine's Milling and Lumber Company v. the Queen: Arguments of Mr. Blake Counsel for Ontario* (Toronto, 1888), 39.

84 *Saloman v. Saloman & Co.*, [1897] A.C. 22 at 38 (H.L.).

85 *City of Winnipeg v. Barrett*, [1892] A.C. 445, reversing *Barrett* v. *City of Winnipeg* (1891), 19 S.C.R. 374.

86 *City of Winnipeg* v. *Barrett*, oral argument, Canada, *Sessional Papers, 1893*, no. 33B, 54–5.

87 *Brophy* v. *A.G. Manitoba*, [1894] A.C. 202 at 215. Thus, although the committee had upheld the validity of the Manitoba Schools Act, it found reasons why an appeal for remedial action under subsection 3 of the Manitoba Act was valid, once again reversing the decision of the Supreme Court which had thought it was bound by the precedent in *Barrett*. Herschell explained the court's dilemma over language during the oral argument in the *Fisheries Reference* when it was argued that an obvious typographical error at London in 1867, which had changed 'River and lake improvements,' into 'Rivers and lake improvements,' had placed all rivers in Canada under federal jurisdiction according to the third Schedule 'Provincial Public Works and Property to be the Property of Canada.' 'Of course, Mr. Blake, there is this, that it happened before now, and one has been obliged to say judicially: We think this was not foreseen and if the Legislature had seen the effect of the words they would not have used them; they have used them and we cannot help it. This is not infrequently said by the Judicial Bench.' (*Jurisdiction over Fisheries, Harbours, and Navigable Waters* [London: 1897], oral argument, 188.) The French text of the 1867 schedule read, 'Amélioration sur les lacs et rivières.' During the argument, Watson had stated categorically that 'surely a French translation of an Imperial Statute can have no meaning.' (Ibid., 69.) Herschell devoted two pages to the question in his decision and concluded, without admitting any extrinsic evidence, that they felt 'justified, therefore, in putting upon the language used the construction which seems to them to be more probably in accordance with the intention of the legislature.' (*A.G. Canada* v. *A.G. Ontario, Quebec and Nova Scotia*, [1898] A.C. 700 at 711.)

88 *Law in the Making* (Oxford, U.K.: Oxford University Press 1964), 417. 'Much of our case-law,' Allen continued, 'certainly suggests that the letter killeth more often than the spirit giveth life.' (Ibid., 418.)

89 Cited in ibid., 426. The experienced parliamentary draughtsman, Sir W. Graham Harrison, recounted experiences which might well have been echoed by the draughtsman of the 1867 constitution. 'We find that when an Act comes before a court it is quite often held to mean something which we never intended, and we are told that this interpretation is inevitable, in view of well-established rules applicable to the construction of statutes; it seems to us, however, that the results are arrived at by subtleties and an excessive ingeniousness of argument which are out of place in construing legal documents prepared as Acts of Parliament necessarily are.' (Ibid., 34.)

90 *A.G. Ont.* v. *A.G. Canada*, [1896] A.C. 348 at 359.
91 *St. Catherine's Milling and Lumber Co.* v. *The Queen* (1887), 13 S.C.R. 577 at 606–7. See Chapter 3, n.17.
92 Viscount Simon, 'The Limits of Precedent,' Holdsworth Club, University of Birmingham (1943), 3.

5 Caesar Speaks, 1874–1888

1 *Citizens Insurance Co. of Canada* v. *Parsons* (1881), 7 A.C. 96 at 109.
2 Of the sixteen cases included by Richard O. Olmsted, *Decisions of the Judicial Committee of the Privy Council relating to the British North America Act, 1867 and the Canadian Constitution* (Ottawa: Queen's Printer 1954) I have excluded three as not properly division-of-power cases: *R* v. *Coote* (1875), *Bourgoin* v. *La Compagnie du Chemin de Fer de Montreal, Ottawa, et Occidental* (1880); and *The Queen* v. *Belleau* (1882) (*Decisions of the Judicial Committee of the Privy Council relating to the British North America Act, 1867 and the Canadian Constitution, 1867–1954 (Ottawa: Queen's Printer 1954) 3 vols). Attorney General of Ontario* v. *Mercer* (1883) will be discussed in Chapter 6.
3 *Valin* v. *Langlois* (1879), 5 A.C. 115 at 118.
4 Including *Mercer.*
5 (1872), 20 *Lower Canadian Jurist*, 29.
6 A.C. 31 at 35. Selborne's comment was frequently cited in aid of the proposition that a provincial law could be valid in the absence of federal legislation, but, when Ottawa 'occupied' the field with legislation within the section 91 enumerations, the provincial law was displaced.
7 *Valin* v. *Langlois* (1879), 5 A.C. 115 at 117. Born in the British Virgin Islands, Benjamin had moved to Louisiana and become an eminent lawyer. Elected to the United States Senate, he became secretary of state and of war in the Confederacy. He escaped to England in 1865 and was called to the bar a year later. When he retired in 1882, William Freshfields of Freshfields and Williams, the solicitors engaged by Mowat, wrote to the future Lord Halsbury: 'Benjamin is gone and you are without flattery, pre-eminent at the bar ... Why don't you take the position he did, throw over all work in the Divisional courts and go nowhere but to the Appeal courts under a special fee of one hundred guineas.' (R.F.V. Heuston, *Lives of the Lord Chancellors* (Oxford, U.K.: Clarendon Press 1964), 28.) Benjamin has been credited with planting the 'states rights theory' of Canadian federalism in the minds of the Judicial Committee, but the speculation is without substance. (Claudius O. Johnson, 'Did Judah P. Benjamin Plant the States Right Doctrine in the Interpretation of the British North America Act?' 45 *Canadian Bar Review*

(1967), 454.) Benjamin lost every Canadian constitutional case but one (*Dow v. Black* (1875), 6 A.C. 272. He appeared with Frances Herschell in *Parsons* (arguing against the validity of the Ontario act), and the text of his oral argument in *Russell* confirms his biographer's comment that in the years before his retirement he 'was obviously more concerned with making money than in establishing a record for the number of suits he had won.' (R.T. Meade, *Judah P. Benjamin: Confederate Statesman* [New York: Oxford University Press 1943], 357.)

8 *Valin* at 118, 119–20.
9 (1880), 5 A.C. 409 at 415–16.
10 *Citizens Insurance Co. v. Parsons* (1881), 7 A.C. 96.
11 National Archives of Canada (NAC), Macdonald Papers, Gwynne to Macdonald, 22 June 1880.
12 Ibid., Galt to Macdonald, 20 November 1880.
13 Ibid., Bompas, Bischoff and Dodgson to Macdonald, 5 July 1881. These men were the solicitors for the federal government and their belief that Macdonald was in one sense a client in the case was revealed when they advised him that, since they were engaged in *Parsons*, it was inadvisable that they also be involved in the pending appeal in *Russell* against him. (Ibid., 4 November 1881.)
14 Archives of Ontario (AO), RG 4–32, file 1881 no. 1 689 (1). Mowat to Freshfields and Williams, 11 January 1881. The rumours apparently were confirmed. (Ibid., draft letter for Mr Scott, 1 February 1881.)
15 Ibid., Freshfields and Williams to Reeve, 28 February 1881; Freshfields and Williams to Mowat, 1 March, 4 March 1881. In their letter of 4 March, the solicitors suggested that, even if the cases were argued *ex parte*, 'we think it probable that our communications with the Registrar would have some effect and the Court would be more than ever careful to see that all the points involved were properly before them.' Mowat was advised to draw up a petition to the crown to be allowed to intervene, which would contain 'an accurate statement of the points affecting your legislation and showing the detriment which will arise to the Province if its Acts are not upheld.' There is no record of such a petition. (Ibid., 689 (2), Freshfields and Williams to Mowat, 17 May 20 May, 1881.)
16 Despite his track record, Mowat was unhappy that Benjamin was not acting for Ontario and asked that his solicitors be informed 'that I would like to retain him in such a way as to prevent his hereafter acting against us whereas in the present case the province is concerned in the question in controversy though not parties ... and authorize them to extend his retainer accordingly.' (AO, RG 4–32 file 1881, no. 1 689 – (1), Memo for Mr Scott,

7 April 1881.) The discussion among the solicitors as to the best counsel led Freshfields to advise Mowat that, while the solicitor general might be the best, he was fully involved in the Irish question. The letter also raises an intriguing question about the role of the two law officers of the crown before the Judicial Committee: 'Had the Government of Ontario interfered [intervened] we should in that case felt no hesitation in selecting first the Attorney General and next the Solicitor General and in a Government matter every attention would have been secured. In the present circumstances if the Solicitor General were selected it would be merely on behalf of the Respondents as civilians and he would only represent the Government very indirectly.' (Ibid., Freshfields and Williams to Mowat, 17 June 1881.)

17 Ontario, *Sessional Papers*, 1882, no. 31, 'Report of the Attorney General with Respect to Certain Proceedings before the Privy Council, Involving the Right of the Provincial Legislature to Pass the Act to Secure Uniform Conditions in Policies of Insurance.'

18 *Citizens Insurance Co.* v. *Parsons* (1881), 7 A.C. 96, at 102–3, 101.

19 Ibid. at 107–9. With reference to mutual modification, Robert Vipond maintains that 'this is arguably the critical methodological statement of the Judicial Committee's early Canadian jurisprudence. Jurisdictional conflict had to be avoided if the exclusive areas of provincial power were to be saved; it could be avoided if the courts defined sections 91 and 92 as spheres of legislative entitlement that were contiguous rather than overlapping, and limited rather than open-ended.' (*Liberty and Community: Canadian Federalism and the Failure of the Constitution* [Buffalo: State University of New York 1991], 161.) Of the aspect and mutual modification doctrines, Paul Weiler observes that, although in *Parsons* it began as a laudable effort to save provincial legislation, 'instead of utilizing the "aspect doctrine" to avoid the converse results on federal power, later courts turned this approach into an abstract formula which struck down subsequent federal legislation with which the judges were neither familiar or overly sympathetic.' ('The Supreme Court and the Law of Canadian Federalism' (1973) 23 *University of Toronto Law Journal*, 307 at 321.)

20 *Citizens Insurance Co.* v. *Parsons* at 111–13. As authority for the last observation, he cited *St. Jacques* and *Cushing*. This observation was picked up by the solicitors who, perhaps as a hint to Macdonald, wrote him: 'You will observe that the Court has taken care not to travel beyond what was necessary for the decision of the case before them, and have left open the question whether it would be within the powers of the Dominion Parliament to pass a General Act relating to all the Provinces of the Dominion for the regulation of matters of a similar character to those provided for by the

Ontario Act ... The great difficulty of the case has obviously been felt by their Lordships, as they have abstained from laying down any general rule for the guidance of the Courts in cases of a similar character.' (NAC, Macdonald Papers, Bompass, Bischoff and Dodgson to Macdonald, 7 December 1881.)

21 *Citizens Insurance Co.* v. *Parsons* at 117.

22 Smith might simply have cited article a. 24668 of the Quebec Civil Code of 1866: 'L'assurance est un contrat par lequel l'un des contractants appelé l'assureur, en considération d'une valeur, s'engage à indemniser l'autre qu'on appelle l'assuré, ou ses représentants, contre la perte ou la responsabilité résultant de certains risques ou périls auxquels l'objet assuré peut être exposé, ou contre la chance d'un événement.'

23 Supreme Court of Canada Library, MSS oral argument, *Russell* v. *The Queen,* first day at 54 (hereafter *Russell,* oral argument).

24 Ibid., second day, at 3, 17. During the oral argument on the *McCarthy Act Reference* in 1885, Herschell observed that the comments on trade and commerce in *Parsons* were not relevant because the matter at issue was so clearly within property and civil rights. Smith agreed: 'If it had not, all that discussion about trade would have been inapplicable.' However perplexing, the observation does nothing to strengthen the authority of Smith's *obiter.* (Supreme Court Library, MSS oral argument, 'Report of the Proceedings before the Judicial Committee of the Privy Council on the Hearing of the Petition of the Governor-General of Canada in relation to the Dominion License Acts of 1883 and 1884,' 120.)

25 *McCarthy Act Reference,* oral argument, 202. The transcript of the oral argument in the Supreme Court is printed in Canada, *Sessional Papers,* 1885, no. 35, 'Return to an Address of the House of Commons, dated 5 February 1885' (hereafter *McCarthy Act Reference,* oral argument).

26 *Ex parte William Russell* (1880), [1880–1] 20 N.B.S.C. 536.

27 In response to O'Keefe's pressure, Macdonald replied that repeal was politically impossible on the eve of en election. 'The true plan is to let the present excitement exhaust itself,' win the election, then pass some 'reasonable measure,' and by the 1885 election the Scott Act 'would be a dead issue.' (NAC, Macdonald Papers, Macdonald to O'Keefe, 22 April 1881.)

28 Ibid., T.T. Brown to Macdonald, 12 October 1881.

29 *Russell,* oral argument, first day, 9.

30 Ibid., second day, 7–9.

31 Ibid., 37–8.

32 Ibid., 64 (italics added).

33 Ibid., 23–4.

34 Ibid., 43, 52.
35 Ibid., 56.
36 Ibid., 56.
37 Ibid., 57–8.
38 Ibid., 100, 91.
39 Ibid., 102. This might be characterized as an early version of Watson's national dimensions or national concern doctrine.
40 Ibid., 107.
41 Ibid., 70, 115.
42 Ibid., 123.
43 Ibid., 132.
44 *Russell* v. *The Queen* (1882), 7 A.C. 829 at 838–42.
45 AO, Campbell Papers, Macdonald to Campbell, 28 August 1882. Campbell, who had doubted the act's constitutionality and had no desire to engage in a jurisdictional and political battle with Mowat over liquor, replied wearily that he had 'laid it aside for the purpose two months ago – but never found myself in the mood for a close examination.' (NAC, Macdonald Papers, Campbell to Macdonald, 2 September 1882.)
46 As Edward Blake pointed out after he had read the decision, it did not 'either expressly or by implication' mean that only the federal government could pas prohibitory legislation. More important, can we suppose that the Judicial Committee of the Privy Council was inspired to know all about the municipal institutions and local laws which were not even alluded to in argument? Can it be seriously argued before a Canadian Parliament, that the single decision of four or five men – when the great question of municipal institutions was never even raised or discussed – has so finally concluded this question that it is not further arguable? It is absurd to say so.' (House of Commons, *Debates*, 1883, 239).
47 A. Margaret Evans, *Sir Oliver Mowat* (Toronto: University of Toronto Press, 1992), 109.
48 NAC, Macdonald Papers, 29 January 1883.
49 House of Commons, *Debates*, 8 February, 1883, 4.
50 Ibid., 25–6.
51 An Act respecting the Sale of Intoxicating Liquors, and the Issue of Licenses Therefore, S.C. 1883, c. 30. Ontario did impose a further tax, in effect doubling it, which was disallowed by Macdonald over the objections of Campbell. (*Globe*, 5 March 1884; W.E. Hodgins, *Correspondence, Reports of the Minsters of Justice and Orders in Council upon the Subject of Dominion and Provincial Legislation 1867–1895* [Ottawa: Government Printing Bureau 1896], 194.) During the oral argument in the 1916 *Insurance Reference*, E.L. New-

combe, deputy minister of justice since 1893, stated during an interchange with Viscount Haldane: 'The Dominion did not think they had the right to enact it; it was a tentative sort of thing; it was simply a lawyers's project, if I may say so, an attempt to see how far in view of the Russell case the Court would go in upholding Dominion legislation to take control of the whole liquor trade. I think no one was better pleased than the Dominion when it was found it was an *ultra vires measure*.' (E.R. Cameron, ed., *Canadian Companies, Proceedings in the Judicial Committee of the Privy Council* [Toronto: Carswell 1917], xxx.) Macdonald's persistence, even after the Supreme Court rejection, would not seem to support Newcombe's view.

52 *Blouin* v. *Corporation of the City of Quebec* (1880), 7 L.C.J. 18 at 22. (The decision was confirmed a year later when Sunday closing was upheld as a matter of police regulations within the power of municipal corporations. (*Poulin* v. *La Corporation de Quebec* (1881), 7 Q.L.R. 337–9.) The case was appealed to the Supreme Court where Ritchie, Strong, and Fournier upheld the statute. The other three did not address the constitutional issue, and the court being divided, the act was *intra vires* (1884), 9 S.C.R. 185.)

53 *Corporation of Three Rivers* v. *Sulte* (1882), 5 Legal News 330 at 333–4.

54 *R.* v. *Hodge* (1880), 46 U.C.Q.B. 141 at 151.

55 *R.* v. *Hodge* (1882), 7 O.A.R. 246 at 251, 253.

56 NAC, Macdonald Papers, O'Keefe to John Small, 28 September 1884. The letter was prompted by a bill to the 'licensed victuallers' for over $2,000 from Blake, Kerr and Cassels. The case had already cost them $5,000.

57 Canada, *Sessional Papers*, 1884, no. 30, 7, 8, Burbidge to Kerr, 13 November 1883; Kerr to Burbidge, 14 January 1884.

58 Davey was a Liberal and Home Ruler. He was then a member of the House of Commons and later served briefly as Gladstone's solicitor general. Before his appointment as a law lord in 1894, he had acted as counsel in nine important constitutional appeals from Canada, acting in eight for the provinces. He lost only one appeal.

59 The brief emphasized the unanimity in Canadian courts of the right to regulate and the importance of municipal institutions. The desired result, the brief read, was 'to maintain the exclusive right of the provinces to regulate the traffic. Should we be unfortunate enough to fail in maintaining that position it is next in importance to secure from the Privy Council a recognition of the Provincial right to regulate in the absence of a Dominion Law on the subject, and it is apprehended that the latter ground alone is sufficient for our purpose in the present appeal.' (AO, Irving Papers, Memorandum by the Attorney General [Ontario] *Hodge* v. *The Queen* [n.d.] [circa June 1883].)

60 *Hodge* v. *The Queen*, oral argument, 106. The oral argument before the Judicial Committee is printed in Canada, *Sessional Papers*, 1884, no. 30, 'Return to an Address of the House of Commons, dated 24 January 1994.' Cartwright edited the definitive text of all Canadian constitutional cases: *Cases Decided on the British North America Act, 1867* (Toronto 1882–97). Mowat and Cartwright were in London on the appeal in *Mercer* when they acted with Davey.

61 Peacock, Collier, and Couch had sat on *Russell* and Hobhouse on *Parsons*. It was Lord Fitzgerald's first Canadian case, but he took the lead in questioning and wrote the decision. He had been appointed the first Irish lord of appeal in June 1882. A Liberal in politics, he was for a time solicitor general for Ireland in Palmerston's ministry and later attorney general.

62 *Hodge*, oral argument, 27.

63 Ibid., 34.

64 Ibid., 108.

65 Ibid., 93.

66 Ibid., 96.

67 Ibid., 100. It is interesting in view of Watson's later *dicta* that Collier interjected that the committee had always held that the deeming clause applied only to 92(16) and Hobhouse and Davey agreed.

68 *Hodge* v. *The Queen* (1883), 9 A.C. 117 at 130.

69 *Hodge*, oral argument, 67.

70 *Hodge* v. *The Queen* (1883), 131.

71 Ibid., 132.

72 Canada, *Sessional Papers*, 1884, no. 30, 142, Lieutenant Governor of Ontario to Secretary of State, 19 January 1884.

73 House of Commons, *Debates*, 1884, 19–20.

74 Ibid., 26–7.

75 House of Commons, *Debates*, 1884, 937; An Act to Amend 'The Liquor License Act 1883, S.C. 1884, ch. 32.

76 The facta and a transcript of the oral argument are printed in Canada, *Sessional Papers*, 1885, no. 85, 'Return to an Address of the House of Commons, dated 5 February 1885.' Quebec, British Columbia, Nova Scotia, and New Brunswick participated in the hearing.

77 As Gwynne stated during the argument, 'it appeared to me that the subject of the Scott Act was what might be said to be more of the character of a national Act, whereas this is of a private character.' (*McCarthy Act Reference*, oral argument, 167.)

78 Ibid., 152.

79 Ibid., 74.

80 Ibid., 75.
81 Ibid., 64.
82 Ibid., 51, 212.
83 Ibid., 75.
84 Ibid., 51. On the same point, Strong later angrily declared, 'I say that advisedly, and it may go upon the record and sent to the Privy Council for all I care.' (Ibid., 128.)
85 Ibid., 221.
86 Ibid., 165.
87 Ibid., 171.
88 Ibid., 173.
89 Ibid., 182.
90 Ibid., 235.
91 Ibid., 64.
92 Ibid., 242.
93 B.L. Strayer, *Judicial Review of Legislation in Canada* (Toronto: University of Toronto Press 1968), 183. Their refusal on this reference led to an amendment to the Supreme Court Act in 1891 which broadened the scope of possible references and provided that the court was obliged to certify its opinion 'with the reasons therefore, which shall be given in a like manner as in a case of a judgement upon appeal to the said Court.' (Ibid., 185.)
94 *McCarthy Act Reference*, oral argument, 212–13.
95 The judgment is appended to n.120.
96 House of Commons, *Debates*, 1885, 1281; An Act respecting 'The Liquor License Act, 1883, S.C. 1885, c. 74.
97 The board was composed of Halsbury, Smith (*Russell, Hodge*), Peacock (*Russell, Hodge*), Couch (*Russell, Hodge*), Hobhouse (*Hodge*), Monkswell (*Russell, Hodge*), and Fitzgerald (*Hodge*).
98 Oral argument 69. Herschell had argued the federal cause in *Mercer and Caldwell* v. *McLaren*, both of which he lost.
99 Ibid., 70. Smith had commented earlier that much of the act consisted of 'minute regulations.' (Ibid., 29.)
100 Ibid., 43.
101 Ibid., 69.
102 Ibid., 97.
103 Ibid., 73. As authority he cited *L'Union St-Jacques* on which three members of the board had sat. (Ibid., 77.)
104 Ibid., 106.
105 Ibid., 107.
106 Ibid., 144.

107 Ibid., 145.

108 Ibid., 155.

109 AO, Irving Papers, 'Memorandum by the Attorney General of Ontario,' 12 October 1885.

110 Oral argument, 166. Peacock later reminded Davey that the declaratory clause stated explicitly that 'notwithstanding anything in section 92 the exclusive legislative power of the Dominion extended to all the enumerated heads in section 91. (Ibid., 224.)

111 Ibid., 168.

112 Ibid., 187.

113 Ibid., 189.

114 Ibid., 192.

115 Ibid., 194.

116 Ibid., 195–6. It was typical of Davey's seemingly self-effacing but arrogant manner that, when Peacock expressed difficulty with his argument, he replied (after disagreeing with Peacock) that 'I am very much obliged to your Lordships because it helps counsel a great deal to know what the difficulties are in your Lordships' mind.' (Ibid., 227.)

117 Ibid., 233.

118 Ibid., 240.

119 NAC, Macdonald Papers, Donald MacMaster to Macdonald, 12 November 1885.

120 Ibid., Burbidge to Macdonald, 12, 13 November 1885.

121 *A.G. Quebec* v. *Queen Insurance Company* (1878), 3 A.C. 1090 at 1095–7. A summary of the Court of Appeal decision is included in the report. The decisions are in Cartwright, ed. *Cases Decided on the British North America Act, 1867*, vol. 3 at 212 (Q.B.), 226 (S.C.).

122 *Reed* v. *Mousseau* (1883), 8 S.C.R. 408; *A.G. Quebec* v. *Reed* (1884), 10 A.C. 141 at 144, 145.

123 In his decision Chief Justice Dorion noted that initially the bill referred to the levies as licences or licence taxes, but the government obviously hoped that the change in nomenclature would bring the taxes within section 92(2). 'It cannot be reasonably concluded that the nature of the tax was thereby altered, ' Dorion observed. 'The name of the tax was changed, but not the substance.' (*North British & Mercantile Fire & Life Insurance Co.* v. *Lambe* (1884), 1 M.L.R [Q.B.] 122 at 145.)

124 Ibid. at 146, 136. Ramsay, Tessier, and Baby delivered impassioned *obiter dicta* about provincial rights. Citing *Hodge* as confirming that the provinces were supreme within their powers, Tessier argued that Confederation was 'but a federal alliance' and the provinces 'should reasonably and liberally

have the right of maintaining themselves and of raising the revenue necessary for their support. If it had been desired to limit the powers of the provincial legislatures to certain particular subjects, why not have defined
these powers and then said afterwards that all other powers belonged to
the federal parliament. On the contrary it has been necessary to specify in
sect. 91 the special powers of this parliament in certain cases, as in a treaty
between two independent parties which specifies the rights belonging to
each' (translation; 166–7). Baby argued that 'even should this tax not be a
direct one, the Legislature of Quebec had the right of imposing it in the
exercise of one of its inherent powers ... The general powers of taxation
cannot be impliedly taken way from them. The enumerations in section 92
'does not imply any abandonment by them of all other rights of taxation,
or a prohibition to them to levy money by any means of taxation within
the province and for provincial ends ... I am aware that this interpretation
of the statute has not been accepted in certain quarters, but I cannot see –
to be practical – how any other can be given' (197–8).

125 *Bank of Toronto* v. *Lambe* (1887), 12 A.C. 575. A friend of John Thompson's
who heard the argument wrote that Peacock 'chiefly seemed possessed
with the idea that it was like an income tax in England. He is an abler man
than George Allison our librarian but not as good a judge as Old Shields
used to be when he was alive. Hobhouse looked exactly like Mackenzie ...
I think he is abler or at least he is harder to convince.' (NAC, Thompson
Papers, Graham Wallace to Thompson, 13 July 1887.)

126 *Bank of Toronto* v. *Lambe* at 583.

127 Ibid. at 584–5.

128 Ibid. at 586.

129 Ibid.

130 Ibid. at 587.

131 Ibid. (italics added).

132 Ibid. at 587.

133 The Supreme Court immediately decided that *Lambe* had overruled *Severn*. (See *Molson* v. *Lambe* (1888), 15 S.C.R. 253, Ritchie at 259.) Strong was
more circumspect: 'Even if the decision in *Severn* v. *The Queen* has not been
over-ruled observations not in accordance with it are to be found in later
decisions of the Privy Council.' (*Pigeon* v. *The Records Court and the City of
Montreal* (1889), [1890] 17 S.C.R. 495 at 505.) *Lambe* would be explicitly confirmed and *Severn* laid to rest in *Brewers and Malsters' Association of Canada*
v. *A.G. Ontario*, [1897] A.C. 231.

134 Peter Hogg, *Constitutional Law of Canada* (Toronto: Carswell 1992), 752.

135 Gérard V. La Forest, *The Allocation of Taxing Power under the Canadian Con-*

stitution (Toronto: Canadian Tax Foundation 1981), 93. Typically, LaForest cautiously suggests that the bank tax was contrary to the distribution of taxing power under the constitution.

136 NAC, Thompson Papers, Macdonald to Thompson, 7 August 1888. Macdonald added that if he went to England to see Lord Salisbury he planned 'to take up the question of Canada being represented on the Judicial Committee of the Privy Council.' Patterson was the first Macdonald appointment since Gwynne in 1879.

137 P.B. Waite, *The Man from Halifax: Sir John Thompson, Prime Minister* (Toronto: University of Toronto Press 1985), 227.

138 NAC, Macdonald Papers, McCarthy to Macdonald, 7 September 1888; Thompson Papers, McCarthy to Macdonald, 9 September 1888; ibid., note from Macdonald to Thompson.

139 Macdonald was indirectly involved in *Parsons*, party in the appeal in *Mercer*, and was responsible for the reference on the McCarthy Act.

140 AO, RG 4–32, file 1891, no. 576, Thompson to Mowat, 22 October 1891. Explaining at the Judicial Committee in 1903 why the federal government had not intervened in the Hamilton Street Railway case in the Ontario Court of Appeal, E.L. Newcombe, deputy minister of justice since 1893, noted: 'Dominion not represented below because it has not been the policy of Dominion to be represented upon these references in the provincial courts. They are made not infrequently & there are other cases where a constitutional point arises upon the pleadings but the Dominion has found it convenient not to take part in these as a rule but to intervene in such proceedings only when it becomes apparent that the revenue or some constitutional rights of Dominion likely to be affected by a final judgement.' (NAC, RG 13, C1, vol. 2098, file Ontario Street Railway [pt 2, 'Mr. Newcombe's notes for argument of appeal, before Jud, Committee'].)

141 NAC, reel A–623, Lansdowne Papers, MG 27, I B6, Lansdowne to Thompson, 17 July 1886.

142 Ibid., reel A–627, Thompson to Lansdowne, 28 July 1886. (The oral arguments before the Judicial Committee suggest a high level of ignorance, often admitted, of Canadian geography and history. After the appeal in *McLaren v. Caldwell* (1884), 9 A.C. 392, D'Alton McCarthy wrote Macdonald: 'I am inclined to think that except in constitutional cases we would be quite as well without an appeal to Her Majesty. It is so hard to impress these Lords with a true notion of our state and condition. In this case they are I think too much influenced by an erroneous notion that they have taken up that Canada is mainly a lumbering country ... and that the

use of its streams as public highways is of the first consequence to us all. And as Blackburn shut me up when I proposed to try and abuse them of this notion saying that such considerations had nothing to do with the construction of a statute they or some of them remain influenced by Bethune's exaggerated statements when moving a year ago for leave to appeal.' (NAC, Macdonald Papers, 7 March 1884.)

143 Ibid., reel A–627, Thompson to Lansdowne, 28 July 1886.
144 *Molson v. Lambe* (1886), 2 M.L.R. (Q.B.) 381 at 397.
145 (1893) 23 S.C.R. 458 at 472.
146 R.C. Risk, 'Canadian Courts under the Influence' (1990) 40 *University of Toronto Law Journal*, 687 at 737.

6 The Watson Era, 1889–1912

1 'Lord Watson' (1899) 11 *Juridical Review*, 272 at 279. See also R.B. Haldane, 'The Appellate Courts of the Empire' (1900) 12 *Juridical Review*, 4.
2 Lord Denning, *Borrowing from Scotland* (Glasgow: Jackson, Son 1963), 34.
3 *The Times*, 15 September 1899.
4 'Lord Watson' (1899) 11 *Juridical Review*, 278 at 279.
5 G.P. Browne, *The Judicial Committee and the British North America Act: An Analysis of the Interpretative Scheme for the Distribution of Legislative Powers* (Toronto: University of Toronto Press 1967).
6 [W.F. O'Connor] Canada, Senate, *Report pursuant to Resolution of the Senate to the Honourable Speaker by the Parliamentary Counsel relating to the Enactment of the British North American Act, 1867, Any Lack of Consonance between Its Terms and Judicial Construction of Them and Cognate Matters* (Ottawa: King's Printer 1939); Bora Laskin, '"Peace, Order and Good Government" Re-Examined' (1947) 25 *Canadian Bar Review*, 1054.
7 Paul Romney, 'The Nature and Scope of Provincial Autonomy: Oliver Mowat, the Quebec Resolutions and the Construction of the *British North America Act*' (1992) 25 *Canadian Journal of Political Science*, 3 at 28.
8 'Why Lord Watson was Right,' in Janet Ajzenstat, ed., *Canadian Constitutionalism, 1791–1991* (Ottawa: Canadian Study of Parliament Group 1991), 177 at 191.
9 'Unity and Diversity in Canadian Federalism' (1975) 53 *Canadian Bar Review*, 597 at 608, 607.
10 'The Judicial Committee and Its Critics' (1971) *Canadian Journal of Political Science*, 301 at 324–5.
11 Ibid., 319.
12 Robert Vipond, *Liberty and Community: Canadian Federalism and the Failure of*

the Constitution (Albany: State University of New York Press 1991), 158–9. On the historiography of the controversy, see also Richard Risk, 'The Scholars and the Constitution: P.O.G.G. and the Privy Council' (1966) 23 *Manitoba Law Journal*, 496; and 'Constitutional Scholarship in the Late Nineteenth Century: Making Federalism Work' (1996) 46 *University of Toronto Law Journal*, 427.

13 'Lord Watson' (1899) 15 *Scottish Law Review*, 235. This obituary is the fullest account of Watson's life. See also the entry in the *Dictionary of National Biography*, vol. 22 (London: Oxford University Press 1901), 1380; and 'E.M.,' 'Lord Watson,' *London Law Times*, reprinted in *Canadian Law Times* (June 1903), 551.

14 Alan Paterson, 'Scottish Lords of Appeal, 1876–1988' (1988) *Juridical Review*, 238.

15 *Dobie v. The Temporalities Board* (1881–2) 7 A.C. 136, appropriately since it involved the Presbyterian Church and the Church of Scotland.

16 See George J. Wheeler, *Confederation Law of Canada: Privy Council Cases on the British North America Act 1867* (London: Eyre and Spottiswoode 1896). T.B. Smith notes that, when preparing the English-language version of the Quebec Civil Code in 1866, 'Scottish legal terminology was used to ensure a civilian construction.' (*British Justice: The Scottish Contribution* [London: Stevens and Sons 1961], 42.)

17 The sixteen are conveniently printed in Richard A. Olmsted, *Decisions of the Judicial Committee of the Privy Council relating to the British North America Act, 1867 and the Canadian Constitution, 1867–1954* (Ottawa: Queen's Printer 1954). The exception was *A.G. Ontario v. A.G. Canada*, [1894] A.C. 189, known as the *Voluntary Assignments* case, which led to the controversial unoccupied-field doctrine. Among the sixteen are two on the Manitoba schools question on which he sat but did not deliver the judgments.

18 *City of Winnipeg v. Barrett*, [1892] A.C. 445. The oral argument is printed in Canada, *Sessional Papers*, no. 33B, 1893.

19 Morris, a prominent Irish Catholic, was appointed in 1889. Described as a Tory of independent temperament, distrustful of democracy and hostile to Home Rule, in the Judicial Committee 'he not infrequently dissented from the majority.' Judging from the oral argument in *Barrett*, he must have dissented in that case. (*Dictionary of National Biography* [supplement, vol. 1, London: Oxford University Press 1912], 653.)

20 *Bank of Montreal v. Lambe* (1887), 12 A.C. 575 at 579.

21 *Citizens Insurance Company v. Parsons* (1881), [1881–2] 7 A.C. 96 at 109.

22 *St. Catherine's Milling and Lumber Company v. The Queen* (1888), 14 A.C. 46. Sidney Harring, in an excellent legal account, described the case as 'one of

the most significant cases on native rights in the common law world.' (Sidney L. Harring, *White Man's Law: Native People on Nineteenth-Century Jurisprudence* (Toronto: University of Toronto Press 1998), 125. The decision is still before the courts. See the judgment of Justice Archie Campbell in *The Chippewa Band of Sarnia* v. *A.G. Canada, A.G. Ontario et al.* [released April 1999], Ontario, Superior Court of Justice, court file no. 95–CU–92484. On the dispute generally, see Christopher Armstrong, *The Politics of Federalism: Ontario's Relations with the Federal Government, 1867–1942* (Toronto: University of Toronto Press 1981), 14–22.

23 Cited in Anthony J. Hall, '*The St. Catherine's Milling and Lumber Company* v. *The Queen*: Indian Land Rights as a Factor in Federal-Provincial Relations in Nineteenth Century Canada,' in Kerry Abel and Jean Friesen, eds., *Aboriginal Land Use in Canada: Historical and Legal Aspects* (Manitoba: University of Manitoba Press 1991), 267 at 271.

24 National Archives of Canada (NAC), Macdonald Papers, McCarthy to Macdonald, 5 January 1885.

25 NAC, Macdonald Papers, 83015, Campbell to Macdonald, 23 October 1885. Campbell had retired as minister of justice a month earlier.

26 Strong's dissenting opinion held that to interpret the BNA Act as 'by implication abolishing all right and property of the Indians in unsurrendered lands ... would attribute to the Imperial Parliament the intention of taking away proprietary rights, without express words and without any adequate reason.' Such an interpretation would constitute a departure from 'the long cherished and most successful policy originally inaugurated by the British Government for the treatment of the Indian tribes ... and must be rejected.' (*St. Catherine's Milling and Lumber Co.* v. *R.* (1887), 13 S.C.R. 577 at 616.) Strong's dissent has become more appealing given the direction of modern decisions on aboriginal rights. See, for example, Hamar Foster, 'Forgotten Arguments: Aboriginal Title and Sovereignty in *Canada Jurisdiction Act* Cases' (1992) 21 *Manitoba Law Journal*, 343.

27 During the hearing on the petition to appeal, opposed by Haldane acting for Ontario, the board requested that the federal government be a formal party to the litigation given the size of the territory at stake. John Thompson reluctantly agreed and retained Sir Richard Webster, who appeared with McCarthy. The transcript of the hearing on appeal and subsequent correspondence is in Archives of Ontario (AO), Irving Papers, MU 1480, file 41/08/5 and 41/06/2. Webster, better known as Lord Alverstone, also acted in *Precious Metals*, *Voluntary Assignments*, and *Barrett*, losing all three. The transcript of the oral argument in *Barrett* confirms John Ewart's bitter comment that he 'didn't look at the brief, knew nothing of the case, and

blundered from start to finish.' (NAC, Thompson Papers, N.C. Wallace to R. White, 6 August 1892, enclosed in White to Thompson, 8 August 1892.) The contributor to the *Dictionary of National Biography* (vol. 24, 1912–31, 562) wrote that 'he was not a clever man, nor a learned lawyer, nor a good speaker – either in the courts or in parliament, his equipment as an advocate consisted mainly in a splendid physique, a forcible personality, and immense industry.' In fact, as attorney general Webster boasted of his large, private practice. (Viscount Alverstone, *Recollections of Bar and Bench* [London: Edward Arnold 1915], 227.)

28 Blake to Margaret Blake, 21 July 1888, cited in Joseph Schull, *Edward Blake: Leader and Exile* (Toronto: Macmillan 1976), 108.

29 Blake printed his argument: *In the Privy Council: The St. Catherine's Milling and Lumber Company v. The Queen: Arguments of Mr. Blake, Counsel for Ontario* (Toronto, 1888).

30 Blake to Margaret Blake, 25 July 1888, cited in Schull, *Blake*, 110.

31 *St. Catherine's Milling and Lumber Co. v. The Queen* (1889), 14 A.C. 46 at 54.

32 *Delgamuukw v. British Columbia*, [1997] 3 S.C.R. 1010 at 1081 (Lamer). See also the judgment of Justice Archie Campbell n.22 above. Of Watson's decision, Harring concludes that while it remains important in modern title cases, 'almost no part of its analysis, taken element by element, is good law.' (Harring, *White Man's Law*, 146–7.)

33 *St. Catherine's Milling* at 59. In *Delgamuukw* (at 1117) the Supreme Court, following Watson's opinion, determined that the provision extended to all 'lands held pursuant to aboriginal title' and that only the federal government could extinguish aboriginal title.

34 Alverstone, *Recollections*, 224–5.

35 *St. Catherine's Milling* at 60.

36 *Dominion of Canada v. Province of Ontario*, [1910] A.C. 637 at 647.

37 Blake, *The St. Catherine's Milling and Lumber Company*, 5–7.

38 *A.G. British Columbia v. A.G. Canada* (1889), 14 A.C. 295.

39 In *Re Earl of Northumberland's Mines*, I Plowd. 310, 75 *English Reports* (1907) 472.

40 *A.G. British Columbia v. A.G. Canada* (1887), 14 S.C.R. 345 at 357–8.

41 Ibid. at 361.

42 Ibid. at 372–3. Fournier believed that the Earl of Nothumberland's case applied, and Henry concluded that title to the land was not vested in the crown.

43 *A.G. British Columbia v. A.G. Canada* (1889), 14 A.C. 295 at 303–4.

44 *B.C. (A.G.) v. Can. (A.G.)* (1989), 45 B.C.L.R (2d) 339 at 358.

45 *British Columbia (Attorney General)* v. *Canada (Attorney General)* (1991), 59 B.C.L.R. (2d) 280 at 302.

46 *A.G. Canada* v. *A.G. British Columbia*, [1994] 2 S.C.R. 41 at 97. Indexed as *British Columbia (Attorney General)* v. *Canada (Attorney General): An Act Respecting the Vancouver Island Railway* (Re). In a lengthy judgment for the court, Iacobucci reviewed the judgments in the lower courts on the railway in question but included the comments on the quality of Watson's reasons. At issue was the federal government's responsibility not only to build but to continue to operate the railway.

47 Ibid.

48 For example, *Molson* v. *Chapleau* (1883), 6 *Legal News* 222 at 224, where Justice Auguste Papineau asserted that if the queen was not part of the provincial government, the province could not be part of the empire.

49 *St. Catherine's Milling and Lumber Company* v. *The Queen* (1886), 13 O.A.R 158 at 165.

50 Lieutenant governor to the secretary of state, 22 January 1886, Ontario, *Sessional Papers*, 1888, no. 37, 20.

51 NAC, Lansdowne Papers, reel 627, Lansdowne to Thompson, 17 July 1886; Thompson to Lansdowne, 28 July 1886. The governor general pressed Thompson to agree to the reference. Thompson refused and replied officially to Mowat that 'so long as the judgement in *Lenoir* v. *Ritchie* is not revised, it is the duty of Governments and individuals in Canada to respect and conform to that judgement.' (Secretary of State to the Lieutenant Governor, 27 September 1886, Ontario, *Sessional Papers*, 1888, no. 37, 27–9.)

52 51 Vict. c. 5. See Paul Romney, *Mr Attorney: The Attorney- General of Ontario in Court, Cabinet, and Legislature, 1791–1899* (Toronto: Osgoode Society/University of Toronto Press 1986), 258.

53 Thompson to Mowat, 4 February 1889, in W.E. Hodgins, comp., *Correspondence, Reports of the Ministers of Justice, and Orders in Council upon the Subject of Dominion and Provincial Legislation, 1867–1895* (Ottawa: Government Printing Bureau 1896), 206.

54 *A.G. Canada* v. *A.G. Ontario* (1890), [1891] 20 O.R. 222 at 247, 249. The arguments and decisions in the courts are fully examined in Suzanne Marthe Birks, 'The Survival of the Crown in the Canadian State: The Political Components of Monarchy' (LLM thesis, Osgoode Hall, 1980), 51–60.

55 Blake's argument was published privately: *The Executive Power Case: Argument* (Toronto: 1892).

56 [1892] A.C. 437. Though the Supreme Court did hear the appeal, Taschereau stated that the appeal should have been abandoned because of Watson's decision or gone directly to the Judicial Committee: 'Constitu-

tional questions cannot be finally determined in this court. They never have been, and can never be under the present system.' *A.G. Canada* v. *A.G. Ontario* (1893), 23 S.C.R. 458 at 472. At the Judicial Committee, where the issue was the validity of acts of Ontario in 1873 to appoint queen's counsel, the case was decided without reference to *Liquidators*.' Assuming it to have been within the competency of the provincial legislature to vest the power in some authority other than the Sovereign,' wrote Watson, 'the Lieutenant-Governor appears to have been very properly selected as its depositary,' citing the provisions of section 65. And under heads 4 and 14 of section 92, it lay within provincial authority to determine who should represent the crown in its courts. (*A.G. Canada* v. *A.G. Ontario* (1897), [1898] A.C. 247 at 253.)

57 The bank also owed money to the federal government but, for purposes of the stated case, it was agreed that the federal government would be regarded as a simple creditor of the bank. This may have been to avoid the question raised in *The Queen* v. *The Bank of Nova Scotia* (1885), 11 S.C.R. 1, where it was argued that, since the federal government was attempting to recover money owed by the bank, only the crown in the right of the province had the prerogative right of preference over other creditors. The argument was rejected by the court and the right of the federal government upheld.

58 *The Provincial Government of New Brunswick* v. *The Liquidators of the Maritime Bank* (1888), 17 N.B.R. 379 at 382, 384.

59 Ibid. at 396.

60 *Liquidators of the Maritime Bank* v. *The Receiver General of New Brunswick* (1889), [1892], 20 S.C.R. 695 at 707.

61 NAC, Gowan Papers, Gwynne to Gowan, 24 December 1889.

62 *Liquidators of the Maritime Bank of Canada* v. *Receiver-General of New Brunswick*, [1892] A.C. 437 at 438–9.

63 Ibid. at 441.

64 Ibid. at 443. Watson neglected to point out that the appointment was made on advice and at no point received royal approval, as did that of the governor general. It also seemed irrelevant to question whether the lieutenant governor's capacity to reserve provincial legislation on the advice of the federal executive compromised his position as a regal representative.

65 Ibid. at 444–5.

66 *A.G. Canada* v. *A.G. Ontario* (1893), 23 S.C.R 458 at 463.

67 Ibid. at 441–2. Italics added. That the provinces were still subject to federal powers of disallowance and reservation, transferred from the imperial authority, obviously did not influence Watson's opinion although his judg-

ment weakened the powers themselves. Watson continued with a long quotation from the decision *Hodge*, cited in chapter 3, n.74, but he conveniently omitted the last clauses – 'would have under like circumstances ...' This suggested the equality of the imperial, Dominion, and provincial governments, something that Fitzgerald may not have intended.

68 See David Smith, *The Invisible Crown* (Toronto: University of Toronto Press 1995). Smith notes that in *Liquidators* 'the courts redefined the nature of Canadian federalism by recourse to the Crown's prerogative' (139).

69 (1893), [1894] A.C. 31 at 35–6. The constitutional question had arisen in the Ontario Court of Appeal but was not discussed because it was at variance with the decision in *Merchants' Bank of Canada* v. *Smith* (1883), 8 S.C.R. 512, which was binding on the provincial court. When it arose at the Judicial Committee in July 1892, further argument on that question was delayed until July 1893 because the Judicial Committee had undertaken to hear the Labrador case. In the interim, the bank had replaced Christopher Robinson with Davey as lead counsel. Since the government of Ontario, whose retainer Davey held, was not party to the litigation, he could plead in support of federal jurisdiction for the only time in his career.

70 Ibid. at 45. Italics added.

71 *Tennant* v. *Union Bank of Canada* at 46.

72 Canada, *Report pursuant to Resolution of the Senate to the Honourable Speaker*, 36; Browne, *The Judicial Committee and the British North America Act*, 43. André Tremblay has also noted that 'à ce moment-là, on n'avait pas encore distingué les pouvoirs énuméres des pouvoirs généraux du Parlement Canadienne.' (*Droit Constitutionnel: Principes* [Montreal: Les Éditions Thémis 1993], 230.)

73 'The substitution is most important,' O'Connor emphasized, 'for the word *extends* indicates that the existing *necessary* exclusiveness of the enacted residuary power *extends* to the 29 declared exemplary enumerations of classes of subjects which all "come within" the enacted general legislative powers of the Dominion, whilst the words "shall extend" imply a new creation and distribution of exclusive powers. O'Connor, *Report*, 37.

74 *A.G. Ontario* v. *A.G. Canada*, [1894] A.C. 189. Legislation similar to An Act Respecting Assignments and Preferences by Insolvent Persons (R.S.O. 1887, c. 124) had existed in Ontario since Confederation.

75 Thompson had refused to agree to a reference to the Supreme Court (AO, RG 4–32, file 1891, no. 576, Mowat to Thompson, 16 October 1891.) Mowat believed that Thompson would agree 'all the more readily because I believe that you approve of the provincial Legislature's dealing with the subject so far as practicable while there is no Dominion legislation respecting Bank-

ruptcy or Insolvency.' (Ibid., file 1892, no. 1052, Mowat to Newcombe 20 May 1893.)

76 *A.G. Ontario* v. *A.G. Canada*, [1894] A.C. 189 at 200–1.

77 *Edgar* v. *Central Bank* (1888), 15 O.A.R. 193 at 197–8.

78 The MSS oral argument is in AO, Irving Papers, MU 1489, file 1027: *The Ontario Insolvency Case in the Privy Council ... Argument of Mr. Blake for the Appellant* (Toronto: Bryant Press 1894). See also Blake, *Ontario Insolvency Case*, 6.

79 Oral argument, 12 December 1893, 75.

80 Ibid., 100.

81 Oral argument, 13 December 1893, 60.

82 Blake, *Insolvency Case*, 21. Nor apparently did other members of the board. Forwarding the transcript of the oral argument, the London solicitors noted that 'you will gather from a perusal of this that there is every reason to believe the judgement will be in favour of your Province.' (AO, RG 4–32, file 1052, Freshfields and Williams to J.R. Cartwright, 15 December 1893.)

83 [1896] A.C. 66, cited in A.H.F. Lefroy, *The Law of Legislative Power in Canada* (Toronto: Toronto Law Book 1897–98), 537n.1.

84 SCC Library, oral argument, 97. *Brewers and Malsters' Association of Ontario* v. *A.G. Ontario* [1897] A.C. 231.

85 *A.G. Canada* v. *A.G. Ontario, Quebec, Nova Scotia*, [1898] A.C. 700 (*Fisheries Reference*) Supreme Court of Canada, Library, oral argument, 135.

86 *Fisheries Reference*, 715.

87 *Canadian Pacific Railway* v. *Corporation of the Parish of Notre Dame de Bonsecours*, [1899] A.C. 367, Supreme Court of Canada Library, oral argument, 30–1.

88 *Union Colliery Company of British Columbia* v. *Bryden*, [1899] A.C. 580.

89 Ibid. at 582.

90 Ibid. at 585, 588. Italics added.

91 See, for example, Peter Hogg, *Constitutional Law of Canada* (Toronto: Carswell 1992), 404; W.R. Lederman, 'The Concurrent Operation of Federal and Provincial Laws in Canada' (1962–3) 9 *McGill Law Journal*, 185 at 188. The British Columbia Supreme Court had reluctantly felt Watson's precedent binding and found *ultra vires* the B.C. elections act denying Japanese, naturalized or not, the right to vote. As Chief Justice McColl stated, 'apart from the decision binding upon me I would have considered that the authority of the Dominion Parliament becomes exhausted with the naturalization.' (In *Re The Provincial Elections Act and in Re Tomey Homma, a Japanese* (1900), 7 B.C.R. 368 at 372.) On appeal, Lord Halsbury found that the exclusivity of federal jurisdiction over naturalization and aliens was trumped by the

power of the provinces, 'notwithstanding anything in this Act,' to 'exclusively make Laws' in relation to the provincial constitution. (*Cunningham* v. *Tomey Homma* (1902), [1903] A.C. 151.) Moreover, in argument, members of the committee insisted that naturalization did not extend to the consequences of naturalization, thus distinguishing *Union Colliery*. (SCC Library, oral argument, *Cunningham* v. *Tomey Homma*.) Watson's decision was distinguished to the point of rejection by the Judicial Committee in *Brooks-Bidlake and Whitall* v. *A.G. British Columbia*, [1923] A.C. 450.

92 In re *Local Option Reference* (1891), 18 O.A.R. 572 at 580.
93 Ibid. at 591.
94 *Globe*, 3 May 1893.
95 NAC, MG 26 D, vol. 187, Thompson Papers, Mowat to Thompson, 10 October 1893.
96 *Huson* v. *South Norwich* (1895), 24 S.C.R. 145.
97 NAC, RG 125, vol. 15, file 147, Supreme Court of Canada, 'Subject Provincial Jurisdiction, Prohibitory Liquor Law. Factum of the Solicitor General of Canada,' 2 April 1894.
98 *A.G. Ontario* v. *A.G. Canada* (1895), 24 S.C.R. 170.
99 *Liquor Prohibition Appeal: An Appeal from the Supreme Court of Canada to Her Majesty the* Queen *in Council* (London: 1895), oral argument at 31.
100 Ibid. at 153.
101 Couch had sat on the three earlier cases; Halsbury on the *McCarthy Reference*; Davey, now on the committee, had been counsel in *Hodge* and *McCarthy*; and Herschell had opposed Davey in *McCarthy*.
102 Maclaren and Blake between them were responsible for more than 250 of the 325 pages of argument.
103 *Liquor Prohibition Appeal* at 114.
104 Ibid. at 77.
105 Ibid. at 224.
106 Ibid. at 242, 239.
107 'Lord Watson' (1899) 15 *Scottish Law Review*, 241. Blake might have taken some comfort in the reply Watson once made to an eminent counsel who complained about his interruptions: 'Eh! man, you should never complain about that for I never interrupt a fool.' *The Times*, 19 September 1899, letter to the editor.
108 *A.G. Ontario* v. *A.G. Canada*, [1896] A.C. 348.
109 *Citizens Insurance Company of Canada* v. *Parsons* (1881), [1881–2] 7 A.C. 96 at 108.
110 *Russell* at 100, 91; *Hodge* at 88; *McCarthy* at 168.
111 *Liquor Prohibition Appeal*, oral argument, 94. See also 163, 185, 194.

112 Ibid., 244.

113 Ibid., 292.

114 Ibid., 256.

115 *A.G. Canada v. A.G. Ontario*, [1896] A.C. 348 at 360. During the oral argu-
     ment in *Fielding* v. *Thomas* in July 1896, Watson elaborated his understand-
     ing of the clause. 'I think that clause plainly shows the consciousness of
     those who framed that Act, that the things given to the one parliament by
     section 92 and the supreme parliament by section 91, did run into each
     other or over-ride each other, and they got rid of the difficulty by the dec-
     laration that nothing done by the supreme legislature under the express
     and exclusive power given them by section 91 should be deemed to come
     within the exclusive power given to the province by section 92. In other
     words, if the Dominion exercise that power, the matter is no longer within
     the exclusive power committed to the province. It is a very wise provision
     and shows a good deal of foresight.' (Cited in A.H.F. Lefroy, *The Law of
     Legislative Power in Canada* [Toronto: 1897–8], 649n.2.) Clearly, Watson con-
     fused the purpose of the declaratory and deeming clauses and virtually
     ignored the former.

116 'Lord Watson' (1899) 11 *Juridical Review*, 270–1.

117 'Lord Watson' (1899) 15 *Scottish Law Review*, 229 at 237.

118 *Liquor Prohibition Appeal* at 141.

119 Ibid. at 45.

120 *A.G. Canada v. A.G. Ontario*, [1896] A.C. 348 at 360–1. Emphasis added. In
     Tennant, Watson had divided section 91 into two distinct grants of legisla-
     tive jurisdiction: the residual clause 'and also exclusive legislative author-
     ity in relation to certain enumerated subjects.' (*Tennant* v. *Union Bank of
     Canada*, [1894] A.C. 31 at 45.) Here he went further and stated that 'these
     sources of jurisdiction are in themselves distinct, and are to be found in
     different enactments' (at 359.) It is impossible to reconcile this with the
     wording of section 91.

121 *Liquor Prohibition Appeal* at 130, 236.

122 *A.G. Canada v. A.G. Ontario*, [1896] A.C. 348 at 361. In fact, he borrowed the
     example from Herschell who had commented that the right to carry arms
     might be purely local, but during a war the federal government might pro-
     hibit the carrying of arms. (Oral argument, 118.) The head-note to the case,
     cited more often than the decision, was misleading: 'The general power
     conferred upon the Dominion Parliament ... in supplement of its therein
     enumerated powers must be strictly confined to such matters as are
     unquestionably of national interest and importance; and must not trench
     on any of the subjects enumerated in s.92 ... *unless* they have attained such

dimensions as to affect the body politic of the Dominion' (at 348). Watson did not go as far as 'unless.'

123 *Liquor Prohibition Appeal* at 303, 296. If Blake had read the oral argument in *Russell*, he would have had a stronger case, citing Smith's own words, although it would have been termed inadmissable. See Chapter 5, n.23.

124 Ibid. at 210. He said precisely the same about the word 'commerce.' Ibid. at 103.

125 Ibid. at 179.

126 Ibid. at 218. In *City of Fredericton v. The Queen* (1880), 3 S.C.R. 505. The Supreme Court had no doubt that the power to prohibit lay within 'The Regulation of Trade and Commerce.' Ritchie did 'not entertain the slightest doubt that the power to prohibit is within the power to regulate' (537) and Taschereau stated emphatically that 'A prohibition is a regulation' (559).

127 Ibid. at 225, 306.

128 Ibid. at 353.

129 *A.G. Canada v. A.G. Ontario*, [1896] A.C. 348 at 362–3. Watson's opinion later caused some difficulty in the Supreme Court in *Gold Seal Limited v. A.G. Alberta* (1921), 52 S.C.R. 424, but Duff found a way around it (457–8). Years later, Chief Justice Rinfret rejected Watson's proposition: 'In my opinion such a contention cannot be supported ... It stands to reason that, if you regulate, you may prohibit things that are not in accordance with those regulations.' (*Re Validity of Section 5 [a] of the Dairy Industry Act*, [1949] S.C.R. 1 at 25.)

130 (1895), [1896] A.C. 88 at 93. The regulation/prohibition issue is thoroughly discussed in two articles by David Schneiderman, who sees it as much more than a refinement necessary to suit the immediate purpose. The decision on that point, he argues, 'reflects the cast of mind of the common lawyer that Dicey so ably captured in *The Law of the Constitution* ... Federal government was meant to mean weak government, and laws were to be tested against the same standards as those of a delegated authority under British constitutionalism [such as a by-law made by a railway company].' ('A.V. Dicey, Lord Watson and the Law of the Canadian Constitution' [1998] 16 *Law and History Review*, 495 at 510.) In an earlier article, using 'a conception of productivity' traceable to John Locke, Schneiderman argued that this aspect of '*Local Prohibition* can best be understood as a manifestation of judicial anxiety about the potential implications of energetic federalism for property and productivity, anxieties which were prevalent in late-nineteenth century legal thought.' ('Constitutional Interpretation in an Age of Anxiety: A Reconsideration of the Local Prohibition Case' [1996] 41 *McGill Law Journal*, 411 at 415.)

131 The comment of Lord Denning to Alan Paterson that within six weeks of the argument he ceased to take an interest in the details of the judgment seems apt. Watson's decision was delivered nine months after the argument. See Chapter 4, n.51. (*The Law Lords* [London: Macmillan 1982], 99.) However, someone on the board or in the registrar's office cared enough to change the answer to the question, had a province 'jurisdiction to prohibit the importation of liquors into the province?' The answer, in Watson's judgment, which was printed in the *Appeal Cases*, was: 'Their Lordships answer this question in the negative. It appears to them that the exercise by the provincial legislature of such jurisdiction in the wide and general terms in which it is expressed, would probably trench upon the executive authority of the Dominion Parliament.' However, the certificate of judgment issued by the clerk of the Privy Council read: 'No useful answer can be given to this question in the absence of a precise statement of the facts to which it is intended to apply. There may be some circumstances in which a Provincial Legislature will and others in which it will not have such jurisdiction.' (The certificate is printed in E.R. Cameron, 'The House of Lords and the Judicial Committee' [1923] 1 *Canadian Bar Review* 223 at 231.)

132 'Lord Watson' (1899) 11 Juridical Review, 278 at 281.

133 Murray Greenwood, 'Lord Watson, Institutional Self-Interest, and the Decentralization of Canadian Federalism in the 1890s' (1974) 9 *University of British Columbia Law Review,* 244 at 261.

134 Birks, 'The Survival of the Crown,' 158–9.

135 Schneiderman, 'A.V. Dicey, Lord Watson, and the Law of the Canadian Constitution' 510, 524.

136 Richard Risk, 'Canadian Courts under the Influence' (1990) 40 *University of Toronto Law Journal,* 687 at 731–2, 733.

137 'Lord Watson' (1902) 4 *Journal of the Society of Comparative Legislation* (new series), 9 at 9. Watson was a member of the Comparative and Historical Jurisprudence Committee of the Society, on which he sat with A.V. Dicey, Sir F. Pollock, and F.W. Maitland.

138 *Nordenfelt* v. *Maxim-Nordenfelt Co.* [1894] A.C. 535 at 553. See T.B. Smith, *The Doctrine of Judicial Precedent in Scots Law* (Edinburgh: Green and Son 1952). It is significant that the catalyst for change in the rigid adherence to precedent in the House of Lords in 1966 came from the Scottish Law Commission, which wanted a statement that the doctrine of precedent in the Lords did not apply in Scottish appeals. The movement resulted in the 1966 practice statement loosening the doctrine of precedent. (See Alan Paterson, *The Law Lords* [London: Macmillan 1982] 149–53).

139 Moir T. Stormont-Darling, 'Lord Watson' (1899) 11 *Juridical Review* 272, 277.

140 T.B. Smith, *British Justice: The Scottish Contribution* (London: Stevens and Son 1961), 205, 202.

141 *Winnipeg v. Barrett*, [1892] A.C. 445. The oral argument is printed in *Sessional Papers*, no. 33, 1893.

142 *Robinson v. Canadian Pacific Railway*, [1892] A.C. 481 at 485, 490.

143 'Lord Watson' (1899) 15 *Scottish Law Review*, 237.

144 George L. Gretton, 'Trust and Patrimony,' in H.L. MacQueen, ed., *Scots Law into the 21st Century* (Edinburgh: Green Sweet 1996), 187.

145 *Brophy v. A.G. Manitoba*, [1895] A.C. 202; *Sessional Papers*, no. 20, 1895, 246.

146 Canada, Department of Labour, *Judicial Proceedings respecting Constitutional Validity of the Industrial Disputes Investigation Act, 1907 and Amendment of 1910, 1918 and 1920: Toronto Electric Commissioners v. Snider et al.* (Ottawa: King's Printer 1925), 116.

147 *A.G. Canada v. A.G. Ontario* (Indian annuities) (1896), [1897] A.C. 199 at 213.

148 Lord Watson, 'Recent Legal Reform' (1901) 13 *Juridical Review*, 1 at 17, a speech given in 1883 and printed after his death.

149 *Ontario Mining Company v. Seybold* (1902), [1903] A.C. 53, following *St. Catherine's*; *A.G. Manitoba v. Manitoba License Holders Association* (1901), [1902] A.C. 73, following *Liquor Prohibition*; and *Canada v. Ontario* [1910] A.C. 637, following *St. Catherine's*.

150 *A.G. British Columbia v. Canadian Pacific Railway*, [1906] A.C. 204; *Burrard Power Company v. The King* (1910), [1911] A.C. 87.

151 *Grand Trunk Railway v. A.G. Canada*, [1907] A.C. 66 at 68. The two doctrines occasioned a good deal of scholarly comment. See Hogg, *Constitutional Law* (1992), 405, 418; W.R. Lederman, 'The Concurrent Operation of Federal and Provincial Laws in Canada' (1962–3) 9 *McGill Law Journal*, 185; Bora Laskin, 'Tests for the Validity of Legislation: What's the "Matter"?' (1944) 11 *University of Toronto Law Journal*, 114.

152 Supreme Court of Canada Library, *Hamilton Street Railway Company*, oral argument, third day, 13.

153 *A.G. Ontario v. Hamilton Street Railway Co.* (1902), 1 Ontario Weekly Reports 312.

154 When one draft bill was appealed to the Privy Council, Lord Davey caustically commented that they had expressed themselves on this 'Sunday question before' and unceremoniously declined the opportunity, as Newcombe requested, to 'set the matter finally at rest.' (AO, RG 4–32, file 1905, no. 458 (2), 'In the Privy Council on Appeal from the Supreme Court of

Canada, July 1905,' transcript of hearing.) The federal-provincial correspondence may be found in RG 4–32, various files in 1903–5.

155 *City of Montreal* v. *Montreal Street Railway*, [1912] A.C. 333. In the Supreme Court, Davies and Anglin dissenting, the majority rejected the 'necessarily incidental' and ancillary powers arguments. (1910), 43 S.C.R. 197.

156 *City of Montreal* v. *Montreal Street Railway* at 343–4.

157 Ibid. at 346.

158 Ibid. at 344. See, for example, Lord Tomlin's abbreviated statement of the accepted propositions in the *B.C. Fish Canneries* case (*A.G. Canada* v. *A.G. British Columbia* (1929), [1930] A.C. 111 at 118.)

7 Viscount Haldane, 1911–1928

1 Sir Almeric Fitzroy, *Memoirs*, 27 April 1911, vol. 2 (London: Hutchinson 1925), 441–2.

2 'Lord Watson' (1899) 11 *Juridical Review*, 278 at 279.

3 J.G. Hall and Douglas Martin, *Haldane: Statesman, Lawyer, Philosopher* (Chichester: Barry Rose 1996), 34.

4 R.V.F. Heuston, *Lives of the Lord Chancellors, 1875–1940* (Oxford: Clarendon Press 1964), 142; Earl of Birkenhead, *Last Essays* (London: Cassel 1930), 280, quotes Campbell-Bannerman: 'We shall see how Schopenhauer gets on in the kailyard.'

5 *The Times*, 11 April 1911.

6 Haldane forced himself on Ramsay MacDonald as lord chancellor in the short-lived Labour government in 1924. See Chapter 9.

7 Cited in Stephen E. Koss, *Lord Haldane: Scapegoat for Liberalism* (New York: Columbia University Press 1969), 96.

8 Haldane, *An Autobiography* (London: Hodden and Stoughton 1929), 254.

9 Laski to Holmes, 15 January 1929, in Mark DeWolfe Howe, ed., *Holmes-Laski Letters: The Correspondence of Mr. Justice Holmes and Harold J. Laski, 1916–1935*, 2 vols. (Cambridge, Mass.: Harvard University Press 1953), 1126. After reading his *Autobiography*, Laski had written to Holmes: 'His vanity is, in a delicate and refined way, colossal; and his power of intrigue evidently very great. He illustrates, too, the variety of truth; for he tells his side of certain episodes in a way that is utterly without relation to the published accounts of others.' Later Laski added: 'It isn't, I think, the book of a first class mind but certainly of one who knew how to make the utmost of the ability he had.' (Ibid. at 26 February 1929, 1136.)

10 Haldane, *Autobiography*, 255.

11 'The Haldane Paradox' *The New Statesman*, 25 August 1928, 30.

12 Barbara Drake and Margaret Cole, ed., *Our Partnership by Beatrice Webb* (London: Longmans Green 1948), 141; Howe, *Holmes-Laski Letters*, Laski to Holmes, 11 March 1922, 410.

13 Cited in Heuston, *Lives of the Lord Chancellors*, 201. The one consolation for Haldane when he was pushed out of the cabinet in 1915 was that he concluded that the pledge of abstinence that he had taken with the king and Lord Kitchener when the war began bound the lord chancellor not Lord Haldane. (Margaret Cole, ed., *Beatrice Webb Diaries, 1912–1924* [London: Longmans 1952] 42.)

14 Howe, *Holmes-Laski Letters*, Laski to Holmes, 11 January 1927, 912. The most fulsome praise of Haldane, in all his personae, was by his friend J.H. Morgan in the *Quarterly Review* (January and April 1929). Perhaps the most vicious was an obituary in the *New Statesman* (25 August 1928) which, while hailing him as the greatest war minister in memory, stated that 'in truth he had no intellect. He was almost as absurdly over-rated in that respect as he was under-rated in his patriotism and his practical abilities ... If life had thrown him into a garage he would have been a first-class motor mechanic.'

15 Birkenhead, *Last Essays*, 283.

16 Drake and Cole, ed., *Our Partnership*, 98; Cole, *Beatrice Webb Diaries*, 137–8.

17 A.G. Gardiner, *Prophets, Priests and Kings* (London: Dent 1914), 283.

18 Fitzroy, *Memoirs*, vol. 1, 354.

19 Duff Cooper, *Old Men Forget* (London: Rupert Hall Davis 1957), 57.

20 Cited in Stephen Wexler, 'The Urge to Idealize: Viscount Haldane and the Constitution of Canada' (1984) 29 *McGill Law Journal*, 630.

21 Haldane, 'Appellate Courts of the Empire' (1900) 12 *Judicial Review*, 2.

22 Ibid.

23 Ibid., 4–5.

24 Ibid., 5.

25 Ibid., 9. Haldane was critical of Chamberlain for caving in to the Australian demands.

26 Haldane's judicial imperialism convinced him that only an imperial court of appeal, combining the Judicial Committee and the appellate jurisdiction of the House of Lords, would satisfy the aspirations of the Dominions since it would level the playing field between the United Kingdom and the colonies. He had proposed the scheme as early as 1900 and tried to secure the consent of his cabinet colleagues and the Dominions at the Imperial Conference of 1911 (Maurice Ollivier, comp., *The Colonial and Imperial Conferences from 1887 to 1937* [Ottawa: Queen's Printer 1954], vol. 2, 82, 84.) Although the result was indecisive and ultimately a failure, Haldane boasted to his mother on 13 June: 'I had an important day yesterday, for I got through the

Imperial Conference the proposals for a reconstitution of the Supreme Court of the Empire at which I have been working for years.' (National Library of Scotland [NLS], Haldane Papers.) See also: Haldane, 'The Cabinet and the Empire (1902–3), *Proceedings of the Royal Colonial Institute*, 331; David B. Swinfen, *Imperial Appeal: The Debate on the Appeal to the Privy Council* (Manchester: University of Manchester Press 1987).

27 See the excellent analysis by Jonathan Robinson, 'Lord Haldane and the British North America Act' (1970) 20 *University of Toronto Law Journal*, 55.

28 Introduction to M.P. Follett, *The New State* (London: Longmans Green 1920), xii.

29 *The Reign of Relativity* (London: John Murray 1921), 351.

30 Robinson, 'Lord Haldane,' 64–5.

31 'The Judicial Committee of the Privy Council' (1923) 38 *Empire Review*, 716–7.

32 Supreme Court Library, oral argument, *In the Matter of the Initiative and Referendum Act*, 15 May 1919, second day, 20.

33 *Holmes-Laski Letters*, 1052, Laski to Holmes, 8 May 1928.

34 My reading agrees with those in Olmsted and Browne. (Richard A. Olmsted, *Decisions of the Judicial Committee of the Privy Council relating to the British North America Act and the Canadian Constitution 1867–1954*, 3 vols. [Ottawa: Queen's Printer 1954]; G.P. Browne, *The Judicial Committee and the British North America Act: An Analysis of the Interpretive Scheme for the Distribution of Legislative Powers* [Toronto: University of Toronto Press 1967].)

35 *John Deere Plow Co. v. Wharton*, [1915] A.C. 330; *A.G. Canada v. A.G. Alberta (Insurance Reference)*, [1916] 1 A.C. 588; *A.G. Ontario v. A.G. Canada (Companies Reference)*, [1916] 1 A.C. 598; *Bonanza Creek Gold Mining Company v. The King*, [1916] 1 A.C. 566; *Great West Saddlery v. The King*, [1921] 2 A.C. 91; *In re the Board of Commerce Act 1919*, and the *Combines and Fair Prices Act, 1919*, [1922] 1 A.C. 191; *Fort Frances Pulp and Paper Co. v. Manitoba Free Press Co.*, [1923] A.C. 695; *A.G. Ontario v. Reciprocal Insurers.* [1924] A.C. 328; *Toronto Electric Commissioners v. Snider*, [1925] A.C. 396.

36 National Archives of Canada (NAC), Duff Papers, Duff to Haldane, 20 December 1923.

37 Dates given are for the argument. *Royal Bank of Canada v. The King* (1912); *Toronto and Niagara Power Company v. The Corporation of the Town of North Toronto* (1912); *A.G. British Columbia v. A.G. Canada (Fisheries Reference)* (1913); *John Deere Plow v. Wharton* (1914); *A.G. Canada v. A.G. Alberta (Insurance Reference)* (1915); *A.G. Ontario v. A.G. Canada (Company Reference)* (1915); *Bonanza Creek Gold Mining Co. v. The King* (1915); *In re the Initiative and Referendum Act* (1919); *Great Western Saddlery v. The King* [1920]; *A.G. British Columbia v. A.G. Canada (Johnny Walker)* (1923); *Toronto Electric Com-*

missioners v. *Snider* (1924). The argument in *Board of Commerce* was at one time in E.R. Cameron's collection in the Supreme Court but now cannot be located (E.R. Cameron, *Canadian Companies and the Judicial Committee* [Toronto: Carswell, 1922], xxxiii.)

38 [1914] A.C. 176. The board consisted of Atkinson and the newly appointed Lord Moulton who wrote the decision. The argument over the Quebec Succession Duties Act, where the Judicial Committee overturned a decision of the Supreme Court and restored the decision of the Quebec Court of King's Bench, lasted for six days.

39 Haldane was concerned that the Judicial Committee was dangerously weak in numbers and, by the Appellate Jurisdiction Act of 1913, obtained the authority to increase the number of law lords and appointed lords Sumner and Dunedin. (NLS, Haldane Papers, MS 5910, 153, Haldane to Fitzpatrick, 29 January 1913 [improperly dated 1915 in MSS]; Fitzpatrick to Haldane, MS 5910, 160, 9 January 1914.) During Haldane's visit to the meeting of the American Bar Association in Montreal in 1913, Fitzpatrick had complained to Haldane that leaves to appeal had been too freely granted 'except in the case of Quebec.' Haldane consulted his colleagues and replied that he had personally 'sat on every leave to appeal from Canada since we resumed sitting in October. If your registrar will look into the records since then he will find that we have very effectively checked the stream of applications. Few of them have succeeded.' (NAC, Fitzpatrick Papers, Haldane to Fitzpatrick, 13 October 1913; NLS Haldane Papers, MS 5910, ff. 153–7, Haldane to Fitzpatrick 29 January 1914.)

40 Ibid. 35.

41 *A.G. Quebec* v. *Reed* (1884), 10 A.C. 141.

42 NLS, Haldane Papers, MS 5920, 'Memoirs,' 28.

43 Ibid. at 29. The brief was for the argument in the Ontario-Manitoba boundary dispute in 1884 when Mowat and David Mills argued Ontario's case. He appeared with Davey in the *McCarthy Act Reference* and *St. Catherine's Milling* but not in *Precious Metals, Liquidators, Barrett,* or *Tennant.*

44 Ibid.

45 'The Appellate Courts of the Empire,' 4.

46 25 January 1887. Haldane was commenting on a public speech Chamberlain had given, not on the substance of his speech in the House of Commons where he had provided this version of Canadian federalism. 'Now, they have each their separate autonomy, under the authority of the Dominion Parliament. In that way you might have Provincial Assemblies in Ireland, under the authority of the Imperial Parliament. Then, again, in the Dominion Parliament there is complete and continuous representation of every part of the Dominion ... In the third place, there is absolute and effec-

tive supremacy of the Dominion Parliament over the Provincial Legislatures. There is a right of veto which can be, and is, used; and the Provincial
Assemblies are subordinate bodies, with distinctly defined rights of subordinate bodies, with distinctly defined rights of legislation, expressly given
to them by Statute.' The Dominion also had control over criminal law and
the appointment of judges, thus freeing the judiciary from local influences.
(U.K., *Parliamentary Debates*, 3rd Series, vol. 306 [1886] 697.)

47 The case cited was *Regina* v. *Horner* (1876) in the Quebec Court of Queen's
Bench, reported in Charles H. Stephens, *The Quebec Law Digest* (Montreal,
Lovell and Son 1882), vol. 2, 451. The Judicial Committee decision cited in
that case, however, was *Regina* v. *Coote*, [1873] A.C. 599, and it would not
appear to bear out Haldane's far-ranging conclusion.

48 Haldane, *Autobiography*, 94–5.

49 Canada, *Sessional Papers*, 1895, no. 20, *Brophy* v. *A.G. Manitoba*, oral argument in the Judicial Committee, 309.

50 U.K., *Parliamentary Debates*, 4th Series, vol. 83 (1900) 98.

51 Oral argument in the Privy Council, *Great West Saddlery* v. *The King*, in Cameron, *Canadian Companies and the Judicial Committee*, 16 at 182.

52 Oral argument, *Bonanza Creek Gold Mining Company* v. *The King*, in E.R.
Cameron, *Canadian Companies: Proceedings in the Judicial Committee* (8–17
December 1915) (Toronto: Carswell 1917), 325. This volume contains the
combined oral arguments in the *Insurance Reference*, *The Companies Reference*, and *Bonanza Creek* (hereafter 'oral argument').

53 Canada, Department of Labour, *Judicial Proceedings respecting Constitutional
Validity of the Industrial Disputes Investigation Act, 1907, and Amendments of
1910, 1918 and 1920: Toronto Electric Commissioners* v. *Snider et al.* (Ottawa:
King's Printer 1925), 190. To which Lewis Duncan sarcastically added,
'Ably assisted by other noble Lords' (hereafter, oral argument, *Snider*).

54 Oral argument, *Great West Saddlery*, 124.

55 Oral argument, *Snider*, 192.

56 Oral argument, *Insurance Reference*, 94. The section referred to in the 1896
decision is quoted in Chapter 6, nn.109–11.

57 Oral argument, *Snider*, 111.

58 Cited in Maurice Ollivier, *Problems of Canadian Sovereignty* (Toronto: Canada
Law Book 1945), 239.

59 *Attorney General for the Commonwealth of Australia* v. *Colonial Sugar Refining
Co.* (1913), [1914] A.C. 237 at 253.

60 Supreme Court Library, oral argument *In the matter of the Initiative and Referendum Act* 15 May 1919, second day, 4.

61 Oral argument, *Great West Saddlery*, 86.

62 Oral argument, *Snider*, 190.

63 Canada, Sessional Papers, 1895, no. 20, 'Judicial Committee of the Privy Council,' *Brophy* v. *Attorney General of Manitoba*, oral argument, 302. Lord Fitzgerald's much quoted statement in *Hodge* v. *R.* (1883), 9 A.C. 117 at 132, that 'within these limits of subject and area the local legislature is supreme and has the same authority as the Imperial Parliament, or the Parliament of the Dominion,' echoed the judgments of Spragge and Burton in the Ontario Court of Appeal in *Hodge* (7 O.A.R. 246). 'Indeed, this doctrine as to the respective powers of the Dominion and local legislatures seems to me to be almost the only one on which there has been entire unanimity of opinion' stated Thomas Ramsay in 1880. *Dobie* v. *Board of Management of the Temporalities Fund* (1880), 3 *Legal News* 244 at 250.

64 Oral argument, *Snider*, 116.

65 Ibid., 166.

66 Ibid., 139.

67 Oral argument, *Bonanza Creek*, 311.

68 Ibid., 220.

69 *Fisheries in the Railway Belt of British Columbia and in Canada Generally* (Victoria: King's Printer, 1914) 176. (*A.G. British Columbia* v. *A.G. Canada*, [1914] A.C. 153.)

70 Oral argument, *Insurance Reference*, 166.

71 Oral argument, *Great West Saddlery*, 61.

72 *A.G. Ontario* v. *A.G. Canada*, [1896] A.C. 348 at 348 (emphasis added). See Chapter 6, at n.111.

73 Oral argument, *Insurance Reference*, 47.

74 Ibid., 89.

75 *In Re: The Board of Commerce Act 1919 and the Combines and Fair Prices Act 1919*, (1921), [1922] 1 A.C. 191 at 197.

76 Oral argument, *Snider*, 148.

77 Ibid., 149.

78 Ibid., 148–9.

79 Ibid., 181.

80 Ibid., 191. Yet years earlier Haldane had written that the 'Constitution of Canada sprang at once into full life and vigour because the Imperial Parliament was in 1867 simply giving effect to exhaustive resolutions passed by the federating provinces.' ('Federal Constitutions within the Empire,' in *Education and Empire* [London: Jarry 1902], 114.)

81 *Toronto Electric Commissioners* v. *Snider*, 'Case for the Respondents before the Judicial Committee of the Privy Council,' in *Judicial Proceedings respecting Constitutional Validity of the Industrial Disputes Investigation Act 1907*, 55. As

interveners, the federal government threw in the criminal law, trade and commerce, and the militia. (Ibid., 'Case for the Attorney-General of Canada before the Judicial Committee of the Privy Council,' 59.) The legislation was upheld with a 4–1 majority in the Ontario Court of Appeal as legislation in relation to trade and commerce and the criminal law, but Justice Ferguson explicitly rejected the argument some drew from *Russell* and *Fort Frances* that the residual clause did not permit any encroachment on the provincial enumerations. *Toronto Electric Commissioners* v. *Snider* (1923–4), 55 O.L.R. 454.

82 Oral argument, *Snider*, 79.

83 Ibid., 82.

84 Ibid., 135.

85 Ibid., 155.

86 *Toronto Electric Commissioners* v. *Snider*, [1925] A.C. 396 at 412, 415–16. The decision in *Russell*, wrote Haldane, 'can only be supported to-day, not on the footing of having laid down an interpretation, such as had sometimes been invoked of the general words at the beginning of s. 91, but on the assumption of Board, apparently made at the time of deciding the case of *Russell* v. *the Queen*, that the evil of intemperance at that time amounted in Canada to one so great and so general that at least for a period it was a menace to the national life of Canada so serious and pressing that the National Parliament was called on to intervene to protect the nation from disaster.' (Ibid. at 412.) It was a strange *obiter* from one who had agreed during argument that the case had not been decided on emergency. Interestingly, it was left to Viscount Simon, who had followed Duncan in the argument, to dismiss the emergency doctrine in *A.G. Ontario* v. *Canada Temperance Federation*, [1946] A.C. 193. However, it did not stay dismissed!

87 Oral argument, *Bonanza Creek*, 214. The reference is to the often cited words in the judgment in *John Deere* v. *Wharton* (1914), [1915] A.C. 330 at 338. 'The language of these sections [91 and 92] and of the various heads which they contain obviously cannot be construed as having been intended to embody the exact disjunctions of a perfectly logical scheme ... It may be added that the form in which provisions in terms overlapping each other have been placed side by side shows that those who have passed the Confederation Act intended to leave the working out and interpretation of these provisions to practice and to judicial decision.'

88 *Liquor Prohibition Appeal, 1895* (London: William Brown 1895), 94–5, 244, 292.

89 *A.G. Ontario* v. *A.G. Canada*, [1896] A.C. 348 at 359.

90 Oral argument, *Great West Saddlery*, 60. 'The effect, as was pointed out in the decision just cited, is to effect a derogation from what might otherwise

have been literally the authority of the Provincial Legislatures, to the extent of enabling the Parliament of Canada to deal with matters local and private where, though only where, such legislation is necessarily incidental to the exercise of the enumerated powers conferred on it by s. 91.' (Ibid. at 99.)

91 Oral argument, *Snider*, 226.

92 Oral argument, *Great West Saddlery*, 187.

93 In *John Deere Plow* v. *Wharton* (1914), [1915].

94 Cameron, *Canadian Companies* (1917), xxxii. It might be noted that, during the argument in the *Insurance Reference* (35), Haldane stated that the 'concluding words of section 91 take anything that falls within section 91 out of section 92 ... Therefore if you get it within regulation of trade and commerce you have got it for the Dominion, notwithstanding that it is an infringement of the property and civil rights in section 92.'

95 *In re the Board of Commerce Act, 1919*, at 198.

96 *Toronto Electric Commissioners* v. *Snider*, [1925] A.C. 396 at 410.

97 *In re the Board of Commerce Act* at 198–9.

98 Oral argument, *Snider*, 118.

99 Supreme Court of Canada Library, MSS oral argument, *John Deere Plow Company* v. *Wharton*, 13 July 1914, fourth day, 23.

100 Oral argument, *Snider*, 150–1.

101 Ibid., 167.

102 Ibid., 179.

103 *In re the Board of Commerce Act, 1919*, at 198. Haldane's concern for liberty was similar to that of A.V. Dicey, the high priest of late Victorian individualism who saw the courts as guardians of individual rights. Arthur Elliott reported to Dicey in 1917 that Haldane had said, '"Dicey is much the best legal mind we have" [–] that from an ex-Chancellor is worth recording.' (Cited in Richard Cosgrove, *The Rule of Law: Arthur Venn Dicey, Victorian Jurist* [Chapel Hill: University of North Carolina Press 1980] 293.)

104 One exception was *In re Marriage Legislation in Canada* where Haldane quickly decided that the provincial power of the 'solemnization of marriage' was intended to be extracted from the federal power over 'marriage and divorce' and could enable the province to enact conditions which could affect the validity of a marriage ([1912] A.C. 880).

105 One example was the securities industry where federally incorporated companies were finally placed under provincial jurisdiction in 1932 with Dunedin's decision in *Lymburn* v. *Mayland*, [1932] A.C. 318.

106 Companies were not mentioned in the initial list of provincial (or federal) powers introduced by Mowat at Quebec, and first appeared in an amendment by A.G. Archibald of Nova Scotia to the provincial enumerations:

'The incorporation of private local companies, except such as relate to matters assigned to the Federal Legislature.' (G.P. Browne, *Documents on the Confederation of British North America* [Toronto: McClelland & Stewart 1969], 83.)

107 *Citizens Insurance Co.* v. *Parsons* (1881), [1881–2] 7 A.C. 96.

108 This was true of all ministers who had occasion to review such legislation from 1867 to 1911: John A. Macdonald, Edward Blake, T-A-R Laflamme, Alexander Campbell, John Thompson, C.H. Tupper, Oliver Mowat, David Mills, Charles Fitzpatrick, and Allen Aylesworth. (See W.E. Hodgins, *Correspondence, Reports of the Ministers of Justice and Canadian Council upon the Subject of Dominion and Provincial Legislation, 1867–1895* [Ottawa: Government Printing Bureau 1896].) As Mowat observed in objecting to a Nova Scotia incorporation in 1896, the words provincial objects have 'been construed to mean objects located within the Province and to be locally carried on by such companies within the Province.' (Francis H. Gisborne and Arthur Hardy, *Correspondence, Reports of the Ministers of Justice and Orders in Council upon the Subject of Provincial Legislation, 1896–1920* [Ottawa: King's Printer 1922], 274.) In office, Mowat had scrupulously kept within provincial borders and objects. There was little argument over the functional limitation and with few exceptions the provinces accepted the restrictions implied by the section 91 enumerations, including the 92(10) exclusions. See also W.J. White, *A Treatise on Company Law* (Montreal: Theoret 1901).

109 The best treatment is by F.W. Wegenast, *Extra-Provincial Corporations* (Toronto: Carswell 1911). By 1916, Ontario had earned $250,000 from licensing fees and the other provinces an estimated $150,000. (AO, RG 40–32, file 1916, no. 415 A [1], E.R. Bayley, *Memorandum: Re Companies Reference*, nd.) Oliver Mowat, David Mills, Charles Fitzpatrick, Allen Aylesworth, and Charles Doherty all objected. (See Gisborne, *Provincial Legislation*, 12, 26, 39–51 [for the Ontario legislation] and 452–7 [for Manitoba].) Provincial courts in a few decisions had upheld the validity of extra-provincial licensing acts, but there was some doubt about their correctness. In 1907 the Supreme Court of Canada, in a specially argued case, decided by majority that provincially incorporated companies were not 'inherently incapable' of insuring property outside the province, but did not answer the question, 'Has a province power to prohibit or impose conditions and restrictions upon extra-provincial companies which transact business within its limits?'

110 Canada, House of Commons, *Debates*, 25 April 1910, 7949. Provincial representatives had met in Ottawa in March 1910 to oppose the reference and

propose instead a constitutional amendment giving the provinces the powers they had been exercising. The federal government refused and ordered the reference. (AO, RG 4–32, file 1910, no. 518 [1].) The provinces responded by challenging the constitutionality of references themselves, and, after losing in the Supreme Court, appealed to the Judicial Committee which affirmed the Supreme Court decision. (In *re Re References by the Governor-General in Council* (1910), 43 S.C.R. 536; *A.G. Ontario and others* v. *A.G. Canada*, [1912] A.C. 571.) When the question of *ultra vires* arose during the argument on the facts, the court ordered a re-argument of the constitutional questions with representatives of the two levels of government present. (*Canadian Pacific Railway Company* v. *Ottawa Fire Insurance Company* (1908), 39, S.C.R. 405.) The two dissenting judges, as often happened in constitutional cases, were the chief justice, Sir Charles Fitzpatrick, and Sir Louis Davies, both exiles from Laurier's cabinet.

111 Supreme Court of Canada Library, MSS oral argument, Newcombe, 25, Lafleur 51, Nesbitt 63, Geoffrion 102. *In re 'Insurance Act 1910'* (1913), 48 S.C.R. 260. In the *Companies Reference*, Fitpatrick and Davies concluded that the words 'Provincial Objects' imposed a territorial limitation and defined the powers which provincial companies could exercise, among which was not the capacity to compel federal companies to obtain a provincial licence. The majority agreed that, although a province could not legislate to interfere with their corporate powers, Dominion companies had to obey general provincial legislation governing corporate activity. (*In re the Incorporation of Companies* (1913), [1914] 48 S.C.R. 331.)

112 *John Deere Plow Co. v. Wharton* (1914), [1915] A.C. 330.

113 Alexander Smith, *The Commerce Power in Canada and the United States* (Toronto: Butterworths 1963), 97.

114 Peter W. Hogg, *Constitutional Law of Canada* (Toronto: Carswell 1992), 203.

115 Jacob S. Ziegel, 'Constitutional Aspects of Canadian Companies,' in Ziegel, ed., *Studies in Canadian Company Law* (Toronto: Butterworths 1967), 160.

116 *Deere* at 343. *Great West Saddlery* v. *The King*, [1921] 2 A.C. was decided on the precedent of *Deere*, and *A.G. Ontario* v. *Reciprocal Insurers*, [1924] A.C. 328 was decided on the precedent of the 1916 *Insurance Reference*.

117 *A.G. Canada* v. *A.G. Alberta and A.G. Ontario*, [1916] 1 A.C. 558 at 596.

118 Ibid. at 597.

119 In *Re Insurance Act of Canada* (1931), [1932] A.C. 41 at 52. Other cases were *A.G. Ontario* v. *Reciprocal Insurers*, [1924] A.C. 328, where Lyman Duff wrote the decision. See Vincent C. MacDonald, 'The Regulation of Insurance in Canada' (1946) 24 *Canadian Bar Review*, 257.

120 *Bonanza Creek Gold Mining Company* v. *The King* (1915), 50 S.C.R. 534.
121 Ibid. at 576.
122 Oral argument, *Bonanza Creek* at 272, 277, 278, 287.
123 *Bonanza Creek Gold Mining Company* v. *The King* (1915), at 583.
124 According to Haldane's doctrine, the words 'with provincial objects' did not 'preclude a province from keeping alive the power of the Executive to incorporate by charter in a fashion which confers a general capacity analogous to that of a natural person.' Since the province had not 'thought fit to restrict the exercise by the Lieutenant-Governor of the prerogative power to incorporate by letters patent with the result of conferring a capacity analogous to that of a natural person,' the company could accept powers and rights conferred by outside authorities. (Ibid. at 584–5.)
125 Haldane's argument was that, since the prerogative power of incorporation entrusted to the governor general before Confederation was by section 65 entrusted to the lieutenant governor 'so far as provincial objects required its exercise ...' Watson's decision on the point was authoritative: Whatever obscurity may at one time have prevailed as to the position of the Lieutenant-Governor appointed on behalf of the crown by the Governor-General has been dispelled by the decision of this Board in *Liquidators of the Maritime Bank of Canada* v. *Receiver-General of New Brunswick'* (581). *Bonanza Creek Gold Mining Company* v. *The King*, [1916] 1 A.C. 566 at 581.
126 Oral argument, *Bonanza Creek* at 303, 306, 309.
127 E.E. Palmer wrote in 1965 that the decision was another illustration of the Judicial Committee's 'desire to expand provincial legislative authority, always to the detriment of commercial life in Canada ... This proclivity was most clearly shown in the area of company law' where the court 'grotesquely twisted the constitutional provisions relating to the authority to incorporate businesses.' Palmer noted that 'few cases have created the degree of alarm and indignant reaction in Canadian law than did Lord Haldane's judgement in this one.' ('Federalism and the Uniformity of Laws: The Canadian Experience' [1965] 30 *Law and Contemporary Problems,* 250 at 252–3.) David Schneiderman, however, does not criticize the judgment or reasoning. On the contrary, he finds that the results in *Bonanza* and the *Companies Reference* were the application of principles 'familiar to British pluralists – that the law had failed to properly reflect the explosive activity of corporate activity and that corporate activity could not be rigidly bound by principles of statutory interpretation. Haldane's language on the corporation cases reflects his understanding of group personality ... All this suggests a fit with pluralist conceptions of associational life that could also be extended to the life of the provinces.' ('Harold Laski, Vis-

count Haldane, and the Law of the Canadian Constitution in the Early Twentieth Century' [1988] 48 *University of Toronto Law Journal*, 521 at 533–4.)

128 Thomas Mulvey, 'Common Law Companies' (1925) 10 *Proceedings of the Canadian Bar Association*, 185–92.

129 Ibid., vii.

130 'Memorandum of Cecil T. Carr' (1925) 10 *Proceedings of the Canadian Bar Association*, 193 at 197.

131 *Waterous Engine Company* v. *Town of Capreol* (1922), 52 O.L.R. 247 at 255. Hodgins's judgment contained not only a scholarly critique of the decision but also an attack on what he regarded as a fundamental 'anomaly' in *Deere* (at 255).

132 *Edwards* v. *Blackmore* (1918), 42 O.L.R. 105 at 123. Mockler believes that the Judicial Committee did not agree with Haldane and in a case in 1918 did not act on the precedent of *Bonanza*. (E.J. Mockler, 'The Doctrine of Ultra Vires in Letters Patent Companies,' in Ziegel, *Canadian Company* Law, citing *Canadian National Fire Insurance Company* v. *Hutchings*. [1918] A.C. 451.) The decision was still a matter of comment as late as 1964 in the Canadian courts. (See *Walton* v. *Bank of Nova Scotia* (1964), 1 O.R. 673.)

133 John S. Ewart, 'The Bonanza Creek Gold Mining Company v. The King' (1916) 36 *Canadian Law Times*, 679 at 683, 697. See also Thomas Mulvey, 'The Companies Act: With Special Reference to the Bonanza Creek Mining Company Case' (1919) 39 *Canadian Law Times*, 79; Bram Thomson, 'The Doctrine of Ultra Vires in relation to Incorporated Companies in Canada' (1920) 40 *Canadian Law Times*, 993. 'It is my contention' wrote Mockler, 'that the wide proposition relating to the doctrine of ultra vires stated in *Bonanza Creek* was not at the time of the case supported by authority and is not now supported.' ('The Doctrine of Ultra Vires,' 231 at 233.)

134 It is difficult, for me at least, to follow Haldane's essays on the crown in Canada both during the argument and in the decision, a decision that he later stated was revised by Lord Sumner. (Oral argument, *Great West Saddlery*, 26.) He was also hopelessly confused about the role of the governor general in disallowance.

135 *Bonanza Creek* at 585.

136 Ibid. at 586–7.

137 *Re the Initiative and Referendum Act*, [1919] A.C. 935.

138 The act did state that if a proposed law had been approved by a majority of the voters it was to take effect 'subject, however, to the same powers of veto and disallowance as are provided in the British North America Act or exist in law with respect to any Act of the Legislative Assembly, as though such law were an Act of the said Assembly.' Ibid. at 940.

139 Ibid., 943. Watson, it should be noted, did not write that the lieutenant governor 'directly' represented the sovereign. See Chapter 6, n.65.

140 James McLeod Hendry, *Memorandum of the Office of Lieutenant-Governor of a Province: Its Constitutional Character and Function* (Ottawa: Department of Justice 1955), 16. *A.G. Canada* v. *A.G. Ontario* (1891), 20 O.R. 222 at 247.

141 (1919) 55 *Canada Law Journal*, 286.

142 The best study of the legislation is Bernard J. Hibbits, 'A Bridle for Leviathan: The Supreme Court and the Board of Commerce' (1989) 21 *Ottawa Law Review*, 65. See also John A. Ball, *Canadian Anti-Trust Legislation* (Baltimore: William and Wilkins 1934); Tom Traves, *The State and Enterprise: Canadian Manufacturers and the Federal Government, 1917–1931* (Toronto: University of Toronto Press 1979). The legislation was a failure regardless of the legal challenge. See R.C. Brown and Ramsay Cook, *Canada, 1896–1921* (Toronto: McClelland and Stewart 1974), 324.

143 Hibbitts argues that the case marked a 'watershed' in Supreme Court jurisprudence because it represented a conflict between the older 'traditionalism,' which 'showed a faith in the state (in its most powerful federal aspect) and a sensitivity to legislative intent, to economic, political and social conditions,' and the newer 'liberal version of law,' where the role of the judiciary was to protect the individual against the state. Law was 'the critical boundary between the two, shielding the one from the power of the other and defining the parameters of their respective spheres.' Hibbits mentions Richards, Taschereau, and Sedgewick in particular and the decisions in *Severn*, *Fredericton*, and *Liquor Prohibition* as representing the traditional vision. However, as he admits, there was little left of the traditional vision by 1918. ('A Bridle for Leviathan,' 104, 106, 108.)

144 *In re Board of Commerce Act* (1920), 60 S.C.R. 456 at 462–71.

145 Ibid. at 494ff, 509–10, 513.

146 AO, RG 4–32, 1920, file 226, J.R. Boyle to W.E. Raney, 29 July 1920.

147 Ibid., E. Bayley to Raney, 23 May 1921: 'I do not think this Province is very specially interested in this appeal but we have gone too far in my opinion to withdraw.' However, he refused to go to the expense of hiring Canadian counsel and shared the cost of Geoffrey Lawrence with Alberta. In fact, Ontario had supported the legislation and co-operated in its enforcement.

148 Ibid., 'In the Privy Council ... Case on behalf of the Attorney General of Canada.'

149 Ibid., 'Case for the Intervenant, the Attorney-General for the Province of Quebec,' 5.

150 *In re The Board of Commerce Act, 1919,* and the *Combines and Fair Prices Act, 1919* (1921), [1922] 1 A.C. 191 at 197–8.

151 Ibid. at 200.

152 [1923] A.C. 695.

153 NLS, Haldane Papers, MS 6006, Haldane to his mother, 27 June 1923.

154 Lord Buckmaster and Lord Phillimore had sat on *Commerce* but Viscount Cave and Lord Carson were replaced by Lord Parmoor and the strong-minded Lord Sumner.

155 [1923] A.C. 695 at 704.

156 Ibid. at 705–6. "The language invoked here resembles that of Haldane's intervention in the debate between monists and pluralists. In *Fort Frances,* Haldane distinguishes between "Government," on the one hand, and the "State as a whole" or "Canada as an entirety," on the other. It is the "State regarded as a whole," he writes, that gives "expression and influence" to "public opinion as such." Recall that for Haldane the real source of sovereignty was "public opinion," which he likened to the general will. Government was merely one manifestation of the general will – elected legislators were mere "temporary rulers." In *Fort Frances,* Haldane refers to the "State as a whole" (meaning, as did Bosanquet, the state in its larger sense) as giving expression to "public opinion," arming Government with extended authority to deal with the extraordinary circumstances of war."' ("Harold Laski, Viscount Haldane, and the law of the Canadian Constitution in the early Twentieth Century" (1998) 48 *University of Toronto Law Journal,* 521 at 527.

157 Ibid., 706–7. Haldane did believe that war necessarily limited individual freedom and, as he wrote, 'in wartime, a highly centralized control may be essential.' ('On Sovereignty' (1922), *The Nation* (25 March 1922), 946 at 946.

158 Oral argument, *Snider,* 186.

159 Ibid., 178.

160 Ibid., *Judicial Proceedings,* 255–8.

161 Canada, House of Commons, *Debates,* 1925, 3154.

162 *Toronto Electric Commissioners* v. *Snider* (1923), [1923–4], 55 O.L.R. 454 at 462.

163 Ibid. at 468.

164 Ibid. at 470.

165 Ibid. at 474–5 and passim.

166 Ibid. at 477.

167 Ibid. at 479, 485, 490, 493. By 1924, boards had dealt with 428 disputes and failed to avert a strike or to end the dispute in 37 cases. (Department of Labour, *Judicial Proceedings,* 281.)

168 Oral argument, *Snider*, 220. After one of Haldane's interjections, the following exchange occurred. Simon: 'I am not discussing some vague and impossible hinterland.' Haldane: 'I am alarmed at that.' Simon: 'I am keeping very close to the coast.' Haldane: 'But a claim to the hinterland often gives rise to warfare though you are not going there.' (Ibid. at 226.)

169 Ibid., 76.

170 Ibid.

171 Ibid., 82.

172 Ibid., 83.

173 NLS, Haldane Papers, MS 6007, 1 December 1924.

174 *Toronto Electric Commissioners v. Snider*, [1925] A.C. 396 at 415.

175 NLS, Haldane Papers, 6007, 7 February 1925. The decision led the *Globe* (5 February 1925) to advocate the abolition of appeals. The act had been useful and there was no demand in Canada for its repeal. 'Yet, after more than seventeen years of working, it is suddenly destroyed by an authority over which the people of Canada have no control, and a blow is struck at industrial peace and progress.' To the argument that the Judicial Committee was 'a link of Empire,' the *Globe* replied that the appeal 'is a source of delay, disturbance, uncertainty and expense,' and as a means of promoting imperial unity 'it is worse than useless.' Justice Lyman Poore Duff wrote Haldane that there 'has been a current of criticism upon the interpretation of the Act by the Judicial Committee, and comparisons have been drawn at times, rather disparagingly, to the Privy Council, with Marshall's development of the American constitution on the National side.' (NAC, Duff Papers, n.d.) To W.F. MacLean, who had attacked the decision and introduced a motion in the House of Commons calling for the amendment of the constitution in Canada, Duff wrote that 'you may take it from me that no court of competent lawyers in Canada would or could honestly have given any other decision as to the Lemeiux Act.' (Letter courtesy of the late David Williams.)

176 Haldane, *Autobiography,* 263–4.

177 J.H. Morgan, 'The Riddle of Lord Haldane' (April 1929) 252 *Quarterly Review*, 339 at 343.

178 Cole, *Beatrice Webb's Diaries*, 130.

179 *Roman Catholic Separate School Trustees v. The King*, [1928] A.C. 363.

180 Morgan, 'Riddle,' 351.

181 Heuston, *Lives of the Lord Chancellors*, 237.

182 NLS, Haldane Papers, MS 6004, 9 July 1921.

183 Ibid., MS 6006, 16 July 1923; Haldane to Elizabeth Haldane, MS 6023, 20 July 1923.

184 Ibid., MS 6007, 19 July, 20 July 1924.

185 *Social Credit and the Federal Power in Canada* (Toronto: University of Toronto Press 1954), 49.

186 'The Urge to Idealize: Viscount Haldane and the Constitution of Canada' (1984) 29 *McGill Law Journal*, 609. In his view of the crown, Haldane followed Watson in *Liquidators* but made the relationship 'direct' without qualification.

187 'Lord Haldane and the British North America Act' (1970) 30 *University of Toronto law Journal*, 55 at 57.

188 R.B. Haldane, *The Reign of Relativity* (London: John Murray 1921), 370, cited in ibid., 63.

189 Ibid., 67.

190 Ibid., 66.

191 'Harold Laski, Viscount Haldane, and the Law of the Canadian Constitution,' 528–9.

192 Ibid. at 535.

193 'Sociologically we must call Hegel a pluralist.' David Nicholls, *The Pluralist State* (London: Macmillan 1975), 77.

194 Ibid., 538 n.115.

195 Ibid., 543.

196 Ibid., 554.

197 Ibid., 559.

198 Ibid., 560.

8 Lord Sankey and 'Progressive Constructionism,' 1929–1935

1 Laski to Holmes, 8 May 1928, in Mark DeWolfe Howe, ed., *Holmes-Laski Letters: The Correspondence of Mr. Justice Holmes and Harold J. Laski, 1916–1935* (Cambridge, Mass.: Harvard University Press 1953), 1052.

2 W. Ivor Jennings, 'Constitutional Interpretation: The Experience of Canada' (1937) 51 *Harvard Law Review*, 36. Federalism cases not discussed here include: *In Re: Insurance Act of Canada* [1932] A.C. 41, finding *ultra vires* sections on the federal Insurance Act requiring insurers in Quebec to acquire a federal licence; *Lymburn* v. *Mayland*, [1932] A.C. 318, finding *intra vires* Alberta securities legislation subjecting federally incorporated companies to provisions applying to all persons trading in securities; *Lower Mainland Dairy Product Sales Adjustment Committee* v. *Crystal Dairy, Limited* (1933), [1932] A.C. 168, finding *ultra vires*, as constituting indirect taxation, adjustment levies designed to regulate the dairy industry.

3 Stephen R. Ward, *James Ramsay MacDonald: Low Born among the High Brows*

(New York: Peter Klaing 1990), 124. Among the reasons he should have the chancellorship, Haldane informed MacDonald, were 'questions of the Judicial Committee of the privy council, over which I have been presiding through nearly the whole of ten years. Certain of the Dominions watch closely, and their aspirations have to be studied.' (Sir Federick Maurice, *Haldane, 1915–1928* [Westport, Conn.: Greenwood Press 1939], 146.)

4 Robert Stevens, *The Independence of the Judiciary: The View from the Lord Chancellor's Office* (Oxford, U.K.: Clarendon Press 1993), 67.

5 David B. Swinfen, *Imperial Appeal: The Debate on the Appeal to the Privy Council, 1833–1986* (Manchester, U.K.: Manchester University Press 1987), 107.

6 Stevens, *Independence of the Judiciary,* 66. The decision did (and still does) arouse intense opposition in Quebec. The lord chancellor, Cave, presided over a board composed of Haldane, Finlay, Sumner, and Sir Thomas Warrington. Macmillan, soon to be a member of the Judicial Committee, acted for Canada and Sir John Simon for Newfoundland.

7 Atkinson felt that he was up to the work and had no intention of resigning, but as he wrote: 'The Chancellor [Cave] asked me to call on him. I did call. He said the scurrilous press of Quebec had abused the Privy Council and said the members were old fogies, that I was the oldest of the old fogies and had better resign. Of course, I would not think of begging not to be dismissed, and answered him that I would resign if he wished it, and did so.' (Cited in R.F.V. Heuston, *Lives of the Lord Chancellors, 1885–1940* [Oxford, U.K.: Clarendon Press 1964], 303–4.)

8 Ibid., 481.

9 *A.G. Canada* v. *A.G. British Columbia* (1929), [1930] A.C. 111 at 118.[Fish canneries].

10 Tomlin, like others, preferred the head-note to *Local Prohibition* to the text of Watson's decision. See Chapter 6, n.107.

11 Writing in 1937, Ivor Jennings commented that the propositions 'have since become as much part of Sections 91 and 92 as if they had actually been enacted. If principles can be set out in this way it is quite impossible to say that *stare decisis* is a pure fiction.' ('Constitutional Interpretation: The Experience of Canada' (1937) 51 *Harvard Law Review,* 1 at 28.)

12 *Reference re Validity of the Combines Investigation Act and of s. 498 of the Criminal Code,* [1929] S.C.R. 409 at 415. Chief Justice Meredith had earlier stated that 'I am unable to reconcile the views expressed in the Board of Commerce case with what was decided in the Lord's Day Act case, for in the latter case I find no warrant for the view that it is only where the subject matter is one which by its very nature belongs to the domain of criminal

jurisprudence that the Parliament of Canada can legislate.' *A.G. Ontario* v. *Wholesale Grocers* (1923), [1922–3] 53 O.L.R. 627 at 636. On another occasion he had been more direct. 'With great respect, in my judgement' to limit the powers of the Parliament of Canada to passing only such laws as come within the ambit suggested by Viscount Haldane, would be to take from Parliament powers which the framers of the Act intended that it should possess and which the words of the provisions are wide enough to include.' (*In re Reciprocal Insurance Legislation* (1922), 53 O.L.R. 195 at 209, both decisions Appeal Division].)

13 *Reference re Validity of the Combines Investigation Act* at 423.

14 *Proprietary Articles Trade Association* v. *A.G. Canada*, [1931] A.C. 310 at 324.

15 Ibid. at 326. Atkin provided support for Chief Justice Anglin's criticism of Haldane a few years earlier. Seldom deferential to the reasoning in the Judicial Committee, Anglin stated that he failed 'to appreciate the reasoning on which this view is based ... But the decisive authority of the judgements which have so determined cannot now be questioned in this court. I defer to it.' However in deferring, Anglin added that but 'for their Lordships' emphatic and reiterated allocation of 'the regulation of trade and commerce' to this subordinate and wholly auxiliary function, my inclination would have been to accord it some independent operation, such as was indicated in *Parsons'* case, and within that sphere, however limited, to treat it as appropriating to the Dominion Parliament an enumerated subject with consequences similar to those which attach to the other twenty-eight enumerative heads of s. 91.' (*King* v. *Eastern Terminal Elevator Co.*, [1925] S.C.R. 434 at 441–2.)

16 *Edwards* v. *A.G. Canada* (1929), [1930] A.C. 124 at 136–7, citing W.H.P. Clements, *The Law of the Canadian Constitution* (Toronto: Carswell 1916), 347.

17 *Reference as to Meaning of the Word 'Persons' in Section 24 of the British North America Act, 1867*, [1928] S.C.R. 276. With women voting and sitting in the House of Commons, 'it seems as though Bumble ["the law is an Ass"] was right,' editorialized the Ottawa *Evening Journal*, reflecting the outrage and ridicule which greeted the decision in Canada. (David Ricardo Williams, *Duff: A Life in the Law* [Vancouver: University of British Columbia Press 1984] 146.)

18 *Edwards* v. *A.G. Canada* (1929), [1930] A.C. 124 at 136.

19 Ibid. at 143

20 'The Privy Council Decisions: A Comment from Great Britain' (1937) 15 *Canadian Bar Review*, 428 at 429.

21 'The Statute of Westminster and Appeals to the Privy Council' (1936) 52 *Law Quarterly Review*, 173 at 181.

22 Supreme Court of Canada Library, oral argument, *In the Supreme Court of Canada: In the Matter of a Reference as to the Respective Legislative Powers under the British North America Act, 1867, of the Parliament of Canada and the Legislatures of the Provinces in relation to the Regulation and Control of Aeronautics in Canada*, 45 (hereafter *Aeronautics Reference*, oral argument).

23 Section 132 reads: 'The Parliament and Government of Canada shall have all Powers necessary or proper for performing the Obligations of Canada or of any Province thereof, as Part of the British Empire, towards Foreign Countries, arising under Treaties between the Empire and such Foreign Countries.'

24 *Reference re Regulation and Control of Aeronautics in Canada*, [1930] S.C.R. 663.

25 *Aeronautics Reference*, oral argument, 140–1. 'We have, therefore, three unhelpful and dubious negatives,' commented John S. Ewart; 'two puzzling uncertainties; and an indivisible subject divided among ten independent legislative jurisdictions. Truly, a sad, sad mess.' ('The Aeronautics Case' [December 1931] 10 *Canadian Bar Review*, 724 at 725.)

26 *In re Regulation and Control of Aeronautics in Canada* (1931), [1932] A.C. 54, summary of arguments at 57–62.

27 Ibid. at 70–1. The 'real object ...' was a direct, but unacknowledged, quotation from Lord Carnarvon's speech introducing the act in the House of Lords in 1867, although Carnarvon had added 'and, at the same time, to retain for each Province so ample a measure of municipal liberty and self-government as will allow, and indeed compel, them to exercise those local powers which they can exercise to great advantage to the community' (*Parliamentary Debates*, 3rd series, vol. 185 [1867] 563–6.) See W.P.M. Kennedy's comment on the skilful way in which Sankey avoided the rule prohibiting reference to Parliamentary debates. ('Our Canadian Letter: Radio: Aviation: Insurance' (1932) 1 *South African Law Times*, 240 at 240–1.

28 Ibid., 71–3. 'Since it was not contended there was in this case any question of emergency,' wrote Ivor Jennings, the reference to emergency 'could have no other purpose than to create the necessary 'atmosphere' for an extension of Dominion powers.' ('Constitutional Interpretation,' 30.)

29 Ibid., 74, 77.

30 Ibid., 77.

31 As reported by John Dafoe to Brooke Claxton, 2 December 1931, cited in Margaret Prang, *N.W. Rowell: Ontario Nationalist* (Toronto: University of Toronto Press 1975), 458.

32 Ewart, 'Aeronautics Case,' 726. Ewart, however, was disturbed by Sankey's description of Confederation as a 'contract.'

33 *In the Matter of a Reference as to the Jurisdiction of Parliament to Regulate and Control Radio Communication*, [1931] S.C.R. 541 at 544.
34 Supreme Court of Canada Library, *Radio Reference*, oral argument, 38.
35 Ibid., 46.
36 Ibid., 55, 75, 59.
37 Ibid., 103.
38 Ibid., 141.
39 *Radio Communication* at 545–6.
40 Ibid. at 565–6.
41 Ibid. at 566. See Gerald LeDain, 'Sir Lyman Duff and the Constitution' (1974) 12 *Osgoode Hall Law Journal*, 261 at 286.
42 'Lord Dunedin' (1942) 92 *Law Journal*, 317.
43 *In re Regulation and Control of Radio Communication in Canada*, [1932] A.C. 304 at 312.
44 Ibid. at 317. The board was not strong. Sitting with Dunedin were lords Blanesburgh, Merrivale, Russell of Killowen, and Sir George Lowndes.
45 'The Radio Case' (1932) 10 *Canadian Bar Review*, 298 at 298–9.
46 'Canada's Power to Perform Treaty Obligations (1933) 11 *Canadian Bar Review*, 664 at 668.
47 *Nadan v. The King*, [1926] A.C. 482. The case in all its aspects is fully discussed in Jacqueline D. Krikorian, 'British Imperial Politics and Judicial Independence: The Judicial Committee's Decision in the Canadian Case *Nadan v. The King*' (2000) 33 *Canadian Journal of Political Science*, 291.
48 *Manitoba Free Press*, 5 April 1926, cited in ibid., 313.
49 *Dunphy v. Croft* (1930), 2 M.P.R. 350.
50 [1931] S.C.R. 531 at 535–6.
51 Ibid. at 540.
52 (1885), 10 A.C. 675 at 678–9.
53 *Croft v. Dunphy* (1932), [1933] A.C. 156 at 163.
54 Ibid., 167. The decision contained *dicta* which alarmed both the British and Canadian governments because Macmillan's opinion could serve to legalize contiguous zones to which the British government was opposed. Attempts were made to get Macmillan and the board to alter the opinion, but an outraged Sankey refused. (A.V. Lowe and J.R. Young, 'An Attempt to Rewrite a Judgement' [1978] 94 *Law Quarterly Review*, 255.)
55 *British Coal Corporation v. The King*, [1935] A.C. 500 at 502–4. The Board was composed of Sankey, Atkin, Tomlin, Macmillan, and Wright.
56 Vincent C. MacDonald,' British Coal Corporation,' 626. MacDonald was wiser than he realized. Five days before the argument began, the cabinet met to discuss a memorandum prepared by the secretary of state for

Dominion affairs that referred to the 'politics of the attorney general on the Irish and Canadian appeals on abolition. Sankey left the discussion. The cabinet then discussed the question at issue with the Attorney General who stated that he had received a report that Lord Atkin had intimated that the Judicial Committee would later wish to have information as to the views of His Majesty's Government in the United Kingdom. He himself could not see how such views could be relevant to the question of law which the Judicial Committee had to decide, and he felt confident that the real intention of the Judicial Committee was only to invite his assistance on the legal and constitutional issues involved. On being asked as to whether he wished to receive any instructions from the Cabinet, the Attorney General made clear that he would prefer to have no instructions and be left with a free hand to exercise his own judgement if he were consulted by the Judicial Committee. The Cabinet took note that if the Attorney General was asked by the Judicial Committee for his assistance in this appeal, he would offer such help as seemed proper as a lawyer dealing with the legal issue, and that no declaration of the view of the Government on any political question was invoked.' (Cabinet Minutes, 13 March 1935, cited in George Vegh, 'Abolition of Appeals to the Judicial Committee of the Privy Council,' Honours thesis, York University, 1985, 35.) The attorney general, Sir Thomas Inskip, was invited to assist the board and argued both that *Nadan* was wrongly decided and that the right to abolish appeals existed in the residual clause.

57 *British Coal Corporation* v. *The King*, [1935] A.C. 517–20. 'That the decision is consonant with Imperial Policy, expediency and sentiment, goes without saying,' wrote Cyril Asquith, who questioned its soundness. 'If it had gone the other way, remedial legislation might well have been needed. Further, it is in full harmony with the general intention of the Statute of Westminster as understood by the man in the street ... The judgement delivered by Lord Sankey on behalf of the Board exhibits a robust adhesion to the common-sense view, and a judicious intolerance of the niceties of legal theory ... The decision of the Privy Council has spared lawyers a lot of judicial contortion-ism by bluffly brushing aside the technical and unreal. Unreal, in a practical sense, some of these legalities unquestionably are, in the sense that elementary statesmanship must prevent their emergence.' ('The Dominion and the Privy Council' [July 1935] 118 *Nineteenth Century and After*, 1 at 7.) Ivor Jennings also questioned whether in law the Statute of Westminister had empowered Canada to abolish appeals. ('The Statute of Westminster and Appeals to the Privy Council' [1936] 52 *Law Quarterly Review*, 173.) Sankey delivered the decision, as well as that in *Moore* v. *A.G. of the Irish Free State*,

[1935] A.C. 484, to the same effect on 6 June, the day before he was replaced as lord chancellor.

58 'Judicial Interpretation of the Canadian Constitution' (1935–6) 1 *University of Toronto Law Journal*, 260 at 276.

59 *Special Committee on British North America Act: Proceedings and* Evidence *and Report* (Ottawa: King's Printer 1935). The committee's mandate was 'to study and report on the the the best method by which the British North America Act may be amended so that while safeguarding the existing rights of racial and religious minorities and legitimate provincial claims to autonomy, the Dominion Government may be given adequate power to deal effectively with urgent economic problems which are essentially national in scope.' (Ibid., iv.)

60 Ibid., 3–4.

61 Ibid., 27.

9 The New Deal at Court and the End of Appeals

1 The transcript was found in the basement of the Supreme Court Library. The pagination is continuous and will be referred to by case and page.

2 The fullest account of the genesis and nature of the reform package is Larry A. Glassford, *Reaction and Reform: The Politics of the Conservative Party under R.B. Bennett 1927–1928* (Toronto: University of Toronto Press 1992).

3 'Crisis in the Canadian Constitution' (September 1934) *Round Table*, 812.

4 House of Commons, *Debates*, 28 January 1935, 223.

5 Ibid. 29 January 1935, 306.

6 National Archives of Canada (NAC), RG 13, vol. 2551, file 134869.

7 House of Commons, *Debates*, 2 March 1935, 123.

8 Stevens to Lapointe, 6 November 1935, Lapointe to Stevens, 14 November 1935, cited in W.H. McConnell, 'The Judicial Review of Prime Minister Bennett's "New Deal"' (1968) 6 *Osgoode Hall Law Journal*, 39 at 47.

9 James G. Snell and Frederick Vaughan, *The Supreme Court of Canada: History of the Institution* (Toronto: University of Toronto Press 1985), 165.

10 McConnell 'Judicial Review,' 82–3. Finlayson told McConnell that he had often been sent by Bennett to 'explain' to Duff the 'different features' of the legislation and why Bennett considered the legislation *intra vires*. Duff, he said, 'welcomed the information this made available.' Bennett may well have thought that Duff was in his debt because he had appointed him chief justice after King had denied him the appointment in 1924 because Duff drank.

11 Gerald LeDain, 'Sir Lyman Duff and the Constitution' (1974) 12 *Osgoode Hall Law Journal*, 261 at 285.

12 Lyman Poore Duff, 'The Privy Council' (1925) 3 *Canadian Bar Review*, 273 at 275.

13 *Re the Board of Commerce Act and the Combines and Fair Prices Act of 1919* (1920), 60 S.C.R. 456 at 509–10.

14 *Canadian National Railways* v. *Nova Scotia*, [1928] S.C.R. 106 at 120.

15 *Reference re Regulation and Control of Aeronautics in Canada*, [1930] S.C.R. 663 at 717.

16 Bennett to C.D. Richards, premier of New Brunswick, 28 January 1932, cited in Snell and Vaughan, *The Supreme Court*, 147. Bennett had concluded that there was 'no one in New Brunswick fitted by training and experience to become a member of the Court of last resort, in this Dominion.' In his closing address as president of the Canadian Bar Association in 1930, Bennett had stated that 'I, speaking as a member of the Bar and as a member of the parliament of this country, 'condemn any departure from the only just rule of selection, and state unequivocally that so long as I have the power to influence it, the appointment of our judges will be made with regard only to their real qualifications for the exalted position they must occupy in the proper administration of our laws, and upon which, in my humble opinion, in no small degree demands the maintenance of our Canadian civilization.' (Cited in W.H. Angus, 'Judicial Selection in Canada: The Historical Perspective' [1966] 3 *Legal Studies*, 220 at 240–1.) Two years later, Bennett observed in the House of Commons that 'the test whether a man is entitled to a seat on the bench has seemed to be whether he has run an election and lost it.' In few cases, he continued 'has the test been the merit of the appointee. To get away from that in a new democracy is not an easy thing. No one knows the difficulty better than I do.' (House of Commons, *Debates*, 17 May 1932, 2999.)

17 McConnell, 'Judicial Review,' 54.

18 NAC, Duff Papers, Duff to Lapointe, 9 November 1935.

19 Toronto *Daily Star*, 15 January 1936.

20 *Reference re Section 498A of the Criminal Code*, [1936] S.C.R. 363 at 366.

21 Ibid. at 370 (Canon), 375, 377 (Crocket)

22 *Reference re Dominion Trade and Industry Commission*, [1936] S.C.R. 380 at 382–3.

23 Described collectively as the Labour Conventions cases, the three statutes were The Limitation of Hours of Work Act, which limited work to eight hours a day or forty-eight hours a week; The Weekly Day of Rest in Industrial Undertakings Act, requiring twenty-four consecutive hours of rest in

every seven-day period for the entire staff in an industrial undertaking; and The Minimum Wages Act, permitting the federal government to establish the machinery to set minimum wages in order that all industrial workers could meet basic living costs.

24 *In the Matter of Legislative Jurisdiction over Hours of Labour*, [1925] S.C.R. 505
25 All factums for the New Deal cases can be found in the Supreme Court Library and in NAC, RG 125, vol. 747.
26 Labour Conventions, oral argument, 710ff.; factum of Canada.
27 Ibid., 847–8.
28 Labour Conventions, oral argument, 740–1.
29 Ibid., 832.
30 Ibid., 844.
31 Ibid., 909.
32 Ibid., 810.
33 Factums of Quebec, Saskatchewan, and British Columbia.
34 Factum of Ontario, 12–16.
35 *References re The Weekly Rest in Industrial Undertakings Act, The Minimum Wages Act and The Limitation of Hours of Work Act*, [1936] S.C.R. 461 at 486.
36 Ibid. at 496.
37 Ibid. at 476–7.
38 Ibid. at 520–1. Duff apparently tried to bring Crocket onside. He told Finlayson that he was 'having his devil's own time with my brother Crocket.' (McConnell, 'Judicial Review,' n.53.) It was unlikely that Crocket could be persuaded: he was ideologically opposed to state intervention and disliked Duff and resented his pre-eminence. Duff's secretary recalled that Crocket 'sometimes felt that Sir Lyman condescended to him. He thought that Sir Lyman lectured him in conferences and treated him as a student-at-law. I do not know what actually happened, but it was quite apparent that there was a clash of opinions and ideas.' (W. Kenneth Campbell, 'The Right Honourable Sir Lyman Poore Duff: The Man as I Knew Him' [1974] 12 *Osgoode Hall Law Journal*, 243 at 252.)
39 *Unemployment Reference*, oral argument, 1428. McConnell's otherwise excellent article is flawed by his failure to use the oral argument, which, to the best of my knowledge, was not discovered in the basement of the Supreme Court Library until the research was done for this study. For instance, of this reference he states: 'Indirection, if not outright deviousness, was also a feature of the argument of federal counsel in the unemployment insurance reference ... in both the I.L.O. and social insurance references they tended to put their cases obliquely – not arguing that the subject matter was in the federal domain necessarily, but that the invocation of other powers, the

treaty power or the taxing power, made the proposed statutes a valid subject-matter for federal enactment.' ('Judicial Review,' 65.) In fact, St Laurent argued that economic conditions justified federal remedial action, as the text reveals. The federal factum contained detailed statistics on unemployment and industrial conditions.

40 *Unemployment Reference,* oral argument, 1447–51.

41 Ibid., 1360.

42 Ibid., 1455–7.

43 Ibid., 1536.

44 *Reference re The Unemployment and Social Insurance Act,* [1936] S.C.R. 427 at 452–4.

45 The federal government had in fact conceded. When a drop in post-war wheat prices led to a demand for a peacetime version of the wartime Wheat Board, E.L. Newcombe, the deputy minister of justice (soon to be appointed to the Supreme Court), stated that all the coercive powers of the board normally fell within property and civil rights, and that the trade and commerce power, although 'comprehensive enough in its mere statement, has been limited by judicial interpretation; and compatibly with the decisions, it does not comprise the powers which would be necessary for the reconstruction of the Wheat Board.' Although most of the wheat was exported and the trade was a matter of 'great dimensions and importance,' that argument had failed to secure Haldane's support in the *Insurance Reference* and *Board of Commerce.* 'We are told,' he added, that Watsons's doctrine 'is to be applied with great caution, and with great reluctance, and that its recognition as relevant can be justified only after scrutiny sufficient to render it clear that circumstances are abnormal. A constitutional power which is beset by these conditions, and which moreover depends upon the dimensions of its subject matter, is not a very safe one to rely upon.' ('Memorandum for the Minister of Justice,' 17 April 1922, House of Commons, *Debates,* 940–2.)

46 Duff found 'two lurking fallacies' in the argument that the federal government could control wheat marketing: the relevance of the principle of percentages and of provincial incapacity. (*The King* v. *Eastern Terminal Elevator Company,* [1925] S.C.R. 434 at 443.) In 1926 the federal government passed the Canada Grain Act, declaring all grain elevators and warehouses to be for the general advantage of Canada. On provincial incapacity, see *Lawson* v. *Interior Tree Fruit and Vegetable Committee of Direction* (1930), [1931] S.C.R. 357; *Lower Mainland Dairy Products Adjustment Committee* v. *Crystal Dairy* (1932), [1933] A.C. 168, affirming a decision of the British Columbia Court of Appeal.

47 Section 5 (4)(a) (b). When St Laurent read 4(b) early in the argument, Duff immediately queried: 'May be?' To which St Laurent replied: 'Yes, My Lord. I am calling your Lordships' attention to it as it reads because it is a difficulty we shall have to discuss ... whether the language of (b) ... would be too inclusive to make that in pith and substance a scheme dealing with export trade.' (Oral argument, 1572–3.)

48 Oral argument, 1619. The Quebec act had not been proclaimed.

49 Ibid., 1592–3.

50 Ibid., 1601.

51 Ibid., 1598.

52 Ibid., 1631.

53 LeDain, 'Sir Lyman Duff and the Constitution,' 289.

54 *Reference re Natural Products Marketing Act*, [1936] S.C.R. 398 at 403–12. Duff emphasized that in *Snider* Haldane had determined that unless the trade and commerce power could 'be invoked in aid of capacity conferred independently under other words in s. 91,' it could not 'be relied upon as enabling the Dominion Parliament to regulate civil rights in the provinces.' For whatever reason, the court overlooked Atkin's repudiation of that doctrine in *P.T.A.* After Atkin had again repudiated the doctrine in 1937, Duff later declared, in his decision in the Alberta banking case, that 'we unanimously expressed the opinion and our judgement proceeded in part, at least, upon the hypothesis that we were bound by this pronouncement in *Snider's* case and by similar pronouncements in the *Board of Commerce* case, as expressing the *ratio decidendi* of those decisions.' (*Reference re Alberta Statutes*, [1938] S.C.R. 100 at 121.)

55 Ibid. at 410.

56 Ibid. at 419–21.

57 Ibid. at 425–6.

58 *Reference re Farmers' Creditors Arrangement Act* 1934, [1936] S.C.R. 384.

59 Cited in R.F.V. Heuston, *Lives of the Lord Chancellors, 1885–1940* (Oxford, U.K.: Clarendon Press 1964), 528.

60 Ibid., 529.

61 Ibid., 531.

62 Hailsham to Atkin, 17 November 1936, cited in Geoffrey Lewis, *Lord Atkin* (London: Butterworths 1983), 217.

63 Hailsham to Atkin, 3 November, 1936, Schuster to Atkin, 2 November 1936, in Lewis, *Lord Atkin*, 213–16. Schuster informed Atkin that the composition of the board was settled by Hailsham 'himself after the very fullest consideration of the nature of the cases to be heard and the work of both Tribunals. No man is more conscious of the importance of the Dominion Appeals

and he gave particular attention to the nature of the Canadian appeals now to be heard.' (Ibid. at 213.)

64 Hailsham to Atkin, 17 November, 1936, cited in Lewis, *Lord Atkin*, 101.

65 Lewis, *Lord Atkin*, 110.

66 Robert Stevens, *Law and Politics: The House of Lords as a Judicial Body, 1800–1976* (Chapel Hill: University of North Carolina Press 1978), 292.

67 Lewis, *Lord Atkin*, 113.

68 *James v. Cowan*, [1932] A.C. 542 at 558. As Lewis comments, 'when issues arose about which he felt profoundly, as in the Australian free trade cases, he was a champion without equal in his time.' (*Lord Atkin*, 117.)

69 R.W. Harding, 'Lord Atkin's Judicial Attitude and Their Illustration in Commercial Law and Contract' (1964) 27 *Modern Law Review*, 443 at 436.

70 Heuston, *Lives of the Lord Chancellors*, 481.

71 Lewis, *Lord Atkin*, 169.

72 Alan Paterson, *The Law Lords* (London: Macmillan 1982), 71.

73 Lewis, *Lord Atkin*, 110.

74 E. Cockburn Millar, 'Some Memories of Lord Atkin,' 23 *GLIM*, 13 at 15.

75 Wright, 'Lord Atkin of Aberdovey' (1946) *Proceedings of the British Academy*, 407 at 416–17.

76 Stevens, *Law and Politics*, 289–90.

77 Harding, 'Lord Atkin's Judicial Attitude,' 436–7.

78 Lewis, *Lord Atkin*, 110.

79 'Constitutional Interpretation – The Experience of Canada' (1937) 51 *Harvard Law Review*, 1 at 36.

80 As noted above, Sankey had replaced the politically appointed law lords 'with the now more traditional type of judge.' Atkinson had been replaced by Atkin; Carson and Shaw by Tomlin, Russell, and Thankerton; Sumner by Macmillan; and Dunedin by Wright. (Brian Abel-Smith and Robert Stevens, *Lawyers and the Courts: A Sociological Study of the English Legal System, 1750–1965* (London: Heinemann 1967), 118.

81 Heuston, *Lives of the Lord Chancellors*, 481.

82 Ibid.

83 Stevens, *Law and Politics*, 281nn.222, 223.

84 Heuston, *Lives of the Lord Chancellors*, 481.

85 Stevens, *Law and Politics*, 294.

86 'A.L.G.,' 'Lord Macmillan on Lord Wright' (1947) 63 *Law Quarterly Review*, 259 at 261.

87 'Precedents' (1942) 4 *University of Toronto Law Journal*, 247 at 265. See also his decision in *James v. Commonwealth of Australia*, [1936] A.C. 578 at 614,

and his brooding over constitutional review in 'Section 92 – A Problem Piece' (1954) 1 *Sydney Law Review,* 145.

88 Robert Stevens, *The Independence of the Judiciary: The View from the Lord Chancellor's Office* (Oxford, U.K.: Clarendon Press 1993), 75.

89 B.J. Mackinnon, 'Correspondence: To The Editor' (1956) 34 *Canadian Bar Review,* 115 at 117.

90 *A.G. Canada* v. *A.G. Ontario,* [1937] A.C. 326 at 341.

91 Ibid. at 328.

92 Ibid. at 330.

93 Ibid. at 330.

94 Ibid. at 335.

95 Ibid. at 338.

96 Ibid. at 350.

97 *References re The Weekly Rest in Industrial Undertakings Act ...,* [1936] S.C.R. 461 at 500.

98 NAC, MG 27, III B 10, vol. 49, file 24, R.S. Robertson to W.S. Edwards, deputy minister of justice, 2 March 1937, enclosed in Edwards, 'Memorandum for the Minister of Justice,' 5 March 1937.

99 *A.G. Canada* v. *A.G. Ontario,* [1937] A.C. at 350.

100 'Memorandum,' Robertson to Edwards, 2 March 1937.

101 *A.G. Canada* v. *A.G. Ontario,* [1937] A.C. at 351.

102 Ibid. Robertson reported that there 'was much discussion of the judgement in the Radio case in the argument ... and while in the course of the argument, as well as in their judgement, their Lordships were not prepared to accept the interpretation of their judgement in the Radio case that would support the legislation in question, the most careful reading of the language used in the Radio case suggests that their Lordships are not prepared to accept all that their Lordships said on that occasion as binding upon them.' ('Memorandum,' Robertson to Edwards, 2 March 1937.)

103 W.R. Lederman, 'Legislative Power to Implement Treaty Obligations in Canada,' in Lederman, *Continuing Canadian Constitutional Dilemmas: Essays on the Constitutional History, Public Law and Federal System of Canada* (Toronto: Butterworths 1981), 350 at 354.

104 *A.G. Canada* v. *A.G. Ontario,* [1937] A.C. at 351–2.

105 Ibid. at 352–3.

106 See, for example, Jacques-Ivan Morin, 'Le Québec et le pouvoir de conclure des accords internationaux' (1966) 3 *Canadian Legal Studies,* 136.

107 *A.G. Canada* v. *A.G. Ontario,* [1937] A.C. 355 at 356–9, 363.

108 Ibid. at 360. Only New Brunswick intervened to oppose the act.

109 Ibid. at 366.

110 *A.G. British Columbia* v. *A.G. Canada*, [1937] A.C. 377. The federal government joined in the appeal that the sections were severable. Ontario, Quebec, and New Brunswick opposed both the act and severance. More than a decade later the Supreme Court would accept the principle of inter-delegation. See Chapter 10.

111 Ibid. at 389. One year later, Atkin affirmed a decision of the Supreme Court of British Columbia upholding a provincial natural products marketing act that was essentially the provincial component of the one held to be *ultra vires*. The act provided for the regulation in all or any respects of natural products produced or sold within the province. Since the act professed what Atkin described as 'a bona fide intention by the Province to confine itself to its own sphere,' it was upheld despite the argument that such regulations must have an effect on inter-provincial and international trade and was thus an encroachment of the federal regulation of trade and commerce. Atkin's reasoning was interesting. Because it was 'well settled' that under 91(2) the federal government did not have the power to regulate 'particular trades or businesses so far as the trade is confined to the Province ... it follows that to the extent that the Dominion is forbidden to regulate within the Province, the Province itself has the right under its legislative powers over property and civil rights within the Province.' (*Shannon* v. *Lower Mainland Dairy Products Board*, [1938] A.C. 708 at 719.)

112 *A.G. British Columbia* v. *A.G. Canada*, [1937] 368 at 375.

113 *A.G. British Columbia* v. *A.G. Canada*, [1937] A.C. 391.

114 *A.G. Ontario* v. *A.G. Canada*, [1937] 405 at 417–18. See above, n.52.

115 *A.G. Canada* v. *A.G. Ontario*, [1937] A.C. 326 at 354 (*Labour Conventions*). Atkin may have borrowed his metaphor from James Bryce who, in his discussion of federalism, had written with a different intent: 'A nation so divided is like a ship built with water-tight compartments. When a leak is sprung in one compartment, the cargo stored there may be damaged, but the other compartments remain dry and keep the ship afloat.' (*The American Commonwealth* [London: Macmillan 1893], vol. 1, 345.)

116 Lord Atkin, 'Appeal in English Law' (1929) 3 *Cambridge Law Review*, 1 at 9.

117 Lord Wright, 'Obituary for the Rt. Hon. Sir Lyman Poore Duff' (1955) 33 *Canadian Bar Review*, 1123 at 1126.

118 Ibid.

119 Mackinnon, 'Correspondence,' 117.

120 Stevens, *Independence of the Judiciary*, 75. Although he did not reveal his own position on the appeal, Wright suggested that the 1940 amendment on unemployment insurance occasioned by the court decisions 'seems to justify Sir Lyman's practical sense, and it may be his sense, of what was

the correct construction and effect of the legislative measures involved.'
The 'pith and substance,' he said, 'would seem to be the nation-wide system of social insurance' and not the 'ordinary consensual insurances
which would normally fall within property and civil rights.' (Wright,
'Obituary for Duff,' 1129.) In fact, the suspicion lingers that, with Sankey
presiding, the labour, unemployment-insurance, and marketing acts
would have been upheld.

121 'The Privy Council Decisions: A Comment from Great Britain' (1937) 15
Canadian Bar Review, 428 at 429, 432. Moreover, he observed, 'it must be
pointed out that it is very difficult to see how the constitutional position of
the provinces could have been safeguarded, had not the Privy Council
drastically limited the operation of the general power of the Federation'
(430). He did acknowledge, however, that while the jurisprudence was
sound, it was 'a completely different question whether the terms of the
Canadian constitution are now consonant with the promotion of the best
interests of the people of the Dominion' (435).

122 (1937) 6 *Fortnightly Law Journal*, 225. As Jacques-Ivan Morin wrote, 'au
Canada anglais, Lord Atkin devint une des cibles préférés des savantes
diatribes juridiques.' ('Le Québec ... et des accords internationaux,' 138.)

123 'The British North America Act: Past and Future' (1937) 15 *Canadian Bar
Review*, 394 at 397–9. The academics, of course, were also nationalists. The
views of other academics were similar: Vincent MacDonald of Dalhousie,
N.A.M. Mackenzie of Toronto, F.C. Cronkite of Saskatchewan, and Frank
Scott of McGill. The fullest treatment of the emergence of the legal realists
is R. Blake Brown, 'Sobering up: The Constitution, the Great Depression,
and the Rebellion against Legal Formalism, 1930–1940' (major research
paper, graduate history, York University 1999). See also his 'Realism, Federalism and Statutory Interpretation during the 1930s: The Significance of
the *Home Oil Distributors* v. *A.G. B.C.*' (2001) 59 *University of Toronto Faculty
Law Review*, 1, R.C. Risk has discussed the legal realists in 'The Scholars
and the Constitution: P.O.O.G and the Privy Council (1996) 23 *Manitoba
Law Journal*, 496, and 'Here Be Cold and Tygers: A Map of Statutory Interpretation in Canada in the 1920s and 1930s' (2000) 63 *Saskatchewan Law
Review*, 195.

124 House of Commons, *Debates*, at 8 April 1938, 2151–2, 2155–7. Before introducing his bill, Cahan had corresponded with W.P.M. Kennedy, who
urged him to make certain that appeals from provincial courts were
abolished. Cahan replied that if 'I sought by express terms to abolish
appeals ... from provincial courts, I would raise such a storm of opposition
from the provincial governments that the bill would probably have to be

abandoned. As it is, I have reason to doubt that the government here will facilitate the measure by providing ample time for its discussion.' (NAC, Cahan Papers, Cahan to Kennedy, 29 January 1938; Kennedy to Cahan, 31 January 1938; Cahan to Kennedy, 15 February 1938.) A Nova Scotian, Cahan was born in 1861 and was provincial Conservative leader from 1890 to 1894. He stated that he 'knew personally the men from the maritime provinces who had to do with the framing of the act. Time and time again in private conversation and in public I have heard them state their belief as to the meaning and intent of section 92(13) and matters such as included in the New Deal legislation were never imagined to fall within the section.' (House of Commons, *Debates*, 1 February 1935, 450.)

125 Ibid., 8 April 1938, 2167. On 30 June 1938, the Senate directed W.F. O'Connor, parliamentary counsel to the Senate, to undertake a study of Judicial Committee jurisprudence. (*Report to the Honourable the Speaker of the Senate relating to the Enactment of the British North America Act, 1867, Any Lack of Consonance between Its Terms and Judicial Construction of Them and Cognate Matters* [Ottawa : 1939].) Published a year later, the 708-page report was, as Bora Laskin wrote, a 'severe raking of the Privy Council [which] probably owed as much to contemporary events ... as it did to his historical research and legal analysis.' (Review of G.P. Browne, *The Judicial Committee and the British North America Act* [1967] 10 *Canadian Public Administration*, 514.) Critics of the Judicial Committee found, and find, the report effective. A contemporary criticism and defence of the committee was offered by V. Evan Gray, who wrote that the report 'is of fascinating piquancy; it joins to law the romance of history; it unites speculation with logic and gives the legalist leave to plunge into that intoxicating stratosphere, the region of "it might have been."' ('The O'Connor Report on the British North America Act' [1939] 17 *Canadian Bar Review*, 309 at 309.) For a current criticism of the report, see Paul Romney, *Getting It Wrong* (Toronto: University of Toronto Press 1999), 170–2, 175–6).

126 House of Commons, *Debates*, 14 April 1939.

127 *Reference as to the Legislative Competence of the Parliament of Canada to Enact Bill No. 9, entitled 'An Act to Amend the Supreme Court Act,'* [1940] S.C.R. 49 at 70 (Duff), 103 (Davis). Cannon did not sit. All provinces except Quebec, Saskatchewan, and Alberta were represented by counsel.

128 Cited in Stevens, *Independence of the Judiciary*, 76.

129 Ibid.

130 Ibid., 151, Massey to Simon, 11 December 1943.

131 Ibid., 152, Churchill to Simon, 2 February 1944.

132 He appointed Chief Justice Rinfret to the Judicial Committee because 'I

hoped – rather against hope' – that his appointment 'might influence the Canadian Government against the abolition of the appeal.' (Ibid., 140, Jowitt to Gordon Walker, Commonwealth Relations Secretary, 7 February 1951.) Rinfret became an embarrassment and attempted to sit with the committee when he was neither invited nor wanted, even after his retirement from the Supreme Court in 1954. Lord Chancellor Simonds felt that his presence was outrageous: 'First because all the Law Lords agree that he is nothing like good enough to sit on the strong board which you take pains to ensure in Canadian appeals. Second because Canadian judicial and other legal opinions are unanimous in the view that he is not good enough.' (Ibid. at 142, Sir George Coldstream to Viscount Kilmuir, 19 April 1955.)

133 Ibid., 152.

134 Ibid., Goddard to Jowitt, 2 November 1945.

135 Ibid., 153, Jowitt to Addison, 9 January 1946. In fact, Jowitt had a memorandum ready for cabinet in December 1945 recommending his proposal at least for Canada. 'The relative ease of travel between this country and Canada, and the particularly strong ties formed during the war between that Dominion and this country make the scheme, prima facie, really practicable in the case of Canada.' Significantly, the memo suggested that provincial opposition to abolition might be counted on, if not cultivated. 'Although the Canadian Bill to abolish the right of appeal to the Privy Council received a fair measure of support in the Canadian Parliament in 1938, it is doubtful whether the situation is not now rather different. In any event, it is questionable whether all the Provinces of the Dominion are really in favour of abolition. If this view of the probable Canadian reaction is right it would surely be worth making soundings in Canada, whatever may be the outcome of the appeal to the Privy Council which will probably not be heard before the late summer of 1945.' (Ibid., 153n.97.)

136 The members were Jowitt, Viscount Simon, Lord Greene, Lord Goddard (all of whom had hoped Canada could be persuaded against abolition), Lord Wright, Lord Macmillan, and Lord Simonds.

137 *A.G. Ontario* v. *A.G. Canada*, [1947] A.C. 127 at 131. Summary of provincial arguments at 130–8. Manitoba and Saskatchewan filed facta in support of the federal government.

138 Ibid. at 140.

139 Ibid. at 148

140 Ibid. at 151.

141 Ibid. at 154.

142 Ibid.

143 National Archives of Canada, King Diary, 30 January, 3 February 1948.

144 Ibid., 5 March 1948.

145 Ibid.

146 13 Geo. VI, c. 37.

147 The only exception in the nine appeals was Atkin's decision that the amalgamation of the city of Windsor and the reorganization of its debt fell within provincial jurisdiction over municipal institutions and affected rights outside the province only 'collaterally and as a necessary incident to their lawful powers of good government within the Province.' (*Ladore* v. *Bennett*, [1939] A.C. 468 at 482.)

148 *A.G. Alberta* v. *A.G. Canada* (1938), [1939] A.C. 117 at 132, 135.

149 *A.G. Alberta* v. *A.G. Canada*, [1943] A.C. 356 at 370. He added that it had been settled since *Voluntary Assignments* in 1894 that, if provincial legislation was only ancillary to a section 91 enumeration, the province could legislate until the federal parliament chose to occupy the field.

150 *Co-Operative Committee on Japanese Canadians* v. *A.G. Canada* (1946), [1947] A.C. 87 at 101.

151 *A.G. Canada* v. *Hallet and Cary Ltd.*, [1952] A.C. 427 at 449–50; *Canadian Wheat Board* v. *Hallet and Carey Ltd. and Jeremiah H. Nolan*, [1950] S.C.R. 81. 'Whether the Privy Council will reverse the decision in the *Nolan* case,' commented John Willis, 'I do not, of course, dare to predict. Whichever way the case goes, I shall have some pangs. If the Supreme Court of Canada is reversed we shall have the distressing spectacle of the court which the Government has now established as the final Canadian court being upset on the threshold of its new authority at the instance of the very Government which created it, but against the Supreme Court's loss of face can be set the vindication of the principle of reality in the interpretation of statutes.' ('Case and Comment' (1951) 29 *Canadian Bar Review*, 296 at 304.)

152 *R.* v. *Jones*, [1937] 1 D.L.R. 193 (Appeal Division).

153 *Re The Canada Temperance Act* (1939), O.R. 570 at 571.

154 *A.G. Ontario* v. *Canada Temperance Federation*, [1946] A.C. 193 at 195, 199–200.

155 Ibid. at 205.

156 Ibid.

157 Ibid. at 207.

158 *Canadian Pacific Railway Co.* v. *British Columbia* (1949), [1950] A.C. 122 at 127–8. Alternatively the appellant argued that the hotel was immune because it also fell under federal jurisdiction under 92(10a).

159 The Supreme Court had, by a 5–2 majority, found the legislation unconstitutional. Chief Justice Rinfret held that it was within agriculture, trade and

commerce, and, following Simon, possibly the residual power. He agreed
with Kerwin that it was also valid as an exercise of the criminal law power.
(*Reference as to the Validity of Section 5(a) of the Dairy Industry Act*, [1948]
S.C.R. 1.)
160 *Canadian Federation of Agriculture* v. *A.G. Quebec* (1950), [1951] A.C. 179 at
193–4.
161 Ibid. at 197–8.

10 Restoring the Balance: The Supreme Court of Canada, 1949–1979

1 'The Role and Function of Judges' (1980) 14 *Law Society of Upper Canada
Gazette*, 139 at 187.
2 'The British North America Act: Past and Future' (1937) 15 *Canadian Bar
Review*, 394 at 399.
3 House of Commons, *Debates*, 1 February, 1938, 434.
4 James G. Snell and Frederick Vaughan, *The Supreme Court of Canada*
(Toronto: University of Toronto Press 1985), 192.
5 *The 1949 Yearbook of the Canadian Bar Association and the Minutes and
Proceedings of the Thirty-First Annual Meeting* (Ottawa: National Printers
1949), 55.
6 House of Commons, *Debates*, 23 September 1949, 190–1, 193.
7 Ibid., 197.
8 Ibid., 496.
9 Ibid., 509 (Canon), 501–2 (Garson). For a full discussion, see Mark R.
MacGuigan, 'Precedent and Policy in the Supreme Court' (1967) 45 *Canadian Bar Review*, 627.
10 The comment of Andrew Joanes ten years later – that the authors of the
1949 act 'must have contemplated, and indeed intended, a substantial
break from the automatic acceptance of English authorities, and to regard
pre-1949 decisions of the Privy Council as being of no more than persuasive authority is simply to give effect to legislative intent' – is not supported by the evidence. ('Stare Decisis in the Supreme Court of Canada'
[1958] 36 *Canadian Bar Review*, 175 at 197.)
11 'The Meaning of Provincial Autonomy' (1951) 29 *Canadian Bar Review*, 1126
at 1128.
12 Ibid., 1135.
13 'The Supreme Court of Canada: A Final Court of and for Canadians'
(1951) 29 *Canadian Bar Review*, 1038 at 1057.
14 Ibid., 1073.
15 Ibid., 1076.

16 *Reference re the Farm Products Marketing Act,* [1957] S.C.R. 198 at 212–13.
   Three years later, after shedding his judicial robes, Rand added that the
   'interpretation of a written constitution limiting jurisdiction within a federal union, with more or less elaborate formalities of amendment, does not
   permit of the perpetuation of unsound judgements.' ('Some Aspects of
   Canadian Constitutionalism' [1960] 38 *Canadian Bar Review,* 135 at 160.)

17 *R. v. George,* [1966] S.C.R. 267 at 278.

18 [1966] 3 All E.R. 77.

19 'Law Reform and the Judiciary's Role' (1972) 10 *Osgoode Hall Law Journal,*
   399 at 403.

20 *Reference re Agricultural Products Marketing Act,* [1978] 2 S.C.R. 1198 at 1291
   (Pigeon), 1257 (Laskin). In its decision the committee had found a British
   Columbia attempt to regulate the marketing of milk unconstitutional
   because the levies charged were in effect indirect taxes. (*Lower Mainland
   Dairy Products Sales Adjustment Committee* v. *Crystal Dairy Ltd.,* [1933] A.C.
   168.)

21 *A.V.G. Management Science Ltd.* v. *Barwell Developments Ltd.,* [1979] 2 S.C.R.
   43 at 57.

22 'Casting off the Mooring Ropes of Precedent' (1980) 58 *Canadian Bar Review,*
   255 at 256. Citations of Judicial Committee decisions fell from 16 per cent in
   1949–54 to 7.7 per cent in 1973–84 and 1.4 per cent in the 1990s. (Peter
   McCormick, *Supreme at Last: The Evolution of the Supreme Court of Canada*
   [Toronto: Lorimer 2000], various tables.)

23 'A Few Reflections upon the Role Which I See the Supreme Court of Can-
   ada, and the Law, Playing in the Last Quarter of Twentieth Century,'
   Address to the Manitoba Law Students Association, 2 May 1981, in
   Supreme Court of Library, Speeches Delivered by the Right Honourable
   Brian Dickson, typescript, vol. 1, 142.

24 Rebecca Johnson and John P. McEvoy, ed., *Gérard La Forest at the Supreme
   Court of Canada, 1985–1997* (Winnipeg: University of Manitoba 2000), 3 at 4.

25 'Role and Function of Judges,' 187.

26 G.V. Nicholls, 'Legal Periodicals and the Supreme Court of Canada' (1950)
   24 *Canadian Bar Review,* 422 at 422. The article in question was Vincent C.
   MacDonald, 'Constitutional Interpretation and Extrinsic Evidence' (1939)
   Canadian Bar Review, 77.

27 Vaughan Black and Nicholas Richter, 'Did She Mention My Name: Citation
   of Academic Authority by the Supreme Court of Canada 1985–1990' (1993)
   16 *Dalhousie Law Journal,* 377 at 383.

28 Peter McCormick, 'Do Judges Read Books Too? Academic Citations by the
   Lamer Court' (1998) 9 *Supreme Court Law Review,* 463 at 473.

29 Initially, five justices employed clerks, but by 1970 all had. Laskin was the first to employ two in 1979, and the rest, some reluctantly, had followed within the next two years. Dickson described the work of his law clerks: 'They can add depth in research, first of all ... go to the learned journals and get a bibliography of what has been written by various legal scholars ... they brought the most recent up-to-date views that were being expressed within the various law faculties in this country. The students were normally chosen from the top one or two in the top law schools – very, very dedicated, very able, very intelligent, sensitive young people who introduced a new dimension, and kept us, I think, from having arteries which were a little bit aged.' (Robert Sharpe, 'Brian Dickson: Portrait of a Judge' [July 1998] 17 *Advocates' Society Journal*, 3 at 25.) It can also be explained by the increase in the full-time complement of law faculties from 44 after the war to over 700 by the end of the century, and the increasing emphasis on scholarly research. In addition, after 1982, Charter appeals initially necessitated more scholarly and American case law research in the absence of Canadian precedents.

30 Bora Laskin, 'A Judge and His Constituencies' (1976) 7 *Manitoba Law Journal*, 1 at 12.

31 'The Role and Function of Judges,' 165. Dickson also questioned the performance of the academic community in daring to say that the 'quantity of good academic writing, published in any year, is meagre in relation to the number of legal scholars to be found in the law schools of the nation. This bears upon judicial performance because the quality of the law achieved by the courts bears a direct relationship to the quality of analysis offered by the academic community' (166).

32 Cited in Gordon Bales, 'W.D. Lederman and the Citation of Legal Periodicals by the Supreme Court of Canada' (1994) 19 *Queen's Law Journal*, 34 at 63.

33 *Reference Re Anti-Inflation Act*, [1976] 2 S.C.R. 373 at 389. See the analysis in Peter Hogg, 'Proof of Facts in Constitutional Cases' (1976) 26 *University of Toronto Law Journal*, 386.

34 'Role and Function of Judges,' 163–4. Of Dickson's personal appeal to history, Katherine Swinton wrote: 'One of the most noteworthy aspects of Dickson's federalism decisions was his use of history ... Again and again, he sought an historical rationale for particular allocations of power, even when the record was sparse.' (*The Supreme Court and Canadian Federalism: The Laskin-Dickson Years* [Toronto: Carswell 1990], 305.) See also S. Beaulac, 'Parliamentary Debates in Interpretation' (1998) 43 *McGill Law Journal*, 289; Gordon Bale, 'Parliamentary Debates and Statutory Interpretation: Switch-

ing on the Light or Rummaging Around in the Ashcans of the Legislative Process' (1995) 74 *Canadian Bar Review*, 1; W.G.H. Charles, 'Extrinsic Evidence and Statutory Interpretation: Judicial Discretion in Context' (1983) 7 *Dalhousie Law Journal*, 7; D.G. Kilgour, 'The Rule against the Use of Legislative History: Canon of Construction or Counsel of Caution?' (1952) 30 *Canadian Bar Review*, 769.

35 [1993] 3 S.C.R. 463 at 484. The overall analysis of Professor H. Scott Fairley is apt. 'The increased, less qualified use of extrinsic materials in constitutional adjudication, where characterizing the "pith and substance" of legislative enactments becomes crucial to the result, indicates a growing if not controlling preference on the part of our highest Court to engage in interpretation rather than construction. This purpose emerges not only for the purpose of characterizing the nature of legislative enactments in relation to constitutional limitations, but also for the better identification of the parameters of constitutional principles where textual prescriptions are hopelessly open-ended or incomplete.' ('Developments in Constitutional Law: The 1983–84 Term [1985] 7 *Supreme Court Law Review*, 63 at 66–7.)

36 Sharpe, 'Brian Dickson,' 4. However, as Dickson said of his papers at the archives, 'it will offer a small addition to that large Canadian jurisprudential heritage that we are all responsible for bequeathing to our grandchildren's grandchildren.' And that may well be when the papers are opened! (Brian Dickson with DeLloyd Guth, 'Serving Canada's Judicial Heritage,' in Guth, ed., *Brian Dickson at the Supreme Court of Canada, 1973–1990* [Winnipeg: University of Manitoba 1998], 321 at 323.) More has been written about Dickson's jurisprudence than of any other Supreme Court justice, with the possible exception of Duff. Robert Sharpe is apparently writing a biography. See his 'The Constitutional Legacy of Chief Justice Brian Dickson' (2000) 38 *Osgoode Hall Law Journal*, 189. The 1991 volume (20) issue of the *Manitoba Law Journal* was devoted entirely to Dickson and the Dickson court, with articles on federalism and the court by Katherine Swinton, Bryan Schwartz, James C. MacPherson, Robert Sharpe, and Peter Russell.

37 *A.G. Nova Scotia* v. *A.G. Canada*, [1951] S.C.R. 31 at 48 (*Nova Scotia Interdelegation*).

38 The oral argument exists only in manuscript in the Supreme Court Library, but Watson's comment was conveniently cited in A.H.F. Lefroy, *Canada's Federal System* (Toronto: Carswell 1913), 70n.10a. The decision aroused considerable negative academic comment. John Ballem was dismayed by a decision which 'unmistakably demonstrated' that the court 'will follow the restricted interpretative process' of the New Deal decisions and will reject the 'living constitution' approach. ('Case and Comment' [1951] 29 *Canadian*

Bar Review, 79 at 86.) Vincent MacDonald commented that the expedient 'might have enabled escape from the concept of "water-tight compartments" as descriptive of legislative jurisdiction.' (*Legislative Power and the Supreme Court,* 14.) The always cautious W.R. Lederman, however, agreed with the court that inter-delegation 'could seriously confuse the basis of political responsibility and accountability' of both levels of government. ('Some Forms and Limitations of Co-operative Federalism' [1967] 45 *Canadian Bar Review,* 409 at 426.) On the question of inter-delegation, see: Paul C. Weiler (who found the reasoning by no means compelling), 'The Supreme Court and the Law of Canadian Federalism' (1973) 23 *University of Toronto Law Journal,* 307 at 311–18; Gérard V. La Forest, 'Delegation of Legislative Power in Canada (1975) 21 *McGill Law Journal,* 131; E.A. Driedger, 'The Interaction of Federal and Provincial Laws' (1976) 54 *Canadian Bar Review,* 695.

39 *P.E.I. Marketing Board* v. *H.B. Willis Inc.,* [1952] 2 S.C.R. 392 at 397. (Atkin cited in *Proprietary Articles* in 1931.) Following the Nova Scotia precedent, the PEI Supreme Court found the scheme invalid.

40 Ibid. at 404.

41 'The Supreme Court and the Law of Canadian Federalism,' 154. John Ballem stated that the two decisions amounted to 'a tacit permission to do *indirectly* what cannot be done *directly.* This last criticism calls for the strictest and most searching re- examination of the *Nova Scotia* case on its appeal to the Privy Council, which now represents, ironically enough, the last avenue of escape from the present judicial impasse.' ('Case and Comment' [1952] 30 *Canadian Bar Review,* 1050 at 1058.) There was no appeal and the apparent impasse was simply ignored.

42 *A.G. Ontario* v. *Israel Winner,* [1954] A.C. 541; *Coughlin* v. *Ontario Highway Transport Board,* [1968] S.C.R. 569 at 576.

43 'Relations between Federal and Provincial Governments: The Role of Canada's Court of Last Resort,' a paper for use at the Trevino Conference, 27–30 August 1986, Supreme Court of Canada Library, Speeches Delivered by the Right Honourable Brian Dickson, typescript, vol. 2, 92.

44 'The Supreme Court and the Law of Canadian Federalism,' 317. See also K. Lysyk, 'Comments' (1969) 47 *Canadian Bar Review,* 271.

45 *Murphy* v. *Canadian Pacific Railway,* [1958] S.C.R. 626 at 632.

46 'Some Aspects of Canadian Constitutionalism' (1960) 38 *Canadian Bar Review,* 135 at 160.

47 *Johannesson* v. *Rural Municipality of West St. Paul,* [1952] 1 S.C.R. 292 at 348. A year earlier, the court had held *Re Wartime Leaseholds* valid as falling within the residual clause. It was hardly a fresh consideration, however, since it

fit easily into the precedents of *Fort Frances of 1923* and the *Co-operative Committee on Japanese Canadians* v. *Canada* of 1947, both of which empowered the government to determine when a wartime emergency was over.

48 *Pronto Uranium Mines Ltd.* v. *Ontario Labour Relations Board*, [1956] 5 D.L.R. (2d) 342 at 348.

49 *Reference re the Industrial Relations and Disputes Investigation Act*, [1955] S.C.R. 529 at 546. Haldane's comment in *Montreal City* v. *Montreal Harbour Commissioners*, [1926] A.C. 300 at 313. Micheline Patenaude later wrote that 'La chose m'a rien de surprenant quand on sait que *Re Stevedoring* s'explique par le désir de Cour Suprême de s'éloigner des décisions du Conseil privé ... Elle l'a fait en élargissant la notion d'enterprise fédérale comme le préconisait et commé de le préconiser une abondante doctrine anglo-canadienne.' The extensions of federal jurisdiction to 'cette catégorie hybride d'entreprises,' she concluded, was 'une fabrication judiciare destinée a renforcir les pouvoirs du Parlement fédérale en matière de relations de travail.' ('L'entreprise qui fait partie intégrante de l'enterprise fédérale' [1991] 32 *Les Cahiers de Droit* 763 at 766, 807.

50 See *Campbell-Bennett Ltd.* v. *Comstock Midwestern*, [1954], S.C.R. 207, where the court held that an interprovincial pipeline was immune from provincial mechanics-lien legislation. The issue is discussed more fully later.

51 *Reference re The Farm Products Marketing Act*, [1957] S.C.R. 198: Rand (208–11), Locke with Nolan concurring (231), and Kerwin (204–5).

52 *Murphy* v. *Canadian Pacific Railway*, [1958] S.C.R. 626 at 632.

53 Ibid. at 638, 640–1.

54 *Regina* v. *Klassen* (1959), 29 W.W.R. 369.

55 'Case and Comment' (1959) 38 *Canadian Bar Review*, 630 at 636. For Idington's comment, see *In re the Board of Commerce Act*, [1920] S.C.R. 456 at 488. The court continued to support exclusive federal control over the grain trade. In 1971 it upheld the sweeping terms of the declaration in 1926 taking over the elevators and warehouses. (*Jorgenson v. A.G. Canada*, [1971] 1 S.C.R. 725.) In *Chamney* v. *The Queen*, [1975] 2 S.C.R. 151, it held that the federal government had complete control over the handling of grain in elevators.

56 'The Supreme Court and the Law of Canadian Federalism,' 331.

57 *Goodyear Tire and Rubber Co.* v. *The Queen*, [1956] S.C.R. 303 at 311.

58 *Industrial Acceptance Co.* v. *The Queen*, [1953] 2 S.C.R. 273.

59 *Johnson* v. *A.G. Alberta*, [1954] S.C.R. 127.

60 *Birks* v. *City of Montreal*, [1955] S.C.R. 799.

61 *Switzman* v. *Elbling*, [1957] S.C.R. 285.

62 *Re Orderly Payment of Debts Act, 1959 (Alta.)*, [1960] S.C.R. 571.

63 *Canadian Bankers' Association* v. *A.G. Saskatchewan* (1955), [1956] S.C.R. 31.

64 'One Step Backward: The Supreme Court and Constitutional Law in the Sixties' (1975) 53 *Canadian Bar Review*, 621 at 621.

65 The figures vary according to the exact time-frame and the definition of federalism cases. See Gibson, 'One Step Backward,' 641ff.; Patrick Monahan, *Politics and the Constitution* (Toronto: Carswell/Methuen 1987), 152; Peter Russell, 'The Supreme Court's Interpretation of the Constitution from 1949 to 1960,' in Paul Fox, ed., *Politics in Canada* (Toronto: McGraw-Hill Ryerson 1977), 523.

66 'Constitutional Trends and Federalism,' in A.R.M. Lower, *Evolving Canadian Federalism* (Durham, N.C.: Duke University Press 1958), 92 at 109.

67 Gibson, 'One Step Backward,' 622–4.

68 'Supreme Court and the Law of Federalism,' 365. Weiler notes that in the 1950s there were 113 opinions in 27 decisions and in the 1960s only 50 in 27 decisions, confirming Gibson's observation that the judges showed 'a much greater tendency to concur silently and to employ the "formal manner" of reasoning with no indication of the policy considerations underlying their decisions.' ('One Step Backward,' 633.)

69 *In the Last Resort: A Critical Study of the Supreme Court of Canada* (Toronto: Carswell Methuen 1974), 227.

70 A study of judicial appointments from 1957 to 1960 by the Association of Canadian Law Teachers revealed that all of the twenty-seven Superior Court appointments in the common law provinces (except Newfoundland and Prince Edward Island) were known political supporters of the party in power. (W.H. Angus, 'Judicial Selection in Canada: The Historical Perspective' [1967] 3 *Canadian Legal Studies*, 220 at 247n.161.)

71 Thomas Stinson, 'Mr. Justice Roland Ritchie: A Biography' (1994) 17 *Dalhousie Law Journal*, 509 at 519, 529, 533.

72 'One Step Backward,' 633.

73 *Supreme at Last*, 66. Professor James MacPherson (as he then was) found that Martland was in the majority in almost 100 per cent of the constitutional cases he had selected for examination, and a later study reported that he had been in the majority in 94.8 per cent of all the constitutional cases during his term. (Randall Balcome, Edward McBride, and Dawn Russell, *Supreme Court of Canada Decision Making: The Benchmarks of Rand, Kerwin and Martland* [Toronto: Carswell 1990], 348.) Ritchie and Martland were in agreement 93.5 per cent of the time before Martland retired in 1982. McCormick finds that they were often allied with the Quebec trio: Taschereau, Fauteaux, and Abbott.

74 *Financial Post*, 27 March 1982.
75 In an interview with Professor James C. MacPherson in 1984. (Balcome, *Supreme Court of Canada Decision-Making*, 354.)
76 *Financial Post*, 27 March 1982.
77 Re s. 92 of the Vehicles Act 1957 (Sask.), [1958] S.C.R. 608.
78 'Supreme Court and the Law of Canadian Federalism,' 356.
79 *O'Grady* v. *Sparling*, [1960] S.C.R. 804; *Stephens* v. *The Queen*, [1960] S.C.R. 923. The reasoning was confirmed in *Mann* v. *The Queen*, [1966] S.C.R. 238, a case which Hogg states decided that 'the negative implication test no longer has any place in Canadian constitutional law' and was to be confirmed in *Ross* v. *Registrar of Motor Vehicles*, [1973] 1 S.C.R. 5 and *Bell* v. *A.G. P.E.I.*, [1973] 1 S.C.R. 25. (Peter Hogg, *Constitutional Law of Canada* [Toronto: Carswell 1992] 426.)
80 *Smith* v. *The Queen*, [1960] S.C.R. 776.
81 78. Hogg, *Constitutional Law*, 429.
82 *A.G. British Columbia* v. *Smith*, [1967] S.C.R. 702 at 703. See Weiler's extended discussion of the decision which undoubtedly expanded federal jurisdiction. ('The Supreme Court and the Law of Canadian Federalism,' 353.) The second was *Batary* v. *A.G. Saskatchewan*, [1965] S.C.R. 465.
83 *Crawford* v. *A.G. British Columbia*, [1960] S.C.R. 346. The cases distinguished were *Lower Mainland Dairy Products* v. *Crystal Dairy Ltd.*, [1933] A.C. 168 and *Lower Mainland Dairy Products Board Bd.* v. *Turner Dairy Ltd.*, [1941] S.C.R. 573. In the 1957 Ontario *Farm Products Reference*, the court had found a comparable fee invalid. The federal government then amended its marketing act to delegate the power to impose equalization levies to provincial marketing boards. *Crawford* rendered the delegation superfluous. (See Peter Russell, 'The Supreme Court's Interpretation of the Constitution from 1949 to 1960,' 529.)
84 *Cairns Construction* v. *A.G. Saskatchewan*, [1960] S.C.R. 619; *Nickel Rim Mines Ltd.* v. *A.G. Ontario*, [1967] S.C.R. 270.
85 *Texada Mines* v. *A.G. British Columbia*, [1960] S.C.R. 713.
86 *Carnation Company Ltd.* v. *Quebec Agricultural Marketing Board*, [1968] S.C.R. 238 at 253. On the decision and Martland's view of the trade and commerce power and Canadian federalism generally, see Balcome, *Supreme Court of Canada Decision-Making*, 347ff., citation at 354.
87 *A.G. Ontario* v. *Barfried Enterprises*, [1963] S.C.R. 570.
88 *Tomell Investments* v. *East Marstock Lands* (1977), [1978] 1 S.C.R. 974. On both cases, see Hogg, *Constitutional Law*, 636–7.
89 *A.G. Ontario* v. *Policyholders of Wentworth Insurance Company*, [1969] S.C.R.

779; Weiler, 'The Supreme Court and the Law of Canadian Federalism,' 339n.55.

90 *Agence Maritime* v. *Canada Labour Relations Board*, [1969] S.C.R. 851. The company's ships made only three trips outside the province in three years and the court held it to be subject to provincial labour laws, thus refining the 1955 *Stevedores* decision.

91 *The Queen in the Right of Ontario* v. *Board of Transport Commissioners* (1967), [1968] S.C.R. 118 at 119. The decision was soundly criticized in I.H. Fraser, 'Some Comments on Subsection 92(10) of the *Constitution Act*, of 1867' (1984) 29 *McGill Law Journal*, 557 at 578.

92 *Commission du Salaire Minimum* v. *Bell Telephone Co.*, [1966] S.C.R. 767 at 774 (Martland). Dale Gibson, among others, was highly critical of what he termed 'a new principle of immunity: that a provincial statute will not be allowed to affect any "essential" part of an enterprise under the exclusive jurisdiction of the federal Parliament.' The principle would give the court a 'wide discretion,' he argued, and was 'neither wise constitutional policy nor sound constitutional law.' ('Interjurisdictional Immunity in Canadian Federalism' [1969] 47 *Canadian Bar Review*, 40 at 53.)

93 *Munro* v. *National Capital Commission*, [1966] 663 at 671. Quebec and Ontario had initially intervened, but Ontario withdrew.

94 *Le Devoir*, 15 July 1966.

95 *Le Fédéralisme Canadien*, vol. 1, *La Loi Constitutionelle de 1867* (Montreal: Québec/Amerique 1983), 329.

96 Martin Robbin, *Pillars of Profit: The Company Province, 1934–1972* (Toronto: McClelland and Stewart 1973), 259–60.

97 *Re Offshore Mineral Rights of British Columbia*, [1967] S.C.R 792 at 793. The question of offshore resources was another example where the legal decision forced the political actors to find some form of political/financial/administrative accommodation. (See David Milne, *Tug of War: Ottawa and the Provinces under Trudeau and Mulroney* [Toronto: Lorimer 1986].) The court reached a similar decision concerning the resources of the continental shelf off Newfoundland, finding that Newfoundland was not a sovereign state when it entered the federation in 1949. (*Re Newfoundland Continental Shelf*, [1984] 1 S.C.R. 86.)

98 Gérard V. La Forest, 'The Labour Conventions Case Revisited' (1974) 12 *Canadian Yearbook of International Law*, 137 at 142.

99 'One Step Backward,' 629.

100 *Regina* v. *Campbell*, [1966] 673. The court agreed with the lower court without giving reasons or calling for argument from the federal govern-

ment. (Weiler, 'The Supreme Court and Law of Canadian Federalism,' 328.)

101 'Le fédéralisme gagne-t-il sa cause devant la Cour Suprême d'aujourd'hui?' (In Gérald Beaudoin, ed., *The Supreme Court of Canada: Proceedings of the 1985 Conference* (Cowansville: Les Éditions Yvon Blais 1986), 35 at 43.)

102 'Reflections on the Canadian Constitution after the First Century' (1967) 45 *Canadian Bar Review,* 395 at 398.

103 McCormick, *Supreme at Last,* 92–3.

104 Sharpe, 'Portrait of a Judge,' 21, 22.

105 Ibid., 84, 94, and 60–3, 83–4 on the appointments. See also Snell and Vaughan, *The Supreme Court of Canada,* 216–25; Ian Bushnell, *The Captive Court: A Study of the Supreme Court of Canada* (Montreal: McGill-Queen's University Press 1992), 342–6. Beetz was well known for his classical federalist views and had written that, although the Judicial Committee had dramatically diminished federal jurisdiction, it was important to Quebec that its constitutional interpretation 'restât inchangée le plus longtemps possible.' ('Les Attitude changeantes du Quebec à l'endroit de la Constitution de 1867,' in P.-A. Crepeau and C.B. Macpherson, ed., *The Future of Canadian Federalism* [Toronto: University of Toronto Press 1965], 113 at 119.)

106 *Caloil Inc.* v. *A.G. Canada,* [1971] S.C.R. 543 at 550.

107 *A.G. Manitoba* v. *Manitoba Egg & Poultry Assn.,* [1971] 689 at 703. Weiler was surprised at a decision which 'produced a very substantial change in the direction of Canadian constitutional law.' ('The Supreme Court and the Law of Canadian Federalism,' 335.) Patrick Monahan believes that the decision was 'surely right. Otherwise, the provincial power over property and civil rights could be used to erect protectionist and discriminatory barriers against goods produced in other provinces, thereby potentially carving up the Canadian economic union into ten separate provincial economies.' (*Constitutional Law* [Toronto: Irwin Law 1997], 267.) The court subsequently found Manitoba's prohibition of meatpackers from processing hogs that had not originated in Manitoba unconstitutional on the same grounds. (*Burns Food* v. *A.G. Manitoba,* [1975] 1 S.C.R. 494.)

108 *Re Agricultural Products Marketing Act,* [1978] 2 S.C.R. 1198 at 1296. The opinions of Laskin and Pigeon agreed that it was proper to overrule what was left of *Crystal Dairy* in 1933 and was a logical development of the decision in *Crawford.* (See above n. 19.)

109 [1980] 1 S.C.R. 844 at 854. Estey wrote for Martland, Pigeon, Beetz, and Pratte, and Laskin, in dissent, wrote for Dickson, Ritchie, and McIntyre. In a strange conclusion, Estey stated that it 'may well be that the state of

interpretation of the *British North America Act*, which I have summarized at the outset with reference to the decisions of the Privy Council, is not now a correct description of the federal power under s.91(2).' It may well be, he continued, that the court would have an occasion to 'deal with the interlocking of the federal and provincial power with reference to local marketing of articles of commerce, both natural products and otherwise, which have entered the interprovincial and international trade stream.' But it was not necessary in the present case, 'and I therefore do no more than reiterate that the disposition which I propose is based entirely on the state of the law as we find it to be in those decisions mentioned at the outset' (866).

110 'Economic Regulation and the British North America Act' (1980–1) 5 *Canadian Business Law Journal*, 172 at 181–3. Hogg is equally critical (*Constitutional Law*, 529), as is Monahan (*Constitutional Law*, 255). Estey also distinguished Atkins's *Canada Standards* decision on dubious grounds.

111 *Labatt Breweries of Canada Ltd.* v. *A.G. Canada* (1979), [1980] 1 S.C.R. 914. Estey wrote for Martland, Dickson, Beetz, and Pratte. Pigeon dissented in an opinion joined by McIntyre. Laskin wrote a separate dissent. Ritchie wrote a separate concurring opinion.

112 Ibid. at 938, 936–7, 938.

113 Ibid. at 919, 921. On Laskin's development of the second-branch argument, see Chapter 11.

114 Ibid. at 942–3.

115 *Constitutional Law*, 473–5, but he feels that the court was correct in rejecting the trade and commerce argument.

116 'Economic Regulation,' 196–7.

117 *Labatt Breweries* at 944–5.

118 Estey replaced Judson in July 1977 but took part in neither decision.

119 *Canadian Industrial Gas & Ltd.* v. *Saskatchewan* (1977), [1978] 2. S.C.R. 545. Martland later told James C. MacPherson that 'I went through a great deal of torment and self-doubt in relation to the *CIGOL* case which to me was an extremely difficult one, which had been drafted by someone with meticulous care to avoid what ultimately happened to it and I was very much concerned but again I was fortified by the fact that a substantial majority of the court seemed to agree with what I had written.' (Balcome, *Supreme Court of Canada Decision-Making*, 362.)

120 *Central Canada Potash Co.* v. *Saskatchewan* (1978), [1979] 1 S.C.R. 42 at 75. At the Saskatchewan Court of Appeal, the attorney general of Canada took 'the unprecedented step of becoming a plaintiff in this action, called witnesses and adduced evidence at the trial[,] thus influencing the set of facts

on which the cases is founded.' (*Report of the Western Premiers' Task Force on Constitutional Trends*, May 1977, 51.)

121 Ibid.

122 Ibid., 76. The two decisions were in part responsible for the addition of section 92A in the Constitution Act, 1867. James MacPherson wrote that the 'cries of anguish following CIGOL were deeply felt and justified' while those following Potash 'were less genuine (one suspects) and certainly less supportable.' ('Developments in Constitutional Law: The 1978–79 Terms' (1980) 1 *Supreme Court Law Review*.) 'For academic comment, see William D. Moull, 'Natural Resources: The Other Crisis in Canadian Federalism' (1980) 18 *Osgoode Hall Law Journal*, 1.

123 *Jones v. A.G. New Brunswick*, [1975] 2 S.C.R. 182.

124 *Interprovincial Co-Operatives Ltd. v. Dryden Chemicals Ltd.*, [1976] 1 S.C.R. 477 at 513–14. Pigeon wrote for Martland and Beetz. Ritchie concurred in the result but not in reasons. Laskin, Judson, and Spence dissented on other grounds. More substantively, the question turned on the issue of recovery for damages from downstream pollution from one province to another.

125 *Reference re Anti-Inflation Act* (1975), [1976] 2 S.C.R. 373. The decision has spawned an enormous academic literature. The political background, the role of the provinces, and the decision are superbly discussed by Peter H. Russell in 'The *Anti-Inflation* Case: The Anatomy of a Constitutional Decision' (1977) 20 *Canadian Public Administration*, 632.

126 *Reference re Anti-Inflation Act* at 116.

127 Ibid. at 419.

128 Ibid. at 425.

129 Ibid. at 432, 439.

130 Ibid. at 458.

131 An aspect of the decision explored and criticized by Edward P. Belobaba, '"Disputed Emergencies" and the Scope of Judicial Review: Yet Another Implication of the Anti-Inflation Act Reference' (1977) 15 *Osgoode Hall Law Journal*, 406.

132 G.J. Brandt, 'Judicial Restraint and Emergency Power: The Anti-Inflation Act Reference' (1977) 15 *University of Western Ontario Law Review*, 191 at 192. Lederman agreed that the decision was 'a good one – no wide-ranging new powers for the Federal Parliament by judicial interpretation, except temporarily to meet outright emergencies. This strikes a good balance, and is a result to which all nine judges contributed, especially Chief Justice Laskin and Mr. Justice Beetz.' 'Continuing Constitutional Dilemmas: The Supreme Court and the Federal Anti-Inflation Act of 1975' (1977) 84 *Queen's Quarterly*, 90 at 98.

133 'The *Anti-Inflation* Case,' 632 at 633.

134 'Les arrêts de la Cour suprême sur le partage des compétences depuis 1973: un commentaire' (1980) 11 *Revue Générale de Droit*, 328 at 331.

135 Bora Laskin, '"Peace, Order and Good Government" Re-examined' (1947) 25 *Canadian Bar Review*, 1054 at 1080.

136 'The *Anti-Inflation* Case: The Shutters Are Closed but the Back Door Is Wide Open' (1977) 15 *Osgoode Hall Law Journal*, 397.

137 François Chevrette and Herbert Marx, 'Comment' (1976) 54 *Canadian Bar Review*, 732 at 743.

138 *The Queen* v. *Hauser*, [1979] 1 S.C.R. 984 at 1000. Martland, Ritchie, and Beetz concurred. Dickson wrote a long dissent. Laskin, who did not sit, later wrote that the majority should not have placed it under the residual power and suggested that there was 'good grounds to reconsider the basis of the decision, resting as it did on a bare majority.' (*Schneider* v. *The Queen*, [1982] 2 S.C.R. 112 at 115.) *Schneider* made the issue moot in deciding that the federal government had the same prosecutorial authority over criminal laws as other federal laws.

139 *Capital Cities Communications Inc.* v. *Canadian Radio-Television Commission*, [1978] 2 S.C.R. 141 at 161.

140 Ibid., 162.

141 *Public Service Board* v. *Dionne*, [1978] 2 S.C.R. 191 at 197.

142 *A-G Quebec* v. *Kellog's Co.*, [1978] 2 S.C.R. 211. Martland wrote for Ritchie, Dickson, Pigeon, Beetz, and de Grandpré. An unrelenting Laskin (Judson and Spence concurring) dissented on the grounds that the regulations were an indirect approach to embrace matters outside provincial competence. In short, the medium included the message. The decision was confirmed a decade later when the court upheld Quebec legislation prohibiting advertising directed at children under thirteen. The court also held (3–2) that the ban was a reasonable limit on freedom of expression under the Charter. (*Irwin Toy Ltd.* v. *Quebec*, [1989] 1 S.C.R. 927.)

143 An exception was *Macdonald* v. *Vapor Canada Ltd.* (1976), [1977] 2 S.C.R 134, which found a section of the federal Trade Mark Act unconstitutional and which was doctrinally important. See chapter 11.

144 *Construction Montcalm Inc.* v. *Minimum Wage Commission*, [1979] 1 S.C.R. 754. Laskin (with Spence) in dissent argued that 'there can be no constitutional distinction between the construction and operation of a federal work and undertaking' (at 759). See James C. MacPherson, 'Developments in Constitutional Law: The 1978–79 Term' (1980) 1 *Supreme Court Law Review*, 77 at 84.

145 *Cardinal* v. *A.G. Alberta*, [1874] S.C.R. 695. Academics generally agreed that

Laskin's rigid view of immunity was overdone. See Katherine Swinton, 'Federalism and Provincial Government Immunity' (1979) 29 *University of Toronto Law Journal*, 1.

146 *Four B Manufacturing Limited* v. *United Garment Workers*, [1980] 1 S.C.R. 1031.

147 *Robinson* v. *Countrywide Factors Ltd.*, [1978] 1 S.C.R. 753. The fault lines were unusual in the decision: Spence, Judson, Ritchie, Pigeon, and Beetz versus Laskin, Martland, Dickson, and de Grandpré.

148 *Ross* v. *Registrar of Motor Vehicles* (1973), [1975] 1 S.C.R. 5; *Bell* v. *A.G. Prince Edward Island* (1973), [1975] 1 S.C.R. 25.

149 *Canadian Indemnity* v. *A.G. British Columbia*, [1977] 2 S.C.R. 504.

150 *Nova Scotia Board of Censors* v. *McNeill*, [1978] 2 S.C.R. 662. Ritchie wrote for Martland, Pigeon, Beetz, and de Grandpré. Laskin (for Judson, Spence, and Dickson) contended that the provision was an invasion of criminal law which 'extends beyond the control of morality, and is wide enough to embrace anti-social conduct or behavior and has, indeed, been exercised in those respects' (ibid. 681). Six provinces intervened to support provincial jurisdiction.

151 *A.G. Canada* and *Dupond* v. *Montreal*, [1978] 2 S.C.R. 770. In dissent, Laskin (for Dickson and Spence) stated that the province was creating a mini-criminal code, for the provision was so 'explicitly directed to breaches of the peace and to the maintenance of public order as to fall squarely within exclusive federal authority in relation to the criminal law (ibid., 775). For an extensive critique of the two decisions, see Joseph J. Arvay, 'The Criminal Law Power in the Constitution: And Then Came McNeil and Dupond' (1979) 11 *Ottawa Law Review*, 1. Avray contends that, with the decisions, 'section 91(27) has become a hefty sword but a puny shield' and that the court fundamentally altered the constitution by 'transforming an exclusive criminal law power into one that is virtually concurrent' (2).

152 *DiIorio* v. *Warden of Montreal Jail* (1976), [1977] 2 S.C.R. 662. Laskin, with the unusual support of de Grandpré, dissented on the grounds that the enforcement of the criminal law, including policing and prosecution, was an exclusive federal responsibility.

153 *A.G. Quebec and Keable* v. *A.G. Canada* (1978), [1979] 1 S.C.R. 218. Two years later the court held that disciplining the RCMP was a federal responsibility. (*A.G. Alberta* v. *Putnam*, [1981] 2 S.C.R. 267.)

154 The numbers differ according to the time-frame and definition of federalism, but the ratio of the outcomes does not vary significantly. Hogg has 102 cases by 1979, with 37 challenges to federal legislation of which 4 were successful in whole or part and 65 challenges to provincial legislation of

which 25 were successful. ('Is the Supreme Court of Canada Biased in Constitutional Cases?' [1979] 57 *Canadian Bar Review*, 721 at 726.) Patrick Monahan found 120 cases which involved federalism issues, even if decided on other grounds, of which 6 of the 40 challenges to federal legislation and 35 of the 80 to provincial legislation were upheld. (*Politics and the Constitution* [Toronto: Carswell Methuen 1987], 151.) Russell located 155 cases by 1982 (of which half were between 1975 and 1982), with a federal victory ratio by 1979 of 54.7 per cent. ('The Supreme Court and Federal Provincial Relations: The Political Use of Legal Resources' [1985] 11 *Canadian Public Policy*, 161 at 161–3.)

155 Cited in Alan C. Cairns, 'Who Should the Judges Be? Canadian Debates about the Composition of a Final Court of Appeal,' in Harry N. Scheiber, *North American and Comparative Federalism: Essays for the 1990s* (Berkeley: University of California, Institute of Governmental Studies Press 1992), 82n.5. Duplessis had made his comment during the Jehovah's Witness case. See Robert Rumilly, *Maurice Duplessis et son temps* (Montreal: Fides 1973), vol. 2, 543.

156 'A Political Scientist's View' (1974) 13 *Osgoode Hall Law Journal*, 293 at 299.

157 'The Political Role of the Supreme Court in Its First Century' (1975) 53 *Canadian Bar Review*, 576 at 590. However, a decade later, citing many decisions from the late 1970s, Russell shifted ground and concluded that 'the Supreme Court's overall record shows an uncanny balance. In so many areas the net outcome of its decisions is to strike a balance between federal and provincial powers.' ('The Supreme Court and Federal-Provincial Relations' 162.)

158 K.M. Lysyk, 'Reshaping Canadian Federalism' (1978) 13 *University of British Columbia Law Review*, 1 at 16.

159 (May 1977), 50.

160 (1979) 58 *Canadian Bar Review*, 721.

161 Ibid., 731.

162 Ibid., 733.

163 Ibid., 739. The word 'bias,' of course, begs the question. In my judgment, the court had strayed far from the path blazed by the Judicial Committee both in doctrine and in decision, and while there had been a notable expansion of federal jurisdiction, provincial authority had also been restricted in some areas and expanded only at the margin in others – particularly with inter-delegation and concurrency.

164 *La Cour suprême du Canada et le partage des compétences 1949–1978* (Québec: Ministère des Affaires Intergouvernementales 1978), 380, 387, 393. L'Écuyer examined over 115 cases in detail. He also offers the following

observations.' À la différence du Comité Judiciaire du Conseil Privé, la Cour Suprême, quant à elle, semble avoir opté pour une analyse fonctionnelle des articles 91 et 92 du B.N.A. Act ainsi que pour une analyse littérale des termes des article 91 et 92 du B.N.A. Act. L'interprétation qui en est résultée paraît, dans l'ensemble, plus conforme à l'esprit du B.N.A. Act ainsi aux intentions centralisatrices de la loi impériale. (390–1).

165 Jacques Brossard, 'La révolution fédéraliste' (1972) 7 *Revue juridique Thémis*, 1 at 2. Francophone scholars are more agreed on both the text and the intentions than anglophones. The most thorough analysis of sections 91 and 92 by André Tremblay is consistent with that in Chapter 1. (*Les compétences législatives au Canada et les pouvoirs provincaux en matière de propriété et de droits civils* [Ottawa: Éditions de l'Université d'Ottawa, 1967], 47ff.) For a review of francophone scholarship, see Roger Chaput, 'La Cour suprême et le partage des pouvoirs: Rétrospective et inventaires' (1981) 12 *Revue générale de droit*, 35.

166 Professor André Bzdera is highly critical of francophone scholarship on judicial review. He questions the general acceptance of the centralist nature of the BNA Act. The conclusion reached by fracophone scholars, as well as Hogg, can be explained because they ask the wrong questions: i.e., 'est-ce que l'interprétation constitutionnel de la Cour suprême est plausible à la lumière des dispositions particulières de l'A.A.N.B.?' Their answer is less an analysis of the impact of the court on the division of powers than 'une démonstration selon laquelle l'interprétation retenue par la Cour suprême est, sinon la meilleure, alors tout au moins plausible dans les limites de la science juridique normative ... [P]oser la question ainsi, c'est y répondre.' (Perspectives québécoises sur la Cour suprême du Canada' [1992] 7 *Canadian Journal of Law and Society*, 1 at 11–12.) Elsewhere Bzdera argued that, like all federal high courts, the Supreme Court is both nationalist and centralist because of the strong institutional links, including the appointment of 'politically correct' judges, with the central government. ('Comparative Analysis of Federal High Courts: A Political Theory of Judicial Review' [1993] 26 *Canadian Journal of Political Science*, 3 at 22, 27.)

167 'Les attitudes changeantes,' in P.-A. Crépeau and C.B. Macpherson, *The Future of Canadian Federalism*, 113 at 119. 'Il est difficile de contester que plusieurs de ces décisions auraient pu être différentes de ce qu'elles ont été, sinon à l'effet inverse,' Beetz added,' et que la discrétion dont jouissait le tribunal a servi l'intérêt des provinces plutôt que celui du pouvoir fédéral.' On the other hand, the 1867 constitution 'est susceptible de se prêter à une expansion presque indéfinie de la compétence fédérale, soit à cause de renversements jurisprudentiels toujours concevables, soit par

suite de l'exploration par la jurisprudence de domaines qu'elle a laissés jusqu'ici intouchés, soit enfin par la pratique ou l'usage plus abondant par le pouvoir fédéral de compétences qui lui sont déjà reconnues.' The residual clause and trade and commerce, in particular, 'sont susceptibles d'être remises en question par la jurisprudence' as anglo-Canadians had long desired. 'Dans certains cas, il serait à peine besoin de renverser la jurisprudence, il suffirait de mettre l'accent sur certains arrêts plutôt que sur d'autres.' (131–3).

168 *Le fédéralisme Canadien*, 1, 258. Jacques Brossard also agreed: unlike the Judicial Committee, the Supreme Court 'a été volontiers fidèle à la lettre et à l'esprit centralisateurs du *B.N.A. Act* de 1867, du moins dans la mesure où la jurisprudence du Conseil privé en a laissé la liberté. C'est ainsi qu'elle a violé plus d'une fois – et particulièrement ces dernières années – les principes du fédéralisme.' (*La Cour suprême et la constitution* [Montreal: Les Presses de l'Université de Montréal 1968], 172.)

169 W.R. Lederman was also concerned about the trend towards judicially created concurrency, which 'must be used with care if we would preserve the balance of our federal constitution – preserve, that is, a proper equilibrium between significant provincial autonomy and adequate central power ... Complete concurrency of federal powers with provincial ones, coupled with the doctrine of paramountcy, would mean the end of a balanced federal system in Canada.' ('The Balanced Interpretation of the Federal Distribution of Legislative Powers in Canada,' in Crépeau and Macpherson, *The Future of Canadian Federalism*, 98, 106.)

170 (1979) 20 *Cahiers de Droit*, 229. 'Les moins que l'on puisse dire,' concluded Gil Rémillard, 'c'est que cette "étanchéité" est maintenant fortement menacée ... De fait, notre fédéralisme est de plus en plus basé sur les compétences mixtes de par l'interprétation judiciaire, ce qui n'est pas sans mettre en danger le respect du principe de l'autonomie des États fédérés, qui est à la base de tout État vraiment fédératif.' *La Loi constitutionnelle de 1867* [Montreal: Québec/Amérique 1983), 307.) See also J.C. Bonenfant, 'L'étanchéité de la A.A.N.B. est-elle menacée? (1977) 18 *Cahiers de Droit*, 383.

171 'A Constitutional Court for Canada' (1965) 43 *Canadian Bar Review*, 545 at 547.

172 Henri Brun and Guy Tremblay, *Droit Constitutionnel*, 3rd ed. (Montreal: Les Éditions Yvon Blais 1997), 427. For a valiant, but unsatisfactory, attempt to relate decisions of the Supreme Court to the changing political/ constitutional environment in Quebec, which appears to assume that there was/could have been/should have been a relationship, see the study by

Andrée Lajoie, Pierrette Mulazzi, and Michelle Gamache. Of the years between 1960 and 1975, they write: 'We would not claim that there is a direct causal relationship between the decentralizing tendencies of the Supreme Court (or in any event those decisions that favoured the provinces) in cases originating in Quebec, and the political events and thought in the province after 1960 ... We would neither be insulting the Supreme Court nor charging it with bias if we concluded that it was sensitive to its social and political context. No more is it able to escape from its environment than is any other institution.' ('Political Ideas in Quebec and the Evolution of Canadian Constitutional Law, 1945–1985,' in Ivan Bernier and Andrée Lajoie, ed., *The Supreme Court of Canada as an Instrument of Political Change* [Toronto: University of Toronto Press 1986], 26.)

173 'Judicial Integrity and the Supreme Court of Canada' (1978) 12 *Law Society of Upper Canada Gazette*, 116 at 118. His address was given before a seminar of journalists whom he accused of being among those 'who should know better' (116).

11 Consolidation and Innovation, 1980–2000

1 In the words of Robert Sharpe, the amendment gave the court a mandate to 'shape and develop the law. These statutory amendments ... presented an implicit parliamentary recognition of this role and bolstered the growing confidence of the court that past decisions should not always stand in the way of the sound development and evolution of the law.' ('The Doctrine of *Stare Decisis*,' in DeLloyd J. Guth, ed., *Brian Dickson at the Supreme Court of Canada*, 1973–1990 [Winnipeg: University of Manitoba 1998], 193 at 197.)

2 Cited in Ian Bushnell, *The Captive Court: A Study of the Supreme Court of Canada* (Montreal: McGill-Queen's University Press 1992), 405. The early effect on the type of appeals heard, a high percentage of which were constitutional, is tabulated in Bushnell, 'Leave to Appeal Applications to the Supreme Court of Canada: A Matter of Public Importance' (1982) 3 *Supreme Court Law Review*, 479.

3 'The Development of a Distinctively Canadian Jurisprudence,' Address to the Faculty of Law, Dalhousie University, 29 October 1983, supreme Court of Canada Library, Speeches Delivered by the Right Honorable Brian Dickson, typescript, vol. 1, 464–7.

4 See James B. Kelly, 'Reconciling Rights and Federalism during Review of the Charter of Rights and Freedoms: The Supreme Court and the Centralization Thesis, 1982 to 1999' (2001) 34 *Canadian Journal of Political Science*, 321.

5   [1984] 2 S.C.R. 145 at 155.

6   Katherine Swinton writes that well into the 1970s the Supreme Court
    'tended to obscure or avoid the important policy considerations that either
    did or should have influenced them. Their reasons were couched in for-
    malistic tones, consisting only of recitations of past cases to justify deci-
    sions about important constitutional, public and private law matters.' She
    attributes much of the change to Dickson. ('Dickson's Style and Sources,'
    in Guth, *Brian Dickson at the Supreme Court*, 185 at 185.) François Chevrette
    also writes that throughout the 1960s and into the 1970s, 'on a souvent
    reproché à la Cour le caractère abstrait et simplificateur de des ses analy-
    ses, un certain nominalisme, un formalisme terminologique.' But in the
    decade beginning in 1975, he concluded that the court had shown 'proba-
    blement plus que jamais auparavant, un triple souci d'éclaircir et d'appro-
    fondir les concepts, d'introduire plus de réalisme dans ses analyses, enfin
    de simplifier le style des jugements.' ('Le fédéralisme gagne-t-il sa cause
    devant la Cour suprême d'aujourd'hui?' in Gérald Beaudoin, ed., *The
    Supreme Court of Canada: Proceedings of the October 1985 Conference* [Cow-
    ansville, Que.: Les Éditions Yvon Blais 1986], 35 at 36–7.)

7   In *Bell Canada* v. *Quebec*, [1988] 1 S.C.R. 749 at 838, Beetz wrote a lengthy
    rebuttal of Peter Hogg's critique of the court's treatment of interjurisdic-
    tional immunity. As Hogg noted, 'Beetz quoted extensively from my book,
    and criticized my views in a detailed fashion more like a law review arti-
    cle than a judgement.' (*Constitutional Law* [Toronto: Carswell 1992],
    398.n.124.)

8   'The Role of the Supreme Court of Canada' (October 1984) *The Advocates'
    Society Journal*, 3 at 5.

9   'Some of you may be surprised to learn that judges were not all enthusias-
    tic about this innovation,' Beetz told the law clerks in 1988. 'The late Mr.
    Justice Judson almost had to be pressured into taking a law clerk. One
    year, he did not even bother hiring one. When he did, he gave them rela-
    tively little to do. Perhaps this explains in part the proverbial conciseness
    of his reasons for judgement.' ('Allocation prononceé par le Juge Beetz 15
    juin 1988,' Supreme Court of Canada Library, Speeches Presented by the
    Honourable Jean Beetz, typescript, 1990.)

10 Dickson, 'Distinctively Canadian Jurisprudence,' 5.

11 *Reference re Canada Assistance Plan*, [1991] 2 S.C.R. 525 at 545. On the ques-
    tion of justiciability, see Lorne Sossin, *Boundaries of Judicial Review: The Law
    of Justiciability in Canada* (Toronto: Carswell 1999).

12 *Reference re Canada Assistance Plan* at 557. There were practical, as well as
    theoretical, reasons for rejecting the legitimacy of the doctrine. 'Such expec-
    tations might be created by statements during an election campaign. The

business of government would be stalled while the application of the doctrine and its effect was argued out in the courts. Furthermore, it is fundamental to our system of government that a government is not bound by the undertakings of its predecessor.' (Ibid. at 559.) Ontario, Saskatchewan, and Alberta intervened.

13 Ibid. at 567. The court also found the federal Goods and Services Tax valid within 91(3) and that any effect on matters within provincial jurisdiction was incidental, dismissing Ontario's bizarre argument that its passage with the use of closure made it invalid. (*Reference re Goods and Services Tax*, [1992] 2 S.C.R. 445.)

14 The exceptions were: *Clarke* v. *Canadian National Railways*, [1981] 2 S.C.R. 690 (finding that a provincial law of general application could apply to a federal undertaking); *A.G. Canada* v. *Law Society of B.C.*, [1982] 2 S.C.R. 307 (determining that the Restrictive Trade Practices commission did not extend to the Law Society because its regulations did not lessen competition); *Central Western Railway* v. *United Transportation Union*, [1990] 3 S.C.R. 1112 (deciding that the short-line railway, although connected to the Canadian National and involved in grain delivery, did not extend beyond the provincial border and thus was not within federal jurisdiction); *Ontario* v. *Canadian Pacific Ltd.*, [1995] 2 S.C.R. 1031 (finding, following Watson in *Bonsecours*, that the railway was not immune from provincial environmental legislation concerning burning slash along the railway).

15 *Northern Telecom Can.* v. *Communication Workers of Canada*, [1983] 1 S.C.R. 733.

16 *OPSEU* v. *Ontario (Attorney General)*, [1987] 2 S.C.R. 17–18.

17 Ibid. at 19.

18 [1988] 1 S.C.R. 749 at 839, 843. In his criticism of the arguments of Hogg (above, n.1) and other academics (and, by implication, of Dickson in *OPSEU*), Beetz elaborated his view at some length. 'In my view ... this theory does not confer on Parliament any power that it does not already have, since it is an integral and vital part of its primary legislative authority over federal undertakings. If this power is exclusive, it is because the Constitution which could have been different but is not, expressly specifies this to be the case; and it is because this power is exclusive that it pre-empts that of the legislatures both as to their legislation of general and specific application, in so far as such laws affect a vital part of a federal undertaking '(840). The other cases in the trilogy were *Canadian National Railways* v. *Courtois*, [1988] 1 S.C.R. 868; *Alltrans Express Ltd.* v. *British Columbia*, [1988] 1 S.C.R. 897. The decisions occasioned considerable comment. See Dale Gibson, 'Case Comment' (1990) 69 *Canadian Bar Review*, 339; Robin Elliott, 'Notes of

Cases' (1988) 67 *Canadian Bar Review*, 523; Yves Tardif, 'Droit Constitutionel (relations de Travail)' (1988) 48 *Revue du Barreau*, 702.

19 *Alberta Government Telephones* v. *Canada (Radio-Television & Telecommunications Commission*, [1989] 2 S.C.R. 225 at 259, 256–7. Wilson had dissented on the issue of crown immunity only. The 1993 Telecommunications Act (S.C. 1993, c. 38) placed all phone companies under federal jurisdiction and stated that the act was binding on the crown in the right of the province. The issue was finally settled when a small local company in Quebec was deemed to be under federal control. (*Telephone G.T.* v. *Quebec (Régie des Telecommunications)*, [1994] 1 S.C.R. 878.) It was all or nothing when the court decided that the requirement to secure a Quebec permit for the sight-seeing bus of the National Battlefield Commission to service the Plains of Abraham was a 'massive and intrusive impact' on the federal undertaking. However, the court rejected a challenge to Quebec's Consumer Protection Act on the grounds that a prohibition against advertising directed at children did not affect a 'vital part' of television operations. *Irwin Toy* v. *Quebec*, [1989] 1 S.C.R. 930.

20 *Ontario Hydro* v. *Ontario (Labour Relations Board)*, [1993] 3 S.C.R. 327 at 370. La Forest wrote for L'Heureux-Dubé and Gonthier. Lamer wrote a concurring opinion in which he emphasized that parliament's jurisdiction over a declared work or under the residual clause should be limited so as to respect provincial powers but remain consistent with the 'appropriate recognition of the federal interests involved' (at 331).

21 Ibid. at 371.

22 Ibid. at 371-2.

23 Ibid. at 374–5. La Forest also stated that the case could be 'equally well disposed of' under the national concern doctrine. 'There can be no doubt that the production, use and application of atomic energy constitute a distinct matter of national concern. It is predominantly extra-provincial and international in character and implications and possesses sufficiently distinct and separate characteristics to make it subject to Parliament's residual power' (379).

24 Ibid. at 399, 403, 427.

25 The National Energy Board had ruled that gas processing and transmission were fundamentally different activities but the Federal Court of Appeal had found that both came within the definition of 'pipelines' and were under federal jurisdiction. Four provinces intervened to support the appeal. In a judgment delivered by Iacobucci and Major, the court was dismissive of the board's findings: 'While appellate courts will generally accord deference to findings of fact by a tribunal, this is not equally true of

findings of law ... It would be particularly inappropriate to defer to a tribunal like the board whose expertise lies completely outside the realm of legal analysis on a question of constitutional interpretation.' (*Westcoast Energy* v. *Canada (National Energy Board)*, [1998] 1 S.C.R. 322 at 353–4.)

26 Ibid. at 394, 396, 398.
27 *Schneider* v. *The Queen*, [1982] 2 S.C.R. 112 at 115.
28 *A.G. Canada* v. *Canadian National Transportation*, [1983] 2 S.C.R. 206 at 223.
29 Ibid. at 279. Beetz and Lamer stayed out of the controversy by finding validity under trade and commerce and thus within federal prosecutorial authority 'whether or not' it could be supported under the criminal law power. (Ibid. at 282.)
30 *R.* v. *Wetmore*, [1983] 2 S.C.R. 284 at 299.
31 Ibid. at 303.
32 Ibid. at 306.
33 Ibid. at 307.
34 Ibid. at 308.
35 See Neil Finkelstein, 'Notes of Cases' (1984) 63 *Canadian Bar Review*, 182; H. Scott Fairley, 'Developments in Constitutional Law: The 1983–84 Term,' in (1985) 7 *Supreme Court Law Review*, 85–93. Laskin's judgments, commented Ross Shamenski of the British Columbia bar, 'have now stood the constitutional authority of the administration of justice on its head.' For an historical analysis critical of Laskin's judgments, see his 'Kripps and C.N. Transportation: The Meaning of "Administration of Justice" before Confederation' (1985) 7 *Supreme Court Law Review*, 441.
36 *Westendorp* v. *The Queen*, [1983] 1 S.C.R. 43 at 52.
37 *R.* v. *Morgentaler*, [1993] 3 S.C.R. 463 at 483.
38 Ibid. at 503.
39 Quebec Court of Appeal: (1993), 102 D.L.R. (4th) 289. Quebec Superior Court: (1991), 82 D.L.R. (4th) 449.
40 *RJR-MacDonald Inc.* v. *Canada (A.G.)*, [1995] 3 S.C.R. 199 at 245. La Forest wrote for Lamer, L'Heureux-Dubé, Gonthier, Cory, McLachlin, and Iacobucci.
41 Ibid. at 240.
42 Ibid. at 258.
43 Ibid. at 364. The court unanimously found that the prohibition on advertising and promotion violated section 2(b) of the Charter, and a 5–4 majority held that it could not be saved under section 1.
44 *R.* v. *Hydro-Quebec*, [1997] 3 S.C.R. 213. La Forest wrote for L'Heureux-Dubé, Gonthier, Cory, and McLachlin. Lamer, Sopinka, Major, and Iacobucci dissented.

45 Ibid. at 285.
46 Ibid. at 297.
47 Ibid. at 296
48 Ibid. at 296-7
49 Ibid. at 314.
50 'Developments in Constitutional Law: The 1997-98 Term – Activism and Accountability,' (1999) 10 (2nd) *Supreme Court Law Review*, 151 at 153–4. (Mitchell was Director of the Constitutional Branch in the Saskatchewan Department of Justice.) Sven Deimann notes that the decision was delivered on 18 September 1997, when the ministers of the environment were about to sign a harmonization initiative designed to secure greater efficiency and effectiveness and to delineate the role of all governments 'within an environmental management partnership by ensuring that specific roles and responsibilities will generally be undertaken by one order of government only ... [and] preventing overlapping jurisdiction and interjurisdictional disputes.' The accord, without Quebec, was released on 29 January 1998. ('R. v. Hydro-Quebec: Federal Environmental Regulation as Criminal Law' [1998].) *See* 43 (1998) *McGill Law Journal*, 923 at 926.
51 *Reference re Firearms Act*, [2000] 1 S.C.R. 782 at 791.
52 Ibid. at 796.
53 Ibid. at 797.
54 Ibid. at 801, 804.
55 Ibid. at 814.
56 Ibid. at 817.
57 *Re Exported Natural Gas Tax*, [1982] 1 S.C.R. 1004. Premier Peter Lougheed's retaliatory threat to reduce oil production drastically led to the most famous bumper-sticker in Canadian history: 'Let the Eastern Bastards Freeze in the Dark.' For the reaction of the producing provinces, and the effect of the NEP on constitutional negotiations, see Roy Romanow, John Whyte, and Howard Lesson, *Canada Notwithstanding: The Making of the Constitution, 1976–1982* (Toronto: Carswell 1984), 114ff. François Chevrette comments that in the decision the court 'avait rappelé que le fédéralisme existait au Canada et qu'il comportait ses avantages et ses contraintes.' (Le fédéralisme gagne-t-il sa cause devant la Cour suprême d'aujourd'hui?' in Beaudoin, *The Supreme Court of Canada*, 51.)
58 *Re Exported Natural Gas Tax* at 1041.
59 Ibid. at 1042–4. See the analysis in John D. Whyte, 'Developments in Constitutional Law: The 1981–82 Term' (1983) 5 *Supreme Court Law Review*, 77 at 124.
60 *R. v. Crown Zellerbach*, [1988] 1 S.C.R. 401.

61 *Northwest Falling Contractors Ltd.* v. *R.*, [1980] 2 S.C.R. 292.

62 *Crown Zellerbach* at 431-2.

63 Ibid. at 434.

64 Ibid. at 457.

65 'L'interprétation du partages des compétences à l'heure du libre-échange' (1990) 21 *Revue de droit de l'université de Sherbrooke*, 1 at 16.

66 *Droit Constitutionnel: Principes* (Montreal: Les Éditions Thémis 1993), 242.

67 'R. v. Crown Zellerbach Ltd.' (1989) 23 *U.B.C. Law Review*, 355 at 370–1.

68 *Friends of the Oldman River* v. *Canada (Minister of Transport)*, [1992] 1 S.C.R. 3.

69 For an analysis of the complex issues involved, see D.F. Bur and J.K. Kehoe, 'Developments in Constitutional Law: The 1991–92 Term' (1993) 4 *Supreme Court Law Review* (2nd) 77 at 93.

70 'Constitutional Jurisdiction over Environmental Management in Canada' (1973) 23 *University of Toronto Law Journal*, 54 at 85.

71 *Oldman River* at 64.

72 Ibid. at 64–5. L'Heureux-Dubé, Sopinka, Gonthier, Cory, McLachlin, and Iacobucci concurred. Stevenson dissented on all grounds.

73 This was also the basis of La Forest's decision for a unanimous court in *Whitbread* v. *Walley*, [1990] 3 S.C.R. 1273. 'Once Canadian waters are conceived of as a single navigational network, the activity of navigation is very akin to the activity of aeronautics and should lead to similar constitutional treatment' (1276).

74 *Morguard Investments Ltd.* v. *Savoye*, [1990] 3 S.C.R. 1077 at 1089.

75 Ibid. at 1100.

76 *Hunt* v. *T&N PLC*, [1993] 4 S.C.R. 289 at 324.

77 Ibid.

78 Ibid. at 326.

79 'Some Impressions on Judging' (1986) 35 *University of New Brunswick Law Journal*, 145 at 156.

80 'The La Forest Years: The Vocation of Judging – A Judge's Perspective,' in Rebecca Johnson and John P. McEvoy, ed., *Gérard La Forest at the Supreme Court of Canada, 1985–1997* (Winnipeg: University of Manitoba 2000), 499 at 506. Professor Elizabeth Edinger wrote that from 'the point of view of constitutional law, the simultaneous expansion and qualification of jurisdiction to determine the constitutional validity of provincial laws, the willingness of the Supreme Court to consider issues not argued at trial or on appeal, the skepticism about the need for governmental intervention and, in particu-lar, the creation of new justiciable constitutional principles and the endorsement of their application to "the Courts" must be regarded with

some astonishment.' ('The Constitutionalization of the Conflict of Laws [1995] 25 *Canadian Business Law Journal*, 38 at 64–5.)

81 G.V. La Forest, 'Judicial Lawmaking, Creativity and Constraints,' in Johnson, *La Forest at the Supreme Court*, 3 at 15.

82 *Multiple Access* v. *McCutcheon*, [1982] S.C.R. 161 at 173.

83 *Quebec (A.G.)* v. *Canada (National Energy Board)*, [1994] 1 S.C.R. 159 at 192.

84 I do not regard as substantive Haldane's opinion regarding its application to the activities of Dominion companies in *John Deere* or Atkin's validation of the Canada Trade Mark Act in 1937 (which had been undermined by Estey's decision in *Dominion Stores*).

85 *Reference re Anti-Inflation Act, 1975*, [1976] 2 S.C.R. 373 at 426. Note also his comments in his dissent in *Labatt's*. See Chapter 10, n.100.

86 *MacDonald* v. *Vapor Canada Ltd.* (1976), [1977] 2 S.C.R. 134.

87 Ibid. at 164.

88 Ibid. at 165. For an extended discussion of the decision, see Peter Hogg, 'Comments' (1976) 54 *Canadian Bar Review*, 361.

89 *A.G. Canada* v. *Canadian National Transportation*, [1983] 2 S.C.R. 206. See above, n.32.

90 Ibid. at 266.

91 Ibid. at 267.

92 Ibid. at 268.

93 H. Scott Fairley, 'Developments in Constitutional Law: The 1983–84 Term' (1984) 7 *Supreme Court Law Review*, 63 at 104.

94 'Notes of Cases' (1984) 62 *Canadian Bar Review*, 182 at 184, 191.

95 *General Motors of Canada Ltd.* v. *City National Leasing*, [1989] 1 S.C.R. 641 at 663.

96 Ibid. at 663ff.

97 Ibid. at 682.

98 Ibid. at 684.

99 Ibid. at 688.

100 Ibid. at 689.

101 Vilaysoun Loungnarath, 'La participation de provinces Canadiens et en particulier du Québec à la négociation de l'Accord de libre-échange entre le Canada et les États-unis' (1987) 4 *Revue Québécoise de droit international*, 9 at 17.

102 'Legislative Power to Implement Treaty Obligations in Canada' (1963), reprinted in Lederman, *Continuing Canadian Constitutional Dilemmas* (Toronto: Butterworths 1981), 350 at 354.

103 See Chapter 9 at n.56.

104 *Francis* v. *The Queen*, [1956] S.C.R. 618 at 621 (Kerwin for Taschereau and Fauteux), 625 (Rand for Cartwright).

105 'Some aspects of Canadian Constitutionalism' (1960) 38 *Canadian Bar Review*, 135 at 142. 'Assuming treaty-making to be an entirety as legislative matter, the transmission or originated faculty finds its only place of reception in the residual power of the Dominion; to attribute any role to the province would require a statutory enlargement of provincial capacity. Every consideration of policy leads to the continued association of the treaty executive with its own legislative organ' (143).

106 'Canadian Federalism, and the Foreign Affairs and Treaty Power: The Impact of Quebec's 'Quiet Revolution (1969) 7 *Canadian Yearbook of International Law*, 3 at 19. 'Since it strains credulity to believe that the Supreme Court of Canada intended ... to overrule the *Labour Conventions* decision *sub silento*, one's conclusion may have to be that the *Labour Conventions* case was not properly presented by counsel ... to a court whose opportunities of ruling on international law issues are few and far between; and that this apparent *non sequitur* ... was therefore arrived at by the court *per incuriam*' (20–1).

107 'The Labour Conventions Case Revisited' (1974) 12 *Canadian Yearbook of International Law*, 137 at 138, 147. Interestingly, the future judge added that the 'general balance of our constitution is after all more strongly secured by historical, cultural, political, and geographical considerations than mere legalisms ... Still, it is desirable that the organized forces that dictate the type of federalism that exists in this country be supported by an adequate constitutional base' (149).

108 *Macdonald* v. *Vapor Canada* (1976), [1977] 2 S.C.R. 134 at 169.

109 [1982] 2 S.C.R 112 at 134–5.

110 'Notes of Cases' (1983) 61 *Canadian Bar Review*, 856 at 858, 865.

111 [1988] 1 S.C.R. 401 (La Forest at 442). See L. Alan Willis, 'The *Crown Zellerbach* Case on Marine Pollution: National and International Dimensions' (1988) 26 *Canadian Yearbook of International Law*, 235.

112 [1989] 1 S.C.R. 641. See Robert Howse, 'The Labour Conventions Doctrine in an Era of Global Interdependence: Rethinking the Constitutional Dimensions of Canada's External Relations' (1989–90) 16 *Canadian Business Law Journal*, 160.

113 'Treaty Making and Implementing Powers in Canada: The Continuing Dilemma,' in B. Cheng and E.D. Brown, *Contemporary Problems in International Law: Essays in Honour of George Schwartzenberger on His Eightieth Birthday* (London: Stevens and Sons 1988), 333 at 348–9.

114 Henri Brun and Guy Tremblay, *Droit Constitutionnel*, 3rd ed. (Montreal: Les Éditions Yvon Blais 1997), 439.

115 Ibid. at 562.
116 'Le role du pouvoir judiciare dans la structuration politico-juridique de la fédération canadienne' (1997) 57 *Revue du Barreau*, 1003 at 1019.
117 Ibid. at 1044.
118 'L'interpretation du partage des compétences,' 74, 76.
119 '"Federalism under Fire" The Role of the Supreme Court of Canada' (1992) 55 *Law and Contemporary Problems*, 121 at 128.
120 Ibid., 136.
121 Ibid., 683.
122 See above at nn.74–81.
123 *Reference Re Authority of Parliament in Relation to the Upper House*, [1980] 1 S.C.R. 54 at 78, 77. Ironically, although the reforms were intended to ensure provincial representation and make the Senate more independent of the federal executive, the court mysteriously concluded that a system of partial election would contradict the intentions of the framers 'to make the Senate a thoroughly independent body which could canvass dispassionately the measures of the House of Commons.'
124 United Kingdom, House of Commons, Foreign Affairs Committee, 1980–1 Session, *British North America Act: The Role of Parliament*, vol. 1, xi–xii, 14:8–10.
125 However, Trudeau had told the *New York Times* (3 April 1981) that he would rather 'lose the whole effort than go on record as saying that legislatures cannot legislate until they get permission from the Supreme Court.'
126 Robert Sharpe, 'Brian Dickson, Portrait of a Judge' (July 1998) 17 *Advocates' Society Journal*, 3 at 28.
127 *Reference re Amendment of the Constitution of Canada (Nos. 1, 2, and 3)*, [1981] 1 S.C.R. 753 at 807. The opinion was signed by Laskin, Dickson, Beetz, Estey, McIntyre, Chouinard, and Lamer.
128 Ibid. at 841, 905, 909, 883, 871. The minority refused to accept the existence of any convention, particularly one so ill-defined as to require only substantial consent. (Ibid. at 871–2.)
129 Years later, Trudeau bitterly declared 'there seems to be little doubt that the majority judges had set their minds to delivering a judgement that would force the federal and provincial governments to seek a political compromise. No doubt believing in good faith that a political agreement would be better for Canada than unilateral legal patriation, they blatantly manipulated the evidence before them so as to arrive at the desired result. They then wrote a judgement which tried to lend a fig-leaf of legality to their preconceived conclusion.' ('Convocation Speech at the Opening of the Bora Laskin Law Library' [1991] 43 *University of Toronto Law Journal*,

295 at 302.) Dickson later stated that he believed Trudeau was wrong in law and added that 'I hesitate to think what might have happened if our judgement had gone the other way.' (Sharpe, 'Brian Dickson,' 29.)

130 *Re Attorney-General of Quebec and Attorney-General of Canada* (1982), 134 D.L.R. (3d) 719.

131 *Re Objection to a Resolution to Amend the Constitution*, [1982] 2 S.C.R. 793 at 812–13, 817.

132 *Reference re Secession of Quebec*, [1998] 2 S.C.R. 217 at 247-8. The court was composed of Chief Justice Lamer and justices L'Heureux-Dubé, Gonthier, Cory, McLachlin, Iacobucci, Major, Bastarache, and Binnie. Lamer was the only veteran of the earlier constitutional wars, having sat on patriation and the Quebec veto references.

133 Ibid. at 265, 260.

134 Ibid. at 269.

135 Ibid. at 294.

Index

1981 David H. Flaherty, ed., *Essays in the History of Canadian Law: Volume I*

1982 Marion MacRae and Anthony Adamson, *Cornerstones of Order: Courthouses and Town Halls of Ontario, 1784–1914*

1983 David H. Flaherty, ed., *Essays in the History of Canadian Law: Volume II*

1984 Patrick Brode, *Sir John Beverley Robinson: Bone and Sinew of the Compact*
David Williams, *Duff: A Life in the Law*

1985 James Snell and Frederick Vaughan, *The Supreme Court of Canada: History of the Institution*

1986 Paul Romney, *Mr. Attorney: The Attorney General for Ontario in Court, Cabinet, and Legislature, 1791–1899*
Martin Friedland, *The Case of Valentine Shortis: A True Story of Crime and Politics in Canada*

1987 C. Ian Kyer and Jerome Bickenbach, *The Fiercest Debate: Cecil A. Wright, the Benchers, and Legal Education in Ontario, 1923–1957*

1988 Robert Sharpe, *The Last Day, the Last Hour: The Currie Libel Trial*
John D. Arnup, *Middleton: The Beloved Judge*

1989 Desmond Brown, *The Genesis of the Canadian Criminal Code of 1892*
Patrick Brode, *The Odyssey of John Anderson*

1990 Philip Girard and Jim Phillips, eds., *Essays in the History of Canadian Law: Volume III – Nova Scotia*
Carol Wilton, ed., *Essays in the History of Canadian Law: Volume IV – Beyond the Law: Lawyers and Business in Canada, 1830–1930*

1991 Constance Backhouse, *Petticoats and Prejudice: Women and Law in Nineteenth-Century Canada*

1992 Brendan O'Brien, *Speedy Justice: The Tragic Last Voyage of His Majesty's Vessel* Speedy
Robert Fraser, ed., *Provincial Justice: Upper Canadian Legal Portraits from the Dictionary of Canadian Biography*

1993 Greg Marquis, *Policing Canada's Century: A History of the Canadian Association of Chiefs of Police*
F. Murray Greenwood, *Legacies of Fear: Law and Politics in Quebec in the Era of the French Revolution*

1994 Patrick Boyer, *A Passion for Justice: The Legacy of James Chalmers McRuer*
Charles Pullen, *The Life and Times of Arthur Maloney: The Last of the Tribunes*
Jim Phillips, Tina Loo, and Susan Lewthwaite, eds., *Essays in the History of Canadian Law: Volume V – Crime and Criminal Justice*
Brian Young, *The Politics of Codification: The Lower Canadian Civil Code of 1866*

1995 David Williams, *Just Lawyers: Seven Portraits*
Hamar Foster and John McLaren, eds., *Essays in the History of Canadian Law: Volume VI – British Columbia and the Yukon*

W.H. Morrow, ed., *Northern Justice: The Memoirs of Mr Justice William G. Morrow*

Beverley Boissery, *A Deep Sense of Wrong: The Treason Trials and Transportation to New South Wales of Lower Canadian Rebels after the 1838 Rebellion*

1996 Carol Wilton, ed., *Essays in the History of Canadian Law: Volume VII – Inside the Law: Canadian Law Firms in Historical Perspective*

William Kaplan, *Bad Judgment: The Case of Mr Justice Leo A. Landreville*

F. Murray Greenwood and Barry Wright, eds., *Canadian State Trials: Volume I – Law, Politics, and Security Measures, 1608–1837*

1997 James W. St.G. Walker, *'Race,' Rights, and the Law in the Supreme Court of Canada: Historical Case Studies*

Lori Chambers, *Married Women and Property Law in Victorian Ontario*

Patrick Brode, *Casual Slaughters and Accidental Judgments: Canadian War Crimes and Prosecutions, 1944–1948*

Ian Bushnell, *A History of the Federal Court of Canada, 1875–1992*

1998 Sidney Harring, *White Man's Law: Native People in Nineteenth-Century Canadian Jurisprudence*

Peter Oliver, *'Terror to Evil-Doers': Prisons and Punishments in Nineteenth-Century Ontario*

1999 Constance Backhouse, *Colour-Coded: A Legal History of Racism in Canada, 1900–1950*

G. Blaine Baker and Jim Phillips, eds., *Essays in the History of Canadian Law: Volume VIII – In Honour of R.C.B. Risk*

Richard W. Pound, *Chief Justice W.R. Jackett: By the Law of the Land*

David Vanek, *Fulfilment: Memoirs of a Criminal Court Judge*

2000 Barry Cahill, *The Thousandth Man: A Biography of James McGregor Stewart*

A.B. McKillop, *The Spinster and the Prophet: Florence Deeks, H.G. Wells, and the Mystery of the Purloined Past*

Beverley Boissery and F. Murray Greenwood, *Uncertain Justice: Canadian Women and Capital Punishment*

Bruce Ziff, *Unforeseen Legacies: Reuben Wells Leonard and the Leonard Foundation Trust*

2001 Ellen Anderson, *Judging Bertha Wilson: Law as Large as Life*

Judy Fudge and Eric Tucker, *Labour before the Law: The Regulation of Workers' Collective Action in Canada, 1900–1948*

Laurel Sefton MacDowell, *Renegade Lawyer: The Life of J.L. Cohen*

2002 John T. Saywell, *The Lawmakers: Judicial Power and the Shaping of Canadian Federalism*

Patrick Brode, *Courted Abandoned: Seduction in Canadian Law*

David Murray, *Gelded Justice: Justice, Morality, and Crime in the Niagara District, 1791–1849*

Barry Wright and F. Murray Greenwood, *Canadian State Trials: Volume II – Rebellion and Invasion in the Canadas, 1837–1839*